Lecture Notes in Computer Sc

T0238611

Commenced Publication in 1973
Founding and Former Series Editors:
Gerhard Goos, Juris Hartmanis, and Jan van Leeuwen

Tiziana Margaria   Bernhard Steffen (Eds.)

Leveraging Applications of Formal Methods, Verification and Validation

Technologies for Mastering Change

5th International Symposium, ISoLA 2012
Heraklion, Crete, Greece, October 15-18, 2012
Proceedings, Part I

 Springer

Volume Editors

Tiziana Margaria
Universität Potsdam, Institut für Informatik
August-Bebel-Straße 89, 14482 Potsdam, Germany
E-mail: margaria@cs.uni-potsdam.de

Bernhard Steffen
Technische Universität Dortmund, Fakultät für Informatik
Otto-Hahn-Straße 14, 44227 Dortmund, Germany
E-mail: steffen@cs.tu-dortmund.de

ISSN 0302-9743   e-ISSN 1611-3349
ISBN 978-3-642-34025-3   e-ISBN 978-3-642-34026-0
DOI 10.1007/978-3-642-34026-0
Springer Heidelberg Dordrecht London New York

Library of Congress Control Number: 2012948288

CR Subject Classification (1998): D.2.4-5, D.2.1-3, D.3.3-4, D.4.1, D.4.5, D.4.7,
F.1.1, F.3.1-2, I.2, C.2

LNCS Sublibrary: SL 1 – Theoretical Computer Science and General Issues

Typesetting: Camera-ready by author, data conversion by Scientific Publishing Services, Chennai, India

Printed on acid-free paper

Springer is part of Springer Science+Business Media (www.springer.com)

Preface

Welcome to ISoLA 2012, the 4th International Symposium on Leveraging Applications of Formal Methods, Verification and Validation, that was held in Heraklion, Crete (Greece) during October 14–18, 2012, endorsed by EASST, the European Association of Software Science and Technology.

This year's event followed the tradition of its forerunners held 2004 and 2006 in Cyprus, 2008 in Chalkidiki, and 2010 in Crete, and the series of ISoLA Workshops in Greenbelt (USA) in 2005, Poitiers (France) in 2007, Potsdam (Germany) in 2009, and in Vienna (Austria) in 2011.

As in the previous editions, ISoLA 2012 provided a forum for developers, users, and researchers to discuss issues related to the adoption and use of rigorous tools and methods for the specification, analysis, verification, certification, construction, test, and maintenance of systems from the point of view of their different application domains. Thus, since 2004 the ISoLA series of events serves the purpose of bridging the gap between designers and developers of rigorous tools on the one hand, and users in engineering and in other disciplines on the other hand. It fosters and exploits synergetic relationships among scientists, engineers, software developers, decision makers, and other critical thinkers in companies and organizations. By providing a specific, dialogue-oriented venue for the discussion of common problems, requirements, algorithms, methodologies, and practices, ISoLA aims in particular at supporting researchers in their quest to improve the usefulness, reliability, flexibility, and efficiency of tools for building systems, and users in their search for adequate solutions to their problems.

The program of the symposium consisted of a collection of special tracks devoted to the following hot and emerging topics

- Adaptable and Evolving Software for Eternal Systems (R. Hähnle, I. Schäfer)
- Approaches for Mastering Change (M. Leucker, M. Lochau, I. Schäfer)
- Bioscientific Data Processing and Modeling (J. Kok, A.-L. Lamprecht, F. Verbeek, M. Wilkinson)
- Formal Methods for the Development and Certification of X-by-Wire Control Systems (A. Fantechi, F. Flammini, S. Gnesi)
- Handling Heterogeneity in Formal Development of HW and SW Systems (Y. Ait-Ameur, D. Mery)
- Learning Techniques for Software Verification and Validation (E.M. Clarke, M. Gheorghiu Bobaru, C. Pasareanu, D. Song)
- Model-Based Testing and Model Inference (K. Meinke, N. Walkinshaw)
- Processes and Data Integration in the Networked Healthcare (A. Braun v. Reinersdorff, T. Margaria, C. Rasche)
- Process-Oriented Geoinformation Systems and Applications (H. Asche)
- Quantitative Modeling and Analysis (J.-P. Katoen, K.G. Larsen)
- Runtime Verification: The Application Perspective (Y. Falcone, L. Zuck)

- Software Aspects of Robotic Systems (J. Knoop, D. Schreiner)
- Timing Constraints: Theory Meets Practice (B. Lisper, J. Nordlander, P. Quinton)

and of the following four events

- LearnLib Tutorial: From Finite Automata to Register Interface Programs (F. Howar, M. Isberner, M. Merten, B. Steffen)
- The RERS Grey-Box Challenge 2012: Analysis of Event-Condition-Action Systems (F. Howar, M. Isberner, M. Merten, B. Steffen, D. Beyer)
- Linux Driver Verification Workshop (D. Beyer, A. Petrenko)
- ITSy Day 2012 (T. Margaria, B. Steffen)

The ISoLA Symposium was itself part of the ISoLA Week, which signaled the steady growth of the community and included the following four co-located events:

- STRESS 2012 — International School on Tool-Based Rigorous Engineering of Software Systems (P.Chalin, J. Hatcliff, Robby, T. Margaria, B. Steffen)
- SEW 2012 — 35th IEEE Software Engineering Workshop (M. Hinchey, J. Bowen, H. Zhu)
- Graduate/Postgraduate Course on Soft Skills for IT Professionals in Science and Engineering (B. Floyd)
- FRCSS 2012 — 2nd Future Research Challenges for Software and Services (T. Margaria)

We thank the track organizers, the members of the Program Committee and their subreferees for their effort in selecting the papers to be presented, the Local Organization Chair, Petros Stratis, and the Easyconference team for their continuous precious support during the week as well as during the entire two-year period preceding the events, and Springer for being, as usual, a very reliable partner in the proceedings production. Finally, we are grateful to Horst Voigt for his Web support, and to Maik Merten, Johannes Neubauer, and Stephan Windmüller for their help with the online conference service (OCS).

Special thanks are due to the following organization for their endorsement: EASST (European Association of Software Science and Technology), and our own institutions — the TU Dortmund, and the University of Potsdam.

October 2012   Tiziana Margaria
                                                    Bernhard Steffen

Organization

Committees

Symposium Chair   Bernhard Steffen

Program Chair   Tiziana Margaria

Program Committee

Yamine Ait-Ameur
Hartmut Asche
Dirk Beyer
Mihaela Bobaru
Edmund Clarke
Ylies Falcone
Francesco Flammini
Stefania Gnesi
Reiner Hähnle
John Hatcliff
Falk Howar
Joost-Pieter Katoen
Joost Kok
Jens Knoop
Anna-Lena Lamprecht
Kim G. Larsen
Martin Leucker

Björn Lisper
Malte Lochau
Karl Meinke
Dominique Mery
Alessandro Moschitti
Johan Nordlander
Corina Pasareanu
Alexander K. Petrenko
Sophie Quinton
Ina Schaefer
Dietmar Schreiner
Dawn Song
Fons Verbeek
Neil Walkinshaw
Mark D. Wilkinson
Lenore Zuck

Table of Contents – Part I

Adaptable and Evolving Software for Eternal Systems

Approaches for Mastering Change

Runtime Verification: The Application Perspective

Model-Based Testing and Model Inference

Learning Techniques for Software Verification and Validation

LearnLib Tutorial: From Finite Automata to Register Interface Programs

RERS Grey-Box Challenge 2012

Table of Contents – Part II

Timing Constraints: Theory Meets Practice

Formal Methods for the Development and Certification of X-by-Wire Control Systems

Quantitative Modelling and Analysis

Software Aspects of Robotic Systems

Process-Oriented Geoinformation Systems and Applications

Handling Heterogeneity in Formal Development of HW and SW Systems

Adaptable and Evolving Software
for Eternal Systems
(Track Summary)

Reiner Hähnle[1] and Ina Schaefer[2]

[1] Department of Computer Science
Technische Universität Darmstadt, 64289 Darmstadt
`haehnle@cs.tu-darmstadt.de`
[2] Institute for Software Engineering and Automotive Informatics
Technical University of Braunschweig, D-38106 Braunschweig
`i.schaefer@tu-braunschweig.de`

1 Motivation and Goals

Modern software systems are extremely long-lived and have to adapt to changing user requirements and evolving environment conditions, such as different hardware or resource constraints [6,9]. Furthermore, they have to remain operational over long periods of time which requires to alter their functional or non-functional behavior without halting the system's operation [3]. These phenomena related to evolving and long-lived software systems pose new challenges for software engineering concepts, methods and tools.

For this track, we have invited a leading researchers to present their solutions to tackle the challenge of software evolution in very long-lived systems. The invited format ensures broad coverage of this important topic: diverse solution approaches (language-based, verification-based, process-based), diverse methodologies (learning, modeling and model-driven development, formal verification), as well as diverse application areas (product line engineering, scientific workflows, compatibility checking, regression testing) are featured in the eight contributions of this track. All papers represent systematic rather than ad-hoc proposals which makes them interesting for a wide audience. Together, the papers in this track provide a comprehensive and up-to-date overview of the research community's response to the challenge of evolving software.

2 Contributions

Bodden et al. [1] present the requirements and challenges for designing a programming language that is capable of expressing dynamic analyses of security properties. Efficiently specifying and guaranteeing security policies is an important issue for long-lived software systems. The proposed analyses can be used to ensure designated security properties and policies, such as access control or secure information flow, at runtime. A well defined relationship between static

T. Margaria and B. Steffen (Eds.): ISoLA 2012, Part I, LNCS 7609, pp. 1–3, 2012.
© Springer-Verlag Berlin Heidelberg 2012

compile time analyses and dynamic runtime analyses ensure that the performance of program execution is in acceptable bounds.

Bosch & Eklund [2] advocate continuous, user- and test-driven software development in an embedded systems scenario. To this end, they introduce the concept of *innovation experiment systems* in the context of long-lived embedded software. Traditional embedded software development strictly follows a waterfall model, but such systems need to evolve continuously to stay competitive and provide value to the customer and end-user, especially in domains where the pace of change is increasing. The paper explores the implications for the architecture to support the ability to continuously evolve and conduct experiences in the deployed product context in a safe and controlled manner.

Hähnle & Schaefer [4] consider the formal verification of variant-rich software systems developed in delta-oriented programming. Delta-oriented programming is a flexible, yet modular approach to implement variable and evolvable software systems. In this paper, the authors provide a foundation for the compositional verification of delta-oriented software product families by providing a set of criteria when it is possible to establish the specification of single product variants from the specification of their shared artifacts.

Lamprecht & Margaria [5] present a framework for realizing variable and evolvable scientific workflows in an agile manner. Their approach is based on the paradigms of extreme model-driven development and loose programming. Service independent building blocks (SIBs) abstract functionality towards the end user and encapsulate implementation-specific details in order to allow a modular response to change, both to the implementation and to the application. The end user serves as application designer by arranging SIBs in workflows. Synthesis algorithms allow agile and evolutionary experimentation with different SIB orchestrations to achieve the same goal.

Lienhardt et al. [7] propose a new component model cast as a conservative extension of the concurrent modeling language ABS. The model is able to describe the structural as well as the behavioral aspects of components, while staying close to a standard OO language. The model is simpler and easier to use than competing approaches, which, together with its formal semantics, makes it amenable to automated analysis. A number of important properties follow directly from the formal semantics.

Merten et al. [8] combine two separate approaches: first, a dependency relation between method calls and potential call parameter changes is constructed by an analysis of the signatures augmented by black-box testing. This information is used to automatize the construction of mappers (from abstract to concrete queries) in an automata-based learner. The point of this construction is to exploit a syntactic, imprecise dependency analysis to automatize the building of an accurate method that is able to learn system behavior.

Poetzsch et al. [10] present an approach to verify backward compatibility of a component with respect to the system behavior. The goal is to check whether a replacement component maintains backward compatibility in an application where components mediate between an environment input layer (e.g., user or sensor input) and a process layer computing a response. Backward compatibility is defined precisely in such a context where all components are formally specified on the basis of the abstract modeling language ABS. Checking backward compatibility/trace equivalence is done after a translation from ABS into component transition systems (CTS).

Zech et al. [11] propose a generic framework for model-based regression testing which is particularly useful to efficiently guarantee correctness of evolving software systems already in early development stages. They take a tool-centric perspective and extend the MoVe modeling framework with generic means for regression test selection and planning. The approach is evaluated using different UML testing profile showing its general applicability.

References

1. Bodden, E., Follner, A., Rasthofer, S.: Challenges in Defining a Programming Language for Provably Correct Dynamic Analyses. In: Margaria, T., Steffen, B. (eds.) ISoLA 2012, Part I. LNCS, vol. 7609, pp. 4–18. Springer, Heidelberg (2012)
2. Bosch, J., Eklund, U.: Eternal Embedded Software: Towards Innovation Experiment Systems. In: Margaria, T., Steffen, B. (eds.) ISoLA 2012, Part I. LNCS, vol. 7609, pp. 19–31. Springer, Heidelberg (2012)
3. Cheng, B.H.C., de Lemos, R., Giese, H., Inverardi, P., Magee, J., Andersson, J., Becker, B., Bencomo, N., Brun, Y., Cukic, B., Di Marzo Serugendo, G., Dustdar, S., Finkelstein, A., Gacek, C., Geihs, K., Grassi, V., Karsai, G., Kienle, H.M., Kramer, J., Litoiu, M., Malek, S., Mirandola, R., Müller, H.A., Park, S., Shaw, M., Tichy, M., Tivoli, M., Weyns, D., Whittle, J.: Software Engineering for Self-Adaptive Systems: A Research Roadmap. In: Cheng, B.H.C., de Lemos, R., Giese, H., Inverardi, P., Magee, J. (eds.) Self-Adaptive Systems. LNCS, vol. 5525, pp. 1–26. Springer, Heidelberg (2009)
4. Hähnle, R., Schaefer, I.: A Liskov Principle for Delta-Oriented Programming. In: Margaria, T., Steffen, B. (eds.) ISoLA 2012, Part I. LNCS, vol. 7609, pp. 32–46. Springer, Heidelberg (2012)
5. Lamprecht, A.-L., Margaria, T.: Scientific Workflows: Eternal Components, Changing Interfaces, Varying Compositions. In: Margaria, T., Steffen, B. (eds.) ISoLA 2012, Part I. LNCS, vol. 7609, pp. 47–63. Springer, Heidelberg (2012)
6. Lehman, M.M.: Software's future: Managing evolution. IEEE Software 15(1), 40–44 (1998)
7. Lienhardt, M., Bravetti, M., Sangiorgi, D.: An Object Group-Based Component Model. In: Margaria, T., Steffen, B. (eds.) ISoLA 2012, Part I. LNCS, vol. 7609, pp. 64–78. Springer, Heidelberg (2012)
8. Merten, M., Howar, F., Steffen, B., Pellicione, P., Tivoli, M.: Automated Inference of Models for Black Box Systems Based on Interface Descriptions. In: Margaria, T., Steffen, B. (eds.) ISoLA 2012, Part I. LNCS, vol. 7609, pp. 79–96. Springer, Heidelberg (2012)
9. Parnas, D.: Software aging. In: ICSE, pp. 279–287 (1994)
10. Poetzsch-Heffter, A., Feller, C., Kurnia, I.W., Welsch, Y.: Model-based Compatibility Checking of System Modifications. In: Margaria, T., Steffen, B. (eds.) ISoLA 2012, Part I. LNCS, vol. 7609, pp. 97–111. Springer, Heidelberg (2012)
11. Zech, P., Felderer, M., Kalb, P., Breu, R.: A Generic Platform for Model-Based Regression Testing. In: Margaria, T., Steffen, B. (eds.) ISoLA 2012, Part I. LNCS, vol. 7609, pp. 112–126. Springer, Heidelberg (2012)

Challenges in Defining a Programming Language for Provably Correct Dynamic Analyses

Eric Bodden, Andreas Follner*, and Siegfried Rasthofer**

Secure Software Engineering Group
European Center for Security and Privacy by Design (EC SPRIDE)
Technische Universität Darmstadt

Abstract. Modern software systems are not only famous for being ubiquitous and large scale but also infamous for being inherently insecure. We argue that a large part of this problem is due to the fact that current programming languages do not provide adequate built-in support for addressing security concerns.

In this work we outline the challenges involved in developing CODANA, a novel programming language for defining provably correct dynamic analyses. CODANA analyses form security monitors; they allow programmers to proactively protect their programs from security threats such as insecure information flows, buffer overflows and access-control violations. We plan to design CODANA in such a way that program analyses will be simple to write, read and prove correct, easy to maintain and reuse, efficient to compile, easy to parallelize, and maximally amenable to static optimizations. This is difficult as, nevertheless, CODANA must comprise sufficiently expressive language constructs to cover a large class of security-relevant dynamic analyses.

For deployed programs, we envision CODANA-based analyses to be the last line of defense against malicious attacks. It is hence paramount to provide correctness guarantees on CODANA-based analyses as well as the related program instrumentation and static optimizations.

A further challenge is effective but provably correct sharing: dynamic analyses can benefit from sharing information among another. We plan to encapsulate such shared information within CODANA program fragments.

Keywords: Runtime verification, inline reference monitors, code synthesis, declarative programming languages, information flow, buffer overflows.

1   Introduction

Modern software systems are ubiquitous and often large scale, however many such systems are also inherently insecure. A large part of this problem is caused by the fact that currently programmers are forced to implement security features

---

* At the time of writing, Andreas Follner was with the Technikum Wien.
** At the time of writing, Siegfried Rasthofer was with the Universität Passau.

T. Margaria and B. Steffen (Eds.): ISoLA 2012, Part I, LNCS 7609, pp. 4–18, 2012.
© Springer-Verlag Berlin Heidelberg 2012

using general-purpose programming languages. While during the requirements elicitation phase of the software development process, software architects formulate security requirements rather concisely on a high level of abstraction, this simplicity becomes lost as appropriate security checks are implemented using generic low-level programming-language constructs.

As an example, consider the same-origin policy, an important security policy in web-based scripting languages such as JavaScript and ActionScript:

> "An origin is defined by the scheme, host, and port of a URL. Generally speaking, documents retrieved from distinct origins are isolated from each other." [35]

The same-origin policy can be concisely and precisely defined in a few paragraphs of English text. Implementing enforcement of the same-origin policy, however, is a whole different story, as is evident by a former violation of the same policy in WebKit [3], the rendering engine used in the Chrome [1] and Safari [2] browsers. Listing 1 shows change set 52401 in WebKit, which fixes a vulnerability that allowed for violations of the same-origin policy. The change comprises a single character; building WebKit involves downloading a software development kit of several gigabytes.[1]

This example shows the challenges involved with implementing security policies in large-scale software systems. Ideally, programming languages would allow for definitions of security policies at a high level and in a modular fashion, and implement the enforcement of those policies through automatic means. Today's reality, however, are low-level security checks in general-purpose languages, written and maintained by hand. The checks are scattered throughout the program, which makes them hard to trace and maintain. Moreover, they are tangled to the program's base functionality.

In this work we outline the challenges involved in developing CODANA, a novel programming language with which we try to rectify some of those problems. CODANA has the goal to be a language for defining provably correct dynamic analyses for security purposes. In this setting, dynamic analyses effectively form security monitors. Thus, they allow programmers to proactively protect their programs from security threats such as insecure information flows, buffer overflows and access-control violations. Opposed to design-time analyses, CODANA-based analyses are meant to remain a part of the program even after deployment; they form an essential security-critical part of the program.

```
1 - if(protocolIsJavaScript(url) ||
2 + if(!protocolIsJavaScript(url) ||
3      ScriptController::isSafeScript(newFrame) {
```

Listing 1. Fix for bug 30660 in WebKit (violation of same-origin policy)

---

[1] Building WebKit: http://www.webkit.org/building/checkout.html

CODANA is not a general-purpose programming language. Instead, we envision functional concerns of programs to be written in a "base language" such as Java or C/C++. CODANA-based analyses then uses aspect-oriented programming techniques to augment those base programs with instrumentation to fulfill the stated security goals.

At the time of writing, the language design for CODANA has not yet been fixed. In this paper we outline the challenges involved in designing such a language. We plan to design CODANA in such a way that program analyses will be simple to write, read and prove correct, easy to maintain and reuse, efficient to compile, easy to parallelize, and maximally amenable to static optimizations. On the other hand, CODANA must comprise sufficiently expressive language constructs to cover a large class of security-relevant dynamic analyses.

Dynamic analyses expressed in the CODANA language are not just supposed to be used to determine whether or not a program fulfills its security guarantees, but rather to implement security features that will establish those guarantees. A formerly insecure program hence becomes secure by augmenting it with dynamic analyses formulated in CODANA. This programming paradigm requires that dynamic analyses be efficient enough to actually remain part of the program even after deployment time. We hence plan to include a wide range of domain-specific static optimizations that restrict runtime checks to a necessary minimum.

In such deployed programs, CODANA-based analyses are likely to be the last line of defense against malicious attacks. It is hence paramount to provide correctness guarantees on CODANA-based analyses as well as the related program instrumentation and static optimizations.

A further challenge is effective but provably correct sharing and reuse: dynamic analyses can benefit from sharing information among another. We plan to encapsulate such shared information within reusable CODANA fragments. This fosters reuse of both CODANA implementations and correctness proofs.

To summarize, this paper provides the following original contributions:

- an outline of the challenges in designing a language for correct dynamic analyses,
- an outline of the impact of the language design on static optimizations to speed up those analyses,
- an outline of the requirements for providing correctness guarantees, and
- an outline of the potential for reuse of dynamic-analysis definitions.

The remainder of this paper is structured as follows. In Section 2, we discuss the trade-offs involved in CODANA's language design. Section 3 provides details about our envisioned static optimizations. Section 4 outlines the challenges involved in providing correctness proofs and guarantees. We discuss our plan to support sharing, reuse and extensions in Section 5. Section 6 discusses related work. We conclude in Section 7.

2   Dynamic Analysis

We next explain the challenges involved in designing a programming language for security-related dynamic analyses. First, one may ask why we opt at all to counter malicious attacks through dynamic and not static program analyses. The problem is that static-analysis tools are always limited in precision, as they have to make coarse-grain assumptions about the way a program is used, and which input a program is provided. In addition, all interesting static-analysis problems are inherently undecidable. In result, analysis result will always be approximate, which leaves static-analysis designers two options: design the analysis to be overly pessimistic or optimistic. An optimistic analysis would not be a viable option in a security-sensitive setting, as it would allow a potentially large class of malicious attacks to go unnoticed. A pessimistic static analysis, however, runs risk of generating false warnings. Such false warnings are a burden to the programmers, who are often under time pressure and have insufficient resources at their disposal to manually tell apart false warnings from actual vulnerabilities.

For those reasons, we base our approach primarily on dynamic runtime analysis. With a dynamic analysis, we can actually guarantee to detect certain classes of vulnerabilities without false warnings and without missed violations. For deployed programs, we envision CODANA-based analyses to be the last line of defense against malicious attacks. The analyses will identify vulnerabilities just in time, as they are about to be exploited. This allows the program to induce countermeasures to prevent the exploit from succeeding.

We would like CODANA-based analyses to be able to detect and mitigate different kinds of attacks, such as attacks based on buffer overflows, insecure information flows and cross-site scripting, circumvention of access control, exploitation of leaked capabilities, and side channels such as timing channels. To this end, CODANA needs to support various language features. To identify buffer-overflows, one must be able to reason about numeric values and operations, as well as pointer assignments. Insecure information flows and cross-site scripting vulnerabilities can only be identified if the sources of sensitive information are known and if values assigned from those sources can be tracked trough all possible program operations. Access-control and object-capabilities require an analysis to be able to associate state with objects. Timing channels require an analysis to reason about real-time data.

In the following, we explain some of those requirements in more detail by given two examples: the detection of buffer overflows and a mechanism for enforcing access control. The reliable detection of buffer overflows during runtime could be realized by comparing the lengths of the buffers right before a vulnerable function like `strcpy` is called.

Listing 2 shows what language constructs in CODANA could look like that could support such a use case. We here use a syntax roughly based on a related static-analysis approach by Le and Soffa [28]. Anytime the `strcpy` function is called, the CODANA program compares the lengths of the two parameters and, in case the length of the source buffer exceeds the length of the destination buffer, raises a violation. To support the user with a concise syntax, the language

```
1 Buffer a,b;
2 at 'strcpy(a,b)' if len(a) < len(b) violation(a)
3 violation(Buffer a) {
4   print("buffer overflow detected in variable " +
5   name(a) + " at " + location); }
```

Listing 2. Detecting buffer overflows with CODANA (based on [28])

will provide built-in constructs such as len, which represents the length of a selected buffer, and location, which represents the current code location. Most of
those constructs will require runtime support. For instance, to be able to tell the
length of a buffer, the CODANA runtime must track this value in the first place.
We plan to provide the necessary program instrumentation through technologies from aspect-oriented programming [27]. The difference between CODANA
and general-purpose aspect-oriented programming languages is that CODANA
requires a more fine-grained approach. For instance, languages like AspectJ [8]
allow users to instrument calls to methods and assignments to fields but not
assignments between local variables. In this respect, CODANA can be seen as a
domain-specific aspect language, for the domain of security monitoring.

As another example of a use case that we envision the CODANA language to
support, consider the problem of access control. To this end, we plan to have
CODANA support specially associative arrays[2] that can be used to keep track of
a user's authorizations.

Listing 3 shows how one could use an enum construct and associative arrays to
model a dynamic analysis detecting access violations. In the security community,
such dynamic analyses are frequently called security automata [33] or inline
reference monitors [23]. Lines 1–2 define two different classes of internal states
that we use to keep track of whether a user is currently logged in and whether
or not the user has been granted access to a given file. Note that we include such
constructs for modeling finite states on purpose. We plan to conduct effective,
domains-specific optimizations to CODANA programs (see Section 3), and those
are easier to conduct when data structures are known to be finite. In lines 4–5,
we use two associative arrays to map users and files to their respective states.
Note that often one will encounter situations in which states must be associated
with combinations of objects such as in line 5, where we associate a state with
a user and file. Line 7 defines local variables u and f. The remainder of the code
uses those typed variables as place holders for runtime objects. Lines 9–12 define
four rules (or pieces of advice) to update the security monitor's state based on a
range of concrete program events. Lines 9–12 define an error handler. Whenever
the underlying program calls the method fgets, we check whether the third
argument, the file f, may be accessed by user u, who is fetched from the current
context.

---

[2] An associative array is an array that can be indexed not just by numbers but by
objects. Although associative array appears syntactically just as normal arrays, they
are typically implemented through map data structures.

```
1  enum LoginState { LOGGED_OUT, LOGGED_IN }
2  enum Access { GRANTED, FORBIDDEN }
3
4  LoginState[User] loginState = LOGGED_OUT;
5  Access[User,File] access = FORBIDDEN;
6
7  User u, File f;
8
9  after 'u=login()' loginState[u] = LOGGED_IN;
10 after 'logout(u)' loginState[u] = LOGGED_OUT;
11 after 'grantAccess(u,f)' access[u,f] = GRANTED;
12 after 'revokeAccess(u,f)' access[u,f] = FORBIDDEN;
13
14 at 'fgets(*,*,f)' with 'u=curr_user()'
15   if loginState[u] != LOGGED_IN ||
16     access[u,f] != GRANTED violation(u,f);
```

Listing 3. Access control with CODANA

Expressiveness vs. Simplicity. We plan to design CODANA in such a way that it is not only simple to use, but also is amenable to correctness proofs and static optimizations. Efficiency is a big concern for CODANA. If no due care is taken, dynamic analysis can slow down a program's execution considerably [14,19]. This calls for a language design that focuses on simplicity. The simpler the language constructs that CODANA supports the easier it will be, both for compilers and for programmers, to prove properties about CODANA-based analyses. Frequently found features in general-purpose programming languages that cause problems for static analyses are infinite state, pointers and aliasing, loops and recursion as well as exceptions. While it may be necessary for CODANA to comprise some of those features, we plan to thoroughly investigate, which features to include, and how to make programmers aware of the performance or maintenance penalties that their use may entail.

Use of infinite state could be excluded or at least discouraged by supporting language constructs like enum, which we mentioned above. Aliasing could be excluded by adapting a pass-by-value semantics for variables. In general, this may increase analysis runtime, as every assignment entails a deep copy. However, static optimizations could counter this effect. Loops could at least be restricted to bounded *for-each*-style loops. Recursion at this point seems unnecessary to include in CODANA altogether.

Another important matter is concurrency. On the one hand, we wish to include constructs that enable CODANA to detect data races [16,17]. On the other hand, our own data structures need to be thread safe, and preferably, for performance reasons, lock-free as well. We plan to design and implement such data structures in the back-end of CODANA, e.g. to implement runtime support for associative arrays.

3   Static Optimization

We envision CODANA to be used to secure end-user programs that are deployed at the user's site. But dynamic program analysis often requires an extensive amount of program instrumentation, which can slow down the analyzed program considerably [14, 19]. The fact that CODANA will support the analysis of data-centric information flows (information-flow analysis) such as insecure information flows or access-control violations yields CODANA programs that have to track a considerable amount of runtime information. Much of the overhead is attributable to the fact that each variable could track different data-centric or security-centric information. To improve the dynamic analysis, we and others have shown in the past that a static analysis can be very effective in speeding up dynamic analyses [15–17, 19, 22, 36]. These approaches, also frequently called hybrid program analyses, usually build on the idea of only instrumenting certain program parts, while at the same time proving that instrumentation of other parts of the program is unnecessary: monitoring those program parts would have no effect on the outcome of the dynamic analysis. Those parts are identified in advance, through static analysis of the program to be monitored with respect to the definition of the dynamic analysis. The static analysis is used to eliminate useless instrumentations which causes a reduction of events dispatched to the dynamic-analysis code, hence reducing its evaluation time. In the past, we have also applied proof techniques to formally show that our static optimizations are correct, i.e., that they do not change the outcome of the dynamic analyses [14, 15]. So far, this approach is based on control-flow analysis, but we plan to extend the approach to information-flow analysis as well.

Let's consider a simple data-centric policy rule which is efficiently enforced by a typestate analysis as described in [14]. The data-centric policy is a modified version of the secure coding guideline *Sanitize the Output* taken from Aderhold et. al [4]. Figure 1 shows the simplified taint-flow finite-state machine which could be used as a runtime monitor for the detection of Cross-Side-Scripting attacks. In CODANA, such state machines could be expressed via enums, such as shown in Listing 3.

This finite-state machine contains three different states whereas s_0 and s_1 are security-irrelevant states, whereas the *error* state symbols a policy violation (Cross-Side-Scripting attack). There are also three different kind of events (*tainted*, *untainted* and *output*) which get activated by different program statements. For example, the event *tainted* gets activated by $_GET['tainted_data'], the *untainted* event by statements which assign definitely untainted values and the *output* event is activated if the data leaks from the program, for instance when data is printed to the browser.

An information-flow analysis would associate such a state machine with each tracked variable. Each variable starts in the initial state (s_0) and performs a transition corresponding to the activated event. Listing 4 shows an example with tainted and untainted data and also one security-relevant flow along line 1 → line 5 → line 7, which could allow a Cross-Side-Scripting attack. With the tracking of the different security events and the corresponding transitions in the

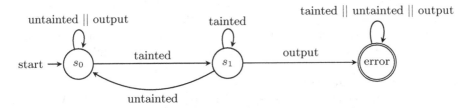

Fig. 1. Simple taint-flow finite-state machine for the prevention of Cross-Side-Scripting attacks

finite-state machine, the analysis is able to identify this kind of attack if one of the variables reaches an error state.

A general, un-optimized dynamical-analysis approach would instrument each assignment, as shown in 4. In this example, however, the instrumentation of the untainted variable *$number* is completely unnecessary: on this variable, no taint violations can take place, and hence the analysis would never report taint violations on this variable. A static information-flow analysis, executed in advance, would allow the CODANA compiler to omit instrumentation for this variable from the dynamic analysis. The result after applying the static analysis and optimization is shown in Listing 5.

```
1  $input1 = $_GET['tainted_data'];
2    makeTransition(input1, tainted);
3  $number = 1;
4    makeTransition(number,
            untainted);
5  $input2 = $input1;
6    propagateTaint(input1, input2);
7  echo($input2);
8    makeTransition(input2, output);
9  echo($number);
10   makeTransition(number, output);
```

```
1  $input1 = $_GET['tainted_data'];
2    makeTransition(input1, tainted);
3  $number = 1;
4  $input2 = $input1;
5    propagateTaint(input1, input2);
6  echo($input2);
7    makeTransition(input2, output);
8  echo($number);
```

Listing 4. Example exposing a Cross-Side-Scripting attack without static optimization

Listing 5. Example exposing a Cross-Side-Scripting attack with static optimization

A significant challenge to such static optimizations are multi-threaded programs. For such programs, multiple control-flows can be interleaved. In consequence, a single control-flow graph is not sufficient to simulate all possible control flows. Moreover, the analysis state quickly grows due to the many possible different schedules that static analyses need to simulate. Many existing whole-program analysis (including some of our own previous work [14]) ignore this problem. A promising escape route are flow-insensitive analyses [19]. Such analyses do not at all take the program's control-flow into account. Because of this, the analyses are, by design, agnostic to the different possible schedules. At the same time, such analyses can be implemented quite efficiently.

We hence plan to follow a staged analysis approach that applies relatively inexpensive flow-insensitive analysis first. As we observed in previous work [19], such analyses can often optimize away already a significant amount of program optimization. We then execute more expensive, potentially thread-aware, flow-sensitive analyses only to such parts of the program in which instrumentation remains after the first analysis stages have been applied.

But multi-threading is not just an annoyance but can also be of help. We plan to investigate to what extent our static-analysis algorithms can be designed to exploit parallelism. Rodriguez and Lhoták have recently shown [31] that such an approach promises significant speed-ups. In addition, parts of the CODANA runtime could be designed to support executing the dynamic analysis in separate threads.

4   Correctness

Dynamic analyses based on CODANA will usually be able to detect bugs and vulnerabilities just as they are about to be exploited. Because of this, the analyses are practically the program's last line of defense. It is hence paramount that analyses written in CODANA be reliable. We plan to prove the correctness of CODANA programs on several levels.

One threat to the correctness of CODANA-based analyses are the static optimizations that we apply. In previous work we have demonstrated how a proof technique based on so-called continuation-equivalent analysis configurations can be used to prove the correctness of such optimizations [15]. In a nutshell, one must prove that if a static optimization removes instrumentation at a statement s, then all possible analysis configurations before and after s must be equivalent with respect to all possible continuations of the control flow that follow s. If they are equivalent, then this means that dynamically executing the instrumentation at s would have no effect, and hence it is sound to omit the instrumentation at this statement. In the past, we have used this approach to prove the correctness of a flow-sensitive static typestate-analysis [13, 14]. This process also revealed bugs in previous approaches [20, 30]. For CODANA, we plan to extend this approach to other classes of static optimizations for dynamic analyses.

CODANA programs consist mainly of program instrumentation and accesses to a runtime library, both of which need to adhere to correctness guarantees. In recent work, we have developed a clean semantics for weaving of aspect-oriented code into Java programs [25]. We assume to be able to reuse some of the results to prove that our instrumentation preserves the behavior of the instrumented program. A challenge in this area are race conditions and side-channel attacks. As the instrumentation caused by our dynamic analysis causes the program to slow down, this may cause certain race conditions or certain information leaks, e.g., through timing channels to disappear due to this slow-down. Such so-called "Heisenbugs" are a general problem in dynamic analysis that cannot be solved without specific modifications to the program's scheduler. Essential parts of CODANA's runtime library could be proven correct through tool-assisted functional-correctness proofs [37].

We plan to aid programmers in proving the correctness of analyses formulated in CODANA. Given a high-level security property, programmers should be able to argue why a given CODANA program establishes this property. To this end, we first plan to keep the language itself as simple as possible (see Section 2), but also plan to include a standard library with CODANA code templates. Along with those templates, we can provide example proofs that prove important properties about those templates. Ideally, those proofs could then be composed to a correctness proof for a CODANA program that uses the respective code templates.

5   Reuse, Sharing and Composition

In the previous section, we have already explained the advantages of a standard library for CODANA programs. In addition to this kind of reuse, we still plan to support reuse on other levels.

For instance, a common use case will be that programs execute augmented not with only one single dynamic analysis but with multiple ones. For instance, one may want to secure a program against information-flow violations and buffer overflows at the same time. Both of those information need to track assignments to certain classes of variables. When both analyses are performed at the same time, it is hence advisable to share information among those analyses. This sharing must be correct, however, it must not lead to unintentional alterations of the analysis information.

There are multiple ways to implement such information sharing. A simple way would be to provide certain common analysis elements as parts of the CODANA runtime library. If multiple analyses include the same elements and are executed at the same time, then this could lead to automatic sharing. A drawback of this approach is that we as CODANA designers must be able to anticipate common use cases for sharing to provide them in such a library. Another, more sophisticated approach, could try to identify the potential for information sharing irrespective of the origin of the analysis code. Such an approach would require a sophisticated analysis of the CODANA programs. In recent work, we have outlined the challenges that arise from composing instrumentations for multiple dynamic analyses [7].

Many of our static analyses and optimizations, although domain specific, may have parts that are reusable also for other static-analysis problems. We plan to encapsulate those analyses such that they can be reused by others. In the past, we have made accessible static analyses through simple domain-specific extensions to AspectJ [16–18, 21]. A similar approach could be taken also in this project.

In addition, we plan to open our compiler implementation up to others. That way, other researchers could extend CODANA with additional language constructs or different static optimizations, such as we and others have previously done with AspectJ [10]. In the past, we have developed the Clara framework, which is explicitly designed to allow analysis extensions by others [18, 21].

6   Related Work

One of the most closely related projects is ConSpec [6], another formal specification language for security policies. As we propose for CODANA, also ConSpec
supports advice-like before/after blocks that allow users to update a finite set of
state variables. ConSpec allows for the definition of two different entities, called
policies and *contracts*, both of which are defined manually by the user and are
written in the ConSpec language. Contracts are application specific and describe
the kinds of security properties that an application guarantees. Contracts can
be checked against applications through a translation into Spec# [11] and subsequent static verification [5]. Policies are more general than contracts. They are
specific with respect to an execution environment, e.g., a device on which the
program is to be executed. ConSpec assumes that both policies and contracts are
finite-state, which allows ConSpec to use simple algorithms for deciding regular-
language inclusion to decide whether a contract complies with a policy. Further,
ConSpec allows the monitoring of policies against applications, either through
an external monitor or through an inline reference monitor [23]. We believe that
the distinction between policy and contract is an interesting and valuable one.
Similar concepts may be useful also for CODANA. On the other hand, CODANA
will go much beyond what is supported by ConSpec, in that it will allow the
generation runtime monitors that are statically optimized, and nevertheless will
provide language constructs like associative arrays, which go beyond finite state.
In previous work, we have developed Join Point Interfaces [24, 25], a mechanism
to establish clean interfaces for aspect-oriented programs. Those interfaces currently focus on establishing the ability to type-check aspects independent of the
base program's code. It may be useful to combine mechanisms of those join point
interfaces with some of those of ConSpec within CODANA to achieve a separation
between policies and contracts.

Le and Soffa present a generative approach that has some similarity to
CODANA [28]. The approach provides a domain-specific specification language
for program analyses. In the case of Le and Soffa, however, this approach is
restricted to purely static analyses. Programmers can use the language to define how static-analysis information needs to be updated at particular classes of
statements, and which conditions on the analysis information signal property violations. Based on the specification, the approach then automatically generates
an appropriate flow-sensitive and path-sensitive static analysis for C/C++ programs. The authors demonstrate the efficacy of their approach by implementing
analyses to detect buffer overflows, integer violations, null-pointer de-references
and memory leaks. Our approach will provide a language that may have similarities with what Le and Soffa propose. However, due to the fact that we focus
on dynamic analysis, we may be able to provide certain language features that
static analyses cannot provide, and vice versa. Moreover, we plan to not focus
on C/C++ programs but rather on an intermediate representation that allows
us to instrument and analyze programs written in a range of different languages.

DiSL, a domain-specific language for bytecode instrumentation by Marek et
al., is another very related project [29]. DiSL is currently implemented not as a

programming language with own, domain-specific syntax, but rather as a set of annotations and conventions over syntactic constructs defined in pure Java. Using DiSL, programmers can define pieces of advice to be applied before or after certain sequences of Java bytecode. DiSL further provides convenience methods for accessing elements on the stack or from other parts of the execution context. As DiSL programs are compiled, accesses to those methods are then automatically replaced by low-level (stack) operations. One important advantage of DiSL over other instrumentation tools is that DiSL allows for the uniform instrumentation of *entire* Java programs, including relevant parts of the Java runtime library. CODANA differs from DiSL in that it will provide domain-specific programming constructs with a simple and well-defined semantics. The intricacies of bytecode instrumentation will be hidden from the user. This not only suggests that CODANA programs may be easier to read and understand that programs written in DiSL, but also that they are more amenable to static optimizations. It may be interesting, though, for CODANA to use DiSL as a back-end instrumentation technology, and we are currently discussing this opportunity with the developers of DiSL.

In the past, the first author has developed the Clara [18, 21] framework for static typestate analysis. Similar to the approach we propose here, also Clara uses static optimizations to speed up dynamic analyses. Also Clara provides a domain-specific aspect language for this purpose. In contrast to CODANA, however, Clara is restricted to finite-state runtime monitors, and hence only supports static typestate analyses. While CODANA will reuse some ideas of Clara, in this paper we showed that implementing a language such as CODANA comes with many challenges that go beyond our previous experience with Clara.

Austin and Flanagan present a purely dynamic information-flow analysis for JavaScript. Their approach "detects problems with implicit paths via a dynamic check that avoids the need for an approximate static analyses while still guaranteeing non-interference" [9]. We plan to investigate whether we can use similar tricks in our implementation of CODANA. Zhivich et al. compare seven different dynamic-analysis tools for buffer overflows [38]. XSS-Guard [12] by Bisht and Venkatakrishnan is a dynamic approach for detecting cross-site scripting attacks. The approached is based on a learning strategy; it learns the set of scripts that a web application can create for any given HTML request. This is different from CODANA in that it gathers information among multiple program runs. We will investigate whether such an extension of the scope of CODANA can be of more general use. Vogt et al. [34] implement a hybrid dynamic/static analysis to find cross-site scripting vulnerabilities. Interestingly, they use static analysis not to enhance efficiency, but to detect attacks that through a purely dynamic analysis may go unnoticed. We plan to investigate whether such analyses would be useful to have within CODANA.

Jones and Kelly propose an approach to dynamically enforce array bounds through the use of a table which holds information about all valid storage elements [26]. The table is used to map a pointer to a descriptor of the object to which it points, which contains its base and extent. To determine whether an address computed off an in-bounds pointer is in bounds, the checker locates the referent object by comparing the pointer with the base and size information stored in the table. Then it checks if the new address falls within the extent of the referent object. The authors implemented their bounds checking scheme in the GNU C compiler (GCC), where it intercepts all object creation, address manipulation and de-reference operations and replaces them with their own routines. A problem observed with their approach is that it sometimes incorrectly crashes working code and that it considerably slows down program execution. Ruwase and Lam took the basic concepts, improved them and created CRED (C Range Error Detector) [32], which eradicated mentioned problems. We will investigate if some of the basic ideas used in either of the approaches could be adapted for CODANA.

7   Conclusion

We have presented a range of important design decisions involving the development of CODANA, a novel programming language for correct dynamic analysis. Challenges arise in the areas of dynamic analysis, static optimization, correctness, as well as reuse, information sharing and analysis composition. CODANA has the goal to allow programmers to write dynamic program analyses that will be simple to write, read and prove correct, easy to maintain and reuse, efficient to compile, easy to parallelize, and maximally amenable to static optimizations. We have explained how we wish to achieve those goals, and which implications those goals will probably have on the language design.

Acknowledgements. This work was supported by the Deutsche Forschungsgemeinschaft within the project RUNSECURE, by the German Federal Ministry of Education and Research (BMBF) within EC SPRIDE and by the Hessian LOEWE excellence initiative within CASED. We thank Andreas Sewe, Walter Binder and Mira Mezini for discussions and suggestions on the topics presented in this paper.

References

1. Chrome Browser, https://www.google.com/chrome
2. Safari Browser, http://www.apple.com/safari/
3. The WebKit Open-Source Project, http://www.webkit.org/
4. Aderhold, M., Cuéllar, J., Mantel, H., Sudbrock, H.: Exemplary formalization of secure coding guidelines. Technical Report TUD-CS-2010-0060, TU Darmstadt, Germany (2010)
5. Aktug, I., Gurov, D., Piessens, F., Seehusen, F., Vanoverberghe, D., Vétillard, E.: Static analysis algorithms and tools for code-contract compliance, Public Deliverable D3.1.2, S3MS (2006), http://s3ms.org
6. Aktug, I., Naliuka, K.: ConSpec–a formal language for policy specification. Electronic Notes in Theoretical Computer Science 197(1), 45–58 (2008)

7. Ansaloni, D., Binder, W., Bockisch, C., Bodden, E., Hatun, K., Marek, L., Qi, Z., Sarimbekov, A., Sewe, A., Tůma, P., Zheng, Y.: Challenges for Refinement and Composition of Instrumentations: Position Paper. In: Gschwind, T., De Paoli, F., Gruhn, V., Book, M. (eds.) SC 2012. LNCS, vol. 7306, pp. 86–96. Springer, Heidelberg (2012)

8. The Aspect J. home page (2003)

9. Austin, T.H., Flanagan, C.: Efficient purely-dynamic information flow analysis. In: Proceedings of the ACM SIGPLAN Fourth Workshop on Programming Languages and Analysis for Security, PLAS 2009, pp. 113–124. ACM, New York (2009)

10. Avgustinov, P., Christensen, A.S., Hendren, L., Kuzins, S., Lhoták, J., Lhoták, O., de Moor, O., Sereni, D., Sittampalam, G., Tibble, J.: Abc: an extensible aspectj compiler. In: Proceedings of the 4th International Conference on Aspect-Oriented Software Development, AOSD 2005, pp. 87–98. ACM, New York (2005)

11. Barnett, M., Leino, K., Schulte, W.: The spec# programming system: An overview. Construction and analysis of safe, secure, and interoperable smart devices, 49–69 (2005)

12. Bisht, P., Venkatakrishnan, V.: Xss-guard: precise dynamic prevention of cross-site scripting attacks. Detection of Intrusions and Malware, and Vulnerability Assessment, 23–43 (2008)

13. Bodden, E.: Verifying finite-state properties of large-scale programs. PhD thesis, McGill University, Available in print through ProQuest (June 2009)

14. Bodden, E.: Efficient hybrid typestate analysis by determining continuation-equivalent states. In: Proceedings of the 32nd ACM/IEEE International Conference on Software Engineering ICSE 2010, vol. 1, pp. 5–14. ACM, New York (2010)

15. Bodden, E.: Continuation equivalence: a correctness criterion for static optimizations of dynamic analyses. In: WODA 2011: International Workshop on Dynamic Analysis, pp. 24–28. ACM (July 2011)

16. Bodden, E., Havelund, K.: Racer: Effective race detection using AspectJ. In: International Symposium on Software Testing and Analysis (ISSTA 2008), Seattle, WA, pp. 155–165. ACM, New York (2008)

17. Bodden, E., Havelund, K.: Aspect-oriented race detection in Java. IEEE Transactions on Software Engineering (TSE) 36(4), 509–527 (2010)

18. Bodden, E., Hendren, L.: The Clara framework for hybrid typestate analysis. International Journal on Software Tools for Technology Transfer (STTT), 1–20 (2010)

19. Bodden, E., Hendren, L., Lhoták, O.: A Staged Static Program Analysis to Improve the Performance of Runtime Monitoring. In: Bateni, M. (ed.) ECOOP 2007. LNCS, vol. 4609, pp. 525–549. Springer, Heidelberg (2007)

20. Bodden, E., Lam, P., Hendren, L.: Finding programming errors earlier by evaluating runtime monitors ahead-of-time. In: 16th ACM SIGSOFT International Symposium on Foundations of Software Engineering (SIGSOFT 2008/FSE-16), pp. 36–47. ACM, New York (2008)

21. Bodden, E., Lam, P., Hendren, L.: Clara: A Framework for Partially Evaluating Finite-State Runtime Monitors Ahead of Time. In: Barringer, H., Falcone, Y., Finkbeiner, B., Havelund, K., Lee, I., Pace, G., Roşu, G., Sokolsky, O., Tillmann, N. (eds.) RV 2010. LNCS, vol. 6418, pp. 183–197. Springer, Heidelberg (2010)

22. Dwyer, M.B., Purandare, R.: Residual dynamic typestate analysis exploiting static analysis: results to reformulate and reduce the cost of dynamic analysis. In: Proceedings of the Twenty-Second IEEE/ACM International Conference on Automated Software Engineering, ASE 2007, pp. 124–133. ACM, New York (2007)

23. Erlingsson, U.: The inlined reference monitor approach to security policy enforcement. PhD thesis, Cornell University (2003)

24. Inostroza, M., Tanter, É., Bodden, E.: Modular reasoning with join point interfaces. Technical Report TUD-CS-2011-0272, CASED (October 2011)
25. Inostroza, M., Tanter, E., Bodden, E.: Join point interfaces for modular reasoning in aspect-oriented programs. In: ESEC/FSE 2011: Joint Meeting of the European Software Engineering Conference and the ACM SIGSOFT Symposium on the Foundations of Software Engineering, pp. 508–511 (2011)
26. Jones, R.W.M., Kelly, P.H.J.: Backwards-compatible bounds checking for arrays and pointers in C programs. In: AADEBUG, pp. 13–26 (1997)
27. Kiczales, G., Lamping, J., Mendhekar, A., Maeda, C., Lopes, C., Loingtier, J., Irwin, J.: Aspect-Oriented Programming. In: Aksit, M., Auletta, V. (eds.) ECOOP 1997. LNCS, vol. 1241, pp. 220–242. Springer, Heidelberg (1997)
28. Le, W., Soffa, M.L.: Generating analyses for detecting faults in path segments. In: Proceedings of the 2011 International Symposium on Software Testing and Analysis, ISSTA 2011, pp. 320–330. ACM, New York (2011)
29. Marek, L., Villazón, A., Zheng, Y., Ansaloni, D., Binder, W., Qi, Z.: Disl: a domain-specific language for bytecode instrumentation. In: AOSD 2012, pp. 239–250. ACM, New York (2012)
30. Naeem, N.A., Lhotak, O.: Typestate-like analysis of multiple interacting objects. In: Proceedings of the 23rd ACM SIGPLAN Conference on Object-Oriented Programming Systems Languages and Applications, OOPSLA 2008, pp. 347–366. ACM, New York (2008)
31. Rodriguez, J., Lhoták, O.: Actor-Based Parallel Dataflow Analysis. In: Knoop, J. (ed.) CC 2011. LNCS, vol. 6601, pp. 179–197. Springer, Heidelberg (2011)
32. Ruwase, O., Lam, M.S.: A practical dynamic buffer overflow detector. In: Proceedings of the 11th Annual Network and Distributed System Security Symposium, pp. 159–169 (2004)
33. Schneider, F.: Enforceable security policies. ACM Transactions on Information and System Security (TISSEC) 3(1), 30–50 (2000)
34. Vogt, P., Nentwich, F., Jovanovic, N., Kirda, E., Kruegel, C., Vigna, G.: Cross-site scripting prevention with dynamic data tainting and static analysis. In: Proceeding of the Network and Distributed System Security Symposium (NDSS), vol. 42 (2007)
35. W3C. Same-Origin Policy, http://www.w3.org/Security/wiki/Same_Origin_Policy
36. Yong, S.H., Horwitz, S.: Using static analysis to reduce dynamic analysis overhead. Form. Methods Syst. Des. 27(3), 313–334 (2005)
37. Zee, K., Kuncak, V., Rinard, M.: Full functional verification of linked data structures. In: PLDI 2008, pp. 349–361. ACM, New York (2008)
38. Zhivich, M., Leek, T., Lippmann, R.: Dynamic buffer overflow detection. In: Workshop on the Evaluation of Software Defect Detection Tools (2005)

Eternal Embedded Software: Towards Innovation Experiment Systems

Jan Bosch and Ulrik Eklund

Chalmers University of Technology
Software Engineering Division, Dept. Computer Science & Engineering
Göteborg, Sweden
`jan.bosch@chalmers.se`

Abstract. The paper discusses the concept of innovation experiment systems in the context of long-lived embedded systems. These systems need to evolve continuously to stay competitive and provide value to the customer and end-user, especially in domains where the pace of change is increasing.

Innovation experiment systems provide a natural mechanism that allows an embedded system, its architecture and underlying platform to continuously evolve in response to changes in the user requirements and system context. It uses a rapid feedback loop to evaluate the benefits of small variations to users with the intent of continuous improvements.

The paper explores the architectural implications as the ability to continuously evolve and conduct experiences in the deployed product context in a safe and controlled manner must be supported by the architecture of the embedded systems.

Finally, the paper illustrates these concepts using a case study concerning an infotainment system in the automotive industry.

Keywords: innovation experiment system, embedded systems, software architecture, automotive software.

1 Introduction

Software has made an amazing journey since its first introduction in the middle of the 20th century. Initially considered as a handy configuration mechanism for electronic systems, it has managed to increasingly become the core of virtually any modern system supporting individuals, companies and entire societies. With the constantly expanding role of software, the lifespan of software systems has extended as well with examples existing where the lifespan of the software is longer than the entire working career of the software developers that initially developed it. This trend occurs not only in the area of information systems, but is starting to become a key challenge for embedded software as well. For the purpose in this paper, there are two main categories of "eternal" embedded software:

The first is infrastructure software, which is completely pervasive today, where the deployment of new systems requires huge investment or effort and therefore

T. Margaria and B. Steffen (Eds.): ISoLA 2012, Part I, LNCS 7609, pp. 19–31, 2012.

occurs very seldom. Examples could be traffic lights in a city, railway signaling, public transport automated ticket systems etc. This category increases since previously "unconnected" systems are becoming software dependent, such as car-to-car and car-to-infrastructure communication.

The second is mass-produced embedded systems, where some domains overlap the first category. Even in the world of fast moving electronics the software platform lives significantly longer than the manufacturing of any individual product, including the microprocessor the software runs on. The extreme example here would be cars, where a single car model could be manufactured for seven years, longer than any CPU, and would have requirements of spare parts availability up to twenty years after the manufacturing has stopped. In many cases the underlying software platform providing end-user functionality evolves beyond the initial purpose, but the services of the platform also reuse existing software from previous product generations.

These kind of systems need to evolve continuously to stay competitive and provide value to the customer and end-user, especially in domains where the pace of change is ever increasing. Whereas earlier this was achieved by period, e.g. yearly, new releases of software, we recognize a trend where continuous testing of new, innovative functionality in deployed systems is increasingly applied in especially on-line, software-as-a-service (SaaS) systems.

In our research, however, we have studied this phenomenon and realized that this can be applied to embedded systems as well and, in fact, allows for significant improvements in the rate of innovation and the ability of systems to adjust to their continuously evolving environment. We refer to this trend as innovation experiment systems (IES) [1].

Common for SaaS software and software in connected embedded systems is that allows for an approach where instead of freezing the requirements before starting product development, the requirements constantly evolve and also affect already deployed systems that are actively used by customers. Consequently, requirements evolve in real-time based on data collected from systems in actual use with customers instead of being frozen early based on the opinions of product management about the likely customer needs 12, 18 or 24 months from now.

The contribution of the paper is a discussion of the concept of innovation experiment systems in the context long-lived embedded systems. In addition, it explores the architectural implications as the ability to continuously evolve and conduct experiences in the actual real setting in a safe and controlled manner must be supported by the architecture of the embedded systems. Finally, it illustrates these concepts using a case study concerning an infotainment system in the automotive industry.

The remainder of the paper is organized as follows. In the next section, we discuss contemporary and future embedded systems. Subsequently, we introduce the concept of innovation experiment systems in more detail. This is followed by a discussion of the application of innovation experiment systems in the embedded systems domain. Then, we present a case study that illustrates the discussed concepts in the context of the automotive domain. Finally, we conclude with a discussion of the relation between innovation experiment systems and "eternal" embedded software and an outline of future work.

2   Characteristics of Current and Future Embedded Systems

It is difficult to identify a single perspective on software development among original equipment manufacturers (OEM) of products with embedded software. The view ranges from focusing on efficient manufacturing of products with the software as difficult necessity to seeing software as a key business differentiator. Software is often an enabler for new innovation in embedded systems, for example in cars [2], and marketed innovative features are often realized by software. One indicator for this is the amount of software is increasing exponentially over time in many embedded domains [4].

A common development approach for embedded systems is using a traditional stage-gate process, where the gates are driven by decisions on investment in the manufacturing of the product, i.e. driven by the hardware, towards a new periodical release. The finalization of software artifacts often correspond to process gate progression, e.g. user requirements, system requirements, software architecture, component requirements, and software implementation, i.e. a waterfall process even if the artifacts are updated as the project progresses.

We define the domain of mass-produced software-intensive embedded systems by four characteristics:

- Deep integration between hardware and software for significant parts of the functionality
- Strong focus on manufacturing aspects of the product in the development (e.g. by development process gates)
- Strong supplier involvement in the form of subcontractors
- Some elements of the system realize safety-critical functionality

Examples of mass-produced embedded products include cars and trucks, washing machines and other home utensils, sewing machines, printers and copying machines [4]. We will give some examples from the automotive industry since cars are arguably the most complex product of this category, both in terms of conflicting requirements and longevity of the platform in production.

Over the last years, cloud computing and SaaS solutions are rapidly becoming the norm and enjoy enormously rapid growth. The key reasons for this include the lower cost for the customer, the simplicity associated with not having to own hardware and the freedom from long-term constraints associated with most licensed software solutions. Interestingly, these benefits extend in part also to software-intensive embedded systems and increasingly companies building connected embedded systems, from mobile phones to cars, are starting to exploit the advantages of frequent, post-deployment updating of software and the collection of usage and other performance data from systems in the field.

3   Concept of Innovation Experiment Systems

Innovation is lifeblood of any organization, but notoriously hard to get right in many companies. Innovation in large organization is often characterized by an enormous imbalance between the number of ideas that, informally or formally, exist in the organization and the number of concepts that are in fact tested with customers. The ratio, depending on the attention the organization puts towards idea generation by its employees, can range from one in a hundred to one in thousands. With that strict selection process and the high cost associated with testing, the importance of selecting the most promising ideas, turning these into concepts and then designing a (prototype) product to test the concept with customers becomes such that it receives significant attention by senior management and many other functions and layers in the organization.

The selection process is, unavoidably, driven by the earlier experiences and beliefs of the people in the selection process. In most organizations, it is the opinions of the more senior persons in the organization that tend to weigh the heaviest. The challenge with this approach is threefold. First, opinions are a very poor substitute for real customer data and the innovation literature has many examples of successful innovations that were resisted for years inside the organization before made successful by a small "skunk works" team working under the radar. Second, even if the organization is sufficiently open minded to explore more innovative ideas and concepts, there is a natural risk avoidance that causes organizations to settle on the safe bets. Human psychology, as has been studied extensively in behavioral economics, experiences a loss much more strongly than it experiences a win, causing a selection process where losses are as much as possible avoided, resulting in mundane innovations. Finally, the demands on the system from its users as well as the overall context in which it operates evolve constantly and this requires continuous validation and experimentation to determine in which direction the system needs to evolve.

The solution is, obviously, to find ways to decrease the dependence on opinions and to increase reliance on real customer or other data. Traditional metrics such as the Net Promoter Score [8] have been used for the last decade or more, but often fail to provide timely feedback during the development process as these are backward looking and focus on the entire product. To collect customer or performance data early in the innovation process, the organization needs to find mechanisms to test more ideas and concepts with customers and in the installed base in real-time and obviously at a much lower cost than earlier. This requires new behaviors at the business level, i.e. involving customers in feature and product concept validation without an, initially clear, business model. Also, it requires changes to the R&D processes as customers need to be involved much earlier and deeper in the R&D process. Finally, this requires changes to the architecture of the products and platforms to facilitate testing versions of screens, components, subsystems and entire products in order to determine customer preference and interest. The mechanisms used for achieving customer involvement and the efficient execution of experiments on the deployed product base depend heavily on the type of experiments, system, stage and purpose.

Connected, software-intensive embedded systems offer a particularly well-suited context for building an innovation experiment system. Connected systems allow for the rapid and low-cost deployment of new functionality. In addition, the collection of customer feedback as well as usage and other performance metrics is simple and the connection to business goals is virtually real-time.

In Figure 1, we present the concept of innovation experiment systems in R&D graphically. The loop between deploying new functionality, measuring usage and other performance metrics and subsequently using the collected data to drive development is the main process. The goal of an innovative product is to maximize the number of iterations that can be executed per time unit, e.g. per quarter. The rationale is that the faster the organization learns about the customer and the real world operation of the system, the more value it will provide and consequently the more successful it will be compared to its competitors.

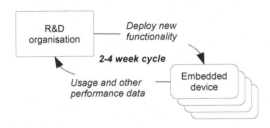

Fig. 1. Overview of the Innovation Experiment System with the iteration of experiments

When embedded systems are network connected and the development teams have adapted to rapid development and deployment i short cycles, allows the manufacturers to have the ability to conduct innovation experiments with the deployed embedded systems on a scale comparable to the full customer base.

A perhaps less obvious but very important advantage of connected products is that the cost of collecting active and passive information from and about the customer is much lower. Active customer feedback is concerned with surveys and other mechanisms where the customer is aware that he or she is providing feedback. Passive feedback and usage data is collected while the customer is using the system. Examples include the amount of time a user spends using a feature, the relative frequency of feature selections, the path that the user takes through the product functionality, etc. The low cost and ease of data collection leads to the next major difference between IES-based and traditional software.

In connected, embedded systems, in addition to usage data, several kinds of other performance data can be collected. For example, connected cars can collect fuel consumption data whereas telecom equipment can collect real-time bandwidth data. In many systems, this data is already collected for operational management purposes, but hardly used in evolution of already deployed systems.

An automotive OEM gains a significant competitive advantage from building products as innovation experiment systems compared to present practices of customer clinics and consumer surveys[1]; with the former being labor-intensive even for a very small sample size and the latter has a very long cycle time from development to survey results. The second advantage is for the customers, who continuously will get a vehicle with new or improved features, and a better retained second-hand value when selling to the 2nd and 3rd customers.

Due to the approach that companies like Google have taking concerning "perpetual beta", customers expect a continuous evolution of product functionality. Customers are becoming increasingly accustomed to frequent, trouble-free updates that provide relevant additional value and consequently this is increasingly an expectation also for traditional embedded products.

4 Applying Innovation Experiment Systems to Modern/Future Embedded Systems

4.1 Overall Implications on R&D Process

Innovative ideas for embedded products are typically collected and prioritized during the roadmapping and requirement management process as part of the yearly release cycle, which usually is determined by manufacturing concerns of the hardware. Feedbacks on innovations from real customers are collected only on new product models, if collected at all.

For a car there is a long innovation cycle for the mechanical parts, involving heavy investment in the manufacturing plants, typically 7-10 years. The electronics have a much shorter innovation cycle owing to the life-cycle of semiconductors, typically 1-3 years. Oddly enough the cycle of software is longer than for electronics, with a common feature being updated maybe once as a mid-cycle action on a car model.

Since more and more embedded products also are connected [5], it is conceivable to develop, deploy and measure usage on new software in iterations which length is determined by the speed of the software development teams instead of the setup of the manufacturing process, going from years to weeks. Such an innovation experiment system would utilize feedback from real customers in a scale comparable to the entire customer base and would require a product architecture embedded in each product together with an infrastructure capable of collecting and analyzing the data.

The driver for having such an innovation experiment system is that business and design decisions should be based on *data*, not opinions among developers, domain experts or managers. The company running the most experiments among the customer base against the lowest cost per experiment outcompetes the others by having the decision basis to engineer products with outstanding customer experience.

---

[1] http://autos.jdpower.com/

Developing software in an innovation experiment system is different from development approaches for traditional embedded software. First, it frequently deploys new versions focusing on continuously evolving the embedded software in short cycles of 2-4 weeks, as seen in Figure 1. Second, the design decisions are based on customers and customer usage data throughout the entire development process. Third, the goal of the development process is to test as many innovations as possible with customers to enhance customer satisfaction and, consequently, revenue growth. Last, it allows for software updates to the customer during the entire life-span of the product thereby counteracting declining customer value as the products becomes older.

4.2 Business Model Implications

One of the main trends affecting several embedded systems industries is the transition from products to services. Whereas companies such as telecom equipment manufacturers, automotive companies as well as others earlier were selling products that were static after leaving the factory, more and more customers are requesting the product to be offered as a service. This means that the company remains the owner of the product and offers the use of the product to its customers. As the switching cost for customers typically is much lower and the company is interested in minimizing total cost of ownership, it is important to exploit the post-deployment evolution of the software in the embedded system. This allows for constantly offering (and hopefully monetizing) new functionality as well as maximizing the useful life of products in the field through new software.

The capability significantly broadens the set of business models available to an organization. In addition to traditional products sales, pure service contracts, hybrid contracts combining product acquisition with service contracts, as well as usage-based pricing become feasible and all of these are exploited by different companies in the embedded systems industry.

4.3 Architecture Implications

The embedded devices are only one part of the innovation experiment system, the other two being the development environment and the experiment infrastructure, as seen in Figure 2.

The experiment infrastructure allows developers to deploy new software and collect data how it behaves in a real-world settings being used by actual users. The infrastructure support deployment of software experiments and collection of data over-the-air on a scale comparable to the entire customer base, for an automotive developer this means devices in the order of 10^5. To lessen the burden on the development teams on experimental design with automated randomization and factorial designs [7], it is supported by the infrastructure, sufficient to draw statistical conclusions from the experimental scenarios.

The architecture on the embedded device must support composability of the applications to be experimented upon. It must be easy to add or exchange applications when running new experiments with minimal impact on the rest of the

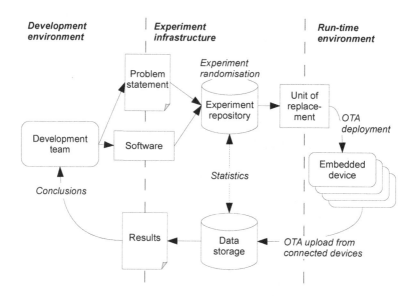

Fig. 2. The infrastructure enabling the innovation experiment system

embedded software. This goes against the current trend for cars which tends to integrate more and more functions [3]. The applications included in an experiment must be possible to activate independently of each other, and the product behavior must not depend on the order in which experiments are carried out.

In order to remove the burdensome control and synchronization of development teams, and allow independent updates of software experiments, there are three dimensions where decoupling between development parties/teams must take place, and which should be supported by the platform and infrastructure:

1. Decoupling between applications, this would otherwise require all experiments to be synchronized and make future feature growth impossible at some point.
2. Decoupling in time, i.e. all software must not be integrated with the product at the time of manufacturing.
3. Decoupling of applications from the underlying hardware, both from choice of e.g. CPUs and by using suitable sensor/actuator abstractions.

The simplest architecture for the embedded device involved in an IES is seen in Figure 3. This architecture is suitable when the memory and processing footprint of the experimental software needs to be kept to a minimum, or when it is desirable to keep the on-board software as simple as possible, at expense of having a more complicated infrastructure.

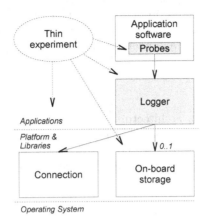

Fig. 3. The architecture for running a thin experiment client on an embedded device with scarce resources or when ease of implementation is desired

The software part under experimentation is usually a small part of embedded software, and all other software parts are kept invariant. If multiple experiments are to be performed in parallel a suitable experiment design has to be used in determining the number of different configurations of the deployed software and how many variants needs to be deployed.

Measurement is done on-board, but analysis is done off-board. This collects more data and requires better connection with the infrastructure, but allows exploration of unforeseen behavior from users and allows for posing additional questions after the application is deployed since more raw data is available.

This architecture can even be combined with a continuous connection: No data is actually stored on the device, all measurement are uploaded as soon as they are made. This may be the only solution if persistent memory is scarce. When the device has no connection all measurements are lost.

Since the management of which experiments are run where and when is done off-board to the devices, this architecture demands the infrastructure to keep track of the individual devices and which software is downloaded to each of them. If A/B testing is performed it is the infrastructure that keeps track of which order to do the tests. If needed to revert to a non-experimental version it must be done by re-deploying a previous unit of software. If the infrastructure does not permit the user to do this it can be detrimental to the user experience.

Many embedded domains have stringent dependability requirements. More specifically this means the architecture of the embedded device must satisfy real-time requirements for the execution of individual applications, integrity requirements, high availability, and mechanisms to eliminate undesired feature interaction if several applications interact with the same actuators. If the experiment should run out-of bounds of what is considered safe it must immediately be disabled and a fallback, safe, version of the software application runs instead.

The safety mechanisms should probably be developed and run independently of the experiment software; otherwise it would inherit the necessary safety integrity level causing unnecessary development effort.

5   Case Study

The case implementing an architecture for an IES was a development project of a prototype to establish a proof-of-concept for some radically different development strategies compared to current software development in the automotive industry. The system was an infotainment system based on an open platform, Android.

The project was executed in an industrial setting, but the resulting embedded system was not intended to go into mass production and be sold to customers. The primary goal of the project was to establish whether it was possible to do feature development with extremely short lead-times from decision to implementation compared to present industrial projects, from a nominal lead-time of 1-3 years to 4-12 weeks. The short lead-times were accomplished by a small development team using Scrum from a consultancy firm with automotive software experience, which had a supplier relationship to Volvo car Corporation as product owner. Working software was continuously validated in "real" environments, i.e. the infotainment system was installed in both a driving simulator and real test cars and users evaluated the system during the project.

5.1   Experimentation

A user story in the first sprint covered measurement / logging how the user uses the system with the purpose to provide input to the product backlog and future sprints, in terms of tuning of current features and new ideas. In a subsequent sprint an A/B experiment was defined evaluating two layouts of the start screen of the infotainment system, implemented as two different launchers in Android. The system was mounted in a vehicle and two set of test drivers were requested to perform some common task with the intent to measure which launcher "worked best".

Even though the test sample was too small to draw any conclusions, 7 drivers in total, the test drives showed that the on-board innovation experiment system worked as intended and collected the required data, which was then analyzed off-board.

5.2   Architecture

The system implemented the experiment architecture with a logger from Section 4.3. Architecture for more advanced experiments in future generations of the systems is in the design phase, but is not yet implemented. The system used a logger in the same layer as the observed application, in this case launcher of the android system, seen in Figure 4. The data from the logger was stored in a text-file with a batch upload of the data pulled by the developers. The logger kept track of the user's actions by storing different strings in the text-file, describing the actions that the user has performed, such as adding widgets to the workspace or starting an application. The logger was initiated from within the Android launcher by creating the logger variable and call the constructor of the generic logger-class developed and provided in the platform.

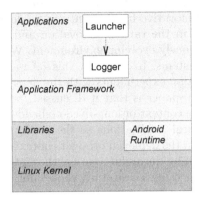

Fig. 4. The launcher, which was deployed in two versions, and the logger were both implemented as Android applications, which minimize changes to the platform and utilizes how easy it is to update Android applications

6   Conclusion

Since its first introduction in the middle of the 20th century, software has evolved from a handy configuration mechanism for electronic systems to the core of virtually any modern system supporting individuals, companies and entire societies. This has causes a significant expansion of the lifespan of software systems to the point that it is measured in decades rather than years. This trend is starting to become a key challenge for embedded software as well. In the context of connected embedded systems, this results in two main categories of "eternal" embedded software, i.e. infrastructure software and mass-produced embedded systems.

Examples of embedded infrastructure software include traffic lights, railway signalling, public transport automated ticket systems etc. Systems previously "unconnected" are becomening more and more software dependent, such as car-to-car and car-to-infrastructure communication, which increses this category of software ssystems. The investments necessary in infrastructure software makes deployment of new systesm a rare occasion.

Mass-produced embedded systems are usually built on a software platform that outlives the hardware platform, e.g. the microprocessor the software runs on. The software platform evolves beyond its initial purpose, and reuse of software is common between product generations. Cars are a typical example of this, where a new car model may reuse software from previous generation, and where the manufacturing life-cycle of a car model, typically seven years, is usually longer than the production of a single micro-controller.

The long life-cycle of these kind of systems demand that they evolve in order to prvide continuous value to the customer, especially if the competition drives an increasing pace of change. The typicla approach to this was to have period releases, e.g. yalry modle changes, but connected embedded systems allow continuous testing of new, innovative functionality to be deployed. This allows for significant improvements in the rate of innovation and the ability to systems to adjust to their continuously evolving environment. We refer to this trend as innovation experiment systems. In practice, this offers product producers the ability to conduct innovation experiments with the deployed systems.

The contribution of the paper is that it discussed the concept of innovation experiment systems in the context of long-lived embedded systems. In addition, it explored the architectural implications as the ability to continuously evolve and conduct experiences in the deployed product context in a safe and controlled manner must be supported by the architecture of the embedded systems. Finally, it illustrates these concepts using a case study concerning an infotainment system in the automotive industry.

Not all embedded systems are suitable for innovation experiment systems, we can identify at least three categories of systems where an IES may be of limited use. The first category are systems which have long lead-times due to heavy verification & validation, such as safety-critical systems and other systems requiring certification before deployment, e.g. nuclear power plants, medical devices etc. Second are embedded domains where the rate of innovation is secondary to other concerns, i.e. very mature domains, from a business or technical perspective.. Third, embedded domains where the product is viewed as a product, i.e. an item which can be bought and owned. The customer is less concerned with the services the product can supply.

The trend towards "eternal" embedded software is strong and is starting to affect many aspects of traditional product development in the industry. Our notion of innovation experiment systems provides a natural mechanism that allows an embedded system, its architecture and its underlying platform to continuously evolve in response to changes in the user requirements and system context. It uses a rapid feedback loop to evaluate the benefits of small variations to users of the product with the intent of continuously improving the system.

6.1   Future Work

In future work, we intend to significantly expand the number of examples in which we study the application of innovation experiment systems to real industrial contexts, to further develop the conceptual framework and to report on our findings. Further validation of IES for software in connected embedded systems would focus on: Investigations of further technical challenges of the embedded platform, beyond what was briefly described in the case in Section 5. Increase the number of involved devices to identify the challenges involved in large scale IES.

Studying the implications for development teams involved in short cycle development and deployment. And finally, investigate the business implications of IES in various embedded domains. These would probably require other methodological approaches besides case studies.

Since the management of which experiments are run where and when is done off-board to the devices, the infrastructure needs to keep track of the individual devices and which software units are downloaded to each of them. This could pose security and specifically privacy issues, which could be an obstacle in widespread acceptance among users, and is thus also some thing that needs to be investigated further. Future work on IES need to address these privacy issues, some possible solutions could be: Adapting present practices, e.g. a modern vehicle has it's software configuration stored in an in an off-device database [6]. Tracking software configurations of connected devices as part of the business model, e.g. as in Apple App Store or Google Play (formerly Android Market). A third option could be getting consent through an opt-in scheme, common in many desktop programs collecting anonymous data. In all of these care must be taken in sufficiently anonymize usage data from the device, and person, identification.

Acknowledgments. The case was financially supported by the Swedish Agency for Innovation Systems (VINNOVA), EIS by Semcon and Volvo Car Corporation within the partnership for Strategic Vehicle Research and Innovation (FFI).

References

1. Bosch, J.: Building Products as Innovation Experiment Systems. In: Cusumano, M.A., Iyer, B., Venkatraman, N. (eds.) ICSOB 2012. LNBIP, vol. 114, pp. 27–39. Springer, Heidelberg (2012)
2. Broy, M.: Challenges in automotive software engineering. In: Proceedings of the International Conference on Software Engineering, pp. 33–42. ACM, Shanghai (2006), http://portal.acm.org/citation.cfm?id=1134285.1134292
3. Di Natale, M., Sangiovanni-Vincentelli, A.L.: Moving from federated to integrated architectures in automotive: The role of standards, methods and tools. Proceedings of the IEEE 98(4), 603–620 (2010), http://dx.doi.org/10.1109/JPROC.2009.2039550
4. Ebert, C., Jones, C.: Embedded software: Facts, figures, and future. Computer 42(4), 42–52 (2009), http://ieeexplore.ieee.org/stamp/stamp.jsp?tp=&arnumber=5054871&isnumber=5054856
5. Koslowski, T.: Your connected vehicle is arriving. Technology Review (January 2012), http://www.technologyreview.com/business/39407/
6. Melin, K.: Volvo s80: Electrical system of the future. Volvo Technology Report 1, 3–7 (1998), http://www.artes.uu.se/mobility/industri/volvo04/elsystem.pdf
7. Montgomery, D.C.: Design and Analysis of Experiments, 3rd edn. Wiley (1991)
8. Reichheld, F.F.: The one number you need to grow. Harvard Business Review 81(12), 46–54 (2003), http://hbr.org/2003/12/the-one-number-you-need-to-grow/ar/1

A Liskov Principle
for Delta-Oriented Programming[*]

Reiner Hähnle[1] and Ina Schaefer[2]

[1] Department of Computer Science
Technische Universität Darmstadt, 64289 Darmstadt
haehnle@cs.tu-darmstadt.de
[2] Institute for Software Systems Engineering
Technical University of Braunschweig, D-38106 Braunschweig
i.schaefer@tu-braunschweig.de

Abstract. In formal verification of software product families one not only analyses programs, but must act on the artifacts and components which are reused to obtain software products. As the number of products is exponential in the number of artifacts, it is crucial to perform verification in a modular way. When code reuse is based on class inheritance in OO programming, Liskov's principle is a standard device to achieve modular verification. Software families, however, employ other variability modeling techniques than inheritance. Delta-oriented programming is an approach to implement a family of programs where code reuse is achieved via gradual transformation of a core program. We define a Liskov principle for delta-oriented programming and show that it achieves modular verification of software families developed in that paradigm.

1 Introduction

Diversity is prevalent in modern software systems in order to meet different customer requirements and application contexts. Formal modeling and verification of software product families have attracted considerable interest recently [23,2,8,4]. The challenge is to devise validation and verification methods that work at the level of families, not merely at the level of a single product. Given the combinatorial explosion in the number of possible products even for small software families, efficient verification techniques for families are essential. For verification techniques to scale, they have to be modular in the artifacts that are reused to build the different variants of the software family.

In the area of object-oriented programming, Liskov's principle of behavioral subtyping [17] is an important means and guideline to achieve modular verification. It is also an important theoretical tool to investigate theories of specification and refinement. However, in the majority of approaches to family-based software development the principles of reuse are not founded on class-based inheritance. Instead, more suitable program modularization techniques, such as

---

[*] Partly funded by the EU project FP7-231620 HATS (http://www.hats-project.eu) and by the German Science Foundation (SCHA1635/2-1).

T. Margaria and B. Steffen (Eds.): ISoLA 2012, Part I, LNCS 7609, pp. 32–46, 2012.

aspect-oriented programming , feature-oriented programming , or delta-oriented programming are applied. For this family of languages, there exist insular approaches to incremental verification [4,23], however, there is no notion corresponding to Liskov's principle for inheritance. As a consequence, there is no approach that would allow modular functional verification for software families.

Here we analyse delta-oriented programming (DOP) of software families [19]. In DOP, a software family is developed from a designated core program and a set of delta modules that alter the core program to realize other program variants. In Sect. 2, we provide background on DOP. We specify functional program properties based on design-by-contract [18] by providing class invariants and method contracts. The core program is specified like any standard program, while the deltas can add or remove method contracts and class invariants to reflect the changes in the code carried out by a delta. As detailed in Sect. 3, by applying the deltas and their specifications to a core program and its specification, a program variant (called *product*) and its corresponding specification is generated.

To support modular reasoning for software families implemented by DOP, we develop a Liskov principle for delta modules in Sect. 4. This principle restricts the changes that a delta module may make to the specification of the core program. Based on this principle, in Sect. 5 we devise a modular proof principle that relies on the approximation of called methods by their first introduced variant. If the Liskov principle for DOP holds, we show that it suffices to analyze the core program and each delta in isolation to establish the correctness of all products. In Sect. 6, we discuss the consequences of DOP for reasoning about invariants. In Sect. 7, we review related work. We conclude and discuss future work in Sect. 8.

2   Delta-Oriented Programming

The basis of this paper is the modeling language ABS (Abstract Behavioral Specification Language) [5] where program variability is represented by DOP. ABS is a class-based, concurrent OO language without class inheritance. Interfaces which are implemented by classes can be extended to provide a taxonomy similar to class inheritance. We consider sequential ABS programs, because there is no standard notion of contract or Liskov principle for concurrent programs.

2.1   Preliminaries

A family of ABS programs is represented by an ABS core program $\mathcal{C}$ and a partially ordered set of deltas $\mathcal{D}$, together called *delta model*. Deltas can add, remove, and modify classes from the core program. Modification of a class changes the internal class structure by adding and removing fields and methods and by changing method implementations. A method implementation can be completely replaced or wrapped using the **original** call. The keyword **original** denotes a call to the most recent version of a method with the same name (possibly already wrapped by a previous **original** call). Calls to **original** are resolved when building a concrete product. It is characteristic of DOP that the selection of features is factored out of the executable code into the product building phase. This makes the code base of a given product smaller and potentially more efficient.

An occurrence of **original** requires to know exactly which delta has been used most recently in order to arrive at the current partial product. Therefore, we define products in such a way that the target of **original** is uniquely determined [5].

To avoid technical complications that are orthogonal to the problem of modular product family analysis treated here, we exclude recursive calls.

A partial order between deltas resolves conflicts if two deltas alter the same entity of an ABS program. This ensures that for a given set of deltas a unique ABS program variant is always generated. Without loss of generality, we assume that the partial order of the deltas is expressed as a total order on a partition [20] denoted as $[\delta_{11} \cdots \delta_{1n_1}] < \cdots < [\delta_{h1} \cdots \delta_{hn_h}]$. We assume that all deltas in one element $[\delta_{j1} \cdots \delta_{jn_j}]$ of the partition are compatible and that the partitions are disjoint. A set of deltas is called *compatible* if no class added or removed in one delta is added, removed or modified in another delta contained in the same set, and for every class modified in more than one delta, the fields and methods added, modified or removed are distinct. Thus, the order of application of the deltas in the same partition element does not matter. The parts of the partition, however, must be applied in the specified order to ensure that a unique product is generated for a selected subset of deltas. We call h the *height* of the delta model and $\max\{n_1, \ldots, n_h\}$ its *width*. The number of possible products in a delta model is bounded by $(2^w)^h$ (the number of subsets that can be selected).

On an abstract level, variability is usually represented by features, that is, user-visible product characteristics. A feature model [12] defines the set of valid feature combinations: the products of the software family. To connect feature models and program variability specified by the delta model, a product line specification is provided where an application condition over the features is attached to each delta. These conditions can be Boolean constraints over the features and specify for which feature configurations a delta can be applied.

A program for a particular feature configuration is generated by selecting the subset of deltas with a valid application condition and applying them to the core program in a linear order compatible to the partial order of the delta model. The generation of a program variant from a core program $\mathcal{C}$ and a delta model $\mathcal{D}$ is written as $\mathcal{C}\delta_1 \cdots \delta_p$ where for all $1 \leq i \leq p$, it holds that $\delta_i = \delta_{kl}$ and $\delta_{i+1} = \delta_{k'l'}$ such that $\delta_i \neq \delta_{i+1}$ and $k \leq k'$. We know that the number of applied deltas is bounded by $p \leq h * w$. We use the following obvious notation to access classes C, fields f, and methods m within (partial) products: $\mathcal{C}\delta_1 \cdots \delta_n.$C.m.f, etc.

It is possible that a sequence of delta applications $\mathcal{C}\delta_1 \cdots \delta_n$ is not a product, for example, when an accessed method or field was not declared before. Since we want to reason only about well-defined products, this causes technical complications. One way to avoid them is to stipulate that all sequences of deltas lead to type-safe products which can be enforced by adding suitably composed intermediate deltas. As this would bloat delta models, we employ a more natural restriction sufficient for our purposes: assume $P = \mathcal{C}\delta_1 \cdots \delta_n$ is any product and $P\delta_{n+1} \cdots \delta_{n+k}$ is a product with a minimal number of deltas obtained

```
module Account;

interface IAccount { Unit deposit(Int x); }

class Account implements IAccount {
  Int balance = 0 ;
  Unit deposit(Int x) { balance = balance + x; }
}
delta DFee(Int fee) {
  modifies class Account {
    modifies Unit deposit(Int x) { if (x>=fee) original(x-fee); }
  }
}
delta DOverdraft() {
  modifies class Account{
    adds Int limit;
    modifies Unit deposit (Int x) { if (balance + x > limit) original(x); }
  }
}
productline AccountPL {
  features Basic, Overdraft, Fee;
  delta DFee (Fee.amount) when Fee;
  delta DOverdraft after DFee when Overdraft;
}
```

Fig. 1. A Bank Account Product Family in ABS [5]

from P (that is, the same product cannot be produced with less deltas); then any method is introduced or modified at most once in $\delta_{n+1}, \ldots, \delta_{n+k}$ (removing and re-introducing a method corresponds to modification). We call a delta model with this property *regular*. In addition, we assume that without loss of generality each delta occurring in a regular delta model is used in at least one product.

2.2   Running Example

We illustrate our ideas with a product family of bank accounts depicted in Fig. 1. The core program contains a class Account implementing an interface IAccount. The class Account contains a field balance for storing the balance of the account and a method deposit to update the balance. The product family contains two deltas. Delta DFee modifies Account by introducing a transaction fee modeled by a parameter that is instantiated when a concrete program variant is generated. Delta DOverdraft adds a limit to the account restricting the possible overdraft.

The feature model for this product family contains the mandatory feature Basic implemented by the Account class. There are optional features Fee (with an integer parameter amount) and Overdraft. The product line declaration in Fig. 1 provides the connection between features and deltas in the **when** clauses.

These state that the delta DFee realizes feature Fee and that delta DOverdraft implements feature Overdraft. The **after** clause provides the application order between the deltas, generally described by an ordered partition (as above). The bank account product family gives rise to four program variants: one with only the Basic features, one with Basic and Overdraft, one with Basic and Fee, and one with all three features where each product containing Fee varies in the concrete value of the fee that is instantiated when a specific product is generated.

3 Specifying Deltas

To reason about behavioral properties of program variants a specification technique for core programs and deltas must be provided that allows generating program variants together with their specification.

3.1 Design by Contract

We use a specification discipline for both core programs and deltas that is derived from design by contract [18] and closely modelled after the JML approach [15].

Definition 1. *A program location is an expression referring to an updatable heap location (variable, formal parameter, field access, array access). Signatures include all locations of a target program. A contract for a method m consists of:*

1. *a first-order formula r called* precondition *or* requires clause*;*
2. *a first-order formula e called* postcondition *or* ensures clause*;*
3. *a set of program locations a (called* assignable clause*) that occur in m and whose value can potentially be changed during execution.*

We extend our notation for accessing class members to cover the constituents of contracts: C.m.r is the requires clause of method m in class C, etc.

Let $m(\bar{p})$ be a call of method m with parameters $\bar{p}$. A *total correctness program formula* in dynamic logic [3] has the form $\langle m(\bar{p})\rangle\Phi$ and means that whenever m is called then it terminates and in the final state Φ holds where Φ is either again a program formula or a first-order formula. One aspect of the semantics of a method contract is expressed as a *total correctness formula* of the form $r \rightarrow \langle m(\bar{p})\rangle e$. (Partial correctness adds nothing to our discussion: we omit it for brevity.) The second aspect of contract semantics is correctness of the assignable clause. It says that m can change only the value of program locations in a. One can encode this property with program formulas [11]. The specifics of the encoding are of no interest: we assume there is a program formula $A(a, m)$ expressing correctness of the assignable clause. The following monotonicity condition holds:

$$a' \subseteq a \ \wedge \ A(a, m) \rightarrow A(a', m) \tag{1}$$

Definition 2. *A method m of class C satisfies its contract if the following holds:*

$$C.m.r \rightarrow \langle m(\bar{p})\rangle C.m.e \ \wedge \ A(C.m.a, C.m) \tag{2}$$

```
class Account implements IAccount {
    Int balance = 0;
    @requires x > 0;
    @ensures balance <= \old(balance) + x;
    @assignable balance;
    Unit deposit(Int x) { balance = balance + x }
}
```

Fig. 2. Specification of Core Bank Account

The presence of contracts makes formal verification of complex programs feasible, because each method can be verified separately against its contract and called methods can be approximated by their contracts. The assignable clause of a method limits the program locations a method call can have side effects on.[1]

We allow first-order formulas i to be attached as *invariants* to classes. We permit to write invariants directly in front of the element they relate to (e.g., a field declaration). However, as we consider all specifications to be globally visible in this paper, these simply are part of the invariant of a class. Hence, we assume that each class C has a unique invariant C.i. As usual, the semantics of invariants requires to establish two properties: (i) after initialization of a class its invariant holds and it does not invalidate the invariant of any other class, and (ii) if an invariant holds just before the execution of a method, then it holds again immediately after termination of that method. As a consequence of global visibility of invariants and of public visibility of fields, the invariants of *all* classes must be maintained by *all* methods. In the absence of modularity constructs, this is the usual situation in specification of object-oriented programs.

Fig. 2 shows the specification of the core program of our example product family. The method deposit is specified with a contract whose precondition in the @requires clause says that the balance should be positive. The postcondition in the @ensures clause expresses that the balance after the method call is at most the balance before the method call (accessed by the JML \old keyword) plus the value of the parameter x. As there is no explicitly specified invariant, the class invariant of Account is simply true.

3.2 Specification Deltas

We want to denote in a structured manner those parts of contracts and invariants that must be modified in order to reflect the changes embodied in a given delta. The specification approach of [4] allows (i) to add and remove invariants as well as (ii) to add and remove whole contracts in deltas. This is too coarse for our purposes, so we make the following refinement:

---

[1] We are aware that this basic technique is insufficient to achieve modular verification. Advanced techniques for modular verification would obfuscate the fundamental questions considered in this paper and can be superimposed later.

```
delta DFee(Int fee) {
  modifies class Account {
    adds @invariant fee >= 0;
    modifies @ensures balance <= \old(balance) + max(x-fee,0) ;
    modifies Unit deposit(Int x) { if (x>=fee) original(x-fee); }
} }
```

Fig. 3. Delta `DFee` with its Specification Delta

- in deltas, the addition, removal, and modification of contracts can be specified separately for requires clauses, ensures clauses, and assignable clauses;
- we permit the usage of the keyword **original** in clauses of contracts with the obvious semantics provided that the contract to which **original** refers can be uniquely determined;
- since the invariant of a (partial) product is always global and the implicit conjunction of all invariants introduced in the core and in the constituent deltas, the modification of invariants and the usage of **original** in invariants does not make any sense. Hence, invariants can only be explicitly added or removed in deltas.

A missing specification clause is equivalent to, for example, "@requires **original**" (or to "@requires true" in the case of the first occurrence of a method). Fig. 3 shows the modification to the specification caused by the delta `DFee`. The contract of method `deposit` is changed by replacing the postcondition. The precondition remains unchanged. Additionally, an invariant for the field `fee` is added to the class `Account` which states that the value of `fee` should be non-negative.

4   Liskov's Principle

Liskov's principle of behavioral subtyping [17] is an important means to achieve modularity for behavioral specification and verification. In this section, we recall Liskov's principle for standard class-based inheritance and transfer it to DOP.

4.1   Standard Object-Oriented Design with Code Inheritance

In standard object-oriented programming with code inheritance Liskov's [17] principle states the following:

1. The invariant of a subclass must imply the invariant of its superclasses.
2. The precondition of a method overridden in a subclass must be implied by the precondition of the superclass method and its postcondition must imply the postcondition of the superclass method.
3. When assignable clauses are present, the assignable locations in a subclass must be a subset of the assignable locations in the superclass.

We distill the essence of the last two points into a relation on contracts:

Definition 3. *For two methods* m, m′ *let* m.r, m.e, m.a, *and* m′.r′, m′.e′, m′.a′ *be different contracts (*m = m′ *allowed). The first contract is* more general *than the second (or the second is more* specific *than the first) if the following holds:*

$$(m.r \rightarrow m'.r') \wedge (m'.e' \rightarrow m.e) \wedge (m'.a' \subseteq m.a) \tag{3}$$

The next lemma is immediate by the definition of contract satisfaction (Def. 2), propositional reasoning, monotonicity of postconditions in total correctness formulas, and monotonicity of assignable clauses (1). It will be tacitly used in the following to establish satisfaction of method contracts.

Lemma 1. *If a method* m′ *satisfies its contract then its satisfies as well any contract that is more general.*

Consequently, if a specification follows Liskov's principle, then *behavioral subtyping* is guaranteed provided that all methods satisfy their contract and maintain the invariants. This means that an object can be replaced by any object with a subtype without changing the behavior of the program.

4.2   Delta-Oriented Specification

We propose delta-oriented programming (DOP) [19] as the fundamental technique for code reuse, in contrast to inheritance. Therefore, it is necessary to understand how Liskov's principle can be ported to a DOP setting.

To cast Liskov principle for DOP we consider the code and specification elements that can be changed by deltas: adding and removing methods together with their contracts is uncritical, since our assumption on type-safety guarantees that such a method has never been called before, respectively, will not be called afterwards. It is sufficient to prove the contract of newly added methods, but that of existing methods cannot be affected. If a newly added method should be integrated into an existing program, modifications of existing methods have to be specified in other applied deltas. This leaves modification of existing methods and contracts as well as the removal and addition of invariants to look at.

To preserve the behavior of a method that is modified by a delta, it is sufficient to follow the same principle as in behavioral subtyping, i.e, to make contracts more specific (Def. 3). This is automatically the case, whenever the modified contract of m has a requires clause of the form C.m.r.**original** ∨ r′, an ensures clause of the form C.m.e.**original** ∧ e′, and for the assignable clause a of the modified contract, a ⊆ C.m.a.**original** holds. The tricky issue is that references to **original**, hence to method calls and contracts are only resolved when a product is being built. In Sect. 5, we show that under certain restrictions one can verify a delta model without having to look at all its exponentially many products.

Regarding removal and addition of invariants, certainly, we must exclude the possibility to remove invariants, because this might invalidate the contracts of arbitary methods added either in the core or in any delta. This would require to reprove all contracts in all exponentially many products. A straightforward counterpart of the first item in Liskov's principle stated at the beginning of

Sect. 4.1 requires adding only invariants implied by previously existing ones. We discuss essentially this situation in Sect. 6.1 below. This approach is restrictive; adding *new* invariants and reproving them in a compositional manner is nontrivial and discussed in Sect. 6.2.

5   Compositional Verification of Delta Models

The advantage of a Liskov principle for the specification of deltas is that one can follow a *compositional* verification approach. This means one can ensure with a polynomial number of proofs the behavioral correctness of an exponential number of products. Clearly, this is a key property for feasibility of product family verification, because even small product families have a vast number of products. In this section, we focus on the verification of method contracts and cover the verification of invariants in Sect. 6. We need to ensure that all methods in any product satisfy their contract. We do this in two steps:

Verification of the Core. This is standard and means simply to prove that all methods m in a core program $\mathcal{C}$ satisfy their contract (Def. 2).

Verification of the Deltas. For each method m added or modified in a delta δ, we must establish its contract. We allow the usage of the keyword **original** in contracts only in the syntactically restricted form mentioned in Sect. 4.2. For each method m, we must show the proof obligation

$$\delta.\text{m}.r \to \langle \text{m}(\overline{\text{p}}) \rangle \delta.\text{m}.e \quad \wedge \quad A(\delta.\text{m}.a, \delta.\text{m}) \tag{4}$$

Additionally, we need to ensure that the contract of each $\delta.\text{m}$ is more specific than the contracts provided and verified for m in all previous deltas used for any product. As the actual set of applied deltas cannot be known before product generation, to get a compositional verification method avoiding the generation of exponentially many products, we have to assume "the worst".

For the verification of (4), let us first analyse the methods called inside $\delta.\text{m}$: if a method n is called[2] in $\delta.\text{m}$ and does not occur in δ itself, then we use the method contract associated with the *first* introduction of n in the given delta model (i.e., in a δ_{ij} with minimal index i). As subsequent contracts of n can only get more specific according to our Liskov principle, this ensures that the call is valid for all possible versions of n. Likewise, we use the "largest" assignable set of locations. If n occurs in δ, we simply use the contract of $\delta.\text{n}$.

Definition 4. *If all methods occurring in a delta δ satisfy their contract, where the contracts of called methods have been selected as outlined above, we say that the δ is* verified.

Next, we ensure that the contract of $\delta.\text{m}$ is more specific than all previous contracts of m. As each method may occur at most once in each part of the partition

---

[2] In case the call is done via the keyword **original** this simply means $n = m$ where m is not the one in δ.

$\mathcal{D}$ (by compatibility of the deltas within that part), it suffices to compare the contract of δ.m with the contract of the most recent (Def. 5) occurrence of m from δ.m, say δ'.m. (If δ.m was the first occurrence in $\mathcal{D}$ there is nothing to do.) It remains to show that the contract of δ'.m is more general than that of δ.m.

Definition 5. *Assume that a method* m *occurs at least twice in a delta model with core* $\mathcal{C}$ *and partition* $\mathcal{D} = ([\delta_{11} \cdots \delta_{1n_1}], \ldots, [\delta_{h1} \cdots \delta_{hn_h}])$, *and one of the occurrences is in* δ_{jk}. *For convenience, we refer to the core as* δ_{00}. *Then an occurrence of* m *in* δ_{il} *is called* most recent *from* δ_{jk}.m *if there is no occurrence of* m *in any* $\delta_{i'r}$ *with* $i < i' < j$.

Together Defs. 4, 5 provide a static (i.e., at the level of the product family) approximation of the deltas used in any possible concrete product. A straightforward induction over the height of a delta model lifts the property that a method contract for a method m is more specific than the contract of the most recent occurrence from m to arbitrary previous occurrences of the method m:

Lemma 2. *Let* $\mathcal{C}$ *and* $\mathcal{D}$ *be a delta model as in Def. 5. Assume that for the core* $\mathcal{C}$ *and for any* δ *occurring in* $\mathcal{D}$ *the following holds: the contract of any method* m *in* δ *is more specific than the contract of the most recent occurrence from* δ.m.
    Then for any two method contracts of a method m *occurring in any* δ_{ik} *and* $\delta_{jk'}$ *such that* $i \le j$ *we have that the contract of* m *in* δ_{ik} *is more general than its contract in* $\delta_{jk'}$.

We formalize the considerations above in the following theorem:

Theorem 1. *Given a regular delta model consisting of a core* $\mathcal{C}$ *and a partition of deltas* $\mathcal{D} = ([\delta_{11} \cdots \delta_{1n_1}], \ldots, [\delta_{h1} \cdots \delta_{hn_h}])$. *Assume the following holds:*

1. $\mathcal{C}$ *satisfies its contract, i.e., equation (2) holds for all its methods.*
2. *For all* δ *occurring in* $\mathcal{D}$:
   (a) δ *is verified.*
   (b) *The contract of each method* m *added or modified in* δ *either is the first occurrence of* m *in the delta model or it must be more specific than the contract of the most recent method in* $\mathcal{D}$ *from* δ.m.

Then every product obtained from the given delta model satisfies its specification, i.e., each of its methods satisfies its contract.

Example. In the bank account product family, the contract of method `deposit` that is modified by the delta `DFee` in Fig. 3 satisfies condition (2b). The contract of method `deposit` in delta `DFee` is more specific than the contract of method `deposit` in the class `Account` given in Fig. 2. Delta `DOverdraft` does not change any specification and fulfills condition (2b) trivially. During the verification of `DFee.deposit` the contract of `Account.deposit` needs to be used. One can apply Thm. 1 to the bank account example and infer that all four products satisfy their respective method contracts.

The significance of Thm. 1 is that the number of proof tasks is polynomial in h, w, and the number M of different methods occurring in $\mathcal{D}$: in the core and in each of at most $h * w$ deltas we need at most three proofs for each modified method which is in $\mathcal{O}(h * w * M)$. This is a clear advantage over providing a separate proof for each product, resulting in $\mathcal{O}(2^{(h*w)} * M)$ many proofs.

Proof (Thm. 1). By induction on the length p of delta sequences where we consider only such sequences that result in a product. The induction hypothesis says: each delta sequence of length p results in a product that satisfies its specification.

The base for $p = 0$ amounts to show the claim for the core $\mathcal{C}$ of the delta model which is taken care of by the first assumption.

Now assume that we have a product $P = \mathcal{C}\delta_1 \cdots \delta_p$ that satisfies its specification and $P' = P\delta_{p+1} \cdots \delta_{p+k}$ is any product with a minimal number of deltas obtained from it. We show that

1. any method m occurring in P', but not in P, satisfies its contract;
2. that the contracts of all other methods called in P' still hold.

Regarding the first item, by regularity of the delta model we can assume that there is exactly one δ in $\delta_{p+1}, \ldots, \delta_{p+k}$ where m is introduced or modified. By assumption (2a), from equation (4) we know that all methods in δ satisfy their contract where the method n called in m can be approximated by the "first", i.e., most general existing contract. In P', these calls to n are replaced by some implementation introduced or modified in a delta.

The actual contract of n was either introduced in δ itself or in a different $\delta_{p+1}, \ldots, \delta_{p+k}$ or somewhere in P. In the first case, since δ is verified, n was proven against its actual contract. If n came from one of the "new" deltas, by assumption (2b) the contract of n is more specific than the contract of the most recent occurrence in the delta model. By Lemma 2, the contract of that occurrence is more specific than the first occurrence of n in the delta model which was used for approximating the contract of n during verification of m. This means that the previous proof supplied by the induction hypothesis still applies.

Finally, assume the contract of n was introduced in P. By Lemma 2, we know that this contract must be either identical to or more specific than the first occurrence of n in the delta model. Since the latter contract was used in verification of m the result holds.

For proving the second item above, assume m is any method that is defined and verified in a $\delta \in P$. The case which we need to check is that m calls a method n whose specification was overridden in $\delta_{p+1}, \ldots, \delta_{p+k}$. From Lemma 2 we know that the contract of the later occurrence is more specific than the contract of m used in P. Therefore, the new contract is still applicable. Together with the assumption that all $\delta_{p+1}, \ldots, \delta_{p+k}$ are verified, this closes the proof.   □

6   Verification of Invariants

Recall that we assume that all invariants are global: each method must satisfy all invariants. Therefore, one can assume there is exactly one invariant for each product. In more fine-grained approaches, one can limit the visibility of invariants by making them private and attaching them to specific class features or restrict their accessibility with type systems, however, this is an orthogonal issue.

Invariants can be viewed as a special case of method contracts where the requires and ensures clause are identical. But this is exactly what makes it difficult to fit invariants into the above framework where contracts become more specific after the application of deltas causing requires and ensures clauses to diverge. For the reason stated in Sect. 4.2 we exclude removal of invariants.

6.1 Core Invariants

The first take on invariants is a direct rendering of the first item in Liskov's principle. As explained in Sect. 4.2, this means only invariants implied by existing ones are added. This amounts to permit the introduction of invariants only in the core. All subsequent deltas use the same invariant. Proof obligations of the kind (2) and (4) are extended with the core invariant $\mathcal{C}.\mathtt{i}$:

$$(\mathtt{m.r} \wedge \mathcal{C}.\mathtt{i}) \rightarrow \langle \mathtt{m}(\overline{\mathtt{p}}) \rangle \mathtt{m.e} \qquad \wedge \qquad \mathcal{C}.\mathtt{i} \rightarrow \langle \mathtt{m}(\overline{\mathtt{p}}) \rangle \mathcal{C}.\mathtt{i} \qquad (5)$$

We continue to use the specification and verification discipline of Sect. 5, but employ proof obligations of the form (5). The number of proofs stays the same, even though some may be harder to establish. The proof of Thm. 1 is done such that at the first occurrence of a method declaration its contract and the invariant is established: the invariant is available in subsequent verification steps.

Even though it may seem rather restrictive to use only core invariants, there are a number of important advantages:

1. The number and complexity of proof tasks stays manageable.
2. Thm. 1 providing a compositional verification approach stays valid.
3. If an invariant $\mathtt{i}'$ in a delta was added, then this invariant must be shown to hold even for the methods not changed in that delta. Hence, either $\mathtt{i}'$ has a signature disjoint from the core or it would have been possible to add and show $\mathtt{i}'$ already in the core. We discuss the first possibility in Sect. 6.2.

6.2 Family Invariants

As soon as invariants can change during delta application, it is no longer possible to reason precisely over product invariants on the level of the delta model. The reason is that invariants behave non-monotonically: if equation (5) holds for $\mathtt{i}$ it may not hold anymore for an $\mathtt{i}'$ that is logically weaker or stronger than $\mathtt{i}$.

It might seem harmless to make existing invariants stronger during delta application, that is, a δ in a delta model may introduce an invariant $\delta.\mathtt{i}$ which is conjoined to the existing invariant. This, however, requires to prove that all methods still satisfy the strengthened invariant. The problem is that at the level of the delta model we do not know which concrete deltas are going to be used to build a product. The best we can do is to approximate the required invariant for

each delta δ by collecting the invariants of all previous deltas. A safe approxima-
tion is to establish the invariant $\mathtt{I}_{\leq\delta} = \bigwedge_{\delta' \leq \delta} \delta'.\mathtt{i}$ for each existing method (not
only for the methods mentioned in the delta) as part of the verification of each
δ in assumption (2a) of Thm. 1. This is more expensive than the core invariant
approach outlined in Sect. 6.1, but there is still only a polynomial number of
proofs in terms of the number of deltas and method calls.

Invariants of a δ whose signature is disjoint relative to previous deltas (such as
invariants about newly introduced fields) trivially satisfy $\mathtt{I}_{\leq\delta}$ and can be added
without penalty in terms of proof effort.

The main drawback of the approach just sketched is not merely the increased
number of proofs, but that the invariant that can be shown on the family level
might be much stronger than necessary for a specific product.

7   Related Work

Behavioral subtyping is often criticized as too restrictive to be practical [21].
This is addressed by a number of relaxations, such as incremental reasoning [22]
or lazy behavioral subtyping [10]. None is directly applicable to DOP.

Product line analysis can be classified in three categories [23]: (i) product-
based analysis considers each product variant separately. Product-based analyses
can use any standard techniques for single products, but are in general infeasible
for product lines due to the exponential number of products. (ii) family-based
analysis checks the complete code base of the product line in a single run to
obtain a result about all possible variants. Family-based product line analyses
are currently used for type checking [1,7] and model checking [6,14] of product
lines. They rely on a monolithic model of the product line which hardly scales
to large and complex product lines. (iii) feature-based analysis considers the
building blocks of the different product variants (deltas in DOP) in isolation to
derive results on all variants. Feature-based analyses are used for compositional
type checking [20] and compositional model checking of product lines [16]. The
compositional verification approach presented here can be classified as feature-
based, since the core and deltas are verified in isolation.

A product-based approach for deductive verification of behavioral properties
is [4]. Assuming one product variant has been verified, the structure of a delta to
generate a new program variant is analyzed to obtain the proof obligations that
remain valid for the new variant and need not be reproven. This does not limit the
variability between two product variants, but requires to consider exponentially
many products. As there is no systematic link between two variants (like the
Liskov principle employed here), it is hard to optimize proof reuse.

In [23], a combination of feature-based and product-based verification for behavioral properties is proposed where for each feature module a partial Coq proof
script is generated. These scripts are composed and checked for single products.
In [2], feature-based proof techniques for type system soundness of language
extensions are proposed where proofs for single language features are incrementally constructed. In [8] Coq proofs for the soundness of a small compiler are

composed feature-wise by modeling the concept of variation points. Composition scripts must be built by hand and it is not clear whether the technique is applicable to functional verification in general. Our approach relies on a compositional proof principle and is modular for behavioral program properties.

Besides DOP, other program modularization techniques have been applied to compositionally implement software variability, for instance, feature modules, aspects, or traits. Apart from initial work regarding modular deductive verification for aspects [13] and traits [9], no compositional verification approach based on an adaptation of a Liskov principle exists.

8   Discussion and Future Work

This is a theoretical and conceptual paper which constitutes the first systematic incremental specification and verification framework for diverse systems implemented in DOP. DOP is amenable to formal analysis, because its granularity is at the method-level which coincides with the best-understood contract-based approaches (JML, Spec#). Another reason is that the result of a delta application is a standard program which has an undisputed correctness semantics.

The main contribution of this paper is to provide a Liskov principle for DOP which gives rise to an efficient, compositional verification approach for software families. As in Liskov's principle for class inheritance, some restrictions are needed to make this work: (i) delta application leads to type-safe products (Sect. 2.1), (ii) the contracts of subsequent deltas must become more specific (Sect. 4.2, item (2b) of Thm. 1), (iii) invariants cannot be removed, but only added (Sect. 4.2, Sect. 6.2), (iv) methods called in deltas use the contract of the first implementation of that method (Def. 4). Restriction (i) is desirable for DOP independently of verification [20]; (ii)–(iii) originate from Liskov's principle for OO programs and restrict the product lines that can be handled as described: future work will consist in devising mitigating strategies similar as in the OO world [10]; (iv) is specific to our approach and to DOP.

References

1. Apel, S., Kästner, C., Grösslinger, A., Lengauer, C.: Type safety for feature-oriented product lines. Automated Software Engineering 17(3), 251–300 (2010)
2. Batory, D.S., Börger, E.: Modularizing theorems for software product lines: The Jbook case study. J. UCS 14(12), 2059–2082 (2008)
3. Beckert, B., Hähnle, R., Schmitt, P.H. (eds.): Verification of Object-Oriented Software. LNCS, vol. 4334. Springer (2007)
4. Bruns, D., Klebanov, V., Schaefer, I.: Verification of Software Product Lines with Delta-Oriented Slicing. In: Beckert, B., Marché, C. (eds.) FoVeOOS 2010. LNCS, vol. 6528, pp. 61–75. Springer, Heidelberg (2011)
5. Clarke, D., Diakov, N., Hähnle, R., Johnsen, E.B., Schaefer, I., Schäfer, J., Schlatte, R., Wong, P.Y.H.: Modeling Spatial and Temporal Variability with the HATS Abstract Behavioral Modeling Language. In: Bernardo, M., Issarny, V. (eds.) SFM 2011. LNCS, vol. 6659, pp. 417–457. Springer, Heidelberg (2011)

6. Classen, A., Heymans, P., Schobbens, P.-Y., Legay, A., Raskin, J.-F.: Model checking lots of systems: Efficient verification of temporal properties in software product lines. In: ICSE. IEEE (2010)
7. Delaware, B., Cook, W., Batory, D.: A Machine-Checked Model of Safe Composition. In: FOAL, pp. 31–35. ACM (2009)
8. Delaware, B., Cook, W., Batory, D.: Theorem Proving for Product Lines. In: OOPSLA 2011 (to appear, 2011)
9. Dovland, J., Damiani, F., Johnsen, E.B., Schaefer, I.: Verifying Traits: A Proof System for Fine-Grained Reuse. In: Workshop on Formal Techniques for Java-like Programs, FTfJP 2011 (2011)
10. Dovland, J., Johnsen, E.B., Owe, O., Steffen, M.: Lazy behavioral subtyping. Journal of Logic and Algebraic Programming 79(7), 578–607 (2010)
11. Engel, C., Roth, A., Schmitt, P.H., Weiß, B.: Verification of modifies clauses in dynamic logic with non-rigid functions. Technical Report 2009-9, Department of Computer Science, University of Karlsruhe (2009)
12. Kang, K., Lee, J., Donohoe, P.: Feature-Oriented Project Line Engineering. IEEE Software 19(4) (2002)
13. Kiczales, G., Mezini, M.: Aspect-oriented programming and modular reasoning. In: ICSE, pp. 49–58. ACM (2005)
14. Lauenroth, K., Pohl, K., Toehning, S.: Model checking of domain artifacts in product line engineering. In: ASE, pp. 269–280 (2009)
15. Leavens, G.T., Poll, E., Clifton, C., Cheon, Y., Ruby, C., Cok, D., Müller, P., Kiniry, J., Chalin, P., Zimmerman, D.M.: JML Reference Manual (September 2009)
16. Li, H., Krishnamurthi, S., Fisler, K.: Modular Verification of Open Features Using Three-Valued Model Checking. Autom. Softw. Eng. 12(3) (2005)
17. Liskov, B., Wing, J.M.: A behavioral notion of subtyping. ACM Trans. Program. Lang. Syst. 16(6), 1811–1841 (1994)
18. Meyer, B.: Applying design by contract. IEEE Computer 25(10), 40–51 (1992)
19. Schaefer, I., Bettini, L., Bono, V., Damiani, F., Tanzarella, N.: Delta-Oriented Programming of Software Product Lines. In: Bosch, J., Lee, J. (eds.) SPLC 2010. LNCS, vol. 6287, pp. 77–91. Springer, Heidelberg (2010)
20. Schaefer, I., Bettini, L., Damiani, F.: Compositional type-checking for delta-oriented programming. In: 10th International Conference on Aspect-Oriented Software Development, AOSD 2011, pp. 43–56. ACM (2011)
21. Soundarajan, N., Fridella, S.: Inheritance: From code reuse to reasoning reuse. In: Proc. 5th Intl Conf. on Software Reuse, pp. 206–215. IEEE Comp. Soc. (1998)
22. Soundarajan, N., Fridella, S.: Incremental Reasoning for Object Oriented Systems. In: Owe, O., Krogdahl, S., Lyche, T. (eds.) From Object-Orientation to Formal Methods. LNCS, vol. 2635, pp. 302–333. Springer, Heidelberg (2004)
23. Thüm, T., Schaefer, I., Kuhlemann, M., Apel, S.: Proof composition for deductive verification of software product lines. In: Proc. Int'l Workshop Variability-Intensive Systems Testing, Validation and Verification, pp. 270–277. IEEE CS (2011)

Scientific Workflows: Eternal Components, Changing Interfaces, Varying Compositions

Anna-Lena Lamprecht and Tiziana Margaria

Chair for Service and Software Engineering
Potsdam University, Germany
{lamprecht,margaria}@cs.uni-potsdam.de

Abstract. We describe how scientific application domains are characterized by the long-term availability of the basic computational components, and how software systems for managing the actual scientific workflows must deal with changing service interfaces and varying service compositions. In this light, we explain how rigorous technical and semantic abstraction, which is key to dealing with huge and heterogeneous application domains in an "extreme model driven design" framework like the jABC, supports the management of workflow evolution. We illustrate the different aspects by means of examples and experiences from the application of the framework in different scientific application domains.

1 Introduction

Evolution of software systems and long-lived applications are currently intensively researched topics under many points of view [1, 2]. In the new field of e-science, workflow management for scientific applications is a key application domain that combines artifacts with very different timelines and life cycles. The basic algorithmic components that perform the individual analysis steps are in fact very long-lived: Many of the popular algorithms, tools, and databases have been available for over a decade and remained mainly unchanged. Their concrete use and composition, however, varies considerably from case to case, according to the current scientific analysis process and the involved data. In fact, progress and novelty in "in silico" experimentation, where experiments and analyses are carried out in computers on the basis of preexisting data and knowledge, thus largely happens "ex aliquo", and not "ex nihilo", i.e. from scratch. Therefore we need to distinguish two fields of progress and evolution: in the *application domain*, that originates from fast-paced evolution of analysis and simulation processes that use preexisting resources, and the progress and evolution of the *IT ingredients*, that makes the first one possible and is itself much less frequent. Process evolution occurs in the frequent case that an existing analysis process has to be adapted to new experimental requirements or data. Standard software evolution on the contrary occurs mainly when existing algorithms, tools and databases are equipped with new interfaces, which happens relatively seldom. The overall setting therefore yields a fairly stable basis of software artifacts,

T. Margaria and B. Steffen (Eds.): ISoLA 2012, Part I, LNCS 7609, pp. 47–63, 2012.

that are combined and recombined at fast pace to try out new analyses in an orchestration or coordination-oriented composition.

In this paper we describe how an extreme model driven approach [3, 4] supports the agile management of process/workflow evolution in the light of such really huge and truly heterogeneous application domains. The core concept is that here different levels of abstraction make a completely symbolic treatment of the involved entities possible. A combination of these abstractions then allows for handling application-level processes and their evolution at a semantic level, within the application domain.

The past decade has seen a lot of research on scientific workflow management in general (see, e.g, [5, 6]) and on the use of semantics-based methods for supporting service composition in particular (see, e.g., [7–10]). We are not aware, however, of any work that looks at the evolution of scientific workflows from the broad service-engineering perspective that we describe in this paper, which is based on the jABC framework [11, 12]. We draw here on the experience of several years of usage for the management of scientific workflows both in teaching and in research projects (cf., e.g., [13–18]),

The paper is structured as follows. Section 2 introduces the abstraction concepts needed to enable and support the fast-paced workflow evolution needed for "in-silico" e-science; Section 3 illustrates the specific jABC-based approach by reporting some exemplary experiences from the bioinformatics and geo-visualization application domains, and Section 4 concludes the paper.

2   Abstraction for Fast-Paced Workflow Evolution

The conceptual framework of *eXtreme Model-Driven Design* (XMDD) [3, 4, 19] aims at an agile yet service-oriented modeling, design, and development of process-style applications within a domain-specific setting. E-science is such a domain, with specific incarnations e.g. for bioinformatics, or geo-visualisation.

The central assets are here a collection of services (implemented by means of software artifacts) and a domain knowledge representation (implemented via taxonomies/ontologies) that can be easily used by domain experts and that are supported by a sophisticated framework that helps the user in the selection, composition, validation, and execution of the resulting workflows. While it is possible to achieve parts of this goal by means of traditional approaches, that use heterogeneous technologies to cover different aspects and subproblems[1], the *jABC* [11, 12] is a concrete framework that supports high automation and consistency in working with processes and workflows by offering a number of special-purpose plugins in an extreme model-driven setting, where the user only works at the model level and the necessary compositions and transformations are largely taken care of by the framework itself via specific plugins.

---

[1] For example, using the standard technologies from the different sub-communities of software engineering, one could have components modeled in UML, wrapped as services in a WSDL, with orchestrations expresses in BPEL or BPMN or Petri nets and domain knowledge expressed in WSMO or OWL ontologies.

user: compositions

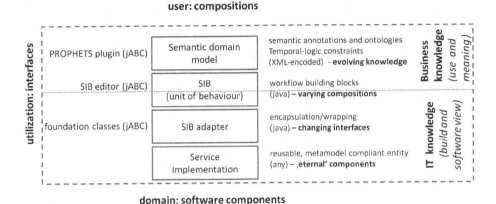

Fig. 1. From the domain knowledge to the IT: Abstraction layers in the jABC framework

In particular, the PROPHETS plugin [20] bundles functionality for semantic annotations, model checking, and automatic synthesis of workflows according to the *Loose Programming* paradigm of [21], which offers abstraction from the concrete workflow (see Sect. 3.4). The basis for the models in jABC are libraries of semantically annotated, behavioral workflow components, called *SIBs* (*Service Independent Building Blocks*). SIBs provide access to encapsulated units of functionality, which can be freely combined into flowchart-like workflow structures called *Service Logic Graphs* (SLGs) that are technically service orchestrations. The concretization of SLGs towards running systems typically happens in a hierarchical fashion via several refinement steps (cf. [22]).

The key to an agile dealing with software evolution is rigorous virtualization/abstraction: striving for a completely symbolic treatment of the involved entities allows one to handle application-level processes at a semantic level, as illustrated in Figure 1. Concretely, given the usual service or component implementation customary in component-based design or in service-oriented architectures, the jABC works with three principal layers of abstraction, which address different challenges of software evolution:

1. The *SIBs* are the actual behavioral entities of the workflow building blocks as defined from the application's/user's perspective. They tailor the single workflow building blocks to the specific needs of the application/user. In essence, a SIB defines an adequate interface for a workflow building block, and connects it to the services that are provided by the SIB adapters. Thus, if something in the SIB adapters changes, the corresponding SIB implementations can be adapted accordingly, but the workflow models themselves are not affected. In the sense of [23], the concept of a SIB is that of a *behavioral metamodel*: it presents all sorts of needed components in a uniform manner to the user and makes them really work in a simple, easy-to-use and composite fashion.

2. The *SIB adapters* absorb the change management of evolving technologies and evolving components by abstracting from the technical details of the underlying platforms and service implementations, which are typically implemented in heterogeneous technologies. Thus, if something in the service implementation changes, the SIB adapters can be changed accordingly, but the SIBs, as workflow building blocks, are themselves not affected: Workflows use only the SIB-level information.

3. *Semantic domain models* on top of the SIB libraries drive the abstraction even further, allowing in particular for the completely symbolic description of the SIBs and their parameters in terms of the application's/user's domain language. As shown in Fig. 1, the user's composition of workflows happens within the "business domain" knowledge, that includes SIB selection and composition, while the IT issues are taken care of within the lower layers [24, 25]. In particular, this organization facilitates "loose" programming of workflows, where parts of the workflow model can be left underspecified, and are only concretized upon request. Thus, if anything in the SIB library changes, the semantic domain model can be independently adapted, and the (loose) workflow models themselves are not affected.

In the following sections we describe these notions of technical and semantic abstraction in greater detail. Together, they lead to two separate levels in workflow development: a *story level*, that takes place between the SIB and the semantic knowledge layers (the upper two in Fig. 1), where one designs and communicates the spirit of the analysis/experiment, and the actual *executable level* (the lower two layers in Fig. 1), where a concretized version takes care of the coherence and consistency of all details.

2.1 Handling Technical Abstraction: The SIBs

The SIBs in the jABC are services in the proper sense, encapsulating units of functionality that are defined from the application's/user's perspective. Instead of being architectural components, as most service component models like in the standard SCA [26], they are *units of behavior* oriented to their use within processes or workflows. As discussed for instance in [25], granularity decisions are essential for the design of SIBs that are adequate for the envisaged applications. While standard services are remote software units that offer a collection of behavior to their users, SIBs only have one behavior and are thus easier to understand, manage, and compose. A single standard (web) service can thus correspond to a collection of SIBs. This explains why they are easy to use for domain experts, much easier than standard services.

Additionally, SIBs provide homogeneous service interfaces that truly abstract from the technical details of the underlying implementation. Their provisioning involves integrating distributed services that are provided via heterogeneous technologies (such as SOAP and REST web services, legacy tools, and specific APIs) into homogeneous libraries of workflow building blocks.

The SIB structure is depicted in the lower three layers of Figure 1:

- The actual *SIB*[2] provides the service interface within the workflow environment. In addition to service documentation and other usability information, it defines the service parameters to be configured by the calling application/workflow.
- The *SIB adapter* handles the service call, using the information from the SIB class that is relevant for its execution (esp. parameters).
- The *service implementation* defines the actual execution behavior. It can be arbitrary functionality in any programming language.

Thus, as the underlying implementation changes, a SIB's adapter has to be exchanged or adapted too, but the SIB class - which is the actual interface to the workflow environment - mostly remains unchanged. In practice, this largely decouples the workflow development in the jABC framework from the evolution of the underlying platforms and of the concrete algorithms.

2.2 Handling Semantic Abstraction: Loose Programming

Loose programming [21] supports a form of model-based *declarative* software development that enables workflow developers to design their application-specific workflows in an intuitive (graphical) style driven by their domain knowledge, rather than from the technicalities of composition and composability. In particular, it aims at making highly heterogeneous collections of services accessible to application experts who have no classical programming skills, but who need to design and manage complex workflows. After an adequate domain modeling, application experts should ultimately be able to profitably and efficiently work with a world-wide distributed collection of services and data, using their own domain language and understanding services at the behavioral metamodel level. In particular, the semantic domain models abstract from the SIB interfaces, making everything in the workflow environment even more symbolic and intuitively comprehensible to the scientist.

Concretely, the semantic domain models are defined on top of the SIB libraries and comprise:

- service and data type taxonomies that provide semantic categories and relations for the involved entities, building the *domain vocabulary*,
- behavioral *interface descriptions*, i.e. input and output annotations, in terms of the domain vocabulary, and
- temporal-logic *constraints* that express additional knowledge about the application domain in general or about the intended workflows in particular.

An example for such models will be discussed in Sect. 3. These semantic domain models are entirely based on symbolic names for services and data types,

---

[2] Technically, the SIB class, which we associate with the part of the SIB that belongs to the IT world in contrast to the view on the SIB from the business domain (from above), which corresponds to concepts in the domain knowledge model.

therefore the user-level semantic service descriptions are completely decoupled from the SIBs that implement the actual functionality. Accordingly, the semantic description(s) provided for a service can be freely defined: it is possible to use custom terminology, use the same service for different purposes, or simply omit unnecessary details in the interface description.

With loose programming users specify their intentions about a workflow in a very sparse way, by just giving an intuitive, high-level rough process flow in terms of ontologically defined semantic entities from the domain model, without caring about types, precise knowledge about the available workflow components or the availability of resources. A synthesis mechanism in the background automatically completes this sketch into a correctly running workflow by inserting missing details. This is achieved by means of a combination of different formal methodologies: Data-flow analysis provides information on available and required resources, which is used by a temporal-logic synthesis algorithm [27] to find sequences of services that are suitable to concretize the loose parts. Additionally, model checking is used to monitor global process constraints continuously.

In loose programming there is thus abstraction from the concrete workflow that implements a particular analysis process: if the set of available SIBs/services changes, the framework can automatically find another suitable composition of services that solves the problem.

In the next section we report some exemplary experiences with software evolution from the application of the jABC framework in the bioinformatics application domain.

3   Examples and Experiences

To show the spread of possible applications and techniques, we focus now on four different aspects: Dealing with the wealth of command line tools (Sect. 3.1), dealing with a technology migration for entire collections of widely used services (Sect. 3.2), dealing with the high volatility of ad-hoc workflow design and evolution (Sect. 3.3), and dealing with a new, declarative way of describing the intentions of a workflow that is automatically synthesized in one or more variants (Sect. 3.4). In the following, we concentrate mainly on examples from bioinformatics, but experiences from the geo-visualization domain are analogous.

3.1   SIBs for "Good Old" Command Line Tools

In scientific application domains, algorithms are often implemented as "small" special-purpose tools that can simply be invoked from the command line, without requiring to cope with "unnecessary" stuff (like fancy GUIs etc.) that is intended to help the user but often hampers programmatic, systematic access to the underlying functionality. Thus, classical command line tools are usually well suited to provide collections of basic building blocks for service compositions. Conveniently, classical command line tools are in fact very popular in the bioinformatics and geo-visualization domains.

Fig. 2. Basic multiple sequence alignment workflow

For example, the European Molecular Biology Open Software Suite (EM-
BOSS) [28][3] is a rich collection of freely available tools for the molecular biology
user community dealing with proteins and amino acids. It contains a number of
small and large programs for a wide range of tasks, such as sequence alignment,
nucleotide sequence pattern analysis, and codon usage analysis as well as the
preparation of data for presentation and publication.

This and similar collections have been used in the respective user community
for quite a long time: the first version of EMBOSS was released around 2000, and
their functionalities are still useful as a basis for new workflow applications. This
is an example of the longevity of basic domain-specific "eternal" components that
support several generations of scientists and serve unchanged the communities
for decades.[4]

Sometimes such service collections are repackaged and provided as "modern"
web services. For example, the EMBOSS tools are provided as web services in
the scope of the EBI's SoapLab project [30, 31]. Often, however, communication
with the web services via these interfaces happens at a quite technical level: the
sheer operations of the web services are not adequate for direct integration as
workflow building blocks.

The jETI technology [32] specifically supports such direct integration for command line tools in the jABC framework. In fact, command line tools are typically
designed to execute specific well-defined tasks, and usually all inputs and configuration options can be provided upon invocation, so that their execution runs
completely autonomous (headless, in bioinformatics terminology). They also typically work on files in a pipe-and-filter transformer fashion, which is per se closer
to the user-level than the programming language entities (such as Java objects)
that are required for the communication with, e.g., Web Service APIs. Accordingly, jETI services, which are designed to provide convenient (remote) access to
file-based command line tools as SIBs, are inherently closer to the user-level than
web services. Entire collections of services can be made available to end-users
this way.

---

[3] http://emboss.sourceforge.net/
[4] As an example from the geo-visualization domain: the Generic Mapping Tools
(GMT) collection [29] (http://gmt.soest.hawaii.edu/) was released around the
year 1990 and is in heavy use since then, also clearly deserving the denomination of
eternal components used in the title.

3.2   SIBs for Bioinformatics Web Services: From SOAP to REST

Large bioinformatics institutions like the DDBJ (DNA Data Bank of Japan), EBI (European Bioinformatics Institute), and NCBI (National Center for Biotechnology Information) have been providing publicly available web services to access databases and computational tools already for a quite long time (that is, since web services became popular).

Currently, many major service providers are abandoning their SOAP-based web service interfaces and follow the general trend towards using REST interfaces. Consequently, the SIBs that had been implemented for accessing the DDBJ and EBI web services [33–35] had to be changed accordingly at some point, to follow this technology shift on the provider's side. Luckily, as discussed in Sect. 2, it was indeed only required to change in the SIB adapters the portion of code that executes the actual service calls. The SIB classes on the contrary were not touched at all by the transition: the user/application-level parameters of the services did not change. Likewise, on the workflow level this change of underlying technology was not perceptible at all.

This is an example of how the "changing interfaces" due to technology migration only locally impact the provisioning of the services. As il lustrated by Fig. 1, technology agnosticism at the behavioral metamodel level guarantees the stable fruition of the SIB for the end-users.

3.3   Agile Models for Variable/Evolving Scientific Workflows

Contrary to the stability of the single services offered, scientific workflows are characterized by being variant-rich and having to be adapted frequently to varying experimental setups and analysis objectives. Actually, in most cases the scientist is even searching for the optimal workflow in a cumbersome cycle of modification, test, analysis, and adaptation. The point of the research is often to find a data analysis or data processing workflow, that is itself the central result of the quest. Working by approximation, the volatility of such workflows is high, yielding series of "varying" compositions.

XMDD as evolution-oriented paradigm explicitly supports these kinds of application evolution and adaptation at a user-accessible level. In jABC, workflows can easily be modified, adapted, customized and tested in its graphical user interface, and (parts of) workflows can be prepared and flexibly (re-)combined according to current analysis objectives.

Example: Multiple Sequence Alignment. In the bioinformatics application domain, the multiple sequence alignment is an example that is particularly suited to illustrate the agility of workflow design (cf. [17] for further details). Figure 2 shows a simple workflow for this computation. In terms of algorithmic computations, it consists of just one SIB that calls an alignment service, here ClustalW. Just this step would however not suffice: it also needs some SIBs that take care of handling the input and output data. The SIB select sequence file (at the left, with the underlined name) lets the user select a file from the local file system and the SIB read sequence file puts the file's content into the execution context.

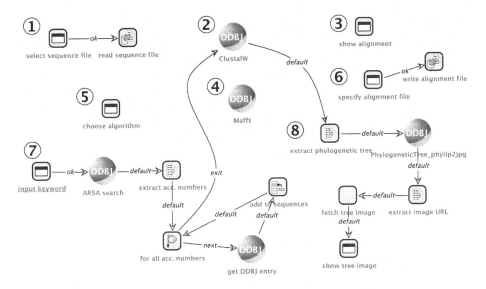

Fig. 3. Flexibly variable multiple sequence alignment workflow

This data is then sent to the DDBJ's ClustalW web service for the alignment computation, and finally show alignment displays the result to the user.

This is the simplest, but certainly not the only way an alignment can be computed. It can be useful to use other algorithms and to manage the input and output in different ways. Figure 3 shows an orchestration of SIBs (a Service Logic Graph) with several preconfigured workflow snippets that in detail provide the following functionalities:

1. Select and read a sequence file from the local file system.
2. Call the DDBJ's ClustalW alignment service.
3. Show an alignment in a simple text dialog window.
4. Call the DDBJ's Mafft alignment service.
5. Let the user choose the service.
6. Save the alignment to the local file system.
7. Let the user enter a keyword, which is used for a DDBJ database search (via the ARSA system). This results in a list of accession numbers (i.e. identifiers) for which the corresponding sequences are fetched from the DDBJ database.
8. Extract the phylogenetic tree that is part of a ClustalW result (using a regular expression) and call the phylip2jpg service of the DDBJ that converts the textual tree representation into an image, followed by retrieving and displaying the image.

These snippets might have arisen from the work of the same scientist in different contexts and stored for reusal, or have been designed by different community members and shared within the community. No matter their origin, they can now be put together to form various alignment workflows simply by connecting them appropriately. For instance, connecting the snippets 1, 2 and 3 results in the basic alignment workflow of Fig. 2. Connecting the snippets 2, 7, and 8 forms a more complex workflow (as depicted in Fig. 3), comprising database search by keyword, sequence retrieval, alignment computation, and visualization of the implied phylogenetic tree.

We see here that variability and a large selection of alternative subprocesses arise naturally in this highly dynamic domain and that artifacts are naturally shared within the community. Variability and reuse at this level, corresponding to the upper two layers of Fig. 1 are the norm in this kind of scientific applications.

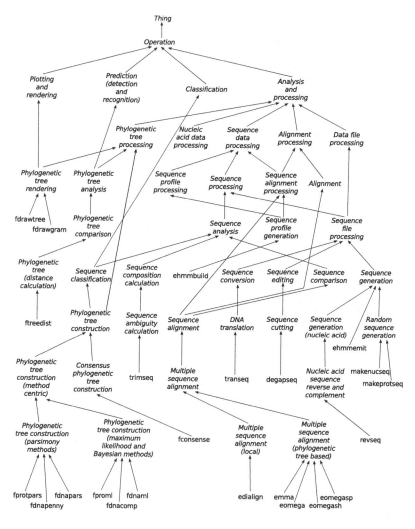

Fig. 4. Part of the service taxonomy of the EMBOSS domain model

3.4   Loose Models for Variable and Evolving Scientific Workflows

While the previous section described how the jABC framework supports building variations of preconfigured workflow snippets consisting of known concrete SIBs, this section demonstrates how the loose programming provided by the jABC framework facilitates creating workflow variants in an exploratory way, without concrete knowledge about the available workflow building blocks. The envisaged workflow is only modeled declaratively, and the framework takes care of translating the specification into a concrete executable workflow based on the available collection of workflow building blocks.

With loose programming, workflow design is not only flexible with regard to changing experimental setups and analysis objectives as described above, but also with regard to evolving service libraries, as the synthesis framework automatically takes into account all changes and extensions of the domain model. This enables even more agile workflow development, as shown in [36] it is not required to pre-define the possible variants. As the underlying constraint language allows fully describing the intended solution space without imposing any overspecification, neither on the structure, nor on the artifacts, our approach may in particular be regarded as a step from the today typical settings with closed-world assumption to one with an *open-world assumption*, where new artifacts are automatically and seamlessly integrated in the domain description and thus in the loose programming solutions as soon as they are available.

Example: Phylogenetic Workflows Based on the EMBOSS Tool Suite. As an example from the field of bioinformatics, we take a look at loose programming of phylogenetic workflows with the EMBOSS tool suite (cf. [37, 38] for further details). Conveniently, as of release 6.4.0 from July 2011, the more than 400 tools of the EMBOSS suite and their parameters are annotated in terms of the EMBRACE Data and Methods Ontology (EDAM) [39], which allows for automatic generation of the semantic domain models that are required for loose programming (cf. [38]).

Figure 4 shows excerpts from the service taxonomy of the domain model. The OWL class *Thing* is always the root of the taxonomies, below which EDAM terms provide groups for concrete and abstract service and type representations. The (part of the) service taxonomy shown there comprises a number of service categories for different *Operations*. Note that the type and service taxonomies comprise 565 and 1425 terms, respectively, directly after being derived from EDAM. They are then automatically reduced to those parts that are relevant for the services and data that appear in the domain model in order to avoid overhead, still covering 236 and 207 terms, respectively. To facilitate the printed presentation, the figure includes only the parts of the service taxonomy relevant for this example.

Table 1 lists the services that are relevant for the following examples, along with their input and output data types. It comprises only 23 of the more than 430 services in the complete domain model. The set of input types contains all mandatory inputs (i.e., optional inputs are not considered), while the set of output types contains all possible outputs. The service interface definitions only

Table 1. Selection of services from the EMBOSS domain model

Service	Input types	Output types
degapseq	*Sequence record*	*Sequence record*
edialign	*Sequence record*	*Sequence alignment, Sequence record*
ehmmbuild	*Sequence record (protein)*	*Hidden Markov Model,* *Sequence alignment (protein)*
ehmmemit	*Hidden Markov Model*	*Sequence record (protein)*
emma	*Sequence record*	*Phylogenetic tree, Sequence record*
eomega	*Sequence record*	*Phylogenetic tree, Sequence record*
eomegash	*Sequence record,* *Sequence-profile alignment (HMM)*	*Phylogenetic tree, Sequence record*
eomegasp	*Sequence record, Sequence-profile*	*Phylogenetic tree, Sequence record,* *Sequence distance matrix*
fconsense	*Phylogenetic tree*	*Phylogenetic tree*
fdnacomp	*Sequence record (nucleic acid)*	*Phylogenetic tree*
fdnaml	*Sequence alignment (nucleic acid)*	*Phylogenetic tree*
fdnapars	*Sequence alignment (nucleic acid)*	*Phylogenetic tree*
fdnapenny	*Sequence alignment (nucleic acid)*	*Phylogenetic tree*
fdrawgram	*Phylogenetic tree*	*Phylogenetic tree*
fdrawtree	*Phylogenetic tree*	*Phylogenetic tree*
fproml	*Sequence alignment (protein)*	*Phylogenetic tree*
fprotpars	*Sequence alignment (protein)*	*Phylogenetic tree*
ftreedist	*Phylogenetic tree*	*Phylogenetic report (tree distances)*
makenucseq	-	*Sequence record*
makeprotseq	-	*Sequence record (protein)*
revseq	*Sequence record*	*Sequence record (nucleic acid)*
transeq	*Sequence record*	*Sequence record (protein)*
trimseq	*Sequence record*	*Sequence record*

consider the data that is actually passed between the individual services, that is, input parameters that are used for configuration purposes are not regarded as service inputs.

Figure 5 (top) shows a simple loosely specified phylogenetic analysis workflow: it begins by generating a set of random nucleotide sequences (using the EMBOSS service makenucseq) and ends by drawing and displaying a tree image (using fdrawtree and the viewer SIB of the jETI plugin), respectively. The first two SIBs are connected by a loosely specified branch (colored red and labeled with a question mark). This loose branch constitutes a synthesis query to the PROPHETS plugin.

The lower part of the figure shows three of the millions of possible service sequences that solve this synthesis problem: The first, which is also one of the shortest solutions, is a single call to emma (an interface to ClustalW), which produces a phylogenetic tree in addition to a multiple sequence alignment. In the second, the reverse complement of the input sequence is built (revseq) and

Loosely specified workflow:

Possible concretizations:

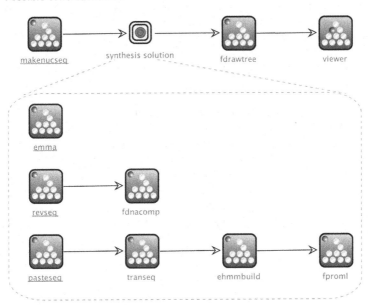

Fig. 5. Loosely specified phylogenetic analysis workflow and possible concretizations

then used for phylogenetic tree construction with **fdnacomp**. In the third, the sequences are translated into protein sequences (**transeq**), which are then aligned via **ehmmbuild** and used for phylogenetic tree estimation with **fprotpars**. The last solution is a four-step workflow where an additional sequence is pasted into the input sequences (**pasteseq**), which are then translated into protein sequences (**transeq**) and aligned via **ehmmbuild** before **fproml** is used for the tree construction.

Since EMBOSS provides various tools for phylogenetic tree construction as well as for the different sequence processing tasks, the solutions contained in the figure are by far not the only possible ones. In fact, millions of logically correct solutions are easily *possible* with the described domain model already when searching only for comparatively short solutions up to length 4. However, they comprise a lot of solutions that are not *desired* or *adequate*. Hence, it is desirable to influence the synthesis process so that it is more focused, returning less solutions that are more adequate. Here we see the advantages of the declarative approach to the problem formulation: we can simply provide temporal-logic constraints that express the corresponding intents by describing more precisely the wished solutions in terms of properties. Conveniently, PROPHETS provides natural-language templates for frequently occurring constraints, so that the workflow designer does not need to be trained in temporal logics. As an example, consider the following three constraints:

- *Do not use services that have no inputs.* Excludes services that distract from the actual synthesis problem: such services require no input but provide new data that is planted into the workflow.)
- *Do not use Sequence editing and alignment services.* (Avoids particular operations that are not wanted for some reason.)
- *Enforce the use of Phylogenetic tree construction (parsimony methods).* (Includes a particular kind of operation.)

With these constraints, manageable sets of adequate solutions are now obtained: there are two solutions of length three and 268 of length four.

This example illustrates how with loose programming workflow models remain robust against evolution of the service infrastructure and the semantic domain model: Loose workflow models and constraints capture the essential properties of the envisaged workflow, and can be synthesized at need into a concrete, executable workflow based on the currently available components using as services the SIBs and in the constraints the concepts of the domain model shown in the upper two layers of Fig. 1.

4   Conclusion

In this paper we focused on a central observation concerning software evolution in scientific application domains: Their basic software components (databases, algorithms, tools) remain available in largely unchanged form for a very long time, even decades, once they have been introduced. New functionality is added to the pool of available components rather than replacing existing assets. Hence, it is the *periphery* of the concrete service interfaces that is subject to sudden changes, for example when an entire suite of algorithms migrates its provisioning from SOAP to REST, and their application-specific use and composition are subject to fast-paced evolution, as the data analysis processes are themselves part of the research work and object of experimentation. In fields like bioinformatics and geo-visualization, e-science seems to have a hard core of stable ingredients (repositories of data and algorithms) and a sizzling outer layer of process-oriented experimental work that yields the progress of the disciplines today.

We have shown how the rigorous abstraction concepts of the extreme model driven design paradigm facilitate dealing with changing service interfaces and varying service compositions and thus with workflow evolution in these application domains. The decoupling of concerns due to adequate abstractions and layers in the semantic service engineering approach we propose, together with the plugin-based tool support offered by the jABC framework is the key to a semantics- (or application domain knowledge-) driven workflow design, that enables scientists (our end-users) to largely work within their domains of competence, without the need of IT knowledge as required by scripting languages that are today considered necessary for any "do it yourself"-style of scientific workflow composition. In particular the declarative loose specification approach, coupled with the automatic synthesis of executable workflows, seems to us to be a promising path towards self-assembling and self-optimizing processes: the declarative top-down approach (plus synthesis) is knowledge-driven and specifies just as much as necessary/wanted (but not more), which leads to an *open-world* assumption, where new components or services or repositories automatically appear in the solutions as soon as they are made available. This contrasts traditional orchestration-based approaches that explicitly define variability as a configuration space, which typically leads to overspecification and a *closed-world* assumption, where one actively deselects from a predefined choice of options.

References

1. Mens, T., Demeyer, S. (eds.): Software Evolution. Springer (2008)
2. : EternalS: EU FET Coordination Action on Trustworthy Eternal Systems via Evolving Software, Data and Knowledge
3. Margaria, T., Steffen, B.: Thinking in User-Centric Models. In: Margaria, T., Steffen, B. (eds.) Leveraging Applications of Formal Methods, Verification and Validation. CCIS, vol. 17, pp. 490–502. Springer, Heidelberg (2009)
4. Margaria, T., Steffen, B.: Service-Orientation: Conquering Complexity with XMDD. In: Hinchey, M., Coyle, L. (eds.) Conquering Complexity, pp. 217–236. Springer, London (2012)
5. Oinn, T., Greenwood, M., Addis, M., Alpdemir, M.N., Ferris, J., Glover, K., Goble, C., Goderis, A., Hull, D., Marvin, D., Li, P., Lord, P., Pocock, M.R., Senger, M., Stevens, R., Wipat, A., Wroe, C.: Taverna: lessons in creating a workflow environment for the life sciences: Research Articles. Concurr. Comput.: Pract. Exper. 18(10), 1067–1100 (2006)
6. Taylor, I.: Workflows for E-Science: Scientific Workflows for Grids. Springer (2007)
7. Chen, L., Shadbolt, N.R., Goble, C., Tao, F., Cox, S.J., Puleston, C., Smart, P.R.: Towards a Knowledge-Based Approach to Semantic Service Composition. In: Fensel, D., Sycara, K., Mylopoulos, J. (eds.) ISWC 2003. LNCS, vol. 2870, pp. 319–334. Springer, Heidelberg (2003)
8. Ludäscher, B., Altintas, I., Gupta, A.: Compiling Abstract Scientific Workflows into Web Service Workflows. In: International Conference on Scientific and Statistical Database Management, p. 251 (2003)
9. Potter, S., Aitken, S.: A Semantic Service Environment: A Case Study in Bioinformatics. In: Gómez-Pérez, A., Euzenat, J. (eds.) ESWC 2005. LNCS, vol. 3532, pp. 694–709. Springer, Heidelberg (2005)
10. Withers, D., Kawas, E., McCarthy, L., Vandervalk, B., Wilkinson, M.: Semantically-Guided Workflow Construction in Taverna: The SADI and BioMoby Plug-Ins. In: Margaria, T., Steffen, B. (eds.) ISoLA 2010, Part I. LNCS, vol. 6415, pp. 301–312. Springer, Heidelberg (2010)
11. Steffen, B., Margaria, T., Nagel, R., Jörges, S., Kubczak, C.: Model-Driven Development with the jABC. In: Bin, E., Ziv, A., Ur, S. (eds.) HVC 2006. LNCS, vol. 4383, pp. 92–108. Springer, Heidelberg (2007)

12. Kubczak, C., Jörges, S., Margaria, T., Steffen, B.: eXtreme Model-Driven Design with jABC. In: CTIT Proc. of the Tools and Consultancy Track of the Fifth European Conference on Model-Driven Architecture Foundations and Applications (ECMDA-FA), vol. WP09-12, pp. 78–99 (2009)

13. Kubczak, C., Margaria, T., Fritsch, A., Steffen, B.: Biological LC/MS Preprocessing and Analysis with jABC, jETI and xcms. In: Proceedings of the 2nd International Symposium on Leveraging Applications of Formal Methods, Verification and Validation (ISoLA 2006), Paphos, Cyprus, November 15-19, pp. 308–313. IEEE Computer Society, Paphos, Cyprus (2006)

14. Margaria, T., Kubczak, C., Njoku, M., Steffen, B.: Model-based Design of Distributed Collaborative Bioinformatics Processes in the jABC. In: Procedings of 11th IEEE International Conference on Engineering of Complex Computer Systems (ICECCS 2006), Stanford, California, Los Alamitos, CA, USA, August 15-17, pp. 169–176. IEEE Computer Society (August 2006)

15. Margaria, T., Kubczak, C., Steffen, B.: Bio-jETI: a service integration, design, and provisioning platform for orchestrated bioinformatics processes. BMC Bioinformatics 9(suppl. 4), S12 (2008)

16. Lamprecht, A.L., Margaria, T., Steffen, B., Sczyrba, A., Hartmeier, S., Giegerich, R.: GeneFisher-P: variations of GeneFisher as processes in Bio-jETI. BMC Bioinformatics 9 (suppl. 4), S13 (2008)

17. Lamprecht, A.-L., Margaria, T., Steffen, B.: Seven Variations of an Alignment Workflow - An Illustration of Agile Process Design and Management in Bio-jETI. In: Măndoiu, I., Wang, S.-L., Zelikovsky, A. (eds.) ISBRA 2008. LNCS (LNBI), vol. 4983, pp. 445–456. Springer, Heidelberg (2008)

18. Lamprecht, A.L., Margaria, T., Steffen, B.: Bio-jETI: a framework for semantics-based service composition. BMC Bioinformatics 10(suppl. 10), S8 (2009)

19. Margaria, T., Steffen, B.: Business Process Modelling in the jABC: The One-Thing-Approach. In: Cardoso, J., van der Aalst, W. (eds.) Handbook of Research on Business Process Modeling. IGI Global (2009)

20. Naujokat, S., Lamprecht, A.-L., Steffen, B.: Loose Programming with PROPHETS. In: de Lara, J., Zisman, A. (eds.) FASE 2012. LNCS, vol. 7212, pp. 94–98. Springer, Heidelberg (2012)

21. Lamprecht, A.L., Naujokat, S., Margaria, T., Steffen, B.: Synthesis-Based Loose Programming. In: Proceedings of the 7th International Conference on the Quality of Information and Communications Technology, QUATIC (September 2010)

22. Steffen, B., Margaria, T., Braun, V., Kalt, N.: Hierarchical Service Definition. Annual Review of Communications of the ACM 51, 847–856 (1997)

23. Jung, G., Margaria, T., Nagel, R., Schubert, W., Steffen, B., Voigt, H.: SCA and jABC: Bringing a Service-Oriented Paradigm to Web-Service Construction. In: Margaria, T., Steffen, B. (eds.) ISoLA 2008. CCIS, vol. 17, pp. 139–154. Springer, Heidelberg (2008)

24. Margaria, T., Steffen, B.: Service Engineering: Linking Business and IT. Computer 39(10), 45–55 (2006)

25. Margaria, T., Bosselmann, S., Doedt, M., Floyd, B. D., Steffen, B.: Customer-Oriented Business Process Management: Visions and Obstacles. In: Hinchey, M., Coyle, L. (eds.) Conquering Complexity, pp. 407–429. Springer London (2012)

26. Service Component Architecture (SCA), http://www.oasis-opencsa.org/sca/ (2012) (online; last accessed July 26, 2012)

27. Steffen, B., Margaria, T., Freitag, B.: Module Configuration by Minimal Model Construction. Technical report, Fakultät für Mathematik und Informatik, Universität Passau (1993)

28. Rice, P., Longden, I., Bleasby, A.: EMBOSS: the European Molecular Biology Open Software Suite. Trends in Genetics: TIG 16(6), 276–277 (2000)
29. Wessel, P., Smith, W. H. F.: Free software helps map and display data. EOS Trans. Amer. Geophys. U. 72(41) (1991)
30. Soaplab, `http://soaplab.sourceforge.net/soaplab1/` (online; last accessed June 25, 2012)
31. Soaplab2, `http://soaplab.sourceforge.net/soaplab2/` (online; last accessed June 25 2012)
32. Margaria, T., Nagel, R., Steffen, B.: jETI: A Tool for Remote Tool Integration. In: Halbwachs, N., Zuck, L.D. (eds.) TACAS 2005. LNCS, vol. 3440, pp. 557–562. Springer, Heidelberg (2005)
33. DDBJ Web API for Biology, `http://xml.nig.ac.jp/workflow/` (online; temporarily suspended since February 15, 2012)
34. Pillai, S., Silventoinen, V., Kallio, K., Senger, M., Sobhany, S., Tate, J., Velankar, S., Golovin, A., Henrick, K., Rice, P., Stoehr, P., Lopez, R.: SOAP-based services provided by the European Bioinformatics Institute. Nucleic Acids Research 33(Web Server issue), W25–W28 (July 2005)
35. Labarga, A., Valentin, F., Anderson, M., Lopez, R.: Web services at the European bioinformatics institute. Nucleic Acids Research 35(Web Server issue), W6–W11 (2007)
36. Lamprecht, A., Margaria, T., Schaefer, I., Steffen, B.: Synthesis-based variability control: correctness by construction. In: Proceedings of FMCO 2011, Software Technologies Concertation Meeting on "Formal Methods for Components and Objects", Torino, Italy (October 2011)
37. Lamprecht, A.L., Naujokat, S., Margaria, T., Steffen, B.: Semantics-based composition of EMBOSS services. Journal of Biomedical Semantics 2(suppl. 1), S5 (2011)
38. Lamprecht, A.L., Naujokat, S., Steffen, B., Margaria, T.: Constraint-Guided Workflow Composition Based on the EDAM Ontology. In: Burger, A., Marshall, M.S., Romano, P., Paschke, A., Splendiani, A. (eds.) Proceedings of the 3rd Workshop on Semantic Web Applications and Tools for Life Sciences (SWAT4LS 2010). CEUR Workshop Proceedings, vol. 698 (December 2010)
39. Pettifer, S., Ison, J., Kalas, M., Thorne, D., McDermott, P., Jonassen, I., Liaquat, A., Fernandez, J.M., Rodriguez, J.M., Partners, I., Pisano, D.G., Blanchet, C., Uludag, M., Rice, P., Bartaseviciute, E., Rapacki, K., Hekkelman, M., Sand, O., Stockinger, H., Clegg, A.B., Bongcam-Rudloff, E., Salzemann, J., Breton, V., Attwood, T.K., Cameron, G., Vriend, G.: The EMBRACE web service collection. Nucl. Acids Res., gkq297 (May 2010)

An Object Group-Based Component Model*

Michaël Lienhardt, Mario Bravetti, and Davide Sangiorgi

Focus Team, University of Bologna, Italy
{lienhard,bravetti,davide.sangiorgi}@cs.unibo.it

Abstract. Dynamic reconfiguration, i.e. changing at runtime the communication pattern of a program is challenging for most programs as it is generally impossible to ensure that such modifications won't disrupt current computations. In this paper, we propose a new approach for the integration of components in an object-oriented language that allows *safe* dynamic reconfiguration. Our approach is built upon *futures* and *object-groups* to which we add: i) output ports to represent variability points, ii) critical sections to control when updates of the software can be made and iii) hierarchy to model locations and distribution. These different notions work together to allow dynamic and safe update of a system. We illustrate our approach with a few examples.

1 Introduction

Components are an intuitive tool to achieve unplanned dynamic reconfigurations. In a component system, an application is structured into several distinct pieces called *components*. Each of these components has dependencies towards functionalities located in other components; such dependencies are collected into *output ports*. The component itself, however, offers functionalities to the other components, and these are collected into *input ports*. Communication from an output port to an input port is possible when a *binding* between the two ports exists. Dynamic reconfiguration in such a system is then achieved by adding and removing components, and by replacing bindings. Thus updates or modifications of parts of an application are possible without stopping it.

Related Work. While the idea of components is simple, bringing it into a concrete programming language is not easy. The informal description of components talks about the structure of a system, and how this structure can change at runtime, but does not mention program execution. As a matter of fact, many implementations of components [1, 3, 5, 15, 2, 11, 13] do not merge into one coherent model i) the execution of the program, generally implemented using a classic object-oriented language like Java or C++, and ii) the component structure, generally described in an annex Architecture Description Language (ADL). This approach makes it simple to add components to an existing standard program. However, unplanned dynamic reconfigurations become hard, as

---

* Partly funded by the EU project FP7-231620 HATS.

T. Margaria and B. Steffen (Eds.): ISoLA 2012, Part I, LNCS 7609, pp. 64–78, 2012.

it is difficult to express modifications of the component structure using objects (since these are rather supposed to describe the execution of the programs). For instance, models like Click [13] do not allow runtime modifications while OSGi [1] allows addition of new classes and objects, but no component deletions or binding modifications. In this respect, a more flexible model is Fractal [3], which reifies components and ports into objects. Using an API, in Fractal it is possible to modify bindings at runtime and to add new components; Fractal is however rather complex, and it is informally presented, without a well-defined model.

Formal approaches to component models have been studied e.g., [4, 8, 14, 12, 10, 9]. These models have the advantage of having a precise semantics, which clearly defines what is a component, a port and a binding (when such a construct is included). This helps understanding how dynamic reconfigurations can be implemented and how they interact with the normal execution of the program. In particular, Oz/K [10] and COMP [9] propose a way to integrate in a unified model both components and objects. However, Oz/K has a complex communication pattern, and deals with adaptation via the use of *passivation*, which, as commented in [7], is a tricky operator — in the current state of the art it breaks most techniques for behavioral analysis. In contrast, COMP offers support for dynamic reconfiguration, but its integration into objects appears complex.

Our Approach. Most component models have a notion of component that is distinct from the objects used to represent the data and the main execution of the software. The resulting language is thus structured in two different layers, one using objects for the main execution of the program, one using components for the dynamic reconfiguration. Even though such separation seems natural, it makes difficult the integration of the different requests for reconfiguration into the program's workflow. In contrast, in our approach we tried to have a uniform description of objects and components. In particular, we aim at adding components on top of the *Abstract Behavioral Specification* (ABS) language [6], developed within the EU project HATS. Core ingredients of ABS are objects, futures and object groups to control concurrency. Our goal is to enhance objects and object groups with the basic elements of components (ports, bindings, consistency and hierarchy) and hence enable dynamic reconfigurations.

We try to achieve this by exploiting the similarities between objects and object groups with components. Most importantly, the methods of an object closely resemble the input ports of a component. In contrast, objects do not have explicit output ports. The dependencies of an object can be stored in internal fields, thus rebinding an output port corresponds to the assignment of a new value to the field. Objects, however, lack mechanisms for ensuring the consistency of the rebinding. Indeed, suppose we wished to treat certain object fields as output ports: we could add methods to the object for their rebinding; but it would be difficult, in presence of concurrency, to ensure that a call to one of these methods does not harm ongoing computations. For instance, if we need to update a field (like the driver of a printer), then we would want to wait first that all current execution using that field (like some printing jobs) to finish first. This way we ensure that the update will not break those computations.

In Java, such consistency can be achieved using the *synchronized* keyword, but this solution is very costly as it forbids the interleaving of parallel executions, thus impairing the efficiency of the program. In ABS, object groups offer a mechanism for consistency, by ensuring that there is at most one task running in an object group. This does ensure some consistency, but is insufficient in situations involving several method calls. A further difference between objects and components is that only the latter talks about *locations*. Locations structure a system, possibly hierarchically, and can be used to express dynamic addition or removal of code, as well as distribution of a program over several computers.

To ensure the consistent modifications of bindings and the possibility to ship new pieces of code at runtime, we add four elements to the ABS core language:

1. A notion of output port distinct from the object's fields. The former (identified with the keyword **port**) corresponds to the objects' dependencies and can be modified only when the object is in a *safe* state, while the latter corresponds to the inner state of the objects and can be modified with the ordinary assignments.
2. The possibility of annotating methods with the keyword **critical**: this specifies that the object, while an instance of the method is executing, is not in a safe state.
3. A new primitive to wait for an object to be in a safe state. Thus, it becomes possible to wait for all executions using a given port to finish, before rebinding the port to a new object.
4. A hierarchy of locations. Thus an ABS program is structured into a tree of locations that can contain object groups, and that can move within the hierarchy. Using locations, it is possible to model the addition of new pieces of code to a program at runtime. Moreover, it is also possible to model distribution (each top-level location being a different computer) and code mobility (by moving a sub-location from a computer to another one).

The resulting language remains close to the underlying ABS language. Indeed, the language is a conservative extension of ABS (i.e., an ABS program is a valid program in our language and its semantics is unchanged), and, as shown in our following example, introducing the new primitives into an ABS program is simple. In contrast with previous component models, our language does not drastically separate objects and components. Three major features of the informal notion of component — ports, consistency, and location — are incorporated into the language as follows: (i) output ports are taken care of at the level of our enhanced objects; (ii) consistency is taken care of at the level of object groups; (iii) the information about locations is added separately.

We believe that the separation between output ports and fields is meaningful for various reasons:

- Output ports represent dependencies of an object towards its environment (functionalities needed by the object and implemented outside it, and that moreover might change during the object life time). As such they are logically different from the internal state of the object (values that the object may have to consult to perform its expected computation).

$$
\begin{array}{llll}
P & ::= & I\ P \ \mid\ C\ P\ \mid\ \{\ \overline{T\ x};\ s\ \} & \qquad\qquad F \quad ::= \quad T\ x \\
T & ::= & \mathtt{I}\ \mid\ \mathtt{Fut}\langle T\rangle & \qquad\qquad S \quad ::= \quad T\ \mathtt{m}(\overline{T\ x}) \\
I & ::= & \mathbf{interface}\ \mathtt{I}\ \{\ \overline{S}\ \} & \qquad\qquad M \quad ::= \quad S\{\ \overline{T\ x};\ s\ \} \\
C & ::= & \mathbf{class}\ \mathtt{C}(\overline{T\ x})\ [\mathbf{implements}\ \overline{\mathtt{I}}]\ \{\ \overline{F}\ \overline{M}\ \} \\
s & ::= & \mathbf{skip}\ \mid\ s;s\ \mid\ e\ \mid\ x = e\ \mid\ \mathbf{await}(g)\ \mid\ \mathbf{if}\ e\ \{\ s\ \}\ \mathbf{else}\ \{\ s\ \} \\
& \mid & \mathbf{while}\ e\ \{\ s\ \}\ \mid\ \mathbf{return}\ e \\
e & ::= & v\ \mid\ x\ \mid\ \mathbf{this}\ \mid\ \mathbf{new}\ [\mathbf{cog}]\ \mathtt{C}\ (\overline{e})\ \mid\ e.\mathtt{m}(\overline{e})\ \mid\ e!\mathtt{m}(\overline{e})\ \mid\ \mathbf{get}(e) \\
v & ::= & \mathbf{null}\ \mid\ \mathbf{true}\ \mid\ \mathbf{false}\ \mid\ 1\ \mid\ \dots \\
g & ::= & e\ \mid\ e?\ \mid\ g \wedge g
\end{array}
$$

Fig. 1. Core ABS Language

- The separation of output ports allows us to have special constructs for them. Examples are the constructs for consistency mentioned above. Moreover, different policies may be used for updating fields and output ports. For instance, in our model while a field of an object o may be updated only by o, an output port of o may be modified by objects in the same group as o. This difference of policy is motivated in Section 3.1
- The separation of output ports could be profitable in reasoning, in particular in techniques of static analysis.
- The presence of output ports may be useful in the deployment phase of a system facilitating, for instance, the connection to local communication resources.

Roadmap. §2 describes the core ABS language. §3 presents our extension to the ABS language. §4 presents the semantics of the language. The main features of core ABS and our extensions are illustrated along the document with several examples.

2   Core ABS

We present in Figure 1 the object core of the ABS language. For the full description of the language, including its *functional* aspect, see [6]. We assume an overlined element to be any finite sequence of such element. A program P is defined as a set of interface and class declarations I and C, with a main function $\{\ \overline{T\ x};\ s\ \}$. The production T types objects with interface names $\mathtt{I}$ and futures with future types $\mathtt{Fut}\langle T\rangle$, where T is the type of the value returned by an asynchronous method call of the kind $e!\mathtt{m}(\overline{e})$ (versus $e.\mathtt{m}(\overline{e})$ representing synchronous calls): the actual value of a future variable can be read with a **get**. An interface I has a name $\mathtt{I}$ and a body declaring a set of method headers S. A class C has a name $\mathtt{C}$, may implement several interfaces, and declares in its body its fields with F and its methods with M. In the following examples: for simplicity we will omit "?" in await guards (in ABS "e?" guards are used for expressions "e" returning a future, instead simple "e" guards are used for boolean expressions) and we will follow the ABS practice to declare the class constructor like a method, named *init*.

```
class Printer {
  Status s;                              int printPhy(File f) {...}
                                         Status getStatus() { return s; }
  int print(File f) {                  }
    int id = s.addToQueue(f);
    await(s!isCurrent(id));             class Status {
                                         ...
    int code = this.printPhy(f);         int addToQueue(File f) {...}
    await(s!popFromQueue(id));           void popFromQueue(int id){...}
    return code;                         void isCurrent(int id) {...}
  }                                      void isCurrentFile(File f) {...}
                                       }
```

Fig. 2. Example, the class Printer

Object Groups and Futures. One of the main features of ABS is its concurrency model which aims to solve data races. Objects in ABS are structured into different groups called *cogs* which are created with the new cog command. These cogs define the concurrency of a program in two ways: i) inside one cog, at most one object can be active (i.e. execute a method); ii) all cogs are concurrent (i.e. all method calls between objects of different cogs must be *asynchronous*). Concurrency inside a cog is achieved with cooperative multitasking using the await statement, and synchronization between concurrent executions is achieved with the await and get statements, based on futures.

We illustrate this concurrency model with a simple class Printer in Figure 2, modeling a printer driver with a job queue stored in a Status s. The principle of the print method of Printer is as follow: i) the printing request is added to the queue of jobs, which returns the identifier for that new job; ii) the method *waits* until all previous jobs have been processed; iii) the method does the actual printing (using the method printPhy) and waits for its completion, which returns a code describing if the printing was successful or not; and iv) the job is removed from the queue and the code is returned to the user.

3   Component Model

3.1   Ports and Bindings

The ABS concurrency model as it is cannot properly deal with runtime modifications of a system, in particular with unplanned modifications. Let us consider the client presented in Figure 3. This class offers a little abstraction over the Printer class with three extra features: i) the possibility to change printer; ii) some notification messages giving the current status of the printing job (count being the identifier of the job); and iii) the possibility to get the number of jobs handled by this object.

```
class PrintClient {
 Printer p;
 int count;

 void setPrinter(Printer pr) { p = pr }

 void print(File f) {
  Fut<int> err = p!print(f);
  count = count + 1;

  System.out.println("Job " + count + ": Waiting to begin");
  await ((get(p!getStatus())!isCurrentFile(f));
  System.out.println("Job " + count + ": Being processed");
  await err;
  System.out.println("Job " + count
          + ": Completed with error code = " + (get(err)));
 }

 int GetNumberOfJobs() { return count; }

 void init() { count = 0; }
}
```

Fig. 3. An evolved Printing Client

This class is actually erroneous: let us consider the scenario where a printing job is requested, followed by the modification of the printer. The `print` method sends the job to the first printer p_1, then waits for the notification from p_1's status. While waiting, the printer gets modified into p_2: the following requests will fail as they will be directed to p_2 and not p_1. A possible solution would be to forbid the interleaving of different methods execution by replacing the `awaits` by `gets`, which corresponds to the *synchronized* in Java.

We overcome this inconsistency problem by forbidding the modification of the field p while it is in use. For this, we combine the notions of *output port* (from components) and of *critical section*. Basically the field p, which references an external service that can change at runtime, is an *output port*; the `print` method that needs stability over this port, creates a critical section to avoid the modification of p while it is executing; the `count` field and the `GetNumberOfJobs` method, that have no link to an external service, remain unchanged.

The syntax for our manipulation of output port and critical section is as follows.

$$
\begin{array}{rcl}
F & ::= & \dots \mid \textbf{port } T \textbf{ f} \\
S & ::= & \dots \mid \textbf{critical } T\, \texttt{m}(\overline{T\ x}) \\
s & ::= & \dots \mid \textbf{rebind } e.x = e \\
g & ::= & \dots \mid \|e\|
\end{array}
$$

Here, a field can be annotated with the keyword **port**, which makes it an output port, supposedly connected to an external service that can be modified at

```
class PrintClient {
 port Printer p;
 int count;

 void setPrinter(Printer pr) {
   await (‖this‖);
   rebind p = pr
 }

 critical void print(File f) { ... }

 int GetNumberOfJobs() { return count; }

 void init() { count = 0 }
}
```

Fig. 4. An improved Printing Client

runtime. Moreover, methods can be annotated with the keyword **critical**, which ensures that, during the execution of that method, the output ports of the object will not be modified.

Output ports differ from ordinary fields in two aspects:

1. output ports cannot be freely modified. Instead one has to use the **rebind** statement that checks if the object has an open critical section before changing the value stored in the port. If there are no open critical sections, the modification is applied; otherwise an error in a form of a dead-lock is raised;
2. output ports of an object o can be modified (using the **rebind** statement) by *any* object in the same object-group of o. This capacity is not in opposition to the classic object-oriented design of not showing the inner implementation of an object: indeed, a port does not correspond to an inner implementation but exposes the relationship the object has with independent services. Moreover, this capacity helps achieving consistency as shown in the next examples.

Finally, to avoid errors while modifying an output port, one should first ensure that the object has no open critical sections. This is done using the new guard $\|e\|$ that waits for the object e not to be in critical section. Basically, if an object o wants to modify output ports stored in different objects o_i, it first waits for them to close all their critical section, and then can apply the modifications using **rebind**.

3.1.1   Examples

Printing Client. In Figure 4 we show how to solve our previous example (from Figure 3). The changes are simple: i) we specify that the field p is a port; ii) we annotate the method **print** with **critical** (to protect its usage of the port p); and iii) we change the method **setPrinter** that now waits for the object to be in a consistent state *before* rebinding its output port p.

```
class OperatorFrontEnd {
  port Operator _op;

  critical Document modify(Document doc) { ... }

  void init(Operator op) { rebind _op = op; }
}

class WFController {
  port Document _doc;
  port Printer _p;
  OperatorFrontEnd _opfe;

  critical void newInstanceWF() { ... }

  void changeOperator(Operator op) {
    await(||this|| ∧ ||_opfe||);
    rebind _opfe._op = op;
  }

  void init(Document doc, Operator op, Printer p) {
    rebind _doc = doc;
    rebind _p = p;
    _opfe = new OperatorFrontEnd(op);
  }
}
```

Fig. 5. Dynamic Reconfiguration Example

Workflow Controller. For the purpose of this example, we suppose we want to define a workflow that takes a document (modeled by an instance of the class Document), modifies it using an Operator and then sends it to a Printer. We suppose that the protocol used by Operator objects is complex, so we isolate it into a dedicated class. Finally, we want to be able to change protocol at runtime, without disrupting the execution of previous instances of the workflow. Such a workflow is presented in Figure 5.

We thus have two classes: the class OperatorFrontEnd implements the protocol in the method modify; the class WFController encodes the workflow. The elements _op, _doc and _p are *ports*, and correspond to dependencies to external resources. In consequence they are annotated as **port**. It is only possible to modify their value using the construct **rebind**, which checks if the object is in a safe state (no critical method in execution) before modifying the port. Moreover, methods modify and newInstanceWF make use of these ports in their code, and are thus annotated as **critical** as it would be dangerous to rebind ports during their execution.

The key operations of our component model are shown in the two lines of code describing the method changeOperator. First is the **await** statement, which waits for the objects **this** and _opfe to be in a safe state. By construction, these objects are in a safe state only when there are no running instances of the workflow: it is then safe to modify the ports. Second is the **rebind** statement; the statement will succeed since the concurrency model of object-groups ensures that no workflow instance can be spawned between the end of the **await** and the end of the method. Moreover, the second line shows that it is possible to rebind a port of another object, provided that this object is in the same group as the one doing the rebinding.

3.2 Locations

The final layer of our language introduces *locations* that are used to model the different elements of our virtual office, like printers, computers, rooms and buildings. The idea is that components stand at a certain location. Thus every location, e.g. a room, is endowed with its own resources/services, e.g. printers, scanners, etc..., and a worker computer that stands at a certain location may exploit the location information to use resources at the same location.

Locations themselves are structured into trees according to a sublocation relation, such that we can have several locations at the top level (roots of trees) and object groups can only occur as leaves of such trees (and not as intermediate nodes).

We modify slightly the syntax of our previous calculus to introduce locations in it. We use l to represent location names. We represent with $(l, \mathbf{g})$ and (l, l') the father-to-son sublocation relation where object groups can only appear as leaves of the location tree. We use $l_\perp$ to stand for a name which is either $\perp$ or l, where $\perp$ is used to represent absence of a father, i.e. $(\perp, \mathbf{g})$ and $(\perp, l)$ mean that $\mathbf{g}$ and l, respectively, do not have a father. We also use n to represent node names which can be location names l or group names $\mathbf{g}$.

The additions are presented as follows.

$$
\begin{aligned}
s &::= \ \ldots \ \mid \ \mathbf{move} \ e \ \mathbf{in} \ e \\
e &::= \ \ldots \ \mid \ \mathbf{new \ loc}
\end{aligned}
$$

First, we add the possibility to create a new location (with a fresh name l) with a command **new loc**, then we add the possibility of modifying the father of a location/group n returned by an expression (or to establish a father in the case n does not possess one, or to remove the father of n) with the command **move** n **in** $l_\perp$: the new father becomes the location $l_\perp$ (returned by an expression). Technically, we also introduce a new type for location values, called location, which is added to the syntax of types T.

3.2.1 Examples

In the Virtual Office case study we use locations to express the movement of a worker from a location to another one. The worker moves with his laptop, in which we suppose a workflow document has been previously downloaded. The worker component has a set of output ports for connection to the services at the current worker location, which are needed to execute the downloaded workflow. Therefore the worker movement from a location to another one requires rebinding all such output ports, which can only be done if the workflow (a critical method) is not executing. Therefore, compared to previous examples, we need to model simultaneous rebinding of multiple output ports.

Example 1. We represent the movement of a worker to a different environment as the movement of the worker to a new location, which includes:

- a set of object groups representing the devices that the worker needs to perform the workflow (here represented by services "*ServiceA*" and "*ServiceB*")
- possibly, a local registry component, providing to the worker laptop component the links to the devices above; this will be modeled in Example 2.

More precisely, whenever the worker moves to a location l, first we wait for possible current workflow executions to be terminated, then we rebind to the (possibly discovered, see Example 2) new devices in the new location.

We represent the worker component as an object group composed by two objects:

- a "*ServiceFrontEnd*" object endowed by all the required output ports (here ports "*a*" and "*b*" for services "*ServiceA*" and "*ServiceB*", respectively),
- a "manager" object, called "*WorkerFrontEnd*" which: changes the ports in the "*ServiceFrontEnd*" object (possibly performing the service discovery enquiring the local service registry, see Example 2).

Finally, in the example code below, we make use of a primitive function "*group*" which is supposed to yield the group of a given object.

```
class ServiceA { ... }
class ServiceB { ... }

class ServiceFrontEnd {
  port ServiceA a;
  port ServiceB b;
  critical void workflow() { ... }
}

class WorkerFrontEnd {

  ServiceFrontEnd s;

  void changeLocation(location l2, ServiceA a2, ServiceB b2) {
    await ‖s‖;
    move group(this) in l2;
    rebind s.a = a2;
    rebind s.b = b2;
  }

  void init(location l, ServiceA a, ServiceB b) {
    move group(this) in l;
    s = new ServiceFrontEnd();
    rebind s.a = a;
    rebind s.b = b;
  }
}
```

Example 2. In this example we also model the local registry component for each location, providing links to the local devices for the worker component, and the global root registry (which has a known address) which, given a location, provides the link to the local register at that location.

More precisely, whenever the worker moves to a location l, first we have a discovery phase via a global root register so to obtain the local registry at location l, then we wait for possible current workflow executions to be terminated, then a discovery phase via the registry component of the new location, and finally a rebinding to the discovered devices in the new location.

```
class ServiceA { ... }
class ServiceB { ... }

class Register {
  ServiceA discoverA() { ... }
  ServiceB discoverB() { ... }
}

class RootRegister {
  Register discoverR(location l) { ... }
}

class ServiceFrontEnd {
  port ServiceA a;
  port ServiceB b;
  critical void workflow() { ... }
}

class WorkerFrontEnd {

  RootRegister rr;
  ServiceFrontEnd s;

  void changeLocation(location l2) {
    Fut<Register> fr=rr!discoverR(l2); await(fr); Register r=get(fr);
    await ‖s‖;
    move group(this) in l2;
    rebind s.a = get(r!discoverA());
    rebind s.b = get(r!discoverB());
  }

  void init(location l, RootRegister rr2) {
    rr = rr2;
    Fut<Register> fr=rr!discoverR(l); await(fr); Register r=get(fr);
    move group(this) in l;
    s = new ServiceFrontEnd();
    rebind s.a = get(r!discoverA());
    rebind s.b = get(r!discoverB());
  }
}
```

$$
\begin{array}{rcl}
N & ::= & \epsilon \mid I \mid C \mid N\,N \\
 & \mid & ob(\mathsf{o}, \sigma, K_{\mathbf{idle}}, Q) \\
 & \mid & cog(\mathsf{c}, \mathsf{o}_\varepsilon) \\
 & \mid & fut(\mathbf{f}, v_\perp) \\
 & \mid & invoc(\mathsf{o}, \mathbf{f}, \mathbf{m}, \overline{v}) \\
 & \mid & (\gamma_\perp, \gamma) \\
Q & ::= & \varepsilon \mid K \mid Q\,Q \\
K & ::= & \{\,\sigma, s\,\} \\
v & ::= & \mathbf{null} \mid \mathsf{o} \mid \mathbf{f} \mid 1 \mid \ \ldots
\end{array}
\qquad
\begin{array}{rcl}
\sigma & ::= & \varepsilon \mid \sigma; T\,x\,v \\
 & \mid & \sigma; \mathbf{this}\ \mathsf{o} \\
 & \mid & \sigma; \mathbf{class}\ \mathsf{C} \\
 & \mid & \sigma; \mathbf{cog}\ \mathsf{c} \\
 & \mid & \sigma; \mathbf{nb}_{cr}\ v \\
v_\perp & ::= & v \mid \perp \\
\mathsf{o}_\varepsilon & ::= & \mathsf{o} \mid \varepsilon \\
K_{\mathbf{idle}} & ::= & K \mid \mathbf{idle} \\
\gamma_\perp & ::= & \gamma \mid \perp
\end{array}
$$

Fig. 6. Runtime Syntax; here o, f and c are object, future, and cog names

4 Semantics

We present in this section the semantics of our language. Our semantics is described as a virtual machine based on i) a runtime syntax that extends the basic language; ii) some functions and relations to manipulate that syntax; and iii) a set of reduction rules describing the evolution of a term.

4.1 Runtime Syntax

The runtime syntax consists of the language extended with constructs needed for the computations, like the runtime representation of objects, groups, and tasks. Figure 6 presents the global runtime syntax. Configurations N are sets of classes, interfaces, objects, concurrent object groups (cogs), futures, invocation messages and hierarchy statements between components. The associative and commutative union operator on configurations is denoted by a whitespace and the empty configuration by ϵ. An object is a term of the form $ob(\mathsf{o}, \sigma, K_{\mathbf{idle}}, Q)$ where o is the object's identifier, σ is a substitution representing the object's fields, $K_{\mathbf{idle}}$ is the active *task* of the object (or $K_{\mathbf{idle}} = \mathbf{idle}$, when the object is idle and it is not executing anything), and Q is the queue of waiting tasks (the union of such queue, denoted by the whitespace, is associative with ε as the neutral element). A cog is a term of the form $cog(\mathsf{c}, \mathsf{o}_\varepsilon)$ where c is the cog's identifier, o_ε is either ε, which means that there is nothing currently executing in the cog, or an object identifier, in which case there is one task of the object o executing in c. A future is a pair of the name of the future f and a place $v_\perp$ where to store the value computed for this future. An invocation message $invoc(\mathsf{o}, \mathbf{f}, \mathbf{m}, \overline{v})$ specifies that some task called the method m on the object o with the parameters $\overline{v}$, this call corresponding to the future f. An hierarchy statement $(\gamma_\perp, \gamma)$ states that the component γ is a child of the component $\gamma_\perp$ ($\perp$ being the name of the top level component). A task K consists of a pair with a substitution σ of local variable bindings, and a statement s to execute. A substitution σ is a mapping from variable names to values. For convenience, we associate the declared type of the variable with the binding, and, in case of substitutions directly included in objects, we also use substitutions to store, the "this" reference, the class, the cog of an object and an integer denoted by $\mathbf{nb}_{cr}$ which, as we will see, will be used for critical section management. Finally, we extend the values v with object and future identifiers.

4.2 Reduction Relation

The semantics of the component model is an extension of the semantics of core ABS in [6]. It uses a reduction relation $\rightarrow$ over configurations, $N \rightarrow N'$ meaning that, in one execution step, the configuration N can evolve into N'. We extend that relation in four different aspects. First, we extend the reduction definition with three reduction rules that define the semantics of the **Rebind** and **subloc** operator.

REBIND-LOCAL
$$\frac{\sigma(\mathbf{nb}_{cr}) = 0}{ob(\mathsf{o}, \sigma, \{\ \sigma', \mathbf{rebind}\ \mathsf{o.f} = v; s\ \}, Q) \rightarrow ob(\mathsf{o}, \sigma[f \mapsto v], \{\ \sigma', s\ \}, Q)}$$

REBIND-GLOBAL
$$\frac{\sigma_{\mathsf{o}}(\mathbf{nb}_{cr}) = 0 \qquad \sigma_{\mathsf{o}}(\mathbf{cog}) = \sigma_{\mathsf{o}'}(\mathbf{cog})}{\begin{array}{c} ob(\mathsf{o}, \sigma_{\mathsf{o}}, K_{\mathbf{idle}}, Q)\ ob(\mathsf{o}', \sigma_{\mathsf{o}'}, \{\ \sigma', \mathbf{rebind}\ \mathsf{o.f} = v; s\ \}, Q) \\ \rightarrow ob(\mathsf{o}, \sigma_{\mathsf{o}}[f \mapsto v], K_{\mathbf{idle}}, Q)\ ob(\mathsf{o}', \sigma_{\mathsf{o}'}, \{\ \sigma', s\ \}, Q) \end{array}}$$

LOC-MOVE
$$(\gamma_{\perp}, \gamma)\ ob(\mathsf{o}, \sigma, \{\ \sigma', \mathbf{move}\ \gamma\ \mathbf{in}\ \gamma'_{\perp}; s\ \}, Q) \rightarrow (\gamma'_{\perp}, \gamma)\ ob(\mathsf{o}, \sigma, \{\ \sigma', s\ \}, Q)$$

The rule REBIND-LOCAL is applied when an object rebinds one of its own ports. The rule first checks that the object is not in a critical section by testing the special field $\mathbf{nb}_{cr}$ for zero and then updates the value of the field. The rule REBIND-GLOBAL is applied when an object rebinds a port of another object and is similar to the previous one. The rule LOC-MOVE moves a location γ (initially put inside the location $\gamma_{\perp}$) inside another location $\gamma'_{\perp}$.

The second aspect of our extension defines the semantics of our new expression, the creation of location **new loc**. In [6], the reduction rules defining the semantics of expressions are written using statements of the form $\sigma \vdash e \rightarrow \sigma \vdash e'$ to say that in the context σ mapping some variables to their values, e reduces to e'. Because expression **new loc** has a side effect (adding the new location to the configuration), we extend this statement to include the configuration: $N, \sigma \vdash e \rightarrow N', \sigma \vdash e'$.

NEW-LOCATION
$$\frac{\gamma\ \text{fresh}}{N, \sigma \vdash \mathbf{new\ loc} \rightarrow N\ (\perp, \gamma), \sigma \vdash \gamma}$$

That rule simply states that the **new loc** commands creates a new location and returns it.

The third aspect of our extension concerns method call. In our system, we indeed have two kinds of methods: normal ones and critical ones, the second ones creating a critical section on the callee. We model opened critical sections with the special hidden field $\mathbf{nb}_{cr}$, that is initialized to zero, incremented each time a critical section is opened, and decremented each time a critical section is closed. Then, when an object calls a method, it creates an *invoc* message describing who is the callee, the method to execute, the parameters and the return future. This message is then reduced into a task in the queue of the callee using the function bind that basically replaces the method by its code. To give the semantics of our critical methods, we extend this bind function to add, to the code of a critical method, some statements that manipulate the $\mathbf{nb}_{cr}$ field.

NM-BIND
$$\frac{\mathbf{class}\ \mathtt{C}\ldots\{\ T\ \mathtt{m}(\overline{T}\ x)\{\ \overline{T'\ x'}\ s\ \}\ \ldots\ \}\in N}{\mathrm{bind}(\mathtt{o},\mathtt{f},\mathtt{m},\overline{v},\mathtt{C})=\{\ \overline{T\ x=v};\overline{T'\ x'=\mathbf{null}};\mathbf{this}=\mathtt{o},s\ \}}$$

CM-BIND
$$\frac{\mathbf{class}\ \mathtt{C}\ldots\{\ \mathbf{critical}\ T\ \mathtt{m}(\overline{T}\ x)\{\ \overline{T'\ x'}\ s\ \}\ \ldots\ \}\in N \qquad s'=\mathbf{nb}_{cr}=\mathbf{nb}_{cr}+1;s;\mathbf{nb}_{cr}=\mathbf{nb}_{cr}-1}{\mathrm{bind}(\mathtt{o},\mathtt{f},\mathtt{m},\overline{v},\mathtt{C})=\{\ \overline{T\ x=v};\overline{T'\ x'=\mathbf{null}};\mathbf{this}=\mathtt{o},s'\ \}}$$

The rule NM-BIND corresponds to the normal semantics of the bind function, while the rule CM-BIND is the one used to bind a critical function. Basically, the first thing a critical method does is to increment the field $\mathbf{nb}_{cr}$, opening the critical section, and the last thing it does is to decrement the field, thus closing it.

Finally, the last aspect of our extension concerns our guard extension $\|e\|$.

CSGUARD1
$$\frac{N,\sigma\vdash e\rightsquigarrow N,\sigma\vdash\mathtt{o} \qquad ob(\mathtt{o},\sigma_\mathtt{o},K_{\mathbf{idle}},Q)\in N \qquad \sigma_\mathtt{o}(\mathbf{nb}_{cr})=0}{\sigma,N\vdash\|e\|\rightsquigarrow\sigma,N\vdash\mathtt{true}}$$

CSGUARD2
$$\frac{N,\sigma\vdash e\rightsquigarrow N,\sigma\vdash\mathtt{o} \qquad ob(\mathtt{o},\sigma_\mathtt{o},K_{\mathbf{idle}},Q)\in N \qquad \sigma_\mathtt{o}(\mathbf{nb}_{cr})\neq 0}{\sigma,N\vdash\|e\|\rightsquigarrow\sigma,N\vdash\mathtt{false}}$$

These two rules simply state that, when the object o has its field $\mathbf{nb}_{cr}$ different from zero, it has a critical section opened.

4.3 Properties

Important properties that show the adequateness of our machinery for port rebinding are: (i) we never modify a port while being in a critical section (this property is a consequence of the reduction rule Rebind: the execution of the rebind expression can only occur when the object's lock is 0) and (ii) when await statements are not used in between, modification of several ports is atomic (due to cooperative concurrency in the object group model): this can be used, like in the second example of the location extension, to ensure consistency.

References

[1] OSGi Alliance. Osgi Service Platform, Release 3. IOS Press, Inc. (2003)
[2] Bhatti, N.T., Hiltunen, M.A., Schlichting, R.D., Chiu, W.: Coyote: A system for constructing fine-grain configurable communication services. ACM Trans. Comput. Syst. 16(4) (1998)

[3] Bruneton, E., Coupaye, T., Leclercq, M., Quema, V., Stefani, J.-B.: The Fractal Component Model and its Support in Java. Software - Practice and Experience 36(11-12) (2006)

[4] Castagna, G., Vitek, J., Nardelli, F.Z.: The Seal calculus. Inf. Comput. 201(1) (2005)

[5] Coulson, G., Blair, G., Grace, P., Joolia, A., Lee, K., Ueyama, J.: OpenCOM v2: A Component Model for Building Systsms Software. In: Proceedings of IASTED Software Engineering and Applications, SEA 2004 (2004)

[6] Johnsen, E.B., Hähnle, R., Schäfer, J., Schlatte, R., Steffen, M.: ABS: A Core Language for Abstract Behavioral Specification. In: Aichernig, B.K., de Boer, F.S., Bonsangue, M.M. (eds.) FMCO 2010. LNCS, vol. 6957, pp. 142–164. Springer, Heidelberg (2011)

[7] Lenglet, S., Schmitt, A., Stefani, J.-B.: Howe's Method for Calculi with Passivation. In: Bravetti, M., Zavattaro, G. (eds.) CONCUR 2009. LNCS, vol. 5710, pp. 448–462. Springer, Heidelberg (2009)

[8] Levi, F., Sangiorgi, D.: Mobile safe ambients. ACM. Trans. Prog. Languages and Systems 25(1) (2003)

[9] Lienhardt, M., Lanese, I., Bravetti, M., Sangiorgi, D., Zavattaro, G., Welsch, Y., Schäfer, J., Poetzsch-Heffter, A.: A Component Model for the ABS Language. In: Aichernig, B.K., de Boer, F.S., Bonsangue, M.M. (eds.) FMCO 2010. LNCS, vol. 6957, pp. 165–183. Springer, Heidelberg (2011)

[10] Lienhardt, M., Schmitt, A., Stefani, J.-B.: Oz/K: A kernel language for component-based open programming. In: GPCE 2007: Proceedings of the 6th International Conference on Generative Programming and Component Engineering, pp. 43–52. ACM, New York (2007)

[11] Miranda, H., Pinto, A.S., Rodrigues, L.: Appia: A flexible protocol kernel supporting multiple coordinated channels. In: 21st International Conference on Distributed Computing Systems (ICDCS 2001). IEEE Computer Society (2001)

[12] Montesi, F., Sangiorgi, D.: A Model of Evolvable Components. In: Wirsing, M., Hofmann, M., Rauschmayer, A. (eds.) TGC 2010, LNCS, vol. 6084, pp. 153–171. Springer, Heidelberg (2010)

[13] Morris, R., Kohler, E., Jannotti, J., Frans Kaashoek, M.: The Click Modular Router. In: ACM Symposium on Operating Systems Principles (1999)

[14] Schmitt, A., Stefani, J.-B.: The Kell Calculus: A Family of Higher-Order Distributed Process Calculi. In: Priami, C., Quaglia, P. (eds.) GC 2004. LNCS, vol. 3267, pp. 146–178. Springer, Heidelberg (2005)

[15] Sun Microsystems. JSR 220: Enterprise JavaBeans, Version 3.0 – EJB Core Contracts and Requirements (2006)

Automated Inference of Models
for Black Box Systems Based on Interface Descriptions*

Maik Merten[1], Falk Howar[1], Bernhard Steffen[1],
Patrizio Pellicione[2], and Massimo Tivoli[2]

[1] Technical University Dortmund, Chair for Programming Systems,
Dortmund, D-44227, Germany
{maik.merten,falk.howar,steffen}@cs.tu-dortmund.de
[2] Università dell'Aquila, Dipartimento di Informatica, Via Vetoio, L'Aquila, Italy
{patrizio.pelliccione,massimo.tivoli}@univaq.it

Abstract. In this paper we present a method and tool to *fully automatically* infer data-sensitive behavioral models of black-box systems in two coordinated steps: (1) syntactical analysis of the interface descriptions, here given in terms of WSDL (Web Services Description Language), for instantiating test harnesses with adequate mappers, i.e., means to bridge between the model level and the concrete execution level, and (2) test-based exploration of the target system by means of active automata learning. The first step is realized by means of the syntactic analysis of StrawBerry, a tool designed for syntactically analyzing WSDL descriptions, and the second step by the LearnLib, a flexible active automata learning framework. The new method presented in this paper (1) overcomes the manual construction of the mapper required for the learning tool, a major practical bottleneck in practice, and (2) provides global behavioral models that comprise the data-flow of the analyzed systems. The method is illustrated in detail along a concrete shop application.

1 Introduction

Documentation of IT-systems is, in well-known practice, usually found to be incomplete and inaccurate or otherwise lacking. This can be a major obstacle for continued development of affected systems, where, e.g., extensions to the systems should not lead to regressions: without an informative specification of the expected behavior it is difficult to ensure that all relevant regressions have been discovered during testing and remedied before product deployment.

Inaccurate specifications also create major challenges when trying to connect remote Networked Systems (NSs). Thus making such specifications precise is one of the major challenges of the CONNECT project [4], which, even more ambitiously, aims at creating an infrastructure where networked connectors can be synthesized fully automatically.

In this paper we present a method and tool to *fully automatically* infer dataflow-sensitive behavioral models of black-box systems based on interface descriptions in WSDL, the Web Services Description Language. This solves the problem of deriving

---

* This work is partially supported by the European FP7 project CONNECT (IST 231167).

T. Margaria and B. Steffen (Eds.): ISoLA 2012, Part I, LNCS 7609, pp. 79–96, 2012.

system specifications of black box systems adequate to, e.g., serve as a basis for the connector synthesis of the CONNECT platform. This is done in two coordinated steps: (1) syntactical analysis of the interface descriptions, here given in terms of WSDL, for instantiating test harnesses with adequate mappers, i.e., means to bridge between the model level an the concrete execution level, and (2) test-based exploration of the target system by means of active automata learning.

The first step is realized by means of StrawBerry, a tool designed for syntactically analyzing WSDL descriptions, and the second step by the LearnLib, a flexible active automata learning framework. The combination of the two tools (1) overcomes the manual construction of the mapper required for the learning tool, a major practical bottleneck in practice, and a show stopper for automated model generation, and (2) provides global behavioral models that comprise the data-flow of the analyzed systems. Thus it is unique in combining the general applicability of StrawBerry, which simply requires WSDL interfaces, with the ability of active automata learning to infer data-sensitive behavioral models.

The presentation of our method is accompanied by a discussion along a concrete shop application, which illustrates the main features and highlights the essence of dataflow sensitive modeling.

The paper is structured as follows. Sect. 2 presents a motivating and running example. Sect. 3 provides background information on StrawBerry and Sect. 4 provides information on LearnLib. The integration of syntactic interface analysis and automata learning is discussed in Sect. 5, for which results are provided and discussed in Sect. 6. Related work is discussed in Sect. 7, before Sect. 8 closes with our conclusions and directions to future work.

2   Motivating Example

The explanatory example that we use in this paper is a web service (WS) called EcommerceImplService. This service simulates a small e-commerce service, where clients can open a session, retrieve a list of products, add products to a shopping cart and finally conclude buying the items previously added to the cart. The following operations are defined in the WSDL interface description:

• openSession: this operation is used by registered users to login into the WS. The operation gets the username and password as input and returns a session. session is a complex type composed of a session id and creationTime.

Input data	Output data
user: string; password: string;	return: session;

• destroySession: this operation gets as input a session, destroys this session, and returns a string denoting success.

Input data	Output data
session: session;	return: string;

• getAvailableProducts: this operation gets no inputs and returns productArray, i.e., a list of products, where a product is a complex type composed of the product id, its description, and its price.

Input data	Output data
	`return: productArray;`

- `emptyShoppingCart`: this operation gets as input a `session`, empties the shopping cart, and returns the current `session`.

Input data	Output data
`session: session;`	`return: session;`

- `getShoppingCart`: this operation gets as input a `session` and returns the current `shoppingCart`. `shoppingCart` is a complex type composed of a cart `id`, a list of products, and the `price`.

Input data	Output data
`session: session;`	`return: shoppingCart;`

- `addProductToShoppingCart`: this operation gets as input a `session` and a `product`, adds the product to the shopping cart, and returns the current `session`.

Input data	Output data
`session: session;`	`return: session;`
`product: product;`	

- `buyProductsInShoppingCart`: this operation gets as input a `session`, buys the array of products contained into the shopping cart and returns this array.

Input data	Output data
`session: session;`	`return: productArray;`

The particular implementation of this service has the following three semantic properties, which we will use for the illustration of our method. We will see that `StrawBerry` fails to detect all of them, but that the integrated approach detects them all:

- The operation `buyProductsInShoppingCart` will only successfully conclude if the shopping cart connected to the current session is not empty. Otherwise an error will be raised.
- In contrast, the operation `emptyShoppingCart` will return successfully even if the shopping cart was empty already, as long as a valid session is provided.
- The shopping cart is emptied on successful invocations of `buyProductsInShoppingCart`.

This behavior was modeled to reflect actual web shops. That is, web shops usually do not allow for empty orders, as sending, e.g., empty packages to customers will nonetheless inflict costs. Performing a clearing operation on an empty shopping cart, however, is not hurtful. Upon concluding a purchase, customers will expect a "fresh" shopping cart, so they can resume shopping without having to worry about potentially shopping items twice.

There are several reasons why we chose to use a simulated e-commerce service over, e.g., an actual e-commerce service available on the Internet. First, public e-commerce services usually do not offer an experimental mode where orders will not actually result in costly deliveries and extensive test runs during the extrapolation of the service will not be interpreted as, e.g., a denial of service attack. Second, the simulated e-commerce service is comparatively small, which allows for easy comparison of the extrapolated models with the actual implementation.

3 StrawBerry

By taking as input a WSDL of a WS (Web Service), `StrawBerry` derives in an automated way a partial ordering relation among the invocations of the different WSDL
operations. This partial ordering relation is represented as an automaton that we call *Behavior Protocol automaton*. It models the interaction protocol that a client has to follow
in order to correctly interact with the WS. This automaton also explicitly models the information that has to be passed to the WS operations. The behavior protocol is obtained
through synthesis and testing stages. The synthesis stage is driven by syntactic interface
analysis (aka data type analysis), through which we obtain a preliminary dependencies
automaton that can be optimized by means of heuristics. Once synthesized, this dependencies automaton is validated through testing against the WS to verify conformance,
and finally transformed into an automaton defining the behavior protocol.

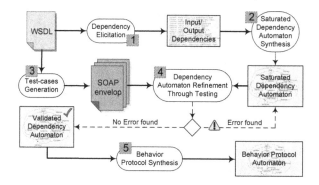

Fig. 1. Overview of the `StrawBerry` method

`StrawBerry` is a black-box and extra-procedural method. It is black-box since it
takes into account only the WSDL of the WS. It is extra-procedural since it focuses
on synthesizing a model of the behavior that is assumed when interacting with the
WS from outside, as opposed to intra-procedural methods that synthesize a model of
the implementation logic of the single WS operations [15,24,25]. Figure 1 graphically
represents `StrawBerry` as a process split in five main activities.

The *Dependencies Elicitation* activity elicits data dependencies between the I/O parameters of the operations defined in the WSDL. A dependency is recorded whenever
the type of the output of an operation matches with the type of the input of another operation. The match is syntactic. The elicited set of I/O dependencies may be optimized
under some heuristics [6].

The elicited set of I/O dependencies (see the *Input/Output Dependencies* artifact
shown in Figure 1) is used for constructing a data-flow model (see the *Saturated Dependencies Automaton Synthesis* activity and the *Saturated Dependencies Automaton*
artifact shown in Figure 1) where each node stores data dependencies that concern the
output parameters of a specific operation and directed arcs are used to model syntactic
matches between output parameters of an operation and input parameters of another

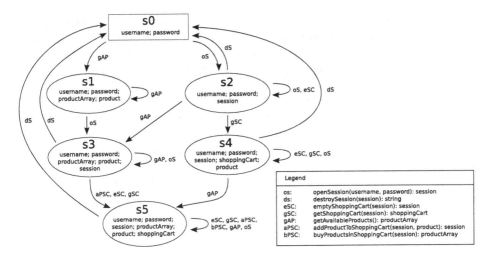

Fig. 2. Model created by `StrawBerry`. The edge labels are abbreviated for improved readability.

operation. This model is completed by applying a *saturation rule*. This rule adds new dependencies that model the possibility for a client to invoke a WS operation by directly providing its input parameters. The resulting automaton is then validated against the implementation of the WS through testing (see *Dependencies Automaton Refinement Through Testing* activity shown in Figure 1).

The testing phase takes as input the SOAP messages produced by the *Test-cases generation* activity. The latter, driven by coverage criteria, automatically derives a suite of test cases (i.e., SOAP envelop messages) for the operations to be tested, according to the WSDL of the WS. In `StrawBerry` tests are generated from the WSDL and aim at validating whether the synthesized automaton is a correct abstraction of the service implementation. Testing is used to refine the syntactic dependencies by discovering those that are semantically wrong. By construction, the inferred set of dependencies is syntactically correct. However, it might not be correct semantically since it may contain false positives (e.g., a string parameter used as a generic attribute is matched with another string parameter that is a unique key). If during the testing phase an error is found, these false dependencies are deleted from the automaton.

Once the testing phase is successfully terminated, the final automaton models, following a data-flow paradigm, the set of validated "chains" of data dependencies. `StrawBerry` terminates by transforming this data-flow model into a control-flow model (see the *Behavior Protocol Synthesis* activity in Figure 1). This is another kind of automaton whose nodes are WS execution states and whose transitions, labeled with operation names plus I/O data, model the possible operation invocations from the client to the WS.

The primary result of `StrawBerry` used in the subsequent learning phase is the set of validated "chains" of data dependencies.

StrawBerry at Work: referring to the example described in Section 2, Figure 4 shows states of the dependencies automaton produced by `StrawBerry`. Each state contains dependencies that each operation has with other operations. Dependencies marked with ✓ represent dependencies that are validated by testing activities. Figure 2 shows the obtained behavioral automaton. In our approach, it is both necessary and reasonable to assume that, for some of the WSDL input parameters, a set of meaningful values, called an *instance pool* [11], is available. Nodes of the behavioral automaton contain the matured "knowledge", i.e., the data that are provided with the instance pool or that are obtained as result of previously invoked operations. The S0 state contains only information that comes from the instance pool, i.e., username and password. In S0 only openSession and getAvailableProducts can be invoked. Once invoked the openSession operation, the service reaches the state S2 in which session is available, since it is returned by the openSession operation. Similarly, by executing getAvailableProducts the service reaches the state S1 in which both productArray and product are available since productArray is the return value of getAvailableProducts and product is nested into the complex type productArray.

Let us now focus on the state S5; in this state each operation can be invoked. Indeed this automaton does not represent an accurate model for EcommerceImplService. In particular the semantic properties introduced above are not revealed. For instance, buyProductsInShoppingCart might fail when the shopping cart is empty. In other words, there exist a sequence of operations that might lead to S5 with an empty cart. The lack of behavioral information in the produced model can be attributed to the fact that web service interfaces are not concerned with describing behavioral aspects and thus provide incomplete information to any analysis approach merely focusing on interfaces. As discussed in the following sections, the approach that we present in this paper overcomes this limitation.

4 LearnLib and Active Automata Learning

LearnLib is a framework for automata learning and experimentation. Active automata learning tries to automatically construct a finite automaton that matches the behavior of a given target automaton on the basis of active interrogation of target systems and observation of the produced behavior.

Active automata learning originally has been conceived for language acceptors in the form of deterministic finite automata (DFAs) (cf. Angluin's L^* algorithm [3]). It is possible, however, to apply automata learning to create models of reactive systems instead. A more suited formalism for this application are Mealy machines:

Definition 1. *A Mealy machine is defined as a tuple* $\langle Q, q_0, \Sigma, \Omega, \delta, \lambda \rangle$ *where*

- Q *is a finite nonempty set of* states *(be* $n = |Q|$ *the size of the Mealy machine),*
- $q_0 \in Q$ *is the* initial state,
- Σ *is a finite* input alphabet,
- Ω *is a finite* output alphabet,
- $\delta : Q \times \Sigma \to Q$ *is the* transition function, *and*
- $\lambda : Q \times \Sigma \to \Omega$ *is the* output function.

Intuitively, a Mealy machine evolves through states $q \in Q$, and whenever one applies an input symbol (or action) $a \in \Sigma$, the machine moves to a new state according to $\delta(q, a)$ and produces an output according to $\lambda(q, a)$.

In the context of reactive systems, the input alphabet contains actions which can be executed on the target system, while the output alphabet is determined by the output the system produces in response to the executed input actions.

Mealy machines are deterministic and thus are not a fitting modeling approach for, e.g., systems with truly erratic behavior, such as slot machines. However, many (if not most) systems serving a specific purpose are deterministic in nature, i.e., provided with a fixed set of inputs applied to a preset internal state, these systems will always produce the same output. Spurious errors (e.g., due to errors in communication) can be detected and eventually corrected by means of repeated experimentation.

When employed to create models in the form of Mealy machines, active automata learning employs two distinct types of queries to gather information on the System Under Learning (SUL):

– Membership Queries (MQs) retrieve behavioral information of the target system. Consisting of traces of system stimuli (each query $mq \in \Sigma^*$), MQs actively trigger behavioral outputs which are collected and analyzed by the learning algorithm. MQs are used to construct a hypothesis, which is subject of a verification by a second class of queries, the equivalence queries.

– Equivalence Queries (EQs) are used to determine if the learned hypothesis is a faithful representation of the target system. If the equivalence oracle handling the EQ finds diverging behavior between the learned hypothesis and the target system a counterexample $ex \in \Sigma^*$ will be produced, which is used to refine the hypothesis after restarting the learning process.

With those two query types, learning algorithms, such as $L^*_{i/o}$ [17], create minimal automata models, i.e., the learned result never contains more states than the minimized representation of the target system, and also guarantee termination with an accurate learned model.

It is worth noting that while MQs are relatively straightforward to employ on actual systems by execution of test runs, EQs pose a more challenging problem: while systems will readily produce output in response to input as normal mode of operation, they usually will neither confirm nor disprove a learned hypothesis in a direct manner. This is easy to see, as systems usually do not possess a formal model of their inner-workings fit for comparison. Thus, in practice, EQs can only be approximated, e.g., by executing additional test runs by means of MQs. Employing approximated EQs does impact the statement on correctness presented above: while the learned model will still be minimal, its accurateness is no longer guaranteed. In certain applications, however, it is possible to construct perfect EQs by employing MQs, e.g., if an upper bound on system size in terms of states is known. For the experiments presented in this paper, however, a simple approximation was used that generates random test runs.

LearnLib contains several learning algorithms fit for learning reactive systems, including EQ approximations, embedded in a flexible framework.

In practice, to learn concrete reactive systems, a *test-driver* has to translate the generated queries composed of abstract and parameterized symbols into concrete system interaction and conduct the actual invocations. In turn, the produced (concrete) system output has to be gathered and translated into abstract output symbols. Figure 3 shows the essential components of such a test-driver, embedded into a learning setup.

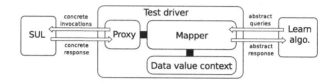

Fig. 3. Schematic view of a test driver for learning a reactive system

- A *mapper* is responsible for translating abstract queries generated by the learning algorithm into concrete queries comprised of actions that can be executed on the SUL. For parameterized actions, fitting valuations have to be inserted. Mappers are discussed, e.g., in [14].
- To fill in values for parameterized actions, a *data value context* maintains a set of value instances, that can be stored, retrieved and updated by the mapper.
- The *proxy* maintains a connection to the SUL and interacts with the SUL on behalf of the test-driver, using the concretized parameterized actions created by the mapper. Invocation results are gathered and returned to the mapper, which creates fitting abstract output symbols. For remote services which deliver an interface description in a standardized format (for instance, WSDL), such proxies can often be generated using specialized tools.

LearnLib at Work: LearnLib employs active automata learning algorithms that belong to the family of L^*-like algorithms. Models are constructed by gathering observations triggered by active infusion of test queries. This approach works without having any knowledge on the syntactic structure of the system's interface. In fact, queries are assembled from a provided alphabet without any notion of syntactic correctness, although having such a notion can speed up the learning process by filtering not well-formed queries (e.g., in the test driver) and only executing syntactically correct on the target system. Even the alphabet from which queries are constructed may be comprised of arbitrary bit-strings, which, of course, do not bode well regarding the chances of creating an insightful model.

To be able to learn models for systems on a sophistication level of the discussed example system, it is necessary to handle data dependencies of the actions to be invoked. This means that the abstract alphabet symbols in fact are parameterized, with fitting valuations being inserted at runtime and returned data values being retained as needed. This is done in the test-driver by the mapper component with data values being organized in a data value context, as discussed in Sect. 4.

In current practice, both the learning alphabet and the according mapper are constructed manually. This can be a time-consuming task, with, for example, more than a

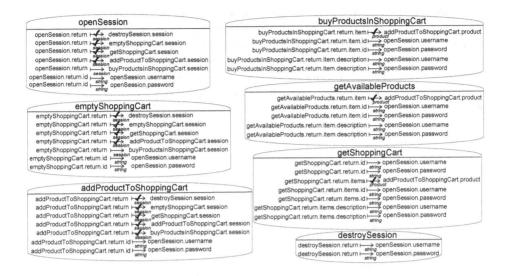

Fig. 4. States of the dependencies automaton produced by `StrawBerry`

quarter of the total effort being attributed to theses tasks in [23]. This manual approach of creating automata learning setups induces clear limitations on where automata learning can be employed. For example, this is unsustainable in scenarios where behavioral models are to be learned automatically for a wide range of systems, which is a requirement, e.g., for automated connector synthesis.

A central bottleneck of current practice is that the test-driver components such as the mapper must be constructed manually for any specific SUL. This is overcome by our approach which uses a generic mapper that is automatically instantiated with information derived from the syntactic interface analysis performed by `StrawBerry`.

5   The Integrated Approach

The integrated approach that is proposed in this paper solves limitations of both `StrawBerry` and `LearnLib`. Conceptually, the new solution integrates learning techniques with syntactic analysis that helps identifying potential dependencies between input and output parameters of different service operations. The integrated approach is an automata learning method, which is automated by a tool, that is realistic since it requires as input only a WSDL interface. As far as we know this is the only method with such minimal input assumption. It is worthwhile to note that, although `StrawBerry` shares the same minimal input assumption, it does not perform automata learning. In fact, it performs a totally different approach (based on data analysis and testing) that is less accurate than automata learning. Accuracy is a key aspect related to the behavioral model inference problem.

As typical usage scenario of the integrated approach let us imagine that a user needs to understand the behavior automaton of an existing black-box WS, such as the Amazon E-Commerce Service (AECS) as shown in [7]. The overall information that the user has to provide are: (i) the URL of the service to be learned; (ii) predetermined data values for an instance pool; (iii) alphabet symbols which refer to parameterized actions on the target system; and (iv) parameters and return variables for each alphabet symbol. Even though in this paper we consider a mock-up service built in house with the aim of carrying out meaningful validation, this usage scenario points it out that our approach is realistic in the sense that it can be applied to third-parties black-box services. As it is usual in the current practice of web-services development, service providers give access to a testing version of the same service that allows developers to extensively test web-services while avoiding negative side effects on the availability of production services. For instance, this is the case for the Amazon case study described in [7] and for other well-known third-parties services, such as PayPal.

The integrated approach enhances `LearnLib` with syntactic analysis that extracts from running services a WSDL enriched with explicit I/O data dependencies. In `LearnLib`, and in general in active learning, this information is assumed to be provided by users and to be part of the learning setup. However, producing this information would be complex and for sure tedious.

Glue connectors have been realized to enable `LearnLib` to take as input the dependency analysis results produced by syntactic analysis. More precisely, glue connectors have been realized to take as input the enriched WSDL and to allow for the automatic construction of a mapper required for the learning tool to bridge between the model level (abstract alphabet symbols) and the concrete execution level (concrete actions outfitted with live data values and return values of invocations).

The syntactic analysis of the integrated approach, which is needed to allow the construction of an alphabet and a mapper accounting for data flow concerns, is inherited by `StrawBerry`. This part of `StrawBerry`, i.e. activities 1 and 2 referring to Figure 1, produces an automaton that is handed over to `LearnLib` in form of an artifact called *setup specification* (an overview is given in Figure 5).

We recall that Figure 4 shows the states of the saturated dependencies automaton produced by `StrawBerry`'s syntactic analysis and syntactic dependencies that each operation has with the other operations. This information is used in the integrated ap-

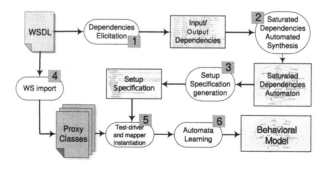

Fig. 5. Integration of `StrawBerry`' syntactic analysis (steps 1-2) and `LearnLib` (steps 4, 5, and 6). Step 3 is a newly added feature. `wsimport` provides proxy classes to interact with the target system.

proach to determine the data-flow between method invocations and to choose parameter and return variables for the setup specification.

This means that information on data dependencies between operations, as deduced by StrawBerry, are used to construct an alphabet of parameterized actions. This allows for carrying enough information so that the mapper can translate abstract alphabet symbols into concrete actions outfitted with live data values and manage return values of invocations.

To illustrate how an automated learning setup can be instantiated with the help of the generated setup descriptor (an activity represented as *Test-driver and mapper instantiation* in Figure 5), it is helpful to recall which concerns have to be addressed:

- Means for instrumentation of the SUL have to be provided, e.g., by means of a proxy that is accessible by the test-driver.
- An alphabet for the learner has to be constructed, as well as a mapping between the abstract alphabet and concrete system actions. This is where the dependency information provided by Strawberry is essential.
- Facilities for handling communicated data-values have to be present and configured to account data-flow between operations.

In the following we will discuss these points in more detail:

5.1 Instrumentation

Within a setup for active automata learning, the instrumentation layer is responsible for injecting system stimuli and gathering the target system's output for every invocation. For WSDL services, injecting system stimuli can be done in a straightforward way, e.g., by using automatically generated proxy classes that expose system functionalities while hiding the specifics of operating the target system through networked messages. For the experiments discussed in this paper, proxy classes for the remote system are generated by the wsimport [18] utility, which can serve as instrumentation layer for the test driver (denoted as *WS import* activity in Figure 5).

5.2 Determining an Alphabet and Mapper Configuration

The interface description is a natural source for the alphabet employed for the learning process, as every message defined in the WSDL description usually has a direct mapping to system features intended for remote consumption. It appears most sensible to choose the names of the defined WSDL messages as abstract alphabet symbols for the learner, which the test-driver concretizes into actual operation invocations of the generated proxy classes. As such the mapping between the abstract learning alphabet and concrete system input is one from operation names to actual invocations of the corresponding operation.

For parameterized operations, abstract alphabet symbols also have to include information for the mapper on how to retrieve values from the data value context to enable actual invocation. Thus the abstract symbols for parameterized operation calls will contain references to this context in form of instructions on how to retrieve data values from it.

To populate the data value context, data values returned by the SUL will be stored as named variables. Thus the abstract symbols also have to contain information on the name of the variable the return value is assigned to. For each stored value the abstract output symbol forwarded to the learner will simply be the variable name in which the return value was stored, abstracting from the actual content of the return message that the system under test produced. A similar approach to abstraction is taken for error messages: if the SUL produces an elaborate error message, the output returned to the learner usually will be a generic "error" symbol, abstracting from all the details related to this error instance. No data value will be stored in this case.

5.3 Storing and Accessing Data-Values

When concretizing learning queries into actual system input, fitting data values have to be inserted into parameterized system messages. Thus the system driver has to be able to store received data values and generate concrete system input by resorting to these stored values.

To accommodate data values, the data value context is realized as an embedded JavaScript environment. The reason for choosing a JavaScript environment over, e.g., a map of variable names and variable values, lies in the ability of a scripted context to access stored data with utmost flexibility. A scripted data value context is, e.g., able to access fields of complex data structures and provide those as parameter values.

Not every parameter can be filled with data values that are results of preceding system invocations. One notable example for this are login credentials, which have to be known beforehand. Such values have to be included in the setup specification and are copied into the data value context.

6 Application to the Example and Discussion

In the following, we will apply the presented approach to the running example.

Figure 6 shows an excerpt of the setup descriptor created by `StrawBerry` as a result of the interface analysis. The `serviceurl` declaration in line 2 provides an URL to the SUL, which can be directly used as an input for `wsimport`. Predetermined values (credentials in this case) are provided in lines 3 to 6 and are used to populate the instance pool.

The remainder of the specification file defines a sequence of symbols. Each `symbol` includes a sequence of `parameter` declarations, which refer to named variables in the data value context. It can be seen that the `symbol` declarations include information on parameters and on the variables where return values are stored. Parameter values stored in the data value context are addressed by named keys that are specified by the `alternative` environment. The reason for having `alternative` declarations is that parameters may have several potential data sources. For example, the second parameter of the symbol `addProductToShoppingCart` may take data values from the variables `productArray` and `shoppingCart`. Each alternative induces the instantiation of additional abstract symbols, meaning that for the presented example the learning alphabet has in fact two `addProductToShoppingCart` symbols, one referring to `productArray` as parameter value, the other referring to `shoppingCart`.

```
1  <learnsetup>
2  <serviceurl>http://vulpis.cs.tu-dortmund.de:9000/ecommerceservice?wsdl
      </serviceurl>
3  <provided>
4   <object name="username" type="string">username</object>
5   <object name="password" type="string">password</object>
6  </provided>
7  <symbols>
8   <symbol name="openSession">
9    <parameters>
10    <parameter>
11     <alternative>username</alternative>
12    </parameter>
13    <parameter>
14     <alternative>password</alternative>
15    </parameter>
16   </parameters>
17   <return>session</return>
18  </symbol>
19  ...
20  <symbol name="getAvailableProducts">
21   <parameters />
22   <return>productArray</return>
23  </symbol>
24  ...
25  <symbol name="addProductToShoppingCart">
26   <parameters>
27    <parameter>
28     <alternative>session</alternative>
29    </parameter>
30    <parameter>
31     <alternative selector="elementOf" field="item">productArray
         </alternative>
32     <alternative selector="elementOf" field="items">shoppingCart
         </alternative>
33    </parameter>
34   </parameters>
35   <return>session</return>
36  </symbol>
37  </symbols>
38 </learnsetup>
```

Fig. 6. Excerpt of the setup descriptor for LearnLib generated by StrawBerry by means of syntactical analysis

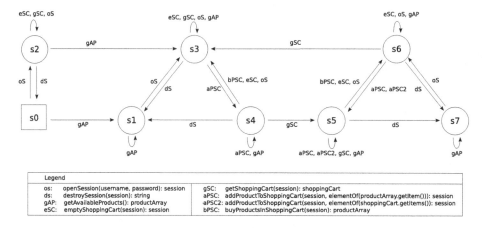

Fig. 7. Model created by `LearnLib` using the setup description created by `StrawBerry`. The edge labels are abbreviated for improved readability.

The parameters of the symbol `addProduct- ToShoppingCart` illustrate why realizing the data value context as scriptable environment is advantageous: the `alternative` declaration in line 31 of Figure 6 includes attributes that specify how the data value for the corresponding parameter has to be extracted from the context. Instead of directly filling in the parameter value with the complete data structure that is pointed by the variable `productArray`, only the `field` "item" of this data structure should be considered. However, the field "item" references a set of products and not a single product. Thus, the `selector` "elementOf" is specified as well. From this information the JavaScript expression `elementOf(productArray.getItem())` is derived and evaluated on the data value context at run time, where the function `elementOf()` is predefined and simply returns the first value of any provided collection.

The result of learning a behavioral model with this setup specification is shown in Figure 7. Please note that this figure presents a view onto the learned Mealy machine that omits error transitions, only showing actions that do not raise an exception during execution. The impact of the experimental semantical analysis is already apparent from the fact that this model contains more states than those created by `StrawBerry` by means of syntactic analysis and test runs, with the effect that all the three properties mentioned in Section 2 are correctly revealed:

- When no products have previously been added to the shopping cart, the operation to purchase products does not conclude successfully: the purchase action only succeeds in states s4 and s5, which can only be reached when adding at least one product to the shopping cart.
- As long as a session is open, it is possible to empty its associated shopping cart: the action to empty the shopping cart succeeds in all states except the states s0, s1 and s7, where the session either has not been openend yet or was subsequently destroyed.

– After a purchase operation it is not possible to immediately trigger another purchase. Instead, it is necessary to put another item into the shopping cart, which implies that the purchase operation does clear the shopping cart. This can be witnessed at the s4/s3 and s5/s6 transitions.

Apart from these facets even more subtle behavioral aspects are captured. For example, once a non-empty shopping cart is retrieved, its contents can be added to another session's shopping cart. This means that the data structure representing products in a shopping cart is not bound to session instances, which is another implementation detail influencing how the service can be operated that is not explicitly contained in the service's interface description.

7 Related Work

Inferring formal properties of software components has been a major research interest for the past decade. Most available approaches fall into one of two classes. One class generates extrinsic properties (e.g., invariants). The other class generates intrinsic properties, e.g., models describing the actual behavior of components. In both classes active and passive approaches, as well as black-box and white-box variants can be found. While StrawBerry falls into the first category, LearnLib is of the second kind.

The class of methods for generating properties can be further subdivided into methods that "mine" statistical models and methods that generate invariants. In the class of methods that generate statistical models, the approaches described in [25,24] mine Java code to infer sequences of method calls. These sequences are then used to produce object usage patterns and operational preconditions, respectively, that serve to detect object usage violations in the code. StrawBerry shares with [24] the way an object usage pattern is represented, i.e., as a set of temporal dependencies between method calls (e.g., $m < n$ means "calls to m precede calls to n").

The work of [19] presents a passive method for the automated generation of specifications of legal method call sequences on multiple related objects from from method traces of Java programs, [9] extends this method by active testing. As for StrawBerry, tests are used to refine the invariants that have been generated inductively from the provided information. However, in contrast to StrawBerry, none of these approaches focuses on data-flow invariants explicitly. A tool that infers invariants from data is Daikon [10].

In the class of methods that generate intrinsic properties, especially automata learning has been used to generate behavioral models of systems. Active learning, as implemented in LearnLib, has been used to infer behavioral models of CTI systems as early as 2002 [12,13]. It has since then been applied in a number of real-life case studies (e.g., [21,20]). In these case studies, however, data has never been treated explicitly but was rather hidden from the learning algorithm. In [22], systems with data parameters are considered. However, this work does not consider relations between different parameters. Recently, automata learning has been extended to deal with data parameters and data dependencies explicitly by means of hand-crafted mappers [14,1]. Our approach is unique in generating mappers automatically.

There are only few approaches that combine inference of behavioral models and invariants on data-flow. The authors of [5] present an approach for inferring state machines (by means of active learning) for systems with parameterized inputs. They first infer a behavioral model for a finite data domain, and afterwards abstract this model to a symbolic version, encoding extrapolated invariants on data parameters as guarded transitions.

The authors of [16,15] demonstrate how behavioral models can be created with passive learning from observations gathered by means of monitoring. In addition, this approach tries to capture the behavioral influence of data values by applying an invariance detector [10]. This approach, however, is subject to the issue of all passive approaches: they are limited to the (possibly small) set of observed executions. If a piece of code or part of the application is not executed, it will not be considered in the generated model.

The work described in [11] (i.e., the SPY approach) aims at inferring a behavioral specification (in this case: graph transformation rules) of Java classes that behave as data containers components by first observing their run-time behavior on a small concrete data domain and then constructing the transformation rules inductively from the observations.

It is common to all these approaches that they work on a large basis of concrete information that by induction is condensed into symbolic behavioral models. Invariants on data values are obtained in a post-processing step after construction of behavioral models.

In [2] an approach is presented that generates behavioral interface specifications for Java classes by means of predicate abstraction and active learning. Here, predicate abstraction is used to generate an abstract version of the considered class. Afterwards a minimal interface for this abstract version in obtained by active learning. This is a white-box scenario, and learning is used only to circumvent more expensive ways of computing the minimal interface.

Our approach, in contrast, provides a solution for the black-box scenario. Similarly, however, we use StrawBerry to compute an interface alphabet, and mapper, which in combination work as an abstraction, and infer a model at the level of this abstraction, using LearnLib.

8   Conclusions and Perspectives

We have presented a method and tool to *fully automatically* infer dataflow-sensitive behavioral models of black-box systems based on interface descriptions in WSDL by combining StrawBerry, a tool for syntactical analysis of the interface descriptions and the LearnLib, a flexible active automata learning framework. This combination allows us to overcome a central bottleneck, the manual construction of the mapper required for the learning tool to bridge between the model level and the concrete execution level.

Our method has been illustrated in detail along a concrete shop application example. The results are promising, but further case studies are required to fully explore the application profile of the approach. Scalability is certainly an issue here, and it has to be seen how stable the approach is concerning varying versions of WSDL-based interface specifications. Particularly interesting is here to investigate how our approach may profit from extra information provided e.g. through semantic annotations, a point explicitly addressed also in the CONNECT context. There, full automation is not sufficient as CONNECT's support is meant to happen fully online. Finally, we are currently working on an extension of our technology to generate even more expressive models in terms of register automata [8]. These models are designed to make the currently only implicitly modeled dataflow information explicit by introducing transitions with explicit conditions and assignments.

References

1. Aarts, F., Jonsson, B., Uijen, J.: Generating Models of Infinite-State Communication Protocols Using Regular Inference with Abstraction. In: Petrenko, A., Simão, A., Maldonado, J.C. (eds.) ICTSS 2010. LNCS, vol. 6435, pp. 188–204. Springer, Heidelberg (2010)
2. Alur, R., Cerný, P., Madhusudan, P., Nam, W.: Synthesis of interface specifications for Java classes. In: POPL, pp. 98–109 (2005)
3. Angluin, D.: Learning regular sets from queries and counterexamples. Inf. Comput. 75, 87–106 (1987)
4. Bennaceur, A., Blair, G., Chauvel, F., Gang, H., Georgantas, N., Grace, P., Howar, F., Inverardi, P., Issarny, V., Paolucci, M., Pathak, A., Spalazzese, R., Steffen, B., Souville, B.: Towards an Architecture for Runtime Interoperability. In: Margaria, T., Steffen, B. (eds.) ISoLA 2010, Part II. LNCS, vol. 6416, pp. 206–220. Springer, Heidelberg (2010)
5. Berg, T., Jonsson, B., Raffelt, H.: Regular Inference for State Machines Using Domains with Equality Tests. In: Fiadeiro, J.L., Inverardi, P. (eds.) FASE 2008. LNCS, vol. 4961, pp. 317–331. Springer, Heidelberg (2008)
6. Bertolino, A., Inverardi, P., Pelliccione, P., Tivoli, M.: Automatic synthesis of behavior protocols for composable web-services. In: ESEC/SIGSOFT FSE, pp. 141–150. ACM (2009)
7. Bertolino, A., Inverardi, P., Pelliccione, P., Tivoli, M.: Automatic synthesis of behavior protocols for composable web-services. In: Proceedings of The 7th Joint Meeting of the European Software Engineering Conference (ESEC) and the ACM SIGSOFT Symposium on the Foundations of Software Engineering (FSE), pp. 141–150 (August 2009)
8. Cassel, S., Howar, F., Jonsson, B., Merten, M., Steffen, B.: A Succinct Canonical Register Automaton Model. In: Bultan, T., Hsiung, P.-A. (eds.) ATVA 2011. LNCS, vol. 6996, pp. 366–380. Springer, Heidelberg (2011)
9. Dallmeier, V., Knopp, N., Mallon, C., Hack, S., Zeller, A.: Generating test cases for specification mining. In: Proceedings of ISSTA 2010, pp. 85–96. ACM, New York (2010)
10. Ernst, M.D., Perkins, J.H., Guo, P.J., McCamant, S., Pacheco, C., Tschantz, M.S., Xiao, C.: The Daikon system for dynamic detection of likely invariants. Sci. Comput. Programming 69(1-3), 35–45 (2007)
11. Ghezzi, C., Mocci, A., Monga, M.: Synthesizing Intentional Behavior Models by Graph Transformation. In: ICSE 2009, Vancouver, Canada (2009)
12. Hagerer, A., Hungar, H., Niese, O., Steffen, B.: Model Generation by Moderated Regular Extrapolation. In: Kutsche, R.-D., Weber, H. (eds.) FASE 2002. LNCS, vol. 2306, pp. 80–95. Springer, Heidelberg (2002)
13. Hungar, H., Margaria, T., Steffen, B.: Test-based model generation for legacy systems. In: Proceedings of the International Test Conference, ITC 2003, September 30-October 2, vol. 1, pp. 971–980 (2003)
14. Jonsson, B.: Learning of Automata Models Extended with Data. In: Bernardo, M., Issarny, V. (eds.) SFM 2011. LNCS, vol. 6659, pp. 327–349. Springer, Heidelberg (2011)

15. Lorenzoli, D., Mariani, L., Pezzè, M.: Automatic Generation of Software Behavioral Models. In: ICSE 2008, pp. 501–510. ACM, NY (2008)
16. Mariani, L., Pezzè, M.: Dynamic Detection of COTS Component Incompatibility. IEEE Software 24(5), 76–85 (2007)
17. Niese, O.: An Integrated Approach to Testing Complex Systems. PhD thesis, University of Dortmund, Germany (2003)
18. Oracle.com. JAX-WS RI 2.1.1 – wsimport, `http://download.oracle.com/javase/6/docs/technotes/tools/share/wsimport.html` (2011) (online; accessed September 13, 2011)
19. Pradel, M., Gross, T.: Automatic generation of object usage specifications from large method traces. In: Proceedings of ASE 2009, pp. 371–382 (November 2009)
20. Raffelt, H., Margaria, T., Steffen, B., Merten, M.: Hybrid test of web applications with webtest. In: Proceedings of TAV-WEB 2008, pp. 1–7. ACM, New York (2008)
21. Raffelt, H., Steffen, B., Berg, T., Margaria, T.: Learnlib: a framework for extrapolating behavioral models. Int. J. Softw. Tools Technol. Transf. 11, 393–407 (2009)
22. Shahbaz, M., Li, K., Groz, R.: Learning Parameterized State Machine Model for Integration Testing, vol. 2, pp. 755–760. IEEE Computer Society, Washington, DC (2007)
23. Shahbaz, M., Shashidhar, K.C., Eschbach, R.: Iterative refinement of specification for component based embedded systems. In: Proceedings of ISSTA 2011, pp. 276–286. ACM, New York (2011)
24. Wasylkowski, A., Zeller, A.: Mining Operational Preconditions (Tech. Rep.), `http://www.st.cs.uni-saarland.de/models/papers/wasylkowski-2008-preconditions.pdf`
25. Wasylkowski, A., Zeller, A., Lindig, C.: Detecting Object Usage Anomalies. In: ESEC-FSE 2007, pp. 35–44. ACM (2007)

Model-Based Compatibility Checking
of System Modifications*

Arnd Poetzsch-Heffter, Christoph Feller, Ilham W. Kurnia, and Yannick Welsch

University of Kaiserslautern, Germany
{poetzsch,c_feller,ilham,welsch}@cs.uni-kl.de

Abstract. Maintenance and evolution of software systems require to modify or exchange system components. In many cases, we would like the new component versions to be backward compatible to the old ones, at least for the use in the given context. Whereas on the program level formal techniques to precisely define and verify backward compatibility are under development, the situation on the system level is less mature. A system component C has not only communication interfaces to other system components, but also to human users or the environment of the system. In such scenarios, compatibility checking of different versions of C needs more than program analysis:

- The behavior of the users are not part of the program, but needs to be considered for the overall system behavior.
- If the user interaction in the new version is different from the old one, the notion of compatibility needs clarification.
- Analyzing the user interface code makes checking technically difficult.

We suggest to use behavioral software models for compatibility checking. In our approach, the underlying system, the old and new component, and the nondeterministic behavior of the environment are modeled with the concurrent object-oriented behavioral modeling language ABS. Abstracting from implementation details, the checking becomes simpler than on the program level.

1   Introduction

Software systems play a key role in the infrastructure for modern societies. The size and cost of these systems forbid to create them "de novo" time and again. Thus, we need to systematically evolve systems and adapt them to new requirements. A typical evolution step is the exchange of a component C by a new version C'. We say that C' is *backward compatible* with C if the behaviors of C are also provided by C'. Backward compatibility is a central notion for quality assurance in software evolution and has different variants. Weaker forms of backward compatibility ensure that some well-defined properties are maintained during evolution steps, but not necessarily all behaviors. Another line of variation is with respect to the contexts in which backward compatibility should

---

* This research is partly funded by the EU project FP7-231620 HATS (Highly Adaptable and Trustworthy Software using Formal Models) and the German Research Foundation (DFG) under the project MoveSpaci in the priority programme RS3 (Reliably Secure Software Systems).

T. Margaria and B. Steffen (Eds.): ISoLA 2012, Part I, LNCS 7609, pp. 97–111, 2012.

be guaranteed. For example, we can require that a component is backward compatible in all possible contexts or just for the use in certain systems.

In this paper, we investigate compatibility of components that have a *bipartite context* consisting of, on the one hand, interactions with users or the environment and, on the other hand, communication with an underlying system. A common example is an application component C with a GUI that talks to an underlying database. Our goal is to show that a new version C', having possibly a very different GUI, can be used instead of C. More precisely, we want to make sure that users of C' can trigger the same interactions with the underlying system as in the old version. That is, we allow modifying the interactions with users or the environment[1], but want to maintain the behavior at the interface to the underlying system. Checking this kind of compatibility is challenging:

- Usual program analysis techniques are not sufficient, because we have to also take the user behavior into account.
- As the user interactions in the new version might be quite different from the old one, we have to be able to compose user and component behavior to derive the behavior at the interface to the underlying system.
- We have to abstract from the complexities of GUI software.

The central contribution of this paper is a new method for reasoning about compatibility of components with bipartite contexts. The method is based on the following framework:

- An executable behavioral modeling technique: Software components and users are modeled using the concurrent, object-oriented modeling language ABS [8]. ABS models abstract from implementation details (e.g., event handling and layout management in GUIs) and capture the concurrent behavior among possibly distributed components. They can faithfully reflect the software structure, simulate the implementation[2] and allow validation of models. ABS also supports modeling internal nondeterminism, which is, e.g., crucial to model the possible behavior of users.
- Component transition systems: The semantics of each component of the ABS model is represented by a component transition system (CTS) receiving and sending messages. In contrast to ABS which is very good for modeling, the CTS-level simplifies composition and reasoning. The consistency between an ABS component and a CTS can be verified by programming logics (see, e.g., [4]).
- A reasoning technique for compatibility with bipartite contexts based on CTS composition and simulation proofs.

In this paper, we describe the framework, use it to model a system with a GUI, and demonstrate a typical evolution step for such systems, in which the GUI and the possible user interactions are modified. Then, we define compatibility of components with bipartite contexts and describe how to check compatibility.

---

[1] For brevity, we will only consider user interactions in the following. However, we claim that our approach can also be used in settings in which sensors and actors are used to communicate with a modeled environment.

[2] ABS also supports code generation.

Overview. Section 2 presents the executable behavioral modeling technique, the language ABS, and our running example. Section 3 describes evolution steps and defines compatibility. Section 4 introduces CTSs, their composition, and compatibility checking. Finally, Sects. 5 and 6 discuss related work and present conclusions.

2   Modeling Software Systems

This section describes our behavioral modeling technique. It is more abstract than implementations, e.g., by abstracting from the event handling mechanisms of GUIs, but still reflects the structure and communication behavior of implementations which is important for component-based reasoning. We illustrate the modeling technique by an example that will also be used to explain our reasoning technique in subsequent sections.

2.1   ABS Modeling

To model software systems, we use the modeling language ABS, an object-oriented language with a concurrency model based on *concurrent object groups* (COGs). COGs follow the actor paradigm [6] and are developed to avoid data races and the complexity of multithreading. COGs are the unit of concurrency and distribution. During execution, each object is a member of exactly one COG for its entire lifetime. This is similar to the Java RMI setting where objects belong to certain JVM instances, which may run distributed on different machines. Groups can be created dynamically and work concurrently. Execution within a single group is sequential. Communication between groups is asynchronous. This concurrency model is used in the abstract behavioral specification language ABS [8] and in JCoBox [11], a Java based realization of COGs.

ABS supports object-oriented concepts using a Java-like syntax and immutable recursive datatypes in the style of functional languages. In ABS, the creation of COGs is related to object creation. The creation expression specifies whether the object is created in the current COG (using the standard **new** expression) or is created in a fresh COG (using the **new cog** expression). Communication in ABS between different COGs happens via *asynchronous method calls* which are indicated by an exclamation mark (!). A reference in ABS is *far* when it targets an object of a different COG, otherwise it is a *near* reference. Similar to the E programming language [10], ABS restricts synchronous method calls (indicated by the standard dot notation) to be made only on near references.

2.2   Example: Flight Booking System

As an example, we consider a simple flight booking system. It follows a two-tier architecture with an application accessing an underlying repository. The application has a GUI with several state-dependent views. The system consists of the two main components:

- Agent, modeling the application and graphical user interface layer, and
- Server, modeling the database upon which the actual booking takes place.

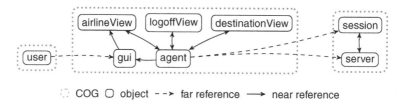

Fig. 1. Runtime structure of ABS model

In addition to these two software components, we provide an explicit user model in ABS. All three components are modeled as COGs. The runtime structure of the system is given in Fig. 1. As the details of the server behavior are not relevant for our model, we represent that part of the system by a generic server object and a session object that handles the connection to the agent. The agent component consists of a main agent object that does the actual booking and various view objects that are used to present the steps of the booking process to the user. For example, the airlineView object presents the user with choices of the bookable airlines and the buttons to select the airline. The gui object is used as a proxy for the various views of the agent. Initially it delegates to the airlineView, but over time, it may delegate to other views. Encapsulating the various views by the gui proxy allows the agent to control which views are presented to the user.

The gui object together with the view objects realize the graphical user interface of the system where the gui object represents the part corresponding to a GUI toolkit. The design of our very simple GUI model is based on two principles:

– The communication between users and the GUI is asynchronous and triggered by the user, and the used methods are application-independent.
– The presentation of views is controlled by the software system.

Asynchronous communication is obtained by using ABS; application independency is achieved by realizing the communication over a generic interface. In our simple model, the interface View (see Fig. 2) allows users to click on buttons (method clickOn where the parameter identifies the button) and to inspect the view: method viewContent returns the shown content and getNbt yields the number of enabled buttons. The user interacts with the system by invoking these methods (the software system cannot call methods on the user). The gui object is the boundary between the software and the user. It delegates calls to the currently visible view and allows the software system to change between views using the setView method (see Fig. 2). Based on the illustrated principles, one can develop more realistic GUI models by providing sufficiently elaborate view interfaces.

The interfaces of the two main components (see Fig. 2) describe a small two-tier system. The server object implements the Server interface which provides a method to create new sessions; session objects implement the Session interface which provides methods to do the actual booking. The method checkAndReserve inquires the price for a certain flight to a certain destination. Note that String, Price, Airline and Destination are *data types* and represent immutable data instead of objects. The agent object implements the Agent interface. For reference types, the type annotations N and F provide enhanced type information, namely whether references of this type point to near or far

```
1   interface Server {
2       SessionN createSession(); }
3   interface Session {
4       Price checkAndReserve(Airline al,
5           Destination dest);
6       Unit buy();
7       Unit cancel();
8       Unit close(); }

9   interface Agent {
10      ViewN getView(); }
11  interface GUI extends View {
12      Unit setView(ViewN v); }
13  interface View {
14      Unit clickOn(Int position);
15      String viewContent();
16      Int getNbt(); }
```

Fig. 2. Interfaces of ABS model

objects (i.e., objects in the same COG or not). For example, the session objects returned by the server are in the same COG as the server, which the type $Session^N$ illustrates for the createSession method. This enhanced typing information can either be manually specified or automatically inferred by the ABS tools [17]. The architecture in Fig. 1 is configured in a *main* COG (that is the reason why all references are far (F)):

```
1   ServerF s = new cog ServerImpl();
2   AgentF a = new cog AgentImpl(s);
3   Fut<ViewF> vfut = a!getView();
4   ViewF v = vfut.get;
5   new cog User(v);
```

The server is passed to the agent in the constructor (line 2). The view is obtained from the agent and passed to the user to enable the interaction with the agent. Asynchronous calls like the call to getView directly return a future. The value of a future is accessed by **get** (line 4) which blocks execution until the futures is resolved. Note that the agent is a component with a bipartite context: It interacts with the user and the server COG.

Users are modeled as nondeterministic and active components. In ABS, active components are described by classes with a run method which is automatically called when a new COG is created. Thus, user behavior is described in the run method of class User (see below). A user looks at the view content (calls viewContent) and at the number of buttons (calls getNbt) and then randomly clicks on one of the available buttons (line 9). The lines 5, 7, and 9 are asynchronous method calls and represent the communication from the user to the agent. The user waits for the futures to the first two calls to be resolved at line 6 and 8, representing the communication from the agent to the user.

```
1   class User(ViewF v) {
2       Unit run() {
3           Bool abort = False;
4           while( ~abort ) {
5               Fut<String> contentfut = v!viewContent();
6               String content = contentfut.get; // look at content
7               Fut<Int> crtNmbBtfut = v!getNbt();
8               Int crtNmbBt = crtNmbBtfut.get;
9               if ( crtNmbBt > 0 ) { v!clickOn(random(crtNmbBt)); } else { abort = True; }
10  }}}
```

The agent COG includes the View objects (see Fig. 1 and below). When a user calls a method on the GUI object, the GUI object delegates the call to the current view (e.g., AirlineView). This specific view can then call the Agent (e.g., slctAirline, slctDestination or buyOffer) which might lead to change the current view (e.g., gui.setView(destinationView) in line 17). Initially, the GUI object delegates to the AirlineView object, which allows the user to select an airline. After the selection (call of the method clickOn), the AirlineView object calls slctAirline method on the AgentImpl object, which then tells the GUI object to *switch* to the DestinationView. After buying a ticket, the connection to the server is closed and the view is changed to the logoffView that does not react to user inputs.

```
1   class AgentImpl(Server^F myserv)          14   ...
2              implements Agent, ... {        15   Unit slctAirline(Airline al) {
3   View^N aView;                             16     slctdAl = al;
4   View^N dView;                             17     gui.setView(dView);
5   GUI^N gui;                                18   }
6   Session^F session;                        19   ...
7   ... {                                     20   Unit buyOffer() {
8     aView = new AirlineView(this);          21     Fut<Unit> f = session!buy();
9     dView = new DestinationView(this);      22     f.get;
10    ...                                     23     session!close();
11    gui = new GUIImpl();                    24     gui.setView(logoffView);
12    gui.setView(aview);                     25   }
13  }                                         26 }
```

We finish this section on modeling with summarizing the five aspects of the modeling technique that are important for our method:

1. The models should be read and written by software developers that might not master formal reasoning. They should be executable for validation.
2. The models should be sufficiently close to realistic implementations, particularly in reflecting the component structure and interfaces. This eases the conformance checking with implementations when they are not generated from the models.
3. The models should express the behavior of the software system and the users/environment in order to define and analyze the overall system behavior.
4. The models should allow for abstraction (e.g., in our example, we abstract from the details of GUI implementations).
5. To allow reasoning, the models need a precise formal semantics that also covers the concurrency aspects.

In the following, we consider evolution steps for components with bipartite contexts.

3   Evolution of Systems

Evolvable systems must be open to change. Often, new component versions should not change the overall behavior of the system. For example, we might want to change the implementation of the agent but still guarantee that the same kind of flight booking operations are possible. Compatibility of the new agent implementation with the old one then means that the *observable* behavior of the system remains the same.

There are different ways to define what should be considered as observable. If we consider all interactions of the agent as its behavior, we could not modify the GUI, because GUI modification in general changes the interactions with the user. Thus, we focus on the communication with the underlying system, namely on the communication between the agent and the server component. This is the communication that leads to the actual flight bookings. More precisely, we allow new components to change the views (different content and buttons) and the way the views are presented and how they react to button clicks. But, we want to guarantee that every behavior at the interface to the underlying system that could be achieved with the old component can also be achieved with the new version. We formalize behavior as traces, that is, sequences of interactions.

Definition 1 (Backward compatibility). *Let U be a nondeterministic user model, C be an application component with a GUI, and D be a component such that Sys=(U,C,D) is a closed system. A component C′ with a GUI is* backward compatible *with C if Sys′=(U,C′,D) is a closed system and the traces between C and D in Sys are a subset of the traces between C′ and D in Sys′.*

To illustrate this definition by our example, let us consider a second implementation of the agent sketched in Fig. 3. For this implementation, the airline view and destination view are combined into a single view that is directly implemented by the agent object itself. This means that the agent class also implements the View interface:

```
1   class AgentImpl(ServerF myserv)
2           implements Agent, View ... { ...
3     { ...
4       gui = new GUIImpl();
5       gui.setView(this);
6     } ...
7   }
```

The new view allows the selection of airlines and destinations in one view and in any order[3]. Thus, the user interactions in the two versions are very different. Nevertheless, the new implementation should allow users to make the same bookings as in the old version. Thus, the new version is backward compatible,although the communication between the user and the agent component is very different. To make this more tangible, consider a concrete trace of events between the agent and the server s:

```
1   ⟨ f1 = s!createSession(), f1!(sess), f2 = sess!checkAndReserve(al,dest),
2     f2!(price), f3 = sess!buy(), f3!(), sess!close() ⟩
```

Here, f!(x) denotes the resolution of future f by value x. One can now see that the order in which the airline al and the destination dest have to be selected is irrelevant for the trace because these choices are transmitted by only one message. So this trace will be a trace for both the old and the new version of the system.

---

[3] For brevity, we do not show the complete ABS description of it.

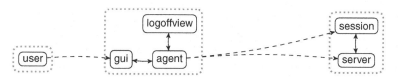

Fig. 3. Runtime structure of ABS model after evolution

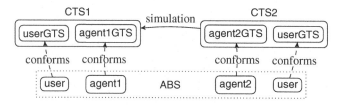

Fig. 4. Reasoning approach

4   Reasoning Approach

At the end of the last section, we postulated that two agent components are backward compatible. In this section, we describe our approach to checking compatibility for such components. The approach is based on three well-known techniques:

- Finite representation of behavior by rule-based transition systems
- Composition of transition systems
- Proving compatibility by using simulation

The ABS language makes it easy to read and write behavioral models of concurrent and distributed software systems. A logic to prove properties about ABS models is under development ([4] presents such a logic for a subset of ABS). As there is no logic to directly prove the compatibility of two COGs, we use a two-step approach:

1. First, we represent the behavior of a COG by a suitable kind of transition systems that we call *group transition systems* (GTS). Logics such as the one in [4] allow us to prove that a GTS faithfully represents the semantics of the corresponding COG.
2. Second, we compose and enclose the GTSs into shells called *component transition systems* (CTS) in order to produce the trace semantics of the component. Then we use composition and simulation techniques for CTSs to reason about compatibility.

Figure 4 illustrates the approach using the flight-booking example: For the ABS model of the user and the two agent models agent1 and agent2, we derived the GTSs userGTS, agent1GTS, and agent2GTS, respectively. We compose each agent GTS with the user GTS to produce CTS1 and CTS2, and show that CTS2 simulates CTS1 in the context of the underlying server. The following subsections explain these steps in more detail.

4.1   Group Transition Systems

GTSs are special labeled transition systems to abstractly represent the behavior of COGs written in ABS. A COG processes an incoming message by executing a corresponding method. The execution outputs a number of messages until the method reaches its end or the COG needs to wait for a future to be resolved. The way a COG processes an incoming message also depends on its current state. Thus, a GTS state should contain an abstract representation of the internal COG state and a bag of incoming messages that the COG must process. The transitions represent an interleaving semantics of the COG, matching nicely the asynchronous nature of the messages. Transitions are labeled by the outgoing messages that the component produces in that transition. As such, the incoming message being processed is obtained from the state information. In general, the state space of GTSs is infinite. To specify GTSs finitely, we utilize first-order logic.

The GTS is based on two sets, namely $\mathbf{O}$ as the set of all object and future instances, or simply names, and $\mathbf{M}$ as the set of all messages that can be produced. A message can be either an asynchronous method call $o!mtd(\overline{p})$ to object o calling method mtd with parameters $\overline{p}$ or a future resolution $f!(v)$ of the future f with value v. In asynchronous method calls, the last parameter is a future name that is used to return the result of the method call. Future names are freshly produced by the sender. Given a message m, the function $target(m)$ extracts the target object o or future f from the message. In this paper, we assume that futures are not passed as parameters and that all COGs are created during program start up. In particular, we do not consider messages for dynamic COG creation.

Definition 2 (GTS). *A group transition system is a quadruple $T = (L, S, R, s_0)$ where*

- *$L \subseteq \mathbf{O}$ is the set of object and future names local to the group,*
- *$S \subseteq Bag(\mathbf{M}) \times \mathbf{O} \times Q$ is the set of states consisting of a message bag, a set of exposed local names and the set of (abstract) local states,*
- *$R \subseteq S \times Bag(\mathbf{M}) \times S$ is a transition relation describing the processing of a message in the incoming message bag by the group, and*
- *s_0 is the initial state.*

The message bag stores the incoming messages that the COG is yet to process. Each transition is labeled with a bag of output messages, sent by the COG when it processes a message. We write $(M, q) \xrightarrow{Mo} (M', q')$ to represent a transition in R, where M, M' and Mo are message bags, and q and q' are local states. The locality of the objects and futures can be guaranteed using the ownership type system as mentioned in Sect. 2.2.

To ensure that a GTS captures the behavioral properties satisfied by all ABS COGs, we enforce a simple *well-formedness* criterium on the states and relations. For this purpose, we need a projection function $M \!\downarrow_L$. This projection function on a message bag M with respect to local names L produces the message bag $M_L \subseteq M$ where each message is targeted to some local object in L or a future resolution of a future in L.

Definition 3 (Well-formed GTS). *A GTS $T = (L, S, R, s_0)$ is* well-formed *if*

1. *$\forall (M, q) \in S \bullet M \!\downarrow_L = M$, and*
2. *$\forall (M, q) \xrightarrow{Mo} (M', q') \bullet \exists m \in M \bullet M' = M \cup Mo \!\downarrow_L - \{m\}$.*[4]

---

[4] We take the union operator on bags as adding all elements from one bag to the other and the difference operator as removing corresponding elements from one bag.

The first item states that the message bag contains only incoming messages. The second states when a transition is taken, the processed incoming message m is taken out from the message bag, while messages produced by the COG directed to the COG are added to the message bag. In other words, every transition of a GTS is a reaction to a method call or a future resolution. Thus, GTSs can represent the behavior of reactive COGs and active COGs that receive messages from other COGs (like User), but they cannot model active COGs that generate infinitely many messages without expecting any response.

We use rules of the form $m_{in} : P \longrightarrow P' \succ Mo$ to describe the transition relation of a GTS where:

- m_{in} is an incoming message contained within the message bag of the COG before the transition occurs and $target(m_{in})$ is in the set of local names L,
- P and P' are boolean expressions over the local state and the message parameters,
- Mo is the bag of outgoing messages resulting from the transition. For each outgoing asynchronous method call, there is always a future created by the component which is represented by **new** f.

A transition $(M,q) \xrightarrow{Mo} (M',q')$ satisfies a rule if $M' = M \cup Mo\!\downarrow_L - \{m_{in}\}$, P evaluates to true for the current state q and the parameters of m_{in}, P' evaluates to true for the post-state q' and the parameters of the messages in Mo. The rules describe the largest transition relation R where each transition satisfies at least one of the rules. Moreover, the transition relation is such that each future name is created fresh. In GTSs that are consistent with ABS models, futures will be resolved at most once.

As an example, let us take a look at the User COG. Users have an application-independent behavior. Local states are pairs of a control state and the GUI reference v. The user looks at the view content and sees a number of buttons. Then, he clicks on some random button (i.e., the nb-th button), unless no buttons are present, indicating the end of the interaction. In the expressions, we use special variable $ to denote the local state:

```
u!run()  : $=(u0,v)            ⟶  $=(u1,v)              ≻ v!viewContent(new f1)
f1!(s)   : $=(u1,v)            ⟶  $=(u2,v)              ≻ v!getNbt(new f2)
f2!(n)   : $=(u2,v) ∧ n>0      ⟶  $=(u3,v) ∧ (0≤nb<n)   ≻ v!clickOn(nb,new f3)
f3!()    : $=(u3,v)            ⟶  $=(u1,v)              ≻ v!viewContent(new f1)
f2!(n)   : $=(u2,v) ∧ n=0      ⟶  $=(u4,v)              ≻ ε
```

For the overall understanding of our method, the details of the GTS construction are not so important. Important are the following three points:

1. GTSs are appropriate for formal analysis, but are not a good language for designing realistic software models (see the requirements mentioned at at the end of Sect. 2).
2. The general theory to verify that a COG, considered as a program, conforms to a GTS, considered as a specification, is available. A specialization of the theory to the particular setting considered here is under development (cf. [4]).
3. Techniques for composition and compatibility checking of transition systems are in general well-developed. A specialization to our setting will be discussed next.

4.2 Component Transition Systems

We introduced GTSs as faithful representations of COGs. In the following, we construct transition systems that exhibit exactly the observable traces that we need for compatibility checking. In particular, they allow us to prove trace inclusion by simulation methods. Technically, we construct a *component transition systems* CTS_T from a set T of GTSs. CTS_T hides internal messages. By composing two CTSs C_1 and C_2, written as $C_1 \mid C_2$, we obtain a closed system that generates the traces at the boundary between C_1 and C_2. Construction and composition can be fully automated.

To illustrate the approach, let us again consider our example with GTS_U being the GTS for the user, GTS_A and $GTS_{A'}$ for the first and second version of the agent, and GTS_D for the underlying system. Compatibility checking is then realized as follows:

- construct $CTS_{\{U,A\}}$ from GTS_U and GTS_A ,
- construct $CTS_{\{U,A'\}}$ from GTS_U and $GTS_{A'}$,
- construct $CTS_{\{D\}}$ from GTS_D , and
- check that $CTS_{\{U,A'\}} \mid CTS_{\{D\}}$ simulates $CTS_{\{U,A\}} \mid CTS_{\{D\}}$.

In summary, construction essentially puts GTSs together and hides internal messages. Composition yields an executable system in which traces at the boundary of the two[5] components are observable, allowing the checking of compatibility as defined in Def. 1. Construction and composition are illustrated in Fig. 5.

Definition 4 (CTS construction). *Let $T = \{T_1, \ldots, T_n\}$ be a set of GTSs where $T_i = (L_i, S_i, R_i, s_{0i})$, $i \in \{1, \ldots n\}$ and L_i pairwise disjoints. Let $s_i = (M_i, q_i), s_i' = (M_i', q_i')$ be states of T_i. The component transition system of T is $CTS_T = (L, S, R, s_0)$ where*

- $L = \bigcup_{i=1}^{n} L_i, \qquad S \subseteq Bag(\mathbf{M}) \times S_1 \times \ldots \times S_n \times Bag(\mathbf{M}), \qquad s_0 = (\emptyset, s_{01}, \ldots, s_{0n}, \emptyset),$
- $R \subseteq S \times (\mathbf{M} \cup \{\tau\}) \times S$ *is the smallest relation such that*

  1. $\forall i, s_i \xrightarrow{Mo}_i s_i' \bullet (I, s_1, \ldots, s_n, O) \xrightarrow{\tau} (I, s_1', \ldots, s_n', O \cup Mo\downarrow_{O-L})$ *where* $\forall j \neq i \bullet s_j' = (M_j \cup Mo\downarrow_{L_j}, q_j);$

  2. $\forall m \bullet \forall (I \cup \{m\}, s_1, \ldots, s_n, O) \in S \bullet (I \cup \{m\}, s_1, \ldots, s_n, O) \xrightarrow{\tau} (I, s_1', \ldots, s_n', O)$ *where if target$(m) \in L_i$ then $s_i = (M_i \cup \{m\}, q_i)$ otherwise $s_i = s_i';$*

  3. $\forall m \bullet \forall (I, s_1, \ldots, s_n, O \cup \{m\}) \in S \bullet (I, s_1, \ldots, s_n, O \cup \{m\}) \xrightarrow{m} (I, s_1, \ldots, s_n, O).$

Similar to GTS, a CTS is described by a set of local names L, a set of states S, a labeled transition relation R and an initial state s_0. L is a union of all local names of the GTSs. S includes not just the states of all GTSs, but also two sets of message bags *IN* and *OUT*, which act as input and output ports of the component, respectively. s_0 is the empty message bags with the initial states of the GTSs. The labels on R can be a message m that is transmitted out of the CTS or an internal transition τ. The relation is built from the transition relation of the GTSs in the following way. For each transition in some T_i (Case 1), we insert a relation labeled with τ to R by distributing the output messages Mo to the corresponding message bags. If a message $m \in Mo$ is targeted to some local name

---

[5] Composition can be easily generalized to a finite set of components.

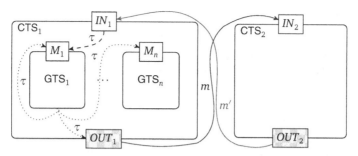

Fig. 5. Component transition systems and their composition

in L_j, that message is inserted into the incoming message bag M_j. Otherwise, m goes to the output port *OUT* of the CTS, as portrayed in the figure by the dotted lines. The second rule (Case 2) states the nondeterministic distribution of messages in the input port to the appropriate incoming message bag. As this is a hidden step, it is labeled with τ (represented by the dashed line). The last rule (Case 3) dispenses nondeterministically the messages in the output port one by one as long as *OUT* is not empty. This message sending is visible from outside of the component, thus the transition is labeled with the corresponding message m (the solid line in Fig. 5). This treatment of output guarantees that outputs from different enclosed GTSs can be interleaved.

To represent CTSs, we use the same rule format as for GTSs. For example, the transition corresponding to the button click in $CTS_{\{User,Agent\}}$ can be formulated as follows where the underscore is a wildcard for any agent state:

f2!(n) : \$=((u2,v),_) $\wedge$ n>0 $\longrightarrow$ \$=((u3,v),_) $\wedge$ (0≤nb<n) $\succ$ v!clickOn(nb,**new** f3)

A CTS represents an open system that needs a context in which it can work. We use another CTS as a context and observe the communication traces between them:

Definition 5 (CTS composition). *Let* $C_i = (L_i, S_i, R_i, s_{0i})$ *for* $i = \{1,2\}$ *be two CTSs. The composed CTS of* C_1 *and* C_2 *is* $C = (C_1 \mid C_2) = (L, S, R, s_0)$ *where*

- $L = L_1 \cup L_2,$ $S \subseteq S_1 \times S_2,$ $s_0 = (s_{01}, s_{02}),$
- $R \subseteq (S_1 \times S_2) \times (\mathbf{M} \cup \{\tau\}) \times (S_1 \times S_2)$ *such that*
  1. $\forall s_1 \in S_1 \bullet \forall s_2 \xrightarrow{\tau}_2 s_2' \bullet (s_1, s_2) \xrightarrow{\tau} (s_1, s_2'),$
  2. $\forall s_2 \in S_2 \bullet \forall s_1 \xrightarrow{\tau}_1 s_1' \bullet (s_1, s_2) \xrightarrow{\tau} (s_1', s_2),$
  3. $\forall (I_2, s_{21}, \ldots, s_{2n}, O_2) \in S_2 \bullet \forall s_1 \xrightarrow{m}_1 s_1' \bullet$

     $(s_1, (I_2, s_{21}, \ldots, s_{2n}, O_2)) \xrightarrow{m} (s_1', (I_2', s_{21}, \ldots, s_{2n}, O_2))$ *where*
     $I_2' = I_2 \cup \{m\}$ *if* $target(m) \in L_2$, *otherwise* $I_2' = I_2$, *and*
  4. $\forall (I_1, s_{11}, \ldots, s_{1n}, O_1) \in S_1 \bullet \forall s_2 \xrightarrow{m}_2 s_2' \bullet$

     $((I_1, s_{11}, \ldots, s_{1n}, O_1), s_2) \xrightarrow{m} ((I_1', s_{11}, \ldots, s_{1n}, O_1), s_2')$ *where*
     $I_1' = I_1 \cup \{m\}$ *if* $target(m) \in L_1$, *otherwise* $I_1' = I_1$.

The composition of two CTSs C_1 and C_2 corresponds to the interaction illustrated in Fig. 5. The local names L are combined from the respective components, the same with the states S and the initial state s_0. The transition relation R lifts up all internal transitions of the components (Cases 1, 2), and for each non-internal transition (Cases 3, 4), we update the input port of the corresponding component if the outgoing message is targeted to that component. The standard computation of the composed CTS provides the necessary ingredients for producing the traces of the components.

Definition 6 (Computation and trace of composed CTS). *A computation of a composed CTS $C = (L, S, R, s_0)$ is a sequence*

$$s_0 \xrightarrow{m_1} s_1 \xrightarrow{m_2} s_2 \xrightarrow{m_3} s_3 \ldots .$$

A trace of the composed CTS is the sequence of the non-internal labels of a computation.

For our flight-booking system, the traces of $CTS_{\{U,A\}} \mid CTS_{\{D\}}$ and $CTS_{\{U,A\}} \mid CTS_{\{D\}}$ are the ones we need for compatibility checking according to in Def. 1.

4.3 Checking Compatibility

As explained in Sect. 3, compatibility is defined based on the traces at the boundary between the combined user and application component on the one side and the underlying system on the other side. The CTSs give us a finite representation of the infinite trace sets and allow us to formally prove compatibility using simulation techniques (cf. [3]).

Essentially, we have to find a simulation relation and show that from two related states we can make a step in both systems and end up again in related states. Simulations for CTSs slightly deviate from the standard simulations because we have to account for the τ-transitions. We write $s \xRightarrow{m} s'$, $m \neq \tau$, if there is a sequence of states $s_0 \ldots s_n$ with $s = s_0$, $s' = s_n$, and an $i < n$ such that

$$s_0 \xrightarrow{\tau} \ldots \xrightarrow{\tau} s_i \xrightarrow{m} s_{i+1} \xrightarrow{\tau} \ldots \xrightarrow{\tau} s_n$$

Definition 7 (Simulation relation on composed CTSs). *Let $C_a = (L_a, S_a, R_a, s_{0a})$ and $C_b = (L_b, S_b, R_b, s_{0b})$ be two composed CTSs. We call $SR \subseteq S \times S'$ a simulation relation on composed CTSs iff*

- *$(s_{0a}, s_{0b}) \in SR$, and*
- *$\forall (s_a, s_b) \in SR \bullet \forall s'_a \bullet s_a \xRightarrow{m}_a s'_a$ implies $\exists s''_a, s'_b \bullet s_a \xRightarrow{m}_a s''_a \wedge s_b \xRightarrow{m}_b s'_b \wedge (s''_a, s'_b) \in SR.$*

If there exists such a simulation relation, we say that C_b simulates C_a.

The initial states have to be in the simulation relation. If a pair (s_a, s_b) of states in C_a and C_b, respectively, is in the relation, then for every computation in C_a starting in s_a that emits a message m there must be corresponding computation in C_b emitting m such that they end up in related states. The following theorem states that we can use simulation to prove compatibility:

Theorem 1. *Let C_a and C_b be two composed CTS, Tr_a and Tr_b the set of traces of C_a and C_b, respectively. If C_b simulates C_a, $Tr_a \subseteq Tr_b$.*

Proof. We show by induction that for all $t \in Tr_a$, $t = m_1 \ldots m_n$, of length n there are sequences of states $s_{0a} \ldots s_{na}$ and $s_{0b} \ldots s_{nb}$ with

$$s_{0a} \xRightarrow{m_1} \ldots \xRightarrow{m_n} s_{na} \quad \text{and} \quad s_{0b} \xRightarrow{m_1} \ldots \xRightarrow{m_n} s_{nb}$$

and $(s_{ia}, s_{ib}) \in SR$ for all $i \in \{0, \ldots, n\}$. In particular, $t \in Tr_b$. This is obviously true for the empty trace and the induction step is directly obtained from the definition of simulation relations.

For our flight-booking system, the simulation relation can include the initial state pairs, the state pairs when the session is requested, the session is returned, checking and reserving a route, getting the price, buying the ticket and closing the session. All the internal state changes of the different versions are hidden.

5 Related Work

Several techniques for modeling the behavior of object-oriented systems are available (e.g., VDM++ [5] or Object-Z [12]). ABS has the advantage that it is easier to handle for programmers, that it is executable, and that it supports a important form of concurrency.

In contrast to the novel approach taken here, where we use an abstract model to reason about compatibility (see Sect. 4). Compatibility or equivalence of components has also been studied directly at the code level [7,9,15]. Using our sound and complete simulation techniques developed in [15] which relate two different implementations, we have made first steps towards automated verification of compatibility for object-oriented libraries [16]. We believe that using a more abstract model like the one in Sect. 4 can further improve the level of automation.

GTS and CTS are a variant to the well-known concept of labeled transition systems tailored to the Actor model [1]. Having all outgoing messages as the label of a single transition in GTS is similar to the big-step semantics of Specification Diagrams [13] without the internal operations. Because the states contain incoming message bags, there is no need to synchronize the messages in the composition. Furthermore it allows lifting up the specification of the subcomponents' GTS to form the specification of the CTS.

Another way to obtain a trace-based interpretation of GTS is by building an independent relation between messages caused by transitions which is produced by different COGs during the composition of GTSs. One can then extract trace equivalence classes that represent the complete behavior of the system as shown in [14]. Coming up with this independent relation, however, is not a trivial task.

6 Conclusion and Future Work

Software maintenance and evolution steps modify some properties of a system and should maintain others. In this paper, we presented a method to reason about modifications of components that have both an interface to users (or an environment) and an interface to other system parts. Whereas changes at the interface to the users should be allowed, we wanted to maintain the behavior at the interface to other system parts. Our approach addresses three challenges:

1. Modeling of user behavior, i.e., of behavior that is not represented by software
2. Abstraction from technical complexities such as GUI frameworks
3. Reasoning about compatibility of two component versions

The first two challenges were met by using the behavioral modeling language ABS. To solve the third challenge, we developed CTS, a special form of transition systems. A CTS finitely represents the semantics of ABS components and is suitable for composition and verifying compatibility of components using simulation proofs.

Our central goal for the future is to develop tools supporting the presented method. We would like to use model mining techniques [2] for automating the constructing of the GTS for a COG. Where full automation is not possible, we need verification support to prove conformance. In addition, we need tools helping with the simulation proofs.

References

1. Agha, G., Mason, I.A., Smith, S.F., Talcott, C.L.: A foundation for actor computation. J. Funct. Program. 7(1), 1–72 (1997)
2. Ammons, G., Bodík, R., Larus, J.R.: Mining specifications. In: POPL, pp. 4–16. ACM, New York (2002)
3. Baier, C., Katoen, J.: Principles of Model Checking, vol. 950. MIT Press (2008)
4. Din, C.C., Dovland, J., Johnsen, E.B., Owe, O.: Observable behavior of distributed systems: Component reasoning for concurrent objects. Journal of Logic and Algebraic Programming 81(3), 227–256 (2012)
5. Dürr, E., Katwijk, J.: VDM++, A Formal Specification Language for Object Oriented Designs. In: COMP EURO, pp. 214–219. IEEE (May 1992)
6. Hewitt, C., Bishop, P., Steiger, R.: A universal modular ACTOR formalism for artificial intelligence. In: IJCAI, pp. 235–245 (1973)
7. Jeffrey, A., Rathke, J.: Java JR: Fully Abstract Trace Semantics for a Core Java Language. In: Sagiv, M. (ed.) ESOP 2005. LNCS, vol. 3444, pp. 423–438. Springer, Heidelberg (2005)
8. Johnsen, E.B., Hähnle, R., Schäfer, J., Schlatte, R., Steffen, M.: ABS: A Core Language for Abstract Behavioral Specification. In: Aichernig, B.K., de Boer, F.S., Bonsangue, M.M. (eds.) FMCO 2010. LNCS, vol. 6957, pp. 142–164. Springer, Heidelberg (2011)
9. Koutavas, V., Wand, M.: Reasoning about class behavior. In: Informal Workshop Record of FOOL (2007)
10. Miller, M.S., Tribble, E.D., Shapiro, J.S.: Concurrency Among Strangers. In: De Nicola, R., Sangiorgi, D. (eds.) TGC 2005. LNCS, vol. 3705, pp. 195–229. Springer, Heidelberg (2005)
11. Schäfer, J., Poetzsch-Heffter, A.: JCoBox: Generalizing Active Objects to Concurrent Components. In: D'Hondt, T. (ed.) ECOOP 2010. LNCS, vol. 6183, pp. 275–299. Springer, Heidelberg (2010)
12. Smith, G.: The Object-Z Specification Language. Kluwer Academic Publishers (2000)
13. Smith, S.F., Talcott, C.L.: Specification diagrams for actor systems. Higher-Order and Symbolic Computation 15(4), 301–348 (2002)
14. Vasconcelos, V.T.: Trace semantics for concurrent objects. MA Thesis, Keio University (March 1992)
15. Welsch, Y., Poetzsch-Heffter, A.: Full Abstraction at Package Boundaries of Object-Oriented Languages. In: Simao, A., Morgan, C. (eds.) SBMF 2011. LNCS, vol. 7021, pp. 28–43. Springer, Heidelberg (2011)
16. Welsch, Y., Poetzsch-Heffter, A.: Verifying backwards compatibility of object-oriented libraries using Boogie. In: FTfJP, Beijing, China (2012)
17. Welsch, Y., Schäfer, J.: Location Types for Safe Distributed Object-Oriented Programming. In: Bishop, J., Vallecillo, A. (eds.) TOOLS 2011. LNCS, vol. 6705, pp. 194–210. Springer, Heidelberg (2011)

A Generic Platform
for Model-Based Regression Testing

Philipp Zech, Michael Felderer, Philipp Kalb, and Ruth Breu

Institute of Computer Science, University of Innsbruck, Austria
{philipp.zech,michael.felderer,philipp.kalb,ruth.breu}@uibk.ac.at

Abstract. Model-based testing has gained widespread acceptance in the last few years. Models enable the platform independent analysis and design of tests in an early phase of software development resulting in effort reduction in terms of time and money. Furthermore, test models are easier to maintain than test code when software systems evolve due to their platform independence and traceability support. Nevertheless, most regression testing approaches, which ensure that system evolution does not introduce unintended effects, are solely code-based. Additionally, many model-based testing approaches do not consider regression testing when applied in practice, mainly due to the lack of appropriate tool support. Therefore, in this paper we present a generic tool platform for model-based regression testing based on the model versioning and evolution framework MoVE. Our approach enhances existing model-based testing approaches with regression testing capabilities aiming at better tool support for model-based regression testing. In a case study, we apply our platform to the model-based testing approaches UML Testing Profile and Telling TestStories.

1 Introduction

In recent years, model-based testing found its way into practice and is still an active area of research [1, 2]. *Model-based testing* (MBT) applies model-based design for the *modeling of test artifacts* and/or the *automation of tests activities*. MBT has several advantages like the abstractness of test cases, the early detection of faults, and the high level of automation that justify the additional effort of test model design and maintenance.

However, if considering existing model-based testing approaches in terms of providing a complete testing process, most of them suffer from one important feature, namely their tool support for regression testing [1]. *Regression testing* is the selective retesting of a system or component to verify that modifications have not caused unintended side effects and that the system or component still complies with its specified requirements [3]. Under consideration of the modeling effort, model-based regression test selection has several advantages to test selection on the code level [4]. The effort for testing can be estimated earlier, tools for regression testing can be largely technology independent, the management of traceability and test automation at the model level is more practical, no complex static and dynamic code analysis is required, and models are smaller compared to the size of modifiable elements because they are more abstract.

T. Margaria and B. Steffen (Eds.): ISoLA 2012, Part I, LNCS 7609, pp. 112–126, 2012.
© Springer-Verlag Berlin Heidelberg 2012

A potential solution to the missing model-based regression testing support dilemma is provided by the Model Versioning and Evolution (MoVE) platform [5]. MoVE provides a platform for versioning various software models based on the well known Subversion versioning system. The versioning procedure of MoVE is based on state machines attached to model elements. When a new version of a model is committed, a change set of modified model elements is identified which triggers change events processed by the attached state machines to calculate a new consistent version of the model in the repository. MoVE is based on the generic machine-readable exchange format XML Metadata Interchange (XMI) and not tailored to any specific type of model representation. Thus, due to its change management, model versioning and model representation capabilities MoVE provides a promising platform for generic model-based regression testing.

In this paper we present an approach for generic model-based regression testing based on the MoVE platform. The approach provides regression testing support for arbitrary XMI-based model representations and can be parameterized with different change identification, impact analysis, and regression test selection strategies defined in the Object Constraint Language (OCL). Additionally, the approach guarantees full traceability between various artifacts for efficient fault detection, and assures model consistency and validity and hence, also test suite validity, due to the change management capabilities of MoVE. To show the applicability of our generic model-based regression platform we apply it to regression testing of two independent model-based testing approaches, namely the UML Testing Profile (UTP) [6] and Telling TestStories (TTS) [7].

The remainder of this paper is structured as follows. Section 2 positions our approach in respect to related work. Section 3 introduces the various technologies underlying the platform and its case study, and Section 4 introduces our generic model-based regression testing platform and its implementation. We then provide a case study applying our approach for regression testing of two different model-based testing approaches, i.e. UTP and TTS in Section 5, and finally conclude in Section 6.

2   Related Work

Rerunning every test after each modification is not feasible, thus a trade-off has to be found between the confidence gained from regression testing, and resources used for it. For this reason, several regression testing techniques for test case minimization, prioritization and selection were proposed over the years [8]. Most regression testing approaches operate on the source code [9], although model-based regression testing has several advantages as mentioned in the introduction [4].

Most model-based regression testing approaches are built on UML and select tests based on change identification and impact analysis [10]. Our platform provides tool support for this important class of model-based regression testing techniques. UML-based system models typically consider class models and a specific type of UML behavior models, such as state machines in Farooq et al. [11], sequence diagrams in Briand et al. [4] or activity diagrams in Chen et al. [12]. Some of the proposed UML-based regression testing approaches have quite mature but very specific tool implementations like START (STAte-based Regression testing Tool) [11] or RTSTool (Regression Test Selection Tool) [4] not providing a generic platform (as MoVE does) applicable to other model-based testing approaches.

Although some industrial model-based testing tools are available and applied in practice, advanced model-based regression testing is still not supported adequately by these tools. A generic model based regression testing platform like MoVE provides additional support for model-based regression testing. For code-based regression testing several industrial and research tools are available. Industrial regression testing tools and platforms used nowadays - both commercial, e.g. [13] and open source (see [14] for an overview) - usually focus only on the automatic execution of tests, the collection of results, and creation of test reports when talking about regression testing. These tools typically do not apply the advanced regression testing techniques supported on the model level. More advanced academic regression testing tools [15, 16] are very specific and only available on the code level. For instance, TestTube [15] has been developed for selective retesting of C programs. It instruments the source code to capture which part of the system is covered by each test, and then computes which tests are needed for a given modification.

Beside MoVE, other platforms have recently been developed for model versioning [17–19]. Differing from MoVE, these platforms focus on a single modeling tool and have not yet been applied to model-based regression testing. The Eclipse Modeling Group provides two solutions for model persistence [20, 21]. These approaches do not provide model versioning support which is needed for model-based regression testing and provided by our approach.

3   Building Blocks

In this section we give an overview of the model versioning framework MoVE which our model-based regression testing approach is based on. Besides, we also introduce two model-based testing approaches, i.e. the UML Testing Profile and Telling TestStories which our model-based regression testing approach is applied to later on in a case study (see Section 5).

3.1   MoVE - Model Versioning and Evolution

MoVE is a model repository supporting versioning of arbitrary models. In the MoVE context we do not only consider models like in UML, but also other models, e.g. an Excel spreadsheet which can be interpreted as instance in tabular representation of a previously specified metamodel. Modeling tools can be integrated into the MoVE tool using MoVE adapters. Adapters consist of two parts: the server side part is responsible to provide the data in a readable format to MoVE. The client side adapter integrates into the modeling tool, using the tool's Application Programming Interface (API), and provides communication methods for the modeling tool with the MoVE server. A minimal requirement for the tool's API is the possibility to access the data stored in the tool and to call an external script or process. Both features are standard features of a tool-API.

MoVE supports a change-driven process as described by Breu [22]. A change-driven process combines three aspects: change-propagation, states and support of state machines. Fig. 3.1 shows the change-driven process in MoVE: on every commit the MoVE repository calculates the changes of the new version of the model to the previous version of the model and generates *change events* for each change. MoVE provides an API to develop plugins and register each plugin for a certain type of event. Each change event is sent to the registered plugin(s) which may trigger further change events and alter the model.

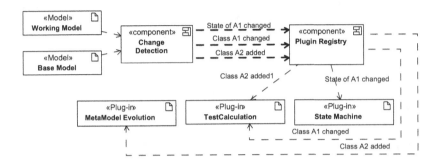

Fig. 1. Change-Driven Process in MoVE

In the MoVE context every model element can have a state machine attached, which is defined in the common metamodel. The state machine can define transitions between states of the model element and also actions that are triggered if a state is reached. This extension of state machines allow us to define a behavior not only on the model element under focus but also on different model elements which have a relation to the current model element. A task system enriches the state machines by user interaction. The change-driven process is used to identify state changes. In case a state change occurred, the state machines are used to calculate the correctness of the state change and derive possible actions belonging to the state change. As part of several industrial projects, the MoVE approach is currently evaluated and enhanced for large models.

3.2 Model-Based Testing Approaches

In this section we describe two actual model-based testing approaches, i.e. the UML Testing Profile and Telling TestStories.

UML Testing Profile. The UML Testing Profile (UTP) [23] provides concepts to develop test specifications and test models for black-box testing. UTP has been standardized by the OMG and mapping rules to the executable test definition languages TTCN-3 and JUnit have been defined. The profile introduces four concept groups for *Test Architecture*, *Test Behavior*, *Test Data* and *Time*.

The concepts of the test architecture are related to the structure and the configuration of tests, each consisting of test components and a test context. Test components interact with each other and the SUT to realize the test behavior. The test context encapsulates the SUT and a set of tests as well as the necessary arbiter and scheduler interfaces for verdict generation and controlling test execution, respectively. The composite structure of the test context is referred to as the test configuration.

The concepts of the test behavior specify a test in terms of sequences, alternatives, loops, stimuli, and observations from the SUT. During execution a test verdict is returned to the arbiter. The arbiter assesses the correctness of the SUT and finally sets the verdict of the whole test.

The test data is supplied via so-called data pools. These either have the form of data partitions (equivalence classes) or as explicit values. The test data is used in stimuli and observations of a test. A Stimulus represents the test data sent to the SUT in order to assess its reaction.

The concepts of test time are related to time constraints and observations within a test specification. A timer controls the test execution and reacts to start and stop requests as well as timeout events. In Baker et al. [24] all UTP concepts and their meaning are explained in detail.

Telling TestStories. Telling TestStories (TTS) [7] is a model-based methodology for the requirements-driven system testing of service centric systems. TTS is based on tightly integrated, yet separated platform-independent *requirements*, *system* and *test* models annotated with a UML profile.

The requirements model is based on a hierarchy of functional and non-functional requirements, attachable to test cases.

The system model describes the system structure and system behavior in a platform independent way. Its static structure is based on the notions of services, components and types.

The test model contains the test scenarios as so called test stories. Test stories are controlled sequences of service operation invocations exemplifying the interaction of components. The necessary test data is provided in a table-based manner to each test story. The manual test design process is supported by validation and coverage checks in and between the requirements, system and test model guaranteeing a high quality of the models. TTS is capable of test-driven development on the model level and provides full traceability between all system and testing artifacts. The test stories are transformed to executable test code in Java invoking running services via adapters which are automatically generated from WSDL files.

Felderer et al. [25] proposed a test evolution management methodology for TTS attaching state machines to model elements and propagating changes. Based on the actual state of model elements regression tests are selected. However, the proposed approach has not been implemented so far. But it can be implemented based on our generic regression testing platform.

4   Model-Based Regression Testing Platform

In this section we unroll our idea of a generic platform for model-based regression testing. Besides discussing the theoretical foundations of our approach we also present an implementation of the framework based on the Eclipse platform.

4.1   A Generic Model-Based Regression Testing Approach

If developing a generic approach for model-based regression testing, the primary issue to overcome and deal with is to not only provide support for a certain type of model but instead for a broad range of different types of (meta)models. This simply comes by the broad diversity of currently existing model-driven and model-based testing approaches [1], using different types of models and metamodels.

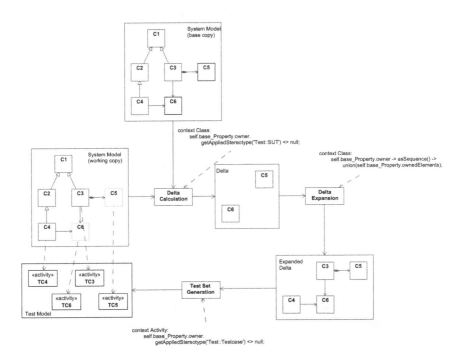

Fig. 2. Overview of the Generic Model-based Regression Testing Approach

Fig. 2 gives an overview of our idea of model-based regression testing. We start by comparing two different versions of the same model, i.e. the *Base Model* (initial development model) and the *Working Model* (current development model) and calculate a *delta* from it, the so called *change set*, containing the differences between the two model versions. As a next step, a regression test selection strategy is used to expand the delta by means of including additional elements from the SUT model. Finally, with the given expanded delta, a new test set is derived by means of *selection*. To support the necessary level of genericity our approach is *completely unaware* of any model, however, by allowing to customize and constrain the calculations in each step by means of OCL queries, we successfully circumvent this problem and enable to support a broad range of existing models. In the following, the three tasks, namely, *delta calculation*, *delta expansion* and *test set generation* are discussed in more detail.

Delta Calculation. The calculation of the *delta* (change set) is the initial task of our model-based regression testing approach. However, prior to calculating the delta, the scope of SUT needs to be defined. For example, if one wants to restrict the scope only to elements of type *Class*, the OCL query shown below the *Base Model* in Fig. 2 achieves this task. This query also assumes, that each SUT element has a stereotype *SUT*, defined in a profile named *Test*, applied. At this point it should be mentioned, that, depending on whether one uses a combined SUT/test model or separated ones, OCL queries at such an early point may be omitted.

With the SUT scope defined, the change set is ready to be calculated. The underlying brainchild hereby is to use the notion of a *left* (Base Model) and a *right* (Working Model) model to calculate the change set from left to right. Put it another way, elements from the right model are compared to elements from the left model by their matching IDs and changes are extracted. If in the right model, an element has been newly added or deleted, this actually poses no difficulty, as in the former case it is already ignored, as it is non-existent anymore in the right model. In the case of a newly created element, it is automatically added to the change set, as no matching already existing element can be found. In case that the IDs of the model elements change, we use a backup strategy based on metrics to define the similarity of model elements from the left and right model, respectively. Section 4.2 gives a detailed description of how this backup strategy works. In the case of Fig. 2, the change set would contain classes *C5* and *C6*, as they had been changed in the Working Model.

Delta Expansion. After successfully calculating the change set, next, the distinct regression test selection strategy enters the stage, as it defines in which way the delta is expanded. Basically, the initially calculated delta already represents a regression test selection strategy, based on the minimal change set, viz., only taking the modified elements but nothing else into account. However, in most cases this clearly does no suffice. Hence, we allow to customize the expansion of the delta by means of OCL queries. For example, the OCL query as depicted at the right picture margin in Fig. 2 would expand the delta by all classes either referring to elements of the delta or refereed to by elements from the delta. Subsequently, the delta would be expanded by adding *C3* and *C4* to it, as both classes either use one or both of *C5* and *C6*. Section 4.2 gives a detailed description of how the expansion actually works in a programmatic way.

Test Set Generation. As a last step, we calculate the new test set based on the expanded delta. As first step, like during the previous tasks, the scope for possible test cases needs to be constrained by means of an OCL-based test set generation strategy. For example, the OCL query shown at the bottom of Fig. 2 searches for possible test cases, based on activity diagrams. Also the query assumes that each test case has a distinct stereotype *Testcase* applied, defined in a profile named *Test*.

With the given set of possible test cases, in a last substep, the new test set is calculated. We evaluate associations between elements of the delta and possible test cases, i.e. we attempt to resolve the links which interconnect each element of the SUT with a given test case. If such a link exists either from an element of the delta to a test case or vice versa (from a test case to an element of the delta), the test case is selected and added to the new test set.

The definition of the OCL queries for each of the above mentioned steps currently happens manually, yet, we are about to create a library of OCL queries to be used for regression testing. In defining any kind of query for the purpose of regression testing, a tester must not follow any requirements posed by our approach, yet solely the application of the respective model-based testing approach must be valid. Hence, our approach also is completely language independent, as it can deal with any kind of model and hence, any kind of target language, used to generate test cases into.

As our approach emerges out of the area of model versioning and not software testing, our terminology slightly differs from a testers' one, defined e.g. in [26]. The delta calculation corresponds to *change identification* in [26], the delta expansion to *impact analysis*, and the test set generation to *regression test selection*.

4.2   A Generic Model-Based Regression Testing Implementation

In the previous section we have given a generic description of our approach. This section provides more details on our implementation and shows how the MoVE tool is used to automate our model-based regression testing approach.

The implementation of our regression testing methodology has two parts, one on the client and one on the server side. On the *client-side* we provide MoVE adapters (as described in Section 3.1), tightly integrated into modeling tools such as MagicDraw, Eclipse or Papyrus. Therefore we support modeling versioning among various tools and do not restrict our approach to a single tool, respectively. Fig. 3 shows a component based view of the MoVE Environment with the testing plugin. In this view MagicDraw is used to model tests with TTS, whereas Papyrus is used to model scenarios with UTP.

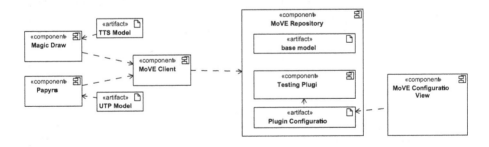

Fig. 3. Architecture of the MoVE Regression Testing Plugin

On the *server-side* MoVE is a repository containing previous versions of the test models (see *Base Model* in Fig. 3). The MoVE server also provides a plugin interface which we used to write and deploy a testing plugin. The Testing Plugin is our implementation for the concepts as explained in Section 4.1. The plugin can be configured with the *MoVE configuration view* which creates a *plugin configuration* for each model or project. The plugin configuration is an XML file that consists of three parts, corresponding to the three tasks identified in Section 4.1, i.e. *delta calculation, delta expansion* and *test set generation*. For each task we define a strategy in the configuration file. Fig. 4 shows the schema of the XML file and shows each part containing an OCL expression which is used in our methodology, respectively.

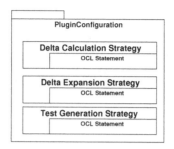

Fig. 4. Schema of Plugin Configuration

Our testing plugin for MoVE follows the workflow shown in Fig. 2. The delta calculation consists of two minor subtasks: the calculation of the change set and the restriction of this very set. MoVE supports *difference calculation* as part of the change-driven process. This calculation is based on a modified version of EMF Compare [27], which was enhanced by several small patches to improve the comparison of UML models. The result is a *delta model* containing all elements which were either changed, added, deleted or moved in the current version of the model compared to the base model in the MoVE repository. The delta model is very fine-grained and usually contains elements that are not relevant for regression testing. To restrict the set of delta model elements we use the OCL expression that was defined in the plugin configuration section *delta calculation strategy*. The result is a sanitized delta, containing only elements which are important for the regression testing strategy.

In the next step the sanitized delta is expanded. Therefore our implementation reads the *delta expansion strategy* from the plugin configuration and iteratively applies the OCL expression to each element of the sanitized delta. This strategy strongly depends on the regression testing method that one wants to apply and is profile independent.

The last step is to identify test cases associated to the elements of the expanded delta. In doing so, we read the *test set generation strategy* from the plugin configuration. Again, this strategy consists of an OCL expression, that returns the affected test cases for the context element. This query is applied to every element of the expanded delta and returns a set of test cases. The final result of the plugin is a map that contains all elements of the expanded delta and the associated test cases.

5   Case Study

In this section we present a case study applying our generic regression testing platform on the two model-based testing approaches UTP and TTS. The goal of the case study is to show that nevertheless which model-based testing approach is used, the regression test sets, as calculated by our approach, do not differ for identical changes in the system model.

5.1 System Under Test

For the purpose of our case study, we use a simple calculator service. Its system model is shown in Fig. 5. The service offers five different components, i.e. `AdderService`, `SubtractService`, `DivideService`, `MultiplyService` and `PowService` (see Fig. 5a). Each of the service components offers a distinct calculation interface with corresponding name (see Fig. 5b) via an implementing class, e.g. the interface `IAdder` is implemented by the class `AdderServiceImpl`, which itself is offered via the component `AdderService`. In case of the `PowService`, its implemented interface `IPow` extends `IMultiply`. Each of the interfaces offers two operations providing the mathematical operation of the declared type name (in this case the interface) for both, integer and float types, e.g. `IAdder` offers the operations `addInt` and `addFloat`.

5.2 Application of the Model-Based Regression Testing Platform

In this section we apply our model-based regression testing platform to UTP and TTS. Due to space limitations we skip the explicit presentation of the modeling fragments of TTS and only print the UTP modeling artifacts in this paper. But for the interpretation of the findings, we consider the results achieved with UTP and TTS. Additionally, we refer to [7] for an in-depth explanation of TTS.

Test Modeling. Fig. 5 shows the model of the SUT with the UTP specific stereotypes applied. As one can see in Fig. 5a each component is tagged as a *SUT*. Yet, the interfaces (see Fig. 5b) and also the classes remain untagged, as they are inherently part of the tagged SUT components.

Fig. 6 shows some of the UTP test artifacts, i.e. a test case and a test context. In the context of the UTP, test cases are often modeled using notions of UML sequence diagrams. The test case in Fig. 6a validates the proper behavior of

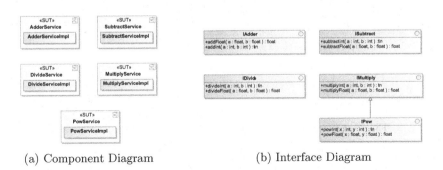

(a) Component Diagram   (b) Interface Diagram

Fig. 5. SUT model with the necessary UTP Stereotypes applied

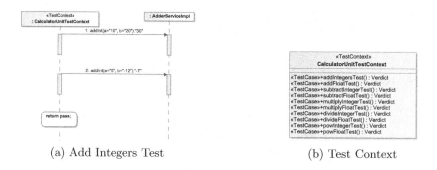

(a) Add Integers Test   (b) Test Context

Fig. 6. UTP Test Model Artifacts

the operation `addInt` of the `AdderService`. Fig. 6b shows the associated testing context as required by the UTP. The test context itself is a collection of test cases which is the basis for the configuration and execution of tests. In our example the test context contains ten test cases, one for each of the operations defined in Fig. 5b.

We skip the presentation of any further UTP specific test artifacts like an arbiter or a scheduler both, due to space restrictions but also as they are hardly relevant for regression testing.

Changing the System Model. We show the derivation of a regression test set by means of expanding the initial delta after a system change. In Section 4.1 the approach is generally introduced, in this section we explain the approach by an example and its interpretation.

The system model shown in Fig. 7 has been changed compared to Fig. 5 by adapting the return type of the operations `divideInt`, `multiplyInt`, and `multiplyFloat`.

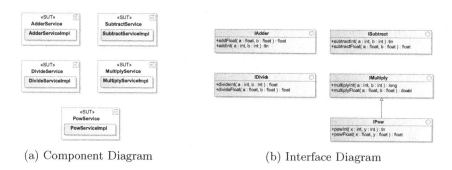

(a) Component Diagram   (b) Interface Diagram

Fig. 7. Changed SUT Model with Applied UTP Stereotypes

Now, with the changed system model, first, the initial change set is calculated (*delta calculation*) with MoVE. As already described before, this set contains the set of model elements of the SUT model with *immediate* changes (compared to model elements, referring change elements, which would be an implicit change). By applying the procedure presented in Section 4.1, the initially calculated delta is as follows:

$$Delta = \{IDivide, IMultiply\}$$

```
1   context  DiffElement :
2            or self . oclIsTypeOf ( ReferenceChange );
3   context  NamedElement :
4            self . ownedElement −>select ( e |
5            e . oclIsKindOf ( DirectedRelationship ))−>
6            collect ( obj :  Element |
7            obj . oclAsType ( DirectedRelationship ). target )−>
8            asSet ()−>iterate ( obj2 :  Element;  result2 :
9            Set ( Element ) = Set {}  |
10           result2 −>union ( obj2−>asSet ())−>
11           union ( obj2 . ownedElement−>
12           select ( e | e . oclIsKindOf ( DirectedRelationship ))−>
13           collect ( obj3 :  Element |
14           obj3 . oclAsType ( DirectedRelationship ). target )));
```

Listing 1. OCL Query for Link-based Delta Expansion Strategy

After the initial delta has been calculated, we expand this very delta by means of applying a delta expansion strategy onto the delta (*delta expansion*). For instance, the query as shown in Listing 1 allows to identify model elements, associated with the elements, contained in the initial delta, by means of *links*. Such an expansion is reasonable, i.e. in the case if a component refers (implements or extends) a changed component.

The link strategy, as depicted in Listing 1, extends the sanitized delta by all components that are linked with an association or inherit from a changed component. Hence, by applying this strategy we retrieve the expanded delta which is as follows:

$$Delta_{exp} = \{IDivide, IMultiply, IPow\}$$

We implemented two more delta expansion strategies for our model-based regression testing approach. (1) The *minimal* strategy does not extend the delta but only retests elements that changed. Therefore, the result is the sanitized delta. It is also possible to use the type of change as impact. (2) The *added* strategy restricts the sanitized delta to all elements that were added to the changed model. Since our case study does not add components or interfaces, the result of the added strategy is an empty set.

Finally, as a last step, based oh the expanded delta, we are ready to derive the new test set (*test set generation*). With the expanded delta and by subsequently applying another OCL query, evaluating the associations between system artifacts and test cases, we retrieve the set of associated test cases which is as follows:

$$TestSet = \{divideIntegerTest, diviveFloatTest, multiplyIntegerTest,$$
$$multiplyFloatTets, powIntegerTest, powFloatTest\}$$

The generated set of regression tests which is equal for UTP and TTS (see Table 1), is then further processed and executed by the respective model-based testing environment. The number of test cases in this case study for sure does not suffice if performing some real world testing of the Calculator system. However, as we are not about to prove that the Calculator system works, but instead to show to proper workings of our approach, the number of test cases clearly suffices.

Table 1. Number of Test Cases for Different Regression Testing Strategies

Number of Testcases	UTP			TTS		
	Minimal	*Link*	*Added*	*Minimal*	*Link*	*Added*
10	4	6	0	4	6	0

Table 1 shows the results of our case study with the delta expansion strategies minimal, link and added as explained before. Each component has two tests (one test for each of its operations). Therefore, the sum of all tests is 10 which is shown in the first column of the table. The minimal strategy results in 4 tests which are the tests for IMultiply and IDivide. The missing errors in the interface IPow are only detected with the link strategy that adds the missing 2 tests of IPow. The added strategy does not execute any tests since no component was added. The results of UTP and TTS profile were equal which shows that our approach delivers the same results for different profiles, i.e. model-based testing approaches.

Table 2. Metrics on the used OCL Queries for Regression Testing

Strategy	UTP			TTS		
	Calculation	*Expansion*	*Generation*	*Calculation*	*Expansion*	*Generation*
Minimal	10/5/18	–	12/10/30	5/3/11	–	15/9/35
Link	10/5/18	19/21/50	12/10/30	5/3/11	19/21/50	15/9/35
Added	10/5/18	25/30/60	12/10/30	5/3/11	25/30/60	15/9/35

The variation points of our regression testing approach, namely the delta calculation, the delta expansion, and the test set generation are controlled purely by OCL-based strategies. Table 2 shows that complexity of the OCL queries for the various phases delta calculation (*Calculation*), delta expansion (*Expansion*), and test set generation (*Generation*), for the approaches UTP and TTS, and for the minimal, link and added delta expansion strategies. Each table entry has the form $x/y/z$, where x denotes the lines of code, y the number of referenced metamodel/profile elements, and z the overall number of words of the respective OCL query. As the delta expansion strategies are independent of the profile or metamodel, the values are equal for UTP and TTS. The OCL queries for delta expansion are the most complex ones, i.e. they have the highest values for lines of code, number of profile elements, and the overall number of words. But the OCL queries for expansion strategies are independent of the metamodel. Thus, there is a trade-off between complexity and genericity of the OCL queries for delta calculation, delta expansion and test set generation.

6 Conclusion

In this paper we presented a generic model-based regression testing platform based on the model versioning tool MoVE. The model-based regression testing approach consists of the three phases delta calculation, delta expansion, and test set generation which are controlled purely by OCL queries. After an overview of the platform's implementation we performed a case study where we applied our platform to the model-based testing approaches UML Testing Profile (UTP) and Telling TestStories (TTS). In the case study, we have applied the minimal, link and added delta expansion strategies to UTP and TTS.

We have shown that our platform derives the same regression test sets for UTP and TTS for each of the three delta expansion strategies providing evidence that our approach is applicable to various model-based testing approaches. On the one side, it turned out that the OCL queries for delta expansion are more complex than the OCL queries for delta calculation and test set generation. On the other side, the delta expansion queries are independent of the applied testing memtamodel.

Our approach is based on the standardized XMI model interchange format and not tailored to a specific test model representation. Currently, our approach only supports selection based regression testing strategies based on delta expansion. As future work, we also consider prioritization based regression testing techniques. Another future research task is to define a library of parameterized OCL queries implementing various regression testing strategies. The queries are parameterized with stereotypes or other metamodel elements. Such a library concept would greatly enhance the applicability of our platform as the tedious task of writing custom OCL queries is reduced to a minimum.

Acknowledgement. This research was partially funded by the research projects MATE (FWF P17380), and QE LaB - Living Models for Open Systems (FFG 822740).

References

1. Dias Neto, A.C., Subramanyan, R., Vieira, M., Travassos, G.H.: A Survey on Model–based Testing Approaches: A Systematic Review. In: 1st ACM International Workshop on Empirical Assessment of Software Engineering Languages and Technologies, pp. 31–36. ACM (2007)
2. Utting, M., Legeard, B.: Practical Model-Based Testing: A Tools Approach. Morgan Kaufmann Publishers Inc., San Francisco (2007)
3. IEEE: Standard Glossary of Software Engineering Terminology. IEEE (1990)
4. Briand, L.C., Labiche, Y., He, S.: Automating Regression Test Selection based on UML Designs. Inf. Softw. Technol. 51(1) (2009)
5. Breu, M., Breu, R., Low, S.: Living on the MoVE: Towards an Architecture for a Living Models Infrastructure. In: The Fifth International Conference on Software Engineering Advances, pp. 290–295 (2010)
6. OMG: OMG UML Testing Profile (UTP), V1.0 (2007)
7. Felderer, M., Zech, P., Fiedler, F., Breu, R.: A Tool–based methodology for System Testing of Service–oriented Systems. In: The Second International Conference on Advances in System Testing and Validation Lifecycle, pp. 108–113. IEEE (2010)

8. Yoo, S., Harman, M.: Regression testing minimization, selection and prioritization: a survey. Software Testing, Verification and Reliability 22(2), 67–120 (2012)
9. von Mayrhauser, A., Zhang, N.: Automated Regression Testing using DBT and Sleuth. Journal of Software Maintenance 11(2) (1999)
10. Fahad, M., Nadeem, A.: A Survey of UML Based Regression Testing. In: Shi, E., Mercier-Laurent, D., Leake, D. (eds.) Intelligent Information Processing IV. IFIP, vol. 288, pp. 200–210. Springer, Boston (2008)
11. Farooq, Q., Iqbal, M., Malik, Z., Riebisch, M.: A model-based regression testing approach for evolving software systems with flexible tool support. In: International Conference and Workshops on Engineering Computer-Based Systems (2010)
12. Chen, Y., Probert, R.L., Sims, D.P.: Specification–based Regression Test Selection with Risk Analysis. In: CASCON 2002 (2002)
13. IBM: IBM Rational Quality Manager (2011), http://www-01.ibm.com/software/rational/offerings/quality/ (accessed: January 5, 2011)
14. Mark Aberdour: Opensourcetesting (2011), http://www.opensourcetesting.org/ (accessed: January 5, 2011)
15. Chen, Y.F., Rosenblum, D.S., Vo, K.P.: TestTube: A System for Selective Regression Testing. In: ICSE, pp. 211–220 (1994)
16. Seidl, H., Vojdani, V.: Region Analysis for Race Detection. In: Palsberg, J., Su, Z. (eds.) SAS 2009. LNCS, vol. 5673, pp. 171–187. Springer, Heidelberg (2009)
17. Aldazabal, A., Baily, T., Nanclares, F., Sadovykh, A., Hein, C., Ritter, T.: Automated Model Driven Development Processes. In: ECMDA Workshop on Model Driven Tool and Process Integration (2008)
18. Altmanninger, K., Kappel, G., Kusel, A., Retschitzegger, W., Schwinger, W., Seidl, M., Wimmer, M.: AMOR — Towards Adaptable Model Versioning. In: 1st Int. Workshop on Model Co-Evolution and Consistency Management (2008)
19. Amelunxen, C., Klar, F., Königs, A., Rötschke, T., Schürr, A.: Metamodel–based tool integration with MOFLON. In: ICSE (2008)
20. Eclipse Teneo, http://wiki.eclipse.org/Teneo#teneo (accessed: April 25, 2012)
21. Eclipse CDO, http://wiki.eclipse.org/CDO (accessed: April. 25, 2012)
22. Breu, R.: Ten Principles for Living Models - A Manifesto of Change-Driven Software Engineering. In: CISIS, pp. 1–8. EIEE Computer Society (2010)
23. OMG: UML Testing Profile, Version 1.0 (2005), http://www.omg.org/spec/UTP/1.0/PDF (accessed: February 25, 2011)
24. Baker, P., Ru Dai, P., Grabowski, J., Haugen, O., Schieferdecker, I., Williams, C.E.: Model-Driven Testing - Using the UML Testing Profile. Springer (2007)
25. Felderer, M., Agreiter, B., Breu, R.: Evolution of Security Requirements Tests for Service–Centric Systems. In: Erlingsson, Ú., Wieringa, R., Zannone, N. (eds.) ESSoS 2011. LNCS, vol. 6542, pp. 181–194. Springer, Heidelberg (2011)
26. Farooq, Q.U.A., Iqbal, M.Z., Malik, Z., Riebisch, M.: A Model-Based Regression Testing Approach for Evolving Software Systems with Flexible Tool Support, pp. 41–49 (2010)
27. EMF Compare Project, http://www.eclipse.org/emf/compare/ (accessed: April 8, 2012)

Approaches for Mastering Change

Ina Schaefer[1], Malte Lochau[2], and Martin Leucker[3]

[1] Institute for Software Engineering and Automotive Informatics
Technical University of Braunschweig, Germany
`i.schaefer@tu-braunschweig.de`
[2] Institute for Programming and Reactive Systems
Technical University of Braunschweig, Germany
`lochau@ips.cs.tu-bs.de`
[3] Institute for Software Engineering and Programming Languages
University of Lübeck, Germany
`leucker@isp.uni-luebeck.de`

1 Motivation

Modern software systems are highly configurable and exist in many different variants in order to operate different application contexts. This is called *static variability* and predominantly considered in software product line engineering [6,14]. Furthermore, software systems have to evolve over time in order to deal with changing requirements which is referred to by the term *temporal evolvability* [10,13]. Additionally, modern software systems are designed to *dynamically adapt* their internal structure and behavior at runtime dependent on their environment in order to efficiently use the available resources, such as energy or computing power [5]. These three dimensions of change, static variability, temporal evolvability and dynamic adaptation, increase the complexity of system development in all phase, from requirements engineering and system design to implementation and quality assurance. In [15], the challenges of static variability and temporal evolution in all phases of the software development process are discussed. In [15], the engineering challenges of self-adaptive systems are described and future research directions are pointed out.

2 Goals

The ISoLA track "Approaches for Mastering Change" focusses on the particular challenges change imposes on efficient quality assurance techniques for software systems. The goal of the track was to bring together researchers and practitioners working in the area of verification and validation for diverse software systems covering all three dimensions of change. In the current state-of-the-art in diverse systems, there are only insulated approaches focussing on one analysis technique, such as testing, type checking, model checking or theorem proving, for one dimension of change. For instance, in [17], a survey and classification of existing analysis techniques for software product lines, i.e., static variability, is presented, but temporal evolution and dynamic adaption are not considered.

T. Margaria and B. Steffen (Eds.): ISoLA 2012, Part I, LNCS 7609, pp. 127–130, 2012.

Thus, his track aimed at identifying and discussing synergies between the existing approaches to develop uniform techniques tackling the challenges of software variability, evolvability and adaptation by the same or similar means.

3   Contributions

Most contributions to the track "Approaches for Mastering Change" address static variability as treated by software product line engineering [14,6]. The first half of these contributions considers different modeling formalisms for describing the (behavioral) variability of product lines. Thoma et al. [16] develop an algebraic specification for capturing the variability structure of product lines. As an instantiation, an extension of the process algebra CCS with variability is presented that lends itself well to analysis via model checking. Asirelli et al. [1] concentrate on behavioral variability modeling with modal transition systems extended with variability constraints in deontic logics. They disucss different ways to obtain such an behavioral model of a product line from the feature model capturing variability at the requirements level. Bodden et al. [3] describe an approach for specifying variable monitors for runtime analysis of product lines. To this end, they adapt the concept of delta modeling for product line variability to the specific case of modeling and realizing runtime monitors.

The second half of the contributions targeting static variability aims at analyzing product line artifacts and implementations. Both Lienhardt et al. [11] and Damiani et al. [7] present type systems for analyzing delta-oriented product line implementations. While Lienhardt et al. [11] concentrate on discovering conflicts during program variant generation via row types, Damiani et al. [7] improve type checking of the actually generated programs via a family-based analysis technique. Devroey et al. [8] propose a comprehensive framework for product line verification and validation by intertwining product-based and product-line-based analysis steps. They exemplify their approach by the analysis of timed properties of product lines in the embedded domain. Lochau et al. [12] consider the challenges of efficiently testing software product lines by test case and test result reuse. They develop a formal framework to reason about commonality of test cases and results with respect to feature-parametric preorder conformance relations.

The last three papers of the track are conceded with either temporal evolution of software and associated documentation or the dynamic adaptation of communicating systems. Autexier et al. [2] consider the evolution of heterogenous documents, code and testing artifacts as required for certification of safety-critical software. They determine the impact of changes in some parts of the documentation to other parts in order to ease the task for maintaining consistency between the documents in case of changes during the development process. Dovland et al. [9] focus on the conflicting aspects between developing and verifying object-oriented software in agile development approaches. In order to allow an interleaving of development and verification steps, they propose an incremental reasoning framework which keeps track of the established and remaining proof obligations during program verification. Bravetti et al. [4] describe a process algebra with explicit operators for updating the behavior of processes at runtime in order to capture reactions of the system to changes in its environment. They provide a logic to formulate general properties about the adaptable system, e.g., that an error can be resolved within a defined number of steps, and prove (un)decidability results for this logic.

References

1. Asirelli, P., ter Beek, M.H., Fantechi, A., Gnesi, S.: A Compositional Framework to Derive Product Line Behavioural Descriptions. In: Margaria, T., Steffen, B. (eds.) ISoLA 2012, Part I. LNCS, vol. 7609, pp. 146–161. Springer, Heidelberg (2012)

2. Autexier, S., Dietrich, D., Hutter, D., Lüth, C., Maeder, C.: SmartTies Management of Safety-Critical Developments. In: Margaria, T., Steffen, B. (eds.) ISoLA 2012, Part I. LNCS, vol. 7609, pp. 238–252. Springer, Heidelberg (2012)

3. Bodden, E., Falzon, K., Pun, K.I., Stolz, V.: Delta-oriented Monitor Specification. In: Margaria, T., Steffen, B. (eds.) ISoLA 2012, Part I. LNCS, vol. 7609, pp. 162–176. Springer, Heidelberg (2012)

4. Bravetti, M., Di Giusto, C., Pérez, J.A., Zavattaro, G.: Towards the Verification of Adaptable Processes. In: Margaria, T., Steffen, B. (eds.) ISoLA 2012, Part I. LNCS, vol. 7609, pp. 269–283. Springer, Heidelberg (2012)

5. Cheng, B.H.C., de Lemos, R., Giese, H., Inverardi, P., Magee, J., Andersson, J., Becker, B., Bencomo, N., Brun, Y., Cukic, B., Di Marzo Serugendo, G., Dustdar, S., Finkelstein, A., Gacek, C., Geihs, K., Grassi, V., Karsai, G., Kienle, H.M., Kramer, J., Litoiu, M., Malek, S., Mirandola, R., Müller, H.A., Park, S., Shaw, M., Tichy, M., Tivoli, M., Weyns, D., Whittle, J.: Software Engineering for Self-Adaptive Systems: A Research Roadmap. In: Cheng, B.H.C., de Lemos, R., Giese, H., Inverardi, P., Magee, J. (eds.) Self-Adaptive Systems. LNCS, vol. 5525, pp. 1–26. Springer, Heidelberg (2009)

6. Clements, P., Northrop, L.: Software Product Lines: Practices and Patterns. Addison-Wesley Longman (2001)

7. Damiani, F., Schaefer, I.: Family-based Analysis of Type Safety for Delta-Oriented Software Product Lines. In: Margaria, T., Steffen, B. (eds.) ISoLA 2012, Part I. LNCS, vol. 7609, pp. 193–207. Springer, Heidelberg (2012)

8. Devroey, X., Cordy, M., Perrouin, G., Kang, E., Schobbens, P.-Y., Heymans, P., Legay, A., Baudry, B.: Towards Behavioural Model-Driven Validation of Software Product Lines. In: Margaria, T., Steffen, B. (eds.) ISoLA 2012, Part I. LNCS, vol. 7609, pp. 208–222. Springer, Heidelberg (2012)

9. Dovland, J., Johnsen, E.B., Yu, I.C.: Tracking Behavioral Constraints During Object-Oriented Software Evolution. In: Margaria, T., Steffen, B. (eds.) ISoLA 2012, Part I. LNCS, vol. 7609, pp. 253–268. Springer, Heidelberg (2012)

10. Lehman, M.M.: Software's future: Managing evolution. IEEE Software 15(1), 40–44 (1998)

11. Lienhardt, M., Clarke, D.: Conflict Detection in Delta-Oriented Programming. In: Margaria, T., Steffen, B. (eds.) ISoLA 2012, Part I. LNCS, vol. 7609, pp. 178–192. Springer, Heidelberg (2012)

12. Lochau, M., Kamischke, J.: Parameterized Preorder Relations for Model-based Testing of Software Product Lines. In: Margaria, T., Steffen, B. (eds.) ISoLA 2012, Part I. LNCS, vol. 7609, pp. 223–237. Springer, Heidelberg (2012)

13. Parnas, D.: Software aging. In: ICSE, pp. 279–287 (1994)

14. Pohl, K., Böckle, G., van der Linden, F.: Software Product Line Engineering - Foundations, Principles, and Techniques. Springer, Heidelberg (2005)

15. Schaefer, I., Rabiser, R., Clarke, D., Bettini, L., Benavides, D., Botterweck, G., Pathak, A., Trujilol, S., Villela, K.: Software Diversity – State of the Art and Perspectives. In: STTT (October 2012)

16. Leucker, M., Thoma, D.: A Formal Approach to Software Product Families. In: Margaria, T., Steffen, B. (eds.) ISoLA 2012, Part I. LNCS, vol. 7609, pp. 131–145. Springer, Heidelberg (2012)

17. Thüm, T., Apel, S., Kästner, C., Kuhlemann, M., Schaefer, I., Saake, G.: Analysis Strategies for Software Product Lines. Technical Report FIN-004-2012, School of Computer Science, University of Magdeburg, Germany (April 2012)

A Formal Approach to Software Product Families

Martin Leucker and Daniel Thoma

Institute for Software Engineering and Programming Languages
Universität zu Lübeck

Abstract. Software product line engineering deals with the combined development of a family of similar software systems. These systems provide a similar set of features and should therefore share a large number of common components. We study the user perspective of features and the engineering perspective of components and present a formal notion of features, component-based product families and their interaction. We then demonstrate using Milner's CCS how our formalism can be applied to extend an arbitrary modelling formalism with support for product lines. To verify that certain products indeed realize certain features, we propose μ-calculus model-checking for multi-valued Kripke-structures. The model checking result in that case no longer is a simple truth-value, but a set of products, conforming to a certain property.

1 Introduction

The vast majority of electronic devices with which we interact is mainly controlled by software—in fact, software-intensive systems pervade our daily life. Typically, not only a single software-intensive system is constructed but rather a family of similar systems that share certain commonalities. Prominent examples of such families of software-intensive systems can be found in a multitude of different application domains, comprising embedded as well as business information systems. For example the model variants of the same model series of a car manufacturer, e.g. the variants of the *7-series BMW*, or the various variants of an operating system, e.g. the various editions of the operating system *Microsoft Windows 7*, constitute such families. Typical commonalities for such systems can be found for example in their (conceptual) functionality, their architectural component structure, or code. To enhance the efficiency of the software development and maintenance process, the integrated development of a family of software-intensive systems by explicitly making use of (reusing) their commonalities in a strategic and planned way seems a promising approach. This is the subject of software product family engineering.

Despite its obvious motivation, the way of constructing a family of systems by taking advantage of commonalities is not sufficiently explored—in particular with respect to its theoretical foundation. How can reuse based on commonalities between system variants take place in a systematic way? What are the fundamental concepts behind commonalities and differences of related systems, and

T. Margaria and B. Steffen (Eds.): ISoLA 2012, Part I, LNCS 7609, pp. 131–145, 2012.

how can we formally represent them? How can commonalities between family members be determined and even schematically computed? How can the relation between family members be modelled, and how are commonalities integrated into the construction of the individual family members? How can we verify correctness properties of a whole software product family instead of looking at the properties of each family member individually?

In this paper we address these questions from a formal point of view and provide an axiomatization of product family concepts using the language of algebraic specification [Wir90]. The axiomatization formalizes the key characteristics of any software product family, where the concept of commonality and the ability to compute the commonalities of an arbitrary subset of family members is the most important aspect for us.

The formal specification may be used as a guidance when defining explicit formalisms supporting the concept of software product families. In this paper, we recall (and slightly simplify) the account of [GLS08] which extends Milner's CCS by a variant operator yielding the product-line aware calculus PL-CCS. With the help of the specification, we can check that PL-CCS is indeed a reasonable product family extension of CCS.

Finally, to make this overview paper self-contained, we recall the model checking approach for PL-CCS that allows to check a whole family of systems with respect to μ-calculus specifications.

2   Related Work

Most of the related approaches which deal with modelling of software product families are found in the area of *Feature Oriented Software Development* (FOSD) [CE00]. FOSD deals with the construction of variable software systems. A common specification technique for software product lines in FOSD are so-called *feature models* [KHNP90]. Feature models are used to model optional, mandatory and variable features, and in particular their dependencies. In that way a feature model allows to restrict the set of possible configurations of a product line, but in general it does not incorporate the information of how to construct the family members, nor does it allow to compute common parts of a given subset of family members. Thus, a feature model serves the same purpose as our dependency model, but does not represent a product family in our sense, i.e. as a construction blueprint that shows how the family members can actually be constructed from the common and variable parts, or how the members are related with respect to reusing common parts. Moreover, feature models usually lack a precise semantics which impedes to reason about features or feature combinations using formal methods.

To make these issues more precise, we recall the concept of features in the next section.

Regarding the algebraic treatment of software product families, there are some approaches which also unify common concepts, techniques and methods of feature-oriented approaches by providing an abstract, common, formal basis.

In this context, we consider especially the approaches [HKM06,HKM11,BO92] to be of interest.

The closest to our axiomatization of a software product family is an approach by Höfner et al. [HKM06,HKM11], introducing the notion of a *feature algebra*, and a *product family*, respectively, which describes the features of a family of products, and their typical operations from a semi-ring, algebraic perspective. The elements of a feature algebra are called product families. A product family corresponds to a set of products, where individual products are considered to be flat collections of features. In general, the structure of a feature algebra largely agrees with the structure of a software product family of type Spf_α, as it can be built using the constructors (cf. Section 4) only. While Höfner et al. nicely characterize the structure of a product line from an algebraic point of view, they do not include operations that describe the manipulation or alteration of product families into their algebraic components. For example, Höfner et al. do not explicitly express the notion of configuration. In contrast, our approach defines functions that characterize how to manipulate and work with a product family, e.g. the functions selL and selR that formalize the act of configuring a product family, or the function is_mand that formalizes the notion of mandatory parts. In our opinion these additional operations are as essential as the basic constructors in order to formalize the notion of a product family.

The first work on verifying software product families via model checking is, to best of our knowledge, in [GLS08]. A slightly different verification approach is given in [CHSL11].

3   Features

Intuitively, a product family subsumes a number of products with similar functionality. From an engineering perspective, organizing products in product families is beneficial, as it allows for a single development process, and eases the identification of common components. While product variants sometimes evolve over time for technical reasons, they are often specifically developed out of marketing concerns or to meet similar but different customer needs. In the latter case, a product family is first designed from an external, user perspective in terms of features without considering their technical structure. A feature in this context is the ability of a product to cover a certain use case or meet a certain customer need. Thus, it is frequently impossible to map features independently to certain technical properties.

An established method to design and structure the feature domain of a product family is the use of feature diagrams [KHNP90]. Feature diagrams do not describe the meaning of different features, since at that stage no common formalism to describe such properties and product behaviour is applicable. Instead they define the compositional structure and dependencies between features from a user perspective.

We use a product family for a fictional windscreen wiper system as running example. Figure 1 shows the corresponding feature diagram. The variants of our

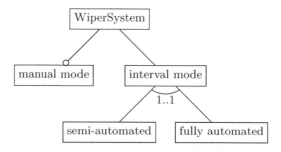

Fig. 1. Feature diagram for a product family of a windscreen wiper system

wiper systems may have a manual mode. They are required to have an interval mode controlled by a rain sensor. This mode can either be semi-automated and control only some operation modi of the wiper or fully automated. Thus, from our feature diagram we can derive four different feature combinations.

There are a lot of different variations of feature diagrams. All of them allow to express the compositional structure and optional, mandatory and alternative features. For most types the semantics can be given by translation into propositional logic with features as atomic propositions [SHT06].

Feature diagrams only describe possible combinations of features. To be able to express statements about products and their technical structure, we need to bind features to products.

Definition 1. $\mathcal{F} : \mathbb{P} \to 2^{\mathbb{F}}$ *is a feature function, mapping products $p \in \mathbb{P}$ to the features $f \in \mathbb{F}$ they have.*

Since feature diagrams only describe feature dependencies from a user or product designer perspective, some possible feature combinations might not actually be feasible, i.e. it is impossible for technological reasons to combine those features.

Definition 2. *The set $F \subseteq \mathbb{F}$ is a feasible feature combination if $\exists p \in \mathbb{P} : F \subseteq \mathcal{F}(p)$.*

Conversely, feasible feature combinations may not be possible with respect to a feature diagram as feasible combinations might be undesirable.

4   Specification of Product Lines

At a technological level, different feature combinations have to be realized by different products. To be able to manage complexity, products are usually described and built in a compositional manner. Consequently, sets of products are usually specified by introducing variation points at different levels of their compositional structure. A concrete product can be derived from such a description by selecting one alternative at each variation point. Widespread instances of these concepts for software development are source code preprocessors and dependency injection frameworks.

Consider again the wiper system introduced above. To specify a certain wiper system, we would compose a wiper and a sensor component into one system.

$$\text{wiper} \| \text{sensor}$$

To realize the different feature combinations, we would use different variations of those components. To do so, we introduce variation points.

$$\text{wiper} := \text{wiper}_1 \oplus_1 \text{wiper}_2; \quad \text{wiper} := \text{sensor}_1 \oplus_2 \text{sensor}_2$$

To support product families in an arbitrary specification formalism, we introduce several generic operators. As we want to define product families following the compositional structure of the underlying formalism, we need an operator $\text{asset}(A)$, that converts an atomic product into a product family. To express shifting operators from products to product families in a generic way, we need an operator $\text{op} \circ \text{arg}$, that applies an operator op (partially) to all products described by arg. In the case of the binary operator $\|$, we would write $(\| \circ A) \circ B$, to express that $\|$ is shifted to product families by applying it to all products described by A using its first parameter. The resulting unary operator is then applied to each product from B.

Using these three operators, it is possible to lift the semantics of any product specification formalism to product families.

We can now add choice points in the same manner as in our example above. A choice operator $A \oplus_i B$ describes the product family, where a left choice for i results in the products from A, and a right choice in the products from B. As the choice between left and right variants is bound to the index i, for every occurrence of an operator with the same index the same choice has to be made. It is thus possible to express dependencies between different choice points in a system.

It is usually the case that not all possible configurations of a product family describe a system that is technologically feasible. Thus, we introduce the empty product family $\bot$, containing no products. Using $\bot$, dependencies on choices may be expressed. For example, we could write $A \oplus_i \bot$ to express, that at some point in our product family specification, only a left choice may be made for i. To ease notation of these dependencies, we introduce a dependency operator $(i_1, L/R), \ldots, (i_k, L/R) \hookrightarrow A$, meaning A requires left or right choices for certain $i_1, \ldots i_k$.

Using the operators described so far a product family can be completely described. To derive products from such descriptions we only need the operator $\text{conf}(A)$, returning all possible products annotated with the choices leading to them. For convenience we further introduce operators $\text{products}(A)$ and $\text{choices}(A)$, yielding the set of all products and choices, respectively.

A further common mechanism observed in product line development is the instantiation of components. Considering our wiper system example, a car might use separate systems to control front and rear wipers, which can be different variants of the same product. Thus, we introduce a renaming operator $A[f]$, which renames all choice indices i in A by applying function f. Consider the description of the above wiper system. To compose two of them in one system allowing independent choices for each, we could write:

$$\text{wipersys} \| \text{wipersys} \, [1/3, 2/4]$$

We give a formal definition of all those operators in Figure 2. We use higher order functions to define the operator $\circ$ and most signatures are defined using a type variable α known from polymorphic function types.

Given our formal notion of both the user and engineering perspective on product families, we are now able to precisely describe their connection.

Definition 3. *The technologically feasible configurations for a product famliy P providing a set of features F with respect to a feature function $\mathcal{F}$ is given by*

$$\mathcal{C}_{P,F,\mathcal{F}} = \{c \mid (c,p) \in \mathit{conf}(P), \mathcal{F}(p) \subseteq F\}$$

There usually is a multitude of possible product family specifications, where the same products can be derived using the same configuration. This observation warrants the following equivalence relation between product family specifications.

Definition 4. *Product family specifications P and Q are called configuration-equivalent*

$$P \equiv_c Q \ \text{ iff } \ \mathit{conf}(P) \equiv \mathit{conf}(Q)$$

Using that equivalence and the axioms from Figure 2 we can prove several laws that facilitate restructuring product family specifications and identifying common parts in different variants.

The operator for lifting operators from an underlying formalism to product families $\circ$ is (left and right) distributive over the choice operator $\oplus_i$.

$$(P \circ Q) \oplus_i (P \circ R) \equiv_c P \circ (Q \oplus_i R)$$
$$(P \circ R) \oplus_i (Q \circ R) \equiv_c (P \oplus_i Q) \circ R$$

Thus all operators of an underlying formalism are distributive over the choice operators. We can therefore pull out common parts.

Choice operators with different index are distributive.

$$(P \oplus_j Q) \oplus_i (P \oplus_j R) \equiv_c P \oplus_j (Q \oplus_i R) \text{ with } i \neq j$$
$$(P \oplus_j R) \oplus_i (Q \oplus_j R) \equiv_c (P \oplus_i Q) \oplus_j R \text{ with } i \neq j$$

It is thus possible to change the way choices are nested and to pull out common choices.

Dependencies between choices can render certain parts of a specification inaccessible. When two dependent operators are directly nested, the following laws can be applied to simplify the specification.

$$P \oplus_i (Q \oplus_i R) \equiv_c P \oplus_i R$$
$$(P \oplus_i Q) \oplus_i R \equiv_c P \oplus_i R$$

SPEC Softwareproductfamily = {

  defines Spf_α

  based_on Bool, Nat, Set, HOFunc

  functions

    $\perp_\alpha :$ Spf_α

    $\mathsf{asset}_\alpha :$ $\alpha \to \mathsf{Spf}_\alpha$

    $\circ_{\alpha,\beta} :$ $\mathsf{Spf}_{\beta\alpha} \times \mathsf{Spf}_\alpha \to \mathsf{Spf}_\beta$

    $\oplus_\alpha :$ $\mathsf{Spf}_\alpha \times \mathbb{N} \times \mathsf{Spf}_\alpha \to \mathsf{Spf}_\alpha$

    $[]_\alpha :$ $\mathsf{Spf}_\alpha \times (\mathbb{N}^\mathbb{N}) \times \mathbb{N} \to \mathsf{Spf}_\alpha$

    $\hookrightarrow_\alpha :$ $2^{\mathbb{N}\times\{L,R\}} \times \mathsf{Spf}_\alpha \to \mathsf{Spf}_\alpha$

    $\mathsf{conf}_\alpha :$ $\mathsf{Spf}_\alpha \to 2^{2^{\mathbb{N}\times\{L,R\}}\times\alpha}$

    $\mathsf{products} :$ $\mathsf{Spf}_\alpha \to 2^\alpha$

    $\mathsf{choices} :$ $\mathsf{Spf}_\alpha \to 2^\mathbb{N}$

    $\mathsf{comp} :$ $2^{\mathbb{N}\times\{L,R\}} \to 2^{2^{\mathbb{N}\times\{L,R\}}\times\alpha}$

    $\mathsf{confd}_\alpha :$ $\{L,R\} \times \mathsf{Spf}_\alpha \to 2^{2^{\mathbb{N}\times\{L,R\}}\times\alpha}$

  axioms

    $\mathsf{comp}(C) = \bigwedge_{(i,d),(i,d')\in C} d = d'$

    $\mathsf{confd}(d,P) = \{(\{(i,d)\}\cup c,p) \mid (c,p) \in \mathsf{conf}(P), \mathsf{comp}(\{(i,d)\}\cup c)\}$

    $\mathsf{conf}(\perp) = \varnothing$

    $\mathsf{conf}(\mathsf{asset}(a)) = (\varnothing, a)$

    $\mathsf{conf}(\mathsf{apply}(F,P)) = \bigcup_{(c_1,f)\in\mathsf{conf}(F),(c_2,p)\in\mathsf{conf}(P),\mathsf{comp}(c_1\cup c_2)}(c_1 \cup c_2, f(p))$

    $\mathsf{conf}(P \oplus_i Q) = \mathsf{confd}(L,P) \cup \mathsf{confd}(R,Q)$

    $\mathsf{conf}(P[f]) = \{(c',p) \mid (c,p) \in \mathsf{conf}(P), c' = \{(f(i),d) \mid (i,d) \in c\}, \mathsf{comp}(c')\}$

    $\mathsf{products}(P) = \bigcup_{(c,p)\in\mathsf{conf}(P)}\{p\}$

    $\mathsf{choices}(P) = \bigcup_{(c,p)\in\mathsf{conf}(P),(i,d)\in c}\{i\}$

    $\varnothing \hookrightarrow P = \perp$

    $(\{(i,L)\}\cup I) \hookrightarrow P = P \oplus_i (I \hookrightarrow P)$

    $(\{(i,R)\}\cup I) \hookrightarrow P = (I \hookrightarrow P) \oplus_i P$

}

Fig. 2. Algebraic specification of a generic product line formalism

Since the configuration of product family specifications is defined inductively replacing a part by a configuration-equivalent expression yields a configuration-equivalent specification.

$$P \equiv_c Q \text{ then } R \equiv_c R[P/Q]$$

Note that in this case $[P/Q]$ refers to the syntactic replacement of a sub-expression.

The empty product family $\bot$ can be used to prohibit certain configurations. The laws involving $\bot$ facilitate the simplification of product family specifications in certain cases. It is possible to reduce expressions without any choices containing $\bot$.

$$P \circ \bot \equiv_c \bot$$
$$\bot \circ P \equiv_c \bot$$
$$\bot[f] \equiv_c \bot$$

It is further possible to eliminate choices yielding $\bot$ for both the left and right choice.

$$\bot \oplus_i \bot \equiv_c \bot$$

When similar components are used at multiple locations in a system, it often is beneficial to factor those components out into a single specification that can then be instantiated appropriately. Using the following laws, renamings of choice indices can be introduced bottom-up.

$$\text{asset}(a)[f] \equiv_c \text{asset}(a)$$
$$(P \circ Q)[f] \equiv_c P[f] \circ Q[f]$$
$$(P \oplus_i Q)[f] \equiv_c P[f] \oplus_{f(i)} Q[f]$$

In doing so, identical sub-expressions using different indices can be defined over the same indices.

The laws discussed so far allow for refactorings of product family specifications that preserve the possible configurations of a product family. Often changes to the configurations are acceptable though, when they allow for more radical refactorings and the derivable products are still being preserved. That observation gives rise to the follow, more relaxed equivalence relation.

Definition 5. *Product family specifications P and Q are called product-equivalent*

$$P \equiv_p Q \text{ iff } products(P) \equiv products(Q)$$

Using this equivalence, we can prove some additional laws.

Obviously, two configuration-equivalent specifications are also product-equivalent.

$$P \equiv_c Q \Rightarrow P \equiv_p Q$$

Leaving out a top level renaming does not change the set of products.

$$P \equiv_p P[f]$$

Choices, resulting in the same set of products, may be left out.

$$P \oplus_i P \equiv_p P$$

While it is possible to apply the laws for configuration-equivalence on any sub-expression, this is no longer the case for product-equivalence as there might be dependencies defined on certain configurations. It is still possible though when respecting some side conditions.

If $F \equiv_p F[P/Q]$ then
$$F \oplus_i G \equiv_p F[P/Q] \oplus_i G \text{ with } i \notin \text{choices}(P, Q)$$
$$G \oplus_i F \equiv_p G \oplus_i F[P/Q] \text{ with } i \notin \text{choices}(P, Q)$$
$$F \circ G \equiv_p F[P/Q] \circ G \text{ with } \text{choices } (P, Q) \cap \text{choices}(G) = \varnothing$$
$$G \circ F \equiv_p G \circ F[P/Q] \text{ with } \text{choices } (P, Q) \cap \text{choices}(G) = \varnothing$$
$$F[f] \equiv_p F[P/Q][f] \text{ with } i \in \text{choices}(P, Q) \Rightarrow i = f(i)$$

5   PL-CCS

In the previous section, we have worked out an algebraic specification for the concept of product families. It is meant to serve as a meta model pointing out the fundamental ideas of any formalism having a notion of families.

In this section, we present a concrete modelling formalism for product families. We enrich Milner's CCS by a variation operator. As the resulting calculus, which we call PL-CCS, is a model of the algebraic specification given in the previous section, it is a valid realization of a product family concept. The approach followed in this section is a slight simplification and extension of the account presented in [GLS08]. The syntax of PL-CCS is given as follows:

Definition 6 (Syntax of PL-CCS)

$$e ::= Q \mid Nil \mid \alpha.e \mid (e + e) \mid (e \parallel e) \mid (e)[f] \mid (e) \setminus L \mid \mu Q.e \mid (e \oplus_i e) \mid (e)[g]$$

Thus, we use a fixpoint-oriented account to CCS as in and enrich CCS by the variant operator $\oplus$, which may cater for additional renaming.

The semantics of PL-CCS may now be given in several, as we will show equivalent, ways. First, one might configure a PL-CCS specification in every possible way to obtain a set of CCS specifications, which may act as the, here called *flat*, semantics of a product family, which is basically a set of Kripke structures. To this end, we recall the definition of a Kripke structure and the semantics of a CCS process.

Definition 7 (KS). *A Kripke structure $\mathcal{K}$ is defined as*

$$\mathcal{K} = (\mathcal{S}, \mathcal{R} \subseteq \mathcal{S} \times \mathcal{A} \times \mathcal{S}, L \subseteq \mathcal{S} \times \mathcal{P})$$

where $\mathcal{S}$ is a set of states, $\mathcal{R}$ is a set of $\mathcal{A}$-labelled transitions, and L labels states by its set of valid propositions.

Next, we recall the definition of CCS. Due to space constraints, it is given according to Figure 3, ignoring the product label ν in the SOS-rules shown.

Now, we are ready to define the notion of a flat semantics for a PL-CCS family.

Definition 8 (Flat Semantics of PL-CCS)

$$[\![P]\!]_{flat} = \{(c, [\![p]\!]) \mid (c, p) \in conf(P)\}$$

Especially for verification purposes, it is, however, desirable, to provide a comprehensive semantics, which we do in terms of a *multi-valued Kripke structure*.

A *lattice* is a partially ordered set $(\mathcal{L}, \sqsubseteq)$ where for each $x, y \in \mathcal{L}$, there exists (i) a unique *greatest lower bound* (glb), which is called the *meet* of x and y, and is denoted by $x \sqcap y$, and (ii) a unique *least upper bound* (lub), which is called the *join* of x and y, and is denoted by $x \sqcup y$. The definitions of glb and lub extend to finite sets of elements $A \subseteq \mathcal{L}$ as expected, which are then denoted by $\bigsqcap A$ and $\bigsqcup A$, respectively. A lattice is called *finite* iff $\mathcal{L}$ is finite. Every finite lattice has a least element, called *bottom*, denoted by $\bot$, and a greatest element, called *top*, denoted by $\top$. A lattice is *distributive*, iff $x \sqcap (y \sqcup z) = (x \sqcap y) \sqcup (x \sqcap z)$, and, dually, $x \sqcup (y \sqcap z) = (x \sqcup y) \sqcap (x \sqcup z)$. In a *DeMorgan* lattice, every element x has a unique *dual* element $\neg x$, such that $\neg\neg x = x$ and $x \sqsubseteq y$ implies $\neg y \sqsubseteq \neg x$. A complete distributive lattice is called *Boolean* iff the $x \sqcup \neg x = \top$ and $x \sqcap \neg x = \bot$.

While the developments to come do not require to have a Boolean lattice, we will apply them only to the Boolean lattices given by the powerset of possible configurations. In other words, given a set of possible configurations N, the lattice considered is $(2^N, \subseteq)$ where meet, join, and dual of elements, are given by intersection, union, and complement of sets, respectively.

Definition 9 (MV-KS). *A multi-valued Kripke structure $\mathcal{K}$ is defined as*

$$\mathcal{K} = (\mathcal{S}, \mathcal{R} : \mathcal{S} \times \mathcal{A} \times \mathcal{S} \to \mathcal{L}, L : \mathcal{S} \times \mathcal{P} \to \mathcal{L})$$

where $\mathcal{S}$ is a set of states, $\mathcal{R}$ is a set of $\mathcal{A}$-labelled transitions, denoting for which product the transition is possible, and L identifies in which state which propositions hold for which product.

Based on this notion, we provide the so-called *configured semantics* of a PL-CCS specification.

Definition 10 (Configured Semantics of PL-CCS). *The* configured seman-tics *of PL-CCS is given according to the SOS-rules shown in Figure 3.*

$$\frac{P \xrightarrow{\alpha,\nu} P'}{\mu Q.P \xrightarrow{\alpha,\nu} P'[Q/\mu Q.P]} \quad \text{(recursion)}$$

$$\frac{P \xrightarrow{\alpha,\nu} P' \quad Q \xrightarrow{\bar{\alpha},\bar{\nu}} Q'}{(P \parallel Q) \xrightarrow{\tau,\nu \cap \bar{\nu}} (P' \parallel Q')} \quad \text{(par. comp. (3))}$$

$$\frac{}{\alpha.P \xrightarrow{\alpha,\mathcal{2}\{R,L\}^n} P} \quad \text{(prefix)}$$

$$\frac{P \xrightarrow{\alpha,\nu} P'}{P[f] \xrightarrow{f(\alpha),\nu} P'[f]} \quad \text{(relabeling)}$$

$$\frac{P \xrightarrow{\alpha,\nu} P'}{P + Q \xrightarrow{\alpha,\nu} P'} \quad \text{(nondet. choice (1))}$$

$$\frac{P \xrightarrow{\alpha,\nu} P'}{(P \setminus L) \xrightarrow{\alpha,\nu} (P' \setminus L)} \, , \, \alpha \notin L$$
$$\text{(restriction)}$$

$$\frac{Q \xrightarrow{\alpha,\nu} Q'}{P + Q \xrightarrow{\alpha,\nu} Q'} \quad \text{(nondet. choice (2))}$$

$$\frac{P \xrightarrow{\alpha,\nu} P'}{P \oplus_i Q \xrightarrow{\alpha,\nu|_{i/L}} P'} \quad \text{(conf. sel. (1))}$$

$$\frac{P \xrightarrow{\alpha,\nu} P'}{(P \parallel Q) \xrightarrow{\alpha,\nu} (P' \parallel Q)} \quad \text{(par. comp. (1))}$$

$$\frac{Q \xrightarrow{\alpha,\nu} Q'}{P \oplus_i Q \xrightarrow{\alpha,\nu|_{i/R}} Q'} \quad \text{(conf. sel. (2))}$$

$$\frac{Q \xrightarrow{\alpha,\nu} Q'}{(P \parallel Q) \xrightarrow{\alpha,\nu} (P \parallel Q')} \quad \text{(par. comp. (2))}$$

$$\frac{P \xrightarrow{\alpha,\nu} P'}{P[g] \xrightarrow{\alpha,\nu[g]} P'[g]} \quad \text{(conf. relabeling)}$$

Fig. 3. The inference rules for the semantics of PL-CCS (and CCS when ignoring the second component of each transition label)

We conclude the introduction of PL-CCS stating that the flat semantics and the configured semantics are equivalent, in the following sense:

Theorem 1 (Soundness of Configured Semantics)

$$\{(c,p) \mid p = \Pi_c([\![P]\!]_{conf})\} = [\![P]\!]_{flat}$$

Here, Π_c denotes the projection of a transition system to the respective configuration c, which is defined in the expected manner.

6   Model-Checking PL-CCS

In this section, we sketch a game-based and therefore on-the-fly model checking approach for PL-CCS programs with respect to μ-calculus specifications.

We have chosen to develop our verification approach for specifications in the μ-calculus as it subsumes linear-time temporal logic as well as computation-tree logic as first shown in [EL86,Wol83] and nicely summarized in [Dam94]. Therefore we can use our approach also in combination with these logics, and in particular have support for the language SALT [BLS06] used with our industrial partners.

Multi-valued modal μ-calculus combines Kozen's modal μ-calculus [Koz83] and multi-valued μ-calculus as defined by Grumberg and Shoham [SG05] in a way suitable for specifying and checking properties of PL-CCS programs. More specifically, we extend the work of [SG05], which only supports unlabelled diamond and box operators, by providing also action-labelled versions of these operators, which is essential to formulate properties of PL-CCS programs.[1]

Multi-valued modal μ-calculus. Let $\mathcal{P}$ be a set of *propositional constants*, and $\mathcal{A}$ be a set of *action names*.[2] A *multi-valued modal Kripke structure* (MMKS) is a tuple $\mathcal{T} = (\mathcal{S}, \{\mathcal{R}_\alpha(.,.) \mid \alpha \in \mathcal{A}\}, L)$ where $\mathcal{S}$ is a set of states, and $\mathcal{R}_\alpha(.,.) : \mathcal{S} \times \mathcal{S} \to \mathcal{L}$ for each $\alpha \in \mathcal{A}$ is a valuation function for each pair of states and action $\alpha \in \mathcal{A}$. Furthermore, $L : \mathcal{S} \to \mathcal{L}^\mathcal{P}$ is a function yielding for every state a function from $\mathcal{P}$ to $\mathcal{L}$, yielding a value for each state and proposition. For PL-CCS programs, the idea is that $\mathcal{R}_\alpha(s, s')$ denotes the set of configurations in which there is an α-transition from state s to s'. It is a simple matter to translate (on-the-fly) the transition system obtained via the configured-transitions semantics into a MMKS.

A Kripke structure in the usual sense can be regarded as a MMKS with values over the two element lattice consisting of a bottom $\bot$ and a top $\top$ element, ordered in the expected manner. Value $\top$ then means that the property holds in the considered state while $\bot$ means that it does not hold. Similarly, $\mathcal{R}_\alpha(s, s') = \top$ reads as there is a corresponding α-transition while $\mathcal{R}_\alpha(s, s') = \bot$ means there is no α-transition.

Let $\mathcal{V}$ be a set of propositional variables. Formulae of the *multi-valued modal μ-calculus* in *positive normal form* are given by

$$\varphi ::= \textit{true} \mid \textit{false} \mid q \mid \neg q \mid Z \mid \varphi \vee \varphi \mid \varphi \wedge \varphi \mid \langle \alpha \rangle \varphi \mid [\alpha]\varphi \mid \mu Z.\varphi \mid \nu Z.\varphi$$

where $q \in \mathcal{P}$, $\alpha \in \mathcal{A}$, and $Z \in \mathcal{V}$. Let $mv\text{-}\mathfrak{L}_\mu$ denote the set of *closed* formulae generated by the above grammar, where the fixpoint quantifiers μ and ν are variable binders. We will also write η for either μ or ν. Furthermore we assume that formulae are well-named, i.e. no variable is bound more than once in any formula. Thus, every variable Z *identifies* a unique sub-formula $fp(Z) = \eta Z.\psi$ of φ, where the set $Sub(\varphi)$ of *sub-formulae* of φ is defined in the usual way.

The semantics of a $mv\text{-}\mathfrak{L}_\mu$ formula is an element of $\mathcal{L}^\mathcal{S}$—the functions from $\mathcal{S}$ to $\mathcal{L}$, yielding for the formula at hand and a given state the *satisfaction value*. In our setting, this is the set of configurations for which the formula holds in the given state.

Then the *semantics* $[\![\varphi]\!]_\rho^\mathcal{T}$ of a $mv\text{-}\mathfrak{L}_\mu$ formula φ with respect to a MMKS $\mathcal{T} = (\mathcal{S}, \{\mathcal{R}_\alpha(.,.) \mid \alpha \in \mathcal{A}\}, L)$ and an *environment* $\rho : \mathcal{V} \to \mathcal{L}^\mathcal{S}$, which explains

---

[1] Thus, strictly speaking, we define a multi-valued and multi-modal version of the μ-calculus. However, we stick to a shorter name for simplicity.

[2] So far, for PL-CCS programs, we do not need support for propositional constants. As adding propositions only intricates the developments to come slightly, we show the more general account in the following.

$$\begin{array}{rcl}
[\![true]\!]_\rho &:=& \lambda s.\top \\
[\![false]\!]_\rho &:=& \lambda s.\bot \\
[\![q]\!]_\rho &:=& \lambda s.L(s)(q) \\
[\![\neg q]\!]_\rho &:=& \lambda s.\overline{L(s)(q)} \\
[\![Z]\!]_\rho &:=& \rho(Z)
\end{array}$$

$$\begin{array}{rcl}
[\![\varphi \vee \psi]\!]_\rho &:=& [\![\varphi]\!]_\rho \sqcup [\![\psi]\!]_\rho \\
[\![\varphi \wedge \psi]\!]_\rho &:=& [\![\varphi]\!]_\rho \sqcap [\![\psi]\!]_\rho \\
[\![\langle\alpha\rangle\varphi]\!]_\rho &:=& \lambda s.\bigsqcup\{\mathcal{R}_\alpha(s,s') \sqcap [\![\varphi]\!]_\rho(s')\} \\
[\![[\alpha]\varphi]\!]_\rho &:=& \lambda s.\bigsqcap\{\neg\mathcal{R}_\alpha(s,s') \sqcup [\![\varphi]\!]_\rho(s')\} \\
[\![\mu Z.\varphi]\!]_\rho &:=& \bigsqcap\{f \mid [\![\varphi]\!]_{\rho[Z\mapsto f]} \sqsubseteq f\} \\
[\![\nu Z.\varphi]\!]_\rho &:=& \bigsqcup\{f \mid f \sqsubseteq [\![\varphi]\!]_{\rho[Z\mapsto f]}\}
\end{array}$$

Fig. 4. Semantics of $mv\text{-}\mathfrak{L}_\mu$ formulae

the meaning of free variables in φ, is an element of $\mathcal{L}^\mathcal{S}$ and is defined as shown in Figure 4. We assume $\mathcal{T}$ to be fixed and do not mention it explicitly anymore. With $\rho[Z \mapsto f]$ we denote the environment that maps Z to f and agrees with ρ on all other arguments. Later, when only closed formulae are considered, we will also drop the environment from the semantic brackets.

The semantics is defined in a standard manner. The only operators deserving a discussion are the $\Diamond$ and $\square$-operators. Intuitively, $\langle\alpha\rangle\varphi$ is classically supposed to hold in states that have an α-successor satisfying φ. In a multi-valued version, we first consider the value of α-transitions and reduce it (meet it) with the value of φ in the successor state. As there might be different α-transitions to different successor states, we take the best value. For PL-CCS programs, this meets exactly our intuition: A configuration in state s satisfies a formula $\langle\alpha\rangle\varphi$ if it has an α-successor satisfying φ. Dually, $[\alpha]\varphi$ is classically supposed to hold in states for which all α-successors satisfy φ. In a multi-valued version, we first consider the value of α-transitions and increase it (join it) with the value of φ in the successor state. As there might be several different α-successor states, we take the worst value. Again, this meets our intuition for PL-CCS programs: A configuration in state s satisfies a formula $[\alpha]\varphi$ if all α-successors satisfy φ.

The functionals $\lambda f.[\![\varphi]\!]_{\rho[Z\mapsto f]} : \mathcal{L}^\mathcal{S} \to \mathcal{L}^\mathcal{S}$ are monotone wrt. $\sqsubseteq$ for any Z, φ and $\mathcal{S}$. According to [Tar55], least and greatest fixpoints of these functionals exist.

Approximants of $mv\text{-}\mathfrak{L}_\mu$ formulae are defined in the usual way: if $fp(Z) = \mu Z.\varphi$ then $Z^0 := \lambda s.\bot$, $Z^{\alpha+1} := [\![\varphi]\!]_{\rho[Z\mapsto Z^\alpha]}$ for any ordinal α and any environment ρ, and $Z^\lambda := \bigsqcap_{\alpha<\lambda} Z^\alpha$ for a limit ordinal λ. Dually, if $fp(Z) = \nu Z.\varphi$ then $Z^0 := \lambda s.\top$, $Z^{\alpha+1} := [\![\varphi]\!]_{\rho[Z\mapsto Z^\alpha]}$, and $Z^\lambda := \bigsqcup_{\alpha<\lambda} Z^\alpha$.

Theorem 2 (Computation of Fixpoints, [Tar55]). *For all MMKS $\mathcal{T}$ with state set $\mathcal{S}$ there is an $\alpha \in \mathbb{O}rd$ s.t. for all $s \in \mathcal{S}$ we have: if $[\![\eta Z.\varphi]\!]_\rho(s) = x$ then $Z^\alpha(s) = x$.*

The following theorem states that the multi-valued modal semantics of the μ-calculus is indeed suitable for checking the different configurations of a PL-CCS program.

Theorem 3 (Correctness of Model Checking). *For all PL-CCS programs P and formulae $\varphi \in mv\text{-}\mathfrak{L}_\mu$, we have*

$$(c, \mathcal{K}) \in [\![P]\!]_{flat} \text{ with } \mathcal{K} \models \varphi \text{ iff } c \in ([\![P]\!]_{conf} \models \varphi)$$

The proof follows by structural induction on the formula.

While Theorem 2 also implies a way for computing the satisfaction value of an $mv\text{-}\mathcal{L}_\mu$-formula and a given MMKS, this naive fixpoint computation is typically expensive. Game-based approaches originating from the work by [EJS93] and [Sti95] allow model checking in a so-called *on-the-fly* or *local* fashion. In the context of multi-valued μ-calculus, the game-based setting becomes technically more involved, as described in detail in [SG05]. Nevertheless, the essence of the game-based approach of computing a satisfaction value based on the so-called *game graph* is similar. For the multi-valued modal μ-calculus, a slight adaptation of the approach taken in [SG05] yields a game-based approach for the full multi-valued modal μ-calculus. Furthermore abstraction-techniques like those presented in [CGLT09] may be applied.

Due to space limitations, we skip details of the game-based model checking approach for the multi-valued modal μ-calculus.

7   Conclusion

In this paper, we have presented a formal foundation for product families, both from a feature as well as a technical perspective and their connection. Based on that foundation we have shown several equivalence laws, that allow for save transformations between different product family specifications. Hence, they facilitate reliable refactorings.

We then applied our formal framework to the well-established, parallel specification formalism, CCS to derive Product-Line-CCS. We have further shown, how PL-CSS can be used to model product lines and efficiently apply model checking to verify properties of a whole product family at once.

We believe this combination of reliable refactorings and verifiable properties yields a robust, formal framework to develop software product families in a safe manner.

References

BLS06.   Bauer, A., Leucker, M., Streit, J.: SALT—Structured Assertion Language for Temporal Logic. In: Liu, Z., Kleinberg, R.D. (eds.) ICFEM 2006. LNCS, vol. 4260, pp. 757–775. Springer, Heidelberg (2006)

BO92.   Batory, D., O'Malley, S.: The design and implementation of hierarchical software systems with reusable components. ACM Transactions on Software Engineering and Methodology 1(4), 355–398 (1992)

CE00.   Czarnecki, K., Eisenecker, U.W.: Generative Programming: Methods, Tools, and Applications. Addison-Wesley (2000)

CGLT09.   Campetelli, A., Gruler, A., Leucker, M., Thoma, D.: *Don't Know* for Multi-valued Systems. In: Liu, Z., Ravn, A.P. (eds.) ATVA 2009. LNCS, vol. 5799, pp. 289–305. Springer, Heidelberg (2009)

CHSL11.   Classen, A., Heymans, P., Schobbens, P.-Y., Legay, A.: Symbolic model checking of software product lines. In: Proceedings of the 33rd International Conference on Software Engineering, ICSE 2011, pp. 321–330. ACM, New York (2011)

Dam94.   Dam, M.: CTL* and ECTL* as fragments of the modal μ-calculus. Theoretical Computer Science 126(1), 77–96 (1994)

EJS93.   Emerson, E.A., Jutla, C.S., Sistla, A.P.: On Model-Checking for Fragments of μ-Calculus. In: Courcoubetis, C. (ed.) CAV 1993. LNCS, vol. 697, pp. 385–396. Springer, Heidelberg (1993)

EL86.   Emerson, E.A., Lei, C.L.: Efficient model checking in fragments of the propositional μ-calculus. In: LICS 1986: Proceedings of the 1st Annual Symposium on Logic in Computer Science, pp. 267–278. IEEE Computer Society Press, Washington, D.C., USA (1986)

GLS08.   Gruler, A., Leucker, M., Scheidemann, K.: Modeling and Model Checking Software Product Lines. In: Barthe, G., de Boer, F.S. (eds.) FMOODS 2008. LNCS, vol. 5051, pp. 113–131. Springer, Heidelberg (2008)

HKM06.   Höfner, P., Khedri, R., Möller, B.: Feature Algebra. In: Misra, J., Nipkow, T., Sekerinski, E. (eds.) FM 2006. LNCS, vol. 4085, pp. 300–315. Springer, Heidelberg (2006)

HKM11.   Höfner, P., Khedri, R., Möller An, B.: algebra of product families. Software and Systems Modeling 10, 161–182 (2011) 10.1007/s10270-009-0127-2

KHNP90.   Sholom, G., Cohen Kyo, C., Kang, J.A., Hess, W.E.: Novak, and A. Spencer Peterson. Feature oriented design analysis (FODA) feasibility study. Technical Report CMU/SEI-90-TR-21-ESD-90/TR-222, Software Engineering Institute, Carnegie Mellon University, Pittsburgh, PA (1990)

Koz83.   Kozen, D.: Results on the propositional μ-calculus. Theoretical Computer Science 27, 333–354 (1983)

SG05.   Shoham, S., Grumberg, O.: Multi-valued Model Checking Games. In: Peled, D.A., Tsay, Y.-K. (eds.) ATVA 2005. LNCS, vol. 3707, pp. 354–369. Springer, Heidelberg (2005)

SHT06.   Schobbens, P.-Y., Heymans, P., Trigaux, J.-C.: Feature diagrams: A survey and a formal semantics. In: 14th IEEE International Requirements Engineering Conference RE 2006, pp. 139–148 (2006)

Sti95.   Stirling, C.: Local Model Checking Games. In: Lee, I., Smolka, S.A. (eds.) CONCUR 1995. LNCS, vol. 962, pp. 1–11. Springer, Heidelberg (1995)

Tar55.   Tarski, A.: A lattice-theoretical fixpoint theorem and its application. Pacific Journal of Mathematics 5, 285–309 (1955)

Wir90.   Wirsing, M.: Algebraic specification. In: Handbook of Theoretical Computer Science, Volume B: Formal Models and Semantics (B), pp. 675–788 (1990)

Wol83.   Wolper, P.: A translation from full branching time temporal logic to one letter propositional dynamic logic with looping (unpublished manuscript)

A Compositional Framework
to Derive Product Line Behavioural Descriptions⋆

Patrizia Asirelli[1], Maurice H. ter Beek[1],
Alessandro Fantechi[1,2], and Stefania Gnesi[1]

[1] ISTI–CNR, Pisa, Italy
[2] DSI, University of Florence, Italy

Abstract. Modelling variability in product families has been the subject
of extensive study in the literature on Software Product Lines, especially
that concerning Feature Modelling. In recent years, we have laid the basis
for the study of the application of temporal logics to the formal modelling
of behavioural variability in product family definitions. A critical point
in this formalization is to give an adequate representation of the elements
of the feature model and their relation with the behaviour of the many
products that are to be derived from the family. To this aim, we propose
a methodology to systematize this step as much as possible, in order to
allow the derivation of behavioural models that are general enough to
capture the behaviour of all consistent products belonging to the family.

1 Introduction

Product Line Engineering (PLE) is a paradigm for the development of a variety of products from a common product platform [23]. Its aim is to lower the production costs of individual products by letting them share an overall reference model of a product family, while allowing them to differ w.r.t. particular features in order to serve, e.g., different markets. Commonality and variability are often defined in terms of *features* and managing variability consists of identifying variation points in a family design as those places where a choice must be made among (optional, mandatory or alternative) features and deciding which combinations of features define valid products. Software Product Line Engineering (SPLE) is a discipline for developing a diversity of software products and software-intensive systems based on the underlying architecture of the product platform [25]. Variability management is what distinguishes SPLE from 'conventional' software engineering.

Since many variability-intensive systems are safety-critical, there is a strong need for rigour and formal modelling and verification (tools). Our contribution in making the development of product families more rigorous consists in an ongoing research effort to investigate upon a suitable formal modelling structure for describing behavioural product variability and a temporal logic than can be

---

⋆ Research supported by the TRACE-IT project funded by the Tuscany Region under
the programme PAR FAS 2007–2013.

T. Margaria and B. Steffen (Eds.): ISoLA 2012, Part I, LNCS 7609, pp. 146–161, 2012.

interpreted over that structure [13,6,7,9]. We opted for Modal Transition Systems (MTSs) [4], which were recognized in [15,20,21] as a useful formal method for describing in a compact way the possible operational behaviour of all products of a product family. We defined a suitable action-based branching-time temporal CTL-like logic over MTSs and developed efficient algorithms to derive valid products from families and to verify properties over products and families alike. We moreover implemented these algorithms in an experimental tool [9].

In this paper, we propose a methodology to systematize the step of formally representing the features from a feature model in relation with the behaviour of the products that can be derived from the family feature model. We also discuss several strategies for the compositional refinement of such behavioural models. We illustrate our approach by means of a simple and intuitive running example.

2   Running Example: A Family of Coffee Machines

For easy comparison, we use the running example from [6,7,11]. It describes a family of (simplified) coffee machines through the following list of requirements:

1. Initially, a coin must be inserted: either a euro, exclusively for European products, or a dollar, exclusively for Canadian products;
2. After inserting a coin, the user has to choose whether (s)he wants sugar, after which (s)he may select a beverage;
3. The choice of beverage (coffee, tea, cappuccino) varies, but coffee must be offered by all products of the family, while cappuccino may be offered solely by European products;
4. Optionally, a ringtone may be rung after delivering a beverage. However, a ringtone must be present in all products offering cappuccino;
5. After the beverage is taken, the machine returns idle.

This list contains a mix of a kind of static constraints defining the differences in configuration (features) between products and more operational constraints defining the behaviour of products through admitted sequences (temporal orderings) of actions/operations implementing features.

The de facto standard variability model in SPLE are *feature diagrams* or *feature models* [19,5] providing compact representations of all products of a product family in terms of their features, and additional constraints among them. Graphically, features are represented as the nodes of a tree, with the family as its root and relations between these features representing constraints. The first three relations below form the tree, the latter two model additional constraints:

Optional features may (but need not) be present only if their parent is present;
Mandatory features are (have to be) present iff their parent is present;
Alternative features are such that only one is present if their parent is present;
Requires is a partial preorder relation indicating that the presence of one feature requires that of the other;
Excludes is a partial symmetric relation indicating the presence of two features to be mutually exclusive.

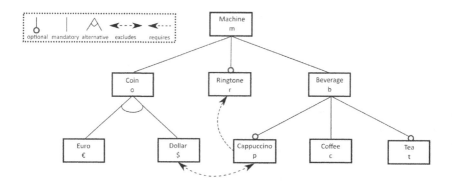

Fig. 1. Feature model of the family of coffee machines (with shorthand names)

Fig. 1 shows a feature model for the coffee machine family, obtained from the list of requirements by considering only the static requirements (1, 3, and part of 4). The behavioural requirements are ignored, since feature models only represent static variability. The feature model defines the following family of 10 products (coffee machines defined by their features):

$$\{m, o, b, c, \in\}, \{m, o, b, c, \in, r\}, \{m, o, b, c, \in, t\}, \{m, o, b, c, \in, t, r\}, \{m, o, b, c, \in, p, r\},$$
$$\{m, o, b, c, \$\}, \{m, o, b, c, \$, r\}, \{m, o, b, c, \$, t\}, \{m, o, b, c, \$, t, r\}, \{m, o, b, c, \in, p, r, t\}$$

A feature model can be characterized by a propositional logic formula [5,26]:

$$(m \Longleftrightarrow true) \wedge (o \Longleftrightarrow m) \wedge ((\in \Longleftrightarrow (\neg \$ \wedge o)) \wedge (\$ \Longleftrightarrow (\neg \in \wedge o))) \wedge (r \Longrightarrow m)$$
$$\wedge (b \Longleftrightarrow m) \wedge ((p \Longrightarrow b) \wedge (c \Longleftrightarrow b) \wedge (t \Longrightarrow b)) \wedge (p \Longrightarrow r) \wedge (\neg(\$ \wedge p))$$

Suppose we have defined two coffee machines with the following sets of features:

$$\text{CM1} = \{m, o, b, c, \in\} \quad \text{and} \quad \text{CM2} = \{m, o, b, c, \in, p\}$$

Without generating all products, it is easy to see that coffee machine CM1 belongs to the product family since it satisfies the characteristic formula of the feature model, whereas CM2 obviously does not: it falsifies the constraint that a cappuccino requires a ringtone ($p \Longrightarrow r$). This can be formally verified by interpreting its set of features as a conjunction of axioms ($m \wedge o \wedge b \wedge c \wedge \in \wedge p$) that when added to the characteristic formula makes it either true or false, according to whether or not the product belongs to the family. In general, the problem of finding a product that satisfies the characterization of a feature model is reduced to the problem of finding a satisfying assignment to a set of boolean variables. Efficient SAT solvers can therefore be used to address this kind of problems [5].

In the next sections, we present the way MTSs can provide behavioural descriptions of product families (based on a combination of their initial lists of requirements and their feature models) over which we can then verify temporal properties. To this end, we first provide their features with a temporal ordering and then step-by-step refine the resulting behavioural descriptions.

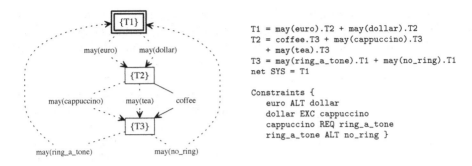

```
T1 = may(euro).T2 + may(dollar).T2
T2 = coffee.T3 + may(cappuccino).T3
   + may(tea).T3
T3 = may(ring_a_tone).T1 + may(no_ring).T1
net SYS = T1

Constraints {
   euro ALT dollar
   dollar EXC cappuccino
   cappuccino REQ ring_a_tone
   ring_a_tone ALT no_ring }
```

Fig. 2. Coffee machine family: MTS (ℓ) and its textual encoding with constraints (r)

3   Modelling Product Family Behaviour with MTSs

Before defining MTSs, we define their underlying Labelled Transition Systems.

Definition 1. *A Labelled Transition System (LTS) is a 4-tuple $(Q, A, \overline{q}, \delta)$, with set Q of states, set A of actions, initial state $\overline{q} \in Q$, and transition relation $\delta \subseteq Q \times A \times Q$; we may write $q \xrightarrow{a} q'$ if $(q, a, q') \in \delta$.*

An MTS is an LTS which distinguishes between *may* and *must* transitions.

Definition 2. *A Modal Transition System (MTS) is a 5-tuple $(Q, A, \overline{q}, \delta^\diamond, \delta^\square)$ such that $(Q, A, \overline{q}, \delta^\diamond \cup \delta^\square)$ is an LTS and $\delta^\square \subseteq \delta^\diamond$. An MTS distinguishes the* may *transition relation $\delta^\diamond$, expressing* admissible *transitions, and the* must *transition relation $\delta^\square$, expressing* necessary *transitions; we may write $q \xrightarrow{a}_\diamond q'$ for $(q, a, q') \in \delta^\diamond$ and $q \xrightarrow{a}_\square q'$ for $(q, a, q') \in \delta^\square$.*

The inclusion $\delta^\square \subseteq \delta^\diamond$ formalises that necessary transitions are also admissible. Reasoning on the existence of transitions is like reasoning with a 3-valued logic with truth values *true*, *false*, and *unknown* [16]: necessary transitions ($\delta^\square$) are *true*, admissible but not necessary transitions ($\delta^\diamond \setminus \delta^\square$) are *unknown*, and impossible transitions ($(q, a, q') \notin \delta^\square \cup \delta^\diamond$) are *false*. Graphically, an MTS is a directed edge-labelled graph where nodes model states and edges model transitions: solid edges are necessary ones and dotted edges are admissible but not necessary ones. Edges are labelled with actions executed as the result of state changes. A sequence of state changes is called a *path*.

An MTS can provide an abstract description of the set of (valid) products of a product family, defining both the behaviour that is common to all products and the behaviour that varies among different products. This requires an interpretation of the requirements of a product family and its constraints w.r.t. certain features as may and must transitions labelled with actions/operations, and a temporal ordering among these transitions.

The methodology we propose in this paper foresees a step-by-step approach, initiated by ordering the features of the feature model. For our running example, the first step of this methodology results in the MTS depicted in Fig. 2(ℓ).

The standard derivation methodology for obtaining a product (which becomes an LTS) from an MTS modelling a product family is defined as including all its (reachable) must transitions and a subset of its (reachable) may transitions; each selection is a product. Unfortunately, MTSs alone are incapable of modelling all common variability constraints. While an MTS is apparently able to model the constraints concerning optional and mandatory features, by means of may and must transitions, no MTS is able to model the constraints regarding alternative features nor those regarding the requires and excludes inter-feature relations. The solution elaborated in [6,7] is to enrich the MTS description with a set of constraints that allow one to define which of the standardly derivable products should be considered as acceptable valid products. In particular, an appropriate variability and action-based temporal logic to formalize these constraints is defined in [6] and an algorithm to derive all and only LTSs describing valid products in [7]. For now, we consider three kinds of (binary[1]) constraints:

F1 ALT F2 Features F1 and F2 are *alternative*;
F1 EXC F2 Feature F1 *excludes* feature F2;
F1 REQ F2 Feature F1 *requires* feature F2.

Their intuitive meaning is as expected: if F1 and F2 are alternative, then all valid products must contain either F1 or F2, but not both; if F1 requires (excludes) F2, then a product which contains F1 must (may not) contain F2. These constraints allow us to define in more detail the set of valid products derivable from the MTS of Fig. 2(ℓ), namely those satisfying each of the constraints specified in Fig. 2(r). Note, however, that these constraints do not imply a temporal ordering among the involved features: a coffee machine that rings a tone before delivering a cappuccino cannot be excluded as a product of the family based on the constraint `cappuccino REQ ring_a_tone`. Such orderings are imposed by the associated behavioural description of a product (family) in the form of an LTS (MTS).

4 Generating and Analyzing Valid Products with VMC

We implemented the above solution in an experimental tool for the modelling and analysis of variability in product lines: the *Variability Model Checker* VMC [9]. Given a product family specified as an MTS, possibly with additional variability constraints, it can automatically generate all the valid products of a family (according to the given constraints), visualize the family/products as MTS/LTSs, and efficiently model check properties expressed in an action- and state-based branching-time temporal CTL-like logic over products and families alike.

VMC takes as input the textual encoding of an MTS in the form of a simple process algebra and an additional set of constraints of the form ALT, EXC, REQ, and IFF (a shorthand for bilateral REQs). The distinction among may and must transitions is encoded in the resulting LTS by structuring action labels of may transitions as `may(·)` (i.e., typed actions). The LTS modelling an MTS through

---

[1] We plan to extend our approach and tool to deal also with n-ary constraints.

typed actions shown in Fig. 2(ℓ) is in fact generated by VMC taking as input the textual representation (without the constraints) depicted in Fig. 2(r).

VMC implements the algorithm in [7] to generate all valid products derivable from an MTS when an associated set of constraints is taken into account. Beyond generating all valid products (LTSs), VMC allows browsing them, verifying whether they satisfy a certain property (a logic formula) and investigating why a specific valid product does (not) satisfy the verified property. To do so, for each product a new window with its textual encoding can be opened.

From the MTS defined in Fig. 2(r) VMC indeed generates the 10 products of the family defined by the feature model depicted in Fig. 1, listing for each product moreover which admitted but not necessary (may) transitions it contains:

```
product14-dollar-ring_a_tone          product23-euro-cappuccino-tea-ring_a_tone
product15-dollar-no_ring               product26-dollar-tea-ring_a_tone
product17-euro-cappuccino-ring_a_tone  product27-dollar-tea-no_ring
product20-euro-tea-ring_a_tone         product8-euro-ring_a_tone
product21-euro-tea-no_ring             product9-euro-no_ring
```

Clicking on a product, its specification appears in a new window. For instance:

```
--------------------------------       -------------------------------------------
-- product14-dollar-ring_a_tone        -- product23-euro-cappuccino-tea-ring_a_tone
--------------------------------       -------------------------------------------

T1 = dollar.T2                         T1 = euro.T2
T2 = coffee.T3                         T2 = coffee.T3 + tea.T3 + cappuccino.T3
T3 = ring_a_tone.T1                    T3 = ring_a_tone.T1
net SYS = T1                           net SYS = T1
```

After having provided an initial temporal ordering of the features, the next step of our methodology is to start refining the behavioural description of a family through the addition of more detailed (operational) information. In our running example, we consider the possibility of distinguishing beverages with and without sugar, as well as different ways of actually mixing the ingredients of beverages:

```
T1 = may(euro).T2 + may(dollar).T2                       Constraints {
T2 = coffee.T3 + may(cappuccino).T4 + may(tea).T5          euro ALT dollar
T3 = may(pour_sugar).T6 + pour_coffee.T11                  dollar EXC cappuccino
T4 = may(pour_sugar).T7 + pour_coffee.T9 + pour_milk.T10   cappuccino REQ ring_a_tone
T5 = may(pour_sugar).T8 + pour_tea.T11                     ring_a_tone ALT no_ring
T6 = pour_coffee.T11                                     }
T7 = pour_coffee.T9 + pour_milk.T10
T8 = pour_tea.T11
T9 = pour_milk.T11
T10 = pour_coffee.T11
T11 = may(ring_a_tone).T12 + may(no_ring).T12
T12 = take_cup.T1
net SYS = T1
```

Given this refined family, VMC generates a total of 36 products. This explosion is due to the way we introduced the possibility of pouring sugar into a beverage, allowing coffee machines in which certain beverages are offered only sugared and others only unsugared. For instance, it allows the two products below: in one only coffee can be sugared while in the other only tea can be sugared. The MTSs of these two products as generated by VMC are shown in Fig. 3; they are obtained by taking as input the following textual representations:

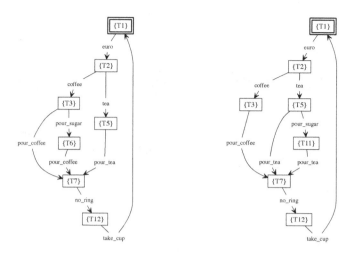

Fig. 3. Valid products of the refined family model as generated by VMC

```
-------------------------------------------
-- product55-euro-tea-pour_sugar-no_ring
-------------------------------------------
T1 = euro.T2
T2 = coffee.T3 + tea.T5
T3 = pour_coffee.T7 + pour_sugar.T6
T5 = pour_tea.T7
T6 = pour_coffee.T7
T7 = no_ring.T12
T12 = take_cup.T1
net SYS = T1
```

```
-------------------------------------------
-- product58-euro-tea-pour_sugar-no_ring
-------------------------------------------
T1 = euro.T2
T2 = coffee.T3 + tea.T5
T3 = pour_coffee.T7
T5 = pour_tea.T7 + pour_sugar.T11
T7 = no_ring.T12
T11 = pour_tea.T7
T12 = take_cup.T1
net SYS = T1
```

There are several ways of resolving this, assuming that coffee machines that offer
sugared versions of only some of the available beverages is not what we want.
One way, leading to the model of [6,7] depicted in Fig. 4, is to further refine
the family by explicitly modelling the choice for sugar upfront (in line with the
requirements), so distinguishing the beverages being sugared, and to extend the
constraints enforcing that all available beverages may but need not be sugared:

```
T1 = may(euro).T2 + may(dollar).T2
T2 = sugar.T3 + no_sugar.T4
T3 = sugared_coffee.T5
   + may(sugared_cappuccino).T6
   + may(sugared_tea).T7
T4 = unsugared_coffee.T8
   + may(unsugared_cappuccino).T9
   + may(unsugared_tea).T10
T5 = pour_sugar.T8
T6 = pour_sugar.T9
T7 = pour_sugar.T10
T8 = pour_coffee.T13
T9 = pour_coffee.T11 + pour_milk.T12
T10 = pour_tea.T13
T11 = pour_milk.T13
T12 = pour_coffee.T13
T13 = may(ring_a_tone).T14 + may(no_ring).T14
T14 = take_cup.T1
net SYS = T1
```

```
Constraints {
    euro ALT dollar
    sugared_tea IFF unsugared_tea
    sugared_cappuccino IFF unsugared_cappuccino
    dollar EXC sugared_cappuccino
    sugared_cappuccino REQ ring_a_tone
    ring_a_tone ALT no_ring
}
```

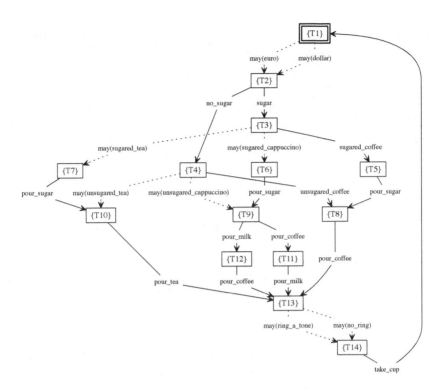

Fig. 4. MTS of refined coffee machine family as generated by VMC

From this refined family MTS, VMC generates the following 10 product LTSs:

```
product11-euro-ring_a_tone
product12-euro-no_ring
product20-dollar-ring_a_tone
product21-dollar-no_ring
product65-euro-sugared_cappuccino-unsugared_cappuccino-ring_a_tone
product77-euro-sugared_tea-unsugared_tea-ring_a_tone
product78-euro-sugared_tea-unsugared_tea-no_ring
product89-euro-sugared_cappuccino-sugared_tea-unsugared_cappuccino-unsugared_tea-ring_a_tone
product95-dollar-sugared_tea-unsugared_tea-ring_a_tone
product96-dollar-sugared_tea-unsugared_tea-no_ring
```

Rather than clicking on the products to analyze them, we can use the model-checking features of VMC to verify whether all valid European products offer both sugared and unsugared cappuccino by checking the following logic formula:[2]

$$[euro]\,((EF\,\langle sugared\_cappuccino\rangle\,true)\ and\ EF\,\langle unsugared\_cappuccino\rangle\,true)$$

VMC produces a table of the above 10 products listing whether or not they satisfy this formula (recall that cappuccino is optional even for European products):

---

[2] Operators $\langle\rangle$ ("possibly") and $[]$ ("necessarily") are the classic diamond and box modalities, while EF ("eventually") is a combination of the classic existential path operator E ("exists") and the classic state operator F ("future").

```
product11-euro-ring_a_tone                                  Formula is FALSE
product12-euro-no_ring                                      Formula is FALSE
product20-dollar-ring_a_tone                                Formula is TRUE
product21-dollar-no_ring                                    Formula is TRUE
product65-euro-(un)sugared_cappuccino-ring_a_tone           Formula is TRUE
product77-euro-sugared_tea-unsugared_tea-ring_a_tone        Formula is FALSE
product78-euro-sugared_tea-unsugared_tea-no_ring            Formula is FALSE
product89-euro-(un)sugared_cappuccino-(un)sugared_tea-ring_a_tone  Formula is TRUE
product95-dollar-sugared_tea-unsugared_tea-ring_a_tone      Formula is TRUE
product96-dollar-sugared_tea-unsugared_tea-no_ring          Formula is TRUE
```

Likewise we can verify whether all valid products offer both sugared and unsugared coffee, in which case VMC reports that this property holds for all 10 products:

$$[euro]\,((EF\,\langle sugared\_coffee\rangle\,true)\,and\,EF\,\langle unsugared\_coffee\rangle\,true)$$

5   Compositional Modelling of Feature Models and MTSs

The step-by-step refinement described in the previous sections is one way to build a large behavioural model of a product family in a bottom-up fashion: a minimal feature model leads to an initial MTS which is subsequently refined by repeatedly adding functionality. Two alternative strategies are based on composition: several minimal feature models, representing different functionalities, are first composed and then interpreted as MTSs or first interpreted and then composed. These strategies require two compositional operators, namely one for feature models and one for MTSs. For feature models, we can use the feature model composition operators described in [1], while for MTSs we can use the classic process-algebraic choice operator (+) and apply it to their textual encodings. Ideally, all strategies should lead to the same refined model. We show that this is not yet the case by applying also the latter two strategies to our running example.

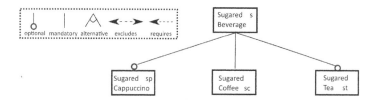

Fig. 5. Sugared Beverage aspect feature model for sugared beverages

Consider the feature model of Fig. 1 and suppose that we want to explicitly add to this configuration the aspect (taken from the list of requirements) that coffee machines come equipped with a functionality that allows the user to choose between sugared and unsugared beverages. Following [1], we can do this by defining the so-called aspect feature model depicted in Fig. 5 and compose it with the feature model depicted in Fig. 1 through the so-called insert operator:

insert(Sugared Beverage, Beverage, And-Mandatory)

Sugared Beverage is the feature to insert (from the aspect feature model), Beverage the target feature (in the base feature model), and And-Mandatory the operator (i.e., the relation defining how the feature is to be included in the tree).

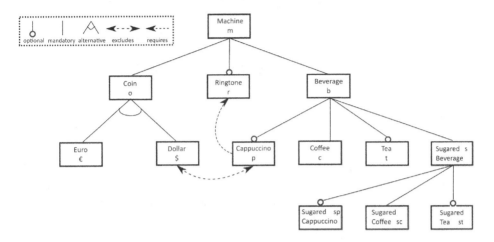

Fig. 6. Aspect inserted into feature model of the family of coffee machines

This composition by insertion results in the feature model depicted in Fig. 6. As before, our methodology now advocates a step-by-step interpretation of the feature model, initially providing a mere ordering of the features. This may result in the MTS depicted in Fig. 7 and its following process-algebraic representation:

```
T1 = may(euro).T2 + may(dollar).T2                         Constraints {
T2 = sugar.T3 + no_sugar.T4                                  euro ALT dollar
T3 = sugared_coffee.T5 + may(sugared_cappuccino).T5         dollar EXC cappuccino
   + may(sugared_tea).T5                                     cappuccino REQ ring_a_tone
T4 = unsugared_coffee.T5 + may(unsugared_cappuccino).T5      ring_a_tone ALT no_ring
   + may(unsugared_tea).T5                                  }
T5 = may(ring_a_tone).T1 + may(no_ring).T1
net SYS = T1
```

Now we run into a problem that is mentioned as future work in [1] and also in later work by the same authors and which — to the best of our knowledge — has not yet been solved: the current composition operators for feature models do not consider inter- and intra-feature constraints between features (such as, e.g., the requires and excludes relations). Translated into our example: composing the feature models depicted in Figs. 5 and 6 should ideally result in a composition (feature model) that incorporates the following constraints:

```
sugared_tea IFF unsugared_tea        sugared_cappuccino IFF unsugared_cappuccino
```

These constraints serve to guarantee that whenever a specific beverage is offered in a valid coffee machine, it can always be obtained sugared as well as unsugared. While this hopefully can be done automatically in the future, for now we have no other choice than to add these constraints by hand.

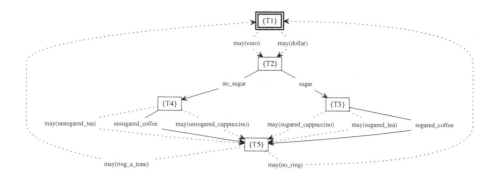

Fig. 7. Coffee machine family interpretation of the feature model of Fig. 6

The next step of our methodology is to refine this behavioural description of the family by adding more detailed (operational) information. If we consider, as before, the different ways of actually mixing the ingredients of the beverages, then this may lead us — once more — to the model of [6,7] depicted in Fig. 4.

This concludes one of the two alternative bottom-up strategies based on composition mentioned in the beginning of this section, namely first composing minimal feature models, representing different functionalities, and then interpreting the resulting composition as an MTS.

The remaining strategy (first interpreting the minimal feature models as MTSs, and then composing these) requires a compositional operator for MTSs.

Consider the MTS and its textual encoding depicted in Fig. 2 (interpreting the feature model depicted in Fig. 1). As before, we want to add the aspect that coffee machines come equipped with a functionality that allows the user to choose between sugared and unsugared beverages as represented by the aspect feature model depicted in Fig. 5. The latter can be interpreted as follows:

```
T = sugared_coffee.Tx + may(sugared_cappuccino).Ty + may(sugared_tea).Tz
```

To compose this with the textual encoding, depicted in Fig. 2(r), of the MTS depicted in Fig. 2(ℓ), we use the well-known process-algebraic choice operator:[3]

```
T1 = may(euro).T2 + may(dollar).T2                Constraints {
T2 = sugar.T3 + no_sugar.T4                          euro ALT dollar
T3 = sugared_coffee.T5 + may(sugared_cappuccino).T5  dollar EXC cappuccino
   + may(sugared_tea).T5                             cappuccino REQ ring_a_tone
T4 = coffee.T5 + may(cappuccino).T5 + may(tea).T5    ring_a_tone ALT no_ring
T5 = may(ring_a_tone).T1 + may(no_ring).T1        }
net SYS = T1
```

In this way, we interpret properly the functionality (originating from the list of requirements) that allows the user to choose between sugared and unsugared beverages after having inserted a coin. However, as before, we need to add constraints to guarantee that whenever a specific beverage is offered in a valid coffee machine, it can always be obtained sugared as well as unsugared.

---

[3] `a.Tx + b.Ty` represents a system which may behave either as `a.Tx` or as `b.Ty`.

After having done so, the next step of our methodology would be — once again — to refine this behavioural description of the family by adding more detailed (operational) information. If we consider, as before, the different ways of actually mixing the ingredients of the beverages, then this may lead us — once again — to the model of [6,7] depicted in Fig. 4.

This concludes the second of two alternative bottom-up strategies based on composition mentioned in the beginning of this section, namely first interpreting minimal feature models, representing different functionalities, as textual encodings of MTSs and then composing the resulting textual encodings into one textual encoding of an MTS.

6   Getting Acquainted with VMC

The core of VMC consists of a command-line-oriented version of the model checker and by a product generation procedure. These programs are stand-alone executables written in Ada and can easily be compiled for the Windows / Linux / Solaris / MacOSX platforms. These core executables are wrapped with a set of CGI scripts handled by a web server; in this way, a graphical html-oriented GUI can easily be built, and the integration with other tools for LTS minimization and graph drawing is easily achieved. (Cf. [9] for further details and references.)

The development of VMC is still in progress, but a prototypical version of the tool is being used at ISTI–CNR for academic and experimental purposes. VMC is publicly usable online (http://fmtlab.isti.cnr.it/vmc/) and its executables are available upon request. The reader is warmly invited to experiment with VMC. The definition of the refined model of the running example used in this paper is available as coffeemodel2.txt from one of the examples.

The current version of VMC is not targeted to the verification of very large systems. Its main limitation, however, lies in generating the model from its process-algebraic input language, while its on-the-fly verification engine and advanced explanation techniques are those of the highly optimized family of on-the-fly model checkers developed during the last decades at ISTI–CNR [8,14]. The on-the-fly nature of their underlying model-checking algorithms means that in general not the whole state space needs to be generated and explored. This feature improves performance and allows to deal with infinite-state systems.

7   Related Work

We first discuss work related to our behavioural modelling and analysis framework based on MTSs and temporal logic, after which we discuss work related to the compositional modelling approach of Archer et alii [1,2,3] that we adopted in the compositional framework presented in this paper.

Behavioural framework. The approach closest to ours is that based on Featured Transition Systems (FTSs) [11,12]. An FTS is a (doubly-labelled) transition system with an associated feature diagram and a specific distinction among its transitions by means of a labelling indicating which transitions correspond to which features. This approach, like ours, thus models product families in terms of specific transition systems that define family behaviour in terms of actions (features). Likewise, both approaches require the addition of further structural relationships between actions to manage (advanced) variability constraints.

In [11], an explicit-state model-checking technique, progressing one state at a time, to verify Linear Temporal Logic (LTL) properties over FTSs is defined. This results in a means to check that whenever a behavioural property is satisfied by an FTS modelling a product family, then it is also satisfied by every product of that family, and whenever a property is violated, then not only a counterexample is provided but so are the products violating the property. In [12], this approach is improved by using symbolic model checking, examining sets of states at a time, and a feature-oriented version of classic CTL (Computation Tree Logic).

SNIP [10] is a model checker for product families modelled as FTSs specified in a language based on that of the well-known SPIN (http://spinroot.com/) model checker. Features are declared in the Text-based Variability Language TVL and are taken into account by the explicit-state model-checking algorithm of SPIN for verifying properties expressed in fLTL (feature LTL) interpreted over FTSs (e.g., to verify a property only over a subset of valid products). Exhaustive model-checking algorithms (continuing their search after a violation was found) moreover allow to verify all the products of a family at once and to output all the products that violate a property. Unlike VMC, SNIP is a command-line tool with no graphical interface. Moreover, it was built from scratch, while VMC profits from numerous optimization techniques that were implemented over the years in the family of on-the-fly model checkers to which it belongs (cf. [8]). SNIP, however, treats features as first-class citizens, with built-in support for feature diagrams, and implements model-checking algorithms tailored for product families.

As said before, MTSs were recognized as a suitable behavioural model to describe product families in [15,20,21]. In [15], a fixed-point algorithm, implemented in a tool, is defined to check whether an LTS conforms to an MTS w.r.t. several different branching relations. In the context of SPLE, it allows to check the conformance of the behaviour of a product against that of its product family.

In [21], variable I/O automata are introduced to model product families. Like modal I/O automata [20], they extend I/O automata with a distinction among may and must transitions. A model-checking approach to verify conformance of products w.r.t. the variability of a family is also defined. This is achieved by using variability information in the model-checking algorithm (while exploring the state space an associated variability model is consulted continuously). Properties expressed in CTL can be verified through explicit-state model checking.

Finally, in [22] an algebraic approach to behavioural modelling and analysis of product families is described, while feature Petri nets are introduced in [24] to model behaviour of product families with a high degree of variability.

Compositional framework. The compositional framework presented in this paper is based on the compositional feature modelling approach of [1]. Archer et alii define a number of operators to separate, relate and compose feature models and semantic properties that must be preserved during such (de)compositions. These operators include the `insert` operator used in Sect. 5 and the more generic `merge` operator built on top of it, as well as the `slice` decomposition operator. To support the manipulation of feature models, they moreover developed the domain-specific language FAMILIAR [3]. For a systematic overview and comparison of their approach with a number of related approaches, we refer to [2]. One of its conclusions is that generic model composition frameworks are outperformed by domain-specific approaches, which convinces us to pursue the development of the compositional framework proposed in this paper.

Two more related domain-specific component-based development approaches are constraint-oriented variability modelling [28], in which behavioural models are constructed by iteratively refining the constraints to determine the admissible solutions, and hierarchical variability modelling [18], which integrates component variability and component hierarchy and is equipped with compositional LTL-based verification techniques for SPL behaviour implemented in a tool set [27]. Compared to our approach, the former uses a top-down rather than a bottom-up approach, while the latter is an architectural rather than behavioural approach to variability modelling.

Finally, in [17] a feature-oriented approach to modelling product families in Event-B by means of a chain of refinements is explored by applying existing Event-B (de)composition techniques to two case studies, using a prototypical feature composition tool. Behavioural variability is not considered, but it would be interesting to explore the feasibility of using this *Feature Event-B* as a high-level specification language on top of the semantic model of our approach.

8   Conclusions and Future Work

We have proposed and illustrated three different methodologies for the derivation of product line behavioural descriptions from feature models, one through refinement and two by means of composition. To complete the variant based on composing MTSs, we are currently working out the details of domain-specific composition operators for MTSs. Subsequently, we intend to implement the resulting compositional framework in VMC.

References

1. Acher, M., Collet, P., Lahire, P., France, R.: Composing Feature Models. In: van den Brand, M., Gašević, D., Gray, J. (eds.) SLE 2009. LNCS, vol. 5969, pp. 62–81. Springer, Heidelberg (2010)
2. Acher, M., Collet, P., Lahire, P., France, R.: Comparing Approaches to Implement Feature Model Composition. In: Kühne, T., Selic, B., Gervais, M.-P., Terrier, F. (eds.) ECMFA 2010. LNCS, vol. 6138, pp. 3–19. Springer, Heidelberg (2010)
3. Acher, M., Collet, P., Lahire, P., France, R.B.: Managing Feature Models with FAMILIAR: a Demonstration of the Language and its Tool Support. In: Heymans, P., Czarnecki, K., Eisenecker, U.W. (eds.) Proceedings 5th Workshop on Variability Modelling of Software-intensive Systems (VaMoS 2011), pp. 91–96. ACM (2011)

4. Antonik, A., Huth, M., Larsen, K.G., Nyman, U., Wąsowski, A.: 20 Years of Modal and Mixed Specifications. Bulletin of the EATCS 95, 94–129 (2008)
5. Batory, D.: Feature Models, Grammars, and Propositional Formulas. In: Obbink, H., Pohl, K. (eds.) SPLC 2005. LNCS, vol. 3714, pp. 7–20. Springer, Heidelberg (2005)
6. Asirelli, P., ter Beek, M.H., Fantechi, A., Gnesi, S.: A Logical Framework to Deal with Variability. In: Méry, D., Merz, S. (eds.) IFM 2010. LNCS, vol. 6396, pp. 43–58. Springer, Heidelberg (2010)
7. Asirelli, P., ter Beek, M.H., Fantechi, A., Gnesi, S.: Formal Description of Variability in Product Families. In: Proceedings 15th International Software Product Line Conference (SPLC 2011), pp. 130–139. IEEE (2011)
8. ter Beek, M.H., Fantechi, A., Gnesi, S., Mazzanti, F.: A state/event-based model-checking approach for the analysis of abstract system properties. Science of Computer Programming 76(2), 119–135 (2011)
9. ter Beek, M.H., Mazzanti, F., Sulova, A.: VMC: A Tool for Product Variability Analysis. In: Giannakopoulou, D., Méry, D. (eds.) FM 2012. LNCS, vol. 7436, pp. 450–454. Springer, Heidelberg (2012)
10. Classen, A., Cordy, M., Heymans, P., Schobbens, P.-Y., Legay, A.: SNIP: An Efficient Model Checker for Software Product Lines. Technical Report P-CS-TR SPLMC-00000003, PReCISE Research Center, University of Namur (2011)
11. Classen, A., Heymans, P., Schobbens, P.-Y., Legay, A., Raskin, J.-F.: Model Checking Lots of Systems: Efficient Verification of Temporal Properties in Software Product Lines. In: Proceedings 32nd International Conference on Software Engineering (ICSE 2010), pp. 335–344. ACM (2010)
12. Classen, A., Heymans, P., Schobbens, P.-Y., Legay, A.: Symbolic Model Checking of Software Product Lines. In: Proceedings 33rd International Conference on Software Engineering (ICSE 2011), pp. 321–330. ACM (2011)
13. Fantechi, A., Gnesi, S.: Formal Modelling for Product Families Engineering. In: Proceedings 12th Software Product Lines Conference (SPLC 2008), pp. 193–202. IEEE (2008)
14. Fantechi, A., Gnesi, S., Lapadula, A., Mazzanti, F., Pugliese, R., Tiezzi, F.: A Logical Verification Methodology for Service-Oriented Computing. ACM Transactions on Software Engineering and Methodology 21(3), article 16, 1–46 (2012)
15. Fischbein, D., Uchitel, S., Braberman, V.A.: A Foundation for Behavioural Conformance in Software Product Line Architectures. In: Hierons, R.M., Muccini, H. (eds.) Proceedings ISSTA 2006 Workshop on the Role of Software Architecture for Testing and Analysis (ROSATEA 2006), pp. 39–48. ACM (2006)
16. Godefroid, P., Huth, M., Jagadeesan, R.: Abstraction-Based Model Checking Using Modal Transition Systems. In: Larsen, K.G., Nielsen, M. (eds.) CONCUR 2001. LNCS, vol. 2154, pp. 426–440. Springer, Heidelberg (2001)
17. Gondal, A., Poppleton, M., Butler, M.: Composing Event-B Specifications - Case-Study Experience. In: Apel, S., Jackson, E. (eds.) SC 2011. LNCS, vol. 6708, pp. 100–115. Springer, Heidelberg (2011)
18. Haber, A., Rendel, H., Rumpe, B., Schaefer, I., van der Linden, F.: Hierarchical Variability Modeling for Software Architectures. In: Proceedings 15th International Software Product Line Conference (SPLC 2011), pp. 150–159. IEEE (2011)
19. Kang, K., Choen, S., Hess, J., Novak, W., Peterson, S.: Feature Oriented Domain Analysis (FODA) Feasibility Study. Technical Report SEI-90-TR-21. Carnegie Mellon University (1990)

20. Larsen, K.G., Nyman, U., Wąsowski, A.: Modal I/O Automata for Interface and Product Line Theories. In: De Nicola, R. (ed.) ESOP 2007. LNCS, vol. 4421, pp. 64–79. Springer, Heidelberg (2007)
21. Lauenroth, K., Pohl, K., Töhning, S.: Model Checking of Domain Artifacts in Product Line Engineering. In: Proceedings 24th International Conference on Automated Software Engineering (ASE 2009), pp. 269–280. IEEE (2009)
22. Leucker, M., Thoma, D.: A Formal Approach to Software Product Families. In: Margaria, T., Steffen, B.(eds.) ISoLA 2012, Part I. LNCS, vol. 7609, pp. 131–145. Springer, Heidelberg (2012)
23. Meyer, M.H., Lehnerd, A.P.: The Power of Product Platforms: Building Value and Cost Leadership. The Free Press (1997)
24. Muschevici, R., Clarke, D., Proença, J.: Feature Petri Nets. Schaefer, I., Carbon, R., (eds): Proceedings 1st Workshop on Formal Methods in Software Product Line Engineering (FMSPLE 2010). Technical Report, University of Lancaster (2010)
25. Pohl, K., Böckle, G., van der Linden, F.: Software Product Line Engineering: Foundations, Principles, and Techniques. Springer (2005)
26. Roos-Frantz, F.: Automated Analysis of Software Product Lines with Orthogonal Variability Models: Extending the FaMa Ecosystem. Ph.D. Thesis, University of Seville (2012)
27. Schaefer, I., Gurov, D., Soleimanifard, S.: Compositional Algorithmic Verification of Software Product Lines. In: Aichernig, B.K., de Boer, F.S., Bonsangue, M.M. (eds.) FMCO 2011. LNCS, vol. 6957, pp. 184–203. Springer, Heidelberg (2011)
28. Schaefer, I., Lamprecht, A.-L., Margaria, T.: Constraint-oriented Variability Modeling. In: Proceedings 34th Annual IEEE Software Engineering Workshop (SEW 2011), pp. 77–83. IEEE (2012)

Delta-Oriented Monitor Specification

Eric Bodden[1], Kevin Falzon[1], Ka I. Pun[2], and Volker Stolz[2,3]

[1] Secure Software Engineering Group,
European Center for Security and Privacy by Design (EC SPRIDE),
Technische Universität Darmstadt, Germany
[2] Dept. of Informatics, University of Oslo, Norway
[3] UNU-IIST, Macau S.A.R.

Abstract. Delta-oriented programming allows software developers to define software product lines as variations of a common code base, where variations are expressed as so-called program deltas. Monitor-oriented programming (MOP) provides a mechanism to execute functionality based on the execution history of the program; this is useful, e.g., for the purpose of runtime verification and for enforcing security policies.

In this work we discuss how delta-oriented programming and MOP can benefit from each other in the Abstract Behavior Specification Language (ABS) through a new approach we call Delta-oriented Monitor Specification (DMS). We use *deltas over monitor definitions* to concisely capture protocol changes induced by feature combinations, and propose a notation to denote these deltas. In addition, we explore the design space for expressing runtime monitors as program deltas in ABS.

A small case study shows that our approach successfully avoids code duplication in monitor specifications and that those specifications can evolve hand in hand with feature definitions.

Keywords: Runtime Verification, Monitor-oriented Programming, Interface Protocols, Software Product Lines.

1 Introduction

Delta-oriented programming (DOP) allows software developers to define software product lines as variations of a common code base. Variations are expressed as *program deltas*, which can add, remove, and re-define units of code such as classes or methods [5]. Delta-oriented programming has been proposed as a way to structure software product lines (SPL) [6] and as a more structured alternative to other conditional-compilation constructs such as `#ifdef` [12].

The application interfaces (APIs) of software products frequently come with implicit or explicit usage contracts that describe how the individual methods of the API are to be called, e.g., in which order or with what parameters. Runtime monitoring is commonly used to verify the adherence to such usage contracts at runtime [3]. In runtime monitoring, the program under test is instrumented with (often stateful) runtime checks that signal an error if clients of the API violate the usage rules at runtime. In practice, the runtime monitoring machinery can be used for other purposes. More specifically, runtime monitors can be seen as

T. Margaria and B. Steffen (Eds.): ISoLA 2012, Part I, LNCS 7609, pp. 162–177, 2012.

a declarative programming paradigm in which code is executed based on events observed in the execution history of the program — a programming style coined Monitor-oriented Programming (MOP) [3].

Subjecting a product line's code to program deltas complicates its monitoring, as the introduction of the deltas may modify or extend usage contracts, or in the more general case of MOP, may expose new or altered execution histories. Thus, it follows that any runtime monitors present in the system may need to be updated as well.

In this work, we describe an initial design of Delta-oriented Monitor Specification (DMS), our approach to updating finite-state-machine based monitor specifications in line with delta definitions for regular program code. DMS allows programmers to deploy monitors as deltas, and to define deltas over monitor definitions comprising additions, removal or replacements of individual transitions, the introduction of new initial states and variable bindings or the additions, removal or replacement of transition guards.

We situate our approach in the context of the Abstract Behaviour Specification language (ABS), a modelling language for active objects [4] that has built-in support for DOP. Concretely, we provide an example based on ABS and propose a tool approach for integration with the ABS platform. We also report on the suitability of ABS for Monitor-oriented Programming.

To assess the viability of our approach, we apply Delta-oriented Monitor Specification to a small case study of a cashier system from the component-based development community. The Common Component Modelling Example (Co-CoME) [15] is given as a use case with optional variabilities, which we treat as features in a software product line. Firstly, we use the example to introduce the ABS language, and then use the same language mechanism to instrument the example program, to monitor and enforce consistent API use through DMS. We give an implementation strategy that generates the necessary deltas which augment every method with monitoring code. As DMS are rather explicit since they describe changes with respect to a base automaton, we also introduce a more accessible, graphical high-level notation, from which one can automatically calculate the delta automaton.

To summarize, this paper contains the following original contributions:

- The idea of and a design for Delta-oriented Monitor Specifications, including a formalization and an implementation strategy.
- A discussion of the suitability of ABS for Monitor-oriented Programming.
- An assessment of the viability of the approach using a small case study.

The remainder of this paper is organized as follows: we present the salient features of the ABS language and its support for SPLs in the context of a running example in Sec. 2. A short motivation for runtime verification and protocols is provided in Sec. 3. We formalize the base automata with variable bindings and delta-automata to capture protocol changes in Sec. 4. Sec. 5 outlines how deltas can be used to enforce protocols as an optional feature in SPL products. Sec. 6 concludes with related work and a few suggested features to improve ABS's support for runtime verification.

2   Overview

ABS is very much in the style of traditional programming languages like Java or C++, but also models asynchronous behaviour, similar to Actors [9]. Every object can be understood as a process receiving and sending messages, with explicit release points in method bodies over boolean guards on the object state. On the static level, ABS uses subtyping through interfaces, but not code inheritance, making formal reasoning in ABS simpler than in other languages that support code inheritance. However, the language supports another important mechanism for reuse, since it directly includes a notion of software product lines (SPL), a feature language, and a low-level assembly mechanism for so-called "deltas".

In an SPL, features are mapped to sets of deltas, each of which may modify the program by removing/adding fields or methods, and overriding method-bodies with new code that can call back into the original code, allowing a construct similar to the `around()`-advice with `super`-calls of aspect-oriented programming. ABS is thus closer to an aspect-oriented programming language, although it lacks the flexibility of, e.g., wildcard matches on method invocation.

In previous work [2], we have used techniques from aspect-oriented programming [10] to instrument applications with runtime checks that enforce a particular *protocol* between objects. In runtime verification, one is generally interested in detecting patterns in the execution history, usually described by linear temporal logic formulas or regular expressions. Additionally, one may specify an action which must be taken when a monitor is triggered. When a monitor matches, the behaviour of the program is overridden with the behaviour annotated to the monitor. Enforcing protocols can be useful to add security aspects to an API, or guard against the misuse of an interface. Monitor specifications are often domain-specific, and can often be derived from the (informal) documentation.

In this paper, instead of using the full power of aspect-oriented programming techniques, we show that the more restricted subset of ABS programs is—in general, save some minor elements which have not yet been implemented in the prototype of the ABS language—sufficient to implement runtime verification.

Most importantly, we lift the notion of deltas to the level of monitoring. This allows us to customize protocols for features and products using a similar mechanism that customizes the code. Deltas are thus used *twice* in our approach: as part of the input, they define the products, and our approach contributes an additional delta which implements the monitoring *per product*.

Next, we give an overview of the ABS language and its support for SPLs.

ABS in the CoCoME Case Study. We illustrate our approach with an example derived from the CoCoME case study [15]. It specifies a simple supermarket system on various levels (single cashdesk, single shop, enterprise) using components (the cashdesk, a store-component providing back-end services, a bank for credit card payments, etc.).

Based on an informal description of the principal use case, we focus here on the design of the cashdesk and how the cashier interacts with it. The scenario also conveniently specifies variabilities which we can express using features.

For each customer, the cashier initiates a new sale, and processes the purchases by scanning them with a barcode scanner. The backend provides necessary information such as price and description. All purchases are aggregated into a sale, and after indicating that the processing has finished, the system calculates the total. The cashier retrieves the money from the customer and enters the amount into the system. The system displays the amount of change to return. After receiving the change, the customer leaves, and the cashier starts over.

We obtain a self-explanatory program for the cashdesk with interface functions `startSale, enterItem, finishSale` and `pay`. In addition to the business logic in the form of methods, data types and (pure) functions over those data types are defined in the functional subset of ABS, e.g., key/value maps.

```
module CoCoME;
class Cashdesk(Store s) implements Cashdesk {
  Store store = s;
  Int total = -1;
  Bool finished = False;
  List<Item> items = Nil;

  Unit startSale() { total = 0; finished = False; items = Nil; }
  Unit enterItem(Int code, Int qty) {
    assert store != null;
    Item item = store.lookup(code);
    total = total + qty*price(item);
    items = Cons(item, items);
  }
  Unit finishSale() { finished = True; }
  Int pay(Int given) {
    assert given >= total;
    return given-total;
  }
}
```

Features of CoCoME. On top of this base program, we define the following optional features: the system should permit credit-card payment as an alternative, and support an express-checkout lane for customers with only a few items. When a cash-desk is in express checkout mode, customers may only purchase a bounded number of products, and only cash payments are allowed.

Instead of changing the program to support those features directly using object-oriented design, we use ABS's software product lines to specify the different products. Delta *Credit* introduces a new method `Bool cardPay(CCData cc)`. Likewise, we ignore the details of refusing a customer should she try to buy too many items when the desk is in express mode—note that the number k of items is configurable by the feature through the delta. We also trigger an assertion when she attempts a credit-card payment while in this mode. The other requirement involving the interaction between both features is specified in delta *ExpressCC*. In express mode, no card payments are allowed:

```
delta Credit {                          delta ExpressCC {
  modifies class Cashdesk {               modifies class Cashdesk {
    adds Bool cardPay(CCData cc)            modifies Bool cardPay(CCData cc) {
      { return store.authorize(cc);}          // Not allowed in express mode
    adds Int cashPay(Int given)              assert ~mode;
      { return this.pay(given); }            return original(cc);
}}                                      }}}
```

It is evident that the sequence in which deltas are applied is relevant, such as when overwriting the `cardPay()` method following its introduction by a previous delta, or when accessing the `mode` attribute. Here, we need ABS's mechanism of explicitly ordering deltas for a particular feature. This is recorded through the `after`-clause in the product-line specification, which assembles the features shown below. We will later show that from our protocol deltas, we can derive a delta which is almost identical to this, since the functionality expressed in the requirement is *exactly* a protocol issue (enabledness of a method based on the execution history).

As a last ingredient, we need to define the valid products in this product line. We have the base product without any features, and both optional features, yielding four possible products in total.[1]

```
productline CoCoME
  features Express, Credit;              product Base();
  delta Credit when Credit;             product Credit(Credit);
  delta Express(10) when Express;       product Ex(Express);
  delta ExpressCC after Credit          product CCEx(Express, Credit);
          when Express && Credit;
```

3 Enforcing Correct Behaviour

The intended use of a programming API, such as our Cashdesk system, is usually not directly inferable from the code. This is problematic, and frequently leads to usage errors. It is therefore desirable to support programmers by documenting and checking usage restrictions.

In [2], we have formalized usage protocols to make their intended use explicit within the code, and to make it automatically checkable. The protocol is specified in a machine-readable notation as annotations in the Java code. *Method invocations*, including constructors, are specified via *atomic propositions* (or equivalently, as transition labels). Any violation of the contract, i.e., a method invocation that is not allowed by the protocol, will terminate the execution. While this is generally undesired for production code (there should not be any runtime errors), this approach is useful for defining testing oracles.

Extension to deltas. As the protocol is clearly application specific, if the application is the product of an SPL, there must be support for various protocols in different products. This gives us two possible options: specifying the full protocol *per product*, or *incrementally changing* the protocol, similarly to how deltas change code. We argue that the latter approach is preferable.

---

[1] ABS supports a product-selection language from, e.g., mutually-exclusive features, or dependencies, which is more than we can make use of in our example. See [6].

To correctly assemble a product from features, which map to sets of deltas, a designer needs intricate knowledge of the internal structure of the program. Features, and consequently their deltas, manipulate a potentially large base application. Clearly, a major focus on the protocol design will be on the base system. Modification of existing methods *may* make it necessary to update the protocol, and new methods *must* be incorporated (unless they require no special interaction protocol). Deletion of methods is straightforwardly handled by removing any occurrence of the method call in the protocol. Thus, we expect that specifying the changes in the protocol per feature is cheaper in terms of syntax and effort than re-specifying the complete protocol for each product.

Base Protocol. The intended API use of our component can be specified through a labelled transition system, where the labels are (guarded) method calls, as shown in Fig. 1. The intended usage, as indicated by the system use case, is that the cashier starts a sale for a new customer, records all items, indicates that all items have been processed, and handles the payment. Correspondingly, the state labels s, b, f are mnemonics for "starting", "buying", "finished". In Sec. 4, we will formalize the automaton construction.

Fig. 1. Base protocol   **Fig. 2.** Credit card payment

Fig. 3. Mode switch   **Fig. 4.** ExCC

For the behaviour of the different products, we informally give the *relative* change in the protocol. Fig. 2 shows that after `finishSale()`, there are now two payment methods available. We have renamed the existing method from `pay` to `cashPay` for clarity, and added the `cardPay` method. The diagram shows wildcard states that the changed transitions attach to; the intention here is to add the new option as an alternative to the existing edge. Any existing edges that are not referred to in the protocol delta are left unchanged. The dashed transitions are used to determine which states in the original protocol to attach to.

Since state names should only be used implicitly, one of our design goals is to *avoid referring to states*, matching, instead, on *existing transitions*. We elaborate on the necessary pointcut expressions in Sec. 4.

Fig. 3 introduces the mode-switch method, which can optionally be called *before* the startSale method. We make use of a *binding occurrence* with formal parameter mode that must match the signature of the operation. Note that the state s before the startSale invocation in the original protocol is an initial state. Therefore, the semantics of "before" should include relocation of the initial state.

Fig. 4 illustrates the interaction between the two available features of credit-card payment and express mode, where the previous mode switch pattern *binds* data (the current mode), and the new, additional part uses the data in the guard. Here, the intention is that the (existing) cardPay transition is only enabled when the mode-flag is not set to express mode. It is obvious that applying the second protocol constraint can only be valid in the presence of the former with the binding occurrence. This corresponds to the delta ExpressCC in our product line from the previous section.

4   Formalization

We model our protocols as finite automata with an extension to *bind* formal parameters of method calls to their instantiated values upon taking a transition. A transition in the automaton refers to variables used as placeholders in its binding function.

4.1   Defining Base Automata

Given that $\Theta := \text{VAR} \rightarrow \text{VAL}$ is a set of functions that resolve the name of a variable to its bound value, a *base automaton* $\mathcal{M}$ is a tuple $\langle Q, \Sigma \times \overrightarrow{\text{VAR}}, q_0, \theta_0, \Gamma \rangle$, with Q states, an alphabet Σ with a list of formal parameters, an initial state $q_0 \in Q$, an initial variable binding $\theta_0 \in \text{VAR} \rightarrow \text{VAL}$ and a set of transitions Γ, where:

$$\Gamma \subseteq \underbrace{Q}_{\substack{\text{current} \\ \text{state}}} \times \underbrace{(\Sigma \times \overrightarrow{\text{VAR}})}_{\substack{\text{method} \\ \text{signature}}} \times \underbrace{(\Theta \rightarrow \mathbb{B})}_{\text{guard}} \times \underbrace{((\Theta \times \overrightarrow{\text{VAL}}) \rightarrow \Theta)}_{\substack{\text{variable-binding} \\ \text{transformation}}} \times \underbrace{Q}_{\substack{\text{next} \\ \text{state}}}$$

Each transition relates a pair of states via a symbol with its parameters, a guard function and a state-binding function. The guard function is evaluated during traversal, with an outgoing transition only being chosen when its guard evaluates to true. The state-binding function will return a new binding function derived from the current bindings s and the input parameters $\vec{c}$. For the sake of brevity, one may forego specifying a guard or a state-binding function, in which case the functions are replaced by an always-true guard and an identity function, respectively. Thus, $(q, e, q') := (q, e, \lambda s.true, \lambda(s, \vec{c}).s, q')$. We also assume correct arity of formal parameters and binding functions.

Configurations. A base automaton *configuration* is a pair consisting of a state and a variable binding. The initial configuration Φ_0 is thus defined as (q_0, θ_0).

Configurations Over Single Transitions. An automaton $\mathcal{M}$ *accepts* an input $a := e(c_0, \ldots, c_n), e \in \Sigma, c_i \in \mathsf{VAL}$ if, given its current configuration, there is an outgoing transition for the input symbol e whose guard evaluates to true. The evolution from a configuration Φ to Φ' within automaton $\mathcal{M}$ on receiving input a is denoted by $\Phi \xrightarrow{a}_{\mathcal{M}} \Phi'$ and is defined as follows:

$$(q, \theta) \xrightarrow{e(c_0, \ldots, c_n)}_{\mathcal{M}} (q', \theta') := (q, e(x_0, \ldots, x_n), guard, binding, q') \in \Gamma$$
$$\wedge \; guard(\theta) \wedge \; binding(\theta, (c_0, \ldots, c_n)) = \theta'$$

Trivially, $\Phi \xrightarrow{\epsilon}_{\mathcal{M}} \Phi' := \Phi = \Phi'$. All states in the automaton are implicitly accepting, and the system is in a correct state as long as a next state is defined for the given input. Conversely, if the automaton cannot progress, then the input is invalid, signalling a *failure*. One can think of such an automaton as being implicitly total, with the complement of the defined transitions leading to a failure state. We define *single step rejection* from configuration Φ on input a:

$$a \notin \mathcal{L}_{\mathcal{M}}(\Phi) := \neg(\exists q' \in Q, \; \theta' \in \mathsf{VAR} \to \mathsf{VAL} \cdot \; \Phi \xrightarrow{a}_{\mathcal{M}} (q', \theta'))$$

Accepting and Rejecting Runs. The notion of accepted and rejected elements can be lifted onto sequences of inputs (or *runs*). Given a run as, with $a \in \Sigma \times \overrightarrow{\mathsf{VAL}}$ and $s \in (\Sigma \times \overrightarrow{\mathsf{VAL}})^*$, one can define the acceptance of a sequence of elements as:

$$(q, \theta) \xRightarrow{as}_{\mathcal{M}} (q', \theta') := \exists q'' \in Q, \; \theta'' \in \mathsf{VAR} \to \mathsf{VAL} \cdot (q, \theta) \xrightarrow{a}_{\mathcal{M}} (q'', \theta'')$$
$$\wedge \; (q'', \theta'') \xRightarrow{s}_{\mathcal{M}} (q', \theta')$$

Trivially, $\Phi \xRightarrow{\epsilon}_{\mathcal{M}} \Phi' := \Phi = \Phi'$.

A rejected sequence w starting from a configuration Φ is denoted as follows:

$$w \notin \mathcal{L}_{\mathcal{M}}(\Phi) := \neg(\exists q' \in Q, \theta' \in \mathsf{VAR} \to \mathsf{VAL} \cdot \Phi \xRightarrow{w}_{\mathcal{M}} (q', \theta'))$$

Thus, a run w is within the base automaton language if $\exists \Phi \cdot \Phi_0 \xRightarrow{w}_{\mathcal{M}} \Phi$. Similarly, a run is not in the language (invalid) if $w \notin \mathcal{L}_{\mathcal{M}}(\Phi_0)$.

4.2   Well-Formedness of Automata

Our use of variables in guards necessitates a notion of well-formedness that ensures that every variable occurring in a guard on a transition has been assigned a value *on all paths* leading to this transition.

Assuming a function $vars : \Gamma \to \overrightarrow{\mathsf{VAR}}$ which yields the used variables in a guard, a transition $\langle S, a, g, b, T \rangle$ is *well-formed*, iff $vars(g) \subseteq defs_{\mathcal{M}}(S)$ where $defs_{\mathcal{M}}(S) : Q \to \overrightarrow{\mathsf{VAR}}$:

$$defs_{\mathcal{M}}(S) := \begin{array}{ll} dom(\theta_0) & \text{iff } s = q_0; \\ \bigcap_{(S^p, e(x_0,\ldots,x_n), g, \theta, S) \in \Gamma} (defs_{\mathcal{M}}(S^p) \cup \{x_0, \ldots, x_n\}) & \text{otherwise} \end{array}$$

where the S^p are the predecessors of the state S. An automaton is well-formed if all its transitions are well-formed.

4.3   Deltas

Deltas are structures that augment a base automaton by adding, modifying or removing transitions. It can also redefine the *initial state* and *variable bindings* of the base automaton.

Defining Deltas. A *delta automaton* is a tuple $\langle Q^{\Delta}, \Sigma^{\Delta} \times \overrightarrow{\mathrm{VAR}}, q_0^{\Delta}, \theta_0^{\Delta}, \Gamma_+^{\Delta}, \Gamma_-^{\Delta} \rangle$, where Q^{Δ} is the set of (possibly new) introduced states, $\Sigma^{\Delta} \times \overrightarrow{\mathrm{VAR}}$ is a set of symbols, q_0^{Δ} is an optional redefined start state, θ_0^{Δ} is a binding function to be composed with any existing initial binding function, and Γ_+^{Δ} and Γ_-^{Δ} are the transitions to be added and removed, respectively. It is assumed that $\Gamma_+^{\Delta} \cap \Gamma_-^{\Delta} = \emptyset$.

Applying Deltas. Given a base automaton $\mathcal{M} = \langle Q^{\mathcal{M}}, \Sigma^{\mathcal{M}} \times \overrightarrow{\mathrm{VAR}}, q_0^{\mathcal{M}}, \theta_0^{\mathcal{M}}, \Gamma^{\mathcal{M}} \rangle$ and a delta automaton $\Delta = \langle Q^{\Delta}, \Sigma^{\Delta} \times \overrightarrow{\mathrm{VAR}}, q_0^{\Delta}, \theta_0^{\Delta}, \Gamma_+^{\Delta}, \Gamma_-^{\Delta} \rangle$, the application of Δ to $\mathcal{M}$ yields a base automaton $\mathcal{M}' := \mathcal{M} \downarrow \Delta$, and is defined as follows:

$$\begin{aligned} Q' &:= Q^{\mathcal{M}} \cup Q^{\Delta} \\ \Sigma' \times \overrightarrow{\mathrm{VAR}} &:= \Sigma^{\mathcal{M}} \times \overrightarrow{\mathrm{VAR}} \cup \Sigma^{\Delta} \times \overrightarrow{\mathrm{VAR}} \\ q_0' &:= q_0^{\mathcal{M}} \text{ if } q_0^{\Delta} = \bot, q_0^{\Delta} \text{ otherwise} \\ \theta_0' &:= \theta_0^{\mathcal{M}} \text{ if } \theta_0^{\Delta} = \bot, \\ & \quad \lambda c.(\texttt{case } \theta_0^{\Delta}(c) = \bot \Rightarrow \theta_0^{\mathcal{M}}(c); \texttt{otherwise}, \theta_0^{\Delta}(c)) \text{ otherwise} \\ \Gamma' &:= (\Gamma^{\mathcal{M}} \cup \Gamma_+^{\Delta}) - \Gamma_-^{\Delta} \end{aligned}$$

where $\bot$ is an undefined element. Deltas can introduce or redefine bindings stated within the initial binding. In the case of redefinitions, the latest updated binding will be used. If the empty base automaton is $\mathcal{M}_{\emptyset} := \langle \emptyset, \emptyset, \bot, \lambda c.\bot, \emptyset \rangle$, one can redefine a base automaton $\mathcal{M}$ as a delta operation on $\mathcal{M}_{\emptyset}$. Formally, $\mathcal{M} := \mathcal{M}_{\emptyset} \downarrow \Delta_{\mathcal{M}}$, where $\Delta_{\mathcal{M}} := \langle Q^{\mathcal{M}}, \Sigma^{\mathcal{M}} \times \overrightarrow{\mathrm{VAR}}, q_0^{\mathcal{M}}, \theta_0^{\mathcal{M}}, \Gamma^{\mathcal{M}}, \emptyset \rangle$. Unreachable states after applying a delta automaton can be pruned implicitly as they can no longer influence the behaviour of the monitor.

Example 1. The delta automaton for the credit card payment (Fig. 2) is

$$\begin{array}{lr} \Delta_{CC} := & \langle \emptyset, \{\texttt{cashPay}, \texttt{cardPay}\} & \text{no new state/new symbols} \\ & \bot, \bot, & \text{no initial state/no new initial binding} \\ & \{(f, \texttt{cashPay}, s), (f, \texttt{cardPay}, s)\}, & \text{transitions added} \\ & \{(f, \texttt{pay}, s)\} \rangle & \text{transition removed} \end{array}$$

As the transitions within the delta do not make use of guards or alter variable bindings, the shorthand transition notation is used.

Example 2. The delta automaton for switching Express mode (Fig. 3) is

$$\Delta_M := \langle \{m\}, \{\texttt{setExpress}\}, m, \qquad \text{new state/symbol/initial state}$$
$$\lambda c.(\texttt{case } c = \text{``mode''} \Rightarrow true), \qquad \text{new initial binding}$$
$$\{(m, \texttt{setExpress}, \lambda s.true, \lambda(s, x). \qquad \text{transitions added}$$
$$(\lambda y.(\texttt{case } y = \text{``mode''} \Rightarrow x_0; \texttt{otherwise}, s(y))), s),$$
$$(m, \texttt{startSale}, b)\},$$
$$\emptyset \rangle \qquad \text{no transitions removed}$$

The newly-added transition redefines the variable binding function, adding a binding for "mode". Its value, x_0, is the first element of the list of values x passed on to the $\texttt{setExpress}$ function.

Example 3. The delta automaton for Fig. 4 is

$$\Delta_{ExCC} := \langle \emptyset, \emptyset, \bot, \bot, \qquad \text{no new state/symbols/initial state/initial binding}$$
$$\{(f, \texttt{cardPay}, \lambda s. \,!s(\text{``mode''}), \lambda(s, \vec{c}).s, m)\}, \qquad \text{transition added}$$
$$\{(f, \texttt{cardPay}, m)\} \rangle \qquad \text{transition removed}$$

The delta effectively modifies a transition in the original automaton, adding a guard on the value of "mode".

Applying all three delta automata to our initial protocol, we obtain the resulting automaton $\mathcal{M}' := \mathcal{M} \downarrow \Delta_{CC} \downarrow \Delta_M \downarrow \Delta_{ExCC}$, as shown in Fig. 5.

4.4   Further Design Decisions

Conceptually, and based on the examples shown, it is clear that explicitly specifying the source- and target states for a transition does not scale very well: in general, a method may be used at various times, and accordingly occur in multiple places in the protocol (our example here is a degenerate case, as every method only occurs once). Ideally, graph-matching, as intended in Sec. 3, will take care of this. Matching the transitions in the base protocol and binding the wild-card states s_i allows us to calculate the set of transitions to add or remove.

The second important feature, that of binding of values during a run, requires a suitable representation of terms and a useful collection of function symbols over primitive types and their interpretation. In [2], we included functions to test object-identities, and allow invoking arbitrary methods over bound values in guards. We refer to the aforementioned paper for a detailed discussion.

The third and last important feature is *quantification*: in our running example, the protocol pertains to exactly one interface (or its implementing classes). A monitor is instantiated *per-object*. Conceivably, a protocol can cover coordinated interaction with several objects. Then, the aforementioned object-identities become a mandatory feature. Labels are then of, e.g., the form o.m(x), and guards could use a more flexible form which allows reference to the variables *just* bound in the current call, e.g. o $\neq$ p & o.m(x), denoting that the invoked object must not correspond to the previously bound p (which could come from either the callee-, or an argument position in a preceding transition).

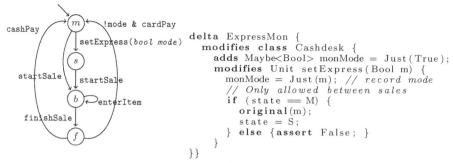

Fig. 5. The resulting automaton   **Listing 6.** Binding of argument value

Instantiation of such a truly crosscutting monitor would then occur on the initial matching transitions, and care must be taken when assigning meaning to a fragment such as $\xrightarrow{\text{o.m}()} \cdot \xrightarrow{\text{p.n}()}$. The "hidden" reference in the second transition to the monitor instantiated by the first one requires *static* access to the monitor, which alas is currently not feasible in the ABS language (see our evaluation of suitability of ABS in Sec. 6).

5   Implementation

In the following, we outline how delta-protocols can be enforced for an interface by keeping track of progress through the state machine and generating assertions, which we naturally deploy using deltas. We will also comment on the use of annotations to make the protocol formally part of the model.

We have two different options for deploying monitors into an existing product line: either we first deploy the base monitor, and then the delta-protocols on top, or we first "flatten" the base protocol automaton and its deltas, and then generate code based on the resulting automaton. The former approach would require subsequent overwriting of previous enforcement code: we can see this clearly in the two different protocols that `cardPay` is involved in, depending on whether express mode is enabled or not. Although in principle the ABS language supports *targeted original calls*, which would aid the implementation, we would like to avoid redundant manipulation, and settle for the latter option.

For a monitor, we first need to introduce a datatype over all states, and a corresponding state variable per class which needs monitoring. Next, we collect all (reachable) transitions from the automaton that a method is involved in. We modify each method to assert that the transition is enabled, execute the original code, and update the state variable before returning from the method, similarly to `around`-advices in aspect-oriented programming (AOP). For ε-transitions, we collect the subsequent transitions. For the bindings, we need to introduce a state variable of the corresponding type, and read (write) the value in guards (binding) events. Listing 6 shows the generated code for binding the `mode`-switch.

As ABS lacks the means to apply deltas to classes *implementing a particular interface*, we also have to designate or compile the list of classes to be instrumented in a preprocessing step as well.

Storing the base protocol and the protocol deltas as part of the model is another problem. ABS has built-in support for annotations, which could be a suitable way of storing the protocol data as part of the file. Annotations attach values over user-defined datatypes to methods or statements. We can then define a datatype to specify the transitions of a protocol as annotations. These are then available during compilation when using the ABS toolchain.

A prototypical implementation of monitoring for the ABS compiler frontend is available from `http://www.mn.uio.no/ifi/english/research/projects/rvabs/`.

6   Related Work and Conclusion

We contrast our work with other works from the areas of aspect-oriented programming, model-driven development, monitor-oriented programming, runtime-verification for software product lines and typestate checking.

Aspect-oriented programming. Both AOP and DOP have in common that they use programming-language elements that allow programmers to insert code into some existing "base code" systems. However, both approaches fundamentally differ in their intent and methodology. The goal of AOP is to modularize concerns that are inherently crosscutting. Most AOP languages therefore support quantification constructs that allow programmers, for instance, to insert code before all method calls or after all field accesses. In addition, most AOP languages have a purely dynamic semantics. While AOP tools typically modify code through static weaving, their semantics are defined through dynamic entities, e.g., the interception of runtime events. Aspects are often intended to be re-used among several software systems. DOP, on the other hand, aims to allow structured compile-time variations of a given piece of software. This is a purely static view; after compilation, deltas are "flattened away", there is no notion of intercepted runtime events. There is also no quantification: in DOP, programmers need to explicitly specify the code elements that need to be modified, and there is no way to specify a whole range of such elements in a declarative style. This lack of quantification makes it less convenient to implement highly crosscutting features such as runtime monitoring. On the other hand, DOP makes it simpler to define delta-oriented monitor specifications, because the code-level effects of applying a delta are immediately obvious. The monitors can thus be defined in terms of the unmodified and modified interface. In AOP, such definitions would be more complex, as the weaving process in AOP is typically hidden from the user, and thus the modified interface is not as easy to deduce.

Model-driven development. The lifting of aspect-oriented techniques to UML models has been done for activity diagrams in [13]. As activity diagrams are syntactically richer than state machines, correspondingly we expect a concrete aspect to be equally verbose. The article does not give a detailed example, but this is confirmed in earlier work, where matching is clearly not based on the diagrammatic representation [14]. In the same paper, the authors also indicate their own and other existing approaches to weave state machines. The manipulations are purely structural, independent of state machine semantics, whereas in contrast, we have well-formedness requirements on the resulting model due to the specific nature of our automata. Similar checks could of course be employed on their resulting models as well.

In the field of SPLs, the Common Variability Language CVL [7] uses an approach to match fragments in the base model which could be useful to implement user-friendly matching on the graphical notation and calculate the delta automata. CVL uses matching on boundary elements (which would be states or transitions in our setting) to define anchor points for substitutions; these anchors are defined in terms of concrete elements of the base model, which indicates that only exactly one substitution can be carried out (a suitable matching mechanism for our purposes should find *all* instances of a pattern in the base automaton). Again, defining delta automata through substitutions will result in a very verbose notation, whereas we envision a more convenient, dedicated notation for adding and removing edges in fragment automata.

Monitor-oriented programming. MOP, prominently advocated by Chen and Roşu [3], is a programming model in which program features can be implemented in a declarative style, as responses to sequences of events in the program's execution history. One natural application of MOP is runtime verification, in which one uses MOP to define testing oracles, notifying the user of a failed test run after having observed a property-violating sequence of program events. However, there are other uses of MOP. For example, one can envision using MOP to implement an auto-save feature that saves a file after every 1000 key strokes. Our delta-oriented monitor specifications allow the delta-oriented adaptation of monitors for the general case of MOP.

Runtime verification for software product lines. Our work on delta-oriented monitor specifications allows monitor specifications to evolve together with delta-oriented code. As explained above, this can be particularly useful in the area of runtime verification. However, there are other ways to combine runtime verification with software product lines. Kim et al. exploit the constraints imposed by a feature model, paired with a static program analysis to restrict runtime verifications only to products that actually have the potential of violating the property in question [11]. This approach could be extended for delta-oriented monitor specifications, and we consider such an extension for future work.

Typestate checking. The stateful patterns that runtime monitors match against can also be checked statically through a mechanism called typestate checking, if appropriate annotations are present in the code. Plaid, for example, is a programming language for implementing software in a typestate-checkable way [1]. In Plaid, programmers annotate methods with the effects that they have on the internal state of a (virtual) state-based monitor. A static type-checker then verifies whether the usage of those methods complies with the given finite-state patterns. The annotations necessary for Plaid bear some similarities to the annotations that we propose in this paper, but in Plaid are much more verbose. In particular, the programmer must add non-trivial aliasing annotations.

General Runtime Verification. In earlier work [2], we have used more general finite alternating automata with variable bindings to support verification of linear-time logics (LTL) properties at runtime. So-called *tracecheck* are defined per Java-interface, and a program is instrumented using AOP. We did not envision variable protocols, and—given their difficult readability—are of the opinion that LTL-specifications are unsuitable candidates to relative modifications.

An interface behaviour specification language for the actor-language Creol was proposed in [8]. It is a regular language over constructor- and method invocations with variable bindings, which *only* supports matching of bound object-identities. In combination with a model checker, a Creol object can then be checked against an interface specification through synchronous parallel composition, with the usual limitations on state space explosion when model checking OO systems. It does not address the runtime of a system, and does not support guards, although this could probably be added.

Conclusion. We have presented a definition and implementation strategy for DMS. Interface protocols, such as [2], for the different products in an SPL can be specified as relative changes to the protocol of the base product, just as relative changes describe a software product in the ABS language. Instrumentation of methods to enforce protocols is done through deltas, as well. Protocol deltas can be generated based on our notion of flattening a base- and delta automaton.

As future work, we will follow up on using annotations to store protocol deltas and develop a preprocessor for the ABS toolchain. Also, we would like to formalize calculation of the delta automata from the (graphical) specification of relative changes as indicated in Sec. 3. This can most likely be discharged by referring to existing graph-matching approaches. Naturally, we are also interested in applying our approach to a non-trivial example.

Currently, one of the limitations of the ABS language is that it neither has constructors, nor can a class-initializer be modified by a delta. This makes it difficult to inject, e.g., a factory for monitor-instances, where many objects communicate with a single monitor. As an immediate workaround, all call-sites of object instantiations would need to be instrumented, which in general cannot be done with simple advice and an `original`-call, but would require code-duplication.

In this paper, we have not made use of ABS as an actor language. Its release points, where execution is suspended until a boolean condition on the object state holds, could be used to alternatively model the protocol: in an actor-based, or even distributed system, in our opinion it would feel much more natural to ignore a "babbling" participant which sends messages out of turn, instead of terminating execution (since, e.g., the assertions which we have used would terminate the *callee*, not the actually misbehaving caller). We could envision `await` statements on the state variable tracking progress through the protocol. Also, the implicit identity of the caller could be incorporated into protocols (avoiding its explicit occurrence in an argument position). In addition, an actor-based setting would encourage the study of the use of protocols in an asynchronous environment.

Acknowledgements. This work was supported by the German Federal Ministry of Education and Research (BMBF) within EC SPRIDE, by the Hessian LOEWE excellence initiative within CASED, the project *Runtime Verification for ABS Product Lines* funded by DAAD and Forskningsrådet, and by the project ARV funded by Macau Science and Technology Development Fund. We thank Franziska Kühn from U. Lübeck for her work on prototyping the implementation.

References

1. Aldrich, J., Sunshine, J., Saini, D., Sparks, Z.: Typestate-oriented programming. In: Proc. 24th ACM SIGPLAN Conf. Companion on Object Oriented Programming Systems Languages and Applications, OOPSLA 2009, pp. 1015–1022. ACM (2009)
2. Bodden, E., Stolz, V.: Tracechecks: Defining Semantic Interfaces with Temporal Logic. In: Löwe, W., Südholt, M. (eds.) SC 2006. LNCS, vol. 4089, pp. 147–162. Springer, Heidelberg (2006)
3. Chen, F., Roşu, G.: MOP: an efficient and generic runtime verification framework. In: OOPSLA 2007, pp. 569–588. ACM (2007)
4. Clarke, D., Diakov, N., Hähnle, R., Johnsen, E.B., Schaefer, I., Schäfer, J., Schlatte, R., Wong, P.Y.H.: Modeling Spatial and Temporal Variability with the HATS Abstract Behavioral Modeling Language. In: Bernardo, M., Issarny, V. (eds.) SFM 2011. LNCS, vol. 6659, pp. 417–457. Springer, Heidelberg (2011)
5. Clarke, D., Helvensteijn, M., Schaefer, I.: Abstract delta modeling. In: Visser, E., Järvi, J. (eds.) GPCE, pp. 13–22. ACM (2010)
6. Clarke, D., Muschevici, R., Proença, J., Schaefer, I., Schlatte, R.: Variability Modelling in the ABS Language. In: Aichernig, B.K., de Boer, F.S., Bonsangue, M.M. (eds.) FMCO 2010. LNCS, vol. 6957, pp. 204–224. Springer, Heidelberg (2011)
7. Fleurey, F., Haugen, Ø., Møller-Pedersen, B., Olsen, G.K., Svendsen, A., Zhang, X.: A generic language and tool for variability modeling. Technical Report A13505, SINTEF, Oslo, Norway (2009)
8. Grabe, I., Kyas, M., Steffen, M., Torjusen, A.B.: Executable Interface Specifications for Testing Asynchronous Creol Components. In: Arbab, F., Sirjani, M. (eds.) FSEN 2009. LNCS, vol. 5961, pp. 324–339. Springer, Heidelberg (2010)
9. Haller, P., Odersky, M.: Scala actors: Unifying thread-based and event-based programming. Theoretical Computer Science 410(2–3), 202–220 (2009)
10. Kiczales, G., Lamping, J., Mendhekar, A., Maeda, C., Lopes, C., Loingtier, J., Irwin, J.: Aspect-oriented programming. In: Aksit, M., Auletta, V. (eds.) ECOOP 1997. LNCS, vol. 1241, pp. 220–242. Springer, Heidelberg (1997)
11. Kim, C.H.P., Bodden, E., Batory, D., Khurshid, S.: Reducing Configurations to Monitor in a Software Product Line. In: Barringer, H., Falcone, Y., Finkbeiner, B., Havelund, K., Lee, I., Pace, G., Roşu, G., Sokolsky, O., Tillmann, N. (eds.) RV 2010. LNCS, vol. 6418, pp. 285–299. Springer, Heidelberg (2010)

12. Liebig, J., Apel, S., Lengauer, C., Kästner, C., Schulze, M.: An analysis of the variability in forty preprocessor-based software product lines. In: ICSE 2010 (1), pp. 105–114. IEEE (2010)
13. Mouheb, D., Alhadidi, D., Nouh, M., Debbabi, M., Wang, L., Pourzandi, M.: Aspect Weaving in UML Activity Diagrams: A Semantic and Algorithmic Framework. In: Barbosa, L.S., Lumpe, M. (eds.) FACS 2010. LNCS, vol. 6921, pp. 182–199. Springer, Heidelberg (2010)
14. Mouheb, D., Talhi, C., Nouh, M., Lima, V., Debbabi, M., Wang, L., Pourzandi, M.: Aspect-Oriented Modeling for Representing and Integrating Security Concerns in UML. In: Lee, R., Ormandjieva, O., Abran, A., Constantinides, C. (eds.) SERA 2010. SCI, vol. 296, pp. 197–213. Springer, Heidelberg (2010)
15. Rausch, A., Reussner, R., Mirandola, R., Plášil, F. (eds.): The Common Component Modeling Example. LNCS, vol. 5153. Springer, Heidelberg (2008)

Conflict Detection
in Delta-Oriented Programming[*]

Michäel Lienhardt[1] and Dave Clarke[2]

[1] University of Bologna, Italy
lienhard@cs.unibo.it
[2] IBBT-DistriNet Katholieke Universiteit Leuven, Belgium
Dave.Clarke@cs.kuleuven.be

Abstract. This paper studies the notion of conflict for a variant of
Delta-Oriented Programming (DOP) without features, separating out
the notions of hard and soft conflict. Specifically, we define a language
for this subset of DOP and give a precise, formal definitions of these
notions. We then define a type system based on row-polymorphism that
ensures that the computation of a well-typed product will always succeed
and has an unambiguous result.

1 Introduction

Delta-oriented programming (DOP) [21,22] is a recent approach to developing
Software Product Lines (SPLs) [6] that addresses several limitations of previous
approaches: it completely dissociates feature models from feature modules (now
called *deltas*), which allows features to be implemented using more than one
delta and deltas to be used by several features, thus improving modularity, reuse
and flexibility; moreover, DOP enables non-monotonic modifications of the core
architecture, including the removal of fields, methods and even classes. DOP is
flexible and enables the modular construction of SPLs. However, tool support
for DOP is not as mature as for other SPL approaches. In particular, the issue
of validating delta-oriented programs has not fully been addressed. Schaefer et
al. [20] propose to generate a collection of constraints for delta-oriented product
lines, ensuring that the manipulations done on the core product are sound and
the resulting products are type safe. However, this work has several limitations:
i) as it is based on constraints, the types do not reflect the structure of the
deltas; ii) it presupposes that the order in which the deltas are applied on a core
is totally specified; and iii) it generates a set of constraints per product, which
means that the complexity is exponential in the number of deltas. More recently,
the present authors proposed an approach [16] that addresses the first of these
limitations using *row polymorphism* [19] to capture the structure of products and
the semantics of deltas in the types. The underlying computational model takes

---

[*] This research is partly funded by the EU project FP7-231620 HATS:
Highly Adaptable and Trustworthy Software using Formal Models
(http://www.hats-project.eu).

T. Margaria and B. Steffen (Eds.): ISoLA 2012, Part I, LNCS 7609, pp. 178–192, 2012.

```
core k {                                delta Sugar {
  class Settings {                        modifies class Settings {
   int coffee;                             adds int sugar;
  }                                       }
                                          modifies class CMachine {
  class CMachine {                          modifies make {...}
    Settings conf;                        }
                                        }
    void make() {...}
    void makeCoffee() {...}             delta ColorPrint {
  }                                       modifies class CMachine {
}                                           modifies make() {...}
                                            modifies makeCoffee() {...}
delta Choco {                               modifies makeChoco() {...}
  modifies class Settings {             }
   adds int chocolate;                 }
  }
  modifies class CMachine {
   adds makeChoco() {...}              product p_s {Choco Sugar} k
   modifies make() {...}               product p_h {Choco ColorPrint} k
  }
}
```

Fig. 1. Soft and Hard Conflicts

a collection of classes as its basis and applies deltas in some order to update them. This paper presents an extension of this approach to deal with the second limitation.

In DOP, if feature modules are applied to a core product in a different order it is not necessarily the case that all computations give the same result. This is illustrated by the code in Figure 1.

This example models a coffee machine with core k comprised of a class Setting storing the type of coffee to brew, and a class CMachine with a generic make method and a method makeCoffee, called by make to prepare coffee. In addition to this core, there are three deltas: Choco adds the capability of brewing hot chocolate; Sugar adds the possibility of setting the quantity of sugar; and ColorPrint changes the make* methods so that messages are printed in color. Finally, there are two different products: p_s applies deltas Choco and Sugar on the core k, and product p_h is constructed by applying deltas Choco and ColorPrint to the core. The order in which the deltas are applied is free in this example, and thus p_s and p_h can either be computed by applying either delta Choco or the other one first.

$$
\begin{array}{ll}
PL ::= & 0 \quad | \quad PLE\ PL \\
PLE ::= & \textbf{core}\ \text{k}\ \{CL\} \\
& | \quad \textbf{delta}\ \text{d}\ \textbf{after}\ DL\ \{COL\} \\
& | \quad \textbf{product}\ \text{p}\ \text{=}\ \{DL\}\ \text{k} \\
COL ::= & CO \quad | \quad CO;\ COL \\
FOL ::= & FO \quad | \quad FO;\ FOL \\
CO ::= & \textbf{adds}\ C \quad | \quad \textbf{removes}\ \text{c} \quad | \\
FO ::= & \textbf{adds}\ F \quad | \quad \textbf{removes}\ \text{f} \quad |
\end{array}
$$

$$
\begin{array}{ll}
DL ::= & \epsilon \quad | \quad \text{d}\ DL \\
CL ::= & \epsilon \quad | \quad C\ CL \\
FL ::= & \epsilon \quad | \quad F;\ FL \\
C ::= & \textbf{class}\ \text{c}\ \{FL\} \\
F ::= & T\ \text{f}\ \mathit{def}
\end{array}
$$

$$
\begin{array}{l}
\textbf{modifies}\ \text{c}\ \{FOL\} \\
\textbf{modifies}\ \text{f}
\end{array}
$$

Fig. 2. Calculus Syntax

Applying first Choco and then Sugar in p_s results in a product with the method make defined by the delta Sugar, whereas if Sugar is applied first, the method make is defined by Choco: the computation of p_s is *ambiguous* (i.e. it can have different results), caused by a *soft conflict* between the deltas Choco and Sugar. Such soft conflicts can be dealt with in two ways: by defining a partial order between delta: for instance, by stating that Choco is always applied after Sugar, the computation of p_s is unambiguous; and by defining another delta to *resolve* the conflict: adding to p_s delta SweetChoco that replaces the method make after applying Choco and Sugar will also make the computation unambiguous.

The product p_h presents another kind of conflict, called *hard conflicts*. While first applying the delta Choco and then ColorPrint, the computation succeeds without any error, first applying ColorPrint results in an error because ColorPrint tries to modify method makeChoco before it exists. Such hard conflicts can only be resolved by imposing an ordering on the deltas specifying that ColorPrint must be applied after Choco. The work on Abstract Delta Modelling discussed only soft conflicts—otherwise hard conflicts did not cause an error—though the theory could easily encompass both [4].

Roadmap. The paper is structured as follows. Section 2 describes a DOP language focusing on deltas and conflicts. Section 3 presents a formal definition of soft and hard conflicts. Section 4 introduces our type system to capture runtime errors and conflicts. Section 5 compares our approach with related work and Section 6 concludes the paper.

2 Delta-Oriented Programming

In the rest of the paper, we will use the term *member* for either a method or a field of a class. The syntax of our delta-oriented programming language is presented in Figure 2. A product line PL is a sequence of element declaration PLE. An element can either be a delta **delta** d **after** DL { COL }, where DL is used to construct the partial order between deltas (see Definition 2) and COL is the body of d; a core product **core** k { CL }, where CL is the set of classes defining the core k; or a product **product** p = { DL } k, where DL are the deltas to be applied to the core k to produce p.

CO and *FO* are the operations on classes and members, respectively. It is possible to add, remove and modify both classes and members. The modification of a class is done with a sequence of operations on members *FOL*, while the modification of members is not specified in our language that only focuses on the manipulation on the structure of the cores, not their behavior.

Free names. The declaration of a new delta d, of a new core k or of a new product p, respectively binds d, k or p in the rest of the program. This notion of binders and free names implicitly creates a form of α-conversion on our *PL* terms. We note $PL =_\alpha PL'$ when *PL* is α-equivalent to PL'. Using this notion of α-conversion, we can assume that all declared deltas, cores and products of a product line *PL* have different names.

Definition 1. *A product line PL with no free names is said to be* closed. *We denote $\mathcal{P}^{cl}$ the set of all closed product lines.*

Semantics. The full semantics of the language is presented elsewhere [5,15]. The principle of the computation of a product in our language is quite simple. The delta names in *DL* are sorted to match the order given by the keyword **after**. When the order is not total, several sequences of deltas are possible, creating the possibility of conflicts. Then, the code of the deltas are applied in order to the core, thus computing the product. The following definition presents the formal construction of the order between deltas, which is necessary to define the notion of conflicts (hard and soft).

Definition 2. *A* general context $\mathbb{G}$ *is a product line with a hole •. Given a product line PL and a term* t *given by one of the productions in Figure 2. Say that* t *is in PL (denoted* $t \in PL$*) if there exists a general context* $\mathbb{G}$ *such that* $PL = \mathbb{G}[t]$. *The relation* $<_{PL}$ *between delta names is defined as the smallest transitive relation satisfying the following property*

$$\textbf{delta d after } d_1 \ldots d_n \ \{COL\} \in PL \Rightarrow d_i <_{PL} d.$$

Finally, the next definition presents the equivalence relation used to sort delta names, which is used in our type system.

Definition 3. *A* relation R *is* closed under general context *iff*

$$\forall \mathbb{G}, x, y, \quad x \: R \: y \quad \Rightarrow \quad \mathbb{G}[x] \: R \: \mathbb{G}[y]$$

Define the relation $\equiv_{dl}$ *as the smallest equivalence relation closed under general context validating the following rule (where* d_1 *and* d_2 *are delta names):*

$$\frac{DL \equiv_{dl} DL'}{d_1 \: d_2 \: DL \equiv_{dl} d_2 \: d_1 \: DL'}.$$

3   Conflicts

Clarke et al. [4] define the notion of conflict for an abstract notion of delta, but they do not capture hard conflicts. This section proposes a more precise definition based on the notion of *action*.

$$act_c(\textbf{adds class } \textsf{c } \{FL\}) \triangleq \overline{\{\textsf{c}\} \cup members(\textsf{c}, FL) \rightarrow \textbf{add}}$$

$$act_c(\textbf{removes class } \textsf{c}) \triangleq \overline{\{\textsf{c}\} \cup \{\textsf{c.f} \mid \textsf{f} \in \mathcal{F}\} \rightarrow \textbf{rem}}$$

$$act_c(\textbf{modifies class } \textsf{c } \{FOL\}) \triangleq \overline{\{\textsf{c}\} \rightarrow \textbf{mod}} \triangleright act_f(\textsf{c}, FOL)$$

$$act_c(CO; COL) \triangleq act_c(CO) \triangleright act_c(COL)$$

$$act_f(\textsf{c}, \textbf{adds } T \textsf{ f } def) \triangleq \overline{\{\textsf{c.f}\} \rightarrow \textbf{add}} \qquad act_f(\textsf{c}, \textbf{removes } \textsf{f}) \triangleq \overline{\{\textsf{c.f}\} \rightarrow \textbf{rem}}$$

$$act_f(\textsf{c}, \textbf{modifies } \textsf{f}) \triangleq \overline{\{\textsf{c.f}\} \rightarrow \textbf{mod}}$$

$$act_f(\textsf{c}, FO; FOL) \triangleq act_f(\textsf{c}, FO) \triangleright act_f(\textsf{c}, FOL)$$

$$A \triangleright \bot = A \qquad \bot \triangleright A = A$$

$\textbf{add} \triangleright \textbf{add} \triangleq \textbf{add}$	$\textbf{add} \triangleright \textbf{rem} \triangleq \bot$	$\textbf{add} \triangleright \textbf{mod} \triangleq \textbf{add}$
$\textbf{rem} \triangleright \textbf{add} \triangleq \textbf{mod}$	$\textbf{rem} \triangleright \textbf{rem} \triangleq \textbf{rem}$	$\textbf{rem} \triangleright \textbf{mod} \triangleq \textbf{rem}$
$\textbf{mod} \triangleright \textbf{add} \triangleq \textbf{mod}$	$\textbf{mod} \triangleright \textbf{rem} \triangleq \textbf{rem}$	$\textbf{mod} \triangleright \textbf{mod} \triangleq \textbf{mod}$

Fig. 3. Actions of Operations

Actions. The following syntax gives the elements E manipulated by a delta and how they can be manipulated:

$$E ::= \textsf{c} \mid \textsf{c.f}$$
$$A ::= \bot \mid \textbf{add} \mid \textbf{rem} \mid \textbf{mod}$$

Given a class $\textsf{c}$ or an member $\textsf{c.f}$ (annotated with its class name $\textsf{c}$), a delta can either do nothing with it ($\bot$); add it (**add**); remove it (**rem**); or modify it (**mod**). Denoting the set of all elements E (resp. all actions A) by $\mathcal{E}$ (resp. $\mathcal{A}$), we define the *effect* (or *action* by language abuse) of a delta d as the function $f : \mathcal{E} \rightarrow \mathcal{A}$ which maps every element E to the action performed by d on E. The action of the code of a delta is defined inductively in Fig. 3, based on the following notions.

Definition 4. *Given a set of elements $S \subseteq \mathcal{E}$ and an action A. Use $\overline{S \rightarrow A}$ to denote the function $f : \mathcal{E} \rightarrow \mathcal{A}$ such that $f(E) = A$ when $E \in S$ and $f(E) = \bot$ for all $E \notin S$. Given two functions $f, g : \mathcal{E} \rightarrow \mathcal{A}$. Use $f \triangleright g$ to denote the function $h : \mathcal{E} \rightarrow \mathcal{A}$ such that $h(E) = f(E) \triangleright g(E)$, where $\triangleright$ is defined in Fig. 3.*

Adding a class corresponds to the action **add** on the class and on all of its members (denoted by the set $members(\textsf{c}, FL)$). Removal corresponds to the action **rem** on the class and on all of its possible members (noted $\mathcal{F}$). Modification corresponds to **mod**, plus all the actions done on the member level. Sequential composition of operators is handled by the operator $\triangleright$.

Finally, the action of a product line that maps all delta names to their actions for a closed product line is defined as follows.

$$
\begin{aligned}
TP &::= \{TCL^\emptyset\} \\
TCL^c &::= \mathbf{Abs}^c \;\mid\; \rho^c \;\mid\; \mathtt{c} : CP; \; CL^{\{c\} \uplus c} \\
CP &::= \mathbf{Pre}_J(TC) \;\mid\; \mathbf{Abs}_J(TC) \\
TC &::= \{FL^\emptyset\} \\
TFL^f &::= \mathbf{Abs}^f_j \;\mid\; \rho^f_\gamma \;\mid\; \mathtt{f} : FP; \; FL^{\{f\} \uplus f} \\
TFP &::= \mathbf{Abs}_J \;\mid\; \mathbf{Pre}_J \\
TD &::= TP \to TP \;\mid\; \forall \alpha. TD \\
TO &::= TC \to TC \;\mid\; \forall \alpha. TO \\
J &::= \gamma \;\mid\; \bot \;\mid\; J; (\mathtt{d}, A) \;\mid\; J; (\mathtt{d}_1 \ldots \mathtt{d}_n)
\end{aligned}
$$

Fig. 4. Type Syntax

Definition 5. *Given a closed product line PL. The action of PL, denoted $act(PL)$, is a function that maps all the deltas declared in PL to their code's action:*

$$
act(PL)(\mathtt{d}) \triangleq \begin{cases} act_c(COL) & \text{if } \mathbf{delta}\ \mathtt{d}\ \mathbf{after}\ DL\ \{COL\} \in PL \\ \mathcal{E} \to \bot & otherwise \end{cases}
$$

Conflicts. The following definition captures the two kinds of conflict:

Definition 6. *Given a closed product line PL, an element E, a product **product** $\mathtt{p} = \{DL\}\ \mathtt{k} \in PL$, and two delta names $\mathtt{d}_1, \mathtt{d}_2 \in DL$ such that $\mathtt{d}_1 \not<_{PL} \mathtt{d}_2 \wedge \mathtt{d}_2 \not<_{PL} \mathtt{d}_1$. Product line PL has a soft conflict, denoted $PL \vDash^E_\mathtt{p} \mathtt{d}_1 \, \natural \, \mathtt{d}_2$, iff E is a member* c.f *and $act(PL)(\mathtt{d}_1)(E) = act(PL)(\mathtt{d}_2)(E) = \mathbf{mod}$. There is a hard conflict, denoted $PL \vDash^E_\mathtt{p} \mathtt{d}_1 \, \natural\natural \, \mathtt{d}_2$, iff both deltas are acting on E and one of them is not doing a simple modification. That is,*

$$
(act(PL)(\mathtt{d}_1)(E), act(PL)(\mathtt{d}_2)(E)) \notin (\{\bot\} \times \mathcal{A}) \cup (\mathcal{A} \times \{\bot\}) \cup \{(\mathbf{mod}, \mathbf{mod})\}
$$

A conflict occurs when two operations on the same element may not produce the same result. An example *soft conflict* results from two modifications of an member: the two possible sequences can produce a different result, thus causing *ambiguity*. Hard conflicts produce an error during the computation of a product. For instance, first modifying an element and then removing it is correct, whereas trying to modify an element that was removed is erroneous. Finally, it is possible to resolve soft conflicts with another delta that acts on the element after the conflict:

Definition 7. *Given a soft conflict $PL \vDash^E_\mathtt{p} \mathtt{d}_1 \, \natural \, \mathtt{d}_2$. This conflict is resolved iff there exists $\mathtt{d} \in dep(\mathtt{p})$ such that $\mathtt{d}_1 <_{PL} \mathtt{d}$, $\mathtt{d}_2 <_{PL} \mathtt{d}$ and $act(PL)(\mathtt{d})(E) \neq \bot$, with*

$$
dep(\mathtt{p}) \triangleq \{\mathtt{d}_1 \ldots \mathtt{d}_n \mid \mathbf{product}\ \mathtt{p} = \{\mathtt{d}_1 \ldots \mathtt{d}_n\}\ \mathtt{k} \in PL\}
$$

Theorem 1. *A closed product line PL with no unresolved conflicts is unambiguous.*

4   Type System

The type system extends our previous work [16] to capture conflicts. Its syntax is presented in Figure 4.

Row types [19] capture the structure of products and classes, *row polymorphism* is used to type deltas and *annotations*, J, capture the action of deltas and conflicts. The type of a product TP consists of a mapping between class names c and presence information that can either be $\mathbf{Pre}_J(TC)$, meaning that the class is present, where TC specifies which members are present and which are absent from the class, and J specifies the previous actions done on the class; or $\mathbf{Abs}_J(TC)$, meaning that the class is not part of the product, where TC specifies all members absent and stores the past actions done to them—normally this component would not be present, but the type system needs to track the previously applied actions, even when a member has been removed. Row polymorphism is enabled with variables ρ which stands for an unknown mapping. The structure of the type TC is similar to TP with two differences: as members do not have an inner structure, presence information for them do not contain an inner type; and empty rows $\mathbf{Abs}_J^f$ (resp. row variables ρ_γ^f) are annotated with a general annotation J (resp. a *conflict* variable γ) to solve the technical difficulty of storing the past actions done on the members of a deleted class. More details can be found in the companion report [15]. Mappings TCL^c (resp. TFL^f) are annotated with sets of class names c (resp. member names f) to ensure that they are just defined once in a type. Deltas are typed with functional types TD where α can either be a row variable ρ or a *conflict* variable γ.

Annotations, J, are used for conflict detection, which is structured into two steps. We first define the action of deltas inductively on their structure: each simple operator acting on an element E is typed with an annotation on E of the form $\gamma; (\mathsf{d}, A)$, where d is the name of the delta performing the operation, A is the performed action, and γ represents past actions done on E. Using type unification, sequential composition of operators on the same element E result in annotations of the form $\gamma; (\mathsf{d}, A_1); \ldots; (\mathsf{d}, A_n)$, which are transformed using a *rewriting relation* into $\gamma; (\mathsf{d}, A_1 \rhd \ldots \rhd A_n)$, corresponding to the action of d on the element E. These annotations are used later, during the typing of products, to detect if they contain conflicts. This detection is done inductively on the structure of the list of delta DL declared in each product: given a list $\mathsf{d}_1 \ldots \mathsf{d}_n$ that result in annotation J on an element E and a delta d that performs the action $A \neq \bot$ on E, using type unification, the list $\mathsf{d}_1 \ldots \mathsf{d}_n \mathsf{d}$ results in annotation $J; (\mathsf{d}, A)$ on E, which is then checked and possibly transformed to record soft conflicts using helper function called $\mathtt{detect}$. Terms of the form $J; (\mathsf{d}_1 \ldots \mathsf{d}_n)$ generally represent soft conflicts involving the n deltas d_i (but can also be used to store delta names in some specific cases). Hard conflicts, corresponding to possible errors, are ill-typed and thus have no syntactic representation in J.

Finally, to ensure the correctness of the conflict detection algorithm, past actions done on deleted members need to be remembered, even when the class itself has been deleted. This means that the type of the deletion of the class c should be able to identify each member f_i in c, take their annotation J_i, and specify that the output product is typed with $c : \mathbf{Abs}(\{\overline{\mathtt{f}_i : \mathbf{Abs}_{J_i;(\mathsf{d},\mathbf{rem})}}\})$. As discussed in the companion report [15], it is not possible using standard unification to compute such a type. We solve this problem by using *local substitutions* [17,15], which allow conflict variables γ to be substituted locally into an element E. For instance, it is possible to type the removal of class c with

$$\{c : \mathbf{Pre}_\gamma(\{\rho_{\gamma'}\})\} \rightarrow \{c : \mathbf{Abs}_{\gamma;(\mathsf{d},\mathbf{rem})}(\{\mathbf{Abs}_{\gamma';(\mathsf{d},\mathbf{rem})}\})\}.$$

It is possible to type the application of this operator to a product with class c by first unifying ρ with the structure of c, producing an input type of the form $\{c : \mathbf{Pre}_J(\{\mathtt{f}_1 : \mathbf{Pre}_{\gamma'}; \ldots; \mathtt{f}_n : \mathbf{Pre}_{\gamma'}; \mathbf{Abs}_{\gamma'}\})\}$, and then unifying each instance of variable γ' with the annotation local to each member.

Relations. We define two relations on our type syntax: a structural equivalence that identifies types with the same semantics, and the rewriting relation used for the computation the action of a delta.

Definition 8. *A type context* $\mathbb{T}$ *is any type term with a hole* $\bullet$. *Moreover, we say that a relation* R *is* closed under type context *iff*

$$\forall \mathbb{T}, x, y, \quad x \, R \, y \quad \Rightarrow \quad \mathbb{T}[x] \, R \, \mathbb{T}[y]$$

The structural equivalence $\equiv$ *between types is the smallest equivalence closed under type context satisfying the following rules, where* a *denotes either a class name or a member name,* K *denotes either* $\mathbf{Abs}$, $\mathbf{Pre}$ *or* $\mathbf{Pre}(TC)$ *and* W^l *denotes either a class list* TCL^c *or a member list* TFL^f:

$$a : K; b : K'; W^l \equiv b : K'; a : K; W^l$$

$$\mathbf{Abs}^{c \uplus \{c\}} \equiv c : \mathbf{Abs}_\bot; \mathbf{Abs}^c \qquad \mathbf{Abs}_J^{f \uplus \{f\}} \equiv \mathtt{f} : \mathbf{Abs}_J; \mathbf{Abs}_J^f.$$

The rewriting relation $\blacktriangleright$ *is the smallest reflexive and transitive relation that is closed under type context satisfying the following rules:*

$$(\mathsf{d}, A); (\mathsf{d}, A') \blacktriangleright (\mathsf{d}, A \rhd A')$$

This equivalence relation states that the order in which the classes and members are typed is not important, and that the empty row $\mathbf{Abs}^l$ corresponds to classes and members being absent. Moreover, the rewriting relation states that when we have two consecutive actions for the same delta d (typically coming from two operators used in the definition of d), we can combine them using the operator $\rhd$, thus computing the action of d. Finally, let $Norm \vdash TD$ denote when the annotations J in TD have been fully reduced with the rewriting relation, i.e. when the actions of the deltas have been computed.

Typing Rules. The rules defining our type system are structured in three parts: classes and core products; operators on classes and products; and product lines, i.e. deltas, core definitions and products.

T:FL
$$\frac{\Phi = \bot \Rightarrow (J = J' = \bot) \qquad \Phi = \mathsf{d}, \gamma \Rightarrow (J = \gamma; (\mathsf{d}, \mathbf{add}) \wedge J' = \gamma)}{\Phi \vdash T_1\ \mathtt{f}_1\ def_1; \ldots; T_n\ \mathtt{f}_n\ def_n : \{\mathtt{f}_1 : \mathbf{Pre}_J; \ldots; \mathtt{f}_n : \mathbf{Pre}_J; \mathbf{Abs}_{J'}\}}$$

T:CL
$$\frac{\Phi \vdash FL_i : TC_i \quad i \in 1..n \qquad \Phi = \bot \Rightarrow J = \bot \qquad \Phi = \mathsf{d}, \gamma \Rightarrow J = \gamma; (\mathsf{d}, \mathbf{add})}{\begin{array}{c} \Phi \vdash \mathbf{class}\ \mathtt{C}_1\ \{FL_1\}\ \ldots\ \mathbf{class}\ \mathtt{C}_n\ \{FL_n\} \\ : \{\mathtt{C}_1 : \mathbf{Pre}_J(TC_1); \ldots; \mathtt{C}_n : \mathbf{Pre}_J(TC_n); \mathbf{Abs}\} \end{array}}$$

Fig. 5. Typing Core Products

Core Products. The typing rules for core products are presented in Figure 5. The rules for cores and classes have the form $\Phi \vdash E : T$, where Φ is a delta context, either a pair (d, γ) or $\bot$, E is the typed term and T its type. When Φ is a pair (d, γ), we are currently typing the addition of some classes performed by delta d, where γ is the previous actions done on the elements. the annotation J is $\gamma; (\mathsf{d}, \mathbf{add})$. Otherwise, when Φ is $\bot$, we are typing a core and the annotation is $\bot$. The rule T:FL types the body of a class with a mapping stating that all the members of the class are present. The rule T:CL types a core product with a mapping stating that all the classes of the core are present, with their bodies typed with the previous rule.

Operators. The typing rules for operators are presented in Figure 6. Our typing statements for operators have the form $\mathsf{d} \vdash E : T$ where d is the delta in which the operators are declared, E is the typed operator and T is its type. The typing rules for operators on members and core products are almost identical to the ones presented in our previous work [16], with the addition of the annotations J describing the actions performed by the operator on the typed element. For instance, the addition of a member $\mathtt{f}$ by a delta d, typed with the rule T:ADDMEM, states that the operator expects: as input, a class with the member $\mathtt{f}$ absent and annotated with a variable γ to capture manipulation done by previous deltas; as output, the same class with member $\mathtt{f}$ added (i.e. present) and with $(\mathsf{d}, \mathbf{add})$ added to γ, thus capturing the addition action performed by d after the previous manipulations stored in γ.

To avoid duplication of typing rules, in the six last typing rules, we use E for any language term, T for any type and Λ for either a delta name d or a typing environments Γ that map delta names and core names to their types (these environments are used to type product lines). The rule T:SEQ types the sequential composition of operators. The rules T:EQUIV and T:REW introduce the usage of the structural equivalence $\equiv$ and rewriting relation $\prec$ in our type system. Finally, the rules T:INST, T:GEN and T:SUBST deal with type generalization and substitution, which can be freely applied.

Product Lines. The type rules for product lines are presented in Figure 7. The typing judgements have the form $\Gamma \vdash E : T$, where Γ is the typing environment storing the type of deltas and cores, E is the typed term and T is its type in the

$$\text{T:ADDMEM} \quad \frac{J = \gamma \qquad J' = \gamma; (\mathbf{d}, \mathbf{add})}{\mathbf{d} \vdash \mathbf{adds}\ T\ \mathtt{f}\ def : \forall \rho, \gamma.\{\mathtt{f} : \mathbf{Abs}_J; \rho_\gamma\} \to \{\mathtt{f} : \mathbf{Pre}_{J'}; \rho_\gamma\}}$$

$$\text{T:DELMEM} \quad \frac{J = \gamma \qquad J' = \gamma; (\mathbf{d}, \mathbf{rem})}{\mathbf{d} \vdash \mathbf{removes}\ \mathtt{f} : \forall \rho, \gamma.\{\mathtt{f} : \mathbf{Pre}_J; \rho_\gamma\} \to \{\mathtt{f} : \mathbf{Abs}_{J'}; \rho_\gamma\}}$$

$$\text{T:MODMEM} \quad \frac{J = \gamma \qquad J' = \gamma; (\mathbf{d}, \mathbf{mod})}{\mathbf{d} \vdash \mathbf{modifies}\ \mathtt{f} : \forall \rho, \gamma.\{\mathtt{f} : \mathbf{Pre}_J; \rho_\gamma\} \to \{\mathtt{f} : \mathbf{Pre}_{J'}; \rho_\gamma\}}$$

T:DELCLASS

$$\frac{J = \gamma \qquad J' = \gamma; (\mathbf{d}, \mathbf{rem})}{\mathbf{d} \vdash \mathbf{removes\ class}\ \mathtt{c} : \forall \rho, \gamma, \rho', \gamma'.\{\mathtt{c} : \mathbf{Pre}_J(\{\rho_{\gamma'}\}); \rho'\} \to \{\mathtt{c} : \mathbf{Abs}_{J'}(\mathbf{Abs}_{\gamma'}); \rho'\}}$$

T:ADDCLASS

$$\frac{J = \gamma \qquad J' = \gamma; (\mathbf{d}, \mathbf{add}) \qquad \mathbf{d}, \gamma' \vdash FL : TC}{\mathbf{d} \vdash \mathbf{adds\ class}\ \mathtt{c}\ FL : \forall \rho, \gamma, \gamma'.\{\mathtt{c} : \mathbf{Abs}_J(\mathbf{Abs}_{\gamma'}); \rho\} \to \{\mathtt{c} : \mathbf{Pre}_{J'}(TC); \rho\}}$$

T:MODCLASS

$$\frac{J = \gamma \qquad J' = \gamma; (\mathbf{d}, \mathbf{mod}) \qquad \mathbf{d} \vdash FOL : TC_1 \to TC_2 \qquad \rho, \gamma\ \text{fresh}}{\mathbf{d} \vdash \mathbf{modifies\ class}\ \mathtt{c}\ FOL : \forall \rho, \gamma.\{\mathtt{c} : \mathbf{Pre}_J(TC_1); \rho\} \to \{\mathtt{c} : \mathbf{Pre}_{J'}(TC_2); \rho\}}$$

$$\text{T:SEQ} \quad \frac{\mathbf{d} \vdash E : T_1 \to T_2 \qquad \mathbf{d} \vdash E' : T_2 \to T_3}{\mathbf{d} \vdash E; E' : T_1 \to T_3} \qquad\qquad \text{T:REW} \quad \frac{\Lambda \vdash E : TP \to TP' \qquad TP' \blacktriangleright TP''}{\Lambda \vdash E : TP \to TP''}$$

$$\text{T:INST} \quad \frac{\Lambda \vdash E : \forall \rho.T}{\Lambda \vdash E : T} \qquad \text{T:GEN} \quad \frac{\Lambda \vdash E : T}{\Lambda \vdash E : \forall \rho.T} \qquad \text{T:SUBST} \quad \frac{\Lambda \vdash E : T}{\Lambda \vdash E : \sigma(T)} \qquad \text{T:EQUIV} \quad \frac{\Lambda \vdash E : T \qquad T \equiv T'}{\Lambda \vdash E : T'}$$

Fig. 6. Typing Operators

context Γ. The type T can either be the type of a delta TD or a mapping Π between product names and their type. The rule T:D types delta declarations by: i) computing the type TD of the delta's body COL; ii) computing the action of the delta: the statement $Norm \vdash TD$ means that the annotations in TD have been completely rewritten by $\blacktriangleright$ (by construction of $\blacktriangleright$, every annotation thus corresponds to the action performed by the delta on the annotated element); and iii) continuing the typing of the product line with the environment Γ extended with a mapping between the delta and its type. The rule T:K types core declarations by typing the declared classes and continuing the typing of PL with the extended typing environment. The rule T:P types a product by typing the list of deltas DL, ensuring that the core $\mathtt{k}$ is a valid input for DL, and adding the type of the product to the rest of the mapping Π. The rule T:NAME is used to type names, where $\mathtt{n}$ is either a core or a delta name.

The type of a list of delta names DL is constructed using the four last typing rules; it works as follows. Using the typing rule T:EQ based on the relation $\equiv_{dl}$,

$$\text{T:D} \quad \frac{\mathtt{d} \vdash COL : TD \quad Norm \vdash TD \quad \Gamma; \mathtt{d} : TD \vdash PL : \Pi}{\Gamma \vdash \textbf{delta d after } DL \ \{COL\} \ PL : \Pi}$$

$$\text{T:K} \quad \frac{\bot \vdash CL : TP \quad \Gamma; \mathtt{k} : TP \vdash PL : \Pi}{\Gamma \vdash \textbf{core k} \ \{CL\} \ PL : \Pi}$$

$$\text{T:P} \quad \frac{\Gamma \vdash DL : TP \to TP' \quad \Gamma \vdash \mathtt{k} : TP \quad \Gamma \vdash PL : \Pi}{\Gamma \vdash \textbf{product p} = \{DL\} \ \mathtt{k} \ PL : \Pi; \mathtt{p} : TP'}$$

$$\text{T:DL-D} \quad \frac{\begin{array}{c} \Gamma \vdash \mathtt{d} : TP_2 \to TP_3 \quad \Gamma \vdash \mathtt{d_1} \ \dots \ \mathtt{d_n} : TP_1 \to TP_2 \\ \forall 1 \leq i \leq n, \mathtt{d} \not<_{PL} \mathtt{d}_i \quad \mathtt{detect}(\mathtt{d}, TP_3) = TP_4 \end{array}}{\Gamma \vdash \mathtt{d_1} \ \dots \ \mathtt{d_n} \ \mathtt{d} : TP_1 \to TP_4}$$

$$\text{T:NAME} \quad\quad \text{T:DL-E} \quad\quad\quad \text{T:EQ}$$
$$\Gamma \vdash \mathtt{n} : \Gamma(\mathtt{n}) \quad\quad \Gamma \vdash \epsilon : \forall \rho.\{\rho\}\{\rho\} \quad \frac{PL \equiv_{dl} PL' \quad PL : \Pi}{PL' : \Pi}$$

Fig. 7. Typing Product Lines

we sort the list of delta names to match $<_{PL}$: DL is thus replaced by DL', corresponding to a valid computation of the product. This sorting is enforced by the statement $\forall \mathtt{d}' \in D_1 \ \dots \ D_n, \mathtt{d} \not<_{PL} \mathtt{d}'$ in rule T:DL-D. Then, the list is typed inductively using T:DL-E for the empty list and T:DL-D to add new deltas to the list. Finally, the rule T:DL-D types the deltas in sequence, with the additional application of the function $\mathtt{detect}(\mathtt{d}, TP_3)$ to detect conflicts added or resolved by $\mathtt{d}$ using the annotations in TP_3. This function traverses type TP_3, applying $\mathtt{detectClass}$ on all annotations at the class level, and $\mathtt{detectMem}$ on all annotations at the member level. We present in Figure 8 these two functions $\mathtt{detectClass}$ and $\mathtt{detectMem}$ (we omit the straightforward presentation of $\mathtt{detect}$) together with an helper function $\mathtt{check}$ which is used to check for hard conflicts between the delta in input and all the previous actions performed on the element. Note that because there are soft conflicts only at the member level, the function $\mathtt{detectMem}$ returns a modified annotation or an error $\mathtt{ERR}$ when an hard conflict is detected; $\mathtt{detectClass}$ returns only either $\mathtt{OK}$ when there are no conflicts, or $\mathtt{ERR}$ otherwise.

Properties. The type system combines the properties of the classic row types system and the conflict detection performed using annotations.

Definition 9. *A type Π is said to be* conflict free *if there are no product name* $\mathtt{p}$, *type context* $\mathbb{T}$ *and annotation J of the form* $J'; (\mathtt{d}_1 \dots \mathtt{d}_n)$ *such that* $\Pi(\mathtt{p}) = \mathbb{T}[J]$.

Definition 10. *A product line PL has a* delta application error *iff during its reduction, either: i) a delta $\mathtt{d}$ that adds an element E is applied on a core that already contains E; ii) a delta $\mathtt{d}$ that removes or modifies an element E is applied on a core that does not contain E.*

```
detectClass(d,J) {                    detectMem(d,J) {
  if  J = J';(d,A) then                 if  J = J';(d,A) then
    if  J' = J'';(d',A') then             if  J' = J'';(d',A') then
      if  d' <_PL d then                    if  d' <_PL d then  J
        OK                                  else if  A = A' = mod then
      else if  A = A' = mod then              if check(d,J'') = OK then
        check(d,J'')                            J'';(d_1,d_2)
      else ERR                              else ERR
    else OK                               else ERR
  else OK                              else if  J' = J'';(d_1...d_n) then
}                                         S ← {d_j | 1 ≤ j ≤ n ∧ d_j ≮_PL d}
                                          if  S = ∅ then
check(d,J) {                                J
  if  J = J';(d',A) then                  else if  A = mod then
    if  d' <_PL d then OK                   if check(d,J') = OK then
    else if  A = mod then                    S' ← {d_j | 1 ≤ j ≤ n} \ S
      check(d,J')                            J'';(S');(d,S)
    else ERR                               else ERR
  else if  J = J';(d_1...d_n) then        else ERR
    if  ∃i, d_i < d then OK             else J
    else check(d,J')                    else J
  else OK                             }
}
```

Fig. 8. Conflict Detection function

Theorem 2 (Soundness). *Given a closed product line PL and type Π such that $\emptyset \vdash PL : \Pi$ holds, there exists PL' with $PL' \equiv_{dl} PL$ such that PL' does not have any delta application error.*

Proof. Consider the derivation K of $\emptyset \vdash PL : \Pi$. K can be transformed it into a derivation K' where we apply the rule T:EQ only once, at the end. Consider the term PL' typed by K' just before the application of T:EQ: this term will not have an error as our type system without T:EQ is more restrictive than [19]. □

Theorem 3 (Freedom). *Given a closed product line PL and conflict free type Π such that $\emptyset \vdash PL : \Pi$ holds. Then PL is conflict free.*

5 Related Work

The goal of type checking the code base of a software product line is to ensure that the generated products are type safe, up to the degree of type safety provided by the base language, *without* having to actually generate the products. Other static analysis techniques can instead be employed to check for other potential deficiencies, without aiming to be ensure complete type safety.

Thaker et al. [23] describe an informally specified approach to the safe composition of software product lines that guarantees that no reference to an undefined class, method or variable will occur in the resulting products. The approach is presented modulo variability given in the feature model and deals especially with the resulting combinatorics. The lack of a comprehensive formal model of the underlying language and type system was rectified with *Lightweight Feature Java* (LFJ) [8]. Underlying LFJ is a constraint-based type system whose constraints describe composition order, the uniqueness of fields and methods, the presence of field and methods along with their types, and feature model dependencies. The soundness of LFJ's type system was validated using theorem prover Coq.

A formal model of a feature-oriented Java-like language called *Featherweight Feature Java* (FFJ) [2] presents a similar base language that also formalizes Thaker et al. [23]'s approach to safe composition, although for this system type checking occurs only on the generated product. *Coloured Featherweight Java* [11], which employs a notion of colouring of code analogous to but more advanced than #ifdefs, lifts type checking from individual products to the level of the product line and guarantees that all generated products are type safe. More recent work [1] refines the work on FFJ, expressing code refinements as modules rather than low-level annotations. The resulting type system again works at the level of the product line and enjoys soundness and completeness results, namely, that a product line is well-typed if and only if all of its derived products are well-typed.

In the above mentioned work the refinement mechanisms are monotonic, so no method/class removal or renaming is possible. Kuhlemann et al. [14] addresses the problem of non-monotonic refinements, though their approach does not consider type safety. They consider the presence of desired attributes depending upon which features are selected. Checking is implemented as an encoding into propositional formulas, which are fed into a SAT solver. Recent work addresses non-monotonic refinement mechanisms that can remove or rename classes and methods. An alternative approach due to Schaefer *et al.* [20] generate detailed dependency constraints for checking delta-oriented software product lines. The checking of the constraint is performed per product, rather than at the level of product lines. This approach to typing delta-oriented programs is complementary to our work, providing part of the checking we have omitted.

A number of static analysis techniques have been developed for the design models or code of software product lines. Heidenreich [10] describes techniques for ensuring that the correspondence between feature models, solution-space models, and problem-space models, which is realised in the FeatureMapper tool. In this tool, models are checked for well-formedness against their meta-model. Similarly, Czarnecki and Pietroszek [7] provide techniques for ensuring that no ill-structured instance of a feature-based model template will be generated from a correct configuration. Apel et al. [3] present a general, language independent, static analysis framework for reference checking—checking which dependencies are present and satisfied. This is one of the key tasks of type checking a software product line. Similar ideas are applied in a language-independent framework for ensuring the syntactic correctness of all product line variants by checking only the product line itself, again without having to generate all the variants [12].

Clarke et al. [4] present an abstract framework for describing about conflicts between code refinements and conflict resolution in the setting of delta-oriented programming. Padmanabhan and Lutz [18] describe the DECIMAL tool, which performs a large variety of consistency checks on software product line requirements specifications, in particular, when a new feature is added to an existing system. Techniques developed for the analysis and resolution of interference of aspects in AOP [13,9] address similar problems to analyses of software product line conflicts, but they do not consider variability.

6   Conclusion

This paper presented a simple language for delta-oriented programming and defines notions soft and hard conflicts, a type system based on row polymorphism to capture errors and on a new concept of annotations to capture conflicts. This paper also shows that, in contrast to Clarke et al. [4], the notion of conflict is not simple and accurately detecting them is not easy. Much work remains to be done. First, we need to extend our type system to ensure type safety not only of delta application, but also of the generated products. Then, we need to extend our calculus and type system to include features models. Whether this can be done while keeping the time complexity of our type system polynomial in the size of the product line remains to be seen.

References

1. Apel, S., Kästner, C., Größlinger, A., Lengauer, C.: Type safety for feature-oriented product lines. Autom. Softw. Eng. 17(3), 251–300 (2010)
2. Apel, S., Kästner, C., Lengauer, C.: Feature Featherweight Java: A calculus for feature-oriented programming and stepwise refinement. In: Smaragdakis, Y., Siek, J.G. (eds.) GPCE, pp. 101–112. ACM (2008)
3. Apel, S., Scholz, W., Lengauer, C., Kästner, C.: Language-independent reference checking in software product lines. In: Proceedings of the 2nd International Workshop on Feature-Oriented Software Development, FOSD 2010, pp. 65–71. ACM, New York (2010)
4. Clarke, D., Helvensteijn, M., Schaefer, I.: Abstract delta modeling. In: Proceedings of the Ninth International Conference on Generative Programming and Component Engineering, GPCE 2010, pp. 13–22. ACM, New York (2010)
5. Clarke, D., Muschevici, R., Proença, J., Schaefer, I., Schlatte, R.: Variability Modelling in the ABS Language. In: Aichernig, B.K., de Boer, F.S., Bonsangue, M.M. (eds.) FMCO 2010. LNCS, vol. 6957, pp. 204–224. Springer, Heidelberg (2011)
6. Clements, P., Northrop, L.: Software Product Lines: Practices and Patterns. Addison-Wesley Longman Publishing Co., Inc., Boston (2001)
7. Czarnecki, K., Antkiewicz, M.: Mapping Features to Models: A Template Approach Based on Superimposed Variants. In: Glück, R., Lowry, M. (eds.) GPCE 2005. LNCS, vol. 3676, pp. 422–437. Springer, Heidelberg (2005)
8. Delaware, B., Cook, W.R., Batory, D.S.: Fitting the pieces together: a machine-checked model of safe composition. In: van Vliet, H., Issarny, V. (eds.) ESEC/ SIGSOFT FSE, pp. 243–252. ACM (2009)

9. Douence, R., Fradet, P., Südholt, M.: A Framework for the Detection and Resolution of Aspect Interactions. In: Batory, D.S., Consel, C., Taha, W. (eds.) GPCE 2002. LNCS, vol. 2487, pp. 173–188. Springer, Heidelberg (2002)
10. Heidenreich, F.: Towards systematic ensuring well-formedness of software product lines. In: Proceedings of the 1st Workshop on Feature-Oriented Software Development, pp. 69–74. ACM, New York (2009)
11. Kästner, C., Apel, S.: Type-checking software product lines - a formal approach. In: ASE, pp. 258–267. IEEE (2008)
12. Kästner, C., Apel, S., Trujillo, S., Kuhlemann, M., Batory, D.: Guaranteeing Syntactic Correctness for All Product Line Variants: A Language-Independent Approach. In: Oriol, M., Meyer, B. (eds.) TOOLS EUROPE 2009. LNBIP, vol. 33, pp. 175–194. Springer, Heidelberg (2009)
13. Katz, E., Katz, S.: Incremental analysis of interference among aspects. In: Clifton, C. (ed.) FOAL, pp. 29–38. ACM (2008)
14. Kuhlemann, M., Batory, D., Kästner, C.: Safe composition of non-monotonic features. In: Siek, J.G., Fischer, B. (eds.) GPCE, pp. 177–186. ACM (2009)
15. Lienhardt, M., Clarke, D.: Conflict detection in delta-oriented programming. Technical report, University of Bologna (2012), http://proton.inrialpes.fr/~mlienhar/reports/2012-Conflict-Detection.pdf
16. Lienhardt, M., Clarke, D.: Row types for delta-oriented programming. In: Proceedings of the Sixth International Workshop on Variability Modeling of Software-Intensive Systems, VaMoS 2012, pp. 121–128. ACM, New York (2012)
17. Lienhardt, M., Mezzina, C.A., Schmitt, A., Stefani, J.-B.: Typing Component-Based Communication Systems. In: Lee, D., Lopes, A., Poetzsch-Heffter, A. (eds.) FMOODS 2009. LNCS, vol. 5522, pp. 167–181. Springer, Heidelberg (2009)
18. Padmanabhan, P., Lutz, R.R.: Tool-supported verification of product line requirements. Autom. Softw. Eng. 12(4), 447–465 (2005)
19. Rémy, D.: Type inference for records in natural extension of ML, pp. 67–95. MIT Press, Cambridge (1994)
20. Schaefer, I., Bettini, L., Damiani, F.: Compositional type-checking for delta-oriented programming. In: Proceedings of the Tenth International Conference on Aspect-Oriented Software Development, AOSD 2011, pp. 43–56. ACM, New York (2011)
21. Schaefer, I., Bettini, L., Bono, V., Damiani, F., Tanzarella, N.: Delta-Oriented Programming of Software Product Lines. In: Bosch, J., Lee, J. (eds.) SPLC 2010. LNCS, vol. 6287, pp. 77–91. Springer, Heidelberg (2010)
22. Schaefer, I., Damiani, F.: Pure delta-oriented programming. In: Proceedings of the 2nd International Workshop on Feature-Oriented Software Development, FOSD 2010, pp. 49–56. ACM, New York (2010)
23. Thaker, S., Batory, D., Kitchin, D., Cook, W.R.: Safe composition of product lines. In: Consel, C., Lawall, J.L. (eds.) GPCE, pp. 95–104. ACM (2007)

Family-Based Analysis of Type Safety
for Delta-Oriented Software Product Lines[*]

Ferruccio Damiani[1] and Ina Schaefer[2]

[1] Università di Torino, Dipartimento di Informatica, C.so Svizzera, 185 - 10149 Torino, Italy
ferruccio.damiani@unito.it
[2] Technische Universität Braunschweig, 38106 Braunschweig, Germany
i.schaefer@tu-braunschweig.de

Abstract. Delta-oriented programming (DOP) is a modular, yet flexible approach for implementing software product lines extending feature-oriented programming. Delta modules allow adding, modifying and removing code for generating product variants. The connection between code modifications and product features and the application ordering of delta modules is less restrictive than in FOP. However, the additional flexibility of DOP increases the complexity for ensuring that all possible product variants of a DOP SPL are well-typed. In previous work, we presented a constraint-based type system which allows analyzing each delta module in isolation, but requires a subsequent analysis step for each product variant. Some FOP SPL type systems generate a representation of all possible product variants and use a family-based analysis to ensure that all possible product variants are type safe. In this paper, we enhance the existing constraint-based type checking approach for DOP by providing a family-based analysis step which improves the product-based analysis of our previous work by making it possible to reuse the intermediate results of the analysis associated to the product variants.

1   Introduction

Delta-oriented programming (DOP) [14,15] is a flexible, modular approach to implement software product lines [13] which can be seen as an extension to feature-oriented programming (FOP) [4] (see [16] for a straightforward encoding of FOP into DOP). In DOP, the product line code base is structured in *delta modules* encapsulating modifications to object-oriented programs. For a particular feature selection, the set of applicable delta module is applied in an ordering given by a product line declaration to the empty product in order to obtain the implementation of the desired product variant. Since delta modules may also contain removals of code, DOP supports proactive product line development, where all possible products are planned in advance, as well as extractive product line development [10] which starts from existing legacy product implementations. The application conditions over the product features that are associated the with delta modules allow handling combinations of features explicitly. This provides an elegant way to counter the optional-feature problem [9] where two optional features require additional glue code to cooperate properly.

---

[*] Authors listed in alphabetical order. Work partially supported by the German Science Foundation (DFG - SCHA1635/2-1) and Italian MIUR (PRIN 2008 DISCO).

T. Margaria and B. Steffen (Eds.): ISoLA 2012, Part I, LNCS 7609, pp. 193–207, 2012.
© Springer-Verlag Berlin Heidelberg 2012

The additional flexibility provided by DOP makes it challenging to ensure that for every feature configuration a unique product can be generated and that all generated products are well-typed. Type checking techniques for software product lines can be classified according to the applied analysis strategy [17]. Product-based strategies consider every possible product of the product line. Family-based analyses check a combined representation of all possible products, i.e., the family, in a single analysis run. In our previous work [15], we have presented a constraint-based type system for DOP SPLs following a product-based analysis strategy. It allows analyzing each delta module in isolation to generate a type abstraction of the delta module expressing the type expectations of the delta modules about the context in which they can safely be used. For each possible product variant, an abstract product generation process is necessary, in order to generate a type abstraction of the product that can be checked to establish whether the corresponding concrete product would be well typed.

In this paper, we enhance the existing constraint-based type checking approach for DOP [15] by providing a family-based analysis step which improves the product-based analysis step by making it possible to reuse the intermediate results of the analysis associated to the product variants. Using the product line declaration, we construct a representation of all possible products in a *product family generation trie*. Type checking all possible product variants amounts to traversing the trie and computing the type abstractions for all (intermediate) products associated to the nodes of the trie. Type abstractions for intermediate products that occur during the generation of several product variants can be reused while the product-based analysis step requires to regenerate the type abstractions of the intermediate products. If the generation of the type abstraction of an intermediate product fails, it can be concluded that the associated product and all products in the underlying subtree are not well typed (without actually generating and checking their type abstractions). If the product line evolves, only subtrees including changed delta modules need to be rechecked to ensure type safety of all possible product variants. The presented family-based analysis approach relies solely on the information contained in the product line declaration and is parametric in both the checked property and the language used to implement the products. Thus, the approach can, for instance, be used to check applicability and context conditions in Δ-MontiArc architectural delta models [7].

2   Recalling Delta-Oriented Programming

In order to illustrate DOP, we use a variant of the *expression product line* (EPL) as described, for instance, in [12,15]. We consider the following grammar:

Exp ::= Lit | Add | Neg   Lit ::= <non−negative integers>   Add ::= Exp "+" Exp   Neg ::= "−" Exp

Two operations can be performed on the expressions described by this grammar: printing, which returns the expression as a string, and evaluating, which returns the value of the expression. The products in the EPL can be described by the features concerned with data Lit, Add, Neg and the features concerned with operations Eval and Print. Lit and Print are mandatory features. The features Add, Neg and Eval are optional. The example aims at illustrating the main DOP concepts, rather than to provide an elegant implementation of the EPL.

```
features Lit, Add, Neg, Print, Eval          delta DLitAddPrint{
configurations Lit & Print                     adds class Exp extends Object { // only used as a type
deltas                                           String toString() { return ""; }
  { DLitAddPrint,                              }
    DNeg when Neg }                            adds class Lit extends Exp {
                                                 int value;
  { DLitEval when Eval,                           Lit setLit(int n) { value = n; return this; }
    DNegPrint when Neg,                           String toString() { return value + ""; }
    DNegEval when (Neg & Eval),               }
    DremAdd when !Add }                        adds class Add extends Exp {
                                                 Exp expr1;
  { DAddEval when (Add & Eval),                   Exp expr2;
    DAddNegPrint when (Add & Neg) }               Add setAdd(Exp a, Exp b)
                                                    { expr1 = a; expr2 = b; return this; }
                                                 String toString()
                                                    { return expr1.toString() + "+" + expr2.toString(); }
                            .                  }
                                             }
```

Listing 1. Left: Declaration of the EPL. **Right:** Delta module for a legacy product.

2.1 Concepts of Delta-Oriented Programming

The main concept of DOP are *delta modules*. A delta module may add, remove or modify classes. Modifying a class means to change the super class, to add or to remove fields or methods or to modify methods. The modification of a method can either replace the method body by another implementation, or wrap the existing method using the `original` construct. The `original` construct expresses a call to the method with the same name before the modifications and is bound at the time the product is generated. The right part of Listing 1 contains a delta module for introducing an existing legacy product, realizing the features Lit, Add and Print. Listing 2 contains the delta modules for adding the evaluation functionality to the classes `Lit` and `Add`, for incorporating the Neg feature by adding and modifying the class `Neg`, for facilitating the two optional features Add and Neg to cooperate properly and for removing the Add feature from the legacy product.

A *delta-oriented product line* consists of its *code base* comprising the delta modules and a *product line declaration*. The product line declaration creates the connection to the product features. The left part of Listing 1 shows a product line declaration for the EPL. The `features` clause lists the features. The `configurations` clause declares the set of valid feature configurations by means of a propositional formula over the set of features [3]. A `when` clause, attached to each delta module, declares (by means of a propositional formula over the set of features) for which feature configurations the delta module has to be applied. Since valid feature configurations are used for product generation, the formula specified by the `when` clause is understood as a conjunction with the formula describing the set of valid feature configurations. Additionally, the possible application orders of the delta modules are described by defining a total order on a partition of the set of delta modules. Deltas in the same part can be applied in any order to the previous product, but the order of the parts is fixed. The order of delta module application is defined by an ordered list of the delta module sets which are enclosed by { .. }.

```
delta DLitEval {                              delta DNegPrint {
  modifies Exp {                                modifies Neg {
    adds int eval() { return 0; }                 adds String toString() { return "-" + expr.toString(); }
  }                                             }
  modifies Lit {                              }
    adds int eval() { return value; }
  }                                           delta DNegEval{
}                                               modifies Neg {
                                                  adds int eval() { return (−1) ∗ expr.eval(); }
delta DAddEval {                                }
  modifies Add {                              }
    adds int eval() { return expr1.eval() + expr2.eval(); }
  }                                           delta DAddNegPrint {
}                                               modifies Add {
                                                  modifies toString { return "(" + original + ")"; }
delta DNeg {                                     }
  adds class Neg extends Exp {                 }
    Exp expr;
    Neg setNeg(Exp a) { expr = a; return this; }  delta DremAdd {
  }                                             removes Add
}                                             }
```

Listing 2. Delta modules for Add, Neg, Print and Eval features

In order to obtain a product for a particular feature configuration, the modifications specified in the delta modules with valid application conditions are applied incrementally to the previously generated product. The first delta module is applied to the empty product. The modifications of a delta model are applicable to a (possibly empty) product if each class to be removed or modified exists and, for every modified class, if each method or field to be removed exists, if each method to be modified exists and has the same header as the modified method, and if each class, method or field to be added does not exist. During the generation of a product, every delta module must be applicable. Otherwise, the generation of the product fails.

2.2   IF∆J: A Core Calculus for Product Lines of JAVA Programs

This section recalls IF∆J (IMPERATIVE FEATHERWEIGHT DELTA JAVA) [15], a core calculus for delta oriented programming of product lines of JAVA programs. IF∆J is based on IFJ, an imperative version of FJ [8].

IFJ: A Core Calculus for JAVA Programs. The abstract syntax of the IFJ constructs is given in Figure 1. Following [8], we use the overline notation for possibly empty sequences. The set of variables includes the distinguished variable this (implicitly bound in any method declaration), which cannot be used as the name of a method's formal parameter. A class table CT is a mapping from class names to class definitions. The subtyping relation <: on classes (types) is the reflexive and transitive closure of the immediate extends relation (the immediate subclass relation, given by the extends clauses in CT). The class Object has no members and its definition does not appear in CT. We assume that a class table CT satisfies the following sanity conditions: (i) $CT(C) = $ class C ... for every $C \in dom(CT)$; (ii) for every class name C (except Object) appearing anywhere in CT, we have $C \in dom(CT)$; and (iii) there are no cycles in the transitive closure of the immediate extends relation.

```
CD ::= class C extends C { FD; MD }                          classes
FD ::= C f                                                    fields
MD ::= C m (C̄ x̄){return e; }                                 methods
e  ::= x | e.f | e.m(ē) | new C() | (C)e | e.f = e | null    expressions
```

Fig. 1. Syntax of classes (x ∈ variable names, including `this` and `original`)

```
DM ::= delta δ {CO}                                          delta modules
CO ::= adds CD | removes C | modifies C [extending C] { AO }  class operations
AO ::= adds FD | adds MD | removes a | modifies MD           attribute operations
```

Fig. 2. Syntax of delta modules (δ ∈ delta module names; a ∈ field or method names)

IFΔJ Delta Modules. The abstract syntax of the IFΔJ constructs is given in Figure 2. The constructs for class definitions CD, field definitions FD and method definitions MD are those of IFJ, given in Figure 1. A delta module DM (see Figure 2) specifies a sequence *class operations*. A class operation CO can add, remove or modify a class. A class-modify operation possibly specifies the change of the super class and specifies a sequence of *attribute operations*. An attribute operation AO can add/remove a field-/method or modify a method. A method-modify operation can either replace the method body by another implementation, or wrap the existing method using the distinguished variable `original` (which can occur only in method-modify operations and cannot be used as the name of a method's formal parameter). In both cases, the modified method must have the same header as the unmodified method. An occurrence of `original` represents a call to the unmodified method where the formal parameters of the modified method are passed implicitly as arguments.

IFΔJ Product Lines. In the following, we use the metavariables φ and ψ to range over feature names. A *delta module table* DMT is a mapping from delta module names to delta modules. An IFΔJ product line is a 5-tuple $L = (\{\overline{\varphi}\}, \Phi, \text{DMT}, \Delta, \Pi)$ consisting of:

1. the set of the features $\{\overline{\varphi}\} = \{\varphi_1, \ldots, \varphi_n\}$ ($n \geq 1$) of the product line,
2. the non-empty set of the valid feature configurations $\Phi \subseteq \mathscr{P}(\{\overline{\varphi}\})$ (abstracting from the concrete representation of the feature model),
3. a delta module table DMT containing the delta modules,
4. a mapping $\Delta : \Phi \to \mathscr{P}(dom(\text{DMT}))$ determining for which feature configurations a delta module must be applied (which is denoted by the when clause in the concrete examples), and
5. a totally ordered partition Π of $dom(\text{DMT})$, determining the order of delta module application.

The 4-tuple $(\{\overline{\varphi}\}, \Phi, \Delta, \Pi)$ represents the *product line declaration*, while the delta module table DMT represents the *code base*.

Product Generation. An *application order* is a total order on the delta modules $\overline{\delta} = \delta_1 \cdots \delta_m$ ($m \geq 0$) of the product line that respects the ordered partition $\Pi = S_1 \ldots S_p$ ($m \geq p \geq 0$) (i.e., for all $i < j \in 1..p$, the elements of S_i occur before the elements of S_j). An application order defines a *product generation mapping*, that is, a partial mapping from each feature configuration $\{\overline{\psi}\}$ in Φ to the class table of the product that is obtained by applying the delta modules in $\Delta(\{\overline{\psi}\})$ to the empty class table according to the application order. The product generation mapping can be partial since a non-applicable delta module may be encountered during product generation, such that the resulting product is undefined. The product line is *unambiguous* if all application orders define the same product generation mapping. The products generated by this product generation mapping are the products of L. We write $CT_{\{\overline{\psi}\}}$ to denote the class table generated for the feature configuration $\{\overline{\psi}\}$ and write $<:_{\{\overline{\psi}\}}$ to denote the subtype relation associated with the class table $CT_{\{\overline{\psi}\}}$.

Strongly Unambiguous and Type-Safe IFΔJ Product Lines. An IFΔJ product line is *strongly unambiguous* if every set S of delta modules in Π is *consistent*. That is, if no class added or removed in a delta module of S is added, removed or modified in another delta module of S, and for every class modified in more than one delta module of S, its direct superclass is changed at most by one delta clause and the fields and methods added, modified or removed are distinct. Strong unambiguity is a sufficient condition for unambiguity, i.e., if a product line is strongly unambiguous, then it is also unambiguous. For strong unambiguity, two delta modules that modify the same method cannot be placed in the same partition even if they are never applied together. An IFΔJ product line is *type-safe* if the following conditions hold: (*i*) it is strongly unambiguous, (*ii*) its product generation mapping is total, and (*iii*) all its products are well-typed IFJ programs.

2.3   Constraint-Based Typing for IFΔJ Product Lines

This section recalls the constraint-based type system for IFΔJ [15]. The system analyzes each delta module in isolation. Afterwards, a type abstraction of every possible product variant needs to be checked.

Constraint-Based Typing for IFJ and Type Abstraction of a Program. A *class signature* CS is a class definition deprived of the bodies of its methods. A *class signature table* CST is a mapping from class names to class signatures. We write *signature*(CT) to denote the class signature table consisting of the signatures of the classes in the class table CT. The subtyping relation $<:$ can be read off from the class signature table such that it is possible to check that there are no cycles in the transitive closure of the extends relation. Moreover, by inspecting a class signature table, it is possible to check, for every class C in *dom*(CST), that the names of the fields defined in C are distinct from the names of the fields inherited from its superclasses, and that the type of each method defined in C is equal to the type of any method with the same name defined in any of the superclasses of C. Therefore, in the following we can safely assume that a class signature table satisfies the following sanity conditions: (*i*) CS(C) = class C ... for every C $\in$ *dom*(CS); (*ii*) for every class name C (except Object) appearing anywhere in CS, we have $C \in dom(CS)$; (*iii*) the transitive closure of the immediate `extends` relation is acyclic; (*vi*) $C_1 <: C_2$ implies that, for all method names m, if a m is available in C_2 then both the version of m available in C_1 and the version of m available C_2 have the same type; and (*v*) $C_1 <: C_2$ and $C_1 \neq C_2$ imply that, for all field names f, if $f \in dom(CST(C_2))$ then $f \notin dom(CST(C_1))$. The constraint-based type system of IFJ [15] infers a set of *class constraints* $\mathscr{C}$ for a given program CT collecting the necessary type checks. These constraints can then be checked against the class signature table *signature*(CT) to establish whether CT is a well-typed IFJ program. Therefore, the pair $\langle signature(\text{CT}), \mathscr{C} \rangle$ suffices to establish whether CT is type safe. We call the pair $\langle signature(\text{CT}), \mathscr{C} \rangle$ the *type abstraction of the program* CT.

Constraint-Based Typing for IFΔJ and Type Abstraction of a Delta Module. A *delta module signature* DMS is the analogue of a class signature for a delta module. The abstract syntax of delta module signatures is obtained from the syntax of delta modules, in Fig. 2, by replacing class definitions (CD) with class signatures (CS) and by replacing method definitions (MD) with method headers (MH). Delta module signatures can be obtained by a straightforward inspection of each delta module in isolation. We write *signature*(δ) to denote the signature of the delta module δ. For each valid feature configuration $\{\overline{\psi}\}$, the class signature table $\text{CST}_{\{\overline{\psi}\}}$ of the product $\text{CT}_{\{\overline{\psi}\}}$ can be generated by applying the signature of the delta modules in $\Delta(\{\overline{\psi}\})$ to the empty class signature table according to the given application order (similarly to product generation). The generation of the product signature succeeds if and only if the generation of the corresponding product would succeed. The constraint-based type system of IFΔJ [15] infers, for each delta module, a *set of class-constraint operations* $\mathscr{D}_\delta$ which transform the class constraints in the same way as the delta module operations transform the class implementations. For each valid feature configuration $\{\overline{\psi}\}$, the set of class constraints $\mathscr{C}_{\{\overline{\psi}\}}$ of the product $\text{CT}_{\{\overline{\psi}\}}$ can be generated by applying the sets of class-constraint operations inferred for the delta modules in $\Delta(\{\overline{\psi}\})$ to the empty set of class constraints. We call the pair $\langle signature(\delta), \mathscr{D}_\delta \rangle$ the *type abstraction of the delta module* δ denoted by *typeAbstraction*(δ).

Product-Based Analysis of Type-Safety for IFΔJ Product Lines. For every valid feature configuration $\{\overline{\psi}\}$, we write *typeAbstraction*($\{\overline{\psi}\}$) to denote the type abstraction of the product $\text{CT}_{\{\overline{\psi}\}}$, which is the pair $\langle \text{CST}_{\{\overline{\psi}\}}, \mathscr{C}_{\{\overline{\psi}\}} \rangle$. A *delta module type abstraction table* is a mapping from delta module names to delta module type abstractions. We write *typeAbstraction*(DMT) to denote the table of the type abstractions of the delta modules in the table DMT. The type abstraction *typeAbstraction*(L) of an IFΔJ product line $L = (\{\overline{\varphi}\}, \Phi, \text{DMT}, \Delta, \Pi)$ is the 5-tuple $(\{\overline{\varphi}\}, \Phi, typeAbstraction(\text{DMT}), \Delta, \Pi)$. Strong unambiguity can be efficiently established by only considering delta module signatures and the declaration of the partition Π (since the consistency of a set of delta modules, cf. the end of Section 2.2, can be checked by only considering delta module signatures). Then, type safety of an IFΔJ product line can be established only based on its type abstraction by a straightforward product-based analysis step that generates the type abstraction of each product (without generating the actual implementation of the product).

3   Family-Based Analysis of Type-Safety for IFΔJ Product Lines

In this section, we present a family-based analysis step which enhances the product-based analysis step illustrated at the end of Section 2 by making it possible to reuse the intermediate results of the analysis associated to the product variants.

In the following, without loss of generality, we assume: a *fixed* IFΔJ product line $L = (\{\overline{\varphi}\}, \Phi, \text{DMT}, \Delta, \Pi)$; the set of feature is non-empty; the set of valid feature configurations in non-empty and does not contain the empty feature configuration; there is at least one delta module; and each delta module is used in at least one valid feature configuration.

3.1   Product Family Generation Trie

For every application order $\overline{\delta} = \delta_1 \cdots \delta_m$ $(m \geq 1)$ and every feature configuration $\{\overline{\psi}\} \in \Phi$, we write $\pi_{\{\overline{\psi}\}}^{\overline{\delta}}$ to denote the *product generation string* of $\{\overline{\psi}\}$, that is, the subsequence of $\overline{\delta}$ obtained by keeping only the delta modules that are in $\Delta(\{\overline{\psi}\})$. The *Product Family Generation Strings* (PFGS) of the product line for the application order $\overline{\delta}$ are the sequences of delta modules required to obtain the valid products of the product line, i.e., the elements of the set $\{\pi_{\{\overline{\psi}\}}^{\overline{\delta}} \mid \{\overline{\psi}\} \in \Phi\}$. We write $\tau^{\overline{\delta}}$ to denote the *Product Family Generation Trie* (PFGT) of the product line for the application order $\overline{\delta}$, that is, the trie [6] that represents the PFGS for $\overline{\delta}$. A trie is a tree that represents a set of strings by factoring out the common prefixes. Its structure is uniquely determined by the set of strings it represents, so the order in which the strings are inserted into the tree does not change its structure. The PFGT can be built from the PFGS by exploiting standard algorithms for trie construction.

Formally, $\tau^{\overline{\delta}}$ is the largest node-labelled, edge-labelled tree such that: each node is labeled by either the empty label or by a valid feature configuration, the edges of the tree are labeled by delta modules names, and the following structural properties are satisfied: (*i*) for each node, the edges that connect the node to its children have pairwise distinct labels; (*ii*) for each node, the labels of the path from the root to the node are a prefix of a sequence $\pi_{\{\overline{\psi}\}}^{\overline{\delta}}$ for some feature configuration $\{\overline{\psi}\} \in \Phi$; (*iii*) each node such that the path from the root to the node is the sequence $\pi_{\{\overline{\psi}\}}^{\overline{\delta}}$, for some feature configuration $\{\overline{\psi}\} \in \Phi$, is labeled by the feature configuration $\{\overline{\psi}\}$; and (*iv*) the other nodes are labeled by the empty label.

By construction, it holds that: the root is labeled with the empty label (since the empty product never corresponds to a valid feature configuration); the leaves are labelled by valid feature configuration corresponding to the respective product variants; and each valid feature configuration labels exactly one node corresponding to the respective product variant. A trie $\tau^{\overline{\delta}}$ describes a strategy for generating the products (or their type abstractions) by reusing the intermediate results obtained during product generation.

Example 1. Consider the EPL example introduced in Section 2. The partition Π is

{ DLitAddPrint, DNeg } { DLitEval, DNegPrint, DNegEval, DremAdd } { DAddEval, DAddNegPrint }

Therefore, there are 96 (= (2!) * (4!) * (2!)) possible application orders. The PFGTs associated to the following three application orders

1.   DLitAddPrint DNeg DLitEval DNegPrint DNegEval DremAdd DAddEval DAddNegPrint
2.   DLitAddPrint DNeg DLitEval DNegPrint DremAdd DNegEval DAddEval DAddNegPrint
3.   DNeg DLitAddPrint DremAdd DNegEval DNegPrint DLitEval DAddEval DAddNegPrint

are listed in Fig.s 3(a), 3(b) and 4, respectively.

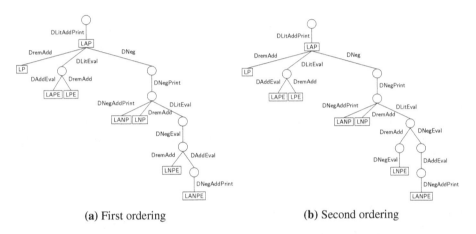

(a) First ordering   (b) Second ordering

Fig. 3. PFGTs for the EPL example

3.2   Checking Type-Safety by Using the Product Family Generation Trie

The type-safety of the product line can be checked by choosing an application order $\overline{\delta}$ and traversing the trie $\tau^{\overline{\delta}}$ in depth-first order to generate and check the type abstractions of all the products as follows:

- when the root is visited, the type abstraction of the empty program is generated;
- when a child node is reached from a parent note by means of an edge with label δ, the delta module type abstraction *typeAbstraction*(δ) is applied to the program type abstractions generated when visiting the parent node;
- when a node labeled by a valid feature configuration $\{\overline{\psi}\}$ is reached, the product type abstraction *typeAbstraction*($\{\overline{\psi}\}$) is used to check whether the associated product is well typed; and
- when a non-applicable delta module abstraction *typeAbstraction*(δ) is encountered, the associated subtree is pruned and the checking of the products associated to the valid feature configurations that occur in the pruned subtree is considered as failed.

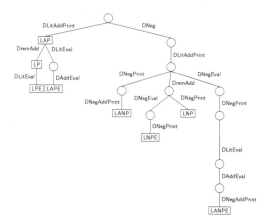

Fig. 4. PFGTs for the EPL example with Third Ordering

In order to reuse the intermediate program type abstractions, it is enough to store only the program type abstractions associated to the nodes that have at least a child that has not yet been visited. Changing the product line declaration and/or the delta modules in the code base of a type safe product line in most cases only affects the checks within a subtree of the PFGT. Therefore, type safety of the new product line can be checked by redoing only the checks within that subtree while for the product-based approach [15] all affected products need to be completely re-generated and checked.

3.3   Minimizing the Size of PFGTs

The number of operations needed to check the type safety of the product line can be minimized by choosing an application order $\overline{\delta}$ that minimizes the number of nodes in the trie $\tau^{\overline{\delta}}$.

Example 2. The PFGTs associated to the first application order, depicted in Figure 3(a), requires to compute 14 type abstractions (excluding the root), the second application order, depicted in Figure 3(b), requires 15 type abstractions, and the third application order, depicted in Figure 4, requires 18 type abstractions. Indeed, the number of nodes of the first PFGT is minimal. As a comparison, the product-based analysis step described at the end of Section 2 requires to compute 30 type abstractions for analyzing each product in isolation.

Given the totally ordered partition $\Pi = S_1 \ldots S_p$ ($p \geq 1$) of the delta modules, there are $(|S_1|!) * \cdots * (|S_p|!)$ possible application orders. Some of these application orders may generate the same PFGT. In order to describe the application orders that minimize the number of nodes of the PFGT, we consider how the delta modules are applied for different feature configurations. For each feature φ in the set of the product line features $\{\overline{\varphi}\}$, we consider a propositional variable with the same name. We say that a propositional formula P *characterizes* a set of feature configurations $\Psi \subseteq \mathscr{P}(\{\overline{\varphi}\})$ to mean that: $\{\,\{\overline{\psi}\} \subseteq \{\overline{\varphi}\} \mid P[\overline{\psi} := \mathbf{true}, (\overline{\varphi}/\overline{\psi}) := \mathbf{false}]\,\} = \Psi$. Additionally, we consider a propositional formula VFC that characterizes the set of valid feature configurations Φ; and for each delta module δ in $dom(\Delta)$, we consider a propositional formula W_δ such that the formula VFC $\wedge W_\delta$ characterizes the set of the feature configurations $\{\overline{\psi}\}$ such that $\delta \in \Delta(\{\overline{\psi}\})$. In the examples in Section 2, the formulas W_δ are introduced by using the when clauses. Furthermore, we consider the abbreviations:

- **implies**$_{\delta',\delta''}$ = VFC $\rightarrow$ $(W_{\delta'} \rightarrow W_{\delta''})$ to say that the application condition of delta δ' implies the application condition of delta δ''.
- **iff**$_{\delta',\delta''}$ = **implies**$_{\delta',\delta''} \wedge$ **implies**$_{\delta'',\delta'}$ to say that both delta modules δ' and δ'' are always applied together.

For the totally ordered partition $\Pi = S_1 \ldots S_p$ $(p \geq 1)$ of the delta modules in a product line, we say that a linear order of the delta modules in one partition S_i is:

- *implication-compliant* to mean that for all $\delta', \delta'' \in S_i$ such that $\delta' \neq \delta''$:
  1. if **implies**$_{\delta',\delta''}$ is a tautology and **implies**$_{\delta'',\delta'}$ is not a tautology, then δ'' precedes δ', and
  2. if **iff**$_{\delta',\delta''}$ is a tautology, then for every delta module δ that occurs between δ' and δ'' also **iff**$_{\delta',\delta}$ is a tautology;
- *implication-determined* to mean that it is implication compliant and all the implication compliant orders of S_i may only differ by permutation of delta modules δ' and δ'' where **iff**$_{\delta',\delta''}$ is a tautology.

An application order is *implication-compliant* if, for each set S_i in Π, the elements of S_i occur in implication-compliant order, and *implication-determined* if, for each set S_i in Π, the elements of S_i occur in implication-determined order.

Example 3. Both the first and the second application order in Example 1 are implication-compliant. The third application order is not implication-compliant (since, e.g., DNeg precedes DLitAddPrint, while **implies**$_{\text{DNeg,DLitAddPrint}}$ is a tautology and **implies**$_{\text{DLitAddPrint,DNeg}}$ is not a tautology).

For every product line such that each delta module is used for at least one valid feature configuration there is at least one implication-compliant application order. However, a product line may not have an implication-determined application order (like in the EPL example in Section 2). The following theorem shows that any application order that minimizes the number of nodes of the PFGT must be implication-compliant.

Theorem 1. *If the application order $\overline{\delta}$ minimizes the nodes of the PFGT $\tau^{\overline{\delta}}$, then $\overline{\delta}$ is implication-compliant.*

Proof (sketch). Assume that $\overline{\delta}$ minimizes the nodes of the PFGT $\tau^{\overline{\delta}}$ and $\overline{\delta}$ is not implication-compliant. Then there are $\delta_1, \delta_2 \in S_i \in \Pi$ such that δ_2 precedes δ_1, **implies**$_{\delta_2,\delta_1}$ is a tautology and **implies**$_{\delta_1,\delta_2}$ is not a tautology. Any generation string that contains δ_1 contains also δ_2, while there is at least one generation string that contains δ_2 and does not contain δ_1. Therefore, swapping δ_1 and δ_2 in the application order decreases the number of nodes in the associated PFGT, which is incompatible with the assumption that $\tau^{\overline{\delta}}$ is minimal. $\qquad\square$

The following theorem shows that any implication-determined application order minimize the number of nodes of the PFGT.

Theorem 2. *If the application order* $\overline{\delta}$ *is implication-determined, then for any other application order* $\overline{\delta}'$ *the number of nodes in the PFGT* $\tau^{\overline{\delta}}$ *is less or equal than the number of nodes in the PFGT* $\tau^{\overline{\delta}'}$.

Proof (sketch). Assume that there is an implication determined application order. Consider $\delta_1, \delta_2 \in S_i \in \Pi$ such that $\delta_1 \neq \delta_2$.

- If $\mathbf{iff}_{\delta_1,\delta_2}$ is a tautology, then any generation string π contains δ_1 if and only if π contains δ_2. Therefore, swapping δ_1 and δ_2 does not change the number of nodes in the associated PFGT.
- If $\mathbf{iff}_{\delta_1,\delta_2}$ is not tautology, then either (*i*) $\mathbf{implies}_{\delta_2,\delta_1}$ is a tautology or (*ii*) $\mathbf{implies}_{\delta_1,\delta_2}$ is a tautology (since the application order is implication-determined). Assume the first case (the second is symmetric). Any generation string that contains δ_1 contains also δ_2, while there is at least one generation string that contains δ_2 and does not contain δ_1. Therefore, putting δ_1 before δ_2 in the application order decreases the number of nodes in the associated PFGT. □

An implication-compliant application order can be computed by building, for each set S_i in Π, a directed graph G_i (that we call the *implication graph* of S_i) where the nodes are the elements of S_i, and for each pair $\delta', \delta'' \in S$ such that $\delta' \neq \delta''$ and $\mathbf{implies}_{\delta',\delta''}$ is a tautology, there is an edge from δ'' to δ'. Any topological order of the strongly connected components of G_i represents a class of implication-compliant orders on S_i (the order of the delta modules in the same strongly connected component does not matter). There exists an implication-determined application order if and only if for every S_i there is a unique topological order of the strongly connected components of G_i.

If there is no implication-determined application order for a product line, the programmer might, for instance:

- change the partition (e.g., by splitting some sets) in order to create an implication-determined application order (this might increase the number of nodes of the minimal PFGT, since some application orders are ruled out), or
- ask the system to iterate over all the classes of implication-compliant application orders to find the PFGT with minimum number of nodes, or
- ask the system to apply some heuristic to select an implication-compliant application order that generates a PFGT with the minimum number of nodes or a number of nodes that approximates the minimum.

3.4 Heuristics

A heuristic can be specified by defining a function $\natural_m$ that associates to each delta module δ a natural number $\natural_m(\delta)$, the measure of δ. Using this measure, the delta modules δ' and δ'' in one partition can be sorted if $\mathbf{implies}_{\delta',\delta''}$ and $\mathbf{implies}_{\delta'',\delta'}$ are not tautologies. We say that a linear order of the delta modules in a partition S_i is *implication-measure-compliant* if it is implication-compliant and, for each $\delta', \delta'' \in S_i$, if **implies**$_{\delta',\delta''}$ and **implies**$_{\delta'',\delta'}$ are not tautologies, then δ' and δ'' are sorted by non-increasing measure order. An application order is implication-measure-compliant if, for each set S_i in Π, the elements of S_i occur in implication-measure-compliant order.

In the following, we define two measures, the height and the size of a delta module δ, giving rise to specific heuristics. The *height* of a delta module $\delta \in S_i$, denoted by $\sharp_h(\delta)$, is the length of the longest PFGS postfix that contains only delta modules in the set $\bigcup_{j \in i..n} S_j$ (that is, in S_i or in a subsequent set of the partition). In a PFGT, this is the length of the longest ascending subpath that starts from a leaf and contains only delta modules in $\bigcup_{j \in i..n} S_j$. Since all application orders respect the total order on the partition Π, the height of a delta module is independent of the actually selected application order.

For defining the *size* of a delta module $\delta \in S_i$, denoted by $\sharp_s(\delta)$, we consider the formula **together**$_{\delta',\delta''} = \mathrm{VFC} \wedge W_{\delta'} \wedge W_{\delta''}$ which states that there are feature configurations in which the two deltas are applied together. The *size* of a delta module $\delta \in S_i$ is the number of delta modules in the set $\bigcup_{j \in i..n} S_j$ that can be applied with δ, which is the number of elements of the set: $\{$ **together**$_{\delta,\delta'}$ satisfiable $\mid \delta' \in S_j$ for some $j \geq i\}$.

The following proposition shows that both the height and the size heuristics refine implication-compliance.

Proposition 1. *Let* $\delta', \delta'' \in S \in \Pi$. *If* **implies**$_{\delta',\delta''}$ *is a tautology, then both* $\sharp_s(\delta') \leq \sharp_s(\delta'')$ *and* $\sharp_h(\delta') \leq \sharp_h(\delta'')$ *hold.*

Proof. Since **implies**$_{\delta',\delta''}$ is a tautology, any path in a PFGT containing δ' contains also δ''. $\qquad\square$

Example 4. For the EPL example given in Section 2, the height and the size heuristics are equivalent (and work well). We have $\sharp_h(\mathsf{DNegEval}) = 5$, $\sharp_h(\mathsf{DremAdd}) = 4$, $\sharp_h(\mathsf{DAddEval}) = \sharp_h(\mathsf{DAddNegPrint}) = 1$, and $\sharp_s(\mathsf{DNegEval}) = 5$, $\sharp_s(\mathsf{DremAdd}) = 4$, $\sharp_s(\mathsf{DAddEval}) = \sharp_s(\mathsf{DAddNegPrint}) = 1$. Thus, the implication-height and implication-size orders are equivalent. The first application order in Example 1, which generates a minimal PFGT, is both implication-height and implication-size compliant, while the second is implication-compliant and not height/size-compliant. The third application order in Example 1 is a (not implication-compliant) reverse height/size-compliant order. Changing the order in the first given application ordering by swapping the delta modules DLitEval and DNegPrint and/or by swapping the the delta modules DAddEval and DAddNegPrint, which are the only delta modules that can be swapped while preserving implication-height/size-compliance, does not change the number of nodes of the associated PFGT.

For each set S_i in Π, let C_i be the set of the strongly connected components of the implication graph G_i, and let D_i be subset of C_i containing only the strongly connected components c such that: for some other c' in C_i, either in G_i there exists no path from c to c' or vice versa. An implication-measure-compliant application order for the delta modules in S_i can be found by computing, for each c in D_i, the measure of one of the delta modules in c, since, by Proposition 1, all delta modules in c have the same measure.

4   Related Work

Type checking techniques for software product lines can be classified according to the applied analysis strategy. Product-based strategies consider every possible product of the product line. Family-based analyses check a combined representation of all possible products, i.e., the family, in a single analysis run. Feature-based analyses consider the building blocks of the products, e.g., the feature or delta modules, one by one.

FEATHERWEIGHT FEATURE JAVA (FFJ) [2] is a calculus for stepwise-refinement. It provides a product-based type system which requires to generate and check all possible products. The FFJ for Product Lines (FFJ$_{PL}$) calculus [1] extends FFJ. In FFJ$_{PL}$, feature-oriented mechanisms, such as class/method refinements, are modeled by the dynamic semantics of the language leading to a family-based representation of all products. The FFJ$_{PL}$ typing rules directly analyze this representation resulting in a family-based type checking strategy. The resulting analysis is not feature-based since each feature module is analyzed by relying on information of the complete product line.

The type system of LIGHTWEIGHT FEATURE JAVA (LFJ) [5] first uses a feature-based analysis step where constraints for the feature modules are generated, similar to the approach presented in this paper. Afterwards, the generated constraints based on propositional formulation of the feature model and the composition ordering are used to construct a propositional formula for the whole family of products. This formula is checked in a single run, leading to a combined feature-family-based analysis strategy. In order to deal with the additional flexibility provided by delta modules, the constraint-based type system for delta-oriented product lines (cf. Section 2) infers more complex constraints (including constraint operations) which seems not suitable to be efficiently encoded by a propositional formula.

In this paper, we enhance the existing constraint-based type checking approach for DOP [15] by providing a family-based analysis step which improves the product-based analysis step by making it possible to reuse the intermediate results of the analysis associated to the product variants. An orthogonal approach to analyzing delta-oriented product lines [11] aims at analyzing the product generation process and the applicability of the delta modules. However, it does not consider the actual type safety of the generated products.

The use of a tree structure for a family-based analysis of delta-oriented product lines is first proposed for architectural variability modeling in Δ-MontiArc [7]. Using a family application order tree (FAOT), it is checked that each delta is applicable in its positions of the possible delta sequences. The FAOT provides an over-approximation of the set of possible products. Instead, PFGTs presented in this paper give an exact representation of all possible product variants and generation sequences.

5   Conclusions and Future Work

The family-based analysis framework presented in Section 3 relies solely on the information contained in the product line declaration (cf. Section 2.2) and is parametric in both the checked property and the language used to implement the products. Thus, the framework can, for instance, be instantiated to check applicability and context conditions in Δ-MontiArc architectural delta models [7]. In future work, we aim at building a tool for managing the generation of a minimal (and/or of an approximation of a minimal) PFGT associated to a given DOP product line declaration. We also plan to refine the notion of PFGT minimality by taking into account, for instance, the number of changes in a single delta module (number of attributes added/modified/removed). In the formulation of DOP considered in this paper, the partial order between delta modules (to be respected by every application order) is specified by means of a totally ordered partition of the set of the delta modules. The original formulation of DOP [14] and the Δ-MontiArc architectural delta models make it possible to specify any partial order between delta modules. Although we believe that from the programmer's point of view the specification by ordered partitions is intuitive to use, the ability to specify an arbitrary partial order might open more possibilities for PFGT minimization.

References

1. Apel, S., Kästner, C., Grösslinger, A., Lengauer, C.: Type safety for feature-oriented product lines. Automated Software Engineering 17(3), 251–300 (2010)
2. Apel, S., Kästner, C., Lengauer, C.: Feature Featherweight Java: A Calculus for Feature-Oriented Programming and Stepwise Refinement. In: GPCE, pp. 101–112. ACM (2008)
3. Batory, D.: Feature Models, Grammars, and Propositional Formulas. In: Obbink, H., Pohl, K. (eds.) SPLC 2005. LNCS, vol. 3714, pp. 7–20. Springer, Heidelberg (2005)
4. Batory, D., Sarvela, J., Rauschmayer, A.: Scaling Step-Wise Refinement. IEEE Trans. Software Eng. 30(6), 355–371 (2004)
5. Delaware, B., Cook, W., Batory, D.: A Machine-Checked Model of Safe Composition. In: FOAL, pp. 31–35. ACM (2009)
6. Fredkin, E.: Trie memory. Commun. ACM 3(9), 490–499 (1960)
7. Haber, A., Kutz, T., Rendel, H., Rumpe, B., Schaefer, I.: Towards a family-based analysis of applicability conditions in architectural delta models. In: VARY: Variability for You (Workshop Co-Located with MODELS 2011) (2011)
8. Igarashi, A., Pierce, B., Wadler, P.: Featherweight Java: A minimal core calculus for Java and GJ. ACM TOPLAS 23(3), 396–450 (2001)
9. Kästner, C., Apel, S., ur Rahman, S.S., Rosenmüller, M., Batory, D., Saake, G.: On the Impact of the Optional Feature Problem: Analysis and Case Studies. In: SPLC, pp. 181–190. ACM (2009)
10. Krueger, C.: Eliminating the Adoption Barrier. IEEE Software 19(4), 29–31 (2002)
11. Lienhardt, M., Clarke, D.: Row types for delta-oriented programming. In: VaMoS, pp. 121–128 (2012)
12. Lopez-Herrejon, R.E., Batory, D., Cook, W.: Evaluating Support for Features in Advanced Modularization Technologies. In: Gao, X.-X. (ed.) ECOOP 2005. LNCS, vol. 3586, pp. 169–194. Springer, Heidelberg (2005)
13. Pohl, K., Böckle, G., van der Linden, F.: Software Product Line Engineering - Foundations, Principles, and Techniques. Springer (2005)
14. Schaefer, I., Bettini, L., Bono, V., Damiani, F., Tanzarella, N.: Delta-Oriented Programming of Software Product Lines. In: Bosch, J., Lee, J. (eds.) SPLC 2010. LNCS, vol. 6287, pp. 77–91. Springer, Heidelberg (2010)
15. Schaefer, I., Bettini, L., Damiani, F.: Compositional Type-Checking for Delta-Oriented Programming. In: AOSD 2011. ACM (2011)
16. Schaefer, I., Damiani, F.: Pure Delta-oriented Programming. In: FOSD 2010 (2010), http://www.fosd.de/2010
17. Thüm, T., Apel, S., Kästner, C., Kuhlemann, M., Schaefer, I., Saake, G.: Analysis Strategies for Software Product Lines. Technical Report FIN-004-2012, School of Computer Science, University of Magdeburg, Germany (April 2012)

A Vision for Behavioural Model-Driven Validation of Software Product Lines

Xavier Devroey[1], Maxime Cordy[1], Gilles Perrouin[1], Eun-Young Kang[1],
Pierre-Yves Schobbens[1], Patrick Heymans[1,2], Axel Legay[3], and Benoit Baudry[3]

[1] PReCISE Research Center, Faculty of Computer Science,
University of Namur, Belgium
[2] INRIA Lille-Nord Europe, Université Lille 1 – LIFL – CNRS, France
[3] INRIA Rennes Bretagne Atlantique, France

Abstract. The Software Product Lines (SPLs) paradigm promises faster development cycles and increased quality by systematically reusing software assets. This paradigm considers a family of systems, each of which can be obtained by a selection of features in a variability model. Though essential, providing Quality Assurance (QA) techniques for SPLs has long been perceived as a very difficult challenge due to the combinatorics induced by variability and for which very few techniques were available. Recently, important progress has been made by the model-checking and testing communities to address this QA challenge, in a very disparate way though. We present our vision for a unified framework combining model-checking and testing approaches applied to behavioural models of SPLs. Our vision relies on Featured Transition Systems (FTSs), an extension of transition systems supporting variability. This vision is also based on model-driven technologies to support practical SPL modelling and orchestrate various QA scenarios. We illustrate one of such scenarios on a vending machine SPL.

Keywords: Software Product Line, Model-Based Testing, Model-Checking.

1 Introduction

The manufacturing industry achieved economies of scope based on the idea that a product of a certain family (e.g., cars) may be built by systematically reusing assets, with some of them common to all family members (e.g., wheels, bodywork, etc.) and others only shared by a subset of the family (e.g., automatic transmission, manual transmission, leather seats, etc.). The Software Product Line (SPL) paradigm [35] applies this idea to software products. In SPL engineering, we usually associate assets with so-called *features* and we regard a product as a combination of features. Features can be designed and specified using modelling languages such as UML, while the set of legal combinations of features (that is, the set of *valid* products) is captured by a *feature model* (FM) [24].

As in single-system development, the engineer will have to improve confidence in the different products of an SPL, using appropriate Quality Assurance (QA) techniques. Two popular QA approaches are *model-checking* and *testing*. Model checking [6] performs systematic analyses on behavioural models in order to assess the satisfaction of

T. Margaria and B. Steffen (Eds.): ISoLA 2012, Part I, LNCS 7609, pp. 208–222, 2012.

the intended temporal and qualitative requirements and properties. As a complement to model-checking, *testing* [27] determines whether or not actual executions of the system behave as expected.

In this SPL context, testing or model checking every possible software product rapidly becomes unfeasible, due to a possibly huge number of different combinations of features. This explains why, despite being identified as a research area for years, the development of practical SPL testing techniques is still in an immature stage [14].

This is not a reason to give up, though. On the one hand, we observe significant progress in the SPL verification area and the emergence of efficient model-checking techniques [2,3,7,9,17,20,25,26]. On the other hand, the testing community has also progressed in this direction by adapting combinatorial interaction testing techniques to the SPL context [32,33,34]. Furthermore, Model-Based Testing (MBT) [39] is a very efficient approach for addressing test concerns for large and complex systems.

These promising results motivate our will to unify MBT and model checking techniques in one framework in order to perform practical, model-based QA of SPLs. It relies upon UML [30] and Featured Transition Systems (FTSs) [8], a formalism for modelling the behaviour of SPLs.

This vision paper sketches this future framework, presenting actual achievements in QA of SPLs and challenges ahead. Section 2 presents a state of the art in variability modelling, model checking and model-based testing. Section 3 gives an overview of the framework and its different QA activities. Section 4 describes how SPL behaviour can be given in UML and how products of interest elicited. Section 5 illustrates QA activities on a running example. Finally, section 6 wraps up with conclusions and outlines future research directions.

2   Background

In this section, we recapitulate theoretical background regarding management of variability and formal verification in SPLs engineering.

2.1   Variability Management

Variability Modelling. Pohl et al. define features in [35] as an end-user visible characteristic of a system. Features are used by the different stakeholders of a project as an abstraction to support reasoning and are generally represented in a FM. The most common representation for a FM is a Feature Diagram (FD) [24]. For example, Fig. 1 presents the FD of a soda vending machine [8]. A product derived from this diagram will correspond to a set of selected features, for example $\{v, b, s, cur, eur\}$ corresponds to a machine that sells soda (and only soda) in euro. Such a set is called a configuration of the FM. Feature models have been equipped with formal semantics [36], automated analyses and tools [24] for more than 20 years.

SPL Behavioural Modelling. Formalisms allowing the description of SPL behaviour can be classified according to the kind of language they rely upon:

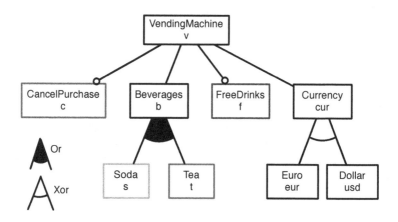

Fig. 1. Example of Feature Diagram: the soda vending machine [8]

- **UML-based approaches.** Several approaches consider using UML to model SPL behaviour. For example, Ziadi and Jézéquel [42] illustrate the usage of UML 2 sequence diagrams and statecharts in the context of product derivation. Czarnecki et al. [12] map features to UML activity diagrams. Our proposal, based on state machines, will be detailed in Section 4.
- **Transition system approaches.** Fischbein et al. propose in [17] to use Modal Transition Systems (MTSs) to model SPLs with some extensions, which were provided by Fantechi and Gnesi in [15,16]. Li et al.[26] model each feature as an independent state machine. The behaviour of a given product is then the state machine that results from the combination of its features.
- **Algebraic Approaches.** Gruler et al. [20,19] augment process algebra with an operator that allows to model variability in the form of alternative choice between two processes.

UML-based approaches are easy to adopt, based on the *lingua franca* of modelling. Since UML has no formal semantics, one should be provided [42], especially for QA purposes. MTSs are transition systems with compulsory and optional transitions. Although they are able to model optional behaviour, they do not include an explicit notion of features. The same issue arises in the approach proposed by Gruler et al. Finally, Li et al. do not consider cross-cutting features that cannot be modelled as an automaton.

To allow the explicit mapping from feature to SPL behaviour, FTSs [8] were proposed. FTSs are Transition Systems (TSs) where each transition is labelled with a feature expression (i.e., a boolean expression over features of the SPL), specifying for a given FD in which products the transition may be fired. Thus it is possible to determine which products are the cause of a violation or a failed test.

The semantics of an FTS is a function that associates each valid product with its set of finite and infinite executions, i.e. all the possible paths in the graph available for this specific product. According to this definition, an FTS is actually a behavioural model of a whole SPL. Fig. 2 presents the FTS modelling a vending machine SPL. For instance,

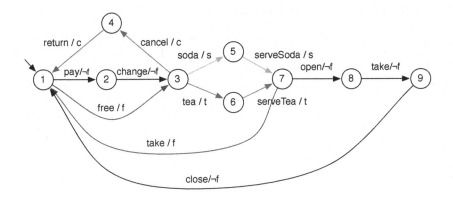

Fig. 2. FTS example: the soda vending machine [8]

transition $①\overset{pay/\neg f}{\longrightarrow}②$ is labelled with the $\neg f$ feature expression. This means that only the products that do not have the feature *FreeDrinks f* are able to execute the transition.

While FTSs can be efficiently analysed and verified [9,7], they are not meant to be designed directly by engineers. In particular, they lack structuring mechanisms. We will illustrate how UML can be combined with FTSs in Section 5.

2.2 Model Checking and Product Lines

Many variability-intensive systems are safety critical. Embedded systems, for instance, are often developed as product lines [13]. The highest levels of QA, including formal verification, are thus needed. Existing verification techniques were mostly developed for single systems. Using those techniques to verify SPLs is tedious, since the number of possible products is exponential in the number of features.

Model checking [6,4] has proven to be a powerful technique for verifying systems against properties expressed in temporal logics. Classical model checking is currently restricted to single systems, but we started to investigate how to use it efficiently on product lines, taking advantage of the fact that large parts of the behaviour are common to many products. This commonality must already be present in the model. We presented above FTSs. Model-checking also requires a specification formula, that must take variability into account. To this purpose, we defined fCTL and fLTL, that are the well-known logics CTL and LTL (resp.) with additional feature symbols. These symbols (called quantifiers) restrict the set of products verified against a given temporal property. As an alternative, one could use the products-restraint operator on FTSs [10]. This operator modifies an FTS so that only the behaviour of specific products is represented in the model. Our model-checking algorithms take the commonality between the products into account and avoid to re-check common behaviour.

Some of the modelling approaches presented above [17,26,20,19] offer model-checking facilities. Yet, because of their feature mapping limitations, they are unable to keep track of the exact behaviour of each product during QA tasks.

2.3 Model-Based Testing and Product Lines

Testing each product of an SPL also faces the same exponential explosion. We therefore need to reason on testing activities at the SPL level, in an abstract manner. MBT [39], like model checking, starts from models of the system under test but provides automated means to derive tests according to test criteria. MBT is thus an excellent candidate to solve this issue. Although behavioural MBT is well established for single-system testing [38], a recent survey [31] shows insufficient support of SPL-based MBT, both in terms of automation and of integration in the development lifecycle. In this paper, we will illustrate a possible integration of testing activities within SPL modelling and QA efforts and focus on the selection of relevant products for testing or/and verification.

3 Overview

Our vision, sketched in Fig. 3, is based on formal model-driven engineering and aims to provide an end-to-end QA framework for SPL. This framework organizes SPL modelling and QA activities within two layers: *modelling* and *design & validation*. These activities are orchestrated by three cooperating roles (roles' interaction is not shown in the figure): *functional architect* who defines SPL behaviour and specifies criteria for selecting products of interest at the requirements level; *QA manager* responsible of QA artifacts and the orchestration of QA tasks; and *Designer* who may refine FTSs with specific behaviour.

Our framework supports the following sequence of activities. First, the SPL is modelled according to its requirements. The functional architect specifies the FM representing the variability of the SPL and expresses SPL behaviour in a *State Diagram Variability Analysis* (SDVA) model. The SDVA formalism is currently under development and will be defined as a UML profile for state machine diagrams. The purpose of the SDVA model is to facilitate behavioural modelling by using a standard notation that offers richer constructions than pure FTSs. Amongst other things, we will support hierarchical constructs (composite states), useful to abstract details during requirements elicitation and orthogonal states used to model parallel behaviours in sub-states. In addition to this SDVA model, criteria for selecting products of interest are defined.

Second, the obtained SPL model is validated. The hierarchical behavioural models (namely, the SDVA) are flattened into FTSs. The QA manager then proceeds with the selection of a specific set of products, test cases, and temporal properties to verify. As we explain in the sequel, the selection of products can be achieved through the specification of conditions over the features, test coverage, or model checking. These criteria have been previously defined by the functional architect. The designer may refine the validation model with product-specific properties. For example, one may refine actions defined on FTS transitions with TSs to obtain a full behavioural model of the SPL (denoted by FTS' in Fig. 3), allowing in-depth analysis of the selected products. Finally, the product QA manager sets various parameters for the application of validation tools and retrieves validation outcomes (not shown in the figure). The selected products are then verified against the chosen temporal properties and refined test cases define the scenarios to be executed on the SPL's implementation.

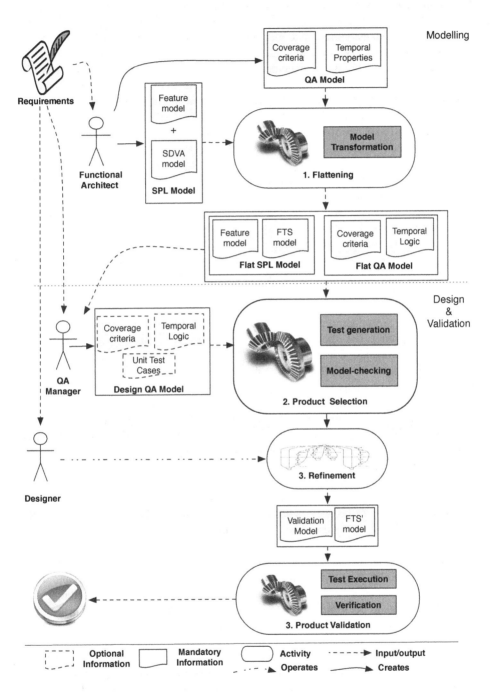

Fig. 3. Framework overview

4   Modelling SPL Behaviour with SDVA

An SDVA is an extension of a state machine diagram with variability operators. As in FTSs, transitions in SDVAs are annotated with constraints over the set of features. A given software product is able to execute a transition if and only if its features satisfy the associated constraint. SDVAs thus combine the modelling constructs of state machines with the conciseness of FTSs (when it comes to representing the behaviour of a *set* of products). Given that the theory surrounding SDVAs is still undergoing, we present here but a small and intuitive instance of this formalism. Fig. 4 presents an example of SDVA for the FM in Fig. 1. The high-level behaviour of the system as described in the diagram entitled SodaVendingMachine is as follows. The vending machine starts in state Idle. It can transit to either state Pay or Free if the feature f is disabled or enabled, respectively. In both cases, the system can move to state Soda (if the feature s is enabled) or to state Tea (if t is enabled). These two features not being exclusive, there exist products able to execute both transitions. Finally, the system reaches state Retrieve and then goes back to Idle.

This small example already gives account of the advantage of SDVAs over a fundamental formalism like FTSs. Indeed, one can observe that this SDVA actually models the same behaviour as the FTS shown in Fig. 2. However, the hierarchical construct in SDVAs allows one to define this behaviour at different levels of abstractions. Indeed, we see that the aforementioned high-level behaviour of the system is detailed in five additional diagrams. The effect of features on the system is thus refined as the model reaches deeper abstraction levels.

In addition to the SDVA, the functional architect also has to specify coverage criteria. For example, one may be interested in the behaviour of all the vending machines where a drink is eventually served. Through coverage criteria, one can thus drive the selection of relevant execution traces. Alternatively, intended requirements for the system can be expressed as temporal properties. Once defined, the SPL model and the criteria will be automatically flattened into an FTS and a suitable QA model. Flattening thus provides the SDVA model with a formal semantics in a transformational way. The transformation is an ongoing work and will be based on the flattening algorithm implemented using Kermeta [28] and proposed by Holt et al. in their state machine flattener Eclipse plug-in [22]. Although it is possible to flatten some of the most advanced UML state machine diagrams features [40], we currently consider only the hierarchical and orthogonal constructs.

By using FTSs as formal semantics for SDVAs, we want our framework to benefits from the accessibility, attractiveness, and usability of UML-based approaches and from the last advances in behavioural SPL model checking techniques. It is an open methodological challenge to determine when to stop detailing the SDVA model and proceed to FTS generation and refinement. We believe the SPL size and roles' skills are important factors impacting this decision. This has to be evaluated in practice.

To define the link between an SDVA and an FM, we propose to use the UML profiling mechanism [30, p. 659–688], which allows one to extend metaclasses to adapt them to specific needs and thus to map variable behaviour with the FM. Ziadi et al. [42] use the same profiling mechanism to introduce variability in UML class and sequence

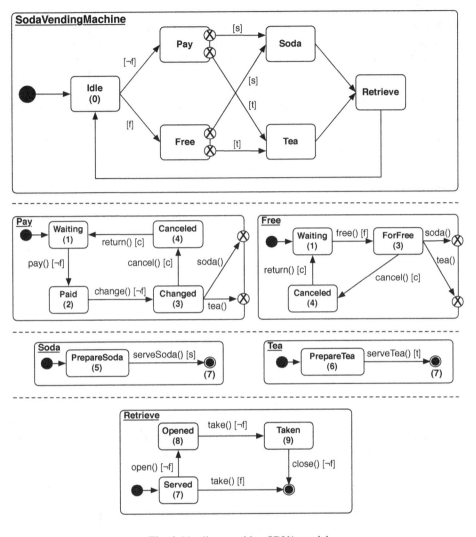

Fig. 4. Vending machine SDVA model

diagrams by "tagging" variants and optional elements and incorporating the constraints expressed in the FM using OCL and algebraic specification. The diagrams are then used to synthesize state machines for a given product of the product line. Contrary to this approach where the UML models may be used as standalone, the purpose of SDVA models is (for now) only to facilitate behavioural modelling by using a standard notation that offers richer constructions than pure FTSs. Amongst other things, we will support hierarchical constructs (composite states), useful to abstract away from details during requirements elicitation and orthogonal states used to model parallel behaviours in sub-states.

From the SPL model, the last step consists in defining the products that will be covered by the validation activities. Various coverage criteria have been proposed for state machines such as *edge coverage* or *location coverage* [29]. One approach to express this coverage is to directly annotate relevant elements of the model. Although pragmatic, this solution has the disadvantage to increase visual clutter and may become error-prone for large models. Rather, we are in favour of an explicit modelling language to specify coverage criteria. In particular, we rely on the *observer automata* concept proposed by Blom et al. [5]. Intuitively, an observer monitors the system under test and "accepts" a trace (a possible execution of the state machine) whenever a coverage item defined by the observer is found. We may thus use an observer to select only the traces of a specific subset of products. For example, we may only be interested in products providing drinks for free. Furthermore, we are not interested in cancelling orders for free drinks. The resulting observer is illustrated in Fig. 5. From the initial location, the observe can reach the accepting location `freeDrinks` if the predicate on the transition evaluates to true, that is if the feature `f` is selected and `c` is not.

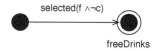

selected(f ∧¬c)

freeDrinks

Fig. 5. An observer covering "free drinks" products

In principle, given an SDVA model and an observer, it would be possible to derive all products satisfying the `freeDrinks` predicate. However, the SDVA model above has only an intuitive semantics and since it is hierarchical, this model raises an issue for the application of the coverage criteria. Indeed, as explained by Weißleder [41], it is not obvious how to traverse outgoing transitions of a composite state. To resolve these issues, we gave our SDVA model a formal semantics by translating it into an FTS. Since FTSs are flat, the application of the coverage criteria can be made more explicit. For example, flattening the SDVA model of Fig. 4 yields the FTS is presented in Fig. 2. The flattening operation usually consists in three steps [1,18,23]. First, the SDVA machine is recursively flattened by replacing all states by their sub-machines. We then have one "expanded state machine" with redundancy (e.g., the `Waiting` state in the `Pay` and `Free` sub-machines) and empty transitions (e.g., from `Retrieve` to `Idle`). The second step consists in simplifying the expanded state machine by merging redundant states (e.g., `Changed` and `ForFree`) and deleting useless ones (e.g., `Idle` since it has only unconstrained incoming transitions). In the last step, the SDVA operations are transformed into FTS actions. The complete mapping of the SDVA states to the FTS is given under each state of Fig. 4. Note that `Idle` state is mapped to 0. It means that this state is useless and will not appear in the FTS. To merge equivalent states in FTS, one could apply algorithms like *simulation quotient* to FTS. Simulation quotient is more complex in FTS than in usual TSs and has been studied in [11]. In the end, we are able to verify the correctness of the flattening transformation and the preservation of properties.

Since the observer's predicate is expressed in terms of feature expressions and does not directly involve composite states (such as Idle, Retrieve on top of Fig. 4), it does not have to be translated. The definition of compact and reusable observers is an open research question.

An alternative to achieve the selection of products is the explicit specification of the desired and forbidden features. In this case, the validation will rely on the use of a formal operator to prune the flattened FTS from the behaviour of the products that must be ignored, as we will explain in the following section.

5   Validation of Refined SPLs

In this section, we consider a validation scenario exemplifying the SPL validation using a design QA model provided by the QA manager and refinements of the validation model provided by the designer. We illustrate this possible scenario on our vending machine example.

5.1   Design and Validation

The first step in the design and validation part is the product selection, solely based on the flat SPL and QA models or on those models with an additional design QA model provided by the QA manager. The selected products are then refined by the designer according to the desired detail level and validated in the last step.

Product Selection. As mentioned in Section 3, product selection can be performed via two ways: by using a test coverage algorithm or a model checker:

1. Considering our observer automata (see Fig. 5), an algorithm computing a TS satisfying this observer has been provided [21,5]. It consists in composing the observer and the TS to systematically explore possible transitions (i.e., transitions whose associated feature expression is compatible with the formula $f \wedge \neg c$) and form "traces", which are in our case the desired products' TSs. There are various strategies to generate such traces (e.g., longest [21]). We also need to ensure the uniqueness of traces. Providing feature-oriented strategies as well as an extension of the observer language (to deal with predicates defined over features as shown above) is a research challenge to be tackled.
2. Use the products-restraint operator defined in [10]. Given an FTS and a feature valuation function (i.e., a partial function that associates features with Boolean values), this operator removes any transition in the FTS whose feature expression is incompatible with the feature valuation function. Also note that the behaviour of an individual product can be extracted from the individual FTS thanks to a total feature valuation function. Applied on our vending machine example and the function that associates f to true and c to false, the products-restraint operator produces the FTS shown Fig. 6. This FTS models exactly the behaviour of the products with free drinks and no possibility to cancel orders.

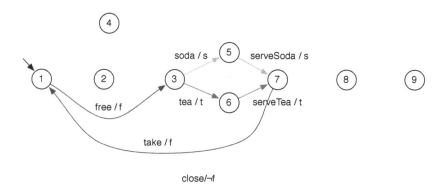

Fig. 6. Restrained FTS for free and non-canceling products

Refinement. Once the products of interest have been selected, we may refine them to perform targeted verification and generate detailed test scenarios. This refinement consists in providing more behaviour to the FTS' actions and adding new transitions. Let us assume that we are interested to validate serveTea behaviour; we detail it by providing three actions, prepare (setting up tea leaves), boil (boil water at the adequate temperature) and pour (having the water pass through the leaves and and pour the tea in the cup when it is infused). The refined FTS is shown Fig. 7.

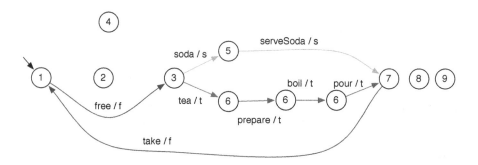

Fig. 7. Refined FTS detailing "serveTea" behaviour

Product Validation. The last step is the validation of the actual products defined in the validation model.

The QA manager is also responsible for designing and managing test cases of the SPL. For instance, the QA manager may want to test that serving tea is correctly handled by the vending machine. To do so, she can provide a new observer as illustrated in Fig. 8. We can reuse the algorithm mentioned above [21,5] to compute traces. However, the role of these traces is different: they form abstract test case scenarios to be applied on the selected products rather than the new set of products to be

Fig. 8. An observer covering all traces where the serveTea action appears

considered. Thus, the algorithm would return a list of actions, like the following one: {free, tea, serveTea, take}.

During selection, relevant observers may be elicited by pruning those related to actions not present in the restrained FTS (or the set of product TSs). During refinement, actions can be detailed. This implies that traces have to be refined as well. However, refining traces directly may represent a huge task and may not be easily automated as selection may affect the un-restrained FTS in many ways. Rather, we propose to derive a refined observer as shown in Fig. 9. This observer is much easier to model by the QA manager and may be generated by an automated model transformation, provided that traceability during refinement is maintained. Once obtained, the observer is enabled to derive traces like {free, tea, prepare, boil, pour, take}.

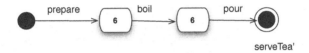

Fig. 9. Refined observer

Generated traces serve as specification for testers to write concrete test cases to be run on the system implementation.

As in single-system engineering, model checking is an alternative validation technique. In our other work, we have designed efficient algorithms to verify FTSs against properties expressed in temporal logic [9,7] or as automata [11]. Given a property, such an algorithm returns the exact set of products that do not satisfy the property. To reduce the overhead of verification, our methods tend to take the commonality between the products into account and to avoid redundant checking. We are still extending our work with the aim of providing a wider range of increasingly efficient techniques for formal verification of SPLs.

6   Conclusion and Perspectives

In this paper, we have presented a vision for a model-based behavioural SPL QA framework. Our approach relies on formal techniques without sacrificing usability in a unified and flexible enough model-driven framework. We believe that this combination will foster the usage of efficient QA techniques for SPLs thus improving the confidence in the SPL paradigm.

By working on domain artefacts with a variability model, we want our framework to be family-based [37]. The output of the whole chain will be a validation model for (potentially) one product, a subset of products or even the whole product line according to the provided select criteria.

Although some achievements have been made in model checking SPL behavioural models [8], there is still a long way to go before having a complete and coherent SPL quality assessment framework. First, we need to completely define SDVA with appropriate hierarchical constructs and its semantics as a mapping function from SDVA to FTS. To do this, we will explore existing UML state machines flattening techniques and see how we can adapt them to our needs.

The second challenge is the definition of observers to generate *relevant* test cases (i.e., interesting traces in the FTS). To define what an "interesting trace" is, we will need to adapt existing test selection criteria and probably create new SPL-dedicated ones.

This leads us to our third challenge: the definition of appropriate test selection algorithms dedicated to SPLs. In addition to well-known criteria like *all-transitions*, we would like to define new ones related to the SPL's features, which may be relevant from the functional architect's perspective.

References

1. Ali, S., Hemmati, H., Holt, N., Arisholm, E., Briand, L.: Model Transformations as a Strategy to Automate Model-Based Testing-A Tool and Industrial Case Studies. Simula Research Laboratory, Technical Report, pp. 1–28 (January 2010)
2. Asirelli, P., ter Beek, M.H., Fantechi, A., Gnesi, S., Mazzanti, F.: Design and validation of variability in product lines. In: Proceedings of the 2nd International Workshop on Product Line Approaches in Software Engineering, PLEASE 2011, pp. 25–30. ACM, New York (2011)
3. Asirelli, P., ter Beek, M.H., Gnesi, S., Fantechi, A.: Formal description of variability in product families. In: Proceedings of the 2011 15th International Software Product Line Conference, SPLC 2011, pp. 130–139. IEEE Computer Society, Washington, DC (2011)
4. Baier, C., Katoen, J.P.: Principles of Model Checking. MIT Press (2007)
5. Blom, J., Hessel, A., Jonsson, B., Pettersson, P.: Specifying and Generating Test Cases Using Observer Automata. In: Grabowski, J., Nielsen, B. (eds.) FATES 2004. LNCS, vol. 3395, pp. 125–139. Springer, Heidelberg (2005)
6. Clarke, E., Grumberg, O., Peled, D.: Model Checking. MIT Press (1999)
7. Classen, A., Heymans, P., Schobbens, P., Legay, A.: Symbolic model checking of software product lines. In: Proceedings 33rd International Conference on Software Engineering (ICSE 2011). ACM Press, New York (2011)
8. Classen, A.: Modelling and Model Checking Variability-Intensive Systems. Ph.D. thesis, PReCISE Research Center, Faculty of Computer Science, University of Namur, FUNDP (2011)
9. Classen, A., Heymans, P., Schobbens, P., Legay, A., Raskin, J.: Model checking lots of systems: efficient verification of temporal properties in software product lines. In: Proceedings of the 32nd ACM/IEEE International Conference on Software Engineering, ICSE 2010, vol. 1, pp. 335–344. ACM, New York (2010)
10. Cordy, M., Classen, A., Heymans, P., Schobbens, P.Y., Legay, A.: Managing evolution in software product lines: A model-checking perspective. In: Proceedings of VaMoS 2012, pp. 183–191. ACM (2012)

11. Cordy, M., Classen, A., Perrouin, G., Heymans, P., Schobbens, P.Y., Legay, A.: Simulation relation for software product lines: Foundations for scalable model-checking. In: Proceedings of the 34th International Conference on Software Engineering, ICSE 2012. IEEE (to appear, 2012)

12. Czarnecki, K., Antkiewicz, M.: Mapping Features to Models: A Template Approach Based on Superimposed Variants. In: Glück, R., Lowry, M. (eds.) GPCE 2005. LNCS, vol. 3676, pp. 422–437. Springer, Heidelberg (2005)

13. Ebert, C., Jones, C.: Embedded software: Facts, figures, and future. Computer 42(4), 42–52 (2009)

14. Engström, E., Runeson, P.: Software product line testing-a systematic mapping study. Information and Software Technology 53(1), 2–13 (2010)

15. Fantechi, A., Gnesi, S.: A behavioural model for product families. In: Proceedings of the the 6th Joint Meeting of the European Software Engineering Conference and the ACM SIGSOFT Symposium on the Foundations of Software Engineering, ESEC-FSE 2007, pp. 521–524. ACM, New York (2007)

16. Fantechi, A., Gnesi, S.: Formal modeling for product families engineering. In: Proceedings of the 2008 12th International Software Product Line Conference, pp. 193–202. IEEE Computer Society, Washington, DC (2008)

17. Fischbein, D., Uchitel, S., Braberman, V.: A foundation for behavioural conformance in software product line architectures. In: Proceedings of the ISSTA 2006 Workshop on Role of Software Architecture for Testing and Analysis, ROSATEA 2006, pp. 39–48. ACM, New York (2006)

18. Gogolla, M., Parisi Presicce, F.: State diagrams in UML: A formal semantics using graph transformations. In: Proceedings PSMT, pp. 55–72 (1998)

19. Gruler, A., Leucker, M., Scheidemann, K.: Calculating and modeling common parts of software product lines. In: Proceedings of the 2008 12th International Software Product Line Conference, SPLC 2008, pp. 203–212. IEEE Computer Society, Washington, DC (2008)

20. Gruler, A., Leucker, M., Scheidemann, K.: Modeling and Model Checking Software Product Lines. In: Barthe, G., de Boer, F.S. (eds.) FMOODS 2008. LNCS, vol. 5051, pp. 113–131. Springer, Heidelberg (2008)

21. Hessel, A., Larsen, K.G., Mikucionis, M., Nielsen, B., Pettersson, P., Skou, A.: Testing Real-Time Systems Using UPPAAL. In: Hierons, R.M., Bowen, J.P., Harman, M. (eds.) FORTEST. LNCS, vol. 4949, pp. 77–117. Springer, Heidelberg (2008)

22. Holt, N.E., Arisholm, E., Briand, L.: Technical report 2009-06: An eclipse plug-in for the flattening of concurrency and hierarchy in uml state machines. Tech. Rep. 2009-06, Simula Research Laboratory AS (2009)

23. Kalnins, A., Barzdins, J., Celms, E.: Model Transformation Language MOLA. In: Aßmann, U., Aksit, M., Rensink, A. (eds.) MDAFA 2003. LNCS, vol. 3599, pp. 62–76. Springer, Heidelberg (2005)

24. Kang, K.C., Cohen, S.G., Hess, J.A., Novak, W.E., Spencer Peterson, A.: Feature-Oriented domain analysis (FODA) feasibility study. Tech. rep., Software Engineering Institute, Carnegie Mellon University (1990)

25. Lauenroth, K., Pohl, K., Toehning, S.: Model checking of domain artifacts in product line engineering. In: Proceedings of the 2009 IEEE/ACM International Conference on Automated Software Engineering, ASE 2009, pp. 269–280. IEEE Computer Society, Washington, DC (2009)

26. Li, H.C., Krishnamurthi, S., Fisler, K.: Interfaces for modular feature verification. In: Proceedings of the 17th IEEE International Conference on Automated Software Engineering, ASE 2002, pp. 195–204. IEEE Computer Society, Washington, DC (2002)

27. Mathur, A.: Foundations of software testing. Pearson Education (2008)

28. Muller, P.-A., Fleurey, F., Jézéquel, J.-M.: Weaving Executability into Object-Oriented Meta-languages. In: Briand, L., Williams, C. (eds.) MoDELS 2005. LNCS, vol. 3713, pp. 264–278. Springer, Heidelberg (2005)
29. Myers, G.: The art of software testing. Wiley (1979)
30. OMG: OMG Unified Modeling Language TM (OMG UML), Superstructure. Tech. Rep. OMG (August 2011), http://www.omg.org/spec/UML/
31. Oster, S., Wöbbeke, A., Engels, G., Schürr, A.: Model-based software product lines testing survey. In: Zander, J., Schieferdecker, I., Mosterman, P.J. (eds.) Model-Based Testing for Embedded Systems. Computational Analysis, Synthesis, and Design of Dynamic Systems, pp. 339–382. CRC Press (September 2011)
32. Oster, S., Zink, M., Lochau, M., Grechanik, M.: Pairwise feature-interaction testing for spls: potentials and limitations. In: Proceedings of the 15th International Software Product Line Conference, SPLC 2011, vol. 2, pp. 6:1–6:8. ACM, New York (2011)
33. Oster, S., Zorcic, I., Markert, F., Lochau, M.: MoSo-PoLiTe: tool support for pairwise and model-based software product line testing. In: Proceedings of the 5th Workshop on Variability Modeling of Software-Intensive Systems, VaMoS 2011, pp. 79–82. ACM, New York (2011)
34. Perrouin, G., Oster, S., Sen, S., Klein, J., Baudry, B., le Traon, Y.: Pairwise testing for software product lines: Comparison of two approaches. Software Quality Journal, 1–39 (August 2011)
35. Pohl, K., Böckle, G., Van Der Linden, F.: Software product line engineering: foundations, principles, and techniques. Springer-Verlag New York Inc. (2005)
36. Schobbens, P.Y., Heymans, P., Trigaux, J.C., Bontemps, Y.: Generic semantics of feature diagrams. Computer Networks 51(2), 456–479 (2007)
37. Thüm, T., Apel, S., Kästner, C., Kuhlemann, M., Schaefer, I., Saake, G.: Analysis Strategies for Software Product Lines. Tech. Rep. FIN-004-2012, School of Computer Science, University of Magdeburg, Germany (April 2012)
38. Tretmans, J.: Model Based Testing with Labelled Transition Systems. In: Hierons, R.M., Bowen, J.P., Harman, M. (eds.) FORTEST. LNCS, vol. 4949, pp. 1–38. Springer, Heidelberg (2008)
39. Utting, M., Legeard, B.: Practical model-based testing: a tools approach. Morgan Kaufmann (2007)
40. Wasowski, A.: Flattening statecharts without explosions. SIGPLAN Not. 39(7), 257–266 (2004)
41. Weißleder, S.: Test models and coverage criteria for automatic model-based test generation with UML state machines. Ph.D. thesis, Humboldt-Universität zu Berlin (2010)
42. Ziadi, T., Jézéquel, J.M.: Product Line Engineering with the UML: Deriving Products. In: Pohl, K. (ed.) Software Product Lines, pp. 557–586. Springer (2006)

Parameterized Preorder Relations for Model-Based Testing of Software Product Lines

Malte Lochau and Jochen Kamischke

TU Braunschweig, Institute for Programming and Reactive Systems, Germany
{m.lochau,j.kamischke}@tu-bs.de

Abstract. Software Product Lines (SPLs) are a promising approach for efficiently engineering similar variants and/or evolving versions of software products. SPLs propagate systematic reuse of design artifacts between variants based on commonality and variability specifications in terms of features. Adopting reuse principles also to methods for behavioral conformance verification of product variants to their formal specifications, e.g., using model-based testing, is still an open problem. The sound reuse of verification artifacts such as test cases and test results is challenging due to the syntax-oriented and cross-cutting nature of recent feature-oriented SPL modeling approaches which obstructs reasoning about the behavioral impact of variability. Therefore, we introduce a formal framework for reasoning about artifact reuse in model-based SPL conformance testing. Based on a modal labeled transition system with explicit feature annotations as semantical ground model, we propose a behavioral notion of commonality by means of parameterized testing preorder relations for decorated trace semantics. Thereupon, applications to the reuse of SPL test artifacts are proposed.

1 Introduction

In many nowadays application domains, the software is an integral part of a dependable system, thus constituting a safety- and/or mission-critical factor, where erroneous implementations may have fatal consequences. Therefore, software implementations are strongly imposed to behave as intended, i.e., to be reliable up to a certain extent. Formally speaking, ensuring the *behavioral conformance* of a software implementation *impl* to a behavioral specification *spec* requires the verification of an *implementation* relation *impl* $\equiv$ *spec* w.r.t. a behavioral equivalence $\equiv$ (cf. [10,9]). In many cases, it is sufficient (or even only possible) to establish a *preorder* relation *impl* $\sqsubseteq$ *spec* requiring the implementation to show *at most* the behaviors as specified. When applying model-based testing for conformance verification, the behavioral specification is given as a *test model*, whereas the implementation under test is considered to be a black-box, solely offering an interface for injecting controllable inputs and observable outputs [26]. Hence, the preorder relation is weakened to a *testing preorder* $\sqsubseteq_{te}$ (cf. [10]), as well as to hold for a finite set behaviors from a usually infinite execution domain by means of finite sets of test cases [12]. Verifying the behavioral conformance in the presence

T. Margaria and B. Steffen (Eds.): ISoLA 2012, Part I, LNCS 7609, pp. 223–237, 2012.

of variability over time and/or space within specifications and implementations is even more challenging. Software Product Lines (SPLs) propagate approaches for the efficient development of families of similar software products based on extensive reuse of engineering artifacts among variants throughout all development phases [8]. Therefore, commonality and variability between different variants is managed in terms of *feature parameters* being explicitly related to artifacts for assembling product variants from reusable components. However, corresponding techniques for efficient, i.e., redundancy-reduced, yet reliable quality assurance of entire SPLs by adapting reuse principles also to verification artifacts is challenging [19,7,11]. Considering model-based SPL testing, the reuse of test cases among product variants is complicated, because (1) different product variants are, in general, incomparable under testing preorder relations and (2) variability modeling based on explicit feature parameters often crosscut semantical entities.

We address these challenges by providing a unifying semantical framework for variability-enriched SPL test models for formal reasoning about test artifact reuse among SPL product variants. Therefore, we define a parameterizable formalism based on labeled transition systems (LTS) as a semantical ground model for SPL test models. The model incorporates explicit modalities as propositional formulas over feature parameters for integrating behaviors of entire product families under test. We introduce different decorated trace semantics for abstract test case specifications and corresponding parameterized testing preorder relations. We correlate product configuration refinement and behavioral refinement w.r.t. those preorders for deriving reusable test cases from *partial* product configurations. We then decompose the sets of decorated traces of different *full* product configurations into subsets of test cases denoting those behaviors commonly specified for these variants. This allows us to reason about the reuse of test cases among arbitrary product variants although being initially incomparable under testing preorders. We also discuss assumptions for the reliable reuse of test results in a model-based SPL test setting.

This paper is organized as follows. In Sec. 2, we review basic notions of model-based testing using decorated LTS trace semantics and define parameterizable testing preorder relations for adopting reuse principles to model-based SPL testing. In Sec. 3, we introduce our LTS-based semantical framework for variability-enriched test models based on explicit feature annotations, which is used in Sec. 4 to reason about the reuseability of SPL test artifacts in a formal way. Sec. 5 discusses related work and Sec. 6 concludes.

2 Model-Based Conformance Testing of SPLs

We introduce basic notions of model-based testing, preorder relations using LTS test models and outline reuse principles in SPL testing.

2.1 Foundations of Model-Based Conformance Testing

In model-based conformance testing, a test model *tm* serves as a formal behavioral specification for an implementation *impl* under test. In practice, high-level modeling languages with rich syntactical constructs like UML state machines are frequently used by test engineers to capture the intended behaviors of the software under test [26]. However, for reasoning about the formal aspects of test case derivations, test case applications and testing equivalences for behavioral conformance verification, a translation of those high-level languages onto a more fundamental model is required that provides formalized semantics [25]. Labeled transition systems [14] offer such a semantical basis.

Definition 1 (Labeled Transition System). *A labeled transition system is a triple* $(Proc, Act, \rightarrow)$*, where*

- *Proc is a countable, non-empty set of* states, *ranged over by* s,
- *Act is a countable set of* actions, *ranged over by* a, b, c,
- $\rightarrow \subseteq Proc \times Act \times Proc$ *is a transition relation and we write* $s \xrightarrow{a} s'$ *if* $(s, a, s') \in \rightarrow$ *holds.*

We write $s \xrightarrow{a}\!\!\!\!\!/\;$ if there is no $s' \in Proc$ such that $s \xrightarrow{a} s'$ and $s \xrightarrow{a}$, otherwise. An *LTS* specifies the behaviors of all its *processes*, i.e., states $s \in Proc$ of the transition system specification. By choosing an *initial state* $s_0 \in Proc$, all behaviors of that process are given by its process graph, i.e., the *LTS* subgraph containing only those states reachable from s_0 via sequences of zero or more transitions. We assume transition labels $a \in Act$ to represent abstract, visible actions performed by the system. We omit τ-transitions representing invisible, i.e., internal behaviors in our following considerations. When using *LTS* specifications as fundamental semantical foundation for concrete test models *tm*, an interpretation of transition labels $a \in Act$ is usually given in terms of disjoint input/output alphabets Act_I, Act_O visible to an *observer process*, i.e., a tester (cf., e.g., [25]). Hence, each transition $s \xrightarrow{a} s'$ denotes a basic *test step*, where $a \in Act_I$ refers to controllable input stimuli injected into the system under test, whereas $a \in Act_O$ refers to expected output behaviors to be observed as system reactions. Due to the black-box view of model-based testing, the internal states of an implementation under test are not accessible to external observers. However, for establishing a preorder relation $\sqsubseteq$ between a specification, e.g., a test model *tm* and the implementation *impl*, a *test assumption* has to be made [4], where the existence of an (imaginary) implementation model *im* is assumed to relate a black-box under test to its test model. As a result, the verification of the preorder relation $im \sqsubseteq tm$ requires the behaviors observed for the (unknown) model *im* of the implementation under test to conform to those specified in the test model *tm*. Here, we assume both, *tm* and *im* to be *LTS* models.

Applying model-based testing to verify the behavioral conformance relation between implementation model and test model imposes a certain *testing preorder relation* $\sqsubseteq_{te}$ based on a testing equivalence relation $\equiv_{te}$ [10]. The choice of a preorder $\sqsubseteq_{te}$ depends, e.g., on the constructs available for test case specifications and their application [1], i.e., to what extent the tester is able to stimulate and investigate the implementation under test. In a black-box setting, we assume the testing preorder to be based on *traces*, i.e., sequences of visible actions, whereas internal actions, choice structures and process states of the implementation are not accessible to the tester. Therefore, we define LTS trace semantics as the basic notion for the definition of testing preorder relations.

Definition 2 (LTS Trace Semantics). *A sequence* $tr = (a_1, a_2, \ldots, a_n) \in Act^*$ *is a* trace *of a process* $s_0 \in Proc$ *of an LTS if there exists a path*

$$s_0 \xrightarrow{a_1} s_1 \xrightarrow{a_2} s_2 \xrightarrow{a_2} \cdots \xrightarrow{a_n} s_n$$

in the process graph of s_0.

We write $s_0 \xrightarrow{tr} s_n$ for short. By $Tr(s_0, spec) \subseteq Act^*$ we denote the set of all traces of process $s_0 \in Proc$ of an *LTS* specification $spec = (Proc, Act, \rightarrow)$. Traces provide the fundamental notion for *LTS* testing preorders such that

$$im \sqsubseteq_T tm :\Leftrightarrow Tr(s_0, im) \subseteq Tr(s_0', tm)$$

where T denotes *trace preorder* as testing preorder, i.e., the implementation behaviors are required to exhibit *at most* the set of traces specified in tm. We assume some process s_0 to be the predefined *initial process* of the implementation under test and s_0' to refer to the corresponding *initial process* of the test model. Conformance testing verifies whether all potential sequences of visible actions of the implementation under test conform those specified in the test model.

In addition to plain traces solely representing action sequences, further *decorated* versions of trace semantics were proposed in the literature [5]. Decorations are, again, based on the notion of visible actions. But, in addition to plain sequences of actions, further details on the enabling and/or disabling of actions in intermediate states reached by traces are taken into account using the notions of *readies* and *failures*. Here, we consider the following decorated trace semantics:

- *Completed traces*: traces $tr \in Tr(s_0, spec)$ are *completed traces* if $s_0 \xrightarrow{tr} s$ and $s \xrightarrow{a}\!\!\!\!\!/\;$ for each $a \in Act$.
- *Failures*: a pair (tr, X) with $tr \in Tr(s_0, spec)$ and $X \subseteq Act$ is a *failure* if $s_0 \xrightarrow{tr} s$ and for each $a \in Act$ with $s \xrightarrow{a} s'$, $a \notin X$.
- *Readies*: a pair (tr, X) with $tr \in Tr(s_0, spec)$ and $X \subseteq Act$ is a *ready* if $s_0 \xrightarrow{tr} s$ and for each $a \in Act$ with $s \xrightarrow{a} s'$, $a \in X$.
- *Failure traces*: a sequence $X_0 a_1 X_1 \cdots a_n X_n$ with $X_i \subseteq Act, 0 \le i \le n$ is a *failure trace* if $s_0 \xrightarrow{a_1} s_1 \xrightarrow{a_2} \cdots \xrightarrow{a_n} s_n$ is a trace of s_0, and for each $a \in Act$ with $s_i \xrightarrow{a} s_{i+1}$, $a \notin X_i$.
- *Ready traces*: a sequence $X_0 a_1 X_1 \cdots a_n X_n$ with $X_i \subseteq Act, 0 \le i \le n$ is a *ready trace* if $s_0 \xrightarrow{a_1} s_1 \xrightarrow{a_2} \cdots \xrightarrow{a_n} s_n$ is a trace of s_0, and for each $a \in Act$ with $s_i \xrightarrow{a} s_{i+1}$, $a \in X_i$.

Inclusion hierarchies on decorated trace semantics can be found, e.g., in [5], where $\sqsubseteq_{te} \subseteq \sqsubseteq_{te'}$ implies that testing preorder te is stricter than te'. We enhance the definition of *LTS* trace semantics accordingly: $Tr_{te}(s_0, spec)$ denotes the set of *decorated traces* of process $s_0 \in Proc$ for testing preorder $te \in \{T, CT, F, R, FT, RT\}$.

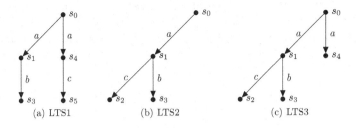

Fig. 1. Sample LTS Specifications

Example 1. Consider the sample *LTS* models in Fig. 1 with $Act = \{a, b, c\}$, where we omit empty traces $\epsilon \in Act^*$ in our discussions. Considering undecorated traces, we have

$$Tr_T(s_0, LTS1) = Tr_T(s_0, LTS2) = Tr_T(s_0, LTS3) = \{a, ab, ac\}$$

thus all three LTS are trace equivalent. For completed trace semantics, we have

$$Tr_{CT}(s_0, LTS1) = Tr_{CT}(s_0, LTS2) = \{ab, ac\}$$

whereas $a \in Tr_{CT}(s_0, LTS3)$, thus $LTS1 \sqsubseteq_{CT} LTS3$ and $LTS2 \sqsubseteq_{CT} LTS3$ holds. Failures further distinguish *LTS1* and *LTS2*, e.g., for trace a we have

$$\{(a, \{a, b\}), (a, \{a, c\})\} \in Tr_F(s_0, LTS1) \text{, whereas } \{(a, \{a\})\} \in Tr_F(s_0, LTS2)$$

thus $LTS2 \sqsubseteq_F LTS1$, because $\{(a, \{a\})\} \in Tr_F(s_0, LTS1)$ as failures are subset closed. In contrast, for readies, we have

$$\{(a, \{b\}), (a, \{c\})\} \in Tr_R(s_0, LTS1) \text{, whereas } \{(a, \{b, c\})\} \in Tr_R(s_0, LTS2)$$

thus no ready preorder relation holds between *LTS1* and *LTS2*.

The verification of a testing preorder relation $\sqsubseteq_{te}$ such that

$$im \sqsubseteq_{te} tm :\Leftrightarrow Tr_{te}(s_0, im) \subseteq Tr_{te}(s_0, tm)$$

requires observation capabilities for a tester to be rich enough to deliver, e.g., failures, readies etc. as required by the decorations of *te*.

So far, we require for testing preorder relations between implementations and specifications the inclusions of complete sets of behaviors in form of a usually infinite number of (decorated) traces. When applying model-based testing as verification method, this notion is to restrictive due the natural limitation of testing campaigns to finite sets of behaviors. Therefore, we further weaken the notion of implementation conformance.

2.2 Parameterized Decorated Trace Preorder Relation

The verification of the behavioral conformance of an implementation *im* and a test model *tm* using model-based testing is done by selecting *finite* sets *TC* of *test cases*, i.e., experimental comparisons of sample behaviors of *im* with those of *tm*. Sets of (abstract) test cases TC correspond to finite subsets $TC \subseteq Tr_{te}(s_0, tm)$ of decorated traces of *finite length* for testing preorder *te* under consideration. To denote the resulting weakened testing preorder relation, we introduce a *parameterized* testing preorder relation (cf. [12]).

Definition 3 (Parametrized Testing Preorder Relation). *A parameterized testing preorder $\sqsubseteq_{te}^{TC}$ is defined such that*

$$im \sqsubseteq_{te}^{TC} tm \;:\Leftrightarrow\; (Tr_{te}(s_0, im) \cap TC) \subseteq (Tr_{te}(s_0, tm) \cap TC)$$

where $TC \subseteq Tr_{te}(s_0, im)$ is a finite set of decorated traces.

The parameterization restricts the inclusion of the preorder relation to a finite subset TC of (decorated) traces. The construction and application of *concrete* observer processes for exercising abstract test cases $tc \in TC$ obtained from a test model *tm* on the implementation under test is discussed elsewhere [1,23]. Parameterized testing preorders help us to characterize behavioral commonality between similar product variants of an SPL, thus building the basis for reuse reasoning in model-based SPL conformance testing.

2.3   Model-Based SPL Conformance Testing

The adaption of model-based conformance testing principles to software product lines requires to cope with a family of similar *product variants under test* [11]. Thus, a set $PC = \{p_1, p_2, \ldots, p_n\}$ of implementations of product configuration variants is to be verified against a set $TM = \{tm_1, tm_2, \ldots, tm_n\}$ of product variant test model specifications using collections $TC = \{TC_1, TC_2, \ldots, TC_n\}$ of product variant specific test cases, such that $im_i \sqsubseteq_{te}^{TC} tm_i$ holds for $1 \leq i \leq n$, where im_i denotes the imaginary implementation model of product p_i.

Besides those families of products, an SPL defines structural capabilities to explicitly specify commonality and variability among the variants [8]. Those structural entities are given as *features*, i.e., product characteristics stating explicit product configuration parameters [13]. Hence, feature-oriented software product line engineering supports the reuse of feature-related artifacts between products throughout all development phases. Due to the crosscutting nature of those feature assets, promoting reuse principles to behavioral commonality and variability w.r.t. semantic artifacts like *LTS* traces is not straight forward. Thus, considering a set P of product variants, we usually have to assume its elements to be incomparable under preorder $\sqsubseteq_{te}$, i.e., for any two variants $p, p' \in P$, neither $tm \sqsubseteq_{te} tm'$, nor $tm \sqsubseteq_{te} tm'$ holds. But, when restricting behavioral conformance relations to parameterized preorders by decomposition into sets of test cases, subsets TC of behaviors common to p and p' may exist, such that $tm \sqsubseteq_{te}^{TC} tm'$ and/or vice versa holds. Although the feature configurations of p and p' provide explicit specifications of commonality and variability between both variants, they do not induce a one-to-one correspondence between test cases and features. Instead, feature parameterizations of product variants usually affect artifact assemblies at the syntactical level. For reasoning about the behavioral impacts of variations, approaches are required for tracing the explicit modalities of syntactical elements onto the semantical level such as decorated traces of *LTS* models. Therefore, three essential challenges concerning the reuse of test artifacts in model-based SPL testing are apparent: (1) provide a generic, reusable SPL test model $tm(p)$ integrating all behavioral variants $tm \in TM$ of any potential product configuration $p \in P$, (2) for the reuse of sets $TC \subseteq Tr_{te}(s_0, tm)$ of test cases selected from a test model tm of variant p for variant p', a subset $TC' \subseteq TC$ is to be identified such that $tm \sqsubseteq_{te}^{TC'} tm'$ holds, and (3) for the reuse of test results obtained from the execution of test cases $TC' \subseteq Tr_{te}(s_0, tm)$ of p for p', a subset $TC'' \subseteq TC'$ is to be identified such that $im \sqsubseteq_{te}^{TC''} im'$ where $TC'' \subseteq TC'$.

3   Parameterized LTS Test Model

We now enhance *LTS* test models with explicit variability using feature parameters organized in feature models. We characterize interrelations among test model variants in terms of a refinement relation similar to modal automata [15].

3.1   Feature Parameters and Feature Models

For enhancing modeling languages with capabilities to express variability, most approaches provide explicit connections to *domain features* by annotating modeling entities with selection conditions over feature parameters [7]. Correspondingly, we propose a description of commonality and variability between different product variant test models in terms of finite sets $F = \{f_1, f_2, \ldots, f_n\}$ of (abstract) feature parameters. This set together with their hierarchical decomposition relation and further constraints are usually captured in *domain feature models* such as FODA feature diagrams [13]. According to [3], we simply assume a feature model to be represented as a propositional formula $FM \in \mathbb{B}(F)$ over feature parameters interpreted as a set of boolean variables $f \in F$. Feature models tailor the *product space* of an SPL by restricting the set of *valid* product configurations. A *product configuration* is a function $\Gamma : F \to \mathbb{B}$ such that $\Gamma \models FM$ holds, i.e., it assigns boolean values to feature parameters denoting either their selection, or deselection within the configuration in a way that complies to the feature model constraints. We distinguish (1) *full* product configurations, i.e., total functions $\hat{\Gamma} : F \to \mathbb{B}(F)$, where every feature parameter is either selected, or unselected and (2) *partial* configurations, i.e., partial functions $\tilde{\Gamma} : F \rightharpoonup \mathbb{B}(F)$, where selection of feature parameters $f \notin dom(\Gamma)$ is undecided.

The product space PC_{FM} of feature model FM contains the set of all full and partial product configurations $\Gamma \in PC_{FM}$ satisfying the feature model. We require a given feature model FM to be *satisfiable* in the following, i.e., $PC_{FM} \neq \varnothing$. We define a refinement relation $\sqsubseteq_{FM}$ on feature models $FM, FM' \in \mathbb{B}(F)$ in terms of product space refinement such that

$$FM' \sqsubseteq_{FM} FM :\Leftrightarrow PC_{FM'} \subseteq PC_{FM}$$

Feature model refinement results from binding feature variables as done in product configurations $\Gamma \in PC_{FM}$. We write

$$\Phi(\Gamma) = \bigwedge_{f \in dom(\Gamma)} \phi(f) \text{ , where } \phi(f) = f \text{ if } \Gamma(f) = true, \phi(f) = \neg f \text{ if } \Gamma(f) = false$$

to represent configuration decisions in Γ as propositional formulas additionally constraining *FM*. We assume feature model refinement to result from staged product (pre-)configurations via Γ which incrementally reduces variability.

Lemma 1. *For $FM' = FM \wedge \Phi(\Gamma)$, where $\Gamma \in PC_{FM}$, $FM' \sqsubseteq_{FM} FM$ holds.*

We use this notion of feature models to enrich LTS-based test models with explicit variability.

3.2   Feature-annotated Labeled Transition Systems

To apply a feature model to annotate an *LTS* test model with variable behaviors, we introduce a function σ that assigns *selection conditions* over sets of feature parameters $f \in F$ of a feature model $FM \in \mathbb{B}(F)$ to transitions. Please note that the abstract syntax of *F-LTS* is similar to those of *FTS* by Classen et al. [7].

Definition 4 (F-LTS). *A feature-annotated labeled transition system (F-LTS) is a 5-tuple $(Proc, Act, \rightarrow, FM, \sigma)$ such that $(Proc, Act, \rightarrow)$ is an LTS, $FM \in \mathbb{B}(F)$ is a feature model over features F and $\sigma : Proc \times Act \times Proc \rightarrow \mathbb{B}(F)$ is an annotation function, where $s \overset{a}{\nrightarrow} s'$ implies $\sigma(s, a, s') \nvDash FM$.*

To annotate *LTS* models with infinite sets of states and transitions, one can assume σ to be a partial function, where triples $(s, a, s') \notin dom(\sigma)$ are implicitly mapped to constant *false*. Similar to modal automata [22], the annotation function σ assigns three potential modalities to transitions (s, a, s'):

- *may*-transitions $\rightarrow_{may} \subseteq \rightarrow$, where $s \overset{a}{\rightarrow}_{may} s' :\Leftrightarrow \exists \Gamma \in PC_{FM} : \Gamma \models \sigma(s, a, s')$
- *must*-transitions $\rightarrow_{must} \subseteq \rightarrow$, where $s \overset{a}{\rightarrow}_{must} s' :\Leftrightarrow \forall \Gamma \in PC_{FM} : \Gamma \models \sigma(s, a, s')$
- *prohibited*-transitions $\nrightarrow \subseteq Proc \times Act \times Proc$, where $s \overset{a}{\nrightarrow} s' :\Leftrightarrow \neg \exists \Gamma \in PC_{FM} : \Gamma \models \sigma(s, a, s')$

The *may*-transitions includes those being annotated with a selection condition that is satisfiable by at least one valid product configuration, whereas annotations of *must*-transition are satisfied by any valid configuration. Annotations of *prohibited*-transitions are never satisfied for any product configuration. The following holds for *F-LTS* models.

Proposition 1. *For an F-LTS, it holds that (1) $\rightarrow_{may} \subseteq \rightarrow$, (2) $\rightarrow_{must} \subseteq \rightarrow_{may}$ and (3) $\nrightarrow \cap \rightarrow_{may} = \varnothing$.*

Proof. Follows from the definition of function σ.

We introduce a *refinement* relation on *F-LTS*. In contrast to the implicit refinement relation of modal automata [15], refinement of *F-LTS* is explicitly coupled to feature model refinement.

Definition 5 (F-LTS Refinement). *An F-LTS $(Proc, Act, \rightarrow, FM', \sigma)$ is a refinement of F-LTS $(Proc, Act, \rightarrow, FM, \sigma)$ if $FM' \sqsubseteq_{FM} FM$.*

We write *F-LTS'* $\sqsubseteq_{F\text{-}LTS}$ *F-LTS* for short. We obtain refinement relationships similar to those of modal automata.

Proposition 2. *For F-LTS' $\sqsubseteq_{F\text{-}LTS}$ F-LTS it holds that* (1) $\rightarrow'_{may} \subseteq \rightarrow_{may}$, (2) $\rightarrow_{must} \subseteq \rightarrow'_{must}$ *and* (3) $\nrightarrow \subseteq \nrightarrow'$.

Proof. Follows from Prop. 1.

The set of *may*-transitions is constantly reduced by refinement, either becoming *must*-transitions, or *prohibited*-transitions. We further have $\rightarrow'_{may} \cap \nrightarrow = \varnothing$, i.e., no previously prohibited transitions may become valid again after refinement, and $\rightarrow_{must} \cap \nrightarrow' = \varnothing$, i.e., no previous *must*-transition may become prohibited after refinement. For associating product configurations $\Gamma \in PC_{FM}$ with *F-LTS* variants, we assign *F-LTS* refinements to product configurations.

Definition 6 (PC-LTS). *The* PC-LTS *of an F-LTS $(Proc, Act, \rightarrow, FM, \sigma)$ for product configuration $\Gamma \in PC_{FM}$ is an F-LTS $(Proc, Act, \rightarrow, FM', \sigma)$ with $FM' = FM \wedge \Phi(\Gamma)$.*

For $(Proc, Act, \rightarrow, FM', \sigma)$ being a *PC-LTS* with $FM' = FM \wedge \Phi(\Gamma)$, we derive the corresponding *LTS* variant $LTS_\Gamma = (Proc, Act, \rightarrow_\Gamma)$ by restricting the set of transitions to $\rightarrow_\Gamma = \{s \xrightarrow{a} s' \mid \sigma(s, a, s') \models FM'\}$, i.e., to those with selections condition satisfying the refined feature model. We have $\rightarrow_\Gamma = \rightarrow_{may} \subseteq \rightarrow$ which follows from the definition of *may*-transitions. The following correspondence holds between *full* configurations and *complete* F-LTS refinement.

Lemma 2. *For a PC-LTS of the F-LTS for a* full *product configuration $\hat{\Gamma}$ it holds that $\rightarrow_{\hat{\Gamma}} = \rightarrow_{may} = \rightarrow_{must}$.*

As a convention, we assume for the *F-LTS* of an unrefined *FM*, i.e., $dom(\Gamma) = \varnothing$, that $\rightarrow_{may} = \rightarrow$ holds.

Example 2. Consider *F-LTS1* in Fig. 2(a), where $FM = f_1 \wedge (f_2 \vee f_3)$. Dashed transitions denote *may*-transitions and feature annotations are written in $[\ldots]$. The *LTS* variants of the three full product configurations $\Phi(\hat{\Gamma}_1) = (f_1 \wedge f_2 \wedge f_3)$, $\Phi(\hat{\Gamma}_2) = (f_1 \wedge \neg f_2 \wedge f_3)$, and $\Phi(\hat{\Gamma}_3) = (f_1 \wedge f_2 \wedge \neg f_3)$ correspond to *LTS1*, *LTS2*, and *LTS3* in Fig. 1. The *F-LTS2* in Fig. 2(b) results from the refined feature model $FM' = FM \wedge (f_1 \wedge f_2)$ for partial configuration $\tilde{\Gamma}$ with $\Phi(\tilde{\Gamma}) = (f_1 \wedge f_2)$, where the transition leading from s_0 to s_4 becomes a *must*-transition, therefore *F-LTS2* $\sqsubseteq_{F\text{-}LTS}$ *F-LTS1* holds.

Feature-annotated *LTS* models build the basis for reasoning about commonality and variability among product variants in terms of decorated trace semantics as reusable (abstract) test cases.

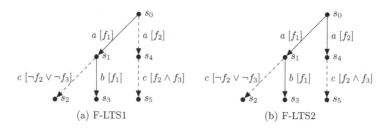

(a) F-LTS1   (b) F-LTS2

Fig. 2. Sample F-LTS and F-LTS Refinement

4   Reuse of LTS Test Artifacts

Based on *F-LTS* refinement, we develop a formal framework for selecting reusable test artifacts w.r.t. different testing preorders.

4.1   Reuse of Test Cases

Sets $TC \subseteq Tr_{te}(s_0, LTS_\Gamma)$ of abstract test cases for product configuration $\Gamma \in PC_{FM}$ are given as sets of (decorated) traces reachable from s_0 via $\to_\Gamma$ of LTS_Γ, where $\to_\Gamma$ coincides with the *may*-transition relation of the corresponding *PC-LTS* for the feature model refined by Γ. To correlate semantics of different product configurations to reason about abstract test case reuse, we first introduce a refinement relation $\sqsubseteq_{PC}$ on configurations Γ such that

$$\Gamma' \sqsubseteq_{PC} \Gamma :\Leftrightarrow dom(\Gamma) \subseteq dom(\Gamma') \wedge \forall f \in dom(\Gamma) : \Gamma'(f) = \Gamma(f)$$

thus imposing a partial ordering on PC_{FM}, where each configuration $\Gamma \in PC_{FM}$ corresponds to a refined feature model $FM' \sqsubseteq_{FM} FM$. We obtain the following relationship between product configuration refinement and *F-LTS* refinement.

Proposition 3. *For product configurations $\Gamma, \Gamma' \in PC_{FM}$ with corresponding PC-LTS and PC-LTS', it holds that $\Gamma' \sqsubseteq_{PC} \Gamma \Rightarrow PC\text{-}LTS' \sqsubseteq_{F\text{-}LTS} PC\text{-}LTS$.*

Proof. Follows from Prop. 2.

For variants LTS_Γ and $LTS_{\Gamma'}$, the refinement relation induces the following correspondence.

Proposition 4. *From $\Gamma' \sqsubseteq_{PC} \Gamma$ it follows that $LTS_{\Gamma'} \sqsubseteq_T LTS_\Gamma$ holds.*

Proof. From Prop. 3 and Prop. 2 it follows that $\to_{\Gamma'} \subseteq \to_\Gamma$ holds, and therefore $LTS_{\Gamma'} \sqsubseteq_T LTS_\Gamma$ as $LTS_{\Gamma'}$ contains at most those traces of LTS_Γ.

The opposite direction does not hold as two product configuration refinements incomparable under $\sqsubseteq_{PC}$ may however yield *LTS* variants related under $\sqsubseteq_T$.

F-LTS refinement causes *may*-transitions to either become (1) *must*-transitions, (2) *prohibited*-transitions, or (3) to stay *may*-transitions. Hence, the sets of traces are successively reduced such that trace inclusion as required for the corresponding trace preorder relation coincides with *F-LTS* refinement. This correspondence does not hold for decorated trace semantics.

Proposition 5. *From* $\Gamma' \sqsubseteq_{PC} \Gamma$ *it does not follow that* $LTS_{\Gamma'} \sqsubseteq_{te} LTS_{\Gamma}$ *if* $te \in \{CT, F, R, FT, RT\}$.

Proof. As stated in Prop. 4, inclusion for traces without decorations holds, whereas the set of completed trace, failures, and failure traces may increase as *may*-transitions may be refined to *prohibited*-transitions. For readies and ready traces, we require maximum sets of actions enabled in the state reached, whereas refinement may lead to reduced readies when prohibiting *may*-transitions.

To obtain a refinement relation that coincides with decorated trace semantics for testing preorder relations, we require actions $a \in Act$ of transitions $s \xrightarrow{a}_{may} s'$ to be not only interpreted as actions that *may* be *ready*, but also to be actions that *may* become *failures* after refinement.

Definition 7 (Decorated May-Trace Semantics). *For the PC-LTS of an F-LTS, decorated* may-trace *semantics is defined as follows:*

- May-Failures: *a pair* (tr, X) *with* $tr \in Tr(s_0, spec)$ *and* $X \subseteq Act$ *is a failure if* $s_0 \xrightarrow{tr} s$ *and for each* $a \in Act$ *with* $s \xrightarrow{a}_{must} s'$, $a \notin X$.
- May-Readies: *a pair* (tr, X) *with* $tr \in Tr(s_0, spec)$ *and* $X \subseteq Act$ *is a ready if* $s_0 \xrightarrow{tr} s$ *and (1) for each* $a \in Act$ *with* $s \xrightarrow{a}_{must} s'$, $a \in X$ *and (2) for each* $a \in Act$ *with* $s \xrightarrow{a} s'$, $a \notin X$

Completed may-traces, may-failure traces and may-ready traces are defined accordingly. We denote *may-testing* preorder relations by $\sqsubseteq_{te\text{-}may}$ and reformulate the *F-LTS* refinement property.

Theorem 1 (F-LTS Refinement coincides with May-Trace Preorders). *If* $\Gamma' \sqsubseteq_{PC} \Gamma$ *then* $LTS_{\Gamma'} \sqsubseteq_{te\text{-}may} LTS_{\Gamma}$ *holds.*

Proof. Prop. 4 still holds for undecorated trace preorder. In addition, completed traces, readies, failures, etc. are now likewise included, because *may*-transitions are now considered to potentially become *enabled* as well as *prohibited*.

Example 3. Consider *F-LTS2* (Fig. 2(b)), *LTS1* (Fig. 1(a)) and *LTS3* (Fig. 1(c)), where $LTS1 \sqsubseteq_{F-LTS} F\text{-}LTS2$ and $LTS3 \sqsubseteq_{F-LTS} F\text{-}LTS2$ holds. For trace $s_0 \xrightarrow{a} s_4 \xrightarrow{c} s_5$, *LTS1* contains, e.g., the completed trace ac, the ready $(a, \{c\})$ and the failure $(a, \{a, b\})$, and *LTS3* contains, e.g., the completed trace a, the ready $(a, \varnothing)$ and the failure $(a, \{a, b, c\})$. Under *may*-trace semantics, *F-LTS2* includes all these decorated traces, as the *may*-transition $s_4 \xrightarrow{c} s_5$ constitutes a potential failures as well as a ready.

The *F-LTS* refinement relates *PC-LTS* of partial product configurations with full product configurations as minimal elements of $\sqsubseteq_{F-LTS}$. As a direct consequence, sets of abstract test cases $TC \in Tr_{te\text{-}may}(s_0, PC\text{-}LTS)$ selected from the *PC-LTS* of a partial product configuration $\tilde{\Gamma}$ can now be refined to sets $TC' \subseteq TC$ for configurations $\Gamma' \sqsubseteq_{PC} \tilde{\Gamma}$. As a consequence, symbolic test cases generated from the *F-LTS* of the unrefined *FM* based on the adapted notion of may-testing preorders suffices to provide appropriate sets of test cases for every product variant $\Gamma \in PC_{FM}$ (cf. [6]).

However, considering test case reuse between *full* product configurations $\hat{\Gamma}, \hat{\Gamma}' \in PC_{FM}$ being unrelated under $\sqsubseteq_{PC}$, so are their corresponding sets of (decorated) traces w.r.t. testing preorder $\sqsubseteq_{te}$. To reason about the reusability of test cases $TC \subseteq Tr_{te}(s_0, LTS_{\hat{\Gamma}})$ of $\hat{\Gamma}$ in the set of test cases $TC' \subseteq Tr_{te}(s_0, LTS_{\hat{\Gamma}'})$ of Γ', we introduce the *least upper bound* of two configurations.

Definition 8 (Least Upper Bound Configuration). *The* least upper bound *of two product configurations* $\Gamma, \Gamma' \in PC_{FM}$ *is defined to be* $lub(\Gamma, \Gamma') = \Gamma'' \in PC_{FM}$ *such that* $\Gamma''(f) = v$ *iff* $\Gamma(f) = \Gamma'(f) = v$, *and* $f \notin dom(\Gamma'')$ *else.*

The least upper bound shares those feature parameter values on which both configurations agree, whereas for contradicting and/or undecided values, the parameter is undecided.

Example 4. F-LTS2 in Fig. 2(b) is *lub* for $\hat{\Gamma}_1$ and $\hat{\Gamma}_3$, but not for $\hat{\Gamma}_2$.

For the least upper bound configuration $\Gamma'' = lub(\Gamma, \Gamma')$ being uniquely defined for any pair $\Gamma, \Gamma' \in PC_{FM}$, it holds that $\Gamma'' \in PC_{FM}$, $\Gamma \sqsubseteq_{PC} \Gamma''$ and $\Gamma' \sqsubseteq_{PC} \Gamma''$. The PC-LTS of that least upper bound then contains the maximum set of behavioral commonality of both variants. More precisely, the behaviors solely referring to *must-* and *prohibited*-transitions are definitely shared by both variants, against what the *may*-behaviors may vary between both variants. Therefore, we introduce the notion of *must-trace* semantics.

Definition 9 (Decorated Must-Trace Semantics). *For an PC-LTS of an F-LTS,* decorated *must-trace* semantics *is defined such that traces* $s_0 \xrightarrow{tr} s_n$ *are* must-*traces, i.e.,* $s_i \xrightarrow{a}_{must} s_{i+1}$, $0 \le i \le n$ *holds, and*

- Must-Failures *are pairs* (tr, X), *where* $s_0 \xrightarrow{tr} s$ *is a* must-*trace and for each* $a \in Act$ *with* $s \xrightarrow{a}_{may} s'$, $a \notin X$, *and*
- Must-Readies *are pairs* (tr, X), $s_0 \xrightarrow{tr} s$ *is a* must-*trace and (1) for each* $a \in Act$ *with* $s \xrightarrow{a}_{must} s'$, $a \in X$, *and (2) there is no* $a' \in Act$ *with* $s \xrightarrow{a'}_{may}$

Again, must versions of completed traces, failure traces and ready traces are defined correspondingly. Condition (2) for readies is required as readies must be maximum sets of enabled actions, thus no undecided transitions are allowed, whereas failures are subset closed. Accordingly, we write $\sqsubseteq_{te\text{-}must}$ for *must-testing* preorder relations. The must-trace semantics of an PC-LTS captures the maximum set of decorated traces common to product variants having the related product configuration as least upper bound.

Theorem 2 (Reuse of Decorated Must-Traces). *For any two PC-LTS, PC-LTS' of an F-LTS and* $\Gamma'' = lub(\Gamma, \Gamma')$, $LTS_\Gamma \sqsubseteq_{te}^{TC} LTS_{\Gamma'}$, *where* $TC = Tr_{te\text{-}must}(s_0, PC\text{-}LTS'')$.

Proof. If Γ and Γ' are related under $\sqsubseteq_{PC}$, then one is the least upper bound of the other and the correspondence holds because of Theorem 1. Otherwise, Γ''

contains the maximum set of commonality in terms of must- and prohibited-transitions, whereas may-behavior refinements are contradicting, because otherwise there would be a more specific least upper bound which contradicts Prop. 3 and $\sqsubseteq_{PC}$ being a partial ordering.

Example 5. Consider *LTS1* in Fig. 1(a), *LTS3* in Fig. 1(c) and *F-TS2* in Fig. 2(b) being their *lub*. *LTS1* has, e.g., failures $(a, \{a, b\})$ and $(a, \{a, c\})$, whereas *LTS3* has failures $(a, \{a, b, c\})$ and $(a, \{a\})$ for trace a. The *must*-failures of *F-LTS2* for trace a are $(a, \{a, b\})$ and $\{a, \{a\}\}$, thus being common to *LTS1* and *LTS3*. The sets of traces of *LTS1* and *LTS3* are both $\{a, ab, ac\}$, whereas the *must*-traces of *F-LTS2* only contains $\{a, ab\}$. This is due to the fact, that the trace ac refers to the same behaviors, but to different paths within *F-LTS2*, thus being unrelated under *F-LTS* refinement.

4.2   Reuse of Test Results

The reuse of sets TC of test cases obtained from the test model tm of product variant p for variant p' requires $tm \sqsubseteq_{te}^{TC} tm'$ to hold. For the reuse of test results observed for test cases TC' when applied to product p also for p', we require (1) $TC' \subseteq TC$, i.e., only results of test cases addressing common behaviors of p and p' may be propagated from p to p' and (2) $im \sqsubseteq_{te}^{TC} im'$, i.e., the test cases refer to equivalent behaviors in the implementations of p and p'. In model-based black-box testing, the second condition is rather complicating as the implementation details are unknown, thus requiring assumptions about the reliability and reproducibility of test execution results [4]. Apart from classical retesting criteria known from regression testing [26] such as *retest-all*, i.e., $TC' = \varnothing$, *retest-none*, i.e., $TC' = TC$ and *retest-random*, i.e., $TC' \subseteq TC$, analytical criteria based on change impact analyses on test models tm and tm' can be taken into account such as test model slicing [18]. Finally, testing preorder hierarchies can be considered for result reuse as follows: select a subset TC' from TC with $tm \sqsubseteq_{te'}^{TC'} tm'$ for retesting on p' such that $tm \sqsubseteq_{te'}^{TC'} tm'$ holds, where $\sqsubseteq_{te'} \subseteq \sqsubseteq_{te}$. Thus, a set of abstract test cases derived for a testing preorder te, e.g., is assumed to show equivalent behaviors on p and p' if the corresponding traces are still related in tm and tm' for a more discriminating preorder te' relation.

5   Related Work

Three approaches are prevalent for reusable test models: (1) selective, i.e., by so-called 150% models with explicit selection condition annotations over feature parameters [6,17], (2) compositional, i.e., by assembling from smaller modules related to specific features [27] and (3) transformative, i.e., by applying variant specific model transformations to a core test model [18]. However, those approaches mainly focus on syntactical variations. Moreover, two major directions for reducing SPL testing efforts exist: (1) subset selection heuristics, and (2) incremental SPL regression-based testing. For (1), i.e., selections of representative products-under-test, feature-model-based combinatorial criteria such as pairwise [20] and

T-wise [21] feature coverage, feature-interaction coverage criteria [17] and SPL test model coverage criteria [6] were proposed. In [6], an annotated SPL test model is used to derive reusable, symbolic, reusable test cases for a set of test goals. For the adaption of incremental approaches for testing SPL product variants (cf. [24]), a specification-based approach is proposed in [27], whereas in [18] test artifact reuse informations are derived by analyzing a delta-oriented SPL test model. In all these approaches, the reuse of test case base a strong notion of identical paths in the test model variants. Recent semantical frameworks for reasoning about behavioral commonality in product families aim at applications to formal verification techniques. The FTS formalism by Classen et al. [7] is a basis for symbolic model-checking complete SPLs using explicit transition annotations over features, thus implicitly considering (weak) bisimulation equivalence. Larsen et al. [15] were the first to propose modal specifications for product line engineering. Asirelli et al. [2] model-check complete SPLs using modal automata combined with deontic logics instead of explicit constraining annotations.

6   Conclusion

We proposed a formal semantical framework for reuse reasoning in model-based testing of software product lines. We use labeled transition systems enhanced with explicit feature parameters to express behavioral commonality and variability between product variants on the basis of decorated trace preorder relations. Thereupon, we developed a notion of refinement that corresponds to that of modal automata to capture behavioral commonality among variants. As a future work, we want to investigate further semantical phenomena and their potential impacts on SPL conformance testing, e.g., τ-transitions, timing, may- vs. must-testing preorders, LTS with state predicates, and further meaningful testing equivalences. We are further interested in experiments to get a better understanding of what sound criteria for of black-box test result reuse might be. Therefore, we plan to translate existing high-level test modeling languages with variability capabilities such as UML state machines [16] into our framework.

References

1. Abramsky, S.: Observation Equivalence as a Testing Equivalence. Theor. Comput. Sci. 53, 225–241 (1987)
2. Asirelli, P., ter Beek, M.H., Fantechi, A., Gnesi, S.: A Model-Checking Tool for Families of Services. In: Bruni, R., Dingel, J. (eds.) FMOODS/FORTE 2011. LNCS, vol. 6722, pp. 44–58. Springer, Heidelberg (2011)
3. Batory, D.: Feature Models, Grammars, and Propositional Formulas, pp. 7–20. Springer (2005)
4. Bernot, G.: Testing against Formal Specifications: A Theoretical View. In: Abramsky, S. (ed.) TAPSOFT 1991. LNCS, vol. 494, pp. 99–119. Springer, Heidelberg (1991)
5. Bloom, B., Fokkink, W., van Glabbeek, R.J.: Precongruence Formats for Decorated Trace Semantics. ACM Trans. Comput. Logic 5(1), 26–78 (2004)
6. Cichos, H., Oster, S., Lochau, M., Schürr, A.: Model-Based Coverage-Driven Test Suite Generation for Software Product Lines. In: Whittle, J., Clark, T., Kühne, T. (eds.) MODELS 2011. LNCS, vol. 6981, pp. 425–439. Springer, Heidelberg (2011)

7. Classen, A., Heymans, P., Schobbens, P.Y., Legay, A., Raskin, J.F.: Model Checking Lots of Systems: Efficient Verification of Temporal Properties in Software Product Lines. In: ICSE 2010 (2010)
8. Clements, P., Northrop, L.: Software Product Lines: Practices and Patterns. Addison-Wesley Longman Publishing Co., Inc. (2001)
9. DeNicola, R.: Extensional Equivalence for Transition Systems. Acta Inf. 24, 211–237 (1987)
10. DeNicola, R., Hennessy, M.C.B.: Testing Equivalences for Processes. Theoretical Computer Science, 83–133 (1984)
11. Engström, E., Runeson, P.: Software Product Line Testing - A systematic Mapping Study. Information and Software Technology 53(1), 2–13 (2011)
12. Grabowski, J., Heymer, S.: Formal Methods and Conformance Testing - or - What are we testing anyway? In: FBT 1998. Shaker Verlag, Aachen (1998)
13. Kang, K.C., Cohen, S.G., Hess, J.A., Novak, W.E., Peterson, A.S.: Feature-Oriented Domain Analysis (FODA) Feasibility Study. Tech. rep., CMU-SEI (1990)
14. Keller, R.M.: Formal Verification of Parallel Programs. Commun. ACM 19(7), 371–384 (1976)
15. Larsen, K.G., Nyman, U., Wąsowski, A.: Modal I/O Automata for Interface and Product Line Theories. In: De Nicola, R. (ed.) ESOP 2007. LNCS, vol. 4421, pp. 64–79. Springer, Heidelberg (2007)
16. Lochau, M., Goltz, U.: Feature Interaction Aware Test Case Generation for Embedded Control Systems. ENTCS 264, 37–52 (2010)
17. Lochau, M., Oster, S., Goltz, U., Schürr, A.: Model-based Pairwise Testing for Feature Interaction Coverage in Software Product Line Engineering. Software Quality Journal, 1–38 (2011) (to appear)
18. Lochau, M., Schaefer, I., Kamischke, J., Lity, S.: Incremental Model-based Testing of Delta-oriented Software Product Lines. In: 6th TAP. Prague (to appear, 2012)
19. Olimpiew, E.M.: Model-Based Testing for Software Product Lines. Ph.D. thesis, George Mason University (2008)
20. Oster, S., Markert, F., Ritter, P.: Automated Incremental Pairwise Testing of Software Product Lines. In: Bosch, J., Lee, J. (eds.) SPLC 2010. LNCS, vol. 6287, pp. 196–210. Springer, Heidelberg (2010)
21. Perrouin, G., Sen, S., Klein, J., Le Traon, B.: Automated and Scalable T-wise Test Case Generation Strategies for Software Product Lines. In: ICST 2010, pp. 459–468 (2010)
22. Raclet, J.B., Badouel, E., Benveniste, A., Caillaud, B., Legay, A., Passerone, R.: Modal Interfaces: Unifying Interface Automata and Modal Specifications. In: EMSOFT, pp. 87–96 (2009)
23. Tschaen, V.: Test Generation Algorithms Based on Preorder Relations. In: Broy, M., Jonsson, B., Katoen, J.-P., Leucker, M., Pretschner, A. (eds.) Model-Based Testing of Reactive Systems. LNCS, vol. 3472, pp. 151–171. Springer, Heidelberg (2005)
24. Tevanlinna, A., Taina, J., Kauppinen, R.: Product Family Testing: A Survey. ACM SIGSOFT Software Engineering Notes 29, 12–18 (2004)
25. Tretmans, J.: Testing Concurrent Systems: A Formal Approach. In: Baeten, J.C.M., Mauw, S. (eds.) CONCUR 1999. LNCS, vol. 1664, pp. 46–65. Springer, Heidelberg (1999)
26. Utting, M., Legeard, B.: Practical Model-Based Testing. A Tools Approach. M. Kaufmann (2007)
27. Uzuncaova, E., Khurshid, S., Batory, D.S.: Incremental Test Generation for Software Product Lines. IEEE Trans. Software Eng. 36(3), 309–322 (2010)

SmartTies –
Management of Safety-Critical Developments*

Serge Autexier, Dominik Dietrich, Dieter Hutter,
Christoph Lüth, and Christian Maeder

Cyber-Physical Systems, DFKI Bremen, Germany

Abstract. Formal methods have been successfully used to establish assurances for safety-critical systems with mathematical rigor. Based on our experience in developing a methodology and corresponding tools for change management for formal methods, we have generalised this approach to a comprehensive methodology for maintaining heterogeneous collections of both formal and informal documents. Although informal documents, like natural language text, lack a formal interpretation, they still expose a visible structure that reflects different aspects or parts of a development and follows explicit rules formulated in development guidelines. This paper presents our general methodology for maintaining heterogeneous document collections and illustrates its instantiation in the SmartTies tool that supports the development of safety-critical systems. SmartTies utilises the structuring mechanisms prescribed in a certification process to analyze and maintain the documents occurring in safety-critical development processes.

1 Introduction

With the advent of sophisticated intelligent systems (so-called cyber-physical systems), there is an increasing need to guarantee the safety of such systems. Formal methods have been successfully used to establish such assurances by providing mathematical proofs that specifications or implementations satisfy required properties. Industrial applications revealed that a flexible, evolutionary formal development approach which efficiently supports changes is absolutely indispensable as it was hardly ever the case that the development steps were correctly designed in the first attempt.

In contrast, standards like IEC 61508 [10] or DO-178B [14] address the problem of establishing trust in such systems by regulating the development process, requiring that all design decisions and safety arguments are documented in meticulous detail. The documents arising during the development mutually depend on each other, and changes in one document typically give rise to changes in others. This makes changes cumbersome, thus decreasing flexibility. Further, the amount of these dependencies explodes with the size of the developed system.

---

* This work was funded by the German Federal Ministry of Education and Research under grants 01 IW 07002 and 01 IW 10002 (projects FormalSafe and SHIP).

T. Margaria and B. Steffen (Eds.): ISoLA 2012, Part I, LNCS 7609, pp. 238–252, 2012.

There is a need for an efficient computer-aided document management that keeps track of the various dependencies in and between documents occurring during the development of safety-critical systems.

Existing tools do not cover this in full generality. They either cover specific aspects of the development process (like DOORS [9], which handles requirements, or the iACMTool [6], which handles UML models), or are specialised to a specific application domain and development methodology (for example, PREEvision [12] to develop safety-critical systems in the automotive industry using a model-based approach); they incorporate specialised knowledge about the underlying domain in fixed rules for maintenance.

Our goal is a generic maintenance and change management tool that can be tailored to deal with heterogeneous document collections, to maintain the corresponding dependencies and relationships, and to exploit them to propagate or to restrict the impact of changes made in the documents [8]. The contribution of this paper is the SmartTies tool, which supports the document types, operations and the workflow typically occurring in the development and certification of safety-critical software.

SmartTies is built on top of the pure document-management system DocTip, which is entirely parametric in the document type and change impact analysis rule systems, and extends it by specific document types, impact analysis rules systems, support for the development and certification workflow, as well as a web-based front-end and mediators converting between the document formats edited by the user and their internal, semantics-oriented representation. In the following, we will not explicitly distinguish between SmartTies and DocTip.

The paper is organised as follows: In Sec. 2 we introduce all the documents, relationships and consistency properties occurring in a software development process regulated by the IEC 61508 and required by a certification authority like the German TÜV. In Sec. 3 we present the different document types and relationships in order to analyse the properties of the whole document collection. Sec. 4 discusses the principles of document-type specific difference analysis and change impact propagation and Sec. 5 presents the structures, relationships and properties maintained in SmartTies as well as the supported workflow.

2   Developing Safety Critical Systems

Our running example here is the development of a system that calculates a *safety zone* for a moving, autonomous robot, thus safeguarding the robot against collisions with static obstacles. It is a very much simplified version of an actual development in the SAMS project [15] which was certified as conforming to IEC 61508 by the German TÜV. The documents occurring in this example are representative of a typical medium-sized certification effort.

Document-type specific structure. Table 1 shows the document types occurring in our example. We mainly have documents in OOXML (Office Open XML, MS-Word's native format) and C source code. All documents have an internal

Table 1. Document types occurring in a safety-critical development process, together with their inherent structure and document format

Document type	Content	Structure	Format
Concept paper	Describe fundamental concepts of the system	Prose	OOXML
FTA	Fault Tree Analysis, models combinations of fault events leading to a safety failure	Table	OOXML
FMEA	Software Failure Modes and Effects Analysis, describes possible causes of failure	Table	OOXML
SRS	Safety Requirement Specification, enumerates requirements that are necessary to guarantee system safety	Table	OOXML
Test plan	Enumerates all test cases, together with their current status	Table	XML
Test suites	Contains the test driver functions	Functions	C code
Implementation	The actual implementation	Functions	C code

structure that results from their designation and the formalisation prescribed by the certification process. The *concept paper* introduces the underlying physical models for computing movement and braking of a vehicle that are used as given assumptions in the software design process. It consists of prose text possibly containing images and mathematical formulae. The *fault tree analysis* (FTA) decomposes the undesired event of a collision with an obstacle down to low-level fault events. The *failure mode and effects analysis* (FMEA) starts from possible failures and analyses how they may contribute to a failure of the safety function. The *safety requirement specification* (SRS) is an enumeration of functional requirements ensuring the safety of the vehicle based on the aforementioned physical models. All these documents are OOXML documents and have document type specific structure and content: a row in a table of the fault tree analysis document describes one undesired event, and a row in the FMEA describes a single failure mode, while a row in a table of an SRS document describes a safety requirement. A table in a concept paper, however, is simply a table without further document type specific semantics. The *test plan* consists of all the test cases, stored in plain XML and edited over the web front-end; *implementation* and *test suites* are MISRA-C source files, structured by the underlying programming language (here, function definitions and declarations).

Document graph. The structure gives rise to relationships within and between documents. Each basic semantic entity, such as safety requirements, fault events, failure modes, test cases, or functions, can be linked to others. This resulting graph structure, visualised exemplarily in Fig. 1, must satisfy a number of properties, which encode the restrictions on the development process prescribed by the certification standard.

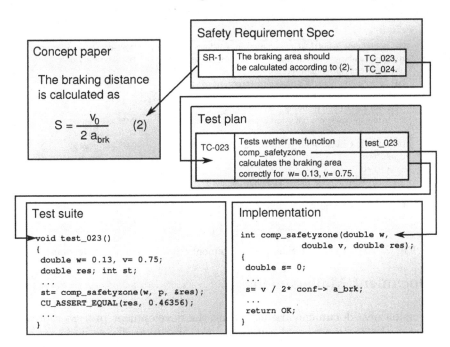

Fig. 1. Example document graph

Document collection properties. As a simple property, identifiers must be unique throughout the whole document collection. Further, each leaf fault event must reference at least one existing requirement. A requirement must either be decomposed into other requirements, or reference an existing function implementing the requirement and an existing test case in the test plan. Each test case must reference the function it is testing and the test driver function implementing the test. For sanity reasons, each test case must serve a purpose, so it must either be directly referenced from a requirement or it must be a precondition of at least one other test case. As a last example, safety requirements are the outcome of a hazard analysis documented in an FTA or FMEA, and we specify that each safety requirement has to be referenced by a fault event or failure mode. Though some automatic testing of properties exists for specific documents, checking all properties is typically done manually and automation is highly desirable. In particular, while we can check the presence of a link automatically, we cannot check that it is justified — we cannot deduce that a test case really tests the desired property. While we can assume that initially manual reasoning and review will be sufficient (if performed and documented properly), it is essential that when changes occur we can pinpoint their effects in terms of the manual reviews necessary.

2. Primäre Sicherheitsanforderungen

SR-1	Das berechnete Schutzfeld muss die gesamte beim Bremsen bis zum Stillstand wie durch das Bremsmodell beschriebene überstrichene Fläche überdecken.	IMPL-compute_safetyzone, TC-test_safetyzone, Testkonzept
SR-2	Das berechnete Schutzfeld muss eine Latenzzeit von ΔT beinhalten, in der das Fahrzeug mit unveränderter Geschwindigkeit und Richtung weiterfährt.	SR-3, SR-4
SR-3	Die Latenzzeit muss die Zykluszeit T des Systems beinhalten.	IMPL-set_config, TC_test-latency_1
SR-4	Die Latenzzeit muss die Ansprechzeit T_{brk} der Bremsen beinhalten	IMPL-set_config, TC_test-latency_2
SR-5	(gestrichen)	
SR-6	Die Bremsverzögerung muss die Abnutzung der Bremsen durch einen geschwindigkeitsabhängigen Zuschlag berücksichtigen	IMPL-set_config, TC_test-brake
SR-7	Die Höchstgeschwindigkeit v_{max} darf nicht überschritten werden.	IMPL-compute_safetyzone, TC-test_vmax

Fig. 2. Excerpt of the Safety Requirements Specification (in German)

3   Document Management

Each version of a document arising during the development process represents the state of the development, documenting and justifying design decisions made at that particular point in time. In early software development methodologies these documents were developed sequentially (waterfall model [13]). While this has the advantage that design decisions once made never have to be reconsidered, and thus assumptions can never become invalid, the underlying premiss that development can be finished successfully with the first attempt has proven highly unrealistic. Therefore, recent methodologies (such as agile development [5]) advocate an intertwined approached resulting in a parallel evolution of numerous documents. In this approach, changes occur frequently, and system support is needed to ensure they do not break the development.

Thus, we need systems which can handle and maintain change. However, as demonstrated in Sect. 2, there are number of different document types and formats, all with different editing tools, accompanied by tools such as compilers, test frameworks which run test suites and analyse the result, or verification tools to analyse and prove formal specifications. To handle change in this setting uniformly, we have developed a document broker called DocTip[1] that maintains and propagates changes and advances of individual documents to related documents. The general idea is that DocTip is notified about changes in documents made in the individual editing or analysis tools, computes their effects on other documents and initiates the necessary changes in the affected documents. DocTip is generic with respect to the document types supported and provides generic mechanisms to add new document types to the system [1,3].

Generic Representation of Documents. We use XML as a common metalanguage to represent explicitly the structure of documents that is intrinsic to their

---

[1] http://www.dfki.de/cps/projects/doctip

```
<Document>
  ...
<srs>
<csrs component="Primäre Sicherheitsanforderungen">
  <reqspec>
    <reqid name="SR-1"/>
    <description>
      <paragraph>
        <text> Das berechnete Schutzfeld muss die gesamte beim Bremsen bis zum Stillstand
               wie durch das Bremsmodell beschrieben überstrichene Fläche überdecken.
        </text>
      </paragraph>
    </description>
    <measures>
      <paragraph> <ref kind="function" name="IMPL-compute_safetyzone"/> </paragraph>
      <paragraph> <ref kind="testcase" name="TC-test_safetyzone"/> </paragraph>
      <paragraph> <ref kind="label" docid="DOK-K-1" name="TestSafetyzone"/> </paragraph>
    </measures>
  </reqspec>
  <reqspec>
    <reqid name="SR-2"/>
    <description><paragraph><text>Das berechnete Schutzfeld muss eine Latenzzeit von </text>
      <formula style="inline">...</formula>
      <text> beinhalten, in der das Fahrzeug mit unveränderter Geschwindigkeit
             und Richtung weiterfährt.</text></paragraph>
    </description>
    <measures><paragraph><ref kind="requirement" name="SR-3"/> <text>, </text>
      <ref kind="requirement" name="SR-4"/></paragraph></measures>
  </reqspec>
    ...
</csrs>
</srs>
</Document>
```

Fig. 3. Corresponding XML version of the excerpt of the Safety Requirement Table

individual types. For instance, consider the safety requirement specifications. While written and edited in MS-Word, DocTip maintains an XML representation that explicitly segments the document in tables of safety requirements and their relations to implementation and environment descriptions. Document type specific parsers encode documents in XML and thus enable DocTip to maintain them but also decode modified XML versions back to the original document language. In SmartTies we developed encoders and decoders for the individual document types that are, for instance, used by MS-Word (which uses a different, richer layout information, but provides less content structure). The corresponding document type specific XML languages provide the structuring mechanisms for both, the generic outline of OOXML documents and the (partial) knowledge about the semantics of the individual document parts. Depending on the degree of natural language understanding and of syntactical restrictions by the document type (e.g. by using domain specific languages), we obtain a more shallow or deep XML encoding of informally written documents containing more or less chunks of non-parseable document fragments. As an example, consider Fig. 2 showing the original document as presented by MS-Word, and Fig. 3 the representing XML document making the implicit structure explicit.

Generic Document Analysis. The key idea to design change impact analysis (CIA) for informal documents is the *explicit semantics method* which represents both the syntax parts (i.e., the documents) and the intentional semantics contained in the documents in a single, typed hyper-graph (see [4] for details). Document-type specific graph rewriting rules are used to extract the intentional semantics of documents and the extracted semantic entities are linked to their syntax source, i.e. their *origin*. The semantic graph is then analyzed to determine and propagate the impact of changes through the semantic graph, which are then projected backwards along the origin links to the syntactic nodes of the graph. A corresponding impact annotation for the syntactic part of the documents is then generated.

Generic Difference Analysis. Changes made to documents are recognised by analysing the differences between the different versions of the corresponding XML documents. Encoding all sorts of documents into different XML-based languages allows us to make use of XML-based tree-difference algorithms to compute differences between different versions of a document and represent the changes in terms of a uniform language and protocol (XML update, [4]). While we use a uniform XML diff algorithm to analyze differences of documents, this algorithm is adjusted to the individual document types by defining individual equivalence relations for each of them. These equivalence relations are used to determine which subtrees in two documents are similar and thus should be related to each other. This allows the diff algorithm to abstract from syntactical presentation issues that would otherwise prohibit the matching of related document parts. Equivalence relations are defined in terms of XML elements, attributes and subelements which identify corresponding XML subtrees.

DocTip relies on the XML update protocol to integrate changes obtained from the user interfaces or supporting analysis systems. Any change reported to DocTip is analyzed by the change management, which computes the impacts of these changes on other parts of a document or even in other documents. The propagated impacts are included in the documents maintained by DocTip, and passed along to the affected user interfaces and support systems.

In general, adding a new document type to DocTip involves the definition of the following:

- an XML language by an *XML schema S* and an additional predicate P to enforce properties of a document that are not covered by schema definitions. A document D is of type S iff D satisfies the scheme S. It is *admissible* with respect to S, P iff D satisfies S and $P(D)$ holds.
- an invertible *extraction function ω* to extract the XML representation from the actual syntax A of the document D, and to generate the actual syntax from the

$$A \xleftarrow{\ \omega\ } D \xleftarrow{\ \simeq\ } T \xrightarrow{\ \varphi\ } \mathbf{Ker} \xhookrightarrow{\ \rho\ } \mathbf{Mod}$$
$$\xleftarrow[\pi]{}$$

Fig. 4. Document type specific analysis: A are the documents of that type in their actual syntax, D the XML sublanguage for those documents, T the corresponding text-graphs, **Ker** the model kernels, and **Mod** the model graphs

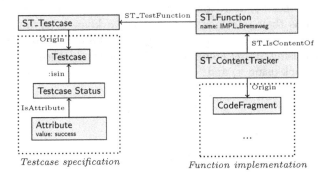

Fig. 5. Examples for text graph, model kernel and full model from the safety-critical software development domain

XML representation. The extraction process then works as follows: Given A, check whether $\omega(A)$ is admissible. If so, a *text graph* is computed. The graph structure correlates to the (parse) tree representation of XML documents. Hence, there is a one-to-one relationship between an XML document and its corresponding text graph, i.e. we can construct the XML document from its text graph and vice versa. A text graph is admissible iff its corresponding XML document is admissible. The subtrees in dotted boxes in Fig. 5 show parts of the text graphs from a testcase specification and an implementation.

- a document type specific *ontology* that describes the semantic concepts and their relationships.
- an *abstraction function* φ that computes the *model kernel* from the text graph. In contrast to the text graph, the model graph operates on semantic entities and their relationships, i.e., it consists of nodes and edges that correspond to the concepts and relationships that are defined in the corresponding ontology. The model kernel has the property that each of its entities is linked to a fragment of the text document, i.e. a node/link in the text graph, that caused its generation. E.g. a safety requirement node in the model kernel graph is linked to the corresponding text (i.e. the corresponding subtree in the XML description, representing the row in a table) defining it. Or the test case node in the model kernel graph is linked to the corresponding textual description, and the source code node in the model kernel graph is linked to the original source code (see Fig. 5). The idea is that the text graph will generate a model kernel which is expanded by semantic analysis to a fully fledged model graph.
- a document type specific *propagation function* ρ that computes the *model graph* by adding new nodes and edges to the model kernel (also from the corresponding ontology), representing derived information. E.g., in Fig. 5 the test case node in the model kernel is related to the tested source code node.
- a document type specific *projection function* π that maps derived information back to the text graph such that it can be presented to the user via ω.
- a document type specific equivalence model $\equiv$ to be able to compute the difference between two documents D and D' of the same type.

Fig. 4 summarises the functions that need to be provided for each document type, as well as their relations. The typical workflow is as follows: (1) Extract the XML representation using ω, (2) generate the text graph, (3) generate the initial model using φ, (4) compute the enriched model using ρ, (5) projecting the changes back using π, and (6) propagating the information back to the user document using ω^{-1}.

4   Change Management

In [2,11] we presented tools to maintain structured specification and verification work in order to minimise the amount of proofs to be redone when modifying a specification. This idea is now extended from theories to heterogeneous document collections and from provers to arbitrary semantic analysis tools: we propagate the syntactical changes observed by the XML diff algorithm towards a change in the semantics and analyse these changes with respect to the deduced or user-postulated properties. In the following we will elaborate in more detail.

As explained in Sec. 3, each document A gives rise to an XML document $\omega(A)$ which induces a text graph T. Changes $A \to A'$ in the document thus result in changes $T \to T'$ of the corresponding text graph, which in turn cause changes $\varphi(T) \to \varphi(T')$ in the model kerneland therefore also changes in the preconditions of derived entities, rendering parts of the old model graph invalid but also potentially enabling the deduction of new entities.

Since we are interested in the development process of documents, it is crucial to encode explicitly what information changed from one version to another. This is because stateful information, e.g., the result of executing a test case, might invalidate due to a change, e.g., a change of the source code of the function that is tested. Therefore, recomputing the model graph from scratch is not an option, as it would not give us information about the changed parts, and therefore restrict our approach to stateless properties.

Our solution consists in specifying graph rewrite rules that adapt a given model graph based on the result of the difference analysis of the text graphs. Thus, applying the rules propagates the differences Δ_T to the kernel, such that they are explicitly represented in Δ_{Ker} (c.f. Fig. 6). Finally, the analysis function ρ is invoked in Δ_{Ker} to change derived properties in the model graph.

The transformation is successful if we reach a model graph that is consistent with the new model kernel and incorporates the same level of analysis as the old model graph. We define consistency by specifying the set of all consistent model graphs by providing a predicate P_{mod}. $P_{mod}(D)$ is true iff D is an element of this set. P_{mod} is invariant with respect to the insertion of derived knowledge, i.e. starting with a consistent model kernel the model graphs that are derived step by step by applying transformation rules (assuming an empty old model graph) will always stay consistent. Typically, P_{mod} is provided by a set of consistency rules defining (sub)graph properties that each model graph has to satisfy.

Adapting an old model graph to a changed model kernel, we have to adjust, delete or insert derived entities in the old graph to match the consistency rules

$$A \xleftarrow{\quad\omega\quad} \omega(A) \xleftarrow{\quad\simeq\quad} T \xrightarrow{\quad\varphi\quad} \mathrm{Ker} \xrightarrow{\quad\rho\quad} \mathrm{Mod}$$

$$\Delta_A \qquad\qquad\qquad \Delta_T \xrightarrow{\quad\varphi\quad} \begin{array}{c}\mathrm{Ker}\cap\mathrm{Ker'}\\+\Delta_{\mathrm{Ker}}\end{array} \xrightarrow{\rho_{\Delta_{\mathrm{Ker}}}} \begin{array}{c}\mathrm{Mod}\cap\mathrm{Mod'}\\+\Delta_{\mathrm{Mod}}\end{array}$$

$$A' \xleftarrow{\quad\omega\quad} \omega(A') \xleftarrow{\quad\simeq\quad} T' \xrightarrow{\quad\varphi\quad} \mathrm{Ker'} \xrightarrow{\quad\rho\quad} \mathrm{Mod'}$$

Fig. 6. Change Management: Changing a document A to A' induces changes in the text graph T, in the model kernel Ker, and in the model graph Mod. The differences Δ_T of the text graph are propagated to determine Δ_{Ker} and finally analyzed to derive the changes of the model graph.

together with the new kernel graph. This transformation process will start at differences between old and new kernel graph and will ripple along the lines of analysis of the old model graph computing implicitly the differences between old and new model subgraphs. This process obviously stops when there is no way to adapt the lines of reasoning appropriately without violating the consistency rules. As usual there are two ways to resolve such a conflict. First, we can drop the further adoption of the old model graph (i.e. throwing away knowledge about old bits that have been changed in the meanwhile). Second, we can speculate about necessary changes in the already computed model (sub)graph in order to satisfy the violated consistency rule and to propagate these required changes back to the model kernel (and further to the text graph). Which way we proceed depends on the character of the violated consistency rule.

Change Management in the Small. The graph transformation process is implemented with the help of a graph rewriting tool GrGen [7], which operates on typed and directed multi-graphs with multiple inheritance on node and edge types. In addition these types can be equipped with typed attributes and connection assertions to formulate restrictions on graphs.

For example, consider the relationship between the code of IMPL_Bremsweg and the corresponding test cases that are used to validate the implementation.

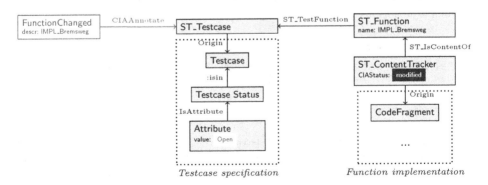

Fig. 7. Excerpt of the document graph and its changes

Changing the implementation, the corresponding tests specified in the test plan have to be redone. Fig. 7 presents the part of the model graph concerning the relation between the implementation of IMPL_Bremsweg and the test case specification. The model kernels of implementation and test cases are indicated by dotted lines. The model graph connects both kernels making the relation between both documents explicit (linking test case and code fragment via ST_Testcase, ST_Function and ST_ContentTracker).

Now suppose the implementation of IMPL_Bremsweg is changed. Comparing the XML versions of old and new version with the help of the XML-diff algorithm SmartTies localises the changes and adds both old and new version of the implementation of IMPL_Bremsweg into the model graph. The propagation of such a change is done with the help of GrGen graph rewrite rules. Since we are not interested in the details of the changes here, the GrGen rewrite rules will simply annotate the new implementation as changed by setting the CIA_Status attribute of ST_ContentTracker to "modified" and removing the old version from the model graph. In a second propagation phase this local change has to be propagated to the entire development using GrGen rewrite rules.

In general, GrGen rules specify rewrite rules on graphs allowing for pattern, replace and modify specification. A pattern matcher performs plain isomorphic subgraph matching as well as homomorphic matching for selectable sets of nodes and edges. Fig. 8 shows the rule used to propagate the modification of the implementation to the status of the tests. The block between iterated and modify constitutes the pattern of subgraphs on which the rule is applicable. Furthermore, the matches can be restricted by arithmetic and logical conditions on attributes and types, in our example we are only interested in changed implementation nodes, i.e if { c.status == CIAStatus::modified; }. Applying this rule to the subgraph printed in black in Fig. 7 results in the red additions: a node FunctionChanged is added to the graph and linked to ST_Testcase. Additionally, the value in the node Attribute is changed to "open", indicating the necessary rerun of the test cases. In a third phase the impacts of the change propagation to individual document parts are computed. Either they are automatically adapted or if this is impossible (because, e.g., manual interaction is required) comments on necessary changes are added (e.g. as comments) to the document (cf. Fig. 10 for such annotations within the Safety Requirement Specification, SRS).

```
rule resetTestsWithChangedFunction {
  iterated {
    stc : ST_Testcase <−:ST_TestcaseFunction− stcused:ST_Function;
    stcused <−l:ST_IsContentOf− c:ST_ContentTracker;
    if { c.status == CIAStatus::modified; }
    stc −:Origin−> tc2:testcase;
    tc2 <−:isin− status:testcasestatus <−:IsAttribute− statusattr:Attribute ;
    modify {
      stc <−:CIAAnnotate− a:ST_FunctionChanged;
      eval { a.description = a.description + stcused.name;
             statusattr.value = "open"; } }
  }
  modify {}
}
```

Fig. 8. Graph Transformation Rule to Actualize Tests

Change Management in the Large. In the following we sketch a typical scenario illustrating the cascade of changes during a development. In our running example, suppose a prototype of the system has been developed, comprising a concept paper, which contains the formula to calculate the braking distance, an FTA and an SRS which state *inter alia* that the braking distance must be calculated according to this formula, an implementation of the calculation of the safety zone, and test cases which check correctness of the calculation for various inputs.

The prototype is presented for internal review to the quality assurance department, and sure enough there is an error in the actual formula calculating the braking distance (it was $s = \frac{v_0}{2a_{brk}}$, and should have been $s = \frac{v_0^2}{2a_{brk}}$). This causes a series of corrections which ripple down the development graph (see Fig. 1):

1. The formula is corrected, and an analysis is triggered. Because there is a reference link to the formula from safety requirement SR-1, the correction in the formula will flag up an annotation in the safety requirement specification at SR-1 to check this event or requirement, respectively. Because we do not deal with the semantics of the formula, we cannot deduce what changes need to be made, but we can ask the specifier to recheck that SR-1 and its handling are still valid.

2. The specifier discovers that SR-1 as written is still valid, because they reference the formula and do not copy it verbatim, but SR-1 references test cases TC-023 and others. Test case TC-023 refers to rest function `test_023`. This test function is now wrong (or rather, the reference link is wrong), because the test data are calculated using the old (wrong) formula. The test functions are corrected, and another document analysis is run. This will invalidate the test results, as the test functions are now newer than the results.

3. The tests are re-run, and the their results uploaded into SmartTies. The changed tests covering SR-1 now fail, because the implementation in function `comp_safetyzone` uses the old formula.

4. The function `comp_safetyzone` is adapted, and assuming this is done in the correct way, the tests will now succeed again. A final document analysis asserts everything is consistent again, and we can re-present the documents for the next internal review.

Of course, in an example as small as this, a circumspect developer might make all changes in one go, but in larger developments, this type of support rippling small changes along the dependencies is the key to handling changes efficiently. Also, the initial error may have been rather obvious, but it is typical of a class errors which occur quite often but have wide-ranging consequences on the development process, namely modelling assumptions that do not quite hold in the real world (normally more subtle).

5   Document Semantics and Implementation

SmartTies supports the documents enumerated Table 1 which occur in the development of safety-critical software in a certification context. We have defined

Fig. 9. The SmartTies web interface

XML schemata which encode the semantic structure described rather straight-forwardly. For these documents, SmartTies provides extraction functions ω as follows:

- For concept papers, FMEAs, FTAs and SRSs, the structured content is extracted by functions which parse OOXML;
- The source code is parsed by the frontend of the SAMS verification framework, and split into a sequence of external declarations;
- The test plan is kept as an XML document, and edited through the web interface.

The consistency checks and change propagation rules have been implemented using 49 graph rewrite rules and 66 graph test patterns.

As tools, SmartTies uses MS-Word for editing the informal text documents, an IDE of the user's choice for the source code, CUnit as the unit test framework (with a simple parser extracting the test results from the log file and inserting them into the test plan), and Subversion as the configuration management and version control backend.

The system architecture is web-based: the SmartTies server allows the user to upload or download documents, trigger the document analysis, and commit and update from a Subversion repository. The user accesses the system by two means: firstly, a plug-in for MS-Word allows to download and upload directly from within MS-Word, and secondly, a web interface allows to download and upload other documents, gives an overview over the current development status, and allows to start internal and external reviewing (Fig. 9). When the user triggers a document analysis, impacts in Word documents are reflected back to

Fig. 10. Annotated Primary Safety Requirement Table (in German)

the user by *annotations* which show up in MS-Word as comments (see Fig. 10). This allows a seamless workflow within MS-Word.

The workflow is further supported by a document status cycling through phases from *in progress* during development to *approved* after a successful external review; SmartTies keeps track of the status, makes sure changes to it are properly documented by review reports, and versions the documents appropriately. The review process is supplemented by a simple ticketing system, which allows reviewers (in particular external) to register a list of open question which the system developers have to account for.

6   Conclusion

This paper presented an application of the generic DocTip-methodology for maintaining heterogeneous document collections in the area of safety-critical systems. While the DocTip engine is generic with respect to document types and operates purely on documents written in XML, SmartTies provides the necessary encodings of the application-depending document types in XML and the graph rewriting rules to propagate local changes in one document to the entire document collection. This allows for flexible development environments in which a user can provide or assemble specifications and corresponding propagation rules for their individually used document types. As a use case we applied SmartTies for a development of a small project with five MS word documents (concept paper, test concept description, FTA, SRS, and a user manual), a test plan with 40 test cases, ca. 650 loc CUnit test suites, and 430 loc implementation in C. We were able to successfully model the consistency rules and uses cases from Sect. 2 and Sect. 4 in our system. The text graph for the whole collection consisted of about 15000 nodes and the model graph of about 900 objects and 1500 relations. The analysis of a change using the graph rewriting rules consists of about 900-1000 graph rewriting rules and takes about 8.7s on an 2.8 GHz Intel Core i7 with 4GB RAM.

Up to now, instantiating the DocTip framework for a specific setting such as SmartTies has been laborious work, especially when formalising the impact analysis in terms of graph rewriting rules. However, we are working on general patterns for such analysis rules that will simplify this process significantly.

References

1. Autexier, S., David, C., Dietrich, D., Kohlhase, M., Zholudev, V.: Workflows for the Management of Change in Science, Technologies, Engineering and Mathematics. In: Conferences on Intelligent Computer Mathematics, CICM 2011 (2011)
2. Hutter, D., Autexier, S.: Formal Software Development in MAYA. In: Hutter, D., Stephan, W. (eds.) Mechanizing Mathematical Reasoning. LNCS (LNAI), vol. 2605, pp. 407–432. Springer, Heidelberg (2005)
3. Autexier, S., Lüth, C.: Adding Change Impact Analysis to the Formal Verification of C Programs. In: Méry, D., Merz, S. (eds.) IFM 2010. LNCS, vol. 6396, pp. 59–73. Springer, Heidelberg (2010)
4. Autexier, S., Müller, N.: Semantics-based change impact analysis for heterogeneous collections of documents. In: Gormish, M., Ingold, R. (eds.) Proc. 10th ACM Symposium on Document Engineering, DocEng 2010 (2010)
5. Beck, K.: Embracing change with extreme programming. IEEE Computer 32(10) (1999)
6. Briand, L.C., Labiche, Y., O'Sullivan, L., Sówka, M.M.: Automated impact analysis of UML models. Journal of Systems and Software 79(3), 339–352 (2006)
7. Geiß, R., Batz, G.V., Grund, D., Hack, S., Szalkowski, A.M.: GrGen: A Fast SPO-Based Graph Rewriting Tool. In: Corradini, A., Ehrig, H., Montanari, U., Ribeiro, L., Rozenberg, G. (eds.) ICGT 2006. LNCS, vol. 4178, pp. 383–397. Springer, Heidelberg (2006)
8. Hutter, D.: Semantic Management of Heterogeneous Documents. In: Aguirre, A.H., Borja, R.M., Garciá, C.A.R. (eds.) MICAI 2009. LNCS (LNAI), vol. 5845, pp. 1–14. Springer, Heidelberg (2009)
9. IBM. Rational DOORS, `http://www-01.ibm.com/software/awdtools/doors/`
10. IEC: IEC 61508 – Functional safety of electrical/electronic/programmable electronic safety-related systems. IEC, Geneva, Switzerland (2000)
11. Mossakowski, T., Autexier, S., Hutter, D.: Development graphs – proof management for structured specifications. Journal of Logic and Algebraic Programming 67(1-2), 114–145 (2006)
12. Reichmann, C.: PREEVision - bridging the gap between electrical/electronic and mechanical areas. Automobile Konstruktion 1, 1–4 (2011)
13. Royce, W.W.: Managing the development of large software systems: Concepts and techniques. In: ICSE, pp. 328–339 (1987)
14. RTCA/DO-178B: Software Considerations in Airborne Systems and Equipment Certification. RTCA, Inc., Washington, D.C. 20036 (1992)
15. Täubig, H., Frese, U., Hertzberg, C., Lüth, C., Mohr, S., Vorobev, E., Walter, D.: Guaranteeing functional safety: design for provability and computer-aided verification. Autonomous Robots 32(3), 303–331 (2012)

Tracking Behavioral Constraints during Object-Oriented Software Evolution⋆

Johan Dovland, Einar Broch Johnsen, and Ingrid Chieh Yu

Department of Informatics, University of Oslo, Norway
{johand,einarj,ingridcy}@ifi.uio.no

Abstract. An intrinsic property of real world software is that it needs to evolve. The software is continuously changed during the initial development phase, and existing software may need modifications to meet new requirements. To facilitate the development and maintenance of programs, it is an advantage to have *programming environments* which allow the developer to alternate between programming and verification tasks in a flexible manner and which ensures correctness of the final program with respect to specified behavioral properties.

This paper proposes a *formal framework* for the flexible development of object-oriented programs, which supports an interleaving of programming and verification steps. The motivation for this framework is to avoid imposing restrictions on the programming steps to facilitate the verification steps, but rather to track *unresolved proof obligations* and *specified properties* of a program which evolves. A *proof environment* connects unresolved proof obligations and specified properties by means of a *soundness invariant* which is maintained by both programming and verification steps. Once the set of unresolved obligations is empty, the invariant ensures the soundness of the overall program verification.

1 Introduction

An intrinsic property of software in the real world is that it needs to evolve. This can be as part of the initial *development* phase, *improvements* to meet new requirements, or as part of a software *customization* process such as, e.g., feature selection in software product lines or delta-oriented programming [1,14]. Requirements to a piece of software also change over time. For this reason we cannot always expect that the specifications are written before the code is developed, and that the verification efforts happen afterwards. As the code is enhanced and modified, it becomes increasingly complex and *drifts away from its original design* [11]. For this reason, it may be desirable to redesign the code base to improve its structure, thereby reducing software complexity. For example, the process of *refactoring* in object-oriented software development describes changes to the internal structure of software to make the software easier to understand

---

⋆ Partly funded by the EU project FP7-231620 HATS: Highly Adaptable and Trustworthy Software using Formal Models (http://www.hats-project.eu).

T. Margaria and B. Steffen (Eds.): ISoLA 2012, Part I, LNCS 7609, pp. 253–268, 2012.

and cheaper to modify without changing its observable behavior [6]. In this paper, the term *adaptable class hierarchies* captures class transformations which occur during object-oriented software evolution, including the development, improvement, customization, and refactoring of class hierarchies.

This paper proposes a formal framework for tracking behavioral constraints during such class transformations to allow incremental reasoning about adaptable class hierarchies, by extending the approach taken by *lazy behavioral subtyping* [4]. We consider a version of Featherweight Java [7] extended with behavioral interfaces, in which methods are annotated with pre/postconditions, and a number of *basic adaptation operations* for manipulating classes and interfaces, reflecting the level of basic program modifications. We consider a series of "snapshots" of a program during software development and evolution, in which the developer applies adaptation and analysis steps. A *proof environment* records both unresolved proof obligations and verified properties, and is manipulated by the different adaptation and analysis steps. Unresolved obligations reflect constraints that are imposed by the analysis, but it remains to ensure that they are satisfied. The purpose of analysis steps is to ensure that unresolved obligations are satisfied, whereas adaptation steps may spawn a number of unresolved obligations, reflecting that the program has changed. The spawned obligations depend on the actual adaptation, and may be inferred from the proof environment.

Paper overview: Sect. 2 motivates our approach, Sect. 3 introduces proof outlines, and Sect. 4 a kernel object-oriented language. Sect. 5 defines a soundness invariant for incremental reasoning, and Sect. 6 explains basic programming and verification tasks in our framework. Sect. 7 presents an example, Sect. 8 discusses related work, and Sect. 9 concludes the paper.

2   Motivation

There is a conflict of interest between the development and verification processes for software: the easier it is to flexibly develop and maintain programs in a language, the harder it is to verify programs in this language. Object-oriented programming, the de facto industry standard for software development, is a case in point: software verification projects have made significant progress in the last decade to support the verification of object-oriented programs, but features such as concurrency, class inheritance, and late binding still pose challenges.

Object orientation offers flexible ways of structuring and restructuring code by means of class inheritance and late binding, but reasoning about the behavior of object-oriented systems is in general non-trivial due to complications which arise from these code structuring mechanisms. Object-oriented software development is based on an open world assumption; i.e., class hierarchies are typically extendable. To have reasoning control under such an open world assumption, it is advantageous to have a framework which controls the properties required of method redefinitions. With *modular reasoning*, a new class can be analysed in the context of its superclasses, such that superclass' properties are guaranteed to be maintained. This has the significant advantage that each class can be fully verified at once, independent of subclasses which may be designed later. The best known modular framework for class hierarchies is *behavioral subtyping* [8], but this framework has been criticized for being overly restrictive and is often violated in practice [15]. It is therefore of interest to investigate approaches which are better aligned with the flexibility expected by the software developer, even if these may have a higher price in terms of verification effort.

Incremental reasoning generalizes modular reasoning by possibly generating new verification conditions for superclasses to guarantee new properties. Additional properties may be established in superclasses after the initial analysis, but old properties remain valid. Incremental reasoning subsumes modularity: if the initial properties of a classes are sufficiently strong (e.g., by adhering to a behavioral contract), it never becomes necessary to add new properties. *Lazy behavioral subtyping* (LBS) is a formal framework for such incremental reasoning, which allows more flexible code reuse than modular frameworks. LBS is based on a separation of concerns between the behavioral *specifications* of method definitions and the behavioral *requirements* to method calls. Both specifications and requirements are manipulated through a bookkeeping framework which controls the analysis and the proof obligations in the context of a given class. Properties are only inherited by need. Inherited requirements on method redefinition are as weak as possible for ensuring soundness. LBS seems well-suited for the incremental reasoning style desirable for object-oriented software development, and can be adjusted to different mechanisms for code reuse. It was originally developed for single inheritance class hierarchies [4], but has later been extended to multiple inheritance [5] and to trait-based code reuse [2].

Adaptable class hierarchies add a level of complexity to proof systems for object-oriented programs, as classes in the middle of a hierarchy can change. Unrestricted, such changes may easily violate previously verified properties in both sub- and superclasses. The management of verification conditions becomes more complicated than for a class hierarchy which is only extended at the bottom. To facilitate program development and maintenance, it is an advantage that programming and verification activities go hand in hand. For this purpose, we need programming environments for flexible alternation between programming and verification tasks. The proposed analysis does not assume that class hierarchies are build top-down; the internal class structures may be revealed during implementation. The proposed analysis technique is developed with the intention to better integrate formal verification with software engineering processes.

3 Proof Outlines and Soundness

The reasoning framework is presented in terms of *proof outlines* [12], which can be explained in terms of Hoare triples. A Hoare triple $\{p\}\, t\, \{q\}$ defines the effect on a state described by the *precondition* p when a statement t executes, leading to a state described by the *postcondition* q (where p and q are assertions). The meaning $\models \{p\}\, t\, \{q\}$ of a triple $\{p\}\, t\, \{q\}$ is here given by a standard partial correctness interpretation: if t is executed in a state where p holds and the execution terminates, then q holds in the state after t has terminated. The derivation of triples can be done in any suitable program logic. Let PL be such a program logic and let $\vdash_{PL} \{p\}\, t\, \{q\}$ denote that $\{p\}\, t\, \{q\}$ is derivable in PL.

A proof outline for t is obtained by decorating t with assertions at selected program points such that the analysis between these program points can be done mechanically. A classical example is to decorate loops in the program with loop invariants. For the purposes of this paper, we are interested in decorating method calls with pre- and postconditions, and we assume that all method calls in the considered proof outlines are decorated. Let $O \vdash_{PL} t : (p, q)$ denote that O is a proof outline for t such that $\vdash_{PL} \{p\}\, t\, \{q\}$ holds, assuming that the decorated statements O are correct. The assertion pair (p, q) is called a *guarantee* for t, and to the decorated call statements in O as *requirements* for the called methods, and we say that these requirements are *imposed* by t. Thus, for a decorated method call $\{r\}\, n()\, \{s\}$ in O, we say that (r, s) is a requirement for n. This terminology can be lifted to method definitions $m(\overline{x})\{t\}$ as follows: If the proof outline O is such that $O \vdash_{PL} t : (p, q)$, we say that m guarantees (p, q) by imposing the requirements in O on the methods that are called by the method body t.

Given a set of methods, proof outlines allow a "divide and conquer" technique in the overall program analysis. For each method we may establish a guarantee by providing a proof outline for the method body. For the overall *soundness* of the program analysis, we need to ensure that each requirement in a proof outline follows from the guarantee of the called method. Let (p, q) be the guarantee for m, and assume that the requirement (r, s) is imposed on m by some proof outline. We essentially need to check the implications $r \Rightarrow p$ and $q \Rightarrow s$ which can be captured by an *entailment relation* $\rightarrowtail$ over assertion pairs, defined as follows [5]:

$$(p, q) \;\rightarrowtail\; (r, s) \triangleq (\forall \overline{z}_0 \,.\, p \Rightarrow q') \Rightarrow (\forall \overline{z}_1 \,.\, r \Rightarrow s')$$

Here, $\overline{z}_0$ and $\overline{z}_1$ denote the logical variables in (p, q) and (r, s), respectively, and the primed assertions q' and s' replace all occurrences of the fields f in q and s by some fresh name f'. This entailment relation may be lifted to sets of assertion pairs [5], e.g., to prove that (r, s) follows from a set of assertion pairs.

Given a closed set of methods (i.e., each method called from the set is defined in the set) and a proof outline establishing a guarantee for each method, the set of proof outlines is *sound* if each requirement follows from the method guarantee in the set. For a proof outline $O \vdash_{PL} t : (p, q)$ in the set, we have $\models \{p\}\, t\, \{q\}$.

4   Proof Outlines for Object-Oriented Programs

In this section the soundness notion for proof outlines is extended to an object-oriented context where the methods are organized in classes in a class hierarchy.

4.1   An Object-Oriented Kernel Language

We consider a kernel object-oriented language with the syntax given in Fig. 1. A program P defines interface and class. An interface I extends superinterfaces

$$
\begin{array}{ll}
P ::= \overline{K}\,\overline{L} & K ::= \textbf{interface } I \textbf{ extends } \overline{I}\ \{\overline{MA}\} \\
T ::= I \mid \textsf{Bool} \mid \textsf{Int} & L ::= \textbf{class } C \textbf{ extends } C \textbf{ implements } \overline{I}\ \{\overline{F};\overline{M}\} \\
F ::= T\,f & MA ::= [T \mid \textsf{Void}]\ m\ (\overline{T\,x}) : (p,q) \\
M ::= MA\ \{\overline{T\,x};t;\textbf{return } e\} & t ::= t;t \mid v := rhs \mid v.m(\overline{e}) \mid \textbf{if } b\ \{t\} \mid \textbf{skip} \\
v ::= f \mid x & rhs ::= \textbf{new } C(\,) \mid v.m(\overline{e}) \mid m(\overline{e}) \mid e
\end{array}
$$

Fig. 1. The language syntax. C is a class name, and I an interface name. Variables v are fields (f) or local variables (x), and e denotes side-effect free expressions over the variables, b expressions of Boolean type, and p and q are assertions. Vector notation denotes lists, as in the expression list $\overline{e}$, interface list $\overline{I}$, and in the variable declaration list $\overline{T\,v}$, otherwise vectors denote sets, as in $\overline{K}, \overline{L}, \overline{MA}$ and $\overline{M}$. To distinguish assignments from equations in specifications and expressions, we use $:=$ and $=$ respectively.

$\overline{I}$ and declares a set of *method constraints* $\overline{MA}$, where a constraint is given by a method signature with pre/post assertions. An interface may extend its superinterfaces with declarations of new methods and with additional constraints for methods already declared in the superinterfaces. We say that I *provides* the methods declared in I or in a superinterface of I. For interfaces I and J, we say that I is *below* J and J is *above* I if I equals J or if J is a superinterface of I.

A class C may inherit from at most one direct superclass B, implement a list $\overline{I}$ of interfaces, and define fields $\overline{F}$ and methods $\overline{M}$. The class may override superclass methods, but we assume no method overloading and no field shadowing (fields with the same name in different classes may be qualified by class names). We say that a method m is *available* in C if m is defined in $\overline{M}$ or a definition is inherited from the superclass B, i.e., the method is available in B. To implement an interface I, each method provided by I must be available in C and the interface constraints must be satisfied. Class C may in addition define *auxiliary* methods for internal purposes. For flexibility, interfaces are not inherited at the class level: The class C may implement different interfaces than those of its superclass B, which leads to a separation of class hierarchies and type hierarchies. Remark that the situation where interfaces are inherited at class level may be considered as the special case where C must implement at least the interfaces of B, leading to behavioral subtyping constraints on class inheritance. *Local calls* in C are late-bound in a standard bottom-up manner following the superclass relation: when a local call $m()$ is executed on an instance of C, the binding is resolved by starting the bottom-up search in C. For classes C and D, we say that C is *above* D and D is *below* C if C equals D or if C is a superclass of D.

Object references are typed by interfaces. Let $v : I$ denote that v is a variable of type I, so v may refer to an instance of any class D, implementing an interface below I. For *external calls* $v.m()$, m must be provided by I, and can bind to any object to which v may refer. Statements t and expressions e are standard.

4.2   Proof Outlines and Inheritance

The notion of proof outlines extends naturally to object-oriented programs; to specify and reason about a program, proof outlines may be provided for the methods implemented in the classes of the program. Each proof outline gives a method guarantee and a set of method call requirements. However, in contrast to the presentation in Sect. 3, there is not a one-to-one correspondence between a call statement and the implementations to which the call may bind. For a requirement $\{r\}\, v.m()\, \{s\}$ with v typed by interface I, we need to ensure that (r, s) follows from each implementation to which the call may bind, i.e, for each class that implements some interface below I. However, proving this directly for each class requires global knowledge about all classes, and contradicts the open world assumption by which classes may be incrementally added.

To enhance the modularity of the reasoning system, we therefore assume that interface constraints are sufficiently strong to analyze external calls. For $\{r\}\, v.m()\, \{s\}$, this means that (r, s) must follow from the constraints for m in I. If a class D implements I or a subinterface of I, the constraints for m in I must be satisfied by the implementation. By transitivity, we then know that the external call requirement is satisfied by all implementations to which the external call can be bound. This reasoning approach is feasible in an open environment where the programmer does not control all parts of the program: Calls to external objects may be done without knowing the detailed implementation of those objects. If the interfaces are fixed, this means that the classes of external objects may be implemented independently from the current class. Also, the approach facilitates e.g., calls to library methods without consulting the library implementation. Remark that interface encapsulation generally leads to incomplete reasoning systems, since an interface represents an abstraction of the actual implementations. This is illustrated by the following example:

Example 1. Consider an interface I with a method m and a class C which implements I. The class D makes a call to m of a newly created instance of C.

```
interface I { Int m() : (true, return ≥0)}
class C implements I {Int m() {return 2} : (true, return = 2)}
class D implements J {Int n() {I x := new C; Int v := x.m(); return v}}
```

The guarantee for m in C satisfies the interface constraint. The question is what we know about the value returned by method n in class D. By inspecting the code, we see that the method will always return the value 2. A proof outline for for n with guarantee (true, **return** = 2) results in a call requirement $\{$true$\}$x.m()$\{$**return** = 2$\}$ but the constraint given by I only promises **return** ≥ 0, which means that the requirement cannot be verified. Remark that a proof outline for n with guarantee (true, **return** ≥ 0) can be verified.

For a language with interface encapsulation, a natural goal for the program analysis is to verify that classes satisfy the constraints of the implemented interfaces. Let $body(C, m)$ denote the implementation of a method m that is available in C. If I gives the constraint (p, q) for m and C implements I, we must ensure $\models_C \{p\}\, body(C, m)\, \{q\}$, where the subscript denotes that the triple must be true when executed on an instance of C. We emphasize that the constraint originates from the fact that C implements I. Especially, the constraint need not be satisfied if $body(C, m)$ is executed on an instance of some subclass D of C, if D does

```
interface  I { Int m() : (true, return=0)}
interface  J { Int m() : (true, return>0)}
interface  K { Int m() : (true, return<0)}

class  C implements I {Int x;
  Int m() {x:=n(); return x}
  Int n() {return 0}}
class  D extends C implements J {Int n() {return 1}}
class  E extends C implements K {Int n() {return −1}}
```

Fig. 2. A small class hierarchy with method overriding

not implement I. Related to C, the binding of a local call to some method n is uniquely determined by the available implementation in C. Given the above constraint (p, q) and a proof outline O such that $O \vdash_{PL} body(C, m) : (p, q)$ and $\{r\} n() \{s\}$ is a requirement in O, it is sufficient to analyze the requirement with respect to the implementation available in C. If the analysis of all requirements succeed, we may then conclude $\models_C \{p\} body(C, m) \{q\}$.

Since locally called methods may be overridden differently in different subclasses, it is natural to allow more than one guarantee for each method. The guarantees may possibly be in conflict as illustrated by Example 2.

Example 2. Consider the code in Fig. 2. For class C, we supply a proof outline for m with the guarantee (true, **return** $= 0$) to ensure that C satisfies the constraints of interface I. This proof outline imposes the requirement $\{true\} n() \{return = 0\}$, which can be verified for n as defined in C. For class D, the method m must satisfy the interface constraint (true, **return** > 0). A proof outline with this guarantee yields the requirement $\{true\} n() \{return > 0\}$, which can be verified for the overriding version of n in D. The verification of class E follows the same pattern as for D. Combined, this leads to three different proof outlines for m, according to the different behavior of the called method. When analyzing each class, we may select the proof outline that fits with the actual interface constraint.

Allowing many proof outlines provides flexibility when analyzing independent properties. For instance, if C implements two interfaces I and J, I declares a constraint (p_I, q_I) for m, and J declares a different constraint (p_J, q_J) for m. The constraints may be verified independently by providing two proof outlines.

Assuming type safety, we formulate the following *soundness conditions* for a class C implementing the interfaces $\overline{I}$: *A set of proof outlines (with guarantees and requirements) for the methods available in C are given such that:*

- *For each method m provided by $\overline{I}$, the guarantees for m ensure all interface constraints.*
- *For external calls $\{r\} v.m() \{s\}$ in some proof outline, the requirement (r, s) follows from the constraints for m in I (where $v : I$).*
- *For each local call $\{r\} m() \{s\}$ in some proof outline, the requirement (r, s) follows from the guarantees for m.*

If a proof outline for m in C with guarantee (p, q) is verified, the soundness constraints ensure $\models_C \{p\}\ body(C, m)\ \{q\}$ (provided that PL is also sound).

5   A Soundness Invariant for the Open World

In this section we generalize the above soundness conditions for an open world assumption for software evolution, by accommodating an interleaving of software evolution and analysis tasks. The generalization is formulated as a *soundness invariant* which is maintained by each individual task. Software evolution tasks are represented as *basic adaptations* which are applied to the classes of an existing program. These adaptations affect the class hierarchy of the program, and are discussed in detail in Sect. 6. Analysis tasks are performed at user request, and the user may select which program properties to analyze.

We assume given a set $\mathcal{U}(C)$ of *unresolved obligations* associated with each class C. This set contains requirements and constraints imposed by the analysis so far, but for which we have not checked that they are satisfied. The set $\mathcal{U}(C)$ is in general extended by the different adaptation tasks, reflecting that proof obligations are spawned if the program is changed. Program analysis removes obligations from $\mathcal{U}(C)$ and perform the actions necessary to maintain the soundness invariant. We identify three kinds of obligations that occur in $\mathcal{U}(C)$:

- $I \rightsquigarrow m : (p, q)$. Here, $m : (p, q)$ is a constraint imposed by I. When this obligation appears in $\mathcal{U}(C)$, the class C is declared to implement I, but it remains to ensure that the implementation actually satisfies the constraint.
- $m \rightsquigarrow n : (r, s)$. Method m is here available in C and the obligation reflects the requirement $\{r\}\ n\ \{s\}$ of a local call statement in a verified proof outline for m. When this obligation appears in $\mathcal{U}(C)$, it remains to ensure that the requirement is satisfied by the called method.
- $m \rightsquigarrow I : n : (r, s)$. This obligation reflects that the requirement $\{r\}\ v.n\ \{s\}$, with $v : I$, is imposed by an external call statement in a verified proof outline for m. When this obligation appears in $\mathcal{U}(C)$, it remains to check that (r, s) follows from the constraints of I.

Remark that the last two obligations include the name of the method which imposes the requirement. As explained in more detail in Sect. 6 this allows us to discard obligations if m changes before the requirements have been analyzed. The soundness invariant is formulated by weakening the above soundness conditions:

Definition 1 (Soundness invariant). *For each class C implementing interfaces $\bar{I}$, the set of proof outlines for the methods available in C are such that:*

- *For each m provided by some I in $\bar{I}$ with constraint (p, q), either (p, q) follows from the guarantees for m, or $I \rightsquigarrow m : (p, q)$ is in $\mathcal{U}(C)$.*
- *For each external call $\{r\}\ v.m()\ \{s\}$ in a proof outline for method n, where $v : I$, either (r, s) follows from the constraints for m in I, or $n \rightsquigarrow I : m : (r, s)$ is in $\mathcal{U}(C)$.*

$$\begin{aligned}
\textit{Class adaptation} ::=\ & \textit{newCls}(C) \mid \textit{remCls}(C) \mid \textit{newFld}(C, F) \\
& \mid \textit{remFld}(C, F) \mid \textit{newMtd}(C, M) \mid \textit{remMtd}(C, M) \\
& \mid \textit{setSup}(C, B) \mid \textit{newImpl}(C, I) \mid \textit{remImpl}(C, I) \\
\textit{Interface adaptation} ::=\ & \textit{newInt}(I) \mid \textit{remInt}(I) \mid \textit{newConstr}(I, m : (p, q)) \\
& \mid \textit{remConstr}(I, m : (p, q)) \mid \textit{newSup}(I, J) \\
& \mid \textit{remSup}(I, J)
\end{aligned}$$

Fig. 3. Basic class and interface adaptations

- *For each local call* $\{r\}\ m()\ \{s\}$ *in a proof outline for method* n, *either* (r, s) *follows from the guarantees for* m, *or* $n \rightsquigarrow m : (p, q)$ *is in* $\mathcal{U}(C)$.

If all unresolved requirements have been verified, i.e., the set $\mathcal{U}(C)$ is empty, the soundness invariant reduces to the soundness conditions given in Sect. 4. The soundness of a class C depends only on declared interfaces and classes above C: i.e., the soundness of C is not affected by modifications of subclasses C.

6 Evolution through Adaptable Class Hierarchies

Object-oriented software evolution can be perceived as a sequence of adaptations to a class hierarchy. The framework allows an interleaving of adaptation and analysis tasks, initiated by the user. A *program environment* $\mathcal{P}$ keeps track of the current definitions of classes and interfaces. In addition to the *unresolved obligations* sets $\mathcal{U}$, each class C and method m available in C will maintain a set $\mathcal{G}(C, m)$ of *verified specifications*. Elements in $\mathcal{G}(C, m)$ are tuples consisting of an assertion pair (the guarantee) and a proof outline (capturing the requirements).

6.1 Basic Program Adaptations

Consider a suite of basic program adaptations as given in Fig. 3, each of which reflects evolution at the level of a single structuring artefact (i.e., a method, class, or interface in the kernel language). We focus on behavioral analysis, so certain behavioral preserving modifications are not considered, such as the consequent renaming of fields or methods within a program. Such renaming is captured by the basic adaptations, but would produce a number of trivial proof obligations. We explain how each adaptation maintains the soundness invariant by recording unresolved obligations, and discuss the verification complexity. Complex adaptations may be constructed by combining basic adaptations (see Sect. 6.2).

Class adaptations. We consider the following basic adaptations for classes:

- **newCls(C) and remCls(C).** The adaptation *newCls*(C) inserts a new class with name C in $\mathcal{P}$. The new class is initially empty (i.e., without inheritance and implements clauses and method definitions), so the soundness invariant is maintained without modifying the sets $\mathcal{U}$ and $\mathcal{G}$. The adaptation *remCls*(C) removes the class C from $\mathcal{P}$. The set $\mathcal{U}(C)$ is erased and all verified proof outlines for C in $\mathcal{G}$ are removed. For this adaptation to be safe, we assume that C has no subclasses and that C does not appear in any **new** statements, which requires global knowledge about the classes.

- **newFld**(C, F) **and remFld**(C, F). The adaptation $newFld(C, F)$ includes the field F in C, and $remFld(C, F)$ removes field F from C. Since there are no field shadowing, we may assume that a new field is not used in classes above or below C. To preserve type safety, a removed field cannot be used in classes below C.

- **newMtd**(C, M). The definition of C is here extended with a method M, or M replaces the old version if a method with the same name was previously defined in C. Let m be the name of M. The soundness invariant is maintained as follows: If m is redefined, the verified specifications for the old version no longer apply, thus the set $\mathcal{G}(C, m)$ is emptied. Consequently, unresolved obligations in $\mathcal{U}(C)$ that are imposed by these specifications are removed. Such obligations are of the forms $m \rightsquigarrow I : n : (r, s)$ and $m \rightsquigarrow n : (r, s)$ for some I, n, and (r, s). We furthermore perform the following steps: *a)* If m is public, the constraints for m, imposed by the implemented interfaces, are added to $\mathcal{U}(C)$ as obligations of the form $I \rightsquigarrow m : (p, q)$ for some I and (p, q); *b)* Verified specifications for other methods in C may impose requirements on m. These requirements are included in $\mathcal{U}(C)$ as obligations of the form $n \rightsquigarrow m : (r, s)$ for some n and (r, s); and *c)* For each subclass D of C which inherits m from C, we perform the corresponding modifications of $\mathcal{U}(D)$ and $\mathcal{G}(D, m)$ as explained for C above.

- **remMtd**(C, M). Removing a method with name m is similar to method redefinition. We empty $\mathcal{G}(C, m)$ and remove unresolved obligations imposed by m from $\mathcal{U}(C)$. However, there may still be calls to m in C if the method is inherited from some superclass B of C. Therefore, $\mathcal{U}(C)$ is extended by interface constraints if m is public, and with requirements imposed by the verified specifications of C. All of these modifications are repeated for each subclass D of C which inherits m from B.

- **setSup**(C, B). This adaptation sets B to be the immediate superclass of C. After the operation, C extends B in $\mathcal{P}$. To maintain the soundness invariant, we consider each available method definition M in B that is not overridden by C. The operations performed to $\mathcal{U}$ and $\mathcal{G}$ correspond to the operations needed by a $remMtd(C, M)$ adaptation, which means that unresolved obligations may also be added to subclasses of C. Remark that the soundness invariant is maintained for the old direct superclass of C, since the soundness of that class does not depend on its subclass C.

- **newImpl**(C, I). This adaptation extends the implements clause of C with interface I. The soundness invariant is maintained by extending $\mathcal{U}(C)$ with all constraints of I. The adaptation has only local effects on C.

- **remImpl**(C, I). This adaptation removes I from the implements clause of C. Locally, this means that we can remove unresolved obligations from $\mathcal{U}(C)$ that are imposed by this interface. However, this is a complicated adaptation to implement, since it requires global knowledge of the system. To be safe, no references to C objects can be typed by an interface above I. Especially, for each statement $v :=$ **new** $C(\ )$, the declared type of v must be implemented by C after reducing the implements clause.

Interface adaptations. We consider these basic adaptations for interfaces:

- **newInt**(I). This adaptation introduces a new empty interface in $\mathcal{P}$, which trivially maintains the soundness invariant.
- **remInt**(I). This adaptation removes the interface I from $\mathcal{P}$. Global concerns must be taken for the adaptation to be safe, ensuring that no other interface is inheriting I and that no class implements I. Thus to perform this adaptation, it may be necessary to first perform a sequence of *remSup* (explained below) and *remImpl* adaptations, which is quite expensive. Remark that as an effect of such a sequence, all references typed by I are removed from the global system, which makes it safe to remove I.
- **newConstr**$(I, m : (p, q))$. The definition of I is here extended by the constraint $m : (p, q)$. The adaptation may be used to add a new constraint to an already provided method, or to extend I such that it provides m. To preserve the soundness invariant, we must find each class C which implements an interface below I, and add $I \rightsquigarrow m : (p, q)$ to $\mathcal{U}(C)$.
- **remConstr**$(I, m : (p, q))$. By removing the constraint $m : (p, q)$ from I, the behavior that can be assumed for external calls made via I is reduced. Thus, to maintain the soundness invariant, a global check must be performed on all requirements imposed on m via I. For each class C with method n, we consider $\mathcal{G}(C, n)$. For any call $\{r\}v.m()\{s\}$ with $v : I'$ in these proof outlines, $\mathcal{U}(C)$ is extended by $n \rightsquigarrow I' : m : (r, s)$, if I' is below I.
- **newSup**(I, J). This adaptation includes interface J in the extends clause of interface I. As a result, we need to check that all constraints above J are satisfied for classes which implement an interface below I. For each such class C and constraint $m : (p, q)$ of J, we extend $\mathcal{U}(C)$ with $J \rightsquigarrow m : (p, q)$
- **remSup**(I, J). This adaptation removes J from the extends clause if I. As for the *remConstr* adaptation, this means that the behavior assumed by external calls via I is reduced. For each constraint $m : (p, q)$ of J, we need to check all classes which make calls to m via I or a subinterface of I, in the same manner as for a *remConstr*$(I, m : (p, q))$ adaptation.

6.2   Combining Adaptations

High-level operations can be defined from the basic adaptations. Adaptations may be lifted to take more than one element as the second argument by flattening the adaptation to a *sequence* of basic adaptations; e.g., $newMtd(C, M \cup \overline{M}) \triangleq newMtd(C, M) \cdot newMtd(C, \overline{M})$ (where $\cdot$ is the sequence append constructor). Extending the program with a *new class definition* may then be defined by:

class C extends B implements $\overline{I}$ $\{\overline{F}; \overline{M}\}$ $\triangleq$
　　$newCls(C) \cdot setSup(C, B) \cdot newImpl(C, \overline{I}) \cdot newFld(C, \overline{F}) \cdot newMtd(C, \overline{M})$

The following adaptation *modifies an existing class definition*, adding support for new interfaces, defining new fields, and (re)defining methods:

modify C implements $\overline{I}$ $\{\overline{F}; \overline{M}\}$ $\triangleq newImpl(C, \overline{I}) \cdot newFld(C, \overline{F}) \cdot newMtd(C, \overline{M})$

The basic adaptations may be further combined to cover common refactoring patterns [6]. For instance, *moving a method M* from class C to class B is captured by the sequence $remMtd(C, M) \cdot newMtd(B, M)$. By applying predefined refactorings defined as sequences of basic adaptations, the user may ensure that program analysis is postponed as appropriate. For instance, if $remMtd(C, M) \cdot newMtd(B, M)$ denotes a simple *pull up method refactoring* from C to a superclass B, program analysis will probably fail between the two adaptations as the proof obligations cannot in general be resolved at that stage.

6.3   Analysis Tasks

An analysis task removes an obligation from $\mathcal{U}(C)$ which is analyzed depending on its structure. This analysis may spawn new proof obligations which are included in $\mathcal{U}(C)$; the size of $\mathcal{U}(C)$ does not necessarily shrink by each task. However, each analysis task maintains the soundness invariant, and the soundness conditions are ensured if all unresolved obligations are successfully analyzed.

- *Obligation* $I \rightsquigarrow m : (p, q) \in \mathcal{U}(C)$. This obligation is resolved if (p, q) follows by entailment from the guarantees in $\mathcal{G}(C, m)$. To ensure entailment, it may be necessary to first extend $\mathcal{G}(C, m)$. Let O be a proof outline such that $O \vdash_{PL} body(C, m) : (p', q')$ for some (p', q'). Extending $\mathcal{G}(C, m)$ by $\langle (p', q'), O \rangle$ means that $\mathcal{U}(C)$ must be extended to maintain the soundness invariant: For each requirement of the form $\{r\} n() \{s\}$ in O, the obligation $m \rightsquigarrow n : (r, s)$ is included in $\mathcal{U}(C)$, and for each requirement of the form $\{r\} v.n() \{s\}$ with $v : I$, the obligation $m \rightsquigarrow I : n : (r, s)$ is included in $\mathcal{U}(C)$. Remark that the supplied guarantee (p', q') may be identical to (p, q).
- *Obligation* $m \rightsquigarrow n : (r, s) \in \mathcal{U}(C)$. This obligation is resolved if (r, s) follows by entailment from the guarantees in $\mathcal{G}(C, n)$. Similar to above, it may be necessary to first extend $\mathcal{G}(C, n)$.
- *Obligation* $m \rightsquigarrow I : n : (r, s) \in \mathcal{U}(C)$. This obligation is resolved if (r, s) follows from the constraints for m in I. One may need to extend the constraints of I before removal, e.g., by the adaptation $newConstr(I, n : (r, s))$.

7   Example

Figure 4 presents a snapshot of a small bank account system under development. A class Account provides basic operations for depositing and withdrawing amounts of money. The balance of the account is stored in a field bal. A class Customer has references to two Account objects; a regular account reg and a savings account sav. The method save implements functionality for transferring an amount from the regular account to the savings account. We consider different adaptations of the code in Fig. 4 and explain the essential parts of the analysis.

Internal modifications of Account. Assume that the programmer extracts the manipulation of bal in Account into one method, defined by the adaptation

$$newMtd(\text{Account, Bool update(Int } y) : (bal = b_0, bal = b_0 + y \land \textbf{return}) \{$$
$$\text{bal} := \text{bal} + y; \textbf{ return true}\}).$$

```
interface IAccount {
  Bool deposit( Int x)   :  (bal = b₀ ∧ x > 0, bal = b₀ + x ∧ return)
  Bool withdraw(Int x)  :  (bal = b₀ ∧ x > 0 ∧ bal − x ≥ 0, bal = b₀ − x ∧ return)
                           (bal = b₀ ∧ x > 0 ∧ bal − x < 0, bal = b₀ ∧ ¬return)
}
class  Account implements IAccount { Int bal  :=  0;
  Bool deposit( Int x) { Bool val  :=  false ;
    if  (x>0) {bal :=  bal+x; val  :=  true}; return val
  }
  Bool withdraw(Int x) {Bool val  :=  false ;
    if  (x>0 ∧ bal−x≥0) {bal :=  bal−x; val  :=  true}; return val}}
class  Customer { IAccount reg, sav;
  Bool save  ( Int amt) {
    Bool res  :=  reg.withdraw(amt); if  ( res ) {sav.deposit (amt)}; return res}}
```

Fig. 4. The initial bank account system, with Account and Customer classes

The guarantee may be verified by a proof outline which imposes no requirements. In the sequel, we assume that this specification is in $\mathcal{G}(\text{Account}, \text{update})$.

Next we consider removing the assignments to bal from deposit and withdraw. For deposit, we may apply the following adaptation:

$$newMtd(\text{Account}, \text{Bool deposit(Int x) \{ Bool val:=false}$$
$$\text{if } (x>0) \{ \text{val} := \text{update(x)}\}; \textbf{return} \text{ val}\}).$$

Since the method definition has changed, we cannot rely on a previous verification of this method; i.e., all elements must be removed from $\mathcal{G}(\text{Account}, \text{deposit})$. However, since deposit is public, the interface constraint for this method is currently unresolved. This means that the following element is added to $\mathcal{U}(\text{Account})$:

$$\text{IAccount} \rightsquigarrow \text{deposit} : (bal = b_0 \land x > 0, bal = b_0 + x \land \textbf{return}).$$

We may consider this constraint as a guarantee for the new version of deposit, and verify a proof outline O with $\{x = y \land bal = b_0\} \text{update} \{bal = b_0 + x \land \textbf{return}\}$ as requirement. The set $\mathcal{G}(\text{Account}, \text{deposit})$ is then extended by

$$\langle (bal = b_0 \land x > 0, bal = b_0 + x \land \textbf{return}), O \rangle$$

and the obligation deposit $\rightsquigarrow$ update : $(y = x \land bal = b_0, bal = b_0 + x \land \textbf{return})$ is included in $\mathcal{U}(\text{Account})$. Now, both elements of $\mathcal{U}(\text{Account})$ follow directly from the specifications of their respective methods. Removing the assignment to bal in withdraw follows the same pattern by applying the adaptation

$$newMtd(\text{Account}, \text{Bool withdraw(Int x) \{ Bool val:=false}$$
$$\text{if } (x>0 \land \text{bal-x} \geq 0) \{ \text{val} := \text{update(-x)}\}; \textbf{return} \text{ val}\}).$$

The interface constraints listed in Fig. 4 are added to $\mathcal{U}(\text{Account})$. These can be analyzed by proof outlines which rely on the verified specification of update.

Adding new functionality. In Customer, the developer adds functionality to save money if the balance of regular account has reached a given value:

$newMtd$(Customer, Bool saveLimit() { Bool res := false; Int rbal := reg.getBal();
if (rbal>limit) {res:=save(rbal-limit)}; **return** res}).

The new method calls a method getBal via IAccount, but getBal has not yet been defined. However, the developer of Customer may assume that the method is there by postponing the adaptation of IAccount. Especially, the new method in Customer may be analyzed before adapting IAccount; new requirements will then be available at the time the interface is extended. We illustrate how such a requirement is tracked, ensuring that both IAccount and the class implementing this interface satisfy the requirement. Assume that the analysis of saveLimit imposes the following requirement on getBal, which is included in $\mathcal{U}$(Customer):

saveLimit $\rightsquigarrow$ IAccount:getBal : $(bal = b_0, bal = b_0 \wedge \textbf{return} = b_0)$.

To resolve this proof obligation, the interface IAccount must be extended, for example by the following adaptation:

$newConstr$(IAccount, Int getBal : $(bal = b_0, bal = b_0 \wedge \textbf{return} = b_0)$).

To preserve the soundness invariant, the framework adds the following obligation to all classes that implement IAccount:

IAccount $\rightsquigarrow$ getBal : $(bal = b_0, bal = b_0 \wedge \textbf{return} = b_0)$.

In this case the obligation is added to $\mathcal{U}$(Account). This obligation is resolved by a straightforward proof outline for the following method addition to Account:

$newMtd$(Account, Int getBal(){**return** bal}).

8   Related Work

Pierik and de Boer [13] present a sound and complete proof outline logic for object-oriented programs. This work is based on a closed world assumption, meaning that the class hierarchy is not open for incremental extensions. To support object-oriented design, proof systems should be constructed for incremental (or modular [3]) reasoning. Most prominent in that context are approaches based on *behavioral subtyping* [8]. Relaxing this approach, *lazy behavioral subtyping* [4,5] facilitates incremental reasoning while allowing more flexible code reuse than traditional behavioral subtyping. We refer to [4,5] for a more comprehensive discussion on incremental reasoning about class extensions.

We have found few systems for the analysis of general class modifications. Two widely discussed topics within model transformations in the context of model-driven development are refactoring and refinement. Different approaches,

Fig. 5. Basic adaptations classified by modularity. Category 1 needs access to a single class; category 2 to the hierarchy below the adapted class; category 3 needs global access to all implements clauses; and category 4 needs global access to all implementations.

Modularity level	Adaptations
1. Class local	*newCls newImpl*
2. Below class	*newFld, remFld, newMtd, remMtd, setSup*
3. Global – implements clause	*remInt, newConstr, newSup*
4. Global – implementation	*remCls, remImpl, remConstr, remSup*

e.g., [9, 10, 17], discuss how to preserve behavioral consistency between different model versions when refinement or refactoring is applied. Program transformations, such as *verification refactoring* [19], may be applied in to reduce program complexity and facilitate verification, e.g., to reduce the size of verification conditions. Contract-based software evolution of aspect-oriented programs is considered in [16], formalizing standard refactoring steps.

Going beyond behavior preserving transformations, *slicing techniques* [18] may be used to describe the effect of updates to determine which properties are preserved and which are potentially invalidated in the new version.

9   Conclusion

As programs evolve, reasoning frameworks for behavioral analysis need to handle shifting proof obligations for different program units. This paper has presented the building blocks of such a framework for object-oriented software evolution. The framework is able to handle program evolution by separating the guarantees of a method from the requirements imposed by calls to the method. The paper formulates a soundness invariant which enables a flexible interleaving of software evolution and reasoning actions by tracking unresolved proof obligations for each class. Software evolution is captured by basic adaptations on existing programs. We describe how each adaptation maintains the soundness invariant and unresolved obligations are tracked automatically. Fig. 5 summarizes the level of modularity supported by the different basic adaptations, a high degree of required global knowledge indicates that the operations may be complex to support in practice. For instance, removing interface constraints may have severe impact on software systems. Proof obligations are resolved by program analysis, and the soundness invariant ensures the overall soundness of the performed analysis when no unresolved proof obligations remain. Whereas many behavioral restrictions to software evolution make sense for manual proof, it is interesting to see to what extent advanced verification systems can be used to alleviate these restrictions by tracking constraints in a more general way. A full formalization of the framework, implementation, and soundness proofs are future work.

Acknowledgment. We thank Olaf Owe for valuable discussions of this work.

References

1. Clarke, D., Diakov, N., Hähnle, R., Johnsen, E.B., Schaefer, I., Schäfer, J., Schlatte, R., Wong, P.Y.H.: Modeling Spatial and Temporal Variability with the HATS Abstract Behavioral Modeling Language. In: Bernardo, M., Issarny, V. (eds.) SFM 2011. LNCS, vol. 6659, pp. 417–457. Springer, Heidelberg (2011)
2. Damiani, F., Dovland, J., Johnsen, E.B., Schaefer, I.: Verifying traits: A proof system for fine-grained reuse. In: Proc. 13th Workshop on Formal Techniques for Java-like Programs (FTfJP 2011), 8:1–8:6. ACM (2011)
3. Dhara, K.K., Leavens, G.T.: Forcing behavioural subtyping through specification inheritance. In: 18th Conf. on Software Engineering. IEEE Press (1996)
4. Dovland, J., Johnsen, E.B., Owe, O., Steffen, M.: Lazy behavioral subtyping. Journal of Logic and Algebraic Programming 79(7), 578–607 (2010)
5. Dovland, J., Johnsen, E.B., Owe, O., Steffen, M.: Incremental reasoning with lazy behavioral subtyping for multiple inheritance. Science of Computer Programming 76(10), 915–941 (2011)
6. Fowler, M.: Refactoring: Improving the Design of Existing Code. Addison-Wesley (August 1999)
7. Igarashi, A., Pierce, B.C., Wadler, P.: Featherweight Java: a minimal core calculus for Java and GJ. ACM TOPLAS 23(3), 396–450 (2001)
8. Liskov, B.H., Wing, J.M.: A behavioral notion of subtyping. ACM TOPLAS 16(6), 1811–1841 (1994)
9. Marković, S., Baar, T.: Refactoring ocl annotated uml class diagrams. Software and Systems Modeling 7, 25–47 (2008)
10. Massoni, T., Gheyi, R., Borba, P.: Synchronizing Model and Program Refactoring. In: Davies, J. (ed.) SBMF 2010. LNCS, vol. 6527, pp. 96–111. Springer, Heidelberg (2011)
11. Mens, T., Tourwé, T.: A survey of software refactoring. IEEE Transactions on Software Engineering 30(2), 126–139 (2004)
12. Owicki, S., Gries, D.: An axiomatic proof technique for parallel programs I. Acta Informatica 6(4), 319–340 (1976)
13. Pierik, C., de Boer, F.S.: A proof outline logic for object-oriented programming. Theoretical Computer Science 343(3), 413–442 (2005)
14. Schaefer, I., Bettini, L., Bono, V., Damiani, F., Tanzarella, N.: Delta-Oriented Programming of Software Product Lines. In: Bosch, J., Lee, J. (eds.) SPLC 2010. LNCS, vol. 6287, pp. 77–91. Springer, Heidelberg (2010)
15. Soundarajan, N., Fridella, S.: Inheritance: From code reuse to reasoning reuse. In: 5th Intl. Conf. on Software Reuse (ICSR5), pp. 206–215. IEEE Press (1998)
16. Ubayashi, N., Piao, J., Shinotsuka, S., Tamai, T.: Contract-based verification for aspect-oriented refactoring. In: Proc. Intl. Conf. on Software Testing, Verification, and Validation, pp. 180–189. IEEE Press (2008)
17. Van Der Straeten, R., Jonckers, V., Mens, T.: A formal approach to model refactoring and model refinement. Software and Sys. Modeling 6, 139–162 (2007)
18. Wehrheim, H.: Slicing techniques for verification re-use. Theoretical Computer Science 343(3), 509–528 (2005)
19. Yin, X., Knight, J., Weimer, W.: Exploiting refactoring in formal verification. In: Proc. Dependable Systems and Networks (DSN 2009). IEEE Press (2009)

Towards the Verification of Adaptable Processes[*]

Mario Bravetti[1], Cinzia Di Giusto[2], Jorge A. Pérez[3], and Gianluigi Zavattaro[1]

[1] Laboratory FOCUS (Università di Bologna / INRIA), Italy
[2] CEA, LIST, France
[3] CITI - Dept. of Computer Science, FCT New University of Lisbon, Portugal

Abstract. In prior work, with the aim of formally modeling and analyzing the behavior of concurrent processes with forms of dynamic evolution, we have proposed a process calculus of *adaptable processes*. Our proposal addressed the (un)decidability of two safety properties related to error occurrence. In order to allow for a more comprehensive verification framework for adaptable processes, the ability to express general properties is most desirable. In this paper we address this important issue: we explain how the proof techniques for (un)decidability results for adaptable processes generalize to a simple yet expressive temporal logic over adaptable processes. We provide examples of the expressiveness of the logic and its significance in relation with the calculus of adaptable processes.

1 Introduction

The notion of *interaction* has been intensively investigated in the last decades of research in computer science. As a result, a number of formal models of interacting computing entities have been proposed; notable examples include Petri nets and process calculi such as CCS [8] and the π-calculus [9]. In process calculi, the notion of interaction has been dominantly related to the idea of (point-to-point) communication: processes interact by producing complementary signals on a designated common medium, possibly exchanging values. While successful, the process calculi approach to concurrent interaction has devoted significantly less attention to forms of interaction not strictly based on communication. Consequently, process calculi abstractions for "non communicating" phenomena such as, e.g., dynamic evolution and reactive behavior, are either unnatural or hard to express in calculi such as CCS. Hence, it is difficult to reason about the fundamental properties of such abstractions. This is unfortunate, as such phenomena are extremely natural and commonly found in actual concurrent systems.

We are interested in *dynamic evolution*, a particularly pervasive phenomenon in concurrent systems nowadays. In fact, dynamic evolution at runtime is a central functional requirement for an increasingly growing class of *evolvable* computing systems. In case of exceptional circumstances (say, failures or low performance), evolvable systems are able to modify their behavior (say, correcting errors or improving performance indicators). This is often expected to occur semi-automatically, without requiring a system-level shutdown. These distinctive features of evolvable systems arise in a number of

[*] Supported by the French projects ANR-2010-SEGI-013 - AEOLUS, ANR-11-INSE-0007 - REVER, by the EU integrated project HATS, and by FCT / MCTES - Carnegie Mellon Portugal Program, grant NGN-44-2009-12 - INTERFACES.

T. Margaria and B. Steffen (Eds.): ISoLA 2012, Part I, LNCS 7609, pp. 269–283, 2012.
© Springer-Verlag Berlin Heidelberg 2012

emerging applications and programming paradigms. For instance, in workflow applications, it is common for activities to be suspended, restarted, and relocated. Moreover, one might also want to replace a running activity without affecting the rest of the workflow. Similarly, in component-based systems we would like to reconfigure a whole component or even groups of components. This is the case of, e.g., distributed systems implemented as collections of interacting web services. Another example are cloud computing infrastructures, in which evolvability corresponds to the crucial ability of acquiring and releasing computing resources depending on the current demand, while observing both performance and business goals.

More concretely, our interest is in effective reasoning/verification techniques for evolvable systems, following the long, fruitful tradition of process calculi in the analysis of concurrent systems. To this end, we have proposed a process calculus of *adaptable processes*, denoted $\mathcal{E}$ [5,4]. The $\mathcal{E}$ calculus extends CCS with *located processes* and a primitive that allows to *update* the part of the system inside a given location. The result of such an update operation is a new process, dynamically constructed by considering both the current state of the location and an *update pattern* described by the update primitive. This way, evolution of $\mathcal{E}$ processes is the result of modifications enforced by update actions on located communicating processes. The power of update actions is thus directly related with the kinds of patterns admitted as part of update actions. For this reason, in [5,4] we have identified three different variants of $\mathcal{E}$, which consider different update patterns: in $\mathcal{E}^3$, the current content of the location must be always preserved by update actions, which insert it into a new context; in $\mathcal{E}^2$, this condition is relaxed: the current content can be removed or duplicated, but it cannot be placed inside prefixes of the language; finally, in $\mathcal{E}^1$, update patterns are completely unconstrained.

We have used $\mathcal{E}$ as a basis to reason about the *correctness* of dynamically evolvable concurrent processes. Our notion of correctness relies on representing *errors* as *barbs*—the standard observability predicates in process calculi. Barbs denote the most basic observation on the behavior of the system. Hence, in our approach a correct state is a state in which error barbs are not observable. This a fairly flexible approach, as barbs can represent errors as well as any kind of exceptional circumstances not necessarily related to failures, such as, e.g., performance alerts. Based on this notion of correctness, in [5,4] we have also studied how to apply formal analysis techniques to study safety properties of $\mathcal{E}$ processes. In particular, we have considered a safety property for *evolvability*. The property is parametric in the maximal number k of steps needed by the system to *manage* the error state (via appropriate update actions). Namely, a system satisfies *k-bounded adaptation* if there is no computation path including more than k *consecutive* error states. In [5,4] we presented a detailed study of the boundaries of decidability of k-bounded adaptation in the three variants of $\mathcal{E}$.

While insightful for understanding the expressiveness of adaptable processes and the challenging interplay of correctness and evolvability, the decidability results of [5,4] are only an initial step towards a *framework* for the formal specification and analysis of dynamically evolvable systems. A particularly pressing issue is the definition of techniques for logic specification and verification, in such a way that correctness guarantees for $\mathcal{E}$ processes can be stated in general terms. Such techniques would put us closer to a practical framework of adaptable processes. This is the topic of the present paper.

Following the approach put forward in [2], in this paper we extend and generalize the (un)decidability results of [5,4] to a logic setting. More precisely, we introduce a temporal logic that allows for the specification of behavioral properties, including the ones presented in [5,4]. Besides the usual conjunction, disjunction, and negation connectives, the logic includes a predicate that checks whether a system can perform a given action, as well as temporal next and eventual modalities, noted $\diamond$ and $\diamond^*$, respectively. This logic is simple and yet expressive enough to assert interesting properties of evolvable processes. For instance, a variant of bounded adaptation with k *non consecutive* errors and a property for *monotone correctness*—representing the fact that once corrected, errors do not reappear—can be easily stated in the logic we propose here.

The main contribution of this paper is in showing the decidability of a fragment of the logic in which negation can be used only at top level (i.e., not under the scope of other operators) and conjunction is applied only between one basic predicate and a formula. The need to restrict to such a fragment is justified by a complementary contribution of the paper, namely the undecidability of formulae like $\diamond^*(\neg w)$ that test the possibility of reaching a state in which action w cannot be executed.

The rest of this paper is structured as follows. In Section 2 we present the calculus of adaptable processes, following [5,4]. The temporal logic over adaptable processes is defined in Section 3. Compelling examples for the framework given by the calculus of adaptable processes and the logic are described in Section 4. The (un)decidability results for the logic and its fragment are detailed in Section 5. Some concluding remarks and directions for further developments are given in Section 6.

2 The $\mathcal{E}$ Calculus

We present the $\mathcal{E}$ calculus, its different variants, and its operational semantics. We refer to [5,4] for further details and discussions.

The $\mathcal{E}$ calculus is a variant of CCS [8] without restriction and relabeling, and extended with constructs for evolvability. As in CCS, in $\mathcal{E}$, processes can perform actions or synchronize on them. We presuppose a countable set $\mathcal{N}$ of names, ranged over by $a, b, \ldots$, possibly decorated as $\overline{a}, \overline{b}$ and $\widetilde{a}, \widetilde{b}$. As customary, we use a and $\overline{a}$ to denote atomic input and output actions, respectively. The syntax of $\mathcal{E}$ processes extends that of CCS with primitive notions of *adaptable processes* $a[P]$ and *update prefixes* $\widetilde{a}\{U\}$:

Definition 1 ($\mathcal{E}$). *The classes of $\mathcal{E}$ processes, prefixes, and update patterns are described by the following grammars:*

$$P ::= a[P] \mid P \parallel P \mid {!}\pi.P \mid \sum_{i \in I} \pi_i.P \qquad \pi ::= a \mid \overline{a} \mid \widetilde{a}\{U\}$$

$$U ::= a[U] \mid U \parallel U \mid {!}\pi.U \mid \sum_{i \in I} \pi_i.U \mid \bullet$$

Intuitively, update patterns above represent a context, i.e., a process with zero or more *holes*. The intention is that when an update prefix $\widetilde{a}\{U\}$ is able to interact, the current state of an adaptable process named a is used to fill the holes in the update pattern U. Given a process P, process $a[P]$ denotes the adaptable process P *located at* a. Notice that a acts as a *transparent* locality: process P can evolve on its own, and interact freely with external processes. Localities can be nested, so as to form suitable hierarchies of adaptable processes. The rest of the syntax follows standard lines. A process $\pi.P$ performs prefix π and then behaves as P. Parallel composition $P \parallel Q$ decrees the concurrent execution of P and Q. We abbreviate $P_1 \parallel \cdots \parallel P_n$ as $\prod_{i=1}^{n} P_i$, and use $\prod^k P$ to denote the parallel composition of k instances of process P. Given an index set $I = \{1, .., n\}$, the guarded sum $\sum_{i \in I} \pi_i.P_i$ represents an exclusive choice over $\pi_1.P_1, \ldots, \pi_n.P_n$. As usual, we write $\pi_1.P_1 + \pi_2.P_2$ if $|I| = 2$, and $\mathbf{0}$ if I is empty. Process $!\,\pi.P$ defines guarded replication, i.e., infinitely many occurrences of P in parallel, which are triggered by prefix π.

Given an update pattern U and a process Q, we write $U \langle\!\langle Q \rangle\!\rangle$ for the process obtained by filling in with Q those holes in U not occurring inside update prefixes (a formal definition can be found in [4]). Hence, $\{\cdot\}$ can be seen as a scope delimiter for holes $\bullet$ in $\widetilde{a}\{U\}$.

We now move on to consider three concrete instances of update patterns U.

Definition 2 (Update Patterns). *We shall consider the following three instances of update patterns for $\mathcal{E}$:*

1. **Full $\mathcal{E}$ ($\mathcal{E}^1$).** *The first update pattern admits all kinds of contexts for update prefixes. This variant, corresponding to the above $\mathcal{E}$ is denoted also with $\mathcal{E}^1$.*
2. **Unguarded $\mathcal{E}$ ($\mathcal{E}^2$).** *In the second update pattern, holes cannot occur in the scope of prefixes in U:*

$$U ::= P \mid a[U] \mid U \parallel U \mid \bullet$$

   The variant of $\mathcal{E}$ that adopts this update pattern is denoted $\mathcal{E}^2$.
3. **Preserving $\mathcal{E}$ ($\mathcal{E}^3$).** *In the third update pattern, the current state of the adaptable process is always preserved (i.e. "$\bullet$" must occur exactly once in U). Hence, it is only possible to add new adaptable processes and/or behaviors in parallel or to relocate it:*

$$U ::= a[U] \mid U \parallel P \mid \bullet$$

   The variant of $\mathcal{E}$ that adopts this update pattern is denoted $\mathcal{E}^3$.

The process semantics is given in terms of a Labeled Transition System (LTS). It is generated by the set of rules in Figure 1. In addition to the standard CCS actions (input, output, τ), we consider two complementary actions for process update: $\widetilde{a}\{U\}$ and $a[P]$. The former represents the possibility to enact an update pattern U for the adaptable process at a; the latter says that an adaptable process at a, with current state P, can be updated. We define $\longrightarrow$ as $\xrightarrow{\tau}$, and write $P \xrightarrow{\alpha}$ if $P \xrightarrow{\alpha} P'$, for some P'.

Definition 3 (LTS for $\mathcal{E}$). *The LTS for $\mathcal{E}$, denoted $\xrightarrow{\alpha}$, is defined by the rules in Figure 1, with transition labels defined as:*

$$\alpha ::= a \mid \overline{a} \mid a[P] \mid \widetilde{a}\{U\} \mid \tau$$

In Figure 1, rules (SUM), (REPL), (ACT1), and (TAU1) are standard. Rule (COMP) represents the contribution of a process at a in an update operation; we use $\star$ to denote

(SUM)
$$\sum_{i \in I} \pi_i.P_i \xrightarrow{\pi_j} P_j \ (j \in I)$$

(REPL)
$$!\pi.P \xrightarrow{\pi} P \ |||!\pi.P$$

(COMP)
$$a[P] \xrightarrow{a[P]} \star$$

(LOC)
$$\frac{P \xrightarrow{\alpha} P'}{a[P] \xrightarrow{\alpha} a[P']}$$

(ACT1)
$$\frac{P_1 \xrightarrow{\alpha} P_1'}{P_1 \ || \ P_2 \xrightarrow{\alpha} P_1' \ || \ P_2}$$

(TAU1)
$$\frac{P_1 \xrightarrow{a} P_1' \quad P_2 \xrightarrow{\bar{a}} P_2'}{P_1 \ || \ P_2 \xrightarrow{\tau} P_1' \ || \ P_2'}$$

(TAU3)
$$\frac{P_1 \xrightarrow{a[Q]} P_1' \quad P_2 \xrightarrow{\tilde{a}\{U\}} P_2'}{P_1 \ || \ P_2 \xrightarrow{\tau} P_1'\{U\langle\!\langle Q \rangle\!\rangle/\star\} \ || \ P_2'}$$

Fig. 1. LTS for $\mathcal{E}$. Rules (ACT2), (TAU2), and (TAU4)—the symmetric counterparts of (ACT1), (TAU1), and (TAU3)—have been omitted.

a unique placeholder. Rule (LOC) formalizes transparency of localities. Rule (TAU3) formalizes process evolvability. To realize the evolution of an adaptable process at a, it requires: (i) a process Q—which represents its current state; (ii) an update action offering an update pattern U for updating the process at a—which is represented in P_1' by $\star$ (cf. rule (COMP)) As a result, $\star$ in P_1' is replaced with process $U\langle\!\langle Q \rangle\!\rangle$. Notice that this means that the locality being updated is discarded unless it is re-created by $U\langle\!\langle Q \rangle\!\rangle$.

We introduce some definitions that will be useful in the following. We denote with $\to^*$ the reflexive and transitive closure of the relation $\to$. We define $Pred(s)$ as the set $\{s' \in S \mid s' \to s\}$ of *immediate predecessors* of s, while $Pred^*(s)$ denotes the set $\{s \in S \mid s' \to^* s\}$ of *predecessors* of s. We will also assume point-wise extensions of such definitions to sets, i.e. $Pred(S) = \bigcup_{s \in S} Pred(s)$ and similarly for $Pred^*(S)$.

3   A Logic for Adaptable Processes

We now introduce the logic $\mathcal{L}$ and its fragment $\mathcal{L}_r$, and illustrate their expressiveness.

Definition 4. *The set* At *of atomic predicates* p *is given by the following syntax:*

$$\mathrm{p} ::= a \mid \bar{a} \mid T.$$

Predicates a and $\bar{a}$ hold true for states/terms that may perform transitions a and $\bar{a}$, respectively. The intention is that the interpretation of atomic predicates should coincide with the notion of *barb* in the process model. T is the true predicate that holds true for every state/term. In the following, we use α to range over labels $a, \bar{a}$, for some name a.

Definition 5. *The set* $\mathcal{L}$ *of logic formulae* $\phi, \psi, \ldots$ *is given by the following syntax, where* p $\in$ At:

$$\phi ::= \mathrm{p} \mid \phi \vee \phi \mid \phi \wedge \phi \mid \neg\phi \mid \Diamond\phi \mid \Diamond^*\phi$$

The set of logical operators includes atomic predicates p $\in$ At, the usual boolean connectives ($\vee$, $\wedge$, and $\neg$), as well as dynamic connectives (the next and eventuality modalities, $\Diamond$ and $\Diamond^*$). The interpretation of $\mathcal{L}$ over LTSs is given below, where each formula is mapped into the set of states/terms satisfying it.

$$[\![\alpha]\!] = \{s \in \mathcal{E} \mid s \xrightarrow{\alpha} \} \quad [\![T]\!] = \mathcal{E} \quad [\![\Diamond\phi]\!] = Pred([\![\phi]\!]) \quad [\![\Diamond^*\phi]\!] = Pred^*([\![\phi]\!])$$
$$[\![\phi_1 \vee \phi_2]\!] = [\![\phi_1]\!] \cup [\![\phi_2]\!] \quad [\![\phi_1 \wedge \phi_2]\!] = [\![\phi_1]\!] \cap [\![\phi_2]\!] \quad [\![\neg\phi]\!] = \mathcal{E} \setminus [\![\phi]\!]$$

Connectives are interpreted as usual. We usually write $s \models \phi$ if $s \in [\![\phi]\!]$.

Definition 6. *A formula ϕ is called* monotone *if it does not contain occurrences of $\neg$.*

Restricted monotone formulae are those monotone formulae in which conjunctions are always of the form $p \wedge \phi$, for some $p \in At$ and a monotone formula $\phi \in \mathcal{L}$.

Definition 7. *A formula ϕ is* restricted monotone *if it is monotone and, for any occurrence of $\phi_1 \wedge \phi_2$ inside ϕ, there exists $i \in \{1, 2\}$ such that ϕ_i is a predicate $p \in At$.*

We now introduce restricted logic as the logic composed by, possibly negated, restricted monotone formulae.

Definition 8. *The restricted logic is composed by the set $\mathcal{L}_r$ of formulae of the form ϕ or $\neg\phi$, where ϕ is a restricted monotone formula.*

We give some examples of formulas in $\mathcal{L}$ and $\mathcal{L}_r$. Below, we take $\Diamond^+\phi \stackrel{\text{def}}{=} \Diamond\Diamond^*\phi$.

1. Possibly the most natural safety property one would like to ensure is the absence of *k consecutive barbs* (representing, e.g., errors):

$$\mathsf{CB}_k(e) \stackrel{\text{def}}{=} \neg\Diamond^*\big(\underbrace{e \wedge \Diamond(e \wedge \Diamond(e \wedge \ldots \wedge \Diamond e))}_{e \text{ appears } k \text{ times}}\big)$$

Observe how $\mathsf{CB}_k(e) \in \mathcal{L}_r$. This basic scheme is easily extendable; below we present a possible variant in which rather than using a single barb e we consider a sequence $\tilde{e} = e_1 \ldots e_k$ of k error barbs that we do not want to observe in sequence:

$$\mathsf{CDB}_k(\tilde{e}) \stackrel{\text{def}}{=} \neg\Diamond^*\big(e_1 \wedge \Diamond(e_2 \wedge \Diamond(e_3 \wedge \ldots \wedge \Diamond e_k))\big)$$

2. A more insightful specialization of $\mathsf{CB}_k(e)$ is the formula below, in which error barbs are *non consecutive*:

$$\mathsf{NCB}_k(e) \stackrel{\text{def}}{=} \neg\Diamond^*\big(\underbrace{e \wedge \Diamond^+(e \wedge \Diamond^+(e \wedge \ldots \wedge \Diamond^+ e))}_{e \text{ appears } k \text{ times}}\big)$$

As $\mathsf{CB}_k(e)$, it is easy to see that $\mathsf{NCB}_k(e) \in \mathcal{L}_r$. Specializations of $\mathsf{NCB}_k(e)$ with different error barbs, as in the previous example, are easy to obtain.

3. Another sensible property to ensure is *monotone correctness*: once solved, errors do not reappear. In $\mathcal{L}$ this can be expressed as:

$$\mathsf{MC}(e) \stackrel{\text{def}}{=} \neg\Diamond^*\big(e \wedge \Diamond^+(\neg e \wedge \Diamond^+ e)\big)$$

Assuming a designated barb *ok*, signaling a correct (error-less) state, the above can be captured in $\mathcal{L}_r$ as follows:

$$\mathsf{MC}^r(ok, e) \stackrel{\text{def}}{=} \neg\Diamond^*\big(e \wedge \Diamond^+(ok \wedge \Diamond^* e)\big)$$

The extension of $\mathsf{MC}^r(ok, e)$ to consider k different error phases (it cannot happen that an error re-appears up to k times) is straightforward:

$$\mathsf{MC}^r_k(ok, e) \stackrel{\mathsf{def}}{=} \neg \Diamond^* \big(\underbrace{e \wedge \Diamond^+(ok \wedge \Diamond^*(e \wedge \Diamond^+(ok \wedge \ldots (ok \wedge \Diamond^* e))))}_{ok \text{ appears } k \text{ times}} \big)$$

4 Two Compelling Examples

We give two examples of adaptable processes. They rely on $\mathcal{E}^2$ processes and properties in $\mathcal{L}_r$. Hence, as we will see, model checking for them is decidable.

Booking a Flight. We model a simple interaction between a travel agency and a client wishing to book a flight. Given a signal from the client, the agency contacts a pool of different airlines. This pool is handled by an external booking service, which controls the airlines the travel agency may choose from. Given a request, each airline may answer positively, or it may emit an error signal, meaning there is no flight as desired by the client, or simply that the airline services are down. If the airline does not provide a positive answer then the booking service removes it from the pool of the airlines to contact. We define the $\mathcal{E}$ process $Sys \stackrel{\mathsf{def}}{=}$ Client $\|$ Agency $\|$ Booking, where:

$$\text{Agency} \stackrel{\mathsf{def}}{=} t[f.(\overline{r} \parallel P[\tilde{n}])] \text{ with } P[\tilde{n}] = \sum_{i=1}^{n} r.\overline{a_i}.A(i) \qquad \text{Client} \stackrel{\mathsf{def}}{=} c[\overline{f} \parallel ok_f.\overline{pay}]$$

$$\text{Booking} \stackrel{\mathsf{def}}{=} \prod_{i=1}^{n} a_i.(e_i.\overline{r_i} + c_i.\overline{ok_f}) \parallel \prod_{i=1}^{n} r_i.\tilde{t}\{t[\overline{r} \parallel P[\tilde{n}/i]]\}$$

For simplicity, we have represented only interaction signals. Both the client and the agency are represented as adaptable processes; this allows for eventual refinements of their specifications (for instance, an update action on t may add new services). The client contacts the agency via a synchronization on f; in turn, this enables a synchronization on r which selects an airline $A(k)$ from the pool of options $P[\tilde{n}]$. As soon as it is selected, before starting its execution $A(k)$, the airline emits a signal $\overline{a_k}$, announcing the selection to the booking service. We associate a signal $\overline{e_i}$ with an error answer from airline $A(i)$, while $\overline{c_i}$ stands for a positive confirmation. Observe how unresponsive airlines are discarded by the booking service, by virtue of update actions affecting the pool of airlines activated by the signal $\overline{r_i}$; $P[\tilde{n}/i]$ denotes the pool $P[\tilde{n}]$ in which $A(i)$ is not included. The booking service above is not very "patient", as it does not give another chance to the selected airline to respond; in case of an error signal, the airline is discarded. With this in mind, it is easy to see that the following holds, for every i:

$$Sys \models \mathsf{MC}^r(\overline{r_i}, \overline{e_i})$$

That is, after an error, an unresponsive airline will never produce new error signals. We could have stated as well $Sys \models \mathsf{MC}(\overline{e_i})$, for every i. However, while $\mathsf{MC}^r(\overline{r_i}, \overline{e_i})$ is a formula in $\mathcal{L}_r$, $\mathsf{MC}(\overline{e_i})$ is a formula in $\mathcal{L}$. As we will see, for $\mathcal{E}^2$ processes the former is a decidable logic, whereas the latter is not.

Scaling in Cloud Computing. In the cloud computing paradigm, applications are deployed in infrastructures offered by external providers. Developers act as clients who pay for the resources they consume (e.g., processor time in remote *instances*) and for associated services (e.g., performance metrics, automated load balancing). A central concern is therefore resource optimization, for clients and providers. To that end, cloud providers such as Amazon's Elastic Cloud Computing (EC2) [3] offer *(auto)scaling* services, which allow cloud applications to add or release resources depending on the current demand. Scaling has a direct influence in the amount of resources supporting the application; correct, reliable scaling policies are thus central to resource optimization.

Below we give a simple model of a cloud computing scenario in $\mathcal{E}$; we focus on scaling, drawing inspiration from autoscaling in EC2 [3]. Each cloud application is composed of a number of *instances* and of active processes implementing the scaling policies. This scenario can be abstracted as process $C \stackrel{\text{def}}{=} P \parallel \text{App}_1 \parallel \cdots \parallel \text{App}_r$, which represents the cloud as a provider P interacting with applications $\text{App}_1, \ldots, \text{App}_r$. In turn, each such applications is defined as $\text{App}_i \stackrel{\text{def}}{=} ap_i [\, I_i \parallel \cdots \parallel I_i \parallel S_i^{dw} \parallel S_i^{up} \,]$. That is, each App_i contains a fixed number of running instances, each represented by $I_i = \text{mid}_i[S_i]$, a process that abstracts an instance as an adaptable process with an identification mid and state S_i. Also, S_i^{dw} and S_i^{up} stand for the processes implementing scaling down and scaling up policies, respectively. In practice, this control relies on external services (e.g., services that monitor cloud usage and produce appropriate *alerts*) present in the provider's infrastructure. Therefore, we will assume P to include a subprocess M which communicates the appropriate alerts. M performs adaptations due to *high* performance (action hi_i) or *low* performance (action lo_i) of App_i and uses a signal e to denote a temporary erroneous situation that remains until the adaptation is performed. Formally, we take M to be $\overline{exec} \parallel M'$, where $\overline{exec}$ triggers the execution of an alerting round in the M' process and M' is:

$$M' \stackrel{\text{def}}{=} !exec.\Big(\sum_{1 \leq i \leq r} lo_i.\overline{\text{alert}_i^d}.(e + ok.\overline{exec}) + \sum_{1 \leq i \leq r} hi_i.\overline{\text{alert}_i^u}.(e + ok.\overline{exec}) \Big)$$

The scaling policies are then defined accordingly (letting $U_i = \text{mid}_i[\bullet] \parallel \text{mid}_i[\bullet]$):

$$S_i^{dw} = s_i^d \big[\, !\,\text{alert}_i^d.(\underbrace{\widetilde{\text{mid}_i}\{0\}. \cdots .\widetilde{\text{mid}_i}\{0\}}_{\text{fixed number of updates on } \text{mid}_i}.\overline{ok}\,)\,\big]$$

$$S_i^{up} = s_i^u \big[\, !\,\text{alert}_i^u.(\underbrace{\widetilde{\text{mid}_i}\{U_i\}. \cdots .\widetilde{\text{mid}_i}\{U_i\}}_{\text{fixed number of updates on } \text{mid}_i}.\overline{ok}\,)\,\big]$$

We assume the provider P to generate errors due to low/high performance by executing an $\overline{lo_i}/\overline{hi_i}$ action triggering the adaptation on application i in M. Given an alert from M, the processes S_i^{dw} and S_i^{up} modify the number of running application instances. Given an output at alert_i^d, process S_i^{dw} destroys a fixed number of instances of the application i: this is achieved by updating localities mid_i with 0. Afterwards, an $\overline{ok}$ action is emitted returning the control to M' and consuming the pending e signal. The observability of $\overline{ok}$ thus represents the fact that the scaling down alert has been properly enforced, and that the involved resources have been released. Process S_{up} implements a scaling up policy in a very similar way: rather than destroying an instance at $\texttt{mid}_i$, each of the update actions creates a new one. Based on the above, we have that by checking

$$C \models \mathsf{MC}_k^r(\overline{ok}, e)$$

we are able to assess whether k adaptations (due to low or high performance) are enough for the adaptation needs of the applications: if this is the case then it will not be possible for the cloud system C to produce an additional error signal e after observing k adaptations (each via an e signal followed by an $\overline{ok}$ signal). As in the previous example, we prefer $\mathsf{MC}_k^r(\overline{ok}, e)$ over the extension of $\mathsf{MC}(e)$ to k error phases: such an extension is a formula of $\mathcal{L}$, which will be shown to be undecidable for $\mathcal{E}^2$ processes.

5 (Un)decidability Results for $\mathcal{L}$ and $\mathcal{L}_r$

Here we present the (un)decidability results for $\mathcal{L}$ and $\mathcal{L}_r$. We first introduce some basic notions on well-structured transition systems and Minsky machines.

5.1 Preliminaries

Well Structured Transition Systems. The decidability of the restricted logic for $\mathcal{E}^2$ and $\mathcal{E}^3$ processes will be shown by appealing to the theory of well-structured transition systems [7,1]. The following notions are from [7], unless differently specified.

Recall that a *quasi-order* (or preorder) is a reflexive and transitive relation.

Definition 9 (Well-quasi-order). *A well-quasi-order (wqo) is a quasi-order $\leq$ over a set X such that, for any infinite sequence $x_0, x_1, x_2 \ldots \in X$, there exist indexes $i < j$ such that $x_i \leq x_j$.*

Thus well-quasi-orders exclude the possibility of having infinite strictly decreasing sequences. Note that if $\leq$ is a wqo then any infinite sequence $x_0, x_1, x_2, \ldots$ contains an infinite increasing subsequence $x_{i_0}, x_{i_1}, x_{i_2}, \ldots$ (with $i_0 < i_1 < i_2 < \ldots$).

The key tool to the decidability of several properties of computations is the notion of *well-structured transition system* [7,1]. This is a transition system equipped with a well-quasi-order on states which is (upward) compatible with the transition relation. Here we will use so-called strong compatibility; hence the following definition.

Definition 10 (Well-structured transition system). *A* well-structured transition system *with strong compatibility is a transition system $TS = (S, \rightarrow)$, equipped with a quasi-order $\leq$ on S, such that the two following conditions hold:*

1. *$\leq$ is a well-quasi-order;*
2. *$\leq$ is strongly (upward) compatible with $\rightarrow$, that is, for all $s_1 \leq t_1$ and all transitions $s_1 \rightarrow s_2$, there exists a state t_2 such that $t_1 \rightarrow t_2$ and $s_2 \leq t_2$ holds.*

In the following, we will just use the term well-structured transition system to stand for a well-structured transition system with strong compatibility.

Given a quasi-order $\leq$ over X, an *upward-closed set* is a subset $I \subseteq X$ such that the following holds: $\forall x, y \in X : (x \in I \wedge x \leq y) \Rightarrow y \in I$. Given $x \in X$, we define its upward closure as $\uparrow x = \{y \in X \mid x \leq y\}$. This notion can be extended to sets as expected: given a set $Y \subseteq X$ we define its upward closure as $\uparrow Y = \bigcup_{y \in Y} \uparrow y$.

Table 1. Reduction of Minsky machines

$$
\frac{(\text{M-INC})}{i : \text{INC}(r_j) \quad m'_j = m_j + 1 \quad m'_{1-j} = m_{1-j}}{(i, m_0, m_1) \longrightarrow_M (i+1, m'_0, m'_1)}
\qquad
\frac{(\text{M-JMP})}{i : \text{DECJ}(r_j, s) \quad m_j = 0}{(i, m_0, m_1) \longrightarrow_M (s, m_0, m_1)}
$$

$$
\frac{(\text{M-DEC})}{i : \text{DECJ}(r_j, s) \qquad m_j \neq 0 \qquad m'_j = m_j - 1 \qquad m'_{1-j} = m_{1-j}}{(i, m_0, m_1) \longrightarrow_M (i+1, m'_0, m'_1)}
$$

Definition 11 (Finite basis). *A* finite basis *of an upward-closed set I is a finite set B such that $I = \bigcup_{x \in B} \uparrow x$.*

We are interested in *effective* pred-bases, as defined below.

Definition 12 (Effective pred-basis). *A well-structured transition system has* effective pred-basis *if there exists an algorithm such that, for any state $s \in S$, it returns the set $pb(s)$ which is a finite basis of $Pred(\uparrow s)$.*

The following proposition is a special case of Proposition 3.5 in [7].

Proposition 1. *Let $TS = (S, \rightarrow, \leq)$ be a finitely branching, well-structured transition system, decidable $\leq$, and effective pred-basis. It is possible to compute a finite basis $\text{pb}^*(I)$ of $Pred^*(I)$ for any upward-closed set I given via a finite basis.*

Minsky machines. A Minsky machine (MM) is a Turing complete model composed of a set of sequential, labeled instructions, and two registers. Registers r_j ($j \in \{0, 1\}$) can hold arbitrarily large natural numbers. Instructions $(1 : I_1), \ldots, (n : I_n)$ can be of three kinds: $\text{INC}(r_j)$ adds 1 to register r_j and proceeds to the next instruction; $\text{DECJ}(r_j, s)$ jumps to instruction s if r_j is zero, otherwise it decreases register r_j by 1 and proceeds to the next instruction; HALT terminates the execution. A MM includes a program counter p indicating the label of the instruction being executed. In its initial state, the MM has both registers set to 0 and the program counter p set to the first instruction. The MM terminates whenever the halting intruction is reached. A *configuration* of a MM is a tuple (i, m_0, m_1); it consists of the current program counter and the values of the registers. Reduction over configurations of a MM, denoted $\longrightarrow_M$, is defined in Table 1.

5.2   Results for $\mathcal{L}$

Here we show that the satisfiability of a formula in the logic $\mathcal{L}$ is undecidable for $\mathcal{E}$ processes. We obtain this result by encoding MMs into $\mathcal{E}^3$ under the non restrictive hypothesis that the MMs end with both registers set to 0. The encoding simulates the behavior of MMs in an unfaithful manner: decrement instructions are simulated by selecting nondeterministically whether to jump or actually execute the decrement. When a jump is executed, a new empty copy of the register is created. The encoding produces

Table 2. Encoding of Minsky machines into $\mathcal{E}^3$

REGISTER r_j
$[\![r_j = 0]\!]_3 = r_j[Reg_j \parallel c_j[0]]$ with $Reg_j = !inc_j.\widetilde{c}_j\{c_j[\bullet]\}.\overline{ack}.u_j.\widetilde{c}_j\{c_j[\bullet]\}.\overline{ack}$
INSTRUCTIONS $(i : I_i)$
$[\![(i : \mathtt{INC}(r_j))]\!]_3 \quad = !p_i.\overline{inc_j}.ack.(\overline{w} \parallel \overline{p_{i+1}})$
$[\![(i : \mathtt{DECJ}(r_j, s))]\!]_3 = !p_i.(\overline{u_j}.ack.w.\overline{p_{i+1}} + \widetilde{c}_j\{\bullet\}.\widetilde{r}_j\{r_j[Reg_j \parallel c_j[\bullet]]\}.\overline{p_s})$
$[\![(i : \mathtt{HALT})]\!]_3 \quad = p_i.w$

an output $\overline{w}$ when an increment is executed, and produces an input w after a decrement. Hence, if the machine executes correctly then there will be an equal number of outputs and inputs at w. Moreover, the execution of the encoding takes place with an additional output $\overline{w}$ in parallel (cf. Definition 13); this signal is meant to be consumed by an input action which is available when the MM reaches a halt instruction. The undecidability result (Theorem 1) thus exploits the ability $\mathcal{L}$ has for checking the absence of a barb: if the MM has a terminating computation then no output $\overline{w}$ is observable.

Definition 13. *Let N be a MM, with registers $r_0 = 0$, $r_1 = 0$ and instructions $(1 : I_1), \ldots, (n : I_n)$. Given the encodings in Table 2, the encoding of N in $\mathcal{E}^3$ (denoted with $[\![N]\!]_3$) is defined as*

$$[\![r_0 = 0]\!]_3 \parallel [\![r_1 = 0]\!]_3 \parallel \prod_{i=1}^{n}[\![(i : I_i)]\!]_3 \parallel \overline{p_1} \parallel \overline{w}$$

A register r_j that stores a number m is encoded as an adaptable process r_j that contains m copies of the unit process $u_j.\widetilde{c}_j\{c_j[\bullet]\}.\overline{ack}$. Such an adaptable process also contains process Reg_j which allows us to create further copies of the unit process when an increment instruction is invoked. Furthermore, we use the collector c_j to store processes which are meant to be isolated. The instructions are defined taking into account this role of c_j. An increment adds an occurrence of $u_j.\widetilde{c}_j\{c_j[\bullet]\}.\overline{ack}$ and outputs a message on w. Notice that it could occur that an output on inc could synchronize with the corresponding input inside a *collected* process. This immediately leads to deadlock as the containment induced by c_j prevents further interactions. The encoding of a decrement is implemented as an internal choice. The process tests if the content of the register is equal or greater than zero. Notice that in $\mathcal{E}^3$ it is not possible to deterministically determine whether the register contains value zero or not. Thus if the process guesses that the register is zero, before jumping to the given instruction, it proceeds at disabling its current content: this is done by putting the collector at top level in the register, the register is then recreated by placing all its previous content in the collector. A decrement instead removes one occurrence of $u_j.\widetilde{c}_j\{c_j[\bullet]\}.\overline{ack}$ and one occurrence of w. As before, it could occur that the output on u_j could synchronize with the corresponding input inside a collected process. Again, this immediately leads to deadlock and no occurrence of w is consumed. Observe that in case of deadlock or a wrong guess some copies of $\overline{w}$ will never be consumed, thus signaling a wrong computation. In case of a correct computation, instead, when the program reaches the halt instruction the

Table 3. Encoding of MMs into $\mathcal{E}^1$

REGISTER r_j $[\![r_j = n]\!]_1 = r_j[(\!|n|\!)_j]$ where $(\!|n|\!)_j = \begin{cases} \overline{z_j} & \text{if } n = 0 \\ \overline{u_j}.(\!|n-1|\!)_j & \text{if } n > 0. \end{cases}$

INSTRUCTIONS $(i : I_i)$

$[\![(i : \mathtt{INC}(r_j))]\!]_1 \quad = !p_i.\tilde{r_j}\{r_j[\overline{u_j}.\bullet]\}.\overline{p_{i+1}}$

$[\![(i : \mathtt{DECJ}(r_j, s))]\!]_1 = !p_i.(u_j.\overline{p_{i+1}} + z_j.\tilde{r_j}\{r_j[\overline{z_j}]\}.\overline{p_s})$

$[\![(i : \mathtt{HALT})]\!]_1 \qquad = p_i.h$

occurrence of $\overline{w}$ present in the initial configuration (cf. Definition 13) is removed. Thus we have that a MM N terminates iff its encoding has no barb on $\overline{w}$.

Theorem 1. $\mathcal{L}$ *is undecidable in* $\mathcal{E}^3$.

Proof (Sketch). Consider a MM N and its encoding $[\![N]\!]_3$. It is easy to see that N terminates iff $[\![N]\!]_3 \models \Diamond^*(\neg\overline{w})$. Thus the undecidability of the satisfiability of formulae in $\mathcal{L}$ follows from undecidability of the termination problem in MMs.   □

As $\mathcal{E}^3$ is a subcalculus of $\mathcal{E}^1$ and $\mathcal{E}^2$ we can immediately conclude the following.

Corollary 1. $\mathcal{L}$ *is undecidable in* $\mathcal{E}^1$ *and* $\mathcal{E}^2$.

5.3   Results for $\mathcal{L}_r$

Undecidability over $\mathcal{E}^1$. Similarly as above, to prove the undecidability of satisfiability of formulae in $\mathcal{L}_r$, we reduce to the termination problem. We resort to a MM similar to the one presented in [5]. The encoding, denoted $[\![\cdot]\!]_1$, is given in Table 3.

Definition 14. *Let* N *be a MM, with registers* $r_0 = 0$, $r_1 = 0$ *and instructions* $(1 : I_1) \ldots (n : I_n)$. *Given the encodings in Table 3, the encoding of* N *in* $\mathcal{E}^1$ *(written* $[\![N]\!]_1$) *is defined as* $[\![r_0 = 0]\!]_1 \parallel [\![r_1 = 0]\!]_1 \parallel \prod_{i=1}^{n} [\![(i : I_i)]\!]_1 \parallel \overline{p_1}$.

A register r_j with value m is represented by an adaptable process at r_j that contains a sequence of m output prefixes on name u_j, ending with an output action on z_j, which represents zero. To encode the increment of register r_j, we enlarge the sequence of output prefixes it contains. The adaptable process at r_j is updated with the encoding of the incremented value (which results from putting the value of the register behind some prefixes) and then the next instruction is invoked. The encoding of a decrement of register j consists of an exclusive choice: the left side implements the decrement of the value of a register, while the right one implements the jump to some given instruction. When the MM reaches a halt instruction the encoding exhibits a barb on h. Thus a MM N terminates iff its encoding has a barb on the distinguished action h.

Theorem 2. $\mathcal{L}_r$ *is undecidable in* $\mathcal{E}^1$.

Proof (Sketch). Consider a MM N and its encoding $[\![N]\!]_1$. It is easy to see that N terminates iff $[\![N]\!]_1 \models \Diamond^* h$. Thus the undecidability of $\mathcal{L}_r$ follows from undecidability of the termination problem in MMs.   □

Decidability over $\mathcal{E}^2$. The decidability of the satisfiability of formulae in the $\mathcal{L}_r$ logic is obtained by resorting to the theory of well-structured transition systems and the pred-basis construction. In [4], we showed a decidable preorder $\preceq$ on processes. Such a preorder is a well-quasi-order, strongly compatible with respect to the reduction in $\mathcal{E}^2$, and with an *effective pred-basis pb*. It is defined over a tree-like representation of processes; below we give intuitions on its definition, see [4] for details.

Given an $\mathcal{E}^2$ process P, we say it is in *normal form* if $P = \prod_{i=1}^m P_i \parallel \prod_{j=1}^n a_j[P_j']$. The tree denotation of P, denoted $\mathsf{Tr}(P)$, is a tree built as follows. The root is labeled ε, and has $m + n$ children: the former m are leaves labeled $P_1, \ldots, P_m$, while the latter n are subtrees recursively built from processes $P_1', \ldots, P_n'$, where the only difference is that their roots are labeled $a_1[\,], \ldots, a_n[\,]$, respectively. Given two processes P and Q, $P \preceq Q$ holds iff there exists an injection f from the nodes of $\mathsf{Tr}(P)$ to the ones of $\mathsf{Tr}(Q)$ such that, let m, n, p be nodes in $\mathsf{Tr}(P)$: (i) If m is an ancestor of n then $f(m)$ is an ancestor of $f(n)$. (ii) If p is the minimal common ancestor of m and n then $f(p)$ is the minimal common ancestor of $f(m)$ and $f(n)$. (iii) The label of n is equal to the label of $f(n)$.

Having defined a suitable preorder on processes, it remains to show how each interpretation $[\![\phi]\!]$ can be described via an effectively computable finite basis.

We begin with the definition of sequential subprocesses.

Definition 15 (Sequential Subprocesses). *Let P be an $\mathcal{E}^2$ process. The set of sequential subprocesses of P, denoted $\mathsf{ss}(P)$, is defined inductively as follows:*

$$\mathsf{ss}(\pi.P) = \{\pi.P\} \cup \mathsf{ss}(P) \quad \text{if } \pi = a \text{ or } \pi = \bar{a}$$
$$\mathsf{ss}(\tilde{a}\{U\}.Q) = \{\tilde{a}\{U\}.Q\} \cup \mathsf{ss}(U) \cup \mathsf{ss}(Q) \qquad \mathsf{ss}(a[P]) = \mathsf{ss}(P)$$
$$\mathsf{ss}(\textstyle\sum_{i \in I} \pi_i.P_i) = \{\textstyle\sum_{i \in I} \pi_i.P_i\} \cup \bigcup_{i \in I} \mathsf{ss}(\pi_i.P_i) \qquad \mathsf{ss}(\bullet) = \emptyset$$
$$\mathsf{ss}(!\pi.P) = \{!\pi.P\} \cup \mathsf{ss}(P) \qquad \mathsf{ss}(P \parallel Q) = \mathsf{ss}(P) \cup \mathsf{ss}(Q)$$

Note that $\mathsf{ss}(\mathbf{0}) = \mathsf{ss}(\sum_{i \in \emptyset} \pi_i.P_i) = \{\mathbf{0}\}$. The definition extends to sets of processes as expected.

The finite basis for a formula ϕ with respect to a process P is defined inductively on the structure of ϕ; see Table 4. The base cases are trivial: the interpretation of a predicate α is given by all sequential subprocesses that can immediately exhibit α, and the interpretation of T is given by all sequential subprocesses (i.e., all processes satisfy T). The finite basis of $\Diamond\phi$ is the pred basis pb of the processes that satisfy formula ϕ; the interpretation of $\Diamond^*\phi$ is the basis given by Proposition 1 of the finite basis of ϕ. The computability of $pb^*()$ derives from Proposition 1. The interpretation of the $\vee$ operator is the union of the interpretation of the two formulae, as expected. In contrast, the calculation of the finite basis for the $\wedge$ operator is more involved, as we cannot simply consider the intersection between the two interpretations. Given a formula $\alpha \wedge \phi$, our aim is to take all the minimal processes which, at the same time, satisfy ϕ and exhibit α. For this reason, we first select from $\mathsf{FB}_P(\phi)$ all processes that can immediately perform α. Then, we modify all the other processes so that they can exhibit α. This is achieved using a function $Add_P(Q, \alpha)$, which adds a sequential subprocess that can exhibit α in parallel at top level and inside every adaptable process. The latter is performed by making use of contexts C, which are simply processes with a hole, such that the process obtained by applying them to a process P is denoted by $C[P]$.

Table 4. Finite basis of a process P for ϕ

$$
\begin{aligned}
\mathsf{FB}_P(\alpha) \quad &= \{R \in \mathsf{ss}(P) \mid R \xrightarrow{\alpha}\} \\
\mathsf{FB}_P(T) \quad &= \mathsf{ss}(P) \\
\mathsf{FB}_P(\Diamond\phi) \quad &= pb(\mathsf{FB}_P(\phi)) \\
\mathsf{FB}_P(\Diamond^*\phi) \quad &= \mathsf{pb}^*(\mathsf{FB}_P(\phi)) \\
\mathsf{FB}_P(\phi_1 \vee \phi_2) &= \mathsf{FB}_P(\phi_1) \cup \mathsf{FB}_P(\phi_2) \\
\mathsf{FB}_P(\alpha \wedge \phi) \quad &= \mathsf{FB}_P(\phi \wedge \alpha) = \mathsf{lb}_P(\mathsf{FB}_P(\phi), \alpha)
\end{aligned}
$$

where:

$$
\begin{aligned}
\mathsf{lb}_P(A, \alpha) \quad &= \{Q \in A \mid Q \xrightarrow{\alpha}\} \cup \{\mathsf{Add}_P(Q, \alpha) \mid Q \in A \text{ and } Q \xrightarrow{\alpha}\!\!\!/\;\} \\
\mathsf{Add}_P(Q, \alpha) \quad &= \{Q \parallel R \mid R \in \mathsf{ss}(P) \text{ and } R \xrightarrow{\alpha}\} \cup \\
&\quad\; \{C\big[a[R \parallel Q']\big] \mid Q = C\big[a[Q']\big], R \in \mathsf{ss}(P) \text{ and } R \xrightarrow{\alpha}\}
\end{aligned}
$$

Theorem 3. $\mathcal{L}_r$ *is decidable in* $\mathcal{E}^2$.

Proof (Sketch). Given a formula $\phi \in \mathcal{L}_r$ and a process $P \in \mathcal{E}^2$. It is easy to see that $\uparrow \mathsf{FB}_P(\phi) = [\![\phi]\!]$. Then as $\mathsf{FB}_P(\phi)$ is computable, in order to decide if P satisfies ϕ it is enough to check if there exists a process S in $\mathsf{FB}_P(\phi)$ such that $S \preceq P$.

As $\mathcal{E}^3$ is a subcalculus of $\mathcal{E}^2$ we can immediately conclude the following.

Corollary 2. $\mathcal{L}_r$ *is decidable in* $\mathcal{E}^3$.

6   Concluding Remarks

This paper has reported initial steps towards the specification and verification of *adaptable processes*, as introduced in [5]. We have presented $\mathcal{L}$, a simple temporal logic that describes the evolution of adaptable processes. The logic $\mathcal{L}$ is shown to be undecidable in the three different variants of $\mathcal{E}$ studied in [5,4]. On the bright side, the satisfiability problem for $\mathcal{L}_r$—a fragment of $\mathcal{L}$ in which negation is allowed only at top level and conjunction is limited—was shown to be decidable for all processes in $\mathcal{E}^2$ and $\mathcal{E}^3$.

The $\mathcal{E}$ calculus is related to *higher-order* process calculi such as, e.g., the higher-order π-calculus [10], Kell [11], and Homer [6]. (Further comparisons between $\mathcal{E}$ and other calculi and languages can be found in [4].) In such calculi, processes can be passed around, and so communication involves term instantiation, as in the λ-calculus. Update actions in $\mathcal{E}$ are a form of term instantiation: they can be seen as a streamlined version of the *passivation* operator of Kell and Homer, which allows to suspend a running process. It would be interesting to investigate if the results and techniques developed in this paper can apply to Kell and Homer (or to some interesting fragments of them).

We comment on a number of extensions of the results here presented. We conjecture that the decidability result can be extended to monotone formulae. This should imply a more involved construction of the finite basis $\mathsf{FB}_P(\phi_1 \wedge \phi_2)$ given in Table 4. Also, all the results shown in this paper can be easily extended to the *static* variants of $\mathcal{E}$, as defined in [4]. Informally speaking, the static characterization of $\mathcal{E}$ processes is related to the tree-like structures obtained by nesting of located processes. In *dynamic* adaptable processes, the class here considered, update actions which modify the nesting structure are allowed; in contrast, in static adaptable processes such actions are disallowed: this guarantees that no adaptable process is created nor destroyed along computation.

It would not be difficult to show that $\mathcal{L}$ is undecidable in the static version of $\mathcal{E}^2$, by resorting to the termination problem, using an MM encoding similar to the one presented here. Furthermore, the undecidability of $\mathcal{L}_r$ in $\mathcal{E}^1$ would hold also when considering static processes, as the encoding reported here already satisfies the static constraints. Finally, by appealing to the machinery based on well-structured transition systems, we can show that $\mathcal{L}$ is decidable for $\mathcal{E}^2$ processes in the static variant.

Also interesting would be to extend $\mathcal{L}$ with recursion. This would allow to express properties like *eventual adaptation*, as considered in [5]. The results in [4] already suggest that $\mathcal{L}_r$ extended with recursion should be undecidable. Indeed, logic satisfiability could be reduced to the termination problem, using encodings of MMs similar to those given in [4]. Nevertheless, some decidability results could be obtained when considering a static version of $\mathcal{E}^3$, using an encoding of Petri nets as the one presented in [4].

References

1. Abdulla, P.A., Cerans, K., Jonsson, B., Tsay, Y.-K.: Algorithmic analysis of programs with well quasi-ordered domains. Inf. Comput. 160(1-2), 109–127 (2000)
2. Acciai, L., Boreale, M., Zavattaro, G.: On the Relationship between Spatial Logics and Behavioral Simulations. In: Ong, L. (ed.) FOSSACS 2010. LNCS, vol. 6014, pp. 146–160. Springer, Heidelberg (2010)
3. Amazon Web Services. Autoscaling (2011),
   http://aws.amazon.com/autoscaling/
4. Bravetti, M., Di Giusto, C., Pérez, J.A., Zavattaro, G.: Adaptable processes. Technical report, University of Bologna (2011), http://www.cs.unibo.it/~perez/ap/
5. Bravetti, M., Di Giusto, C., Pérez, J.A., Zavattaro, G.: Adaptable Processes (Extended Abstract). In: Bruni, R., Dingel, J. (eds.) FORTE 2011 and FMOODS 2011. LNCS, vol. 6722, pp. 90–105. Springer, Heidelberg (2011)
6. Bundgaard, M., Godskesen, J.C., Hildebrandt, T.: Bisimulation congruences for homer — a calculus of higher order mobile embedded resources. Technical Report TR-2004-52, IT University of Copenhagen (2004)
7. Finkel, A., Schnoebelen, P.: Well-structured transition systems everywhere! Theor. Comput. Sci. 256(1-2), 63–92 (2001)
8. Milner, R.: Comunication and Concurrency. Prentice Hall (1989)
9. Milner, R., Parrow, J., Walker, D.: A Calculus of Mobile Processes, I. Inf. Comput. 100(1), 1–40 (1992)
10. Sangiorgi, D.: Expressing Mobility in Process Algebras: First-Order and Higher-Order Paradigms. PhD thesis CST–99–93, University of Edinburgh, Dept. of Comp. Sci. (1992)
11. Schmitt, A., Stefani, J.-B.: The Kell Calculus: A Family of Higher-Order Distributed Process Calculi. In: Priami, C., Quaglia, P. (eds.) GC 2004. LNCS, vol. 3267, pp. 146–178. Springer, Heidelberg (2005)

Runtime Verification: The Application Perspective*

Yliès Falcone[1] and Lenore D. Zuck[2]

[1] University of Grenoble I (UJF), Laboratoire d'Informatique de Grenoble
`ylies.falcone@ujf-grenoble.fr`
[2] University of Illinois at Chicago
`lenore@cs.uic.edu`

Abstract. In the past decade, Runtime Verification (RV) has gained much focus, from both the research community and practitioners. Roughly speaking, RV combines a set of theories, techniques and tools aiming towards efficient analysis of systems' executions and guaranteeing their correctness using monitoring techniques. Major challenges in RV include characterizing and formally expressing requirements that can be monitored, proposing intuitive and concise specification formalisms, and monitoring specifications efficiently (time and memory-wise).

With the major strides made in recent years, much effort is still needed to make RV an attractive and viable methodology for industrial use. In addition, further studies are needed to apply RV to wider application domains such as security, bio-health, power micro-grids.

The purpose of the "Runtime Verification: the application perspective" track at ISoLA'12 was to bring together experts on runtime verification and potential application domains to try and advance the state-of-the-art on how to make RV more attractive to industry and usable in additional application domains. This introductory paper proposes an overview of the contributions brought by the papers selected at the track.

1 Introduction

In the past decade Runtime Verification (RV) has gained much focus from both research community and practitioners [26,17,24,21]. Roughly speaking, RV combines a set of theories, techniques and tools aiming towards efficient analysis of systems' executions and guaranteeing their correctness using monitoring techniques. While the techniques used in RV are not novel and have been applied in several areas, mainly by the testing community, the term *runtime verification* had been coined only in 2001 by a workshop (now a conference) carrying that name initiated by Klaus Havelund (who authors a paper in this track) and Grigore Rosu. Since then, RV had become a first-class citizen in the formal method community, being combined with techniques such as learning, model checking, theorem proving, and more.

Obviously, static methods can guarantee program correctness. They are, however, not always applicable to a variety of systems and properties. Often the size of the system

---

* The work of the first author was funded in part by the French-government Single Inter-Ministry Fund (FUI) through the IO32 project. The work of the second author was funded in part by NSF award CCF-0916438.

T. Margaria and B. Steffen (Eds.): ISoLA 2012, Part I, LNCS 7609, pp. 284–291, 2012.

renders static methods prohibitively expensive. Systems to which static techniques are applied are those where correctness is to be proven under all circumstances, such as safety critical systems. In contract, many "real-life" systems may be occasionally faulty, especially when the fault is not catastrophic (or even very expensive) and the system can recover from it. Similarly, static techniques are applicable to systems that are built top down and are often applied at the design stages. In contrast, many "real-life" systems are developed ad-hoc so that their properties are not always known à priori, yet, they may be learnt during the system' execution. For these and many other reasons, RV offers an interesting alternative to static methods. Yet, in spite of the major strides made in research of RV methods during recent years, much effort is still needed to make it an attractive and viable methodology for industrial use. In addition, many domains, such as security and bio-health monitoring, can gain from RV methodologies, yet, their use is scarce.

The purpose of the "Runtime Verification: the application perspective" track at ISoLA'12 is to bring together experts on runtime verification and potential application domains to try and advance the state-of-the-art on how to make RV more usable and attractive to industry and other disciplines.

This introductory paper briefly presents the research directions addressed by the articles in the "Runtime Verification: the application perspective" track at ISoLA'12. These research directions aims at making runtime verification a more viable and effective technique in the industrial context for more application domains. More specifically, the topics addressed by the articles can be grouped in three following general directions:

– Reducing the overhead induced by monitoring systems (Section 2);
– Combining RV with other validation techniques (Section 3);
– Applying RV to new application domains (Section 4).

2   Towards More Efficient RV

Monitoring the execution induces a penalty in terms of execution time on the monitored system. Parametric properties are especially expensive because observed events carry data values and the monitor has to compute and evaluate possible combinations and monitor the coherent ones. Many frameworks have been proposed to monitor parametric properties (cf. [2,28,9,5,4,3]). There exists a spectrum of available solutions that differ in the expressiveness of the specification formalisms and the efficiency of the monitors at runtime [3]. As one could expect, the rule of thumb is that the more expressive the formalism is, the more costly (resource-wise) it is to monitor the specifications.

The performance issue also arises when monitoring information-flow properties using taint analysis [27,29]. In information-flow analysis, the addressed question is whether dangerous information can potentially flow from input variables (or API) to the vulnerable points in the program. Contrarily to standard monitoring, it entails to monitor a large number of execution points and several executions of the program. Moreover, when performed at the assembly level, the monitoring overhead gets multiplied, and becomes prohibitive.

What Does AI Have to Do with RV? [16] (Havelund). Havelund proposes to use Artificial Intelligence techniques to help monitoring parametric specifications. Several runtime verification frameworks and tools are rule-based systems. Intuitively, in such frameworks, a specification consists more or less of rules of the form left-hand-side ⇒ right-hand-side. A monitoring state is a set of facts that is matched against the left-hand side of each rule which, in turn, possibly produces new facts. Each new event that is received augments the current set of facts. A problem that arises when monitoring parametric specifications is that complex and multiple matching are required depending on the effective parameters carried out by events, and, against the formal parameters in the left-hand side part of rules.

Havelund proposes an original solution inspired from Artificial Intelligence where knowledge systems are similarly modeled using rule-based productions. In such a context, the RETE algorithm provides efficient matching by intuitively maintaining a network of connected facts. Havelund proposes (i) an RV version of this algorithm, (ii) its Scala implementation, (iii) exploration of its use for runtime verification, and (iv) empirical assessment of the algorithm it against state-of-the-art solutions.

A Case for "piggyback" Runtime Monitoring [14] (Hallé et al.). As already mentioned, devising algorithms and implementations to monitor parametric properties is notoriously difficult because of the extremely large state-space created at runtime. Roughly speaking, multiple possible associations between parameters need to be tracked by multiple instances of monitors. Such algorithms usually involve complex additional data structures in the monitoring code to efficiently access and update the state associated with a runtime monitor. When parametric properties rule the order of method calls on objects, the authors point out that objects already maintain some form of internal state machine that can keep track of the evaluation of the property. Using directly this internal data-structure in monitoring is referred to as "piggy-back monitoring." To attain piggy-back monitoring, the authors study the design a systematic method to determine whether a property is monitorable using the embedded state-machine, propose a systematic translation between the field values and the state of the underlying machine, and empirically asses the gain of using such state machine versus traditional techniques using additional data-structures.

3   Combining RV with Other Techniques

In the past few years, research endeavors have been combining runtime verification with other validation techniques so to obtain the benefits of several worlds. Classically, runtime verification has been combined with the static techniques, and more particularly with static analysis techniques [20,19,8], and more recently with model-checking [18]. Objectives of such combination include reducing overhead and improving coverage.

The track "Runtime Verification, the application perspective" contais three original combinations of RV with other techniques. Ahrendt et al. propose to combine RV with theorem proving. Bensalem et al. propose to introduce statistical model-checking techniques on the BIP component framework. Statistical model-checking can be understood as the combination of RV with statistics. Thus, following a previous paper on runtime verification of BIP systems, the authors use statistical algorithms over the verdicts collected during monitoring of systems. Havelund's paper, described above, can also be considered in this category since it employs AI techniques to improve the efficiency of monitoring parametric properties.

A Unified Approach for Static and Runtime Verification: Framework and Applications [1] (Ahrendt et al.). The paper addresses the main limitations of RV that hinders its use in industrial applications: RV is a partial validation technique and the overhead induced by monitoring is still too important to be acceptable. To overcome these difficulties, the authors propose a unified specification and validation framework that combines static and runtime verification methods. The targeted specification are ppDATE, i.e., communicating timed automata with functional unit specifications that allows to combine control and data-centric specifications. In this framework, the static and verification part rely on the Key theorem prover and the LARVA tool, respectively. The pre- and post- conditions of methods referred in a specification are extracted and transmitted to the theorem prover for a tentative proof. Parts of the specification that were statically proved are removed to spare the runtime verifier from those checks. Partial proofs are leveraged to specialize pre-conditions and monitors. The authors propose two applications of this framework: (runtime) verification of the absence of conflicts in contracts and validation of systems handling transactions.

Statistical Model Checking QoS Properties of Real Time Systems in BIP [6] (Bensalem et al.). Statistical model checking extends runtime verification capabilities by exploiting statistical algorithms in order to get some evidence on property satisfaction or violation. Concretely, the outcome of monitoring several runs is used in a mathematical algorithm to compute the probability that the system will satisfy a property with a given confidence level.

In a series of recent works, the authors introduced BIP (Behavior Interaction and Priorities), a component-based framework supporting rigorous design of embedded systems. BIP proposes several monitoring and simulation facilities. However, its verification capabilities are limited. This paper presents SBIP, an extension of BIP that relies on a new stochastic semantics that enables verification of large-size systems by combining existing features of BIP with Statistical Model Checking. The approach is illustrated on several industrial case studies.

4   (New) Application Domains for RV

In the last few years, much progress has been made on the theoretical parts of RV. Applying RV to new domains is now possible and was the topic of some papers of the track. Four application domains are addressed by the papers: security and information flow [11,23], home-automation [7], system biology [10], OSGi services [7], and power-micro grids.

4.1   Information-Flow Properties and Concurrent Programs

Monitoring Temporal Information Flow [11] (Dimitrova et al.). RV methods have been applied to security protocols for several decades. This paper focuses on one of the important yet elusive challenges of security – information-flow. One of the challenges of applying dynamic techniques for enforcement of information-flow policies is that such techniques must not only account for the executions that occur, but also for others that do *not* occur. The authors have recently developed a temporal logic, SecLTL, that extends liner-time temporal logic an new modal operator, "Hide," which captures the property of a certain part of the input remaining secret within some time frame. Here, Dimitrova et al. show how to use SecLTL for the specification of runtime monitors of information-flow control properties.

Dynamic Information-Flow Analysis for Multi-threaded Applications [23] (Mounier and Sifakis). A particularly demanding domain for validation is multi-threaded applications. In this context, analyzing information-flow properties is challenging and costly because of communicating channels between running processes. Dynamic validation of security properties is particularly appealing because static techniques are limited either in scalability or expressiveness of the analyzed properties. Mounier and Sifakis overview existing dynamic approaches to this problem and propose a window-based information flow analysis. It assumes that interleaving of processes is limited to a series of local and restricted time periods, namely epochs. Compared to existing approaches, the window-based analysis is hardware-independent, and enjoys a lower overhead.

Bounded-Interference Sequentialization for Testing Concurrent Programs [25] (Razavi et al.). Similar to Mounier et al, this work studied the problem of multi-threaded programs, here with a shared memory model where threads communicate by means of shared variables. These programs are challenging because they incorporate two types of non-determinism, that imposed by the scheduler and that imposed by the input. Indeed, testing methodologies for such programs focus primarily on the former (with context switching, e.g.) usually ignoring the nondeterminism imposed by the input. In this work, Razavi et al propose a methodology that addresses both types of nondeterminism: A multithreaded program is transformed into a sequential one with *bounded-interference*, that, roughly speaking, bounds the interference of other threads in terms of number of critical accesses to the shared variables. Once a sequential program is obtained, the more traditional testing tools can be applied to it to guarantee good coverage. The methodology was implemented and successfully applied to concurrent C# programs.

4.2   System Biology

Runtime Verification of Biological Systems [10] (David et al.). The paper explores a combination of two statistical model checkers, UPPAAL-SMC and PLASMA to demonstrate the advantages of runtime verification of complex systems whose description may not be available to the verifier. The studied system is a model of biological oscillation whose description is a system of ordinary differential equations. Using UPPAAL-SMC, the system could be modeled as a stochastic one, and several (bounded time) linear temporal logics properties were proven using PLASMA. The paper thus demonstrates the power of runtime verification for system whose state space in not explicitly described, and shows a nice interaction of two powerful model checkers.

4.3 OSGi Services

Behavioral Specification Based Runtime Monitors for OSGi Services [7] (Blech et al.).
The paper proposes a vision of a tool framework and process for component-based systems and presents directions for related research topics and applications. Abstract specifications are used as a basis for runtime monitors and additional checks which can be performed during runtime. RV frameworks dedicated to component-based systems already exist (cf. [12,13]), however, the tool framework suggested here focuses on systems where components can be exchanged, added or removed during runtime. Special emphasis is put on the OSGi framework as an application component system and an Eclipse based realization of an integrated tool framework supporting multiple development phases.

4.4 Power-Micro Grids

Modelling and Decentralised Runtime Control of Self-stabilising Power Micro Grids [15] (Hartmanns and Hermanns). In the past decade or so there has been much effort to develop a "Smart Grid" where networks of automated systems are used to improve efficiency of distribution and use of powers. In 2009, President Obama announced a $10B plan to invest on the smart grid. This paper focuses on the German efforts towards a smart grid. It gives an overview of the modeling aspects of a decentralized power grid, and the challenges towards modeling and allaying such systems so to guarantee their correct operation. The paper then offers several approaches to improve on the unstable system that is currently used. It offers a set of properties that a properly designed system should have, and proposes some models for systems that satisfy those requirements.

5 Concluding Remarks

The "Runtime Verification: the Application Perspective" track at ISoLA 2012 focused on making RV more efficient, combining it with other techniques as to obtain better validation, and applying RV to new application domains. It includes ten papers on state-of-the-art research topics that cover a wide range of topics that are being actively pursued by the RV community and lay the ground for much future work.

We thank all the authors who contributed to the track.

References

1. Ahrendt, W., Pace, G., Schneider, G.: A unified approach for static and runtime verification: framework and applications. In: Margaria, Steffen [22]
2. Allan, C., Avgustinov, P., Christensen, A.S., Hendren, L.J., Kuzins, S., Lhoták, O., de Moor, O., Sereni, D., Sittampalam, G., Tibble, J.: Adding trace matching with free variables to AspectJ. In: Johnson, R.E., Gabriel, R.P. (eds.) OOPSLA, pp. 345–364. ACM (2005)
3. Barringer, H., Falcone, Y., Havelund, K., Reger, G., Rydeheard, D.: Quantified Event Automata: Towards Expressive and Efficient Runtime Monitors. In: Giannakopoulou, D., Méry, D. (eds.) FM 2012. LNCS, vol. 7436, pp. 68–84. Springer, Heidelberg (2012)

4. Barringer, H., Havelund, K.: TRACECONTRACT: A Scala DSL for Trace Analysis. In: Butler, M., Schulte, W. (eds.) FM 2011. LNCS, vol. 6664, pp. 57–72. Springer, Heidelberg (2011)

5. Barringer, H., Rydeheard, D.E., Havelund, K.: Rule systems for run-time monitoring: from Eagle to RuleR. J. Log. Comput. 20(3), 675–706 (2010)

6. Bensalem, S., Bozga, M., Delahaye, B., Jegourel, C., Legay, A., Nouri, A.: Sbip: A statistical model checking extension for BIP. In: Margaria, Steffen [22]

7. Blech, J.O., Falcone, Y., Rueß, H., Schäetz, B.: Behavioral Specification based Runtime Monitors for OSGi Services. In: Margaria, Steffen [22]

8. Bodden, E., Hendren, L.J.: The Clara framework for hybrid typestate analysis. STTT 14(3), 307–326 (2012)

9. Chen, F., Roşu, G.: Parametric Trace Slicing and Monitoring. In: Kowalewski, S., Philippou, A. (eds.) TACAS 2009. LNCS, vol. 5505, pp. 246–261. Springer, Heidelberg (2009)

10. David, A., Larsen, K.G., Legay, A., Seadwards, S., Poulsen, D.: Systems biology, runtime verification and more. In: Margaria, Steffen [22]

11. Dimitrova, R., Finkbeiner, B., Rabe, M.: Monitoring temporal information flow. In: Margaria, Steffen [22]

12. Dormoy, J., Kouchnarenko, O., Lanoix, A.: Using Temporal Logic for Dynamic Reconfigurations of Components. In: Barbosa, L.S., Lumpe, M. (eds.) FACS 2010. LNCS, vol. 6921, pp. 200–217. Springer, Heidelberg (2010)

13. Falcone, Y., Jaber, M., Nguyen, T.-H., Bozga, M., Bensalem, S.: Runtime Verification of Component-Based Systems. In: Barthe, G., Pardo, A., Schneider, G. (eds.) SEFM 2011. LNCS, vol. 7041, pp. 204–220. Springer, Heidelberg (2011)

14. Hallé, S., Tremblay-Lessard, R.: A case for "piggyback" runtime monitoring. In: Margaria, Steffen [22]

15. Hartmanns, A., Hermanns, H.: Modelling and decentralised runtime control of self-stabilising power micro grids. In: Margaria, Steffen [22]

16. Havelund, K.: What does AI have to do with RV. In: Margaria, Steffen [22]

17. Havelund, K., Goldberg, A.: Verify Your Runs. In: Meyer, B., Woodcock, J. (eds.) VSTTE 2005. LNCS, vol. 4171, pp. 374–383. Springer, Heidelberg (2008)

18. Hinrichs, T., Sistla, P.A., Zuck, L.D.: Model checking meets run-time verification. In: Voronkov, A., Korovina, M. (eds.) HOWARD-60: Proceedings of the Higher-Order Workshop on Automated Runtime verification and Debugging (to appear, 2012)

19. Huang, X., Seyster, J., Callanan, S., Dixit, K., Grosu, R., Smolka, S.A., Stoller, S.D., Zadok, E.: Software monitoring with controllable overhead. STTT 14(3), 327–347 (2012)

20. Kim, C.H.P., Bodden, E., Batory, D., Khurshid, S.: Reducing Configurations to Monitor in a Software Product Line. In: Barringer, H., Falcone, Y., Finkbeiner, B., Havelund, K., Lee, I., Pace, G., Roşu, G., Sokolsky, O., Tillmann, N. (eds.) RV 2010. LNCS, vol. 6418, pp. 285–299. Springer, Heidelberg (2010)

21. Leucker, M., Schallhart, C.: A brief account of runtime verification. Journal of Logic and Algebraic Programming 78(5), 293–303 (2008)

22. Margaria, T., Steffen, B.: ISoLA 2012, Part I. LNCS, vol. 7609. Springer, Heidelberg (2012)

23. Mounier, L., Sifakis, E.: Dynamic information-flow analysis for multi-threaded applications. In: Margaria, Steffen [22]

24. Pnueli, A., Zaks, A.: PSL Model Checking and Run-Time Verification Via Testers. In: Misra, J., Nipkow, T., Sekerinski, E. (eds.) FM 2006. LNCS, vol. 4085, pp. 573–586. Springer, Heidelberg (2006)

25. Razavi, N., Holzer, A., Farzan, A.: Bounded-interference sequentialization for testing concurrent programs. In: Margaria, Steffen [22]

26. Runtime Verification (2001-2012), http://www.runtime-verification.org
27. Sabelfeld, A., Myers, A.C.: Language-based information-flow security. IEEE Journal on Selected Areas in Communications 21(1), 5–19 (2003)
28. Stolz, V., Bodden, E.: Temporal assertions using AspectJ. Electr. Notes Theor. Comput. Sci. 144(4), 109–124 (2006)
29. Terauchi, T., Aiken, A.: Secure Information Flow as a Safety Problem. In: Hankin, C., Siveroni, I. (eds.) SAS 2005. LNCS, vol. 3672, pp. 352–367. Springer, Heidelberg (2005)

What Does AI Have to Do with RV?

(Extended Abstract)

Klaus Havelund[*]

Jet Propulsion Laboratory
California Institute of Technology
California, USA

Runtime Verification (RV) consists of monitoring the behavior of a system, either on-the-fly as it executes, or post-mortem after its execution for example by analyzing log files. Within the last decade several systems have been developed to address this issue. These systems usually implement specification languages which are based on formalisms such as state machines [11,14,8,12,5], regular expressions [1,8], temporal logic [16,10,15,3,19,9,18,8,5], or grammars [8].

Some systems are based on some form of rewriting. In the Java PathExplorer (JPAX) system [15] a property is represented as an LTL [17] term. The semantics of LTL is in turn specified by a set of rewrite rules of the form $lhs \Rightarrow rhs$, for example, it contains a rewrite rule reflecting the semantics of the until operator (p until q): $p \cup q = q \vee (p \wedge \bigcirc(p \cup q))$. Each new event causes the current LTL term to be rewritten into a new term representing the formula that holds in the next step. For example, a formula on the form "always, an a implies eventually b": $\square(a \rightarrow \Diamond b)$, on an event a is rewritten into $\Diamond b \wedge \square(a \rightarrow \Diamond b)$. Properties in JPAX are propositional in the sense that formulas cannot refer to events that carry data. The TRACECONTRACT SCALA API lifts this principle to the SCALA programming language, while also handling data parameterization as well as state machines. Other systems based on this form of LTL-rewriting include [10,3,19,18].

The RULER system [6,7], and its state machine oriented derivative LOGSCOPE [4], implement rule-based systems. The state of such a system at any point in time is a set of facts, for example $\{open(file_1), closed(file_2)\}$. An incoming event is a new fact that is added to this set. A RULER specification is in principle a set of rules of the form: $lhs \Rightarrow rhs$, where the left hand side (lhs) is a set of conditions on the current monitoring state (set of facts), and the right hand side rhs is a set of actions to be taken in case the conditions are satisfied, for example adding or deleting facts. RULER's inspiration comes from imperative (executable) temporal logics, as for example found in METATEM [2]. The key problem in evaluating a set of rules given a set of facts is to perform *efficient* matching of facts against conditions in rules. It is not difficult to imagine, that

---

[*] Part of the work described in this publication was carried out at Jet Propulsion Laboratory, California Institute of Technology, under a contract with the National Aeronautics and Space Administration.

T. Margaria and B. Steffen (Eds.): ISoLA 2012, Part I, LNCS 7609, pp. 292–294, 2012.
© Springer-Verlag Berlin Heidelberg 2012

in the case where many facts are stored this matching process can be costly if not performed in a smart manner.

The field of Artificial Intelligence (AI) has itself studied a problem very similar to the runtime verification problem, namely *rule-based production systems*, used for example to represent knowledge systems. In such systems a specification is likewise a set of rules *lhs ⇒ rhs*, with a similar interpretation as in RULER. The classic AI approach to efficient matching is the RETE algorithm [13]. This algorithm maintains a network of facts, avoiding to re-evaluate all conditions in each rule's left hand side each time the fact database changes. We have implemented the rather sophisticated RETE algorithm in the SCALA programming language and are exploring its utility for the RV problem. We address its functionality (is it a solution for implementing runtime monitors) and its efficiency (how does it compare with state-of-the-art RV systems). Dynamic program visualization is used to demonstrate the algorithm and the modifications needed for it to apply to the RV problem.

References

1. Allan, C., Avgustinov, P., Christensen, A.S., Hendren, L., Kuzins, S., Lhoták, O., de Moor, O., Sereni, D., Sittamplan, G., Tibble, J.: Adding trace matching with free variables to AspectJ. In: OOPSLA 2005. ACM Press (2005)
2. Barringer, H., Fisher, M., Gabbay, D.M., Gough, G., Owens, R.: MetateM: An introduction. Formal Asp. Comput. 7(5), 533–549 (1995)
3. Barringer, H., Goldberg, A., Havelund, K., Sen, K.: Rule-Based Runtime Verification. In: Steffen, B., Levi, G. (eds.) VMCAI 2004. LNCS, vol. 2937, pp. 44–57. Springer, Heidelberg (2004)
4. Barringer, H., Groce, A., Havelund, K., Smith, M.: Formal analysis of log files. Journal of Aerospace Computing, Information, and Communication 7(11), 365–390 (2010)
5. Barringer, H., Havelund, K.: TRACECONTRACT: A Scala DSL for Trace Analysis. In: Butler, M., Schulte, W. (eds.) FM 2011. LNCS, vol. 6664, pp. 57–72. Springer, Heidelberg (2011)
6. Barringer, H., Rydeheard, D.E., Havelund, K.: Rule Systems for Run-Time Monitoring: From EAGLE to RULER. In: Sokolsky, O., Taşıran, S. (eds.) RV 2007. LNCS, vol. 4839, pp. 111–125. Springer, Heidelberg (2007)
7. Barringer, H., Rydeheard, D.E., Havelund, K.: Rule systems for run-time monitoring: from Eagle to RuleR. J. Log. Comput. 20(3), 675–706 (2010)
8. Chen, F., Roşu, G.: Parametric Trace Slicing and Monitoring. In: Kowalewski, S., Philippou, A. (eds.) TACAS 2009. LNCS, vol. 5505, pp. 246–261. Springer, Heidelberg (2009)
9. D'Amorim, M., Havelund, K.: Event-based runtime verification of Java programs. In: Workshop on Dynamic Program Analysis (WODA'05). ACM Sigsoft Software Engineering Notes, vol. 30(4), pp. 1–7 (2005)
10. Drusinsky, D.: The temporal rover and the ATG rover. In: Havelund, K., Penix, J., Visser, W. (eds.) SPIN 2000. LNCS, vol. 1885, pp. 323–330. Springer, Heidelberg (2000)
11. Drusinsky, D.: Modeling and Verification using UML Statecharts, 400 pages. Elsevier (2006) ISBN-13: 978-0-7506-7949-7

12. Falcone, Y., Fernandez, J.-C., Mounier, L.: Runtime Verification of Safety-Progress Properties. In: Bensalem, S., Peled, D.A. (eds.) RV 2009. LNCS, vol. 5779, pp. 40–59. Springer, Heidelberg (2009)
13. Forgy, C.: Rete: A fast algorithm for the many pattern/many object pattern match problem. Artificial Intelligence 19, 17–37 (1982)
14. Havelund, K.: Runtime verification of C programs. In: Suzuki, K., Higashino, T., Ulrich, A., Hasegawa, T. (eds.) TestCom/FATES 2008. LNCS, vol. 5047, pp. 7–22. Springer, Heidelberg (2008)
15. Havelund, K., Rosu, G.: Monitoring programs using rewriting. In: 16th ASE Conference, San Diego, CA, USA, pp. 135–143 (2001)
16. Lee, I., Kannan, S., Kim, M., Sokolsky, O., Viswanathan, M.: Runtime assurance based on formal specifications. In: PDPTA, pp. 279–287. CSREA Press (1999)
17. Pnueli, A.: The temporal logic of programs. In: 18th Annual Symposium on Foundations of Computer Science, pp. 46–57. IEEE Computer Society (1977)
18. Stolz, V., Bodden, E.: Temporal assertions using AspectJ. In: Proc. of the 5th Int. Workshop on Runtime Verification (RV 2005). ENTCS, vol. 144(4), pp. 109–124. Elsevier (2006)
19. Stolz, V., Huch, F.: Runtime verification of concurrent Haskell programs. In: Proc. of the 4th Int. Workshop on Runtime Verification (RV 2004). ENTCS, vol. 113, pp. 201–216. Elsevier, Amsterdam (2005)

A Case for "Piggyback" Runtime Monitoring

Sylvain Hallé and Raphaël Tremblay-Lessard

Department of Computer Science and Mathematics
Université du Québec à Chicoutimi, Canada

Abstract. A runtime monitor enforcing a constraint on sequences of method calls on an object must keep track of the state of the sequence by updating an appropriate state machine. The present paper stems from the observation that an object's member fields must already contain an encoding of that state machine, and that a monitor essentially duplicates operations that the object performs internally. Rather than maintain a state machine in parallel, the paper puts forward the concept of "piggy-back" runtime monitoring, where the monitor relies as much as possible on the object's own state variables to perform its task. Experiments on real-world benchmarks show that this approach greatly simplifies the monitoring process and drastically reduces the incurred runtime overhead compared to classical solutions.

1 Introduction

Most non-trivial classes in an object-oriented language expect their methods to be called following a specific pattern. Despite the fact that these methods always have public visibility, the internal state of the object may mandate a program to use only a well-defined subset of all these methods at any given time. As we shall see in Section 2, the allowed sequences of method calls on an object form a kind of "interface" that can often be formalized as a finite-state machine. In the past decade, monitoring tools have been developed and applied to the enforcement of such interfaces at runtime. By intercepting method calls during the execution of a program, these tools can make sure that objects are used according to their finite-state machine specification, and block any non-compliant attempt at accessing an object's methods.

In all monitoring frameworks for Java known to date, such as MOP [20], LARVA [10], BeepBeep [14] and Tracematches [6], the monitor is responsible for keeping a copy of the finite-state machine specification, and for updating its current state based on the method calls it intercepts. Since the storage and updating of such a state machine requires supplemental resources, a central point in current research is to minimize the overhead incurred by using an independent runtime monitor. The basic process can be optimized in various ways —for example, by keeping a single state machine with multiple pointers for each object instance. However, it is common practice to monitor sequences of method calls with a separate data structure.

The present paper challenges this state of things. In Section 5, it shall show through simple examples how in some situations, an object's own member fields

T. Margaria and B. Steffen (Eds.): ISoLA 2012, Part I, LNCS 7609, pp. 295–311, 2012.

contain all the information necessary to determine that a method call is invalid. In other words, if a class imposes a sequence of method calls represented by a finite-state machine, it may already contain a monitor for that machine, encoded somewhere in its member fields. It follows that in those situations, current monitor implementations, which maintain and update their own finite-state machine, essentially duplicate operations that the object itself already performs internally.

The paper then draws the natural conclusions from this observation. In Section 5 it puts forward the idea that, rather than updating its own state, a monitor should rely as much as possible on the monitored object's member fields. Such a monitor effectively "piggybacks" on the object's own state information to make its decisions —hence the term *piggyback runtime monitoring*.

This idea, albeit simple, raises a number of important questions that must be addressed for piggyback runtime monitoring to become useful in practice.

1) How hard is it to find the appropriate mapping between member fields' values and monitor states? We first provide a theoretical answer, by showing in Section 4 that this problem reduces to the directed graph homomorphism problem, known to be NP-complete. Although the desired finite-state machine can theoretically be encoded through a complex combination of multiple member fields, in our empirical study of the OpenJDK we found that the state machine involved at most *two* primitive member fields in the most complex case.

2) How often is a property already "embedded" in an object's member fields? In Section 5, we provide a first empirical answer to this question through a manual inspection of the relevant classes inside the actual source code of the OpenJDK 6, looking for member fields encoding 13 properties used in past literature and benchmarks [5–7, 9, 15, 19]. We found that 10 out of the 13 properties can be equivalently monitored by piggybacking on some of their member fields. This entails that properties that needed to save and track state information across method calls have been reduced to a simple, stateless property that requires no additional data apart from the object's own.

Upon further study, we discovered that the remaining three properties that were not monitorable using the piggyback approach present an interesting dichotomy in the types of constraints one may want to monitor, depending on what happens upon an invalid method call. We call *syntactical* properties the ones that, when violated, create an error in the program: exception thrown, null pointer dereferencing, division by zero, etc. By contrast, *semantic* properties relate to the meaning and integrity of the object's functionality, and do not cause immediate runtime errors. We shall see, through examples taken from the OpenJDK, how these two classes exactly determine if a property is verifiable with piggyback runtime monitoring.

3) How much overhead savings can piggyback monitoring bring? We performed an empirical testing of piggyback monitoring on the DaCapo Benchmark [4] (release 9.12), which consists of a set of open source, *real world* applications with non-trivial memory loads. This is the benchmark used in all past papers in the field [5–7, 9, 15, 19]. Hence the computed measurements can be deemed as a fair basis for comparison to related works. Our results, described in Section 6, reveal that this approach yields a very low runtime overhead (up to 20 times lower than the current best results) and a virtually inexistent memory overhead.

For a majority of the properties we studied, the piggybacked member fields do not have public visibility. We argue in Section 7 that the most important hurdle to piggyback runtime monitoring is not technical, but rather stems from a design issue that can be observed in a number of basic Java classes. The paper ends by suggesting the principle of *design for monitoring*, according to which objects should purposefully provide methods for querying their state, when that information conditions the methods one can call at a given time.

2 State-of-the-Art in Java Runtime Monitoring

Runtime monitoring is the process of observing an actual run of a program and dynamically checking and enforcing constraints while it is executing. A body of literature has focused on the runtime monitoring of so-called *behavioural* properties, i.e. constraints that characterize appropriate use of objects, particularly for the Java language. Behavioural properties can be seen as a generalization of the notion of type; not only does an object have a set of allowed methods, but what methods can be called also depends on the context (i.e. the object's state). A runtime monitor may intercept method calls on each instance of an object and prevent invalid sequences from happening by blocking method calls that do not fit the current state of the the object.

2.1 Stateful Properties of Java Objects

We made an exhaustive compilation of properties studied in Java runtime monitoring in related papers published over the past five years, concentrating on those expressing constraints over objects taken from the Java API (mostly the `java.io` and `java.util` packages) [5–7, 9, 15, 19]. This set of papers relies on a total of 13 properties, sometimes referred to by different names in different papers. A few of them are worthy of mention. For example, property HASNEXT requires tat any call to `next()` must always be immediately preceded by a call to `hasNext()` that returned `true`; property HASHMAP forbids one to change an object's `hashCode()` while it is in a `HashMap`.

Monitoring these properties presents three challenges. First, each of them expresses a *stateful* constraint on objects: the set of method calls that can be invoked on an object depends on the history of previous method calls; hence property REMOVE forbids the user of an `Iterator` to call method `remove()` if it follows a previous call to the same method without a call to `next()` in between.

Second, these properties specify constraints on a per-instance basis (also called "parametric" in [15]). It does not suffice to record all calls to `remove()` and `next()`: each must be tied to the proper instance of `Iterator` to keep track of their respective history.

Finally, some of the properties correlate method calls on *multiple* objects; this is the case of e.g. SAFEENUM, which forbids any call on an `Iterator` if its parent `Vector` has been modified using methods like `put()` or `remove()`. For these properties one cannot simply keep track of each instance's history separately.

2.2   Current Monitoring Methods

In virtually all known monitor implementations, such as JavaMOP [20], LARVA [10], BeepBeep [14], Tracematches [6], J-Lo [23], PQL [18], PTQL [13], SpoX [11], PoET [12], Eagle and RuleR [3], the monitor is responsible for keeping a copy of the finite-state machine specification in memory across each method call to the same object. Method calls are intercepted during execution using purpose-built instrumentation techniques, or by writing pointcuts in an aspect-oriented framework such as AspectJ [17].

In between these calls, the machine is stored into a cell of an "array" containing the state machines of all the current instances of the object. Upon each method call, the appropriate monitor must be located and retrieved. Special data structures to optimize this process have been described (e.g. [2]). Yet this task reportedly amounts to a very large portion of the total overhead incurred by the classical approach.

Moreover, the monitor must also keep track of instances of objects that have been garbage-collected, in order to delete their corresponding automata. Otherwise, unnecessary monitor instances can be kept for the entire length of a program. This issue is a research topic in itself, and ultimately amounts to programming a mini-garbage collector inside the monitor [15].

This inherent inefficiency can be mitigated by inserting the monitor instance directly into the objects whenever possible. The Tracematches tool [6] has had for several years now such an optimization feature, which takes advantage of so-called *inter-type declarations*. However, inter-type declarations are difficult to implement when the property to monitor correlates method calls across multiple objects, as is the case for SAFEENUM described above.

Despite these challenges, runtime monitoring techniques have been steadily improving in the past decade. One of the latest studies on the topic [15] reports that the "most efficient monitoring system to date" incurs a time overhead below 5% for a large number of properties; yet, for some others, execution time almost *triples* when the monitor is added to the program.

3   A Monitor in the Program

Barring their varying performance, a common point of all existing monitoring approaches is their reliance on a monitor that is *independent* from the objects to observe. To the best of our knowledge, this design choice has never been questioned, and alternatives to this approach have never been sought. In this section, we challenge this fact and observe that an object's existing member fields, in many cases, may already contain an encoding of the monitor's finite-state machine that can be put to good use.

3.1   A Simple Example

Consider the Java class `Stateless` object shown in Figure 1. This class defines three methods `a()`, `b()`, and `c()`, and is designed in such a way that `a()` and `b()` can be called at any time, but `c()` always throws an error.[1] It is straightforward to devise a constraint on the invocation of methods on a `Stateless` object:

```
class Stateless {
  void a() { }
  void b() { }
  void c() { throwError(); }
}
```

```
class Stateful {
  private int s = 1;
  void a() { s = s + 1; }
  void b() { s = 0; }
  int c() { return 1 / s; }
  boolean getS() { return s; }
}
```

Fig. 1. Two simple Java classes: `Stateless` and `Stateful`

C1. You should never call `c()`.

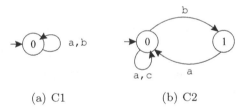

(a) C1   (b) C2

Fig. 2. Two finite-state automata representing constraints C1–C2

This constraint on sequences of method calls can be represented by a state machine shown in Figure 2(a), where edge labels represent method calls, and where output values are ignored. We say that a `Stateless` object O imposes this state machine M, meaning that it throws an error if a sequence of method calls is not in $\mathcal{L}(M)$, the language accepted by M. This state machine is *minimal*, in the sense that no machine with a smaller set of states can be made to accept the same language.

The situation is different if we consider the `Stateless` object class and the following constraint, depicted in Figure 2(b):

---

[1] We use method `throwError()` as a placeholder for any undesirable event or behaviour that should be prevented from happening.

C2. You should never call c() right after b().

This time, the property is not correlated with possible errors resulting from the object's usage. A Stateless object has no way to detect how one calls c() with respect to previous calls to a() and b(), for the simple reason that it has no memory —that is, no state variable or member object that can differentiate between any sequence of method calls. In contrast, the Stateful object shown in Figure 1 has a member variable s. Calls to methods a(), b() and c() update that variable in such a way that, according to constraint C2, c() can be called exactly when s is greater than 0 —in this case, C2 prevents a division by zero.

It turns out that there is a straightforward relationship that can be established between an object's state space and the properties of its valid sequences of method calls. By *state space*, we mean the subset of the Cartesian product of all values of the object's member variables, reachable from the object's initial state through any sequence of method calls. If the object contains member objects, its possible values are the set of its own states, and so on recursively.

Theorem 1. *Let S_O be the set of states of an object O having a set of method names L. Let $M = (S_A, \delta, s_{0,A}, L)$ be a minimal state machine with states S_A, initial state $s_{0,A}$, and a labelled transition function $\delta : S_A \times L \to S_A$. If O imposes a set of valid sequences of method calls encoded by M, then there exists a mapping $H : S_O \to S_A$ such that calling method $\ell \in L$ in state s leads to state s' in O entails $H(s') = \delta(H(s), \ell)$.*

Proof. Define the mapping H as follows: for a sequence $\overline{m}$, let $s_O \in S_O$ be the state in which O is after calling each method of $\overline{m}$ in sequence, and let $s_M \in S_M$ be the state of the state machine after reading the same sequence. Let $H(s_O) \triangleq s_M$.

We must now show that H is well-defined, i.e. that any sequence of methods $\overline{m}$ where O ends in s_O has M ending in the same state s_M. Suppose the contrary; then there exists some $s_O \in S_O$ such that $H(s_O)$ can be defined for two different values s_M and s'_M. This is only possible if there exist two method sequences, $\overline{m}$ and $\overline{m}'$, such that both end in s_O in O, but reach different states s_M and s'_M in M.

Consider a sequence of method calls $\overline{m}''$ resuming from s_O. Since δ_O is a function, then $\delta_O(\overline{m}\overline{m}'') = \delta_O(\overline{m}'\overline{m}'')$. Hence if $\overline{m}\overline{m}''$ ends in an error, then so is $\overline{m}'\overline{m}''$; in reverse if if $\overline{m}\overline{m}''$ does not end in an error, then so is $\overline{m}'\overline{m}''$. But since by hypothesis O imposes M, this entails that then $\overline{m}\overline{m}'' \in \mathcal{L}(M)$ if and only if $\overline{m}'\overline{m}'' \in \mathcal{L}(M)$. Since $\overline{m}''$ is arbitrary, then either $s_M = s'_M$ (contradicting our hypothesis), or $s_M \neq s'_M$, yet the same method calls are accepted from each (contradicting the fact that M is minimal).

In the case of constraint C2 on the Stateful class, the desired homomorphism maps all states of the object where $s \neq 0$ to state 0 of the FSM, and the single state where $s = 0$ to state 1.

3.2   Consequences for Traditional Monitoring

Despite recalling well-known facts about a program's state and execution traces, the previous observations have an important and sometimes overlooked consequence on the actual purpose of performing runtime monitoring on an object's sequences of method calls.

Corollary 1. *Performing runtime monitoring of a property encoded by a finite-state machine M either: 1) duplicates the work of an identical state machine contained within (and updated by) the object itself, or 2) enforces a property on sequences that the object itself cannot correctly discriminate.*

The proof of this assertion follows directly from Theorem 1. If an object imposes a sequence of method calls, it must have all the information within its own state variables to distinguish between valid and invalid sequences —therefore, the combination of its state variables contain an encoding of the same state machine M that the runtime monitor uses to track method calls.

This duplication is obvious in the case of an external monitor. However, even in frameworks that use inter-type declarations, which insert the monitor as an object's member field, the monitor itself is still an autonomous structure that has no interaction with its host object: it maintains its own state, using internal variables that are separate from that of the object to monitor, and which must be externally updated upon each method call.

Of course, this corollary rules out the eventuality where one might want to enforce a constraint on the use of an object, despite the fact that the object itself cannot observe it. For example, one might still want to monitor constraint C2 on a `Stateless` object, perhaps for semantic reasons (the object can be used without causing errors, but provides meaningless results outside of the specification). However, it should be clear that this enforcement cannot be justified by the prevention of errors that the `Stateless` object itself could throw. We shall see in Section 5.2 that some of the aforementioned properties are of that kind.

4   Finding a Suitable Mapping

Based on Corollary 1, it appears that most of the work incurred when performing runtime monitoring using current frameworks actually amounts to an independent recomputation of a state machine that already exists inside the monitored program. Furthermore this state machine, when identified, can be trusted, since by point 2 above the object itself relies on that state information to reject or accept sequences of method calls. [2]

Surprisingly, the consequences of this seemingly simple observation have never been rigorously examined. It is indeed possible to design a runtime monitoring framework that does not require persisting a state machine during a run of the program and updating its state upon each method call —this should be (and

---

[2] The information, however, may not be made *visible* by the object; this case will be discussed in Section 7.

actually is) done by the program itself. Rather, it suffices to *query* the state machine available inside the program's own state, and merely apply simpler, "stateless" conditions on that machine to decide on the validity of the intended method call. In a way, such a runtime monitoring system "piggybacks" on the program's already available variables to perform its task, rather than maintaining its separate data.

The motivating example in Section 3.1, and the ensuing workflow derived from it, rests on some important assumptions: we knew what member fields in the object encoded to the state machine of the corresponding monitor; there was only one member field necessary, and it was of a primitive data type; finally, we knew how to express the condition to monitor as a function of this member field, and that condition was simple. As a matter of fact, we can devise a workflow to be applied in a systematic way to a monitoring problem. If we let S_O be the set of states of an object O, and S_M be the set of states of the state machine M, we shall follow these steps:

1. Find the mapping H between S_O and S_A, as defined in Theorem 1.
2. If no such mapping exists, the process is over. Indeed, by Corollary 1, then we are trying to monitor a constraint that the object itself does not recognize.
3. Otherwise, we still do not have a guarantee that the constraint is followed by the program; only that the object's state *can* be used to monitor it. One must then devise a condition on the object's member fields that is equivalent to the transition function of M.

Steps 2 and 3 are trivial; the bulk of the monitoring problem is now transferred to the search for an appropriate mapping of the object's states to the state machine M, satisfying the conditions of Theorem 1. However, the complexity of this problem can be determined.

Theorem 2. *Identifying the monitor within the object's member fields is NP-complete.*

Proof. Given the notation from Theorem 1, we know that S_O and S_A are labelled (by method names) multigraphs (their edges are directed). The problem in Step 1 above consists of finding a mapping $H : S_O \to S_A$ such that if calling method $\ell \in L$ in state s leads to state s' in O, then $H(s') = \delta(H(s), \ell)$. This is nothing but finding a homomorphism between two labelled multigraphs, a problem shown to be NP-complete [8, Definition 5.6].

5   Piggyback Monitoring on Java Objects

Designing a full-fledged automatic method of digging the proper monitor inside a class' state space is currently an open problem. In general, however, we hypothesize that the appropriate mapping H should not appear out of the blue from unsuspected member fields, and that one should hence have a relatively clear idea, in advance, of what this mapping should be by a simple inspection of the source code. To assess the interest in developing such techniques, as a preliminary step, we tested this conjecture empirically by trying to create, by hand, the piggyback constraints equivalent to each of the properties described in Section 2; the resulting monitors will be then experimentally evaluated in Section 6.

5.1 Stateful Properties Revisited

To this end, we obtained and manually inspected the source code of the Open-JDK 6 [1], the latest open source implementation of the complete Java environment. Apart from primitive data types and the `Object` top-level class, all the standard API classes bundled in a Java Runtime Environment are themselves written in Java. The first step was to determine the member fields inside the objects that could harbour the internal state machine required to monitor these properties.

We give an example of the methodology we followed by showing how to devise the piggyback constraint for property SAFEFILEREADER. An Input-StreamReader is instantiated by passing as an argument to its constructor an `InputStream`. Property SAFEFILEREADER stipulates that an `InputStream-Reader`'s methods should not be used after the `InputStream` passed at its construction has been closed.

Monitoring this property using classical approaches is not a trivial task. The process is described in e.g. [7]. One is required to capture calls to `InputStream-Reader`'s constructor, and instantiate a new monitor $M(r, i)$, where r is the instantiated `Reader` and i the `InputStream` given to its constructor. Calls to r.read() and i.close() must then be trapped, and an error occurs whenever the former is invoked after an occurrence of the latter.

As our inspection of the source code files revealed, an `InputStreamReader` contains as a member object a `StreamDecoder` called `sd`.[3] This decoder is created from the `InputStream` passed at construction; it contains a boolean member field `isOpen`[4] which gets updated in the obvious way. Hence, when calling `read()` on an `InputStreamReader` r, one must simply ensure that r.`sd`.`isOpen` is true to obtain the equivalent monitoring of the property.

One may suspect that for some properties, especially those that correlate the state of two different objects, it may not be possible to simply query an object's state and deduce from it the relevant methods that may be called. In particular, reviewers of an earlier draft of this paper conjectured that the SAFEENUM property could not be verified using the piggyback approach, and concluded that independent monitors where hence unavoidable under these circumstances. We give in the following an example of the methodology we followed by showing how to devise the piggyback constraint for property SAFEENUM, thereby showing that this claim is false.

`Vector`'s parent class, `AbstractList`, contains a `protected` integer member variable called `modCount`, which "counts the number of times this list has been

---

[3] The reader is referred to the OpenJDK 6 source file `InputStreamReader.java`, line 64.

[4] `StreamDecoder.java`, line 42.

structurally modified. Structural modifications are those that change the size of the list, or otherwise perturb it in such a fashion that iterations in progress may yield incorrect results".[5]

Iterators returned by an `AbstractList`'s `iterator()` method are instances of an inner class called `Itr`.[6] Upon creating a new `Itr`, the list populates its internal member field `expectedModCount` to the current value of its own `modCount` field. Whenever a method is called on this `Itr`, its internal value of `expectedModCount` is compared to the parent `AbstractList`'s `modCount`. If the two differ, which occurs when the list has been modified without passing through the iterator's methods, a `ConcurrentModificationException` is thrown, and property SAFEENUM is violated.

Therefore, to monitor the SAFEENUM property, it suffices, whenever a method is called on some `Itr` i, to check that i.`expectedModCount` is equal to $i\$0$.`modCount`. (When i is an instance of an inner class, the Java expression $i\$0$ designates the instance of the outer class object that created i.) Note how the object contains a very explicit encoding of the required monitor using dedicated member fields labelled as such.

It turned out that 10 of the 13 properties mentioned in Section 2 have a piggyback equivalent. We emphasize the fact that all these properties, in their piggyback form, are *stateless*: one is not required to persist any information between method calls. In each case, a simple condition on the current state of the object is sufficient, dismissing the need for an external monitor. One can see the potential for large gains in terms of performance and simplicity of the procedure resulting from this fact —this will be studied in Section 6.

5.2   Syntactical vs. Semantic Properties

There are only three properties for which a piggyback equivalent does not exist. Two of them are actually the same property reformulated for two different classes, which leaves only two *unique* properties for which the proposed approach cannot be applied.

Property HASHMAP requires the comparison of an object's `hashCode` at two moments in time: when it is added to the `HashSet`, and when it is removed from that set or when the set is otherwise queried for the presence of that object. Using the classical approach, a monitor instance must be created for every object added to every `HashSet`, and upon every call to `contains()` or `remove()`, the relevant monitor must check that the involved object returns the same `hashCode` value as when it was added to the set.

It turns out that this information is *not* directly being kept track of inside the `HashMap` itself. `HashMap`, contains an array of elements, called `table`, from an inner class `Entry`.[7] When an `Entry` $e = \langle K, V \rangle$ is added to the HashMap, it is stored in `table`'s row index computed from K.`hashCode()`.

---

[5] Quote taken from the OpenJDK's source code documentation for the `AbstractList` class.

[6] `AbstractList.java`, line 330.

[7] `HashMap.java`, line 149.

Querying the presence of an object or removing an object both amount to calling method `getEntry(K)`. This method computes the `table` row to look for based on K.`hashCode()`, and iterates over the linked list of entries until the one corresponding to K is found. If K's hash code has been changed since its addition to the map, the method will likely look in the wrong row and not find the item asked for. Discovering that an object's hash is inconsistent with the row it sits in would require scanning each row upon every call, which defeats the purpose of using a `HashMap` in the first place.

Property HASHSET is the same property rephrased on instances of `HashSet`. In Java, a `HashSet` is just a wrapper around an internal instance of `HashMap` called `map`, whose key-value pairs are made of the set's objects paired with a simple dummy `Object`; hence we are facing the same situation with class names merely changed. A similar situation occurs with UNSAFESYNCCOLL, which we leave out of the discussion due to lack of space.

These findings may seem to contradict Theorem 1, yet they do not. We remind the reader of the *two* alternatives of Corollary 1: either an independent monitor duplicates an equivalent one inside the object, or it enforces a property on executions that this object cannot discriminate. That second alternative applies to the case of HASHSET, HASHMAP and UNSAFESYNCCOLL. Indeed, nothing prevents a user from changing an object's hash code after putting it into a set; no *execution* error will ever be created by `HashSet` for that reason. Simply put, at no time modifications to hash codes have an impact on what *valid* (i.e. error-free) methods can be called on a `HashSet`. Similarly, nothing prevents a user from modifying a `Collection` after a synchronized wrapper has been created, i.e. these modifications do not have any impact on what methods can or cannot be called on the synchronized collection.

Of course, these modifications do have an impact on the validity of the results returned by the classes. In a worst-case scenario, a `HashSet` may reply that an object does not exist even though it does, but is located in the wrong row according to its current hash code. Therefore, HASHSET is a property we shall call *semantic*, as it relates to the meaning and integrity of the object's functionality. This is opposed to all the previous, *syntactical* properties, which deal with the prevention of sequences of method calls that cause an execution error.

The SAFEENUM property is also essentially a semantic constraint: adding or removing elements to a `Vector` may cause existing `Iterator`s not to enumerate all the elements as they should. However, in that case, concurrent modifications are actively tracked using internal integers `modCount` and `expectedModCount`; an exception is deliberately thrown by the object in case they do not match. This is an example of a semantic constraint that has been integrated into the object at the syntactical level, and explains why, contrarily to HASHSET, it can be piggyback-monitored.

6   Experiments

For the 10 properties where a piggyback version was found, we performed an experimental evaluation of the resulting monitor. The goal was to measure time and memory overhead to provide a basis of comparison of similar tests conducted in related work using "classical" runtime monitors. The selected measurements are: 1) runtime overhead; 2) memory usage; 3) number of events handled by the monitor. These evaluation points are identical to e.g. [19]. Memory usage and event count are by definition system-independent; the same applies for relative runtime overhead, since it compares running times of the same program, both with and without the monitor, on the same machine.

The monitors for each of the properties were executed against the DaCapo Benchmark [4] (release 9.12), which consists of a set of open source, *real world* applications with non-trivial memory loads. This is the benchmark used in all past papers in the field [5–7, 9, 15, 19]. Hence the computed measurements can be deemed as a fair basis for comparison to related works.

6.1   Experiment Setup

It turns out that a number of the member fields required for piggyback monitoring have `protected` or `package` access. To allow our monitor to query them, we added public accessor methods to the classes under study, so that the relevant part of their state can be queried externally.

This design was preferred over the simpler use of privileged aspects that would have bypassed visibility qualifiers so that the monitor could access any member fields of any object. This was made to emphasize the fact that piggyback monitoring does not require an object to jeopardize its functionality or its integrity by granting arbitrary access to its internal state. Rather, it shows that properties on an object can be piggyback-monitored by providing appropriate access to its state in a clean way. It may even be argued that an object *should* provide accessor methods to query its state when that state information determines which method calls are appropriate, by virtue of good design, and irrelevant of whether monitoring is considered. In that sense, adding accessor methods to the Java objects makes our experiment more representative of what is envisioned as a typical piggyback monitoring scenario.

Since all the member fields required in the properties are of primitive data types (boolean or integer), the values returned by the accessor methods are, by the semantics of the Java language, *copies* (not references) of the object's actual member fields. Hence, despite the fact that some classes are modified to reveal some of their internals, we emphasize the fact that the piggyback monitor, like any classical monitor, only needs strict, read-only access to the object and free of side effects.

We modified the source code of the OpenJDK 6 and recompiled the whole Java suite to integrate these changes to the Java environment. We shall stress that these modifications simply amount, for each class, to adding a single public accessor method to a single member field. No computation or functionality of any kind is added to the classes. Similar changes have been made to classes pertaining to the remaining properties. The monitor for each property is a simple AspectJ file that intercepts relevant method calls and evaluates the corresponding condition stated in Section 5.1.

Table 1. Experimental results: a) relative runtime overhead (in %); b) relative memory overhead (in %); c) additional number of Java objects created; d) number of events processed

Benchmark	HasNext (a)	(b)	(c)	(d)	HasNextElem (a)	(b)	(c)	(d)	SafeEnum (a)	(b)	(c)	(d)	UnsafeIter (a)	(b)	(c)	(d)
avrora	-3.5	-0	-7.5k	1.7M	0.6	-0	-7.5k	180	-1.4	-1	-7.7k	0	-1.2	1	-6.5k	1.7M
eclipse	-1.7	0	34k	119k	1.2	0	34k	1.5k	-3.7	-0	-355k	452	1.3	0	-96k	6.1k
fop	2.7	0	758	2.3M	-1.9	0	758	196	-0.2	0	740	580	0.8	1	2.1k	2.1M
h2	0.8	-0	-13k	13M	1.4	-0	-13k	180	-2.3	3	2.2M	0	-2.4	3	2.2M	1.0M
jython	3.1	-1	-298k	1.5M	-0.0	-1	-298k	3.6k	0.9	-1	-362k	0	-0.6	-1	-376k	86k
luindex	-6.2	0	603	1.2k	4.4	0	603	180	-1.9	1	2.2k	0	-8.7	3	2.4k	688
lusearch	-3.7	0	35k	2.1k	3.8	0	35k	180	-3.4	0	36k	0	-0.9	0	36k	299
pmd	0.5	0	2.3k	14M	-1.0	0	2.3k	180	0.2	0	3.1k	616	-0.6	1	11k	5.2M
sunflow	4.2	-0	-7.4k	6.4M	-0.3	-0	-7.4k	180	-3.5	-0	-7.5k	0	1.2	0	-6.7k	237
tomcat	-2.7	0	4.9k	688k	4.6	0	4.9k	186	-2.2	0	11k	0	-3.7	0	1.7k	686k
tradebeans	0.4	-1	-533k	263	-2.7	-1	-533k	180	1.9	-3	-1.2M	0	0.7	-1	-472k	250
tradesoap	0.2	1	854k	329	-0.6	1	854k	180	-0.2	1	997k	0	1.5	0	92k	281
xalan	0.7	0	1.0k	443	-18.4	0	1.0k	442k	20.6	0	2.4k	0	-4.4	0	745	423

6.2   Runtime Overhead

The impact of runtime overhead is shown in Table 1, column a, for each of the benchmarks.[8] We show results for a selection of four properties due to lack of space; however, experiments for the remaining properties produced similar results. The number of events processed remains in the same order of magnitude as for the values reported in related works (Table 1, column d).

Each benchmark was run five times for each property, both with and without the piggyback monitor, and the first two runs were discarded in each case as they were significantly slower.[9] Runtime overhead is the difference between the average running time of the remaining "piggyback" runs vs. the remaining "plain" runs.

One can see that overhead remains close to negligible for most properties and most benchmarks. Only two runs of the benchmark have an overhead over 10%, and only one over 20%. These figures should be contrasted with numbers reported in, e.g. [15]. For example, property UnsafeIter on benchmark "pmd" exhibits a 20-fold improvement over the best relative overhead recorded in that paper; the same property on benchmark "avrora" reported an overhead of 118%; using piggyback monitoring, it decreases to less than 1%. Similarly, benchmark "fop" shows a 10-fold decrease in relative overhead for property HasNext.

In general, runtime overhead can be deemed negligible, as in most instances it lies within the error margin due to the inherent variability in benchmark running times (at least ±3%).

6.3   Memory Usage

Since our monitor relies on objects' existing member fields, by definition the benchmark is expected to require very few additional memory to run when the

---

[8] Benchmark "batik" could not be run, as it is not compatible with the OpenJDK (it relies on classes that are only available in the Oracle implementation of the JDK).

[9] Discarding the first runs of the benchmark is a standard practice that was also done in related papers.

monitor is enabled. We computed memory usage by reading the total memory consumed by allocated objects, and number of objects created by each benchmark, using the Java `hprof` profiler [21], both with and without the piggyback monitor. The difference between the piggyback and plain benchmarks, for each property, is shown in columns b and c of Table 1.

The piggyback approach incurred, in the worst case, an increase of 1% on the number of Java objects created and an increase of 6% on memory consumed compared to the plain benchmark. All but one of the benchmarks added less than 42 megabytes to the overhead. As a rule, there is as much variability ($\pm 2\%$) between runs with the same parameters than between monitored and non-monitored programs: this explains why many of the benchmarks show a negative difference in memory allocated, indicating that the piggybacked program used less memory than the plain program. Again, these values should be contrasted with memory consumption reported in other works [15]: for example, property HASNEXT on benchmark "h2" required between 267 and 565 megabytes, depending on the monitor used.

7   Monitoring as a Design Rule

The piggyback approach assumes that all the state variables necessary to correctly enforce a property can be queried, and at a reasonable cost. The next step is to take these considerations at design time and to build classes amenable to piggyback monitoring by construction.

7.1   A Formal Definition

We shall say that a class providing proper means of querying its state, when such information matters to the methods that can be called, follows a principle that could be dubbed "design for monitoring". In the same way that automatic test pattern generation is much easier if appropriate *design for test* rules and suggestions have been implemented, runtime enforcement of interface properties is facilitated if the object is designed for monitoring. Formally:

Definition 1 (Design for monitoring). *Let O be an object with a set of methods $M = \{m_1, \ldots, m_n\}$ subject to a sequencing constraint C. The object O is* designed for the monitoring of C *if, for any method $m_i \in M$, there exists a set of methods $G_i \subseteq M$ for which there exists a* Boolean *condition on g's return value that decides whether m_i can be called at any moment.*

Such a design philosophy should stand to reason: if calling methods on an object alter that object's state, and if the set of valid methods one can call depends on the state, then the object should provide means of querying its state to allow its consumers to use it properly.

Should the opposite occur, consumers of the object must resort to external means of deducing the object's state (such as keeping track of it in parallel), which is counterproductive (cf. Theorem 1). The situation can be compared to an automobile maker that would ask drivers not to exceed a maximum speed while driving the car, yet does not provide a speedometer so that people can check for themselves. In this case, one would have to resort to external means of determining one's speed, just to comply with the car's requirements —and despite the fact that this "information" is known to the car, yet not made publicly available.

7.2 Design for Monitoring in the Java API

Some stateful objects provided by the Java language exactly follow this philosophy. One example is the `Mixer` interface. Some `Mixer` methods, such as `getSourceLineInfo()`, can only be called if the `Mixer` is open, i.e. after a call to `open()`, but before a call to its `close()` method. To correctly use the Mixer (and monitor this constraint), the classical approach would involve tracking calls to `open()` and `close()` and make sure that `getSourceLineInfo()` is only called at appropriate moments. Thankfully, the Mixer interface implements a method `isOpen()` that returns the state of the mixer; upon every call to `getSourceLineInfo()`, it therefore suffices to check whether `isOpen()` returns true. This allows us to "piggyback" on the Mixer's own state to enforce constraint C2 at runtime.

Yet, surprisingly, our study of piggyback runtime monitoring revealed that some Java classes do *not* follow this design principle. One notable example is `InputStream`. This class provides a number of methods to read and query information about the stream, such as the number of bytes remaining to be read. From its part, method `close()` closes this input stream and releases any system resources associated with the stream. From that point on, none of the other methods methods can be called on an InputStream, at the risk of provoking an `IOException`. However, `InputStream` does not provide any method to determine whether a given stream is open or closed. That design decision appears to us as curious, as this information exists inside the object, and moreover the consumer of the `InputStream` needs to know about it to avoid creating errors. Other classes, such as `Iterator`, present the same characteristics.

7.3 A Threat to Information Hiding?

A possible explanation for these observations was suggested by early readers of this paper, who feared that providing accessor methods to an object's state would completely defeat the purpose of *information hiding* and would thus be very questionable from a software maintenance perspective.

The concept of information hiding has first been defined by Parnas [22]: "one begins [to decompose a system] with a list of difficult design decisions or design decisions that are likely to change. Each module is then designed to hide such a decision from the others." Hence information hiding attempts to prevent external users of an object from relying on implementation decisions that may change.

However, the open or closed state of a File object has nothing to do with an implementation choice; it is part of the nature of a file to be in either such state. Information hiding must not be debased to imply that class developers have arbitrary freedom over whatever state information they wish to conceal. If a file cannot be read after it is closed, then a public method must allow people to know if a file is closed. More generally, an object expecting its consumers to use it in some ways that depend on its state should provide a way for consumers to query that state.

8   Conclusion

While it is generally accepted that member fields inside an object may duplicate the state machine used in a runtime monitor, the leveraging of *existing* internal object data to perform monitoring has never been considered as a line of research in its own right. Yet, piggyback runtime monitoring appears to be a fertile concept that sheds a different light on the task of runtime enforcement of constraints on method calls.

The successful experimental results we present on a body of well-studied properties of the Java API call for the development of piggyback runtime monitoring techniques and tools as a complementary approach to existing approaches. Some open problems that should be addressed are the development of a tool to search for an homomorphism to a state machine inside an object's source code, the study of the impact of arguments inside method calls, and the establishment of programming practices favoring design for monitoring. In conclusion, it is hoped that the paper opens the way to novel ways of investigation in runtime monitoring.

References

1. Java OpenJDK version 6, http://openjdk.java.net/projects/jdk6/
2. Avgustinov, P., Tibble, J., de Moor, O.: Making trace monitors feasible. In: Gabriel, R.P., Bacon, D.F., Lopes, C.V., Steele Jr., G.L. (eds.) OOPSLA, pp. 589–608. ACM Press, New York (2007)
3. Barringer, H., Rydeheard, D.E., Havelund, K.: Rule systems for run-time monitoring: from Eagle to RuleR. J. Log. Comput. 20(3), 675–706 (2010)
4. Blackburn, S.M., Garner, R., Hoffman, C., Khan, A.M., McKinley, K.S., Bentzur, R., Diwan, A., Feinberg, D., Frampton, D., Guyer, S.Z., Hirzel, M., Hosking, A., Jump, M., Lee, H., Moss, J.E.B., Phansalkar, A., Stefanović, D., VanDrunen, T., von Dincklage, D., Wiedermann, B.: The DaCapo benchmarks: Java benchmarking development and analysis. In: OOPSLA 2006: Proceedings of the 21st Annual ACM SIGPLAN Conference on Object-Oriented Programing, Systems, Languages, and Applications, pp. 169–190. ACM Press, New York (2006)
5. Bodden, E., Chen, F., Roşu, G.: Dependent advice: a general approach to optimizing history-based aspects. In: Sullivan, K.J., Moreira, A., Schwanninger, C., Gray, J. (eds.) AOSD, pp. 3–14. ACM (2009)
6. Bodden, E., Hendren, L.J., Lam, P., Lhoták, O., Naeem, N.A.: Collaborative runtime verification with Tracematches. J. Log. Comput. 20(3), 707–723 (2010)

7. Bodden, E., Hendren, L.J., Lhoták, O.: A Staged Static Program Analysis to Improve the Performance of Runtime Monitoring. In: Ernst, E. (ed.) ECOOP 2007. LNCS, vol. 4609, pp. 525–549. Springer, Heidelberg (2007)
8. Chein, M., Mugnier, M.-L.: Graph-based Knowledge Representation. Computational Foundations of Conceptual Graphs. Springer (2009)
9. Chen, F., Meredith, P.O., Jin, D., Roşu, G.: Efficient formalism-independent monitoring of parametric properties. In: ASE, pp. 383–394. IEEE Computer Society (2009)
10. Colombo, C., Pace, G.J., Schneider, G.: LARVA — safer monitoring of real-time java programs (tool paper). In: Seventh IEEE International Conference on Software Engineering and Formal Methods (SEFM), pp. 33–37. IEEE Computer Society (November 2009)
11. Erlingsson, Ú., Pistoia, M. (eds.): Proceedings of the 2008 Workshop on Programming Languages and Analysis for Security, PLAS 2008, Tucson, AZ, USA, June 8. ACM (2008)
12. Erlingsson, Ú., Schneider, F.B.: IRM enforcement of Java stack inspection. In: IEEE Symposium on Security and Privacy, pp. 246–255 (2000)
13. Goldsmith, S., O'Callahan, R., Aiken, A.: Relational queries over program traces. In: Johnson, Gabriel [16], pp. 385–402
14. Hallé, S., Villemaire, R.: Runtime enforcement of web service message contracts with data. IEEE Trans. on Services Computing 5(2), 192–206 (2011)
15. Jin, D., Meredith, P.O., Griffith, D., Roşu, G.: Garbage collection for monitoring parametric properties. In: Hall, M.W., Padua, D.A. (eds.) PLDI, pp. 415–424. ACM (2011)
16. Johnson, R.E., Gabriel, R.P. (eds.): Proceedings of the 20th Annual ACM SIGPLAN Conference on Object-Oriented Programming, Systems, Languages, and Applications, OOPSLA 2005, October 16-20. ACM, San Diego (2005)
17. Kiczales, G., Hilsdale, E., Hugunin, J., Kersten, M., Palm, J., Griswold, W.G.: Getting started with AspectJ. Commun. ACM 44(10), 59–65 (2001)
18. Martin, M.C., Livshits, V.B., Lam, M.S.: Finding application errors and security flaws using PQL: a program query language. In: Johnson, Gabriel [16], pp. 365–383
19. Meredith, P.O., Jin, D., Chen, F., Roşu, G.: Efficient monitoring of parametric context-free patterns. Autom. Softw. Eng. 17(2), 149–180 (2010)
20. Meredith, P.O., Jin, D., Griffith, D., Chen, F., Roşu, G.: An overview of the MOP runtime verification framework. International Journal on Software Techniques for Technology Transfer (to appear, 2011)
21. O'Hair, K.: HPROF: A heap/CPU profiling tool in J2SE 5.0 (2004), http://java.sun.com/developer/technicalArticles/Programming/HPROF.html
22. Parnas, D.L.: On the criteria to be used in decomposing systems into modules. Commun. ACM 15(12), 1053–1058 (1972)
23. Stolz, V., Bodden, E.: Temporal assertions using AspectJ. Electr. Notes Theor. Comput. Sci. 144(4), 109–124 (2006)

A Unified Approach for Static and Runtime Verification: Framework and Applications

Wolfgang Ahrendt[1], Gordon J. Pace[2], and Gerardo Schneider[1,⋆]

[1] Dept. of Computer Science and Engineering,
Chalmers, Univ. of Gothenburg, Sweden
[2] Dept. of Computer Science, University of Malta, Malta
{ahrendt,gersch}@chalmers.se, gordon.pace@um.edu.mt

Abstract. Static verification of software is becoming ever more effective and efficient. Still, static techniques either have high precision, in which case powerful judgements are hard to achieve automatically, or they use abstractions supporting increased automation, but possibly losing important aspects of the concrete system in the process. Runtime verification has complementary strengths and weaknesses. It combines full precision of the model (including the real deployment environment) with full automation, but cannot judge future and alternative runs. Another drawback of runtime verification can be the computational overhead of monitoring the running system which, although typically not very high, can still be prohibitive in certain settings. In this paper we propose a framework to combine static analysis techniques and runtime verification with the aim of getting the best of both techniques. In particular, we discuss an instantiation of our framework for the deductive theorem prover KeY, and the runtime verification tool LARVA. Apart from combining static and dynamic verification, this approach also combines the data centric analysis of KeY with the control centric analysis of LARVA. An advantage of the approach is that, through the use of a single specification which can be used by both analysis techniques, expensive parts of the analysis could be moved to the static phase, allowing the runtime monitor to make significant assumptions, dropping parts of expensive checks at runtime. We also discuss specific applications of our approach.

1 Introduction

There is a significant quest from the software industry for *lightweight formal methods* — methods which achieve a high degree of confidence in desired (sub-) system properties, while satisfying high demands on usability and automation. There are various reasons for this increasing need in software development, including the following recent parallel trends:

⋆ Corresponding author.

T. Margaria and B. Steffen (Eds.): ISoLA 2012, Part I, LNCS 7609, pp. 312–326, 2012.

- *Model driven development.* There is an ever more dominant role of models in the software development process.
- *Automated software engineering.* There is a trend to (partly) automate even more steps in the development cycle.
- *Exploding complexity of embedded software.* The demands on the safety of the increasingly complex embedded units is typically extremely high.
- *Concurrency and distribution.* Distributed architectures led to an increase in the possible causes of failure. On a more fine-grained level, concurrency is also becoming more important due to the rise of multi-core processors.
- *Software standards and certification.* In certain domains (e.g., avionics, automotive, medical), standards for architecture, interfaces, and processes are becoming very important.
- *Application focus of program verification.* Fundamental concepts of program verification have been around for decades, but only lately have arisen many techniques that are tailored to widely used languages and platforms.
- *Increased efficiency of program verification.* Verification technology has become a lot more efficient, and automation has increased significantly.

Even if *static verification* of software has become more relevant, effective and efficient, overcoming certain inherent limitations has proved to be hard. Certain static verification techniques have high precision, in which case powerful judgements are still too hard to achieve automatically, while others use abstractions to enable increased automation, in which case important, or even critical, aspects of the real, concrete system are easily missed, not to speak of the fundamental difficulty of crafting the right abstraction. In reaction to this, there is a recent trend towards more *lightweight* formal methods, which are easier to exploit but give limited guarantees. One such lightweight method is *runtime verification* which, compared to static verification, has complementary strengths and weaknesses. Runtime verification combines the full precision of the execution model (even including the real deployment environment) with full automation. On the other hand, it only ever judges observed runs, and cannot judge alternative and future runs. Another drawback is the computational overhead of monitoring the running system which, although typically not very high, can still be prohibitive in certain settings.

In this paper, we propose a unified static and runtime verification framework for object-oriented software. The aim is to provide a unified, lightweight to use but powerful in result, method for specifying and verifying, with a variety of confidence levels, properties of parallel object-oriented software systems.

The paper is organised as follows. We first give some background on static and dynamic verification techniques/tools. In Section 3 we present our framework, and in Section 4 we provide an example to illustrate how our framework could be applied in practice. We briefly describe some application domains of our framework in Section 5. We discuss related work in Section 6 and we conclude in the last section.

2   Background

2.1   Static Verification of Software

Principles

Static software verification reasons about properties of *all possible runs* of a program. There are basically two families of approaches, deductive verification and model checking. Deductive program verification has been around for nearly 40 years [41], however, a number of developments during the last decade brought dramatic changes to how deductive verification is being perceived and used.

– The era of verification of individual algorithms written in academic languages is over: contemporary verification tools support commercial programming languages such as Java [20,52,29,11] or C# [8] and they are ready to deal with industrial applications [39,47,51,38].
– Earlier, deductive verification tools used to be stand-alone applications that were usable effectively only after years of academic training. Nowadays, one can see a new tool generation that can be used after limited investment in training [1], and that is integrated into modern IDEs [8,11]. On the other hand, full automation is still rarely achieved when verifying functional properties of programs with loops, for instance.
– Perhaps the most striking trend is that deductive verification is emerging as a base technology. It is not only employed for correctness proofs, but in automatic test generation [19,34,30,10], and bug finding [50,36].

Among the state of the art efforts is the KeY tool [2], which it is close to complete coverage of the Java programming language [9]. In contrast to verifiers based on higher order logics, the prover of the KeY system provides a state-of-the-art user interface, high automation, and an easy mechanism for extending its rule base. We describe KeY in more details below.

Apart from deductive verification, model checking has been applied extensively and successfully for the static verification of both hardware and software systems. The adaptation of this technique to object-oriented software is progressing but still in an early stage.

KeY: A System for Static Verification of Java Programs

KeY is a deductive verification system for data centric *functional correctness* properties of Java source code. From Java code augmented with specifications given in JML (Java Modelling Language [43]), KeY generates proof obligations in a program logic, called *dynamic logic* (DL) for Java [11]. DL extends first-order logic with two additional operators, $\langle p \rangle \phi$ and $[p]\phi$, where p is a program and ϕ is another DL formula. A formula $\langle p \rangle \phi$ is true in a state s if there *exists* a terminating run of p, started in s, which results in a state where ϕ is true. As for the other operator, a formula $[p]\phi$ is true in a state s if *all* terminating runs of p, started in s, result in a state where ϕ is true. For deterministic programs p, the difference between $\langle p \rangle \phi$ and $[p]\phi$ is only termination. Hoare logic [37], can be seen as a special case, as the Hoare triple $\{\phi\}p\{\psi\}$ is equivalent to the DL formula $\phi \rightarrow [p]\psi$.

The core of KeY is a theorem prover for validity of Java DL formulas, using a sequent calculus. We cannot introduce the calculus here, but we mention a typical pattern of sequents. If Γ is a list of formulas, the sequent $\Gamma \vdash \langle p \rangle \phi$ means that p, if started in a state fulfilling all Γ, terminates in a state fulfilling ϕ. For instance, $\mathtt{x < y} \vdash \langle \mathtt{tmp:=x;x:=y;y:=tmp;} \rangle \mathtt{y < x}$ is a valid sequent. The calculus uses the *symbolic execution* paradigm. For that, DL is extended by 'explicit substitutions'. During symbolic execution of p, the effects of p are *gradually*, from the front, turned into explicit substitutions. Meaning that after some proof steps, a certain prefix of p has turned into a substitution σ, representing the effects so far, while a 'remaining' program p' is yet to be executed. While verifying p, an intermediate proof node may look like $\Gamma \vdash \sigma \langle p' \rangle \phi$, telling that, if Γ was true before p, and σ is the accumulated effect up to now, then ϕ will be true after executing the remaining program p'. Note that most proofs branch over case distinctions, largely triggered by Boolean decisions in the source code. The branching happens by applying rules like the following, simplified[1] if rule:

$$\text{if} \quad \frac{\Gamma, \sigma(b) \vdash \sigma \langle s_1 \ \omega \rangle \phi \qquad \Gamma, \sigma(\neg b) \vdash \sigma \langle s_2 \ \omega \rangle \phi}{\Gamma \vdash \sigma \langle \mathtt{if} \ b \ s_1 \ \mathtt{else} \ s_2 \ \omega \rangle \phi}$$

Unlike the explicit substitutions preceding the diamond modalities "$\langle \ldots \rangle$", the notation $\sigma(b)$ indicates that σ is *applied* to b, and thereby resolved. Similar for $\sigma(\neg b)$. Through rules like the above, the left side of any sequent, on any branch of the symbolic execution proof, lists conditions for the current execution path to be taken (in addition to the original precondition, in case there is any).

2.2   Runtime Verification of Software

Principles
Runtime verification is a technique for monitoring the execution of a software system, detecting violations as they appear at runtime. In recent years researchers have implemented monitoring tools which usually compile high-level (temporal) properties into monitor implementation (e.g., [21,40,27,28,5,26]). There are two main concerns when using runtime verification:

1. In order to minimise the possibility of erring it is desirable that monitors are automatically synthesised from formally specified properties.
2. Though a minimal runtime overhead is acceptable, it is of course desirable to reduce them as much as possible.

The above concerns are obviously interdependent: properties should be written in a formal language that is expressive enough as to represent meaningful properties, but not too much as to avoid efficient monitoring.

There are two main flavours of runtime verification — *synchronous monitoring*, in which, after each performed action, the system does not proceed further until the monitor confirms that the action did not violate the specification, and *asynchronous monitoring*, in which the system logs all relevant events, which are

---

[1] The simplified rule ignores side effects or exceptions possibly caused by b.

processed independently by the monitor, possibly on a separate address-space. While the latter is attractive in that it induces minimal overheads on the system, the *a posteriori* nature of the analysis makes it useless if one wants to discover and address problems in real-time. Although in-between solutions have been proposed (e.g., see [24]), they are far from being universally applicable, and thus, if one wants to have a guarantee that the system does not proceed beyond a violation, one has no choice but to pay the cost in terms of overheads induced by synchronous monitoring.

Different solutions based on optimisations have been presented to alleviate the overhead problem, e.g. [13,14]. Further approaches aim at obtaining small monitors by construction [45], or use some kind of overhead guarantee, as proposed in [23]. Despite the advance of the state-or-the-art with such approaches there is still need to improve runtime monitoring techniques as motivated by the development of specific techniques to improve monitor efficiency [18].

In the following, we give a brief overview over state-of-the-art runtime monitoring tools developed in recent years, without claiming completeness. ConSpec [3] inlines a runtime monitor into applications on mobile devices based on observed contract violations. JavaMOP [21] is a monitoring-oriented development environment where parts of the system's functionality are designed as monitor-triggered code. Java-MaC [40] enables automatic instrumentation to have access to system events. Higher-level activities are processed by the runtime checker to raise an alarm if any of the specified properties are violated. Eagle [33] is a runtime verification tool supporting future and past time logics, interval logics, extended regular expressions, state machines, real-time and data constraints and statistics. Lola [28] guarantees bounded memory to perform online monitoring, and differs from most other synchronous languages in that it is able to refer to future values in a stream. Tracematches [5] is an extension to AspectJ allowing the specification of trace patterns, also supporting parametrisation of events. This work has been extended in [15] to improve efficiency by making a temporal and spatial partitioning among collaborative users.

Larva: A Runtime Verification tool for Java

Larva (*Logical Automata for Runtime Verification and Analysis*) [26], is a tool tailored to verify untimed and real-time properties of Java programs. Properties can be expressed in a number of notations, including timed-automata enriched with stopwatches (DATEs —*Dynamic Automata with Timers and Events*), Lustre, and a subset of the duration calculus.

As an example of the kind of properties one can express in DATEs and verify with Larva let us consider a system where one needs to monitor the number of successive bad logins and the activity of a logged in user. By having access to *badlogin*, *goodlogin* and *interact* events, one can keep a successive bad-login counter and a clock to measure the time a user is inactive. Fig. 1 shows the property that allows for no more than two successive bad logins and 30 minutes of inactivity when logged in, expressed as a DATE. Upon the third bad login or 30 minutes of inactivity, the system reverts to a bad state. In the figure, transitions

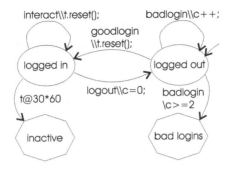

Fig. 1. The DATE of the bad logins scenario

are labelled with events, conditions and actions, separated by a backslash. It is assumed that the bad login counter is initialised to zero.

The tool has been successfully used on a number of case-studies, including an industrial system handling financial transactions. LARVA also performs analysis of real-time properties, and whenever possible to calculate an upper-bound on the memory and temporal overheads induced by monitoring.

3   A Proposed Framework for Integrated Static and Runtime Verification

In this section we present our framework. We start by discussing a unified language for specifying both static and runtime properties, we then describe our framework in general terms, and we finally discuss some interesting features that could be added to enhance our framework.

Though the conceptual model underlying our framework is general and tool-independent, we use LARVA and KeY as a basis to the proposed unified language, and as instances of some of the modules to be used in the framework.

3.1   A Unified Specification Language for Static and Dynamic Verificaion

In order to explore the proposed framework, we are investigating a concrete instantiation — combining the deductive verification tool KeY with the runtime verification tool LARVA. One of the first main challenges is that of identifying a unified specification language. While KeY uses pre- and postconditions for specifications, LARVA uses DATEs — essentially symbolic automata, with timers (allowed to be used also as stopwatches) and the means for dynamic replication of properties (for instance, a property which will be replicated for each user in the system).

As briefly described in the previous section, while KeY addresses the behaviour of a method as a relation, DATEs are less structured and are triggered with events happening in the system, which may refer to method entry and

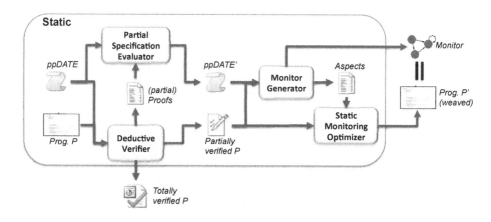

Fig. 2. High-level description of the framework

exit points (although with no native notion of identifying the entry and related exit of a single call), but also to exceptions raised by the system. To combine the approach, we propose *ppDATEs*, an extension of DATEs with the notion of pre- and postconditions, enabling transitions from a state to another whenever a method call satisfying the precondition terminates with the postcondition holding. Notationally, pre-/postconditions are additional elements of transition labels, put in the front/end of the other label elements: $s \xrightarrow{pre\backslash...\backslash post} s'$

ppDATEs enable the co-specification of data centric, control centric, and real time aspects of a system in a unified way. Concretely, ppDATE describes communicating automata with event-triggered transitions, timers, and functional unit specifications. Events are actions on objects (foremost method calls), timer events, primitives for synchronising with different automata, or a combination thereof. In addition, events are potentially augmented with conditions, actions, plus logic based, data centric specifications of the pre-post behaviour of the called method.

3.2   Description of the Framework

An abstract view of the proposed framework, taking as input an object-oriented program P and a specification of the desired properties, can be found in Fig. 2. We describe our framework in what follows based on the figure.

Deductive verification tools typically rely on user input to difficult proof steps, like finding loop invariants. However, the proposed framework is designed for fully automated use of the verifier, represented in the figure by the *Deductive Verifier* module. Therefore, not all proof attempts will lead to complete proofs. The workflow makes use of both, complete and partial, proofs, when specialising the ppDATE specification.

The purpose of the *Partial Specification Evaluator* is to spare the runtime verification (at the end of the workflow) from checking properties that were proved statically. For instance, postconditions that were completely proved (relatively to a certain method and precondition) do not need to be checked at runtime at all. The more interesting question is how to still make use of the information contained in *partial* proofs for the run-time verification phase. Here, the basic idea is to construct, from the open proof goals, specialisations of the precondition to the cases where the postcondition could, respectively could not, be proved. For instance, suppose the original ppDATE automaton features a transition $s \xrightarrow{pre\backslash m()\backslash post} s'$ (where *pre* and *post* are the pre- and postcondition of calling method m). Suppose further the deductive verifier produces a partial, i.e., unfinished proof for $pre \vdash \langle m() \rangle post$ (ignoring s for simplicity.) Then, it is possible, by analysis of the open proof goals, to construct two specialisations pre_1 and pre_2 of *pre*, with $pre_1 \wedge pre_2 \leftrightarrow pre$, such that pre_1 corresponds to the open and pre_2 to the closed proof branches, respectively, and $pre_2 \vdash \langle m() \rangle post$ is a consequence of the partial proof. This can be used by the partial specification evaluator to replace s' with two clones s_1' and s_2', and instead of the above transition have $s \xrightarrow{pre_1\backslash m()\backslash post} s_1'$ and $s \xrightarrow{pre_2\backslash m()\backslash true} s_2'$. Thereby, during runtime verification, only the transition to s_1' will trigger a checking of the postcondition *post*, but not the other transition, as *post* is ensured there statically.

The *Monitor Generator* takes as main input the specialised specification, ppDATE'. From such a specification, it uses aspect-oriented programming techniques to capture relevant system events, and implements runtime checks to ensure no violation takes place. The current approach to automata based monitor generation used in LARVA [25], cannot deal in a satisfactory manner with the data-centric parts of the specification that could not be (fully) ensured statically. This is particularly true for postconditions as in most cases they involve some kind of procedural checking (e.g., to check that an array is indeed sorted). Here we will pursue alternative approaches, like dedicated nested automata (for checking postconditions), and logic based runtime assertion checking of the kind done for JML specifications [22].

Before weaving the generated aspects into the code to be monitored, further static optimisations will be applied in the *Static Monitoring Optimizer* module, using, and expanding on, recent results in the area of combining static analysis (other than verification) with runtime verification. In particular, CLARA [18] is a good candidate to base our static monitor optimizer. Note that the optimisations can also affect the monitor itself giving the possibility to reduce its size and thus enhancing performance (this part is not shown in Fig. 2).

The final step in the workflow is the actual runtime verification, which executes the weaved program P' in parallel with the resulting monitor. Suitable forms of reporting and analysing the results of runtime verification, in certain cases including error recovery mechanisms, are natural extensions of the framework. They will be addressed in future work, without aiming at full generality, however. Rather, these issues are specific for the demands of a deployment scenario and application area, and will be tailored for specific deployments and case studies.

3.3   Additional Features

In addition to what is discussed above, a crosscutting concerns is the treatment of real-time properties. On the runtime side, LARVA already supports timers. On the static verification side, there is recent research on loop bound analysis using a combination of KeY and COSTA [4]. Yet, these two are very different aspects of real-time.

The framework has further potentials outside the main workflow as sketched above. One is the possibility of a feedback loop from the runtime verification to the (static) deductive verifier. For instance, there is work on discovering likely invariants by dynamic analysis [31] or testing [35], and the proposed framework could well be ideal for dynamic-to-static feedbacks of similar kind. Another issue is the broadening of our current deductive test case generation approach [30] to control related aspects, like call-graph related test coverage criteria.

4   An Illustrative Example

Let us reconsider the login-scenario, extending on Fig. 1, introduced in section 2.2 when describing the tool LARVA. We assume now that whenever a user logs in, she is added to a set of current users. A specification of this scenario will consist of a number of parallel ppDATEs specifying different properties. Such ppDATEs could be activated by mutual synchronisation or by events. For instance the high level property about the login will consist of a modified version of the DATE shown in Fig. 1, where the good-/bad-login events are augmented with the user's identity as a parameter. Additionally we will have, in parallel, another ppDATE which includes pre/post-conditions of data sensitive operations, like the method call users.add(u) which is activated whenever the event goodlogin(u) happens. An according transition will look like $s \xrightarrow{pre \backslash \mathtt{add()} \backslash post} s'$.

Before giving details about *pre* and *post*, let us discuss the Java implementation of the set of users. We assume the set is implemented with help of an array arr, using hashing for fast look-up. Hash conflicts are resolved by open addressing, meaning the method add first tries to put the object into arr at the position of the computed hash code. If that index is occupied, however, add searches for the nearest following index which is free. The set has a capacity limited by the length of arr. To enable easy checking whether or not the capacity is reached, a field size keeps track of the number of stored objects.

The ppDATE specifying the behaviour of the user set will therefore contain a transition $s \xrightarrow{\mathtt{size<arr.length} \backslash \mathtt{add()} \backslash \exists i.\, \mathtt{arr}[i]=\mathtt{o}} s'$, among others. To deal with the postcondition, the runtime verifier may use a technique known as 'runtime assertion checking', where logical formulas are operationalised [22]. For our example, $\exists i.\, \mathtt{arr}[i] = \mathtt{o}$ would be turned into a loop walking through the array.

Checking the postcondition needs to be done each time the transition fires. However, we can optimise away this runtime check for certain cases, using static verification with KeY. If one tries to statically prove, with KeY, that add's implementation is correct with respect to some JML specification, KeY first will generate proof obligations in form of DL sequents. One of them could look like the following:

$$\texttt{size} < \texttt{arr.length} \vdash \langle \texttt{add(o)} \rangle \, \exists i. \, \texttt{arr}[i] = \texttt{o}$$

When constructing a proof of this sequent, KeY will branch over case distinctions in the code of `add`, such as whether the initial hash index is free or occupied. The two sequents resulting from that branching look like:

$$\texttt{size} < \texttt{arr.length}, \; \texttt{arr[o.hashCode()\%arr.length]} = \texttt{null} \vdash \; \dots$$

and

$$\texttt{size} < \texttt{arr.length}, \; \neg \, \texttt{arr[o.hashCode()\%arr.length]} = \texttt{null} \vdash \; \dots$$

The first branch will be easier to automatically close by KeY than the second, which requires handling a loop searching for the next free index. Therefore, if KeY runs in auto-mode, excluding using interaction, it might only close the first branch.

As we have managed to prove one of the branches, there will be no need to monitor the case when the initial hash index is free, and only the branch when this is not the case will be monitored. Therefore, we can replace the transition given above by two transitions:

$$s \xrightarrow{\texttt{size<arr.length, arr[o.hashCode()\%arr.length]=null}\backslash\texttt{add()}\backslash true} s'_1$$

and

$$s \xrightarrow{\texttt{size<arr.length, } \neg\,\texttt{arr[o.hashCode()\%arr.length]=null}\backslash\texttt{add()}\backslash \exists i. \, \texttt{arr}[i]=\texttt{o}} s'_2$$

Thereby, during runtime verification, only the transition to s'_2 will trigger a checking of the postcondition, but not the other transition, as *true* is ensured trivially. Given a hashtable that is well dimensioned, the cheaper case will be more frequent at runtime.

5 Applications

5.1 Electronic and Legal Contracts

The term 'contract' has mostly been used in software systems as a metaphor and not according to the common meaning of the word. The first use of the term in connection with software programming and design was done by Meyer in the context of the language Eiffel (*programming-by-contracts*, or *design-by-contract*) [46]. Software contracts can appear as integrated part of a programming language, like in Eifel, or phrased in a special contract language, like JML [42] (supported by KeY) and Code Contracts [44]. Similarly, as a metaphor, the term has been used to describe interfaces of component-based systems or service-oriented architectures.

In the following, however, the word *contract* will be used as a general term to describe any kind of normative document, including contracts in the legal sense and other agreements where the different parties involved engage on certain obligations. Here, we are primarily interested in *electronic agreements*, which form an electronic version of legal contracts, and the role of static and dynamic verification plays in their analysis.

As a simple example consider agreements in the context of installing application on a mobile phone. In such cases the contract is shown in natural language (e.g., English) and the user must accept the terms and conditions stipulated there; otherwise the application is not installed. Ideally, each user would read and understand the agreement, and foresee the consequences in case of violation of certain clauses. Reality is different, though. So how else could one validate a contract between two parties before accepting it? This requires that the contract is fully formalised, which is not an easy task as witnessed by a number of current research papers on the topic (see for instance [48,49] and references therein).

One solution is to monitor the system using a contract as the specification, possibly giving a notification before allowing actions which may lead to a violation to go through. Our proposal is that a third party would statically verify the application software against the agreement, leaving as little as possible to be verified at runtime in the form of a monitor provided with the application. This ensures contract adherence, whilst keeping overheads low.

5.2   Transaction-Handling Systems

Systems which handle transactions (such as financial payments) are becoming increasingly prevalent. Although various design patterns are used to control the complexity of their development, they still pose various challenges to their verification:

- *Concurrency.* Typically, a transaction-handling system handles many transactions concurrently, and unless appropriate design principles are adhered to, this can lead to an overload in complexity. The main principle is to structure transactions to act in a manner which externally is perceived to be atomic — the operation takes place without the possibility of interference. While being a sound design principle, ensuring that the transactions are internally built to satisfy this is rarely easy.
- *Long-lived transactions.* Whenever transactions have to communicate with real-life systems, they may end up with a substantial increase of their lifespan. This means that the complete locking of all necessary resources for the duration of the transaction is not an option. This requires the use of more complex design patterns to engage and use resources in a rational way.
- *Handling failure.* Various transactions interact with external systems (e.g., a payment transaction may have to communicate with a bank) over which the system has no control. One of the side-effects of these interactions is that the external systems may fail. Handling such failure is not trivial, and although approaches such as compensations have been proposed and used, entwining the logic of normal and exceptional (failing) behaviour induces an overhead in complexity.
- *Varying system loads.* Although typically transactions are not individually computationally expensive, the concurrent nature of the handling of transactions introduces a varying load on the machine processing them. In many domains, this load frequently features regular surges in activity, during which performance becomes an important issue. For example, in an online betting system, the number of incoming bets per minute may peak in the last minutes before an important football match.

The first three issues indicate that such systems are ideally verified, even if runtime verification may introduce unacceptable overheads. We thus believe that transaction-handling systems can be an ideal domain on which to apply our proposed framework.

6   Related Work

The combination of different verification techniques in order to get the best from each, is not new. In particular there have been some successful stories combining different static analysis techniques. This is the case for instance of the SLAM project [7], where symbolic model checking, program analysis and theorem proving are combined on a novel fashion to verify drivers written in C. Another example is InVeSt [12] integrating algorithmic and deductive verification techniques, using abstraction, to verify invariance properties.

More recently, some research has been conducted aiming at a combination of static *analysis* (other than *verification*) and runtime verification in different ways. Arhto and Biere describes an architecture based on JNuke where Java programs can be statically and dynamically analysed [6]. In this framework, a static analyser tries to detect faults which are manually checked by a user who writes test cases for each fault found. The program is then run many times against those test cases confirming, or not confirming, the failure. In the latter case, a log is kept for future runs of the static analyser.

In [16] static analysis is used to improve the performance of runtime monitoring based on tracematches. The paper presents a static analysis to speed up trace matching by reducing the runtime instrumentation needed. The static analysis part is based on 3 stages in order to: rule out some tracematches, eliminate inconsistent instrumentation points, and finally further refine the analysis taking into account certain execution order.

In [17] Bodden et al present ahead-of-time techniques to statically prove the absence of *all* program errors, or mark specific parts of the programs where such errors are likely to occur at runtime. The approach is based on tracematches.

CLARA is a framework to statically optimise runtime monitoring [18], which uses static analysis techniques to operate on the monitors themselves with the aim of improving performance, as opposed to the combination of static analysis and verification with runtime verification techniques to verify software.

As opposed to [6], we are not concerned with testing faults found by a static analyser but to prove as much as we can with a static verifier, and only the non-provable parts are verified during the real execution of a program. Besides we do not extract test cases to test the system but perform runtime verification. Like [16] our proposed approach also aim at improving the efficiency of runtime verification but our techniques are completely different. While Bodden *et al.* use static *analysis* we use deductive *verification*. This distinction is crucial as the kind of properties we can prove is not the same.

A related structure to ppDATEs has already been explored in [32], a work supervised by one of the authors of this paper.

7   Conclusion

We have presented the conceptual model of a framework for the verification of object-oriented systems. The proposed framework is based on a suitable combination of static and dynamic verification techniques, in particular based on the underlying approaches of KeY and LARVA. We have proposed ppDATEs as a unified specification language for describing both static and dynamic properties, and we have shown an example to illustrate how our approach could be used. We have also described two application domains that we believe could benefit from our approach.

This is a position paper and as such much work is still to be done, starting with a formal definition of ppDATEs and ending with a full implementation of the framework, including proving interesting properties about the approach and applying it to real case studies.

References

1. Ahrendt, W.: Using KeY. In: Beckert et al. [11], pp. 409–451
2. Ahrendt, W., Baar, T., Beckert, B., Bubel, R., Giese, M., Hähnle, R., Menzel, W., Mostowski, W., Roth, A., Schlager, S., Schmitt, P.H.: The KeY tool. Software and System Modeling 4, 32–54 (2005)
3. Aktug, I., Naliuka, K.: Conspec: A formal language for policy specification. In: FLACOS 2007, Oslo, Norway, pp. 107–109 (October 2007)
4. Albert, E., Arenas, P., Genaim, S., Puebla, G., Zanardini, D.: COSTA: Design and Implementation of a Cost and Termination Analyzer for Java Bytecode. In: de Boer, F.S., Bonsangue, M.M., Graf, S., de Roever, W.-P. (eds.) FMCO 2007. LNCS, vol. 5382, pp. 113–132. Springer, Heidelberg (2008)
5. Allan, C., Avgustinov, P., Christensen, A.S., Hendren, L., Kuzins, S., Lhoták, O., de Moor, O., Sereni, D., Sittampalam, G., Tibble, J.: Adding trace matching with free variables to aspectj. SIGPLAN Not. 40, 345–364 (2005)
6. Artho, C., Biere, A.: Combined static and dynamic analysis. In: *AIOOL 2005*. Electr. Notes Theor. Comput. Sci., vol. 131, pp. 3–14 (2005)
7. Ball, T., Levin, V., Rajamani, S.K.: A decade of software model checking with slam. Commun. ACM 54(7), 68–76 (2011)
8. Barnett, M., Leino, K.R.M., Schulte, W.: The spec# programming system: An overview. In: Barthe, G., Burdy, L., Huisman, M., Lanet, J.-L., Muntean, T. (eds.) CASSIS 2004. LNCS, vol. 3362, pp. 49–69. Springer, Heidelberg (2005)
9. Beckert, B.: A Dynamic Logic for the Formal Verification of Java Card Programs. In: Attali, I., Jensen, T. (eds.) JavaCard 2000. LNCS, vol. 2041, pp. 6–24. Springer, Heidelberg (2001)
10. Beckert, B., Gladisch, C.: White-Box Testing by Combining Deduction-Based Specification Extraction and Black-Box Testing. In: Gurevich, Y., Meyer, B. (eds.) TAP 2007. LNCS, vol. 4454, pp. 207–216. Springer, Heidelberg (2007)
11. Beckert, B., Hähnle, R., Schmitt, P.H. (eds.): Verification of Object-Oriented Software. LNCS (LNAI), vol. 4334. Springer, Heidelberg (2007)
12. Bensalem, S., Lakhnech, Y., Owre, S.: InVeST: A tool for the verification of invariants. In: Vardi, M.Y. (ed.) CAV 1998. LNCS, vol. 1427, pp. 505–510. Springer, Heidelberg (1998)
13. Bhargavan, K., Gunter, C.A., Kim, M., Lee, I., Obradovic, D., Sokolsky, O., Viswanathan, M.: Verisim: Formal analysis of network simulations. IEEE Trans. Software Eng. 28(2), 129–145 (2002)

14. Bodden, E., Hendren, L.J., Lam, P., Lhoták, O., Naeem, N.A.: Collaborative Runtime Verification with Tracematches. In: Sokolsky, O., Taşıran, S. (eds.) RV 2007. LNCS, vol. 4839, pp. 22–37. Springer, Heidelberg (2007)
15. Bodden, E., Hendren, L.J., Lam, P., Lhoták, O., Naeem, N.A.: Collaborative runtime verification with tracematches. J. Log. Comput. 20(3), 707–723 (2010)
16. Bodden, E., Hendren, L., Lhoták, O.: A Staged Static Program Analysis to Improve the Performance of Runtime Monitoring. In: Bateni, M. (ed.) ECOOP 2007. LNCS, vol. 4609, pp. 525–549. Springer, Heidelberg (2007)
17. Bodden, E., Lam, P., Hendren, L.J.: Finding programming errors earlier by evaluating runtime monitors ahead-of-time. In: SIGSOFT FSE 2008, pp. 36–47. ACM (2008)
18. Bodden, E., Lam, P., Hendren, L.J.: Clara: A Framework for Partially Evaluating Finite-State Runtime Monitors Ahead of Time. In: Barringer, H., Falcone, Y., Finkbeiner, B., Havelund, K., Lee, I., Pace, G., Roşu, G., Sokolsky, O., Tillmann, N. (eds.) RV 2010. LNCS, vol. 6418, pp. 183–197. Springer, Heidelberg (2010)
19. Brucker, A.D., Wolff, B.: Interactive Testing with HOL-TestGen. In: Grieskamp, W., Weise, C. (eds.) FATES 2005. LNCS, vol. 3997, pp. 87–102. Springer, Heidelberg (2006)
20. Burdy, L., Requet, A., Lanet, J.-L.: Java Applet Correctness: A Developer-Oriented Approach. In: Araki, K., Gnesi, S., Mandrioli, D. (eds.) FME 2003. LNCS, vol. 2805, pp. 422–439. Springer, Heidelberg (2003)
21. Chen, F., Roşu, G.: Java-MOP: A Monitoring Oriented Programming Environment for Java. In: Halbwachs, N., Zuck, L.D. (eds.) TACAS 2005. LNCS, vol. 3440, pp. 546–550. Springer, Heidelberg (2005)
22. Cheon, Y., Leavens, G.T.: A runtime assertion checker for the Java Modeling Language (JML). In: SERP 2002, pp. 322–328. CSREA Press (2002)
23. Colombo, C.: Practical runtime monitoring with impact guarantees of Java programs with real-time constraints. Master's thesis, University of Malta (2008)
24. Colombo, C., Pace, G.J., Abela, P.: Safer asynchronous runtime monitoring using compensations. Formal Methods in System Design 40, 1–26 (2012)
25. Colombo, C., Pace, G.J., Schneider, G.: Dynamic Event-Based Runtime Monitoring of Real-Time and Contextual Properties. In: Cofer, D., Fantechi, A. (eds.) FMICS 2008. LNCS, vol. 5596, pp. 135–149. Springer, Heidelberg (2009)
26. Colombo, C., Pace, G.J., Schneider, G.: Larva - a tool for runtime monitoring of java programs. In: SEFM 2009, pp. 33–37. IEEE Computer Society (2009)
27. d'Amorim, M., Havelund, K.: Event-based runtime verification of Java programs. SIGSOFT Softw. Eng. Notes 30(4), 1–7 (2005)
28. D'Angelo, B., Sankaranarayanan, S., Sánchez, C., Robinson, W., Finkbeiner, B., Sipma, H.B., Mehrotra, S., Manna, Z.: Lola: Runtime monitoring of synchronous systems. In: TIME 2005, pp. 166–174. IEEE Computer Society Press (June 2005)
29. Deng, X., Lee, J., Robby: Bogor/Kiasan: a k-bounded symbolic execution for checking strong heap properties of open systems. In: ASE 2006, pp. 157–166. IEEE Computer Society (2006)
30. Engel, C., Hähnle, R.: Generating Unit Tests from Formal Proofs. In: Gurevich, Y., Meyer, B. (eds.) TAP 2007. LNCS, vol. 4454, pp. 169–188. Springer, Heidelberg (2007)
31. Ernst, M., Cockrell, J., Griswold, W., Notkin, D.: Dynamically discovering likely program invariants to support program evolution. IEEE Transactions on Software Engineering 27(2), 99–123 (2001)
32. Falzon, K.: Combining runtime verification and testing techniques. Master's thesis, University of Malta (2010)

33. Goldberg, A., Havelund, K.: Automated runtime verification with eagle. In: MSVVEIS (2005)

34. Grieskamp, W., Tillmann, N., Schulte, W.: XRT — exploring runtime for.NET architecture and applications. In: Proc. Workshop on Software Model Checking (SoftMC 2005), Edinburgh, UK. Electr. Notes Theor. Comput. Sci, vol. 144(3), pp. 3–26 (2006)

35. Gupta, A., Majumdar, R., Rybalchenko, A.: From Tests to Proofs. In: Kowalewski, S., Philippou, A. (eds.) TACAS 2009. LNCS, vol. 5505, pp. 262–276. Springer, Heidelberg (2009)

36. Hähnle, R., Baum, M., Bubel, R., Rothe, M.: A visual interactive debugger based on symbolic execution. In: ASE 2010, pp. 143–146. ACM, New York (2010)

37. Hoare, C.A.R.: An axiomatic basis for computer programming. Commun. ACM 12(10), 576–580, 583 (1969)

38. Hunt, J.J., Jenn, E., Leriche, S., Schmitt, P., Tonin, I., Wonnemann, C.: A case study of specification and verification using JML in an avionics application. In: JTRES 2006, pp. 107–116. ACM Press (2006)

39. Jacobs, B., Marché, C., Rauch, N.: Formal Verification of a Commercial Smart Card Applet with Multiple Tools. In: Rattray, C., Maharaj, S., Shankland, C. (eds.) AMAST 2004. LNCS, vol. 3116, pp. 241–257. Springer, Heidelberg (2004)

40. Kim, M., Viswanathan, M., Kannan, S., Lee, I., Sokolsky, O.: Java-mac: A run-time assurance approach for java programs. Formal Methods in System Design 24(2), 129–155 (2004)

41. King, J.C.: A program verifier. PhD thesis, Carnegie-Mellon University (1969)

42. Leavens, G.T., Baker, A.L., Ruby, C.: JML: a java modeling language. In: Formal Underpinnings of Java Workshop, at OOPSLA 1998 (1998)

43. Leavens, G.T., Poll, E., Clifton, C., Cheon, Y., Ruby, C., Cok, D., Müller, P., Kiniry, J., Chalin, P.: JML Reference Manual. Draft Revision 1. 200 (2007)

44. Logozzo, F.: Our Experience with the CodeContracts Static Checker. In: Joshi, R., Müller, P., Podelski, A. (eds.) VSTTE 2012. LNCS, vol. 7152, pp. 241–242. Springer, Heidelberg (2012)

45. Meredith, P.O., Jin, D., Chen, F., Rosu, G.: Efficient monitoring of parametric context-free patterns. Autom. Softw. Eng. 17(2), 149–180 (2010)

46. Meyer, B.: Design by Contract. Technical Report TR-EI-12/CO, Interactive Software Engineering Inc. (1986)

47. Mostowski, W.: Formalisation and Verification of JAVA CARD Security Properties in Dynamic Logic. In: Cerioli, M. (ed.) FASE 2005. LNCS, vol. 3442, pp. 357–371. Springer, Heidelberg (2005)

48. Pace, G.J., Schneider, G.: Challenges in the Specification of Full Contracts. In: Leuschel, M., Wehrheim, H. (eds.) IFM 2009. LNCS, vol. 5423, pp. 292–306. Springer, Heidelberg (2009)

49. Prisacariu, C., Schneider, G.: A dynamic deontic logic for complex contracts. J. Log. Algebr. Program 81(4), 458–490 (2012)

50. Rümmer, P.: Generating counterexamples for Java Dynamic logic. In: Prel. Proc. of Workshop on Disproving at CADE 2005, pp. 32–44 (2005)

51. Schmitt, P.H., Tonin, I.: Verifying the Mondex case study. In: SEFM 2007, pp. 47–56. IEEE Press (2007)

52. Stenzel, K.: Verification of Java Card Programs. PhD thesis, Fakultät für angewandte Informatik, University of Augsburg (2005)

Statistical Model Checking QoS Properties of Systems with SBIP⋆

Saddek Bensalem[1], Marius Bozga[1], Benoit Delahaye[2],
Cyrille Jegourel[3], Axel Legay[3], and Ayoub Nouri[1]

[1] UJF-Grenoble 1 / CNRS VERIMAG UMR 5104, Grenoble, F-38041, France
[2] Aalborg University, Denmark
[3] INRIA/IRISA, Rennes, France

Abstract. BIP is a component-based framework supporting rigorous design of embedded systems. This paper presents SBIP, an extension of BIP that relies on a new stochastic semantics that enables verification of large-size systems by using Statistical Model Checking. The approach is illustrated on several industrial case studies.

1 Introduction

Expressive modeling formalism with sound semantical basis and efficient analysis techniques are essential for successful model-based development of embedded systems. While expressivity is needed for mastering heterogeneity and complexity, sound and rigorous models are mandatory to establish and reason meaningfully about system correctness and performance at design time.

The BIP (Behaviour-Interaction-Priority)[3] formalism is an example of a highly expressive, component-based framework with rigorous semantical basis. BIP allows the construction of complex, hierarchically structured models from atomic components characterized by their behavior and their interfaces. Such components are transition systems enriched with variables. Transitions are used to move from a source to a destination location. Each time a transition is taken, component variables may be assigned new values, possibly computed by C functions. Atomic components are composed by layered application of interactions and priorities. Interactions express synchronization constraints between actions of the composed components while priorities are used both to select amongst possible interactions and to steer system evolution so as to meet performance requirements e.g. to express scheduling policies. BIP is supported by an extensible toolset which includes tools for checking correctness, for model transformations and for code generation. Correctness can be either formally proven using invariants and abstractions, or tested using simulation. For the latter case, simulation is driven by a specific middleware, the BIP engine, which allows to generate and

⋆ Research supported by the European Community's Seventh Framework Programme [FP7] under grant agreements no 248776 (PRO3D), no 288917 (DALI), no 287716 (DANSE), no 257414 (ASCENS), the ARTEMIS JU grant agreement 2009-1-100208 (ACROSS), and Regional CREATIVE project ESTASE.

T. Margaria and B. Steffen (Eds.): ISoLA 2012, Part I, LNCS 7609, pp. 327–341, 2012.
© Springer-Verlag Berlin Heidelberg 2012

explore execution traces corresponding to BIP models. Model transformations allow to realize static optimizations as well as special transformations towards distributed implementation of models. Finally, code generation targets both simulation and implementation models, for different platforms and operating systems support (e.g., distributed, multi-threaded, real-time, etc.). The tool has been applied to a wide range of academic case studies as well as to more serious industrial applications [5].

BIP is currently equiped with a series of runtime verification [8] and simulation engines. While those facilities allow us to reason on a given execution, they cannot be used to assess the overall correctness of the entire system. This paper presents SBIP, a stochastic extension of the BIP formalism and toolset. Adding stochastic aspects permits to model uncertainty in the design e.g., by including faults or execution platform assumptions. Moreover, it allows to combine the simulation engine of BIP with statistical inference algorithms in order to reason on properties in a quantitative manner. Stochastic BIP relies on two key features. The first is a stochastic extension of the syntax and the semantics of the BIP formalism. This extension allows us to specify stochastic aspects of individual components and to produce execution traces of the designed system in a random manner. The second feature is a Statistical Model Checking (SMC) [25,28,16,23,4,30,29,17] engine (SBIP) that, given a randomly sampled finite set of executions/simulations of the stochastic system, can decide with some confidence whether the system satisfies a given property. The decision is taken through either a Monte Carlo (that estimates the probability) [9], or an hypothesis testing algorithm [28,25] (that compares the probability to a threshold). Due to SMC restrictions, these properties must be evaluated on bounded executions. Here, we restrict ourselves to Bounded Linear Temporal Logic (BLTL). As it relies on sampling executions of a unique distribution, SMC can only be applied to pure stochastic systems i.e., systems without non-determinism. The problem is that most of component-based design approaches exhibit non-determinism due to interleaving semantics, usually adopted for parallel execution of components and their interactions. SBIP allows to specify systems with both non-deterministic and stochastic aspects. However, the semantics of such systems will be purely stochastic, as explained hereafter. Syntactically, we add stochastic behaviour to atomic components in BIP by randomizing individual transitions. Indeed, it suffices to randomize the assignments of variables, which can be practically done in the C functions used on transition. Hence, from the user point of view, dealing with SBIP is as easy as dealing with BIP.

Our approach is illustrated on several case studies that cannot be handled with existing model checkers for stochastic systems [20,15]. The presentation restricts to the analysis of a clock synchronization protocol [1] and an MPEG decoder. Other examples can be found in [2].

Structure of the paper. Section 2 presents the BIP framework. The stochastic extension for BIP and its associated semantics are introduced in Section 3. Section 4 describe the Probabilistic Bounded Linear Time Logic, the statistical model checking procedure as well as the implementation of our extension in BIP. Finally, Sections 5 and 6 present experiments and conclusion, respectively.

2 Background on BIP

The BIP framework, presented in [3], supports a methodology for building systems from *atomic components*. It uses *connectors*, to specify possible interactions between components, and *priorities*, to select amongst possible interactions.

Atomic components are finite-state automata that are extended with variables and ports. Variables are used to store local data. Ports are action names, and may be associated with variables. They are used for interaction with other components. States denote control locations at which the components await for interaction. A transition is a step, labeled by a port, from a control location to another. It has associated a guard and an action that are, respectively, a Boolean condition and a computation defined on local variables. In BIP, data and their related computation are written in C. Formally:

Definition 1 (Atomic Component in BIP). *An atomic component is a transition system extended with data* $B = (L, P, T, X, \{g_\tau\}_{\tau \in T}, \{f_\tau\}_{\tau \in T})$, *where:*

- (L, P, T) *is a transition system, with* $L = \{l_1, l_2, \ldots, l_k\}$ *a set of control locations,* P *a set of ports, and* $T \subseteq L \times P \times L$ *a set of transitions,*
- $X = \{x_1, \ldots, x_n\}$ *is a set of variables over domains* $\{\mathbf{x_1}, \mathbf{x_2}, \ldots, \mathbf{x_n}\}$ *and for each* $\tau \in T$ *respectively,* $g_\tau(X)$ *is a guard, a predicate on* X, *and* $X' = f_\tau(X)$ *is a deterministic update relation, a predicate defining* X' *(next) from* X *(current) state variables.*

For a given valuation of variables, a transition can be executed if the guard evaluates to true and some *interaction* involving the port is enabled. The execution is an atomic sequence of two microsteps: 1) execution of the interaction involving the port, which is a synchronization between several components, with possible exchange of data, followed by 2) execution of internal computation associated with the transition. Formally:

Definition 2 (Semantics of atomic component). *The semantics of* $B = (L, P, T, X, \{g_\tau\}_{\tau \in T}, \{f_\tau\}_{\tau \in T})$ *is a transition system* (Q, P, T_0) *such that*

- $Q = L \times \mathbf{X}$ *where* $\mathbf{X}$ *denotes the set of valuations* v_X *of variables in* X.
- T_0 *is the set including transitions of the form* $((l, v_X), p, (l', v'_X))$ *such that* $g_\tau(v_X) \wedge v'_X = f_\tau(v_X)$ *for some* $\tau = (l, p, l') \in T$. *As usual, if* $((l, v_X), p, (l', v'_X)) \in T_0$, *we write* $(l, v_X) \xrightarrow{p} (l', v'_X)$.

Composite components are defined by assembling sub-components (atomic or composite) using *connectors*. Connectors relate ports from different sub-components. They represent sets of interactions, that are, non-empty sets of ports that have to be jointly executed. For every such interaction, the connector provides the guard and the data transfer, that are, respectively, an enabling condition and an exchange of data across the ports involved in the interaction. Formally:

For a model built from a set of component $B_1, B_2, \ldots, B_n$, where $B_i = (L_i, P_i, T_i, X_i, \{g_\tau\}_{\tau \in T_i}, \{f_\tau\}_{\tau \in T_i})$ we assume that their respective sets of ports and variables are pairwise disjoint, i.e. for any two $i \neq j$ in $\{1 \ldots n\}$, we require that $P_i \cap P_j = \emptyset$ and $X_i \cap X_j = \emptyset$. Thus, we define the set $P = \bigcup_{i=1}^n P_i$ of all ports in the model as well as the set $X = \bigcup_{i=1}^n X_i$ of all variables.

Definition 3 (Interaction). *An interaction a is a triple (P_a, G_a, F_a) where $P_a \subseteq P$ is a set of ports, G_a is a guard, and F_a is a data transfer function. We restrict P_a so that it contains at most one port of each component, therefore we denote $P_a = \{p_i\}_{i \in I}$ with $p_i \in P_i$ and $I \subseteq \{1 \ldots n\}$. G_a and F_a are defined on the variables available on the interacting ports $\bigcup_{p \in a} X_p$.*

Given a set of interactions γ, the composition of the components following γ is the component $B = \gamma(B_1, \ldots, B_n) = (L, \gamma, \mathcal{T}, X, \{g_\tau\}_{\tau \in \mathcal{T}}, \{f_\tau\}_{\tau \in \mathcal{T}})$, where $(L, \gamma, \mathcal{T})$ is the transition system such that $L = L_1 \times \ldots \times L_n$ and $\mathcal{T} \subseteq L \times \gamma \times L$ contains transitions of the form $\tau = ((l_1, \ldots, l_n), a, (l'_1, \ldots, l'_n))$ obtained by synchronization of sets of transitions $\{\tau_i = (l_i, p_i, l'_i) \in T_i\}_{i \in I}$ such that $\{p_i\}_{i \in I} = a \in \gamma$ and $l'_j = l_j$ if $j \notin I$. The resulting set of variables is $X = \cup_{1 \leq i \leq n} X_i$, and for a transition τ resulting from the synchronization of a set of transitions $\{\tau_i\}_{i \in I}$, the associated guard (resp. update relation) is the conjunction of the individual guards (resp. update relations) involved in the transition.

Finally, *priorities* provide a means to coordinate the execution of interactions within a BIP system. They are used to specify scheduling or similar arbitration policies between simultaneously enabled interactions. More concretely, priorities are rules, each consisting of an ordered pair of interactions associated with a condition. When the condition holds and both interactions of the corresponding pair are enabled, only maximal one can be executed. Non-determinism appears when several interactions are enabled. In the following, when we introduce probabilistic variables, we will thus have to make sure that non-determinism is resolved in order to produce a purely stochastic semantics.

3   SBIP: A Stochastic Extension for BIP

The stochastic extension of BIP allows (1) to specify stochastic aspects of individual components and (2) to provide a purely stochastic semantics for the parallel composition of components through interactions and priorities.

Stochastic Variables. Syntactically, we add stochastic behaviour to atomic components in BIP by allowing the definition of probabilistic variables. Probabilistic variables x^P are attached to given distributions μ_{x^P} implemented as C functions. These variables can then be updated on transition using the attached distribution. The semantics on transitions is thus fully stochastic. We first define atomic components and interaction between them in SBIP, and then define the corresponding stochastic semantics.

(a) Component B in SBIP   **(b)** Semantics of B according to SBIP

Fig. 1. Example of an abstract component B and its semantics in SBIP

Definition 4 (Atomic Component in SBIP). *An atomic component in SBIP is a transition system extended with data* $B = (L, P, T, X, \{g_\tau\}_{\tau \in T}, \{f_\tau\}_{\tau \in T})$, *where* $L, P, T, \{g_\tau\}_{\tau \in T}$ *are defined as in Definition 1, and*

- $X = X_D \cup X_P$, *with* $X_D = \{x_1, \ldots, x_n\}$ *the set of deterministic variables and* $X_P = \{x_1^P, \ldots, x_m^P\}$ *the set of probabilistic variables.*
- *For each* $\tau \in T$, *the update function* $X' = f_\tau(X)$ *is a pair* $(X_D' = f_\tau^D(X), R_\tau)$ *where* $X_D' = f_\tau^D(X)$ *is an update relation for deterministic variables and* $R_\tau \subseteq X_P$ *is the set of probabilistic variables that will be updated using their attached distributions. Remark that the current value of the probabilistic variables can be used in the update of deterministic variables.*

In the following, given a valuation v_X of all the variables in X, we will denote by v_Y the projection of v_X on a subset of variables $Y \subseteq X$. When clear from the context, we will denote by v_y the valuation of variable $y \in X$ in v_X.

Some transitions in the associated semantics are thus probabilistic. As an example, consider an atomic component B with a transition τ that goes from a location l to a location l' using port p and updates a probabilistic variable x^P with the distribution μ_{x^P} over the domain $\mathbf{x^P}$. In the associated semantics, assuming the initial value of x^P is v_{x^P}, there will be several transitions from state (l, v_{x^P}) to states (l', v_{x^P}') for all $v_{x^P}' \in \mathbf{x^P}$. According to the definition of probabilistic variables, the probability of taking transition $(l, v_{x^P}) \xrightarrow{p} (l', v_{x^P}')$ will then be $\mu_{x^P}(v_{x^P}')$. This example is illustrated in Figure 1. When several probabilistic variables are updated, the resulting distribution on transitions will be the product of the distributions associated to each variables. Since these distributions are fixed from the declaration of the variables, they can be considered independent, ensuring the correctness of our construction. The syntactic definitions of interactions and composition are adapted from BIP in the same manner. For the sake of simplicity, we restrict data transfer functions on interactions to be deterministic.

Purely Stochastic Semantics. Adapting the semantics of an atomic component in BIP as presented in Definition 2 to atomic components with probabilistic variables leads to transition systems that combine both stochastic and non-deterministic aspects. Indeed, even if atomic transitions are either purely deterministic or purely stochastic, several interactions can be enabled in a given system state. In this case, the choice between these potential transitions is non-deterministic. In order to produce a purely stochastic semantics for components defined in SBIP, we thus propose to resolve any non-deterministic choice left after applying the priorities by applying uniform distributions. Remark that other distributions could be used to resolve this non-determinism and that using uniform distributions is the default choice we made. In the future, we will allow users to specify a different way of resolving non-determinism.

Consider a component $B = (L, P, T, X, \{g_\tau\}_{\tau \in T}, \{f_\tau\}_{\tau \in T})$ in SBIP. Given a state (l, v_X) in $L \times \mathbf{X}$, we denote by $\mathsf{Enabled}(l, v_X)$ the set of transitions in T that are enabled in state (l, v_X), i.e. transitions $\tau = (l, p, l') \in T$ such that $g_\tau(v_X)$ is satisfied. Since priorities only intervene at the level of interactions, the semantics of a single component does not take them into account. Remark that the set $\mathsf{Enabled}(l, v_X)$ may have a cardinal greater than 1. This is the only source of non-determinism in the component. In the semantics of B, instead of non-deterministically choosing between transitions in $\mathsf{Enabled}(l, v_X)$, we will choose probabilistically using a uniform distribution. Formally:

Definition 5 (Semantics of a single component in SBIP). *The semantics of $B = (L, P, T, X, \{g_\tau\}_{\tau \in T}, \{f_\tau\}_{\tau \in T})$ in SBIP is a probabilistic transition system (Q, P, T_0) such that $Q = L \times \mathbf{X}$ and T_0 is the set of probabilistic transitions of the form $((l, v_X), p, (l', v'_X))$ for some $\tau = (l, p, l') \in \mathsf{Enabled}(l, v_X)$ such that $v'_{X_D} = f_\tau^D(v_X)$, and for all $y \in X_P \setminus R_\tau$, $v'_y = v_y$.*

In a state (l, v_X), the probability of taking a transition $(l, v_X) \xrightarrow{P} (l', v'_X)$ is the following:

$$\frac{1}{|\mathsf{Enabled}(l, v_X)|} \left[\sum_{\substack{\{\tau \in \mathsf{Enabled}(l, v_X) \\ s.t. \ \tau = (l, p, l')\}}} \left(\prod_{y \in R_\tau} \mu_y(v'_y) \right) \right].$$

The probability of taking transition $(l, v_X) \xrightarrow{P} (l', v'_X)$ is computed as follows. For each transition $\tau = (l, p, l') \in \mathsf{Enabled}(l, v_X)$ such that $v'_{X_D} = f_\tau^D(v_X)$ and for each $y \in X_P \setminus R_\tau$, $v'_y = v_y$, the probability of reaching state (l', v'_X) is $\prod_{y \in R_\tau} \mu_y(v'_y)$. Since there may be several such transitions, we take the sum of their probabilities and normalize by multiplying with $\frac{1}{|\mathsf{Enabled}(l, v_X)|}$.

Stochastic Semantics for Composing Components. When considering a system with n components in SBIP $B_i = (L_i, P_i, T_i, X_i, \{g_\tau\}_{\tau \in T_i}, \{f_\tau\}_{\tau \in T_i})$ and a set of interactions γ, the construction of the product component $B = \gamma(B_1, \ldots, B_n)$ is defined as in BIP. The resulting semantics is given by Definition 5 above, where $\mathsf{Enabled}(l, v_X)$ now represents the set of *interactions* enabled in global state (l, v_X) that are maximal with respect to priorities. By construction, it follows that the semantics of any (composite) system in SBIP is purely stochastic.

Example 1. Consider SBIP components B_1 and B_2 given in Figures 2a and 2b. B_1 has a single probabilistic variable x_1^P, to which is attached distribution μ_1

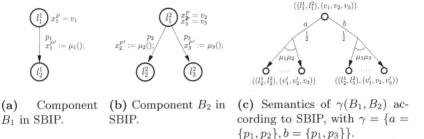

(a) Component B_1 in SBIP. **(b)** Component B_2 in SBIP. **(c)** Semantics of $\gamma(B_1, B_2)$ according to SBIP, with $\gamma = \{a = \{p_1, p_2\}, b = \{p_1, p_3\}\}$.

Fig. 2. Illustration of the purely stochastic semantics of composition in SBIP

and a single transition from location l_1^1 to location l_2^1 using port p_1, where x_1 is updated. In location l_1^1, the variable x_1^P is assumed to have value v_1. B_2 has two probabilistic variables x_2^P and x_3^P, to which are attached distributions μ_2 and μ_3 respectively. B_2 admits two transitions: a transition from location l_1^2 to location l_2^2 using port p_2, where x_2 is updated, and a transition from location l_1^2 to location l_3^2 using port p_3, where x_3 is updated. In location l_1^2, the variables x_2^P and x_3^P are assumed to have values v_2 and v_3 respectively. Let $\gamma = \{a = \{p_1, p_2\}, b = \{p_1, p_3\}\}$ be a set of interactions such that interactions a and b have the same priority. The semantics of the composition $\gamma(B_1, B_2)$ is given in Figure 2c. In state $((l_1^1, l_1^2), (v_1, v_2, v_3))$ of the composition, the non-determinism is resolved between interactions a and b, choosing one of them with probability $1/2$. After choosing the interaction, the corresponding transition is taken, updating the corresponding probabilistic variables with the associated distributions. Remark that this gives rise to a single purely stochastic transition. As an example, the probability of going to state $((l_2^1, l_2^2), (v_1', v_2', v_3))$ with interaction a is $1/2 \cdot \mu_1(v_1') \cdot \mu_2(v_2')$, while the probability of going to state $((l_2^1, l_3^2), (v_1', v_2, v_3'))$ with interaction b is $1/2 \cdot \mu_1(v_1') \cdot \mu_3(v_3')$.

An execution π of a BIP model is a sequence of states that can be generated from an initial state by following a sequence of (probabilistic) transitions. From the above, one easily sees that the semantics of any SBIP (composite) system has the structure of a discrete Markov chain. Consequently, one can define a probability measure μ on its set of executions in the usual way [22].

4   SMC Approach and Implementation

In this section, we present Probabilistic Bounded Linear Temporal Logic (PBLTL), a formalism for describing stochastic temporal properties. We then introduce a model checking procedure for this logic and discuss its implementation in SBIP. We first recap Bounded Linear Temporal Logic and then define its probabilistic extension. The Bounded LTL formulas that can be defined from a set of atomic propositions $\mathbb{B}$ are the following.

- **T**, **F**, p, $\neg p$, for all $p \in \mathbb{B}$;
- $\phi_1 \vee \phi_2$, $\phi_1 \wedge \phi_2$, where ϕ_1 and ϕ_2 are BLTL formulas;
- $\bigcirc\phi_1$, $\phi_1 \mathcal{U}^t \phi_2$, where ϕ_1 and ϕ_2 are BLTL formulas, and t is a positive integer.

As usual, $\Diamond^t \phi = \mathbf{T}\mathcal{U}^t\phi$ and $\Box^t\phi = \neg(\mathbf{T}\mathcal{U}^t(\neg\phi))$. A Probabilistic BLTL formula is a BLTL formula preceded by a probabilistic operator P.

The semantics of a BLTL formula is defined with respect to an execution $\pi = s_0 s_1 \ldots$ in the usual way [7]. Roughly speaking, an execution $\pi = s_0 s_1 \ldots$ satisfies $\bigcirc\phi_1$, which we denote $\pi \models \bigcirc\phi_1$, if state s_1 satisfies ϕ_1. The execution π satisfies $\phi_1 \mathcal{U}^t \phi_2$ iff there exists a state s_i with $i \leq t$ that satisfies ϕ_2 and all the states in the prefix from s_0 to s_{i-1} satisfy ϕ_1.

Definition 6. *A SBIP system B satisfies the PBLTL formula $\psi = P_{\geq\theta}\phi$ iff $\mu\{\pi \mid \pi \models \phi\} \geq \theta$, where π are executions of B and μ is its underlying probability measure.*

4.1   Statistical Model Checking

Runtime verification (RV) [10,8,24] refers to a series of techniques whose main objective is to instrument the specification of a system (code, ...) in order to disprove potentially complex properties at the execution level. The main problem of the runtime verification approach is that it does not permit to assess the overall correctness of the entire system.

Statistical model checking (SMC) [4,28,25] extends runtime verification capabilities by exploiting statistical algorithms in order to get some evidence that a given system satisfies some property.

We now present a model checking procedure to decide whether a given SBIP system B satisfies a property ψ. Consider an SBIP system B and a BLTL property ϕ. *Statistical model checking* refers to a series of simulation-based techniques that can be used to answer two questions: (1) **Qualitative:** is the probability for B to satisfy ϕ greater or equal to a certain threshold θ? and (2) **Quantitative:** what is the probability for B to satisfy ϕ? Both those questions can serve to decide a PBLTL property.

The main approaches [28,25] proposed to answer the qualitative question are based on *hypothesis testing*. Let p be the probability of $B \models \phi$, to determine whether $p \geq \theta$, we can test $H : p \geq \theta$ against $K : p < \theta$. A test-based solution does not guarantee a correct result but it is possible to bound the probability of making an error. The *strength* (α, β) of a test is determined by two parameters, α and β, such that the probability of accepting K (respectively, H) when H (respectively, K) holds is less or equal to α (respectively, β). Since it impossible to ensure a low probability for both types of errors simultaneously (see [28] for details), a solution is to use an *indifference region* $[p_1, p_0]$ (with θ in $[p_1, p_0]$) and to test $H_0 : p \geq p_0$ against $H_1 : p \leq p_1$. Several hypothesis testing algorithms exist in the literature. Younes[28] proposed a logarithmic based algorithm that given p_0, p_1, α and β implements the *Sequential Ratio Testing Procedure (SPRT)* (see [26] for details). When one has to test $\theta \geq 1$ or $\theta \geq 0$, it is however better to use *Single Sampling Plan* (*SSP*) (see [28,4,25] for details) that is another algorithm whose number of simulations is pre-computed in advance. In general, this number is higher than the one needed by *SPRT*, but is known to be optimal for the above mentioned values. More details about hypothesis testing algorithms and a comparison between *SSP* and *SPRT* can be found in [4].

In [11,21] Peyronnet et al. propose an estimation procedure (*PESTIMATION*) to compute the probability p for B to satisfy ϕ. Given a *precision* δ, Peyronnet's procedure computes a value for p' such that $|p' - p| \leq \delta$ with *confidence* $1 - \alpha$. The procedure is based on the *Chernoff-Hoeffding bound* [12].

The efficiency of the above algorithms is characterized by the number of simulations needed to obtain an answer. This number may change from system to system and can only be estimated (see [28] for an explanation). However, some generalities are known. For the qualitative case, it is known that, except for some situations, *SPRT* is always faster than *SSP*. *PESTIMATION* can also be used to solve the qualitative problem, but it is always slower than *SSP* [28]. If θ is unknown, then a good strategy is to estimate it using *PESTIMATION* with a low confidence and then validate the result with *SPRT* and a strong confidence.

4.2   The SBIP Tool

The SBIP tool implements the statistical algorithms described above, namely, *SSP*, *SPRT*, and *PESTIMATION* for SBIP systems. Figure 3 shows the tool structure and execution flow. SBIP takes as inputs a system written in SBIP, a PBLTL property to check, and a series of confidence parameters needed by the statistical test. Then, the tool creates an executable model and a monitor for the property under verification. From there, it will trigger the stochastic BIP engine to generate execution traces (Sampling) which are iteratively monitored. This procedure is repeated until a decision can be taken by the SMC core. As our approach relies on SMC, we are guaranteed that the procedure will eventually terminate.

Due to SMC restrictions, the properties must be evaluated on bounded executions. Here, we restrict to BLTL. We note that the monitoring procedure is an implementation of the work proposed in [10].

5   Case Studies

While still at prototype level, SBIP has been already applied to several case studies coming from serious industrial applications.

5.1   Accuracy of Clock Synchronization Protocol IEEE.1588

Model Description. The case study concerns a clock synchronization protocol running within a distributed heterogeneous communication system (HCS) [1]. This protocol allows to synchronize the clocks of various devices with the one of a designated server. It is important that this synchronization occurs properly,

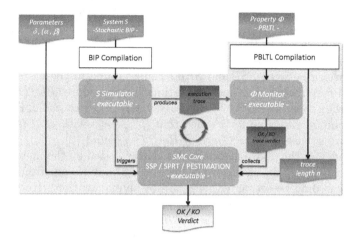

Fig. 3. SBIP tool architecture and work flow

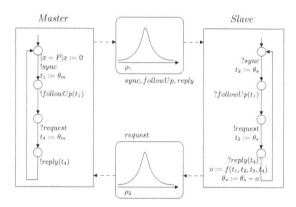

Fig. 4. PTP Stochastic Model

i.e., that the difference between the clock of the server and the one of any device is bounded by a small constant.

To verify such property, we build the stochastic model depicted in Figure 4. This model is composed by two deterministic components namely *Master*, *Slave* and two communication channels. In the PTP model, the time of the master process is represented by the clock variable θ_m. This is considered the reference time and is used to synchronize the time of the slave clock, represented by the clock variable θ_s. The synchronization works by messages exchange between the server and a device where each saves the message reception time $(t_i)_{i=1,4}$ w.r.t. its local clock. In termination, the slave computes the offset between its time and the master time and updates its clock accordingly. Communication channels have been modeled using stochastic components. These components model communication delays over network w.r.t empirical distributions obtained by simulating a detailed HCS model.

The accuracy of the synchronization is defined by the absolute value of the difference between the master and slave clocks $|\theta_m - \theta_s|$, during the lifetime of the system we consider (in this case, 1000 steps). Our aim is to verify the satisfaction of the formula $\phi = \Box^{1000}(|\theta_m - \theta_s| \leq \Delta)$ for arbitrary fixed non-negative Δ.

Experiments and Results. Two types of experiments are conducted. The first one is concerned with the bounded accuracy property ϕ. In the second one, we study average failure per execution for a given bound.

Property 1: Synchronization. To estimate the best accuracy bound, we have computed, for each device, the probability for synchronization to occur properly for values of Δ between $10\mu s$ and $120\mu s$. Figure 5a gives the results of the probability of satisfying the bounded accuracy property ϕ as a function of the bound Δ. The figure shows that the smallest bound which ensures synchronization for any device is $105\mu s$ (for Device $(3,0)$). However, devices $(0,3)$ and $(3,3)$ already satisfy the property ϕ with probability 1 for $\Delta = 60\mu s$. For this experiments, we have used SPRT and SSP jointly with PESTIMATION for a higher degree of confidence. The results, which are presented in Table 1 for Device $(0,0)$, show that SPRT is faster than SSP and PESTIMATION.

Table 1. Number of simulations / Amount of time required for PESTIMATION, SSP and SPRT

Precision	10^{-1}		10^{-2}		10^{-3}	
Confidence	10^{-5}	10^{-10}	10^{-5}	10^{-10}	10^{-5}	10^{-10}
PESTIMATION	4883	9488	488243	948760	48824291	94875993
	$17s$	$34s$	$29m$	$56m$	$> 3h$	$> 3h$
SSP	1604	3579	161986	368633	16949867	32792577
	$10s$	$22s$	$13m$	$36m$	$> 3h$	$> 3h$
SPRT	316	1176	12211	22870	148264	311368
	$2s$	$7s$	$53s$	$1m38s$	$11m$	$31m$

Property 2: Average failure. In the second experiment, we try to quantify the average and worst number of failures in synchronization that occur *per simulation* when working with smaller bounds. Our goal is to study the possibility of using such bounds. For a given simulation, the *proportion of failures* is obtained by dividing the number of failures by the number of rounds of PTP. We will now estimate, for a simulation of 1000 steps (66 rounds of the PTP), the average value for this proportion. To this purpose, we have measured for each device this proportion on 1199 simulations with a different synchronization bounds Δ between $10\mu s$ and $120\mu s$. Figures 5b gives the average proportion of failure as a function of the bound.

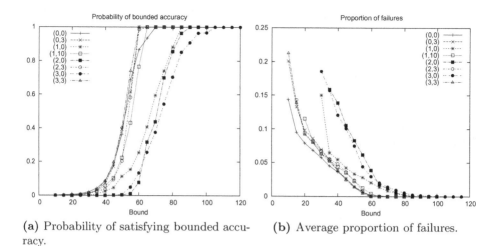

(a) Probability of satisfying bounded accu-   (b) Average proportion of failures.
racy.

Fig. 5. Probability of satisfying the bounded accuracy property and average proportion of failures as functions of the bound Δ

5.2 Playout Buffer Underflow in MPEG2 Player

In multimedia literature [27], it has been shown that some quality degradation is tolerable when playing MPEG2-coded video. In fact, a loss under two consecutive frames within a second can be accepted. In this example, we want to check that an MPEG2 player implementation guarantees this QoS property.

Model Description. We illustrate the multimedia player set-up that has been modeled using the stochastic BIP framework. The designed model captures the stochastic system aspects that are, the macro-blocks arrival time to the input buffer and the their processing time.

The stochastic system model is shown in Figure 6. It consists of three functional components namely *Generator*, *Processor*, and *Player*. In addition to these, the buffers between the above functional components are modeled by explicit *buffer* components, namely *Input buffer* and *Playout buffer*. The transfer of the macro-blocks between the functional blocks and the buffers are described using interactions.

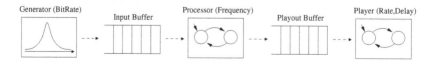

Fig. 6. MPEG2 stochastic Model

The *Generator* is a stochastic component which models macro-blocks production based on a probabilistic distribution. It generates an MPEG2-coded stream with respect to a fixed Group-of-Pictures (GOP) pattern [18,19] and simulates the arrival time of macro-blocks to the *input buffer*. The *Processor* reads them sequentially, decodes them and write them to the *Playout buffer*. The *Player* starts to read macro-blocks from the *Playout buffer* after a defined initial delay namely *Playout Delay*. Once this delay ends, the consumption is performed periodically with respect to a fixed consumption rate. Each period, the *Player* sends a request of N macro-blocks to the *Playout buffer*, where $N = 1$ the first time. Then it gets a response of M macro-blocks, where $0 \leq M \leq N$. We say that we have an underflow if $M < N$. In this case, the next request N will be $(N - M) + 1$. That is, the player will try to read all the missed macro-blocks.

Experiments and Results. To check the described model with respect to the desired QoS property, we used the SBIP tool. The BLTL specification of the QoS property to check is $\phi = \Box^{1500000}(\neg fail)$, where *fail* denotes a failure state condition corresponding to the underflow of two consecutive frames within a second.

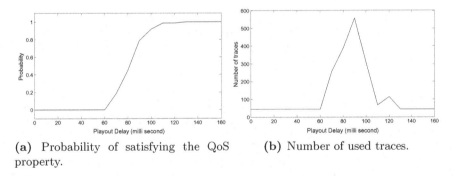

(a) Probability of satisfying the QoS property.

(b) Number of used traces.

Fig. 7. Illustration of results

The obtained results are shown in Figure 7a where we can see that until $60ms$, the probability of satisfying ϕ is 0, that is, for small *Playout delays*, the number of underflow exceeds 2 frames. For delays between 70 and 100, the probability of satisfying the QoS property increases to attain 1 for high *Playout delays* ($\geq 110ms$). Figure 7b shows the amount of needed traces for each *Playout delay* where the average simulation time is about 8 seconds.

6   Conclusion and Future Work

Stochastic systems can also be analyzed with a pure stochastic model checking approach. While there is no clear winner, SMC is often more efficient in terms of memory and time consumption [13]. The above experiments are out of scope of stochastic model checking. Also, there are properties such as clock drift in Clock

Synchronization Protocols (see [1]) that could not have been analyzed with a pure formal approach. The PRISM toolset [20] also incorporates a stochastic model checking engine. However, it can only be applied to those systems whose individual components are purely stochastic. Moreover, probability distributions are described in a very simple and restrictive language, while we can use the full fledged C to describe complex distributions. Nevertheless, we have observed that PRISM can be faster than our tool on various case studies such as those where the same process is repeated a certain number of times. Solutions to considerably enhance the efficiency of SMC in particular cases have recently been developed [14], but have not yet been implemented in SBIP. In a recent work [6], it has been proposed to use partial order to solve non-determinism when applying SMC (which rarely works). In SBIP, the order is directly given in the design through priorities specified by the user.

We shall continue the development by implementing new heuristics to speed up simulation and to reduce their number. We shall also implement an extension of the stochastic abstraction principle from [1] that allows to compute automatically a small stochastic abstraction from a huge concrete system.

References

1. Basu, A., Bensalem, S., Bozga, M., Caillaud, B., Delahaye, B., Legay, A.: Statistical Abstraction and Model-Checking of Large Heterogeneous Systems. In: Hatcliff, J., Zucca, E. (eds.) FMOODS 2010, Part II. LNCS, vol. 6117, pp. 32–46. Springer, Heidelberg (2010)
2. Basu, A., Bensalem, S., Bozga, M., Delahaye, B., Legay, A., Sifakis, E.: Verification of an AFDX Infrastructure Using Simulations and Probabilities. In: Barringer, H., Falcone, Y., Finkbeiner, B., Havelund, K., Lee, I., Pace, G., Roşu, G., Sokolsky, O., Tillmann, N. (eds.) RV 2010. LNCS, vol. 6418, pp. 330–344. Springer, Heidelberg (2010)
3. Basu, A., Bozga, M., Sifakis, J.: Modeling Heterogeneous Real-time Systems in BIP. In: SEFM 2006, pp. 3–12 (September 2006)
4. Bensalem, S., Delahaye, B., Legay, A.: Statistical model checking: Present and future. In: RV. Springer (2010)
5. Bensalem, S., de Silva, L., Griesmayer, A., Ingrand, F., Legay, A., Yan, R.: A Formal Approach for Incremental Construction with an Application to Autonomous Robotic Systems. In: Apel, S., Jackson, E. (eds.) SC 2011. LNCS, vol. 6708, pp. 116–132. Springer, Heidelberg (2011)
6. Bogdoll, J., Ferrer Fioriti, L.M., Hartmanns, A., Hermanns, H.: Partial Order Methods for Statistical Model Checking and Simulation. In: Bruni, R., Dingel, J. (eds.) FORTE 2011 and FMOODS 2011. LNCS, vol. 6722, pp. 59–74. Springer, Heidelberg (2011)
7. Clarke, E.M., Grumberg, O., Peled, D.A.: Model Checking. MIT Press (1999)
8. Falcone, Y., Jaber, M., Nguyen, T.-H., Bozga, M., Bensalem, S.: Runtime Verification of Component-Based Systems. In: Barthe, G., Pardo, A., Schneider, G. (eds.) SEFM 2011. LNCS, vol. 7041, pp. 204–220. Springer, Heidelberg (2011)
9. Grosu, R., Smolka, S.A.: Monte Carlo Model Checking. In: Halbwachs, N., Zuck, L.D. (eds.) TACAS 2005. LNCS, vol. 3440, pp. 271–286. Springer, Heidelberg (2005)
10. Havelund, K., Roşu, G.: Synthesizing Monitors for Safety Properties. In: Katoen, J.-P., Stevens, P. (eds.) TACAS 2002. LNCS, vol. 2280, pp. 342–356. Springer, Heidelberg (2002)

11. Hérault, T., Lassaigne, R., Magniette, F., Peyronnet, S.: Approximate Probabilistic Model Checking. In: Steffen, B., Levi, G. (eds.) VMCAI 2004. LNCS, vol. 2937, pp. 73–84. Springer, Heidelberg (2004)
12. Hoeffding, W.: Probability inequalities. Journal of the American Statistical Association 58, 13–30 (1963)
13. Jansen, D.N., Katoen, J.-P., Oldenkamp, M., Stoelinga, M., Zapreev, I.: How Fast and Fat Is Your Probabilistic Model Checker? An Experimental Performance Comparison. In: Yorav, K. (ed.) HVC 2007. LNCS, vol. 4899, pp. 69–85. Springer, Heidelberg (2008)
14. Jegourel, C., Legay, A., Sedwards, S.: Cross-Entropy Optimisation of Importance Sampling Parameters for Statistical Model Checking. In: Madhusudan, P., Seshia, S.A. (eds.) CAV 2012. LNCS, vol. 7358, pp. 327–342. Springer, Heidelberg (2012)
15. Jegourel, C., Legay, A., Sedwards, S.: A Platform for High Performance Statistical Model Checking – PLASMA. In: Flanagan, C., König, B. (eds.) TACAS 2012. LNCS, vol. 7214, pp. 498–503. Springer, Heidelberg (2012)
16. Katoen, J.-P., Zapreev, I.S.: Simulation-based ctmc model checking: An empirical evaluation. In: QEST, pp. 31–40. IEEE Computer Society (2009)
17. Katoen, J.-P., Zapreev, I.S., Hahn, E.M., Hermanns, H., Jansen, D.N.: The ins and outs of the probabilistic model checker mrmc. In: QEST, pp. 167–176. IEEE Computer Society (2009)
18. Krunz, M., Sass, R., Hughes, H.: Statistical characteristics and multiplexing of MPEG streams. In: INFOCOM, pp. 455–462 (April 1995)
19. Krunz, M., Tripathi, S.K.: On the characterization of VBR MPEG streams. In: SIGMETRICS, pp. 192–202 (June 1997)
20. Kwiatkowska, M.Z., Norman, G., Parker, D.: Prism 2.0: A tool for probabilistic model checking. In: QEST, pp. 322–323. IEEE (2004)
21. Laplante, S., Lassaigne, R., Magniez, F., Peyronnet, S., de Rougemont, M.: Probabilistic abstraction for model checking: An approach based on property testing. ACM TCS 8(4) (2007)
22. Parzen, E.: Stochastic Processes. Holden Day (1962)
23. El Rabih, D., Pekergin, N.: Statistical Model Checking Using Perfect Simulation. In: Liu, Z., Ravn, A.P. (eds.) ATVA 2009. LNCS, vol. 5799, pp. 120–134. Springer, Heidelberg (2009)
24. Roşu, G., Bensalem, S.: Allen Linear (Interval) Temporal Logic – Translation to LTL and Monitor Synthesis. In: Ball, T., Jones, R.B. (eds.) CAV 2006. LNCS, vol. 4144, pp. 263–277. Springer, Heidelberg (2006)
25. Sen, K., Viswanathan, M., Agha, G.: Statistical Model Checking of Black-Box Probabilistic Systems. In: Alur, R., Peled, D.A. (eds.) CAV 2004. LNCS, vol. 3114, pp. 202–215. Springer, Heidelberg (2004)
26. Wald, A.: Sequential tests of statistical hypotheses. Annals of Mathematical Statistics 16(2), 117–186 (1945)
27. Wijesekera, D., Srivastava, J.: Quality of Service (QoS) Metrics for Continuous Media. Multimedia Tools and Applications 3(2), 127–166 (1996)
28. Younes, H.L.S.: Verification and Planning for Stochastic Processes with Asynchronous Events. PhD thesis, Carnegie Mellon (2005)
29. Zuliani, P., Baier, C., Clarke, E.M.: Rare-event verification for stochastic hybrid systems. In: HSCC, pp. 217–226. ACM (2012)
30. Zuliani, P., Platzer, A., Clarke, E.M.: Bayesian statistical model checking with application to simulink/stateflow verification. In: HSCC, pp. 243–252. ACM (2010)

Monitoring Temporal Information Flow

Rayna Dimitrova, Bernd Finkbeiner, and Markus N. Rabe

Universität des Saarlandes, Germany

Abstract. We present a framework for monitoring information flow in security-critical reactive systems, such as communication protocols, cell phone apps, document servers and web browsers. The secrecy requirements in such systems typically vary over time in response to the interaction with the environment. Standard notions of secrecy, like noninterference, must therefore be extended by specifying precisely *when* and *under what conditions* a particular event needs to remain secret. Our framework is based on the temporal logic SecLTL, which combines the standard temporal operators of linear-time temporal logic with the modal *Hide* operator for the specification of information flow properties. We present a first monitoring algorithm for SecLTL specifications, based on a translation of SecLTL formulas to alternating automata, and identify open research questions and directions for future work.

1 Introduction

Runtime monitoring and enforcement of security properties has been an active area of research in the last four decades [1], and its importance continues to grow as *security-critical systems* such as communication protocols, cell phone apps, document servers and web browsers become more and more ubiquitous. The canonical property of interest in such systems is *noninterference* [2], which requires that the public output of the system does not depend on secret input. In this paper we address the problem of monitoring information flow in *reactive systems*. We argue that in the realm of reactive systems, considering classical noninterference is of limited interest: the secrecy requirements of a reactive system typically vary over time in response to the interaction with the environment.

Consider, for example, the flow of information in a system for managing clinical data. Ethical guidelines, such as those by the Caldicott Committee [3], state that patient information is confidential and should not be disclosed without the patient's consent unless justified for a lawful purpose. For example, a release of information without the patient's consent may be allowed (and even required) in certain cases of food poisoning and other notifiable diseases. On the other hand, many secondary uses of the information, for example for research purposes, are only allowed while the patient has given and not (yet) revoked explicit consent.

Due to the nature of information flow, monitoring mechanisms for noninterference and related properties must not only consider the monitored trace, but also additional traces that were *not* observed. For example, if the result of a medical test is to be kept secret, and the test result turns out to be positive in the monitored trace, then we must not only track the computation path corresponding to

T. Margaria and B. Steffen (Eds.): ISoLA 2012, Part I, LNCS 7609, pp. 342–357, 2012.
© Springer-Verlag Berlin Heidelberg 2012

the positive result, but also the computation path corresponding to the negative result in order to check that both traces are observably equivalent. To reduce the runtime overhead resulting from having to analyze parts of the actual system, hybrid approaches that combine dynamic and static analysis techniques have been developed [4,5]. There exist, however, no means of imposing restrictions on which parts the system should be considered while still performing a semantically justified security analysis. This can be achieved by specifying precisely *when* and *under what conditions* noninterference has to hold.

In runtime verification, the usual specification language to describe such temporal contexts is temporal logic. In this paper, we therefore propose an approach for runtime monitoring of information flow in reactive systems that integrates the dynamic analysis of information flow into the monitoring of temporal properties. Our approach is based on the temporal logic SecLTL, which we recently introduced as a specification language for model checking [6]. SecLTL extends linear-time temporal logic (LTL) with the *Hide* operator $\mathcal{H}$ for the specification of information flow properties. The SecLTL formula $\mathcal{H}_{H,I,O}\,\varphi$ specifies that a certain secret, expressed as the current valuation of the variables in H, will not become observable before the endcondition φ evaluates to true. The observer from whom we wish to hide the secret is characterized by the subsets I and O of the input and output variables that are visible to the observer. Applications of the Hide operator can be embedded into a temporal context, for example in the formula $\Box\,(\neg c \rightarrow \mathcal{H}_{\{t\},I,O}\,false)$, which specifies that *whenever* the patent does not give consent c to release the information, then the test result t must be kept confidential *forever* with respect to the variables in I and O, representing the interface to potential secondary users of the information.

The challenge in using SecLTL as a specification language for runtime monitors is to integrate the monitoring of noninterference into the runtime verification of the temporal formula. In the paper, we show that a seamless integration is indeed possible by using alternating automata as an intermediate data structure. Alternating automata combine the disjunctive branching of nondeterministic automata with the conjunctive branching of universal automata. As a result, alternating automata are exponentially more succinct than nondeterministic or universal automata. LTL specifications can be translated in linear time into equivalent alternating automata that closely match the structure of the formula: the states of the automaton correspond to subformulas of the specification [7]. In monitoring, this conciseness can be exploited by an efficient on-the-fly construction, which delays the unfolding of the alternating automaton until new positions of the trace become available [8].

The universal branching available in alternating automata can also be used to concisely express the noninterference requirements in SecLTL specifications. Overall, the automaton for a SecLTL formula has the same structure as the automaton for an LTL formula. If the Hide operator occurs as a subformula, we need to check that *all* alternative traces (corresponding to different values of the secrets) in the system result in the same observation. To verify this condition, the automaton branches *universally* into a separate check for *each* alternative trace, where the subautomaton for each alternative trace keeps track of both the state of the system for the main trace and the state of the system for the alternative trace, and ensures that the observations are the same until the endcondition becomes true on the main trace.

The embedding of the noninterference check into the alternating automaton leads to an efficient monitoring algorithm. Using the standard on-the-fly unfolding technique [8], we only consider that part of the automaton that corresponds to the monitored trace. In particular, the decision which alternative traces to track is delayed until the moment when the temporal context has already been evaluated with respect to the currently available prefix of the monitored trace.

In the following sections, we present the ingredients of our monitoring approach in more detail. In Section 2, we formalize our system model and review the syntax and semantics of SecLTL. In Section 3 we describe the translation of SecLTL specifications to alternating automata. Based on this foundation, we then present our monitoring algorithm for SecLTL specifications. We conclude with a discussion of open research questions and future directions in Section 4.

2   The Specification Language SecLTL

2.1   System Model

Definition 1. *A transition system $\mathcal{S} = (S, s^0, \mathcal{V}_\mathcal{I}, \mathcal{V}_\mathcal{O}, \Sigma, \delta)$ consists of:*

- *a finite set of states S with an initial state s^0,*
- *finite sets $\mathcal{V}_\mathcal{I}$ and $\mathcal{V}_\mathcal{O}$ of boolean input and output variables respectively, with $\mathcal{V}_\mathcal{I} \cap \mathcal{V}_\mathcal{O} = \emptyset$, and alphabet Σ defined as $\Sigma = 2^{(\mathcal{V}_\mathcal{I} \cup \mathcal{V}_\mathcal{O})}$,*
- *a transition function $\delta : S \times \Sigma \to S$, which is a partial function.*

We consider input-enabled *systems, that is, we require for every $s \in S$ and $a \in 2^{\mathcal{V}_\mathcal{I}}$ that there exists an $o \in 2^{\mathcal{V}_\mathcal{O}}$ such that $\delta(s, a \cup o)$ is defined. We define the size of the transition system $\mathcal{S}$ as $|\mathcal{S}| = |S| + |\Sigma|$.*

For a set A, A^* is the set of all finite sequences of elements of A and A^ω is the set of all infinite sequences of elements of A. For a finite or infinite sequence π of elements of A and $i \in \mathbb{N}$, $\pi[i]$ is the $(i+1)$-th element of π, $\pi[0, i)$ is the prefix of π of up to (excluding) position i, $\pi[0, i]$ is the prefix of π up to (including) position i and, if π is infinite, $\pi[i, \infty)$ is its infinite suffix starting at position i. We denote the length of a sequence π with $|\pi|$ (where $|\pi| = \infty$ for $\pi \in A^\omega$).

Definition 2 (Trace). *A trace in a transition system $\mathcal{S} = (S, s^0, \mathcal{V}_\mathcal{I}, \mathcal{V}_\mathcal{O}, \Sigma, \delta)$ is a finite or infinite sequence π of elements of Σ: $\pi \in \Sigma^* \cup \Sigma^\omega$.*

Definition 3 (Execution). *Given a state $s \in S$ and a finite or infinite trace π, there exists at most one (finite or infinite, respectively) sequence of states $s_0, s_1, \ldots$ such that $s_0 = s$ and $s_i = \delta(s_{i-1}, \pi[i-1])$ for all $0 < i < |\pi|$.*

We call this sequence of states (whenever it exists) an execution *of $\mathcal{S}$ from s on π and denote it with $\mathsf{Exec}_\mathcal{S}(s, \pi)$. Given a state s, we denote the set of infinite (finite) traces in $\mathcal{S}$ for which an execution of $\mathcal{S}$ from s exists (i.e., for which $\mathsf{Exec}_\mathcal{S}$ is defined for the state s) by $\mathsf{Traces}_{\mathcal{S}, s}$ (respectively $\mathsf{TracesFin}_{\mathcal{S}.s}$).*

Example 1. We use a simple application for managing clinical data as our running example. The application processes medical test results for a patient and reports the results in accumulated form, here simply stating whether or not some test has been positive, to an external agency. The application takes into account whether the patient agrees to the release of information. Figures 1(a) and 1(b) show two transition systems modeling variations of such an application. In both $\mathcal{S}_A$ and $\mathcal{S}_B$, the set of input variables is $\mathcal{V}_I = \{c, t\}$ and the set of output variables is $\mathcal{V}_O = \{p, d\}$. Thus, the alphabet of edge labels is $\Sigma = 2^{\{t,c,p,d\}}$.

The variable t indicates the positive or negative outcome of the current test, the variable p indicates whether the system reports that some test was positive, the variable c indicates the patient's current consent status, and the variable d indicates whether the patient is included in an ongoing drug study. For clarity, we use the valuations of the boolean variables in $\mathcal{V}_I \cup \mathcal{V}_O$ to represent the elements of Σ, for example the edge label $\bar{c}t\bar{p}d$ stands for $\{c, p, d\}$.

If the patient consents to the release of information, p is truthfully set to *true* if some test result has been positive. If there is no consent, p is always set to *false*. The behaviors of the two systems differ with respect to test results that occurred while the patient did not consent to the release of information. In $\mathcal{S}_A$, once an execution reaches state s_2 or state s_4 (when some test result is positive), it stays in the set of states $\{s_2, s_4\}$ forever. The test results are therefore recorded accurately, even if there is no consent to release the information. System $\mathcal{S}_B$, on the other hand, goes to state s_3 whenever the patient changes the consent status from *false* to *true* (i.e., c becomes *true*) and the current test result is negative, thus discarding the information about any positive test results up to that point.

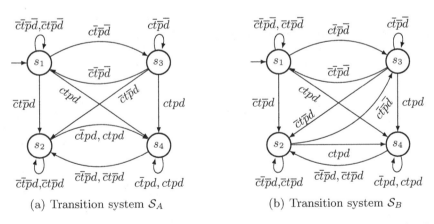

(a) Transition system $\mathcal{S}_A$ (b) Transition system $\mathcal{S}_B$

Fig. 1. Transition systems with input variables c, t and output variables p, d. They model two simple systems for managing clinical data, which report on the accumulated result of a series of medical tests administered to a patient. The input variable t indicates the positive or negative outcome of the current test, the output variable p indicates whether the system reports that some test in the past has been positive, the output variable d indicates whether the patient is included in a drug study, the input variable c indicates whether the patient currently consents to the release of information.

In addition to that, in this case, the patient's participation in the drug study is suspended until possibly a positive test result comes in the future.

The patient can be included in the drug study (i.e, the variable d can be set to *true*) only if some test result was positive. As long as the patient does not consent to the release of information he may or may not be included in the drug study. In the latter case, positive test results are not recorded.

A possible finite trace of $\mathcal{S}_A$ is $\pi = \bar{c}\bar{t}\bar{p}\bar{d}, \bar{c}\bar{t}\bar{p}\bar{d}, \bar{c}t\bar{p}\bar{d}, \bar{c}\bar{t}pd$. The corresponding execution of $\mathcal{S}_A$ from the initial state s_1 is $\mathsf{Exec}_{\mathcal{S}_A}(s_1, \pi) = s_1, s_3, s_1, s_2, s_4$. This trace is not possible in the system $\mathcal{S}_B$ (i.e., there exists no corresponding execution), because there is no transition for $\bar{c}\bar{t}pd$ from state s_2 in $\mathcal{S}_B$.

2.2   SecLTL: Syntax and Semantics

The logic SecLTL, introduced in [6], extends LTL with the *Hide* operator $\mathcal{H}$.

Formally, the SecLTL formulas over a set of input variables $\mathcal{V}_\mathcal{I}$ and a set of output variables $\mathcal{V}_\mathcal{O}$ are defined according to the grammar below. Here, $p \in \mathcal{V}_\mathcal{I} \cup \mathcal{V}_\mathcal{O}$, φ and ψ are SecLTL formulas, $H \subseteq \mathcal{V}_\mathcal{I}$ and $I \subseteq \mathcal{V}_\mathcal{I}$ are sets of input variables with $H \subseteq I$, and $O \subseteq \mathcal{V}_\mathcal{O}$ is a set of output variables:

$$\varphi \quad ::= \quad p \mid \neg\varphi \mid \varphi \vee \psi \mid \varphi \wedge \psi \mid \bigcirc\varphi \mid \varphi\,\mathcal{U}\,\psi \mid \varphi\mathcal{R}\psi \mid$$
$$\mathcal{H}_{H,I,O}\varphi \mid \mathcal{L}_{H,I,O}\varphi.$$

The *Leak* operator $\mathcal{L}$ is the dual of $\mathcal{H}$. Additionally, we introduce the common abbreviations $\mathsf{true} = v \vee \neg v$, $\mathsf{false} = \neg\mathsf{true}$, $\Diamond\varphi = \mathsf{true}\,\mathcal{U}\,\varphi$ and $\Box\varphi = \neg\Diamond\neg\varphi$.

Intuitively, $\mathcal{H}_{H,I,O}\varphi$ requires that the observable behavior of the system does not depend on the initial values of the *secret variables* H in the desired timeframe, that is, before the formula φ is satisfied. The operator specifies the power of the observer associated with it, by providing two sets of variables that are *visible to this observer*: a set I of *input* variables and a set O of *output* variables.

The Hide operator thus specifies what is to be considered the secret, what we consider to be observable, and when the secret may be released.

Example 2. We illustrate the use of SecLTL by providing examples of formal requirements for the clinical data management system from our running example.

The Hide operator allows us to specify precisely at which points some input variable is considered to be secret. If, for example, we are only interested in the first test result, then we can use the SecLTL formula $\mathcal{H}_{\{t\},\{t,c\},\{p\}}\mathsf{false}$ to express the requirement that the first test result has to remain secret forever. The observer in this scenario is specified to see the patient's consent status and the output variable p, which represents whether the system reports that some test in the past has been positive. He cannot observe the output variable d.

We can also restrict the traces on which a variable has to be kept secret, i.e, the traces on which a $\mathcal{H}$ formula needs to hold. The formula (1) below specifies the property that only if the user never gives consent during the execution of the system, the first test result must never be revealed.

$$(\Box\neg c) \rightarrow \mathcal{H}_{\{t\},\{t,c\},\{p\}}\mathsf{false}. \tag{1}$$

By nesting LTL operators and $\mathcal{H}$, we can place $\mathcal{H}$ in an appropriate temporal context and thus also refer to secrets introduced in multiple points of interest during the execution of the system. The following formula represents the property that every test result produced at a moment when the patient currently does not consent to the release of information must remain secret forever.

$$\Box\big(\neg c \rightarrow \mathcal{H}_{\{t\},\{t,c\},\{p\}}\mathsf{false}\big). \tag{2}$$

A different policy for dealing with patient data might require that a test result is treated as confidential until (at some future point) the patient gives consent and that, at that future point in time, information about all test results from the past may be revealed in the system's public output p:

$$\Box\big(\mathcal{H}_{\{t\},\{t,c\},\{p\}}c\big). \tag{3}$$

The formulas (1), (2) and (3) above show that SecLTL allows formalizing different security policies, in particular ones that involve temporal requirements. In formula (2), the values of the input variable t that are considered confidential depend on the temporal context. The temporal aspect of (3) is in the condition c, which determines from what point on *declassification* of the secret is allowed.

Since SecLTL is an extension of LTL, secrecy requirements can be combined with classical requirements on the system's behavior. For example, in addition to the first requirement above one can require that if the current test result is positive and the patient eventually consents in the future, then the existence of a positive test result is eventually reflected in the system's output. Formally:

$$\Box\big(t \wedge \Diamond c \rightarrow \Diamond p\big) \wedge \Box\big(\neg c \rightarrow \mathcal{H}_{\{t\},\{t,c\},\{p\}}\mathsf{false}\big). \tag{4}$$

$\Box$

Although SecLTL specifications are linear-time properties, their semantics, more precisely the semantics of the Hide operator, is defined using a *set of alternative traces* and involves comparison of each of these traces to the *main trace*, i.e., the trace over which the SecLTL formula is interpreted.

Definition 4 (Equivalences). *Given a set of variables $V \subseteq \mathcal{V}_I \cup \mathcal{V}_O$, we define two elements a and a' of Σ, to be* observationally equivalent w.r.t. V, *noted $a \sim_V a'$, iff $a \cap V = a' \cap V$. Observational equivalence w.r.t. V is extended to traces by pointwise comparison.*

Definition 5 (Alternative traces). *The set of alternative traces for an infinite trace $\pi \in \Sigma^\omega$ in $\mathcal{S}$ and a state $s \in S$ with respect to a set of secret variables $H \subseteq \mathcal{V}_I$ and a set of input variables $I \subseteq \mathcal{V}_I$ with $H \subseteq I$, is the set of traces starting with a possibly different valuation of the variables H in the first position, but otherwise adhering to the same values for the observable input variables I.*

$\mathsf{Alt}_{\mathcal{S}}(s, \pi, H, I) = \{\; \pi' \in \mathsf{Traces}_{\mathcal{S},s} \mid \pi[0] \sim_{I \setminus H} \pi'[0] \text{ and } \pi[1,\infty) \sim_I \pi'[1,\infty) \;\}.$

Definition 6 (Semantics of SecLTL). *Let* $\mathcal{S} = (S, s^0, \mathcal{V}_{\mathcal{I}}, \mathcal{V}_{\mathcal{O}}, \Sigma, \delta)$ *be a transition system and* $s \in S$ *be a state in* $\mathcal{S}$. *We say that the infinite trace* $\pi \in \mathsf{Traces}_{\mathcal{S},s}$ *and the state* s *satisfy a given SecLTL formula* φ, *denoted* $\mathcal{S}, s, \pi \models \varphi$ *when the following conditions are satisfied:*

- *For an atomic proposition, i.e, a variable* $p \in \mathcal{V}_{\mathcal{I}} \cup \mathcal{V}_{\mathcal{O}}$:

$$\mathcal{S}, s, \pi \models p \text{ iff } p \in \pi[0].$$

- *For the boolean connectives:*

$$\begin{aligned}
\mathcal{S}, s, \pi &\models \neg\psi & &\text{iff } \mathcal{S}, s, \pi \not\models \psi, \\
\mathcal{S}, s, \pi &\models \varphi_1 \vee \varphi_2 & &\text{iff } \mathcal{S}, s, \pi \models \varphi_1 \text{ or } \mathcal{S}, s, \pi \models \varphi_2, \\
\mathcal{S}, s, \pi &\models \varphi_1 \wedge \varphi_2 & &\text{iff } \mathcal{S}, s, \pi \models \varphi_1 \text{ and } \mathcal{S}, s, \pi \models \varphi_2.
\end{aligned}$$

- *For classical temporal operators, where* $\sigma = \mathsf{Execs}(s, \pi)$:

$$\begin{aligned}
\mathcal{S}, s, \pi &\models \bigcirc\psi & &\text{iff } \mathcal{S}, \sigma[1], \pi[1, \infty) \models \psi, \\
\mathcal{S}, s, \pi &\models \varphi_1 \mathcal{U} \varphi_2 & &\text{iff for some } i \geq 0, \text{ we have } \mathcal{S}, \sigma[i], \pi[i, \infty) \models \varphi_2 \\
& & &\text{and for all } 0 \leq j < i \text{ we have } \mathcal{S}, \sigma[j], \pi[j, \infty) \models \varphi_1, \\
\mathcal{S}, s, \pi &\models \varphi_1 \mathcal{R} \varphi_2 & &\text{iff for all } i \geq 0, \text{ we have } \mathcal{S}, \sigma[i], \pi[i, \infty) \models \varphi_2, \text{ or} \\
& & &\text{for some } i \geq 0, \mathcal{S}, \sigma[i], \pi[i, \infty) \models \varphi_1 \text{ and} \\
& & &\text{for all } 0 \leq j \leq i \text{ we have } \mathcal{S}, \sigma[j], \pi[j, \infty) \models \varphi_2.
\end{aligned}$$

- *For the modal operators* $\mathcal{H}$ *and* $\mathcal{L}$, *where* $\sigma = \mathsf{Execs}(s, \pi)$:

$$\begin{aligned}
\mathcal{S}, s, \pi &\models \mathcal{H}_{H,I,O}\psi \text{ iff for every } \pi' \in \mathsf{Alt}_{\mathcal{S}}(s, \pi, H, I) \text{ we have } \pi \sim_O \pi', \\
& \text{ or for some } i \geq 0 \text{ we have } \mathcal{S}, \sigma[i], \pi[i, \infty) \models \psi \\
& \text{ and } \pi[0, i) \sim_O \pi'[0, i) \text{ for every } \pi' \in \mathsf{Alt}_{\mathcal{S}}(s, \pi, H, I), \\
\mathcal{S}, s, \pi &\models \mathcal{L}_{H,I,O}\psi \text{ iff for some } \pi' \in \mathsf{Alt}_{\mathcal{S}}(s, \pi, H, I) \text{ and } i \geq 0, \pi[i] \not\sim_O \pi'[i] \\
& \text{ and for all } 0 \leq j \leq i, \mathcal{S}, \sigma[j], \pi[j, \infty) \models \psi.
\end{aligned}$$

Remark 1. Note that the secret specified by each (semantic) occurrence of the Hide operator in a SecLTL formula consists of the individual valuation of the variables in the set H at the current point of the trace. Thus, for example, the formula $\mathcal{H}_{\{h\},\{h\},\{o\}}\mathsf{false} \wedge \bigcirc \mathcal{H}_{\{h\},\{h\},\{o\}}\mathsf{false}$ specifies that the first value of h must be secret forever and the second value of h must be secret forever. Thus, on a trace that satisfies this formula each of the inputs is kept secret *individually*, but some *correlation* between them might never the less be revealed.

Example 3. Let us consider again the SecLTL formulas (1), (2), (3) and (4) and the transition systems from Figures 1(a) and 1(b). The formula (1) is satisfied on every trace allowed by $\mathcal{S}_A$, because on all traces where the variable c never becomes *true*, the value of p is also always *false*. Since the alternative traces defined by $\mathcal{H}_{\{t\},\{t,c\},\{p\}}$ agree with the main trace on the values of c, the same holds for them and, hence, they agree with the main trace on the value of p.

To see that formula (2) does not hold for some trace allowed by $\mathcal{S}_A$, consider the infinite trace $\pi_1 = c\bar{t}\bar{p}d, \bar{c}\bar{t}\bar{p}d, \bar{c}tpd, \bar{c}tpd, (\bar{c}tpd)^\omega$, whose corresponding execution from the initial state s_1 in S_A is $\mathsf{Execs}_{\mathcal{S}_A}(s_1, \pi_1) = s_1, s_3, s_1, s_2, s_4, s_4^\omega$. The formula $(\neg c \rightarrow \mathcal{H}_{\{t\},\{t,c\},\{p\}})$ is violated at position 2, since $\pi_1[2, \infty) \models \neg c$

and $\pi_1[2, \infty) \not\models \mathcal{H}_{\{t\},\{t,c\},\{p\}}$, since there exists an alternative trace, $\pi_1' \in$ $\mathsf{Alt}_{\mathcal{S}}(s_1, \pi_1[2, \infty), \{t\}, \{t, c\})$ on which the system's output is different. Such a trace is $\pi_1' = \overline{ct}\bar{p}d, \overline{ct}\bar{p}d$, with corresponding execution $\mathsf{Exec}_{\mathcal{S}_A}(s_1, \pi_1') = s_1, s_1, s_3$.

The formula (3) is clearly satisfied on each possible trace allowed by $\mathcal{S}_A$, because for each position where p is satisfied, the variable c is $true$ as well.

Since the formula (2) is one of the conjuncts in formula (4), formula (4) is also not satisfied by the trace π_1. Note, however that the other conjunct, i.e., $\square(t \wedge \Diamond c \to \Diamond p)$ is satisfied by every trace in $\mathsf{Traces}_{\mathcal{S}_A, s_1}$, because for all executions on which the left hand side of the implication is true visit state s_4 (and hence p is eventually true on the corresponding trace).

Using the same arguments as above, one can see that the formulas (1) and (3) are satisfied by each trace in $\mathsf{Traces}_{\mathcal{S}_B, s_1}$ as well.

In the system $\mathcal{S}_B$, the trace π_1 is not possible, i.e., $\pi_1 \notin \mathsf{Traces}_{\mathcal{S}_B, s_1}$, as we saw earlier (looking at a finite prefix of π_1). While formula (2) is satisfied by each trace in $\mathsf{Traces}_{\mathcal{S}_B, s_1}$, for (4) there exists a counterexample trace, because all information about the existence of a positive test in the past is lost when the edge from state s_2 to state s_3 is taken.

2.3   Finite-Trace Semantics

For runtime monitoring we must interpret temporal formulas on *finite* traces.

In the case of SecLTL, we first have to adapt the definition of alternative traces. For a finite trace $\pi \in \Sigma^*$, state $s \in S$, and sets of variables $H, I \subseteq \mathcal{V}_\mathcal{I}$ with $H \subseteq I$, we define the set of *finite* alternative traces as follows:

$$\mathsf{AltFin}_{\mathcal{S}}(s, \pi, H, I) = \{ \pi' \in \mathsf{TracesFin}_{\mathcal{S},s} \mid |\pi'| = |\pi|, \pi[0] \sim_{I \setminus H} \pi'[0] \text{ and}$$
$$\pi[1, |\pi|) \sim_I \pi'[1, |\pi'|) \}.$$

We can again define inductively $\mathcal{S}, s, \pi \models \varphi$ for a finite trace π, state s and a SecLTL formula φ. The interpretation of propositional variables and boolean operators remains unchanged. The interpretation of the classical LTL operators coincides with the standard finite-trace interpretation[1]. For the $\mathcal{H}$ operator, the finite-trace semantics is similar to that of the LTL weak until ($\mathcal{W}$) operator.

– For classical temporal operators, where $|\pi| = n$ and $\sigma = \mathsf{Exec}_{\mathcal{S}}(s, \pi)$:

$\quad \mathcal{S}, s, \pi \models \bigcirc \psi \quad$ iff $n > 1$ and $\mathcal{S}, \sigma[1], \pi[1, n) \models \psi$,

$\quad \mathcal{S}, s, \pi \models \varphi_1 \mathcal{U} \varphi_2 \quad$ iff for some $0 \le i < n$, we have $\mathcal{S}, \sigma[i], \pi[i, n) \models \varphi_2$ and for all $0 \le j < i$ we have $\mathcal{S}, \sigma[j], \pi[j, n) \models \varphi_1$,

$\quad \mathcal{S}, s, \pi \models \varphi_1 \mathcal{R} \varphi_2 \quad$ iff for all $0 \le i < n$, we have $\mathcal{S}, \sigma[i], \pi[i, n) \models \varphi_2$, or for some $0 \le i < n$, $\mathcal{S}, \sigma[i], \pi[i, n) \models \varphi_1$ and for all $0 \le j \le i$ we have $\mathcal{S}, \sigma[j], \pi[j, n) \models \varphi_2$.

---

[1] We use a simple two-valued finite-trace semantics, as described for example in [8]. For an overview on other finite-trace semantics used in runtime verification, we refer the reader to [9].

- For the modal operators $\mathcal{H}$ and $\mathcal{L}$, where $|\pi| = n$ and $\sigma = \mathsf{Exec}_{\mathcal{S}}(s, \pi)$:

$$\mathcal{S}, s, \pi \models \mathcal{H}_{H,I,O}\psi \text{ iff } \pi \sim_O \pi' \text{ for every } \pi' \in \mathsf{AltFin}_{\mathcal{S}}(s, \pi, H, I), \text{ or}$$
$$\text{for some } 0 \le i < n, \mathcal{S}, \sigma[i], \pi[i, n) \models \psi \text{ and for all}$$
$$\pi' \in \mathsf{AltFin}_{\mathcal{S}}(s, \pi, H, I), \pi[0, i) \sim_O \pi'[0, i),$$
$$\mathcal{S}, s, \pi \models \mathcal{L}_{H,I,O}\psi \text{ iff for some } \pi' \in \mathsf{AltFin}_{\mathcal{S}}(s, \pi, H, I) \text{ and } 0 \le i < n,$$
$$\pi[i] \not\sim_O \pi'[i] \text{ and for all } 0 \le j \le i, \mathcal{S}, \sigma[j], \pi[j, n) \models \psi.$$

Example 4. According to the finite trace semantics, formulas (1) and (3) are satisfied by all traces in $\mathsf{TracesFin}_{\mathcal{S}_A, s_1}$ and $\mathsf{TracesFin}_{\mathcal{S}_B, s_1}$. The argument for (3) from before directly applies, because the only temporal operators that occur in it are $\square$ and $\mathcal{H}$. For (1), the argument is that the formula $\mathcal{H}_{\{t\},\{t,c\},\{p\}}\mathsf{false}$ is satisfied on every finite trace on which the formula $\Diamond c$ does not hold (according to our finite trace semantics, if we have not seen a c yet, $\Diamond c$ is not satisfied).

For formula (2), a trace in $\mathsf{TracesFin}_{\mathcal{S}_A, s_1}$ for which the formula does not hold is obtained by taking the finite prefix $\pi_1[0, 3]$ of the infinite counterexample trace π_1 considered earlier. Again, (2) is satisfied by each trace in $\mathsf{TracesFin}_{\mathcal{S}_B, s_1}$.

3   Monitoring SecLTL

Our monitoring algorithm is based on a translation of the SecLTL specification and the transition system into an alternating automaton, which we call the *monitoring automaton*. The monitoring automaton keeps track of the temporal specification and ensures the observational equivalence of the alternative traces. In the following two subsections, we first describe the construction of the automaton and then define the monitoring algorithm, which constructs the possible run trees of the monitoring automaton on-the-fly while reading the trace.

3.1   From SecLTL Formulas to Automata

We now describe a translation from SecLTL formulas and transition systems to alternating automata, applying the finite-trace semantics defined in Section 2.3. A similar construction for the infinite-trace semantics is given in [6].

Definition 7 (Alternating automaton). *An alternating automaton is a tuple* $\mathcal{A} = (Q, q_0, \Sigma, \rho, F)$, *where*

- Q *is a finite set of states and* $q_0 \in Q$ *is the initial state,*
- Σ *is the finite alphabet of the automaton,*
- $\rho : Q \times \Sigma \to \mathcal{B}^+(Q)$ *is a transition function that maps a state in* Q *and a letter from* Σ *to a positive boolean combination of states, i.e., formulas built from the formulas* true, false *and the elements of* Q *using* $\wedge$ *and* $\vee$,
- $F \subseteq Q$ *is the set of accepting states.*

The run of an alternating automaton $\mathcal{A}$ is in general a tree. A finite Q-labeled tree (T, r) for a finite set Q consists of a finite tree T and a labelling function $r : T \to Q$ which labels every node of T with an element of Q. The tree T can be represented as a finite subset of $\mathbb{N}_{>0}^*$, where each node τ in the tree is a sequence of positive integers and for every $\tau \in \mathbb{N}_{>0}^*$ and $n \in \mathbb{N}_{>0}$, if $\tau \cdot n \in T$ then:

- $\tau \in T$ (i.e., T is prefix-closed) and there is an edge from τ to $\tau \cdot n$, and
- for every $m \in \mathbb{N}_{>0}^*$ with $m < n$ it holds that $\tau \cdot m \in T$.

The root of T is the empty sequence ϵ and for a node $\tau \in T$, $|\tau|$ is the distance of the node τ from the root of the tree.

Definition 8 (Run). *A* run *of an alternating automaton* $\mathcal{A} = (Q, q_0, \Sigma, \rho, F)$ *on a finite word* $\pi \in \Sigma^*$ *is a finite Q-labeled tree (T, r) such that:*

- $r(\epsilon) = q_0$, *that is, the root of the tree is labeled with the initial state, and*
- *for every node τ in T with children $\tau_1, \ldots, \tau_k$ it holds that $k \leq |Q|$ and if $q = r(\tau)$ is the label of τ and $i = |\tau|$ is its distance from the root, then the set of labels of its children $\{r(\tau_1), \ldots, r(\tau_k)\}$ satisfies the formula $\rho(q, \pi[i])$.*

Definition 9 (Language). *A* run *of $\mathcal{A}$ on a finite word π is* accepting *if every path through the tree ends in an accepting state. A finite word π is* accepted *by $\mathcal{A}$ if there exists an accepting run of π in $\mathcal{A}$. We denote the* language *of $\mathcal{A}$, that is, the set of finite sequences accepted by $\mathcal{A}$, by $\mathcal{L}^*(\mathcal{A})$.*

Let $\mathcal{S} = (S, s^0, \mathcal{V}_I, \mathcal{V}_O, \Sigma, \delta)$ be a transition system and φ be a SecLTL formula over the set of input variables $\mathcal{V}_I$ and the set of output variables $\mathcal{V}_O$. We can assume that all negations in the formula have been pushed to the level of the atomic propositions. For propositional and classical LTL operators this can be achieved using standard rewrite rules and for the $\mathcal{H}$ operator using $\mathcal{L}$ [6].

The alternating automaton $\mathcal{A}_{\mathcal{S}}(\varphi) = (Q, q_0, \Sigma, \rho, F)$ for the transition system $\mathcal{S}$ and the SecLTL formula φ is defined as follows.

The set of states Q consists of states corresponding to the subformulas of φ together with special states corresponding to the $\mathcal{H}$ and $\mathcal{L}$ subformulas of φ:

$$Q = \{ (\psi, s) \mid \psi \text{ is a subformula of } \varphi \text{ and } s \in S \} \cup \{ accept \}$$
$$\cup \{ ((\tilde{s}, I, O, \mathcal{H}, \psi), s) \mid \tilde{s}, s \in S \text{ and } \exists H. \, \mathcal{H}_{H,I,O}\psi \text{ is subformula of } \varphi \}$$
$$\cup \{ ((\tilde{s}, I, O, \mathcal{L}, \psi), s) \mid \tilde{s}, s \in S \text{ and } \exists H. \, \mathcal{L}_{H,I,O}\psi \text{ is subformula of } \varphi \}.$$

The initial state of $\mathcal{A}_{\mathcal{S}}(\varphi)$ is $q_0 = (\varphi, s^0)$, where s^0 is the initial state of $\mathcal{S}$.

The set F of accepting states, that contains the state *accept*, is defined as

$$F = \{ accept \} \cup \{ (\varphi_1 \mathcal{R} \varphi_2, s) \in Q \} \cup$$
$$\{ (\mathcal{H}_{H,I,O}\psi, s) \in Q \} \cup \{ ((\tilde{s}, I, O, \mathcal{H}, \psi), s) \in Q \}.$$

The transition function ρ of the automaton is defined recursively as follows.

For $s \in S$ and $a \in \Sigma$ such that $\delta(s, a)$ is undefined, we define $\rho((\psi, s), a) = \text{false}$, $\rho(((\tilde{s}, I, O, \mathcal{H}, \psi), s), a) = \text{false}$, $\rho(((\tilde{s}, I, O, \mathcal{L}, \psi), s), a) = \text{false}$.

Below we consider only the cases when $\delta(s, a)$ is defined.

For an atomic proposition $p \in \mathcal{V}_\mathcal{I} \cup \mathcal{V}_\mathcal{O}$:

$$\rho((p, s), a) = accept \text{ if } p \in a \text{ and } \rho((p, s), a) = \mathsf{false} \text{ otherwise,}$$
$$\rho((\neg p, s), a) = accept \text{ if } p \notin a \text{ and } \rho((\neg p, s), a) = \mathsf{false} \text{ otherwise.}$$

For SecLTL formulas φ_1, φ_2 and ψ:

$$
\begin{aligned}
\rho((\varphi_1 \wedge \varphi_2, s), a) &= \rho((\varphi_1, s), a) \wedge \rho((\varphi_2, s), a), \\
\rho((\varphi_1 \vee \varphi_2, s), a) &= \rho((\varphi_1, s), a) \vee \rho((\varphi_2, s), a), \\
\rho((\bigcirc \psi, s), a) &= (\psi, \delta(s, a)), \\
\rho((\varphi_1 \mathcal{U} \varphi_2, s), a) &= \rho((\varphi_2, s), a) \vee \big(\rho((\varphi_1, s), a) \wedge (\varphi_1 \mathcal{U} \varphi_2, \delta(s, a))\big), \\
\rho((\varphi_1 \mathcal{R} \varphi_2, s), a) &= \rho((\varphi_2, s), a) \wedge \big(\rho((\varphi_1, s), a) \vee (\varphi_1 \mathcal{R} \varphi_2, \delta(s, a))\big).
\end{aligned}
$$

For SecLTL formula ψ and sets $H, I \subseteq \mathcal{V}_\mathcal{I}$ and $O \subseteq \mathcal{V}_\mathcal{O}$:

$$
\begin{aligned}
\rho((\mathcal{H}_{H,I,O}\psi, s), a) &= \rho((\psi, s), a) \vee (\mathsf{check}(O, a, \mathsf{Alt}_\Sigma(s, a, H, I)) \wedge \\
&\quad \bigwedge_{\tilde{a} \in \mathsf{Alt}_\Sigma(s,a,H,I)}((\delta(s, \tilde{a}), I, O, \mathcal{H}, \psi), \delta(s, a))), \\
\rho((\mathcal{L}_{H,I,O}\psi, s), a) &= \rho((\psi, s), a) \wedge (\neg\mathsf{check}(O, a, \mathsf{Alt}_\Sigma(s, a, H, I)) \vee \\
&\quad \bigvee_{\tilde{a} \in \mathsf{Alt}_\Sigma(s,a,H,I)}((\delta(s, \tilde{a}), I, O, \mathcal{L}, \psi), \delta(s, a))),
\end{aligned}
$$

where for $s \in S$, $a \in \Sigma$, and $H, I \subseteq \mathcal{V}_\mathcal{I}$ and $O \subseteq \mathcal{V}_\mathcal{O}$ we define:

$$\mathsf{Alt}_\Sigma(s, a, H, I) = \{\tilde{a} \in \Sigma \mid \tilde{a} \sim_{I \setminus H} a \text{ and } \exists s' \in S.s' = \delta(s, \tilde{a})\},$$

$$\mathsf{check}(O, a, A) = (\forall \tilde{a} \in A : \tilde{a} \sim_O a).$$

For $((\tilde{s}, I, O, \mathcal{H}, \psi), s) \in Q$ and $((\tilde{s}, I, O, \mathcal{L}, \psi), s) \in Q$ we define:

$$
\begin{aligned}
\rho(((\tilde{s}, I, O, \mathcal{H}, \psi), s), a) &= \rho((\psi, s), a) \vee (\mathsf{check}(O, a, \mathsf{Alt}_\Sigma(\tilde{s}, a, \emptyset, I)) \wedge \\
&\quad \bigwedge_{\tilde{a} \in \mathsf{Alt}_\Sigma(\tilde{s},a,\emptyset,I)}((\delta(\tilde{s}, \tilde{a}), I, O, \mathcal{H}, \psi), \delta(s, a))), \\
\rho(((\tilde{s}, I, O, \mathcal{L}, \psi), s), a) &= \rho((\psi, s), a) \wedge (\neg\mathsf{check}(O, a, \mathsf{Alt}_\Sigma(\tilde{s}, a, \emptyset, I)) \vee \\
&\quad \bigvee_{\tilde{a} \in \mathsf{Alt}_\Sigma(\tilde{s},a,\emptyset,I)}((\delta(\tilde{s}, \tilde{a}), I, O, \mathcal{L}, \psi), \delta(s, a))).
\end{aligned}
$$

Finally, we define $\rho(accept, a) = accept$.

Definition 10 (Monitor automaton). *Given a transition system $\mathcal{S} = (S, s^0, \mathcal{V}_\mathcal{I}, \mathcal{V}_\mathcal{O}, \Sigma, \delta)$ and a SecLTL formula φ, the* monitor automaton *for φ is the automaton $\mathcal{A}_\mathcal{S}(\varphi)$ defined above.*

The monitor automaton $\mathcal{A}_\mathcal{S}(\varphi)$ has the property that for every finite trace $\pi \in \Sigma^*$, it holds that $\pi \in \mathcal{L}^*(\mathcal{A}_\mathcal{S}(\varphi))$ iff $\pi \in \mathsf{TracesFin}_{\mathcal{S},s^0}$ and $\mathcal{S}, s^0, \pi \models \varphi$.

Example 5. We now give the alternating automaton $\mathcal{A}_{\mathcal{S}_A}(\varphi)$ for the SecLTL property $\varphi = (\square\neg c) \to \mathcal{H}_{\{t\},\{t,c\},\{p\}}\mathsf{false}$ and the transition system $\mathcal{S}_A$. The set of states and the transition relation of $\mathcal{A}_{\mathcal{S}_A}(\varphi)$ are given in Figure 2.

In the initial state the automaton can either decide to refute the left side of the implication (by waiting for a c in state t_1 or state t_2) or it has to validate the hide operator in which case it has to check whether the corresponding pairs of main and alternative traces in $\mathcal{S}_A$ are observationally equivalent w.r.t. the output variable p. The equivalence check is integrated in the transition relation.

label	state		label	state
q_0	$((\square\neg c) \to \mathcal{H}_{\{t\},\{t,c\},\{p\}}\text{false}, s_1)$		$accept$	$accept$
q_1	$(\lozenge c, s_1)$		q_2	$(\lozenge c, s_2)$
q_3	$((s_1, \{t,c\}, \{p\}, \mathcal{H}, \text{false}), s_1)$		q_4	$((s_2, \{t,c\}, \{p\}, \mathcal{H}, \text{false}), s_1)$
q_5	$((s_1, \{t,c\}, \{p\}, \mathcal{H}, \text{false}), s_2)$		q_6	$((s_2, \{t,c\}, \{p\}, \mathcal{H}, \text{false}), s_2)$
q_7	$((s_3, \{t,c\}, \{p\}, \mathcal{H}, \text{false}), s_3)$		q_8	$((s_4, \{t,c\}, \{p\}, \mathcal{H}, \text{false}), s_4)$

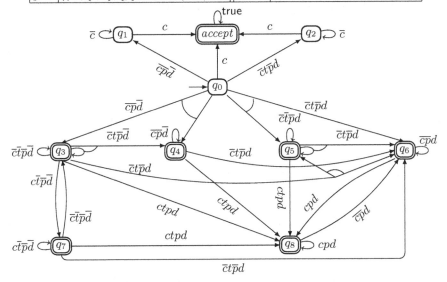

Fig. 2. The alternating automaton $\mathcal{A}_{\mathcal{S}_A}(\varphi)$ for the transition system $\mathcal{S}_A$ from Figure 1(a) and the SecLTL formula $\varphi = (\square\neg c) \to \mathcal{H}_{\{t\},\{t,c\},\{p\}}\text{false}$. Branchings with arcs represent conjunctions, branchings without arcs are to be interpreted disjunctively. The states drawn with double line are the accepting states of $\mathcal{A}_{\mathcal{S}_A}(\varphi)$.

3.2   The Monitoring Algorithm

Trace checking algorithms for alternating automata attempt to construct an accepting run tree. Different traversal strategies, such as depth-first, breadth-first, or bottom-up, result in trace checking algorithms with different performance characteristics [8]. For monitoring, where the trace becomes available incrementally, a good strategy is to construct the run tree in a breadth-first manner. Conceptually, the monitoring algorithm maintains a set of candidate trees and adds a new layer at the leaves whenever a new position in the trace becomes available. However, since neither the construction of the next layer nor the verification of acceptance condition refer to any non-leaf nodes of the tree, it in fact suffices to keep track of the states on the leaves. The state of the monitor is therefore represented by a set D of sets C of states, where each set C corresponds to the states on the leaves of some partially constructed run tree. For a more detailed explanation of the breadth-first strategy, we refer the reader to [8].

The monitoring algorithm shown in Figure 3 applies the breadth-first strategy to the monitoring automaton defined in the previous section. Initially, there is only one candidate tree, consisting of a single node labeled with the initial

MONITOR-SECLTL($\mathcal{S}, \varphi, \pi$)

$\quad$ $(Q, q_0, \Sigma, \rho, F) \leftarrow \mathcal{A}_\mathcal{S}(\varphi)$
$\quad$ $D \leftarrow \{\{q_0\}\}$
$\quad$ **for** $n = 0$ **to** $|\pi| - 1$ **do**
$\quad\quad$ $D' \leftarrow \emptyset$
$\quad\quad$ **for each** $C \in D$ **do**
$\quad\quad\quad$ $D' \quad\leftarrow\quad D' \cup$
$\quad\quad$ $successors(C, \pi[n])$
$\quad\quad$ **end for**
$\quad\quad$ $D \leftarrow D'$
$\quad$ **end for**
$\quad$ **return** ACCEPT(D, F)

ACCEPT(D, F)

$\quad$ $D' \leftarrow \emptyset$
$\quad$ **for each** $C \in D$ **do**
$\quad\quad$ **if** $accepting(C, F)$ **then**
$\quad\quad\quad$ $D' \leftarrow D' \cup \{C\}$
$\quad\quad$ **end if**
$\quad$ **end for**
$\quad$ **return** $(D' \neq \emptyset)$

Fig. 3. Monitoring algorithm for a transition system $\mathcal{S}$, a SecLTL formula φ, and a finite trace $\pi \in$ TracesFin$_{\mathcal{S}, s^0}$. The algorithm returns *true* iff $\mathcal{S}, s^0, \pi \models \varphi$.

state q_0 of $\mathcal{A}_\mathcal{S}(\varphi)$. Variable D is therefore initialized with a singleton set containing the singleton set which consists of q_0. For each position of the trace, the successor sets of the elements $C \in D$ are computed by the *successors* function, where $successors(C, a) = \bigotimes_{q \in C} next(\rho(q, a))$, $\otimes$ denotes the crossproduct $\{C_1, \ldots, C_n\} \otimes \{C'_1, \ldots, C'_m\} = \{C_i \cup C'_j \mid i = 1 \ldots n, j = 1 \ldots m\}$, and function *next* computes the set of sets of successors defined by the positive Boolean combination in the transition function as follows:

$$\begin{aligned} next(q) \quad &= \{\{q\}\} \text{ for } q \in Q, \\ next(\theta_1 \wedge \theta_2) &= next(\theta_1) \otimes next(\theta_2), \\ next(\theta_1 \vee \theta_2) &= next(\theta_1) \cup next(\theta_2). \end{aligned}$$

At any point, we can check if there exists a run tree for the trace seen so far, by searching for an element C of D that consists entirely of accepting states. In the algorithm shown in Figure 3, it is assumed that we are only interested in the result at the end of the trace, after $|\pi|$ steps. Function *accepting* checks if all states are accepting, and the algorithm keeps only those elements of D that satisfy this check. If the resulting set D' is non-empty, we know that there exists a run tree, and the algorithm returns *true*.

Example 6. We monitor the SecLTL formula $(\Box \neg c) \to \mathcal{H}_{\{t\}, \{t,c\}, \{p\}}$false and the transition system $\mathcal{S}_A$ from Figure 1(a) on prefixes of the trace π shown below using the monitoring automaton depicted in Figure 2. The row marked "result" indicates in the ith column the monitoring result obtained after monitoring the prefix $\pi[0, i)$ of π consisting of the first i positions.

step	1	2	3	4
π :	$\overline{c}t\overline{p}d$	$\overline{c}t\overline{p}d$	$c\overline{t}pd$	$\overline{c}t\overline{p}d$
D	$\{\{q_1\}, \{q_3, q_4\},$ $\{q_2\}, \{q_5, q_6\}\}$	$\{\{q_1\},$ $\{q_2\}, \{q_5, q_6\}\}$	$\{\{accept\},$ $\{accept\}\}$	$\{\{accept\},$ $\{accept\}\}$
result	*true*	*true*	*true*	*true*

3.3   Towards Stronger Security Guarantees

Previous approaches to monitoring information flow [1,4,5] only consider *sequential* programs that read all their inputs at the beginning of the execution, and thus the secrets are only introduced at the initial state. For this case, monitoring the SecLTL property $\mathcal{H}_{H,I,O}$false using the algorithm from Section 3.2 provides the same security guarantees as these approaches.

However, SecLTL allows for specifying more complex information flow properties for reactive programs - in particular ones that refer to multiple secrets, which may be introduced at different points of time. A prominent example is noninterference [2] for reactive systems. A reactive system is noninterferent, if for any two executions that have indistinguishable sequences of inputs the observer cannot distinguish the sequences of outputs. We can characterize noninterference by the SecLTL formula $\varphi_{ni} = \square \mathcal{H}_{H,I,O}$false , where H is the input that must be hidden from the observer and I and O are the input and output revealed to him. A system satisfies noninterference if and only if φ_{ni} holds on *all traces* of the system. Thus, when monitoring noninterference we must verify φ_{ni} along more than a single trace in order to be sure to detect every violation.

The SecLTL semantics guarantees that after successfully monitoring a single trace, none of the secrets specified in the formula is revealed. However, this does not exclude disclosure of correlations between different secrets.

Consider the program shown in Figure 4(a), which reads, in each iteration of the loop, a binary input and it outputs whether the sum over the input bits seen so far exceeds 1. The transition system generated by the program, which is shown in Figure 4(b), does not satisfy noninterference, because an observer cannot draw a distinction between the two streams of inputs corresponding to, for example, the left-most and the right-most trace, but the same observer can certainly draw a distinction between the streams of outputs. However, if we monitor φ_{ni} only on the left-most trace with constant input 0 (shown with black nodes in Figure 4(b)), we will not detect this violation, because the alternative

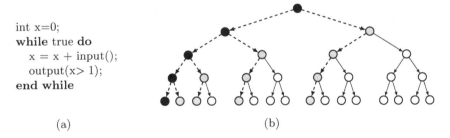

```
int x=0;
while true do
    x = x + input();
    output(x> 1);
end while
```

(a)   (b)

Fig. 4. (a) Program that reads, in each iteration of its loop, a binary input and outputs whether the sum over the input bits seen so far exceeds 1. (b) The corresponding transition system branches to the left on input 0 and to the right on input 1. The dashed arrows indicate output 0, the solid arrows output 1. The black nodes identify the execution corresponding to the monitored trace, with constant input 0. The gray nodes identify the paths corresponding to the alternative traces.

traces (depicted with gray nodes) produce the same sequence of outputs. In order to detect the violation, we must monitor at least one additional trace.

A possible solution would be to monitor, in addition to the given trace, the set of traces that have the same history of observable inputs. Clearly, the efficiency of such an algorithm depends on the representation of the resulting monitor state, and there is room for optimizations and heuristics. We discuss some ideas for future work in this direction in the following section.

4   Outlook and Conclusions

SecLTL is an attractive specification language for security-critical reactive systems, because it allows us to state precisely *when* and *under what conditions* an event must remain secret. For large systems, where SecLTL model checking [6] might be too expensive, the monitoring approach presented in this paper provides a much more practical alternative. Monitoring is dramatically cheaper than model checking, because the on-the-fly construction only explores that part of the system that corresponds to the observed trace and its alternatives as defined by the SecLTL specification. In general, however, the monitor may also need to traverse a substantial part of the system's state space. In this case, the explicit state representation of our monitoring algorithm is a limitation, and an important direction for future work is to integrate symbolic state representations and abstraction techniques from software model checking and abstract interpretation into the monitoring algorithm.

Another research direction concerns the extension of the monitoring algorithm towards more general security guarantees as discussed in Section 3.3. Monitoring sets of traces, as suggested there, may turn out to be too expensive if variations in the secrets force the monitor to explore a significant portion of the system state space in parallel. In practice, it may be possible to trade some loss of precision for a substantial gain in efficiency. In a probabilistic setting, for example, it might be possible to select a small set of traces that guarantee a reasonable limit on the loss of entropy from the observer's point of view.

Acknowledgements.   This work was partially supported by the German Research Foundation (DFG) under the project SpAGAT (grant no. FI 936/2-1) in the priority program "Reliably Secure Software Systems – RS3".

References

1. Sabelfeld, A., Russo, A.: From Dynamic to Static and Back: Riding the Roller Coaster of Information-Flow Control Research. In: Pnueli, A., Virbitskaite, I., Voronkov, A. (eds.) PSI 2009. LNCS, vol. 5947, pp. 352–365. Springer, Heidelberg (2010)
2. Goguen, J.A., Meseguer, J.: Security policies and security models. In: Proceedings of S&P, pp. 11–20 (1982)

3. Caldicott, F.: Department of Health, The Caldicott Committee, Report on the review of patient-identifiable information. Department of Health, London (1997)
4. Russo, A., Sabelfeld, A.: Dynamic vs. static flow-sensitive security analysis. In: Proc. CSF 2010, pp. 186–199. IEEE Computer Society (2010)
5. Le Guernic, G., Banerjee, A., Jensen, T., Schmidt, D.A.: Automata-Based Confidentiality Monitoring. In: Okada, M., Satoh, I. (eds.) ASIAN 2006. LNCS, vol. 4435, pp. 75–89. Springer, Heidelberg (2008)
6. Dimitrova, R., Finkbeiner, B., Kovács, M., Rabe, M.N., Seidl, H.: Model Checking Information Flow in Reactive Systems. In: Kuncak, V., Rybalchenko, A. (eds.) VMCAI 2012. LNCS, vol. 7148, pp. 169–185. Springer, Heidelberg (2012)
7. Vardi, M.Y.: An Automata-Theoretic Approach to Linear Temporal Logic. In: Moller, F., Birtwistle, G. (eds.) Logics for Concurrency. LNCS, vol. 1043, pp. 238–266. Springer, Heidelberg (1996)
8. Finkbeiner, B., Sipma, H.: Checking finite traces using alternating automata. Form. Methods Syst. Des. 24(2), 101–127 (2004)
9. Bauer, A., Leucker, M., Schallhart, C.: Comparing LTL semantics for runtime verification. Journal of Logic and Computation 20, 651–674 (2010)

Dynamic Information-Flow Analysis for Multi-threaded Applications

Laurent Mounier and Emmanuel Sifakis

VERIMAG Laboratory, University of Grenoble
2 Av. Vignate, 38610 Gieres, France
{mounier,esifakis}@imag.fr

Abstract. Information-flow analysis is one of the promising techniques to leverage the detection of software vulnerabilities and confidentiality breaches. However, in the context of multi-threaded applications running on multicore platforms, this analysis becomes highly challenging due to data races and inter-processor dependences. In this paper we first review some of the existing information-flow analysis techniques and we discuss their limits in this particular context. Then, we propose a dedicated runtime predictive approach. It consists in extending information-flow properties computed from a single parallel execution trace to a set of valid serialisations with respect to the execution platform. This approach can be applied for instance in runtime monitoring or security testing of multi-threaded applications.

1 Introduction

On-going advances in processor technology and computer design allow to drastically reduce the cost of computing power and make it available to a large audience. As an example, multi-core architectures are now commonly used in many end user domains, ranging from small embedded devices like smart-phones to powerful personal computers. To correctly exploit the huge computing capabilities of these machines, applications are conceived as a set of asynchronous tasks (or *threads*), able to execute on distinct processors, and cooperating each others to provide the desired functionalities. An example of such a parallel programming model is based on *shared memory* to implement inter-thread communications and synchronisations.

However, exploiting efficiently and correctly this hardware-supplied parallelism is notoriously difficult. In fact, the primitives offered by many classical programming languages to control asynchronous parallel executions are still basic and error prone. As a consequence, it is necessary to develop suitable techniques and tools allowing to analyse this kind of applications.

An important class of analysis is based on the notion of *information flow*. Their purpose is to track how data processed by a program can transit inside the memory at execution time. Such analysis are useful for many validation purposes, and it is a central issue in computer security. In particular it allows to detect *information leakage* (from a confidentiality point of view), or to compute *taint*

T. Margaria and B. Steffen (Eds.): ISoLA 2012, Part I, LNCS 7609, pp. 358–371, 2012.

propagation (to check how user inputs may influence vulnerable statements). Information inside applications can flow in various ways, some of which being obvious and some others being more tedious to identify. *Explicit flows*, corresponding to assignments between variables, are the most commonly analysed. On the other hand, implicit flows using *covert channels* such as control flow and timing delays are much harder to detect.

As many program analysis techniques, information-flow analysis is much more challenging when considering parallel executions. This difficulty comes from several sources, including for instance:

- the extra flows introduced by inter-thread communication channels;
- the conflicting accesses to shared resources or memory locations between concurrent threads (e.g., race conditions);
- the non-determinism introduced by the execution platform (hardware and operating system), which makes some program executions hard to reproduce;
- etc.

Various software analysis techniques have been proposed so far to address these problems. These techniques are either *static* (they do not require any program execution), like data-flow analysis or model-checking, or *dynamic*, like runtime monitoring or test execution. The main difficulty here is to extend the analysis techniques used for sequential programs while avoiding the so-called "interleaving problems". These problems are related to the exponential blow-up occurring when considering all possible serialisations of a parallel execution.

More recent proposals, like *predictive runtime-analysis*, are based on ad hoc combinations of static and dynamic approaches. These techniques consist in extending the results obtained at runtime when observing a given parallel execution to a set of valid serialisations, corresponding to execution sequences that have not been observed, but that could have occurred. Thus, this set can be seen as a *slice* of the target program, computed from a single execution. However, most of the existing predictive runtime-analysis techniques focus on the effects of *coarse-grain* parallelism, introduced by inter-thread scheduling. This scheduling influences the execution order of concurrent eligible threads. Its decisions depend on non-controllable events (e.g., I/O latency), and therefore other interleavings could occur and they are taken into account by the analysis.

Another source of conflict is produced by the "simultaneous" execution of multiple instructions by several processors. Here, the conflicting accesses are (implicitly) solved by the execution platform, and this behaviour escapes from the program level. A possible way to handle this *fine-grain* parallelism is to rely on dedicated hardware elements, allowing to monitor the current execution at a very low level. Thus, specific architectures for dynamic information-flow tracking have been proposed.

In this paper we review some representative works (section 2) illustrating the information-flow analysis techniques stated above and we identify their benefits and limitations. The focus is essentially put on dynamic analysis techniques, and therefore we present some of the monitoring techniques available (section 3) and their use in the context of multi-core executions. Then, we propose a predictive approach (section 4) to address fine-grain parallelism effects, without requiring a specific architecture. Finally, we give some conclusions and perspectives (section 5).

2   Information-Flow Analysis of Multi-threaded Programs

The importance of information flow has captured the interest of researchers working in various domains of computer systems. Starting from hardware, where special architectures have been conceived ([1,2,3]) to operating systems ([4]) and up to the application layer which is dominated by *static* and *dynamic* approaches detailed hereafter.

2.1   Static Analysis Techniques

Static approaches usually reason on source code level. For instance, a possible approach to secure a program execution against information leakage is to promote *type-safe* languages, as proposed by [5,6], to guarantee *by construction* secure information flows. In some cases these languages include primitives for multi-threaded development ([7,8]).

Regarding general static analysis techniques, a work direction was to extend the data-flow analysis techniques used for sequential code while avoiding the "interleaving explosion problem" mentioned in the introduction. A first way to address this problem was to take into account restricted forms of parallelism, like in [9] (no parallel loops) or in [10] (*cobegin/coend* primitives). However, an important step was made in [11]. In this work the authors proposed to consider a sub-class of data-flow analysis problems, the so-called *bit-vector problems*. They define an efficient generalisation of (unidirectional) bit-vector analysis to static parallel programs which faithfully captures the effect of inter-thread dependencies without requiring to enumerate each possible interleavings. The key assumption is to consider bit-vector properties that are *generated* on an execution trace by a *single* transition of the control-flow graph (and not by a combination of transitions). This allows to reduce the effects of inter-thread dependencies at the instruction level, without taking into account whole execution paths occurring in other threads. Note that this category of bit-vector problems is large enough to encompass many interesting properties, including information-flow analysis. More recently, this solution has been extended to deal with dynamic synchronisation primitives [12].

Other existing solutions for information-flow analysis rely on the computation of so-called "Program Dependency Graphs" (PDGs) to express data dependencies. PDGs for concurrent programs were first proposed in [13], based on the computation of *may-happen-in-parallel* (MHP) relations to approximate the effects of concurrent access to shared variables. Precise computations of MHP relations are known to be expensive. However, this static approach has been used in several works dedicated to information flow analysis ([14,15]).

2.2 Dynamic Analysis Techniques

Dynamic approaches may look more appealing for analysing multi-threaded applications. However, they require some instrumentation facilities to track information flows at execution time. There are several frameworks available (such as [16,17,18]) that facilitate the implementation of dynamic monitoring tools. More details about these frameworks are presented in section 3.

An interesting class of dynamic analysis techniques is the so-called *predictive runtime-analysis* category. They consist in observing/monitoring a single parallel execution sequence σ (as for sequential programs), and then to *generalise* the results obtained to other execution sequences corresponding to possible interleavings of σ (i.e., that could have been observed if another valid schedule occurred). This gives a kind of *program slice* of reasonable size, that can be handled by various techniques like static analysis [19], or even test generation [20]. Depending on the approach chosen to generalise the observed trace (and to represent the resulting set of serialisations), the program slice obtained may over-approximate or under-approximate the concrete program behaviour. A short survey on such runtime prediction techniques is provided in [21], together with a precise trace generalisation model.

Dynamic analysis techniques are widely used in the context of multi-threaded applications for runtime error detection like deadlocks ([22,23]) and data races ([24,25]. Although detecting data races could be useful for information-flow analysis, it is not sufficient as such. Hence, more focused analyses are developed to deal with malware detection ([26,27]) and enforcement of security policies ([28,29]).

3 Building Tools for Dynamic Analysis

Building dynamic analysis tools necessitates integrating some monitoring facilities to the analysed application. Monitoring features are added either at source code level or binary level, either statically or dynamically. Waddington et al. [30] present a survey on these techniques.

Instrumentation code is often added statically in applications as implicit logging instructions. It necessitates access to the source code and can be added accordingly by the developers (which is a tedious and error-prone procedure) or automatically. To automate this process source-to-source transformations can be applied, for instance using aspect-oriented programming. Apart from the source level, static instrumentation can also be applied directly at the binary level, e.g., using frameworks like Dyninst [17]. Hereafter we take a closer look to dynamic binary instrumentation (DBI) techniques.

3.1 Dynamic Binary Instrumentation

In general, DBI frameworks consist of a front-end and a back-end. The front-end is an API allowing to specify instrumentation code and the points at which it should be introduced at runtime. The back-end introduces instrumentation at the specified positions and provides all necessary information to the front-end.

There are two main approaches for controlling the monitored application: *emulation* and *just-in-time* (JIT) instrumentation. The emulation approach consists in executing the application on a *virtual machine* while the JIT approach consists in linking the instrumentation framework dynamically with the monitored application and inject instrumentation code at runtime.

Valgrind [18] is a representative framework applying the emulation approach. The analysed program is first translated into an intermediate representation (IR). This IR is architecture independent, which makes it more comfortable to write generic tools. The modified IR is then translated into binary code for the execution platform. Translating code to and from the IR is time consuming. The penalty in execution time is approximately four to five times (with respect to an un-instrumented execution).

Pin [16] is a widely used framework which gains momentum in analysing multi-threaded programs running on multi-core platforms. Pin and the analysed application are loaded together. Pin is responsible of intercepting the applications instructions and analysing or modifying them as described by the instrumentation code written in so-called pintools. Integration of Pin is almost transparent to the executed application.

The pintools use the frameworks front-end to control the application. Instrumentation can be easily added at various granularity levels from function call level down to processor instructions. An interface exists for accessing abstract instructions common to all architectures. If needed more architecture specific analyses can be implemented using specific APIs. In this case the analysis written is limited to executables of that specific architecture.

Adapting a DBI framework to parallel architectures is not straight forward. Hazelwood et al. [31] point out the difficulties in implementing a framework that scales well in a parallel environment and present how they overcame them in the implementation of Pin. As mentioned in their article, extra care is taken to allow frequently accessed code or data to be updated by one thread without blocking the others. Despite all this effort in some cases the instrumenter will inevitably serialise the threads execution or preempt them.

Another challenging issue is writing parallel analysis. The monitored data must also be updated in parallel, and data races on the monitored data should be eliminated.

3.2 Hardware-Based Monitoring Techniques

The software instrumentation techniques described in the previous section suffer from practical limitations in a multi-thread context. In particular:

- they may introduce a rather huge time overhead (making the execution between 10 and 100 times slower [32,18,33]);
- they do not take into account the specific features of a multi-core execution;
- they do not exploit as much as possible all the computational resources of the execution platform.

To overcome these limitations, especially in the context of instruction-grain monitoring, several proposals have been made to introduce some dedicated hardware mechanisms. We discuss here some of these proposals.

First of all, let us recall that instruction grain monitoring is based on several steps:

- capturing the relevant events after each executed instruction;
- propagating these events to the monitor process (event streaming);
- updating the meta-data (or shadow memory);
- executing the appropriate checks.

Each of these steps is a potential source of overhead, and techniques have been proposed to optimise them at the hardware level.

Some of these acceleration techniques are not specific to multi-core executions. For instance Venkataramani et al. [34] proposes to add some extra pipeline stage to perform metadata updates and checks, [35,36] improves the management of metadata through micro-architectural changes. Another option is to reduce the binary instrumentation cost by means of special registers [37], or using cache line tags to trigger event handlers [38].

Regarding multi-core platforms, one of the main proposals is to take advantage of the processors availability to dedicate one (or several) cores to the monitoring task. This idea has been implemented for two typical instruction-level monitoring problems.

Shetty et al. [39] propose in their work a monitoring technique dedicated to memory bugs (e.g., memory leaks, unallocated memory errors, etc.). Its principle is to associate a *monitoring thread* to each *application thread*. On a multi-core platform, both threads can run in parallel on distinct cores. To improve the 2-way communication between these threads, dedicated FIFO buffers are used (instead of using shared memory): one buffer for check requests, and one buffer for check reports. When one of these buffers is full/empty the application/monitoring thread is stalled. Moreover, since the duty cycle of the monitoring thread may be low[1], it can be suspended at any time. Other optimisations include the use of a separate L2 cache for the monitoring thread in order to reduce cache contention. Evaluation results show a monitoring overhead less than 50%, depending on the considered architecture.

The work of Nagarajan et al. [40] aims to *enforce* taint-based security policies. The idea is to use a dedicated thread as a "shadow execution" to keep the taint value of each register and memory locations of the application thread. This monitoring thread interrupts the application thread when the taint policy is violated. Here again, the main difficulties are to keep synchronised both threads and to ensure communication between them. As in [39], a FIFO buffer is used. A specific problem is to correctly react in case of policy violation to ensure fail-safety (i.e., to stop the execution as soon as possible). The solution proposed uses a 2-way communication between the two threads before each *critical* operation (with respect to the policy considered).

---

[1] It may not be the case when monitoring other properties.

Finally, a more recent work [41] advocates the use of so-called *log-based architecture* as a suitable trade-off between *efficiency* (how reduced is the monitoring overhead) and *genericity* (how general is the monitoring support). In this proposal, each core is considered as a log producer/consumer during the execution. When an instruction is executed on producer core, a (compressed) *record* is computed to store relevant information (program counter, instruction type, operand identifiers and/or addresses). Each record may correspond to one or more events on the consumer side. Record transmission is achieved using a large (up to 1MB) log buffer. As a consequence, an implicit synchronisation occurs between producer and consumer threads when the buffer is full or empty (in the former case the application is stalled). This may introduce a (bounded) lag between the time a bug occurs, and the time it is detected. To improve metadata (e.g., taint values) tracking, another feature is to associate a (small) shadow register to each data register in order to store the addresses from which it inherits (rather than the data itself). This choice makes the tracking more general (suitable for more applications) while keeping it efficient. In addition, to reduce the numbers of checks, a dedicated event cache is used (when an event hits the cache it is considered as redundant and discarded). Finally, a rather sophisticated metadata memory layout is provided, with a new instruction allowing to directly translate a data address to its metadata counterpart.

Experiments performed in [42] with this architecture on several monitoring applications (taint analysis, data race detection, memory checking) show an overhead smaller than 50% can be obtained for CPU-intensive applications.

4   Extended Information-Flow Analysis

We present in this section an alternative approach to perform dynamic analysis on a multi-core execution. This approach fits in the category of (over-approximative) predictive runtime-analysis. Its purpose is to extend the results obtained from the observation of a (parallel) execution sequence $\sigma_{\parallel}$ to the set of all serialised execution sequences corresponding to valid interleavings of $\sigma_{\parallel}$. The interleaving we consider here are essentially the ones produced by "side effects" introduced by the execution platform. The goal is to extend an observed execution $\sigma_{\parallel}$ such that the effects of the hardware it was executed on are captured.

In fact, when executing an application in parallel on several cores, platform-related effects may "obfuscate" the observed execution trace $\sigma_{\parallel}$. This may happen for instance due to a cache miss which could delay the effect of an observed instruction to a shared memory location. Similarly, small local overheads introduced by the monitoring probes or by I/O operations may slightly perturb the execution schedule (i.e., the sets of concurrently executed instructions), changing the sequence of (shared) memory updates. As a result, one can legitimately consider that the observation of $\sigma_{\parallel}$ does not fully nor accurately represent a real (non monitored) parallel execution.

A possible way to take into account this uncertainty in the observed execution sequence, is to assume the existence of a bounded time interval δ, during which the effects of instructions executed by concurrent threads may interleave. This value δ depends on the execution platform we consider. We present hereafter the method we propose for taking into account all these possible serialisations of $\sigma_{\parallel}$ during a dynamic information-flow analysis.

4.1   The "butterfly" Approach

The method we propose is partially inspired by the work proposed in [42]. We summarise here what are the main similarities and differences between these two approaches.

The main objective of [42] is to provide a *lifeguard* mechanism for (multi-threaded) applications running on multi-core architectures. It is a runtime enforcement technique, which consists in monitoring a running application to raise an alarm (or interrupt the execution) when an error occurs (e.g., writing to an unallocated memory). The main difficulty is to make the lifeguard reasoning about the *set* of parallel executions. To solve this issue, the authors considered (monitored) executions produced on specific machine architectures [41] on which *heartbeats* can be sent regularly as *synchronisation barriers*, to each core. This execution model can be captured by a notion of *uncertainty epochs*, corresponding to code fragments such that a *strict happens-before* execution relation holds between non-adjacent epochs. These assumptions allow to define a conservative data-flow analysis, based on sliding window principle, taking into account a superset of the interleaving that could occur in three consecutive epochs. The result of this analysis is then used to feed the lifeguard monitor. This approach can be used to check various properties like use-after-free errors or unexpected tainted variable propagation.

Our objectives are not the same. Our intention is to provide some *verdict* to be used in a property oriented test-based validation technique for multi-core architectures. As such, our solution does not need to be necessarily conservative: false negatives are not a critical issue. A consequence is that we do not require any specific architecture (nor heartbeat mechanism) at execution time. Another main distinction is that we may proceed in a *post-mortem* approach: we first produce log files which record information produced at runtime, then this information is analysed to provide various test verdicts (depending on the property under test). This makes the analysis more flexible by decoupling the execution part and the property checking part. From a more technical point of view, we also introduced some differences in the data-flow analysis itself. In particular we considered a sliding window of two epochs (instead of three). From our point view, this makes the algorithms simpler, without sacrificing efficiency. Finally, a further contribution is that we take into account the information provided by mutex locks to reduce the number of false positives.

4.2 A Window-Based Information Flow Analysis

We present here the basis of our window-based dynamic information-flow analysis. More details can be found in [43]. Its goal is to extend the analysis verdict of σ_0 (the observed serialisation) to a set of valid serialisations σ_δ, where δ is a platform-dependent time interval representing the (maximal) overlap between instruction sequences executed in parallel. The main concern is to avoid the whole enumeration of this set. To that end, we use a *sliding window-based* approach. Each window contains a set of concurrent instruction sequences belonging to the active threads (the ones currently executing on a given core). The analysis technique consists in summarising the parallel execution up to the current window $\mathcal{W}$, and to update this summary by taking into account the effects of possible serialisations of the execution sequences belonging to $\mathcal{W}$. This update is performed by means of iterative fix-point algorithms, as explained below.

To properly define each window, we time slice σ_0 using arbitrary time intervals greater than δ. We call these time slices *epochs*. However, instructions at the boundaries of adjacent epochs (hence within a time distance smaller than δ) may interleave, according to our hypothesis. To take this into account we define windows of size two epochs, and we extend the interleaving assumption such that all instructions of a window may interleave. This extension ensures that our analysis results will actually capture the serialisations of a set σ_s, where $\sigma_s \supseteq \sigma_\delta$.

Fig 1 illustrates the parallel execution of two threads (A and B). The dots represent instructions. Each instruction can be identified by a triplet (l, t, j) where l is the epoch it was executed in, t is the thread that executed it and j is an identifier of the instruction inside t. Instructions executed by the same thread in an epoch are surrounded by a box which is a basic block identified as (l, t). The arrows originating from the (highlighted) instruction (l_b, B, i) illustrates our interleaving assumptions. We can note at the boundary between epochs l_h and l_b the definition of the time interval δ. The solid arrows capture the serialisations of (l_b, B, i) for all σ_δ and the dashed arrows the extended serialisations of (l_b, B, i) in σ_s.

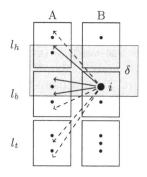

Fig. 1. Interleaving assumptions

4.3 Iterative Information Flow Computation

As explained above, processing a window of two epochs means computing the effects produced by all possible serialisations of the parallel instruction sequences it contains (since all these serialisations are considered as valid). To do so, we use an iterative fix-point computation algorithm. This algorithm proceeds as follows:

- First, we define a sequential data-flow analysis of the property under check. This property could be for instance a taint-analysis, a memory consistency checking, a null-pointer analysis, etc. An important requirement is that this data-flow analysis should be expressed as a bit-vector problem (which is in fact the case for most of the analysis used in practice). Running this sequential data-flow analysis on a single thread t allows to update a given initial summary S_0 (expressed as a *state vector*) into a a new summary S_1^t.
- Since threads are not independent (they may share memory locations), the sequential analysis ran on each thread should be combined with the others. In other words, results produced by executing instruction (l, t, i) should be made available to all instructions (l, t', j) of the window for $t \neq t'$ (according to our assumptions). This could be achieved by *running again* each sequential analysis on each thread t, starting now from an initial state $S_1 = \cup_{t \neq t'} S_1^t$.
- This step is repeated as long as the summary is changed. Since we consider bit-vector problems, this process will eventually reach a fix-point.

This algorithm can be implemented using two generic procedures: a first one (vertical step) iterates the sequential analysis over each thread, the second one (horizontal step) runs the vertical step along the two epochs of the window. Since adjacent epochs may also interleave, the vertical step should be repeated until a (window-level) fix-point is reached. Depending on the analysis under consideration, further processing may be required to "clean up" the results produced (removing the effects of some non valid execution sequences).

It has been showed in [43] that for a taint-analysis:

- this algorithm detects all tainted variables;
- the set of variables detected can be split into *strongly tainted* variables (corresponding to variables really tainted), and *weakly tainted* variables (potential false positives). These false positives are due to our sliding window techniques which may over-approximate the set of valid serialisations across several windows.

4.4 Experimental Results

The window-based methodology we presented can be applied both at runtime or off-line as a post-mortem analysis. We have implemented a tool chain for taint analysis using a post-mortem approach. The tool necessitates the source code of the multi-threaded application (written in C using *pthreads* library). Instrumentation code is added as logging instructions via a source to source transformation. At execution time log files are generated containing address information on assignments.

For taint analysis the summary actually contains variables that can be tainted through a valid serialisation up to the preceding window. The window analysis must hence infer local serialisations (of instructions in window) which either taint new variables or untaint some existing. The serialisations are discovered through the iterative algorithm. Some special care must be taken though on how *gen/kill* information is propagated and how the summary of a window is computed.

Experimental results on small handcrafted benchmarks using five threads racing for access to a shared data structure show an overhead of 50% for producing the log files. The taint-analysis then takes less than 1 second to analyse about 5000 log lines on a Intel i3 CPU @2.4GHz with 3GB of RAM.

5 Conclusion

In this work we have discussed some issues regarding dynamic information-flow monitoring of multi-thread applications running on multi-core architectures. We gave a brief overview of the main existing techniques and underlying tools considered so far to address this issue. The general concerns are to limit the monitoring overhead at runtime, to avoid the explicit exploration of all possible execution sequence interleavings, and to propose general enough frameworks (able to handle various kinds of analysis). In our opinion, two directions are rather promising:

- runtime-prediction techniques, which allow to extend the results produced by a single (parallel) execution to a whole program slice consisting of valid "neighbour" executions;
- hardware-level optimisations of the monitoring techniques.

The former solution can be used in a general context, for instance in a test-based approach where the goal is to evaluate the "robustness" of the application on various execution conditions. The later solution is better suited for specific applications (e.g., with strong security or reliability requirements), and it provides an integrated hardware/software monitoring and enforcement framework.

We also proposed a prospective runtime-prediction technique. Its purpose is to deal explicitly with fine-grain interleavings produced by the multi-core execution platform. Experimental results obtained so far for taint-analysis are encouraging in terms of performance. Further work is now required to extend the prototype and consider other kinds of analysis.

References

1. Chow, J., Pfaff, B., Garfinkel, T., Christopher, K., Rosenblum, M.: Understanding data lifetime via whole system simulation. In: Proceedings of the 13th Conference on USENIX Security Symposium, SSYM 2004, vol. 13, pp. 22–22. USENIX Association, Berkeley (2004)

2. Crandall, J.R., Wu, S.F., Chong, F.T.: Minos: Architectural support for protecting control data. ACM Trans. Archit. Code Optim. 3(4), 359–389 (2006)

3. Suh, G.E., Lee, J.W., Zhang, D., Devadas, S.: Secure program execution via dynamic information flow tracking. SIGARCH Comput. Archit. News 32(5), 85–96 (2004)

4. Clemente, P., Rouzaud-Cornabas, J., Toinard, C.: Transactions on computational science xi, pp. 131–161. Springer, Heidelberg (2010)

5. Volpano, D., Smith, G.: A type-based approach to pro-gram security. In: Proceedings of the 7th International Joint Conference on the Theory and Practice of Software Development, pp. 607–621. Springer (1997)

6. Sabelfeld, A., Myers, A.C.: Language-based information-flow security. IEEE Journal on Selected Areas in Communications 21 (2003)

7. Barthe, G., Rezk, T., Russo, A., Sabelfeld, A.: Security of multithreaded programs by compilation. ACM Trans. Inf. Syst. Secur. 13(3), 21:1–21:32 (2010)

8. Smith, G., Volpano, D.: Secure information flow in a multi-threaded imperative language. In: Proceedings of the 25th ACM SIGPLAN-SIGACT Symposium on Principles of Programming Languages, POPL 1998, pp. 355–364. ACM, New York (1998)

9. Grunwald, D., Srinivasan, H.: Data flow equations for explicitly parallel programs. In: PPOPP. ACM (1993)

10. Krinke, J.: Static slicing of threaded programs. SIGPLAN (1998)

11. Knoop, J., Bernhard, S., Vollmer, J.: Parallelism for free: efficient and optimal bitvector analyses for parallel programs. ACM Trans. Program. Lang. Syst. (1996)

12. Farzan, A., Kincaid, Z.: Compositional Bitvector Analysis for Concurrent Programs with Nested Locks. In: Cousot, R., Martel, M. (eds.) SAS 2010. LNCS, vol. 6337, pp. 253–270. Springer, Heidelberg (2010)

13. Krinke, J.: Context-sensitive slicing of concurrent programs. SIGSOFT (2003)

14. Hammer, C.: Information flow control for java based on path conditions in dependence graphs. In: Secure Software Engineering. IEEE Computer Society (2006)

15. Liu, Y., Milanova, A.: Static information flow analysis with handling of implicit flows and a study on effects of implicit flows vs explicit flows. In: Software Maintenance and Reengineering. IEEE Computer Society (2010)

16. Luk, C.K., Cohn, R., Muth, R., Patil, H., Klauser, A., Lowney, G., Wallace, S., Reddi, V.J., Hazelwood, K.: Pin: building customized program analysis tools with dynamic instrumentation. In: Proceedings of the 2005 ACM SIGPLAN Conference on Programming Language Design and Implementation, PLDI 2005, pp. 190–200. ACM, New York (2005)

17. Buck, B., Hollingsworth, J.K.: An api for runtime code patching. The International Journal of High Performance Computing Applications 14, 317–329 (2000)

18. Nethercote, N., Seward, J.: Valgrind: A framework for heavyweight dynamic binary instrumentation. In: Proceedings of ACM SIGPLAN 2007 Conference on Programming Language Design and Implementation (PLDI 2007), San Diego, California, USA, pp. 89–100 (June 2007)

19. Ganai, M.K., Wang, C.: Interval Analysis for Concurrent Trace Programs Using Transaction Sequence Graphs. In: Barringer, H., Falcone, Y., Finkbeiner, B., Havelund, K., Lee, I., Pace, G., Roşu, G., Sokolsky, O., Tillmann, N. (eds.) RV 2010. LNCS, vol. 6418, pp. 253–269. Springer, Heidelberg (2010)

20. Kundu, S., Ganai, M.K., Wang, C.: CONTESSA: Concurrency Testing Augmented with Symbolic Analysis. In: Touili, T., Cook, B., Jackson, P. (eds.) CAV 2010. LNCS, vol. 6174, pp. 127–131. Springer, Heidelberg (2010)

21. Wang, C., Ganai, M.: Predicting Concurrency Failures in the Generalized Execution Traces of x86 Executables. In: Khurshid, S., Sen, K. (eds.) RV 2011. LNCS, vol. 7186, pp. 4–18. Springer, Heidelberg (2012)

22. Li, T., Ellis, C.S., Lebeck, A.R., Sorin, D.J.: Pulse: a dynamic deadlock detection mechanism using speculative execution. In: Proceedings of the Annual Conference on USENIX Annual Technical Conference, ATEC 2005, p. 3. USENIX Association, Berkeley (2005)

23. Castillo, M., Farina, F., Cordoba, A.: A dynamic deadlock detection/resolution algorithm with linear message complexity. In: Proceedings of the 2012 20th Euromicro International Conference on Parallel, Distributed and Network-based Processing, PDP 2012, pp. 175–179. IEEE Computer Society, Washington, DC (2012)

24. Savage, S., Burrows, M., Nelson, G., Sobalvarro, P., Anderson, T.: Eraser: a dynamic data race detector for multithreaded programs. ACM Trans. Comput. Syst. 15(4), 391–411 (1997)

25. Serebryany, K., Iskhodzhanov, T.: Threadsanitizer: data race detection in practice. In: Proceedings of the Workshop on Binary Instrumentation and Applications, WBIA 2009, pp. 62–71. ACM, New York (2009)

26. Bayer, U., Kirda, E., Kruegel, C.: Improving the efficiency of dynamic malware analysis. In: Proceedings of the 2010 ACM Symposium on Applied Computing, SAC 2010, pp. 1871–1878. ACM, New York (2010)

27. Egele, M., Scholte, T., Kirda, E., Kruegel, C.: A survey on automated dynamic malware-analysis techniques and tools. ACM Comput. Surv. 44(2), 6:1–6:42 (2008)

28. Zhu, D.Y., Jung, J., Song, D., Kohno, T., Wetherall, D.: Tainteraser: protecting sensitive data leaks using application-level taint tracking. SIGOPS Oper. Syst. Rev. 45(1), 142–154 (2011)

29. Cristia, M., Mata, P.: Runtime enforcement of noninterference by duplicating processes and their memories. In: WSEGI (2009)

30. Waddington, Roy, Schmidt: Dynamic analysis and profiling of multi-threaded systems

31. Hazelwood, K., Lueck, G., Cohn, R.: Scalable support for multithreaded applications on dynamic binary instrumentation systems. In: Proceedings of the 2009 International Symposium on Memory Management, ISMM 2009, pp. 20–29. ACM, New York (2009)

32. Nethercote, N.: Dynamic Binary Analysis and Instrumentation. PhD thesis, Computer Laboratory, University of Cambridge, United Kingdom (November 2004)

33. Uh, G.R., Cohn, R., Yadavalli, B., Peri, R., Ayyagari, R.: Analyzing dynamic binary instrumentation overhead. In: Workshop on Binary Instrumentation and Application, San Jose, CA (October 2007)

34. Venkataramani, G., Roemer, B., Solihin, Y., Prvulovic, M.: Memtracker: Efficient and programmable support for memory access monitoring and debugging. In: Proceedings of the 2007 IEEE 13th International Symposium on High Performance Computer Architecture, HPCA 2007, pp. 273–284. IEEE Computer Society, Washington, DC (2007)

35. Suh, G.E., Lee, J.W., Zhang, D., Devadas, S.: Secure program execution via dynamic information flow tracking. SIGPLAN Not. 39(11), 85–96 (2004)

36. Venkataramani, G., Doudalis, I., Solihin, Y., Prvulovic, M.: Flexitaint: A programmable accelerator for dynamic taint propagation. In: 14th International Symposium on High Performance Computer Architecture (2008)

37. Corliss, M.L., Lewis, E.C., Roth, A.: Dise: a programmable macro engine for customizing applications. SIGARCH Comput. Archit. News 31(2), 362–373 (2003)

38. Zhou, Y., Zhou, P., Qin, F., Liu, W., Torrellas, J.: Efficient and flexible architectural support for dynamic monitoring. ACM Trans. Archit. Code Optim. 2(1), 3–33 (2005)
39. Shetty, R., Kharbutli, M., Solihin, Y., Prvulovic, M.: Heapmon: a helper-thread approach to programmable, automatic, and low-overhead memory bug detection. IBM J. Res. Dev. 50(2/3), 261–275 (2006)
40. Nagarajan, V., Kim, H.-S., Wu, Y.: Gupta, R.: Dynamic information flow tracking on multicores. In: Workshop on Interaction between Compilers and Computer Architectures, Salt Lake City (February 2008)
41. Chen, S., Kozuch, M., Strigkos, T., Falsafi, B., Gibbons, P.B., Mowry, T.C., Ramachandran, V., Ruwase, O., Ryan, M., Vlachos, E.: Flexible hardware acceleration for instruction-grain program monitoring. In: Proceedings of the 35th Annual International Symposium on Computer Architecture, ISCA 2008, pp. 377–388. IEEE Computer Society, Washington, DC (2008)
42. Goodstein, M.L., Vlachos, E., Chen, S., Gibbons, P.B., Kozuch, M.A., Mowry, T.C.: Butterfly analysis: adapting dataflow analysis to dynamic parallel monitoring. In: Proceedings of the Fifteenth Edition of ASPLOS on Architectural Support for Programming Languages and Operating Systems, ASPLOS 2010, pp. 257–270. ACM, New York (2010)
43. Sifakis, E., Mounier, L.: Extended dynamic taint analysis of multi-threaded applications. Technical Report TR-2012-08, VERIMAG, University of Grenoble (June 2012)

Bounded-Interference Sequentialization
for Testing Concurrent Programs*

Niloofar Razavi[1], Azadeh Farzan[1], and Andreas Holzer[2]

[1] University of Toronto
[2] Vienna University of Technology

Abstract. Testing concurrent programs is a challenging problem: (1) the tester
has to come up with a set of input values that *may* trigger a bug, and (2) even
with a bug-triggering input value, there may be a large number of interleavings
that need to be explored. This paper proposes an approach for testing concurrent
programs that explores both input and interleaving spaces in a systematic way. It
is based on a program transformation technique that takes a concurrent program
P as an input and generates a sequential program that simulates a subset of behaviours of P. It is then possible to use an available sequential testing tool to test
the resulting sequential program. We introduce a new interleaving selection technique, called *bounded-interference*, which is based on the idea of limiting the degree of interference from other threads. The transformation is sound in the sense
that any bug discovered by a sequential testing tool in the sequential program is a
bug in the original concurrent program. We have implemented our approach into
a prototype tool that tests concurrent C# programs. Our experiments show that
our approach is effective in finding both previously known and new bugs.

1 Introduction

Testing concurrent programs is notoriously difficult. There is often a large number of interleavings that need to be tested and an exhaustive search is mostly infeasible. Several
recent heuristics have been proposed to limit the search in the set of concurrent interleavings, to a manageable subset. Focusing on interleavings that contain races [17,15,7]
or violate atomicity [14,22,19,23,13] are examples of these heuristics. These techniques
have been successful in finding bugs in concurrent programs. However, there are currently two main limitations in concurrent testing techniques: (1) they do not include
any input generation mechanisms, and have to rely on a given set of inputs as a starting
point, and (2) they usually do not provide meaningful coverage guarantees to the tester
in the same sense that sequential testing tools provide various standardized coverage
guarantees.

Recent successful sequential testing tools, such as DART [8] and PEX [20], have
mostly overcome both limitations mentioned above. They employ symbolic execution
techniques to explore the space of possible inputs in a *systematic* way [11]. This enables
these tools to explore the program code (or code parts such as branches, statements, and

---

* Supported in part by the Austrian National Research Network S11403-N23 (RiSE) of the Austrian Science Fund (FWF), and by the Vienna Science and Technology Fund (WWTF) grant
PROSEED.

T. Margaria and B. Steffen (Eds.): ISoLA 2012, Part I, LNCS 7609, pp. 372–387, 2012.

sometimes even paths) in a *systematic* way by generating custom input values, which in turn makes it possible for them to provide guarantees for standard code coverage criteria such as branch coverage or statement coverage.

Most concurrency testing tools expect a set of inputs to be available as a starting point for the testing process, and do not contain a mechanism to generate new inputs to use. This has two important ramifications: (i) These techniques have to rely on the provided input (or set of inputs) to have the potential to lead to existing program errors; otherwise, errors will be overlooked. (ii) Since the input set is not generated in a *systematic* way, the testing tool can hardly quantify the extent of coverage that the testing provides. In fact, the latter problem goes beyond the input space for most concurrency testing techniques, that scarcely perform a *systematic* exploration of the interleaving space of concurrent programs, even if we overlook the input problem. By relying on a given set of inputs, the best guarantee that they can provide is of the form: "no errors exist in the program if executions are limited to the selected set of interleavings (by the heuristic of choice) and inputs are limited to the set which was used for testing".

The goal of our work is to provide a systematic way of testing concurrent programs. We introduce a new interleaving selection heuristic called *bounded-interference*, that incrementally explores the space of concurrent program interleavings by increasing the degree of *interference* from other threads. When a thread reads from a shared variable a value written by another thread, we consider that an *interference* from the writer thread. A remarkable property of *bounded-interference* is that, since it is defined from the point of view of flow of data between threads (in contrast to the control-based notions such as bounded context-switching), it can be very naturally incorporated into a setting in which the search for the right input and the suitable interleaving can be conducted side by side. This will allow our testing approach to provide a greater assurance of correctness and reliability of the tested program, in the form of (clearly defined) coverage measures for our testing approach. Moreover, we take advantage of the great progress that has been made in sequential testing, by formulating the solution as *sequentializaiton* technique. We transform the concurrent program (under test) into a sequential program that can be tested using standard sequential testing tools. Our program transformation effectively defers both the input generation and interleaving selection tasks to the sequential testing tool, by effectively encoding both as inputs to the newly generated sequential program. All interleavings with a certain degree of interference are encoded into the generated sequential program, but the choice of which interleaving to follow is left as a choice determined by values of newly introduced input variables. This way, we employ the systematic testing algorithm of a sequential tester to achieve a more systematic testing technique for concurrent programs.

The idea behind the program transformation is as follow. Consider a concurrent program P consisting of two threads T and T'. Let us assume that testing T sequentially leads to no error, but composed with T', an error state can be reached in T. How can T' help direct the execution of T into an error state? A natural scenario is that T' can write certain values to shared variables that let T pass conditional statements (that would have been blocked otherwise) and execute down a path to an error state. One can imagine that these values are injected into the sequential execution of T when the shared variable reads are performed by T. This simple idea is the inspiration behind our program transformation. We choose a number k, and then select k shared variable reads in T to be the only ones among all reads of shared variable in T that are allowed to observe a value written by a write in T' (we call these reads *non-local reads*). This number k, in a sense, indicates a measure of diversion from a fully sequential execution of T towards a more concurrent execution and can be gradually incremented to find concurrent bugs involving more interference from T', i.e. higher number of non-local reads. Moreover, we do not choose these k non-local reads a priori; the specific selection becomes part of the resulting sequential program input and therefore, the sequential testing tool has the freedom to choose different non-local reads (through input selection) that will help find the error. Since the original program inputs (to P) are also preserved as inputs to the sequential program, the sequential testing tool has the potential to find the bug triggering values for these inputs as well.

We have implemented our program transformation technique into a prototype tool and tested a benchmark suite of concurrent C# programs. We found all previously known errors in these benchmarks, and found some new errors all within a very reasonable time and for $k \leq 3$.

In summary, the contributions of this paper are:

- A novel sequentialization approach tailored specifically towards testing concurrent programs, which does not assume a fixed input for concurrent programs and provides coverage guarantees after the testing process is finished.
- A novel interleaving selection technique, called bounded-interference, based on iteratively allowing more non-local reads, and the appropriate incorporation of this idea so that a backend sequential testing tool can explore all possibilities for the non-local reads and their corresponding writes, through the input generation.
- An effective way of encoding all feasible interleavings for a set of non-local reads and their corresponding writes as a set of constraints, and the use of SMT solvers to ensure the soundness of the approach (every error found is a real error) and to accommodate the reproducibility of the errors found.
- A prototype implementation that confirms the effectiveness of the approach and reports no false positives.

2   Motivating Examples

We use the Bluetooth driver (from [16]) as an example to illustrate the high level idea behind the bounded-interference approach. Figure 1 shows a simplified model of the Bluetooth driver. There are two dispatch functions called `Add` and `Stop`. `Add` is called by the operating system to perform I/O in the driver and `Stop` is called to stop the device. There are four shared variables: `pendingIO`, `stoppingFlag`, `stoppingEvent`, and `stopped`. The integer variable `pendingIO` is initialized to 1 and keeps track of the number of concurrently executing threads in the driver. It is incremented atomically whenever a thread enters the driver and is decremented atomically whenever it exits the driver. The boolean variable `stoppingFlag` is initialized to false and will be set to true to signal the closing of the device. New threads are not supposed to enter the driver once `stoppingFlag` is set to true. Variable `stoppingEvent` is initialized to false, and will be set to true after `pendingIO` becomes zero. Finally, stopped is initialized to false and will be set to true once the device is fully stopped; the thread stopping the driver sets it to true after it is established that there are no other threads running in the driver. Threads executing Add expect stopped to be false (assertion at line l_7) after they enter the driver.

```
Add
vars: int status, pIO;
l1 :  if (stoppingFlag)
l2 :      status = -1;
l3 :  else {
l4 :      atomic{ pendingIO++; }
l5 :      status = 0; }
l6 :  if (status == 0) {
l7 :      assert(stopped==false);
l8 :      //do work here }
l9 :  atomic {
l10 :     pendingIO--;
l11 :     pIO = pendingIO; }
l12 : if (pIO == 0)
l13 :     stoppingEvent = true;
```

```
Stop
vars: int pIO;
l'1 :  stoppingFlag = true;
l'2 :  atomic {
l'3 :    pendingIO--;
l'4 :    pIO = pendingIO; }
l'5 :  if (pIO == 0)
l'6 :    stoppingEvent = true;
l'7 :  assume(stoppingEvent==true);
l'8 :  stopped = true;
```

Fig. 1. The simplified model of Bluetooth driver [16]

Consider a concurrent program with two threads. Thread T executes Add and thread T' executes Stop. The assertion at l_7 in Add ensures that the driver is not stopped before T starts working inside the driver. It is easy to see that this assertion always passes if T is executed sequentially, i.e. without any interference from T'. Therefore, if the assertion at l_7 is to be violated, it will have to be with some help from T', where a shared variable read in T reads a value written by a write in T'; we call these reads *non-local* reads.

We start by digressing *slightly* from the fully sequential execution of T, by letting *one* read of a shared variable in T to be *non-local*. If the read from stoppingFlag in T reads the value written by T' at l'_1 then the assert statement at l_7 is not reachable. Selecting the read from pendingIO at l_4 as the non-local read, forces the read from stop in the assertion statement to read the initial value (i.e. false) and hence the assertion will be successful. If we select the read from stopped in the assertion statement as a non-local read (reading the value written by T' at l'_8), then the read from pendingIO in one of the threads has to be non-local as well. Therefore, the assertion cannot be violated by making only *one* read non-local, and we decide to digress more by allowing *two* reads of shared variables in T to be non-local.

With two non-local reads, the assertion can be falsified if the reads from pendingIO at l_4 and stopped at l_7 read the values written by T' at l'_3 and l'_8, respectively. Moreover, there exists a feasible interleaving (a real concurrent execution of the program) in which all other reads (in both T and T') are local; the execution is $l_1, l'_1, l'_2, l'_3, l'_4, l_3, l_4, l_5, l'_5, l'_6, l'_7, l'_8, l_6, l_7$.

We propose a sequentialization technique that for any k, transforms the concurrent program P, consisting of two threads T and T', into a sequential program $\widehat{P}_k$ such that every execution of $\widehat{P}_k$ corresponds to an execution of P in which exactly k reads of T are *non-local*, while all other reads are *local*. We then use a sequential testing tool to test $\widehat{P}_k$ for errors such as violations of assertions. In the above example, no errors can be found in $\widehat{P}_1$, but the assertion is violated in $\widehat{P}_2$. We will make these notions precise in the remainder of this paper.

3 Preliminaries

Sequential and Concurrent Programs. Figure 2 (a) presents the syntax of simple bounded sequential programs for the purpose of the presentation of ideas in this paper. We consider bounded programs while loops are unrolled for a bounded number of times. We handle dynamically allocated objects in our implementation, but for simplicity here we will limit the domains to integer and boolean types.

	$< seq\_pgm >$	::=	$< input\_decl >< var\_list >< method >^+$
	$< input\_decl >$	::=	inputs: $< var\_decl >^*$
	$< var\_list >$	::=	vars: $< var\_decl >^*$
	$< var\_decl >$	::=	int x; $\mid$ bool x; $\mid$ int[c] x; $\mid$ bool[c] x;
(a)	$< method >$	::=	$f(\overline{x}) \{ < var\_list >< stmt >; \}$
	$< stmt >$	::=	$< stmt >; < stmt >$ $\mid$ $< simple\_stmt >$ $\mid$ $< comp\_stmt >$
	$< simple\_stmt >$	::=	skip $\mid$ $x =< expr >$ $\mid$ $x = f(\overline{x})$ $\mid$ return x $\mid$ assume(b_expr) $\mid$ assert(b_expr)
	$< complex\_stmt >$	::=	if($< b\_expr >$) $\{< stmt >;\}$ else$\{< stmt >;\}$
(b)	$< conc\_pgm >$	::=	$< input\_decl >< var\_list >< init >< seq\_pgm >^+$
	$< init >$	::=	$< method >$
	$< complex\_stmt >$	::=	if ($< b\_expr >$) $\{ < stmt >; \}$ else $\{ < stmt >;\}$ $\mid$ lock (x) $\{< stmt >;\}$

Fig. 2. (a) Sequential (b) Concurrent Program Syntax

A sequential program has a list of inputs, a list of variables, and a list of methods that access the inputs and variables. We assume that every sequential program has a method, named `main`, from which it starts the execution. Each method has a list of input parameters, a list of local variables, and a sequence of statements. Statements are either simple (i.e. skip, assignment, call-by-value function call, return, assume, and assert) or complex (i.e. conditional statement).

We define a concurrent program (Figure 2 (b)) to be a finite collection of sequential programs (called threads) running in parallel. The sequential programs share some variables, and their inputs are included in the inputs of the concurrent program. Here, definition of the complex statement is augmented by lock statements as a synchronization mechanism for accessing shared variables. A lock statement consists of a sequence of statements which are executed after acquiring a lock on a shared variable x.

Each concurrent program has a method, `init` for initializing shared variables, and also for linking the inputs of the concurrent program to the inputs of the individual sequential programs (threads). The semantics of locking mechanism is standard; whenever a thread obtains a lock on a variable, other threads cannot acquire a lock on the same variable unless the thread releases the lock.

Program Traces. A concurrent program has a fixed number of threads $T = \{T_1, T_2, .., T_n\}$ and a set of variables shared between the threads, represented by SV. We also fix a subset of shared variables to be lock variables $L \subset SV$. The actions that a thread T_i can perform on the set of shared variables SV is defined as: $\Sigma_{T_i} = \{T_i{:}rd(x),\ T_i{:}wt(x) \mid x \in SV - L\} \cup \{T_i{:}acq(l),\ T_i{:}rel(l) \mid l \in L\}$.

Actions $T_i : rd(x)$ and $T_i : wt(x)$ are read and write actions to shared variable x, respectively. Action $T_i{:}acq(l)$ represents acquiring a lock on l and action $T_i{:}rel(l)$ represents releasing a lock on l by thread T_i. We define $\Sigma = \bigcup_{T_i \in T} \Sigma_{T_i}$ as the set of all actions. A word in Σ^*, which is an action sequence, represents an *abstract* execution of the program. The *occurrence* of actions are referred to as *events* in this paper. An event,

e_i, is a pair $\langle i, a \rangle$ where i is a natural number and a is the action performed. A program trace is a word $\langle 1, a_1 \rangle \ldots \langle m, a_m \rangle$ where $a_1 \ldots a_m$ is an action sequence of the program. A *feasible* trace of a concurrent program is a trace that corresponds to a real execution of the program. Any feasible trace respects the semantics of locking (is lock-valid), and implies a partial order on the set of events in the trace, known as program order. These are captured by the following two definitions ($\sigma|_A$ denotes the corresponding action sequence of σ projected to the letters in A).

Definition 1 (Lock-validity). *A trace $\sigma \in \Sigma^*$ is* lock-valid *if it respects the semantics of the locking mechanism. Formally, let $\Sigma_l = \{T_i: acquire(l), T_i: release(l) \mid T_i \in T\}$ denote the set of locking actions on lock l. Then σ is lock-valid if for every $l \in L$, $\sigma|_{\Sigma_l}$ is a prefix of $\left[\bigcup_{T_i \in T} (T_i: acquire(l) \; T_i: release(l)) \right]^*$*

Definition 2 (Program Order). *We define a total order on the set of events of each thread T_i, represented by $\sqsubseteq_i$. For any $e_j, e_k \in E$, if $e_j = \langle j, a \rangle$ and $e_k = \langle k, a \rangle$ belong to thread T and $j \leq k$, then $e_j \sqsubseteq_i e_k$. The union of the total orders in the threads form the program order $\sqsubseteq = \cup_{T_i \in T} \sqsubseteq_i$.*

4 From Concurrent to Sequential Programs

Let P be a bounded concurrent program consisting of two threads T and T', with an input set I. The goal is to check if the shared memory values produced by T' can be used to direct the execution of T to an error state. Given k, the number of *non-local* reads of shared variables in T, we transform P into a sequential program $\widehat{P}_k$, with an input set $\widehat{I}_k$ where $I \subset \widehat{I}_k$. Every execution of $\widehat{P}_k$ corresponds to at least one execution of P with exactly k non-local reads in T that observe values written by T' while all other reads are local. As we explain in Section 4.1, once k is fixed, there is a choice of which k reads to choose in T and which k writes to choose as their corresponding writes in T'. Program $\widehat{P}_k$ takes all of these choices as inputs. This means that any sequential testing tool that explores the input space to expose bugs will naturally try all possible combinations (within computation limits) to find the one leading to a bug.

The Figure on the right demonstrates the high level idea behind our transformation. The sequential program $\widehat{P}_k$ has two copies of shared variables; each thread reads/writes on its own copy. The dashed path in the figure illustrates how $\widehat{P}_k$ simulates the executions of P with k non-local reads in T. First, $\widehat{P}_k$ simulates the execution of T up to the first *non-local* read specified by the inputs (part (1) in the Figure). It then stops simulating T, and starts simulating the execution of T'

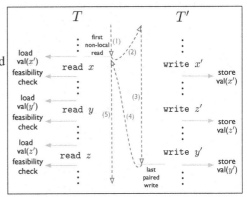

from the beginning until the first lock-free point where all writes that are supposed to produce values for non-local reads have occurred (parts (2) and (3)). Since T' is being executed using its own copy of shared variables, we need to remember the values written by such *paired* writes in some auxiliary variables and later load these values while the corresponding non-local reads are being performed. Then, $\widehat{P}_k$ goes back to simulating T, retrieving the value stored in the corresponding auxiliary variable as each non-local read is being performed (parts (4) and (5)).

Note that for some pairs of non-local reads and writes specified by the inputs of $\widehat{P}_k$ there may not exist any corresponding feasible trace of P. Therefore, we have to ensure that there exists a feasible trace of P which (1) *consists of the same events as in the execution of $\widehat{P}_k$*, (2) observes for each non-local read in T the value written by the corresponding write in T', and (3) where all reads other than the non-local reads are indeed local. To achieve this, all *global* events (accesses to shared variables, and synchronization events) are logged during the execution of $\widehat{P}_k$, and a set of constraints is generated that corresponds to the existence of a feasible trace. Every time that T performs a read from a shared variable, we use a call to an SMT solver to check for the satisfiability of these constraints (these points are marked as feasibility checks in Figure 4). If the feasibility check passes, it means that there exists a trace, with the same set of global events, in which the previous non-local reads are paired with the corresponding writes, and all other reads are paired with local writes. In this case, the execution of $\widehat{P}_k$ continues. Otherwise, the execution is abandoned to prevent exploring unreachable states. Note that the feasible trace may be different from the illustrated trace in Fig. 4 but since the interferences are limited to the non-local reads, the state of the program after passing each feasibility check in the illustrated trace would be the same as the state of the program in the corresponding feasible trace at that point. Therefore, it is just enough to ensure the existence of a feasible trace to be able to proceed the execution soundly.

In the remainder of this section, we precisely define the transformation that was informally described here.

4.1   Transformation Scheme

The Figure below illustrates the sequential program $\widehat{P}_k$ constructed based on P consisting of two threads T and T'. We assume that both T and T' are bounded sequential programs, and therefore, all reads from shared variables in T and all writes to shared variables in T' can be enumerated and identified. The input set of $\widehat{P}_k$ consists of I (inputs of P), and two arrays, rds and $wrts$, of size k where $rds[i]$ stores the id of the ith non-local read in T and $wrts[i]$ stores the id of the write in T' which is supposed to provide a value for $rds[i]$. These two arrays determine what reads in T will be non-local and what writes in T' will provide the values for them.

The sequential program $\widehat{P}_k$ has two copies of shared variables, G and G', so that T and T' operate on

```
inputs:  I; int[k] rds, wrts;    main() {    init() {
vars:    G; G';                  init();     //read-write assumptions
int[k] vals; bool allWsDone;     τ[T];       ...
bool[k] rDone, wDone;            }           initialize G and G';
                                             }
```

their own copy. Variable $vals$ is an array of size k, where $vals[i]$ stores the value written by $wrts[i]$. There are also two arrays of size k, named $rDone$ and $wDone$ such that $rDone[i]$ and $wDone[i]$ indicate whether the ith non-local read and its pairing write have occurred, respectively. The elements of these arrays are initialized to false. $wDone[i]$ and $rDone[i]$ become true when the write $wrts[i]$ and the read $rds[i]$ are performed, respectively. Later, we will explain how these arrays are used to ensure that the corresponding reads and writes show up in the execution of $\widehat{P}_k$.

As mentioned earlier, not all values provided by inputs for rds and $wrts$ arrays are acceptable. Therefore, the validity of the values of rds and $wrts$ is ensured through a set of assumption statements in the $init$ method, first. The assumptions ensure: (1) the non-local reads are ordered, i.e. $rds[i] < rds[i+1]$ for $1 \leq i < k$, and (2) for each non-local read ($rds[i]$) from shared variable x, the pairing write candidate ($wrts[i]$) should write to the same variable x. Note that in our transformation scheme, one always has the option of limiting the search space by allowing only a subset of reads in T to be non-local, and also by selecting only a subset of writes to the corresponding variable in T' as candidates for each non-local read.

The sequential program $\widehat{P}_k$ first calls the $init$ method which ensures that rds and $wrts$ satisfy the above assumptions and initializes both G and G' according to the $init$ method of P. Then, $\widehat{P}_k$ executes the transformed version of T (represented by $\tau[T]$). The transformed versions of T and T' use functions $append$ and $isFeasible$ that are required to check the existence of a feasible trace. Function $append$ adds to a log file the information about a global event, i.e. the identifier of the thread performing it, its type (read, write, lock acquiring and releasing), and the corresponding variable. At any point during the execution of $\widehat{P}_k$, this log provides the exact sequence of global events that occurred up to that point. Function $isFeasible$ checks whether the log can correspond to a *feasible* trace of program P (explained in Section 4.2). Figure 3 gives the transformation function τ for the statements of T.

Transformation Scheme for T.   The goal of the transformation is to let each read of a shared variable in T be a candidate for a *non-local* read, observing a value provided by a write in T'. When handling a (boolean) expression, we perform for each read r from a shared variable x a case distinction:

- r is selected as one of the non-local reads by inputs; in this case we distinguish the first such read ($rds[1]$) from all the other non-local reads, since T' has to be called before the first of the non-local reads is performed (see the dashed schedule presented in Figure 4). If r is the first non-local read, i.e., $r == rds[1]$ is true, the transformed version of T' is called first (represented by $\tau'[T']$). Then, by $\mathtt{assume}(allWsDone)$ we ensure that all writes in $wrts$ occurred during the execution of $\tau'[T']$. If r is the jth non-local read ($1 \leq j \leq k$), then x will read the value $vals[j]$ written by $wrts[j]$. Then, $rDone[j]$ is set to true (which is required when read $rds[j+1]$ is performed) and we log a write to x and a read from x to simulate a local write to x just before it is read. The read $rds[j]$ and the write $wrts[j]$ are now *paired*, and we need to ensure that a feasible concurrent trace exists. Therefore, we call $isFeasible(log)$ and stop the execution if no such feasible concurrent trace can be found.
- r is treated as a *local* read, since r doesn't belong to the input set rds; nothing needs to be done in this case other than calling $isFeasible(log)$, to make sure that a concurrent trace in which this read is paired with the most recent local write (while all previous non-local reads are paired with the corresponding writes) exists.

For each assignment statement we first transform the right-hand side expression, execute the assignment, and in case we write to a shared variable, we log a write event afterward. For a lock statement on variable x, a lock acquire and lock release event are logged just before and after the transformation of the lock body, respectively. Assume and assert

Fig. 3. Transformation scheme for T and T'

Left side:

Statement/expr S	Transformation $\tau[S]$

$(b\_)expr$	`//for each read r = read(x) in`
	`//(b_)expr and x is a shared var`
	
	`if (r == rds[1]) {`
	`  τ'[T'];`
	`  assume(allWsDone);`
	`  x = vals[1];`
	`  rDone[1] = true;`
	`  append(log, (T, WT, x, 1));`
	`  append(log, (T, RD, x, 1));`
	`  assume(isFeasible(log));`
	`} else if (r == rds[2]) {`
	`  x = vals[2];`
	`  assume(rDone[1]);`
	`  rDone[2] = true;`
	
	`  append(log, (T, WT, x, 2));`
	`  append(log, (T, RD, x, 2));`
	`  assume(isFeasible(log));`
	`}`
	`  ⋮`
	`else if (r == rds[k]) {`
	`  x = vals[k];`
	`  assume(rDone[k − 1]);`
	`  append(log, (T, WT, x, k));`
	`  append(log, (T, RD, x, k));`
	`  assume(isFeasible(log));`
	`} else {`
	`  append(log, (T, RD, x));`
	`  assume(isFeasible(log));`
	`}`

$x = (b\_)expr$ (x is a local var)	`τ[(b_)expr];` `x = (b_)expr`

$x = (b\_)expr$
(x is a shared var)
	`τ[(b_)expr];`
	`x = (b_)expr;`
	`append(log, (T, WT, x))`

$lock(x)\{S\}$	`append(log, (T, AQ, x));`
	`τ[S];`
	`append(log, (T, RL, x))`

$assume(b\_expr)$	`τ[b_expr];` `assume(b_expr)`
$assert(b\_expr)$	`τ[b_expr];` `assert(b_expr)`

$if(b\_expr)\{S_1\}$
$else\{S_2\}$
	`τ[b_expr];`
	`if(b_expr){τ[S_1]}`
	`else{τ[S_2]}`

$S_1; S_2$	`τ[S_1]; τ[S_2]`
$skip$	`skip`

Right side:

Statement/expr S	Transformation $\tau'[S]$
$x = (b\_)expr$ (x is a local variable)	`τ'[(b_)expr];` `x = (b_)expr'`

$x = (b\_)expr$
(x is a shared var
where w is the id
of this write)
	`τ'[(b_)expr];`
	`x' = (b_)expr';`
	`if (w == wrts[1]) {`
	`  vals[1] = x';`
	`  wDone[1] = true;`
	`  append(log, (T', WT, x, 1));`
	`  if (returnCondition()) return;`
	`} else if (w == wrts[2]) {`
	`  vals[2] = x';`
	`  wDone[2] = true;`
	`  append(log, (T', WT, x, 2));`
	`  if (returnCondition()) return;`
	`}`
	`  ⋮`
	`else if (w == wrts[k]) {`
	`  vals[k] = x';`
	`  wDone[k] = true;`
	
	`  append(log, (T', WT, x, k));`
	`  if (returnCondition()) return;`
	`}`

$(b\_)expr$	`// for each read r = read(x) in`
	`// (b_)expr where x is a shared var`
	`append(log, (T', RD, x));`

$lock(x)\{S\}$	`append(log, (T', AQ, x));`
	`τ'[S];`
	`append(log, (T', RL, x));`
	`if (returnCondition()) return;`

$assume(b\_expr)$	`τ'[b_expr];` `assume(b_expr')`
$assert(b\_expr)$	`τ'[b_expr];` `assert(b_expr')`

$if(b\_expr)\{S_1\}$
$else\{S_2\}$
	`τ'[b_expr];`
	`if(b_expr'){τ'[S_1]}`
	`else{τ'[S_2]}`

$S_1; S_2$	`τ'[S_1]; τ'[S_2]`
$skip$	`skip`

statements remain the same unless we transform the corresponding boolean expressions before these statements. Analogously, we transform conditional statements as well as sequences of statements. Skip statements stay unchanged.

Transformation Scheme for Statements in T'. The transformed program $\tau'[T']$, which is called from $\tau[T]$ before the first non-local read is performed, is executed until the first lock-free point in which all writes specified in $wrts$ have occurred. Note, log contains all information necessary to determine which locks are held at any point in the execution. We continue the execution of T' up to a lock-free point after the last write in $wrts$ to increase the possibility of finding a feasible trace, by having the option to release some locks before context-switching to T. The function $returnCondition$, used in $\tau'[T']$, returns true if T' is at a lock-free point and all writes in $wrts$ were performed ($returnCondition$ sets the flag $allWsDone$ accordingly). As mentioned before, T' operates on its own copy of shared variables, G'. For each shared variable x, let x' denote the corresponding copy for thread T' and let $(b\_)expr'$ be a (boolean) expression in which each shared variable x is replaced by x'.

If an assignment statement writes to a shared variable, we first check whether the write is in $wrts$ or not. In case the write is supposed to provide a value for the jth non-local read, i.e. $w == wrts[j]$ holds, the value of the shared variable is stored in $vals[j]$ and the flag $wDone[j]$ is set to true. Then, a write event to the corresponding shared variable is logged and function $returnCondition$ is called to return when T' gets to an appropriate point. The transformation of lock statements in T' is the same as in T unless after logging a lock release event we call function $returnCondition$ to check whether we should stop executing T'. For assert, assume, assignment, and conditional statements, we log a read event for each read from a shared variable in the corresponding expressions just before these statements.

4.2   Checking Feasibility of Corresponding Concurrent Runs

The log ρ is used to check for the existence of a feasible trace of the concurrent program, in which all reads other than the non-local reads are reading values written by local writes while each non-local read $rds[i]$ in ρ is paired with the write $wrts[i]$ for $1 \le i \le k'$, where k' is the number of non-local reads appearing in ρ and $k' \le k$. We generate a constraint, PO $\wedge$ LV $\wedge$ RW, encoding all such feasible traces, consisting of the events that appear in ρ, and use SMT solvers to find an answer. For each logged event e, an integer variable t_e is considered to encode the *timestamp* of the event. The constraints required for such feasible traces are captured using timestamps.

Program Order (PO):   A feasible concurrent trace has to respect the order of events according to each thread. Let $\rho|_T = e_1, e_2, ..., e_m$ and $\rho|_{T'} = e'_1, e'_2, ..., e'_n$ be the sequence of events in ρ projected to threads T and T', respectively. The constraint $PO = \bigwedge_{i=1}^{i=m-1} (t_{e_i} < t_{e_{i+1}}) \bigwedge_{i=1}^{i=n-1} (t_{e'_i} < t_{e'_{i+1}})$, ensures that the order of events in T and T' is preserved.

Lock-Validity (LV):   In a feasible concurrent trace, threads cannot hold the same lock simultaneously. The set of events between a lock acquire event e_{aq} and its corresponding lock release event e_{rl} in the same thread is defined as a lock block, represented by $[e_{aq}, e_{rl}]$. We denote the set of lock blocks of a lock l in threads T and T' by L_l and L'_l, respectively. The following constrains ensure that two threads cannot simultaneously be inside a pair of lock blocks protected by the same lock, by forcing the lock release event of one of the lock blocks to *happen before* the lock acquire event of the other:

$$LV = \bigwedge_{lock\ l} \bigwedge_{[e_{aq},e_{rl}] \in L_l} \bigwedge_{[e'_{aq},e'_{rl}] \in L'_l} \left(t_{e_{rl}} < t_{e'_{aq}} \vee t_{e'_{rl}} < t_{e_{aq}} \right)$$

Read-Write (RW):   These constraints ensure that reads and writes are paired as required. Note that in the transformation, whenever the non-local read $rds[i]$ is performed, we *inject* a *new* write event by T in the program and log it before logging a read event from the corresponding variable. This is to simulate the write $wrts[i]$ as to be a local write in T and hence the consequent reads of the same variable in T will be paired locally with this new local write. Therefore, it is sufficient to ensure that each read is paired with a local write (RW_1 expresses these constraints). However, to guarantee that an injected write event w simulates the corresponding write w' in T', we need to ensure that w' happens before w and no other write to the corresponding variable should occur between these two writes (RW_2 encodes this constraint).

We define an x-*live* block, $[e_w, e_r]$, to be a sequence of events in *one* thread starting from a write event e_w (to variable x) until the last read event (from x) e_r, before the next write to x by the same thread. An x-live block should execute without interference from any write to x by the other thread so that all the reads (of x) in it are paired with the write event e_w. For each x-live block $[e_w, e_r]$ and every write e'_w to x by the other thread, e'_w should happen either before the write event e_w or after the read event e_r. Let Lv_x and Lv'_x represent the set of all x-live blocks in T and T', and W_x and W'_x represent the set of all write events to x in T and T', respectively. Then $RW_1 =$

$$\bigwedge_{var\ x} [\bigwedge_{[e_w,e_r]\in Lv_x} \bigwedge_{e'_w\in W'_x} (t_{e'_w} < t_{e_w} \lor t_{e_r} < t_{e'_w}) \land \bigwedge_{[e'_w,e'_r]\in Lv'_x} \bigwedge_{e_w\in W_x} (t_{e_w} < t_{e'_w} \lor t_{e'_r} < t_{e_w})]$$

are true if none of the x-live blocks are interrupted. We also need constraints to ensure $rds[i]$ observes the value written by $wrts[i]$. Let $wrts[i] = e'_{w,i}$, and assume that $e_{w,i}$ is the *new* local write event injected during the transformation of $rds[i]$. Suppose e_r is a read in T after $e_{w,i}$ such that $[e_{w,i}, e_r]$ forms an x-live block. Let $e''_{w,i}$ be the next write event to x after $e'_{w,i}$ in T'. Then, $e'_{w,i}$ should happen before the x-live block, $[e_{w,i}, e_r]$, while forcing $e''_{w,i}$ to happen after the block: $RW_2 = \bigwedge_{[e_{w,i},e_r]} \left(t_{e'_{w,i}} < t_{e_{w,i}} \land t_{e_r} < t_{e''_{w,i}}\right)$. Finally, $RW = RW_1 \land RW_2$.

4.3   Soundness and Reproducibility

Here, we discuss the soundness of our sequentialization, i.e. every error state in the resulting sequential program corresponds to an error in the concurrent program. Let P be a concurrent program with threads T and T', and $\widehat{P}_k$ be the corresponding sequential program which allows k reads in T to read values written by T'. The soundness of our technique is stated in the following theorem:

Theorem 1. *Every error in the sequential program $\widehat{P}_k$ corresponds to an error in the concurrent program P, i.e. there exists a feasible trace in P which leads to the error.*

In case an error is found in $\widehat{P}_k$, the SMT solution from the latest feasibility check can be used to extract the bug-triggering concurrent trace in P, and hence effectively reproducing the error.

5   Concurrency Bug Coverage

The ultimate goal of our sequentialization technique is using standard sequential testing tools to test $\widehat{P}_k$ to find errors in P. Here, we discuss what coverage guarantees our testing approach can provide, based on the assumptions that can be made about the coverage guarantees that the backend sequential testing tool provides. We characterize a class of bugs that our tool can fully discover, if the underlying sequential tool manages to provide certain coverage guarantees.

k-coupled Bugs. We define a function λ that given a trace σ and a read event e (from a shared variable x) in σ, returns the identifier of the thread that has performed the most recent write to the same shared variable before e. When there is no such write, value $init$ is returned by λ.

A trace σ is $\mathcal{T}$-sequential if all reads in thread $\mathcal{T}$ are local (i.e. either read the initial values or values written by writes in $\mathcal{T}$). Formally, for all event $e = \langle i, \mathcal{T} : rd(x) \rangle$ (see Section 3 for the formal definition of events), we have $\lambda(\sigma, e) \in \{\mathcal{T}, init\}$. A trace σ is $\mathcal{T}$-k-coupled if there are exactly k non-local reads in $\mathcal{T}$, and all the other reads are local. Formally, we have $|\{e = \langle i, \mathcal{T} : rd(x) \rangle : \lambda(\sigma, e) \notin \{\mathcal{T}, init\}\}| = k$.

Consider a concurrent program that consists of threads T and T'. Let Δ be the set of feasible traces which are T-k-coupled and T'-sequential. We define the set of bugs that can be discovered by testing all traces in Δ to be the *k-coupled bugs in T*.

Coverage Criteria. Let us consider some commonly used (by the state-of-the-art sequential testing tools) coverage criteria and discuss how these coverage criteria in the underlying sequential testing tools can result in the coverage of all k-coupled bugs of the concurrent programs by our technique.

First, we first discuss *path coverage* which gives us the strongest theoretical results. Since path coverage is expensive to achieve, we also discuss *control flow coverage* which is often used as the more practical alternative by testing tools.

The goal of path coverage is to explore all possible program paths. Several testing tools such as DART [8], EXE [6], and CUTE [18] aim to provide full path coverage. The following theorem formalizes the bug coverage guarantees provided by our technique:

Theorem 2. *Let P be a concurrent program and $\widehat{P}_k$ be the corresponding sequential program allowing k non-local reads in thread T. Suppose that a sequential testing tool,* SEQTOOL, *provides full path coverage for $\widehat{P}_k$. Then,* SEQTOOL *can discover all k-coupled bugs in T.*

Achieving a full path coverage can be expensive in practice. Therefore, some testing tools focus on control-flow coverage, and its variations such as basic block coverage and explicit branch coverage. Control-flow coverage is in general weaker than full path coverage in the sense that it can miss some of the bugs that can be caught by targeting full path coverage. Targeting control-flow coverage for the resulting sequential programs may lead to overlooking some feasible pairings of read-writes since not all feasible paths are guaranteed to be explored. We used PEX [20], which is based on control-flow coverage, as the sequential testing tool in our experiments and managed to find all known bugs and some new bugs.

6   Experiments

We have implemented our approach into a prototype tool for concurrent $C\#$ programs. The source-to-source transformation is performed by augmenting a $C\#$ parser,

CSPARSER [1], to generate the corresponding sequential programs using the proposed sequentialization method in Section 4. We used Microsoft PEX [20] as our backend sequential testing tool and Z3 [3] as the underlying SMT solver while searching for feasible traces.

We performed experiments on a benchmark suite of 15 programs. Table 1 contains information about the programs, their sizes (number of lines of code), and the results of tests. Bluetooth is simplified model of the bluetooth driver presented in Figure 1. Account is a program that creates and manages bank accounts. Meeting is a sequential program for scheduling meetings and here, like in [10], we assumed that there are two copies of the program running concurrently. Vector, Stack, StringBuffer, and Hashset are all classes in Java libraries. To test these library classes, we wrote programs with two threads, where each thread executes exactly one method of the corresponding class. Series, SOR, and Ray are Java Grande multi-threaded benchmarks [5]. We used a Java to $C\#$ converter to transform the corresponding Java classes to $C\#$. FTPNET [4] is an open source FTP server in $C\#$ and Mutual is a buggy program in which threads can be in a critical section simultaneously due to improper synchronization.

In Table 1, we present the number of k-coupled bugs (i.e. bugs caught by allowing k non-local reads) found for $1 \leq k \leq 3$ in each program. The bug in Account resides in the *transfer* method which acquires a lock on the account transferring money without acquiring the corresponding lock on the target account. The bug in Meeting corresponds to the fact that there are two versions of a sequential program running concurrently without using any synchronization mechanism to prevent the threads from interfering each other. The bugs/exceptions in Java library classes and Mutual are due to improper synchronization of accesses to shared objects. Series and SOR seems to be bug-

Table 1. Experimental Results. (*: new bugs found)

Program	#Lines	1-coupled Bugs	2-coupled Bugs	3-coupled Bugs	Total Time[s]
Bluetooth	55	0	1	0	26
Account	103	1	0	0	28
Meeting	101	1	0	0	16
Vector1	345	0	1	0	104
Vector2	336	0	1	0	80
Vector3	365	0	1	0	102
Stack1	340	0	1	0	100
Stack2	331	0	1	0	74
Stack3	361	0	1	0	98
HashSet	334	1	0	0	22
StringBuffer	198	1	0	0	12
Series	230	1	0	0	10
SOR	214	0	1	0	490
Ray	1002	1	0	0	18
FTPNET	2158	2*	0	0	56
Mutual	104	1	0	0	10

free for two threads. Therefore, we injected bugs in them by fiddling with the synchronization and our approach was able to catch them. The bug in Ray, corresponds to a data race on the shared variable checksum1. In FTPNET we found two previously unknown bugs that are due to ignoring the situations in which a connection can be closed before a file transformation is completed.

It is important to note that all bugs were found by allowing only one or two reads to be non-local. In all cases, no new error was found when k was increased to 3. Since these benchmarks have been used by other tools before, we know of no (previously found) bugs that were missed by our tool. Moreover, we found new bugs (that were not previously reported) in FTPNET. The last column in Table 1 represents the total time, for all $1 \leq k \leq 3$, spent by our tool. We can see that in many cases the bugs were found in less than one minute. On most benchmarks (except SOR) our tool spent less than two minutes. For SOR, the majority of time (about 7 minutes) was spent testing for 3-coupled bugs. Note that since this type of testing can be done in batch mode, as long as the full search is successfully performed, the speed of the process is not a great concern. The reason that it takes longer to test SOR is that there are many shared variables reads (more than 100) and many options for the coupling of writes for each read.

Mutual is a good example of the distinction between the idea of bounded context-switch and bounded interference. Here, 3 context switches are required to discover a bug while our approach can find the bug by considering only one non-local read. In fact, CHESS [12] and Poirot [2] (tools based on bounded context-switching) failed to catch the bug with 4GB of memory within 15 minutes while our approach found the bug in a few seconds. However, one can find examples in which bounded context-switch approaches perform better. We believe that these two approaches are not comparable and are complementary as interleaving selection heuristics.

7   Related Work

Sequentialization: There are several proposed approaches on sequentializing concurrent programs with the aim of reducing verification of concurrent programs to verification of sequential programs. Lal and Reps [10] showed that given a boolean concurrent program with finitely many threads and a bound k, a boolean sequential program can be obtained that encodes all executions of the concurrent program involving only k context-rounds. Lahiri et al [9] adapted the sequentialization of Lal and Reps for C. They used a verification condition generator and SMT solvers instead of a boolean model checker. A *lazy* sequentialization for bounded context switches was proposed by La Torre et al [21] that requires multiple execution of each context. None of these techniques can be used to sequentialize and then test a concurrent program using a sequential tester. In fact, these sequentialization techniques are aimed to be used in static analysis (as opposed to testing). However, if one still chooses to use them for testing, there are various complications; some [10,21] require fixed inputs (to guarantee the correctness of their transformation) and will not function properly if the input changes, some [10] may produce unreachable states in their search and could generate false-positives, and some only work for a small number of context switches [16].

Interleaving Selection: To tackle the interleaving explosion problem, recent research has focused on testing a small subset of interleavings that are more probable in exposing bugs. The CHESS tool [12] from Microsoft, for instance, tests all interleavings that use a bounded number preemptions. RaceFuzzer [17] and CTrigger [14] use race/atomicity-violation detection results to guide their interleaving testing. We use a different interleaving selection scheme that incrementally increases the number of non-local reads to explore more interleavings. More generally, these detectors are based on a single execution of the program provided a fixed input, while we have the option of finding the right input. Also, they suffer from false-positives while our approach generates no false-positives.

The ConSeq tool [24] detects concurrency bugs through sequential errors. Although the idea of forcing critical reads to read different values in ConSeq looks similar to our approach, there are major differences between them: ConSeq works on programs with fixed inputs, ConSeq only considers a single execution while we work at program level, and, ConSeq is not precise (ignoring data) and the executions may diverge from the plan, while we provide guarantees (modulo the back-end sequential testing tool) to simulate all feasible concurrent executions in a certain category.

References

1. http://csparser.codeplex.com/
2. http://research.microsoft.com/en-us/projects/poirot/
3. http://research.microsoft.com/en-us/um/redmond/projects/z3/
4. http://sourceforge.net/projects/ftpnet/
5. http://www.epcc.ed.ac.uk/research/java-grande/
6. Cadar, C., Ganesh, V., Pawlowski, P.M., Dill, D.L., Engler, D.R.: Exe: Automatically generating inputs of death. ACM Trans. Inf. Syst. Secur. 12, 10:1–10:38 (2008)
7. Flanagan, C., Freund, S.N.: Fasttrack: efficient and precise dynamic race detection. Commun. ACM 53, 93–101 (2010)
8. Godefroid, P., Klarlund, N., Sen, K.: Dart: directed automated random testing. In: PDLI, pp. 213–223. ACM (2005)
9. Lahiri, S.K., Qadeer, S., Rakamarić, Z.: Static and Precise Detection of Concurrency Errors in Systems Code Using SMT Solvers. In: Bouajjani, A., Maler, O. (eds.) CAV 2009. LNCS, vol. 5643, pp. 509–524. Springer, Heidelberg (2009)
10. Lal, A., Reps, T.: Reducing concurrent analysis under a context bound to sequential analysis. Form. Methods Syst. Des. 35, 73–97 (2009)
11. Miller, J.C., Maloney, C.J.: Systematic mistake analysis of digital computer programs. Commun. ACM 6, 58–63 (1963)
12. Musuvathi, M., Qadeer, S., Ball, T., Basler, G., Nainar, P.A., Neamtiu, I.: Finding and reproducing heisenbugs in concurrent programs. In: OSDI, pp. 267–280 (2008)
13. Park, C.-S., Sen, K.: Randomized active atomicity violation detection in concurrent programs. In: Proceedings of the 16th ACM SIGSOFT International Symposium on Foundations of Software Engineering, SIGSOFT 2008/FSE-16, pp. 135–145. ACM, New York (2008)
14. Park, S., Lu, S., Zhou, Y.: Ctrigger: exposing atomicity violation bugs from their hiding places. In: ASPLOS, pp. 25–36 (2009)
15. Pozniansky, E., Schuster, A.: Multirace: efficient on-the-fly data race detection in multi-threaded c++ programs: Research articles. Concurr. Comput.: Pract. Exper. 19, 327–340 (2007)
16. Qadeer, S., Wu, D.: Kiss: keep it simple and sequential. SIGPLAN Not. 39, 14–24 (2004)
17. Sen, K.: Race directed random testing of concurrent programs. In: PLDI, pp. 11–21 (2008)
18. Sen, K., Agha, G.: CUTE and jCUTE: Concolic Unit Testing and Explicit Path Model-Checking Tools. In: Ball, T., Jones, R.B. (eds.) CAV 2006. LNCS, vol. 4144, pp. 419–423. Springer, Heidelberg (2006)
19. Sorrentino, F., Farzan, A., Madhusudan, P.: Penelope: weaving threads to expose atomicity violations. In: FSE 2010, pp. 37–46. ACM (2010)
20. Tillmann, N., de Halleux, J.: Pex–White Box Test Generation for.NET. In: Beckert, B., Hähnle, R. (eds.) TAP 2008. LNCS, vol. 4966, pp. 134–153. Springer, Heidelberg (2008)
21. La Torre, S., Madhusudan, P., Parlato, G.: Reducing Context-Bounded Concurrent Reachability to Sequential Reachability. In: Bouajjani, A., Maler, O. (eds.) CAV 2009. LNCS, vol. 5643, pp. 477–492. Springer, Heidelberg (2009)

22. Wang, C., Limaye, R., Ganai, M., Gupta, A.: Trace-Based Symbolic Analysis for Atomicity Violations. In: Esparza, J., Majumdar, R. (eds.) TACAS 2010. LNCS, vol. 6015, pp. 328–342. Springer, Heidelberg (2010)
23. Yi, J., Sadowski, C., Flanagan, C.: Sidetrack: generalizing dynamic atomicity analysis. In: PADTAD 2009, pp. 8:1–8:10. ACM, New York (2009)
24. Zhang, W., Lim, J., Olichandran, R., Scherpelz, J., Jin, G., Lu, S., Reps, T.: Conseq: detecting concurrency bugs through sequential errors. In: ASPLOS, pp. 251–264 (2011)

Runtime Verification of Biological Systems*

Alexandre David[1], Kim Guldstrand Larsen[1], Axel Legay[2], Marius Mikučionis[1],
Danny Bøgsted Poulsen[1], and Sean Sedwards[2]

[1] Computer Science, Aalborg University, Denmark
[2] INRIA Rennes – Bretagne Atlantique, France

Abstract. Complex computational systems are ubiquitous and their study increasingly important. Given the ease with which it is possible to construct large systems with heterogeneous technology, there is strong motivation to provide automated means to verify their safety, efficiency and reliability. In another context, biological systems are supreme examples of complex systems for which there are no design specifications. In both cases it is usually difficult to reason at the level of the *description* of the systems and much more convenient to investigate properties of their executions.

To demonstrate runtime verification of complex systems we apply statistical model checking techniques to a model of robust biological oscillations taken from the literature. The model demonstrates some of the mechanisms used by biological systems to maintain reliable performance in the face of inherent stochasticity and is therefore instructive. To perform our investigation we use two recently developed SMC platforms: that incorporated in UPPAAL and PLASMA. UPPAAL-SMC offers a generic modeling language based on stochastic hybrid automata, while PLASMA aims at domain specific support with the facility to accept biological models represented in chemical syntax.

Keywords: runtime verification, synthetic biology, statistical model checking, genetic oscillator, MITL, frequency domain analysis, UPPAAL-SMC, PLASMA.

1 Introduction

It is conceivable to design systems in such a way that makes their analysis easier, but it is most usually the case that they are optimised for other constraints (efficiency, size, cost, etc.) and that they evolve over time, developing highly complex and unforeseen interactions and redundancies. These phenomena are epitomised by biological systems, which have absolutely no inherent need to be understandable or analysable. The discovery that the genetic recipe of life is written with just four characters (nucleotides Adenine, Cytosine, Guanine and Thymine) that are algorithmically transcribed and translated into the machinery

---

* Work partially supported by VKR Centre of Excellence – MT-LAB and by the CREATIVE project ESTASE.

T. Margaria and B. Steffen (Eds.): ISoLA 2012, Part I, LNCS 7609, pp. 388–404, 2012.

of the cell (RNA and proteins) has led scientists to believe that biology also works in a computational way. The further realisation that biological molecules and interactions are discrete and stochastic then suggests the idea that biological systems may be analysed using the same tools used to verify, say, a complex aircraft control system.

Using formal methods to investigate natural systems can thus be seen as a way to challenge and refine the process of investigating man-made systems. It is very difficult to reason about systems of this type at the level of their descriptions, however. It is much more convenient to directly analyse their observed behaviour. In the context of computational systems we refer to this approach as runtime verification, while in the case of biological systems this generally takes the form of monitoring the simulation traces of executable computational models.

To demonstrate runtime verification of biological systems we apply advanced statistical model checking (SMC) techniques to a model of robust biological oscillations taken from the literature. SMC works by verifying multiple independent simulation traces of a probabilistic model against a property specified in linear temporal logic. The results are then used in an hypothesis test or to estimate the probability of the property. In adopting this approach, SMC avoids constructing the generally intractable explicit representation of the state space of the system. The price paid is that results are only known within confidence intervals, however these may be made arbitrarily tight by increasing the number of simulation runs. SMC can thus be seen as a specific instance of runtime verification.

The model we have chosen to investigate demonstrates some of the mechanisms used by biological systems to maintain reliable performance in the face of inherent stochasticity. These mechanisms are literally vital and have relevance beyond biology (e.g. amorphous computing). To perform our investigation we use two recently developed SMC platforms: that incorporated in UPPAAL and PLASMA. UPPAAL-SMC offers a generic modelling language based on stochastic hybrid automata, while PLASMA aims at domain specific support and here accepts biological models represented in chemical syntax. Although our chosen model was conceived to be stochastic, its original description and analysis were in the continuous (ODE) domain. We therefore compare the behaviour of deterministic and stochastic models by performing a frequency domain analysis, taking advantage of UPPAAL's recently implemented ability to work with ODE representations. We verify various interesting temporal properties of the model and compare PLASMA's direct implementation of bounded LTL with UPPAAL's monitor- and rewrite-based implementations of weighted MITL.

2   Beyond Runtime Verification with SMC

Runtime verification (RV) [10,21] refers to a series of techniques whose main objective is to instrument the specification of a system (code, ...) in order to disprove potentially complex properties at the execution level. The main problem of the runtime verification approach is that it does not permit to assess the overall correctness of the entire system.

Statistical model checking (SMC) [4,26,23] extends runtime verification capabilities by exploiting statistical algorithms in order to get some evidence that a given system satisfies some property. Given a program B and a trace-based property[1] ϕ , Statistical model checking refers to a series of simulation-based techniques that can be used to answer two questions: (1) **Qualitative:** is the probability for B to satisfy ϕ greater or equal to a certain threshold θ (or greater or equal to the probability to satisfy another property ϕ')? and (2) **Quantitative:** what is the probability for B to satisfy ϕ?

We briefly review SMC approaches, referring the reader to [4,26] for more details. The main approaches [26,23] proposed to answer the qualitative question are based on *hypothesis testing*. Let p be the probability of $B \models \phi$, to determine whether $p \geq \theta$, we can test $H : p \geq \theta$ against $K : p < \theta$. A test-based solution does not guarantee a correct result but it is possible to bound the probability of making an error. The *strength* (α, β) of a test is determined by two parameters, α and β, such that the probability of accepting K (respectively, H) when H (respectively, K) holds is less or equal to α (respectively, β). Since it impossible to ensure a low probability for both types of errors simultaneously (see [26] for details), a solution is to use an *indifference region* $[p_1, p_0]$ (with θ in $[p_1, p_0]$) and to test $H_0 : p \geq p_0$ against $H_1 : p \leq p_1$. Several hypothesis testing algorithms exist in the literature. Younes[26] proposed a logarithmic based algorithm that given p_0, p_1, α and β implements the *Sequential Ratio Testing Procedure* (*SPRT*) (see [25] for details). When one has to test $\theta \geq 1$ or $\theta \geq 0$, it is however better to use *Single Sampling Plan* (*SSP*) (see [26,4,23] for details) that is another algorithm whose number of simulations is pre-computed in advance. In general, this number is higher than the one needed by *SPRT*, but is known to be optimal for the above mentioned values. More details about hypothesis testing algorithms and a comparison between *SSP* and *SPRT* can be found in [4].

In [11,17] Peyronnet et al. propose an estimation procedure (*PESTIMATION*) to compute the probability p for B to satisfy ϕ. Given a *precision* δ, Peyronnet's procedure computes a value for p' such that $|p' - p| \leq \delta$ with *confidence* $1 - \alpha$. The procedure is based on the *Chernoff-Hoeffding bound* [13].

3   Model and Properties

3.1   A Genetic Oscillator

It is well accepted that molecules are discrete entities and that molecular interactions are discrete. It is further accepted that molecules move randomly as a result of collisions with other molecules (thermal noise). From this it can be inferred that chemical reactions are the result of random interactions and can be modelled as stochastic processes. Biological organisms based on chemical reactions are thus supreme examples of complex stochastic systems. The means by which they overcome low level non-determinism and achieve apparent high level

---

[1] i.e., a property whose semantics is trace-based.

determinism is the subject of much ongoing research and informs such fields as amorphous computing [1].

Oscillation, arising from the execution loops in computer programs, is of great relevance to runtime verification of automated systems. Oscillation also plays a crucial role in biology - life being an essentially cyclic process. One of the key oscillatory behaviours in biology is the circadian rhythm that allows an organism to take advantage of periods of day and night to optimise when to maximise activity and recovery. In light of this, we have chosen the genetic circadian oscillator of [3,24] as the focus of our analysis. This synthetic model distils the essence of several real circadian oscillators and demonstrates how a reliable system can be constructed in the face of inherent stochasticity. In particular, the model has been shown in [12] to exhibit a kind of regularity referred to as *stochastic coherence*.

Though the authors of the model were interested in its stochastic properties, they nevertheless chose to represent it in the form of a system of ordinary differential equations (ODEs, reproduced in Figure 1). Each of the equations describes the infinitesimal rate of change of a particular molecular species; the functions being the sums of the rates of all reactions involving the species, weighted by the direction (positive or negative, corresponding to creation and consumption) and size of the corresponding change. ODEs are commonly used to represent the dynamics of chemically reacting systems and it is traditional to consider concentrations (numbers of molecules per unit volume). Trajectories of ODEs can closely approximate stochastic dynamics when the system operates near to *the thermodynamic limit* (infinite population sizes). This is rarely the case with biological models of cellular processes, which frequently consider molecular species in very low copy numbers. An obvious example is that within a cell there is often just a single copy of a particular gene (as in the case of the genetic oscillator we describe here). The ODE trajectory is often considered (informally) to be the 'average' of the stochastic traces, implying that the noise is somehow superimposed on top of a deterministic trajectory. In fact, the noise is *an inherent part* of the stochastic trajectory and the ODE describes the behaviour of the *limit* of the stochastic process as populations are taken to infinity while maintaining the same concentrations [7,9]. We demonstrate this using frequency domain analysis in Section 3.4.

Using a standard translation between deterministic and stochastic semantics of chemically reacting systems (see, e.g., [8]), it is possible to transform the ODEs given in Figure 1 into the chemical reaction syntax of Equations (1-16). These can then be visualised as a stochastic Petri net (Figure 2). The model comprises two genes (D_A and D_R) that are *transcribed* (Equations (5-8)) to produce two micro-RNA molecules (M_A and M_R, respectively) that are *translated* (Equations (9,10)) to produce two proteins (A and R, respectively). A acts as a promoter for its own gene (Equation (1)) and for that of R (Equation (3)) by reacting with D_A and D_R to produce their more efficient active forms D'_A and D'_R. A and R *dimerise* (Equation (11)) to form complex protein C that eventually degrades back to D. Oscillation arises from the fact that A is part of a positive feedback

$$dD_A/dt = \theta_A D'_A - \gamma_A D_A A$$
$$dD_R/dt = \theta_R D'_R - \gamma_R D_R A$$
$$dD'_A/dt = \gamma_A D_A A - \theta_A D'_A$$
$$dD'_R/dt = \gamma_R D_R A - \theta_R D'_R$$
$$dM_A/dt = \alpha'_A D'_A + \alpha_A D_A - \delta_{M_A} M_A$$
$$dM_R/dt = \alpha'_R D'_R + \alpha_R D_R - \delta_{M_R} M_R$$
$$dA/dt = \beta_A M_A + \theta_A D'_A + \theta_R D'_R$$
$$\quad - A(\gamma_A D_A + \gamma_R D_R + \gamma_C R + \delta_A)$$
$$dR/dt = \beta_R M_R - \gamma_C A R + \delta_A C - \delta_R R$$
$$dC/dt = \gamma_C A R - \delta_A C$$

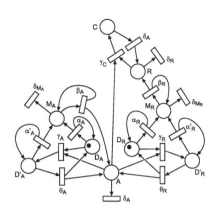

Fig. 1. System of ordinary differential equations describing the genetic oscillator example

Fig. 2. Petri net representation of the initial state of the genetic oscillator example

loop involved in its own production and promotes the production of R that, in turn, sequesters A (i.e., removes it) via the production of C (Equation (11)). This mechanism and other mechanisms of biological oscillation are discussed in more detail in a recent review of synthetic oscillators [19].

$$A + D_A \xrightarrow{\gamma_A} D'_A \quad (1)$$

$$D'_A \xrightarrow{\theta_A} D_A + A \quad (2)$$

$$A + D_R \xrightarrow{\alpha_R} D'_R \quad (3)$$

$$D'_R \xrightarrow{\theta_R} D_R + A \quad (4)$$

$$D'_A \xrightarrow{\alpha'_A} M_A + D'_A \quad (5)$$

$$D_A \xrightarrow{\alpha_A} M_A + D_A \quad (6)$$

$$D'_R \xrightarrow{\alpha'_R} M_R + D'_R \quad (7)$$

$$D_R \xrightarrow{\alpha_R} M_R + D_R \quad (8)$$

$$M_A \xrightarrow{\beta_A} M_A + A \quad (9)$$

$$M_R \xrightarrow{\beta_R} M_R + R \quad (10)$$

$$A + R \xrightarrow{\gamma_C} C \quad (11)$$

$$C \xrightarrow{\delta_A} R \quad (12)$$

$$A \xrightarrow{\delta_A} \emptyset \quad (13)$$

$$R \xrightarrow{\delta_R} \emptyset \quad (14)$$

$$M_A \xrightarrow{\delta_{M_A}} \emptyset \quad (15)$$

$$M_R \xrightarrow{\delta_{M_R}} \emptyset \quad (16)$$

Each equation describes a possible productive interaction between types of molecules (molecular *species*). Monomolecular reactions of the form $A \xrightarrow{k} \cdots$ have the semantics that a molecule of type A will spontaneously decay to some product(s) following a time delay drawn from an exponential distribution with mean k. Bimolecular reactions of the form $A + B \xrightarrow{k} \cdots$ have the semantics that if a molecule of type A encounters a molecule of type B they will react to become some product(s) following a time delay drawn from an exponential distribution with mean k. It is usually assumed that the system is 'well stirred' [8,7,9], such that the probability of a molecule occupying a particular position is uniform over the physical space of the system. This rarely represents reality in the case of biological cells, however it is a widely used mathematical expedient that is common to both deterministic and stochastic treatments. The consequence is that molecules lose their individuality (populations are treated as multisets) and the rate of molecular interactions is simply the product of a rate constant (k in the examples) and a combinatorial factor arising from population sizes [8,7,9]. This is known as *mass action kinetics* [8,7,9]. Referring to molecular species A and B in the example reactions given above, for populations of instantaneous size A and B the overall rates of monomolecular and bimolecular reactions are given by kA and kAB, respectively.

3.2   Properties

The language we use to describe properties is based on the dense timed logic MITL, having the form

$$\phi = \phi \vee \phi \mid \phi \wedge \phi \mid \neg\phi \mid \top \mid \bot \mid \phi U_{[a;b]}\phi \mid \phi R_{[a;b]}\phi \mid X\phi \mid \alpha$$

where $a, b \in \mathbb{N}$, $a < b$ and $alpha$ is a proposition of the model. In the case of the genetic oscillator we consider in this paper, the propositions are numeric comparisons of the variables in question.

An expression as $\phi_1 U[a; b]\phi_2$ means that ϕ_1 should be true until ϕ_2 is true and this should occur between a and b time units. The expression $\phi_1 R[a; b]\phi_2$ means ϕ_2 should be true until either b time units has passed or both ϕ_1 and ϕ_2 is true and that occurs between a and b time units. $X\phi$ means that ϕ should be true in the next state of the system. The remaining operators have their standard interpretation from propositional calculus. The derived eventuality operator $\Diamond_{[a;b]}\phi$ is introduced as short for $\top U_{[a;b]}\phi$ and the always operator $\Box_{[a;b]}\phi$ as short for $\bot R_{[a;b]}\phi$.

3.3   Properties of the Oscillator

The model exhibit an oscillatoric behaviour in which a peak of one protein is followed by the increase of another protein. The increase of one protein also appears to be governed by highly regularity in the sense that one peak level is followed by another peak level in a specific amount of time.

In order to detect peaks we first define the shape of a peak. We say there is a peak if the protein level is above a threshold $thres_L$ and within l time units drops below another threshold $thres_R$.

Using $MITL_<$ we can express that we at the given time is in a peak of the N variable as

$$\phi_{peakN} \equiv N > thres_L \wedge \Diamond_{[0;l]} N < thres_R.$$

Expressing that there is a periodicity in the peaks of a single variable N within the first 1000 time units can be done using the formula:

$$\Box_{\leq 1000}(\phi_{peakN} \implies \Diamond_{\leq p}\phi_{peakN}),$$

where p is the maximum time between peaks. The same form of expression can of course also be used to express that a peak on the N variable should be followed by a peak on the M variable.

3.4   Frequency Domain Analysis

Frequency domain analysis provides a rigorous yet intuitive means to quantify the behaviour of stochastic systems from observations of their executions. This methodology is particularly relevant for oscillatory biological systems [14], but is not limited to these and is able to characterise the distance in behaviour between different models, different systems and different parts within the same system. It can also measure the difference between different simulation algorithms or semantics applied to the same system.

Our technique is to generate N simulation traces sampled at constant time intervals, δt, resulting in K sampled points per simulation. From each set of sampled points and for each state variable of interest we calculate a complex frequency spectrum using a 'fast Fourier transform' (FFT) algorithm. From these we generate N corresponding magnitude spectra and then calculate the pointwise average magnitude spectrum. The average magnitude spectrum often gives a visually compact notion of the complex stochastic behaviour of the system and can also be used to quantify a distance between behaviours using standard statistical metrics.

K and δt are chosen according to the temporal characteristics of the phenomenon of interest: $K\delta t$ is the maximum observed simulated time; $(K\delta t)^{-1}$ is the low frequency resolution (the spacing between spectral components) and $(2\delta t)^{-1}$ is the maximum observable frequency. It is generally desirable to increase K and reduce δt, but note that an optimal value of δt is usually significantly greater than the minimum time between successive update events, since these often do not apply to the same variable and the highest part of the spectrum is often uninformative. N is chosen according to the stochasticity of the system in relation to the desired discrimination of the metric; large N being desirable.

4   UPPAAL-SMC

The verification tool Uppaal [18] provide support for modeling and efficient analysis of real-time systems modeled as networks of timed automata [2]. To ease modeling, the tool comes equiped with a user-friendly GUI for defining and simulating models. Also, the modelling formalism extends basic timed automata with discrete variable over basic, structured and user-defined types that may be modified by user-defined functions written in a Uppaal specific C-like imperative language. The specification language of Uppaal is a fragment of TCTL supporting a range of safety, liveness and bounded liveness properties.

Uppaal-smc is a recent branch of Uppaal which support statistical model checking of *stochastic hybrid systems*, based on a natural stochastic semantics. Uppaal-smc extends the basic timed automata formalism of Uppaal by allowing rates of clocks to be defined by general expressions possibly including clocks, thus effectively defining ODEs. An overview of the architecture is given in Figure 3. The GUI of the tool allows the user to draw automata templates in the editor, instantiate and compose these into a system, simulate the system for easy validation, verify queries, and visualize quantitative answers in the form of plots in the plot composer. The execution engine of UPPAAL-SMC implements the stochast semantics of interacting hybrid automata, and includes a proprietary virtual machine for the execution of imperative code of the model.

The specification formalism of UPPAAL-SMC is that of (weighted) MITL, with respect to which four different statistical model checking components are offered: hypothesis testing, probability estimation, probability comparison and simulation. Here the user may control the accuracy of the analysis by a number of statistical parameters (size of confidence interval, significance level, etc.). UPPAAL-SMC also provides distributed implementations of the hypothesis testing and probability estimation demonstrating linear speed-up [5].

The results generated by the analyses can be processed for visualization in various ways: Gantt charts for individual runs monitoring desired variables, plots of density functions and accumulated distribution functions with respect to given (W)MITL properties. Typically the simulation results in gigabytes of data which are filtered on-the-fly to plot only the relevant points.

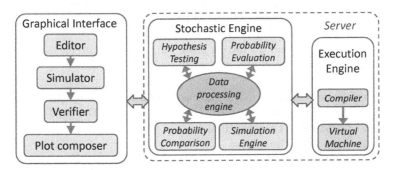

Fig. 3. Architecture of UPPAAL-SMC

4.1 Modeling and Checking in UPPAAL-SMC

A Bouncing Ball Example. To illustrate the expressive power of the stochastic hybrid automata language supported by UPPAAL-SMC, we consider a simple, yet interesting variant of a bouncing ball. Figure 4(a) gives the principle of a ball bouncing on a floor and being hit by a piston. The hybrid model of the ball is given in Fig. 4(b) where three cases are visible: (i) it can be hit while going up (v<=0), (ii) hit while going down (v<0), or (iii) it bounces on the floor. The invariant on the location describes the trajectory of the ball in the form of two differential equations (v' and p'). The piston in Fig. 4(c) can hit the ball only if its position is high enough (p>=6). The ball will rebound with a random dampening coefficient both on the floor and the piston (given by the **random** function). The delays between hits of the piston are chosen stochastically according to an exponential distribution of rate $5/2$. Semantically, the effect of ODE expressions is achieved by an implicit auxiliary process integrating the values based on a given fixed time step and thus directly competing with the rest of processes when the rest of invariant and guard expressions are evaluated.

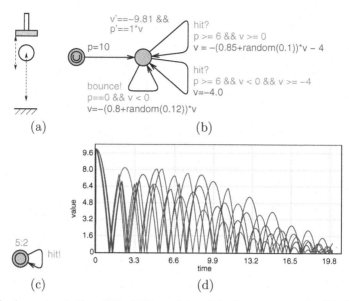

Fig. 4. The bouncing ball and the hitting piston (a), the automata for (b) the ball and (c) the piston, and (d) 5 trajectories of the ball in function of time

Five different trajectories of the ball are obtained by the query simulate 5 [<=20]{p} and shown in Fig. 4(d). We may also ask the model-checker to estimate the probability that the ball is still bouncing above the height of 4 after 12 time units with the query:

$$\texttt{Pr[<=20](<>(time >= 12 \&\& p >= 4))}$$

Here <>(time>=12 && p>=4) is the UPPAAL-SMC syntax for the MITL property $\psi = \Diamond(\text{time} \leq 12 \wedge p \geq 4)$ and Pr[<=20]ψ denote the probability π that ψ will hold within 20 time-units for a random run. Given this query, the interval $[0.152, 0.163]$ is returned as an estimate for π with confidence 99.9% after generating 152020 runs. We can also test the hypothesis:

$$\texttt{Pr[<=20](<> time >= 12 \&\& p >= 4) >= 0.15}$$

with a region of indifference of ± 0.005 and level of significance of 0.1% after generating 18543 runs.

For the analysis of more general MITL properties properties, UPPAAL-SMC generates monitoring automata to be put in parallel with the system. Statistical model checking requires that these monitors are determinstistic timed automata. Unfortunately, not all MITL properties may be monitored by determinstic timed automata. Thus UPPAAL-SMC offers a safe confidence interval based on two monitors corresponding to under- and over-approximations of the set of runs satisfying the particular formula [5]. Experimental results have shown that we obtain an exact monitor, and most recently this method has been replace by an exact rewrite technique.

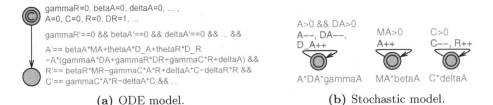

(a) ODE model.   **(b)** Stochastic model.

Fig. 5. Snippets of the UPPAAL models of the genetic oscilator

Figure 5a shows a snippet from an ODE model of the genetic oscilator, where the coefficients (`gammaR, betaA, deltaA`) and variables (`A, C, R, DR`) are initialized with the first urgent transition and then the trajectories are computed based on the ODEs (the last three equations from Fig. 1). A snippet from stochastic genetic oscilator model is shown in Fig. 5b, where each reaction (from Eq. 1, 9 and 12) is modeled by a separate automaton. For example, the first automaton can be read as follows: reaction requires positive quantities of `A` and `DA` (guard conditions), one of each is consumed (`A--` and `DA--`), and one `D_A` is produced (`D_A++`) with an exponential rate `gammaA` times the available quantities of `A` and `DA`.

5   PLASMA

PLASMA is designed to be a high performance and flexible platform for statistical model checking, able to work with multiple modelling and property specification languages. Its basic architecture is shown in Figure 6 and comprises a user interface, a simulation management module, a virtual machine and modules that compile the model and property specifications. Models and properties are compiled into proprietary bytecode and executed on PLASMA's inbuilt virtual machine. Overall control of the verification process is maintained by the simulation management module according to the options specified by the user. The simulation management module contains various statistical model checking algorithms that implement confidence bounds, such as the Chernoff bound of [11]

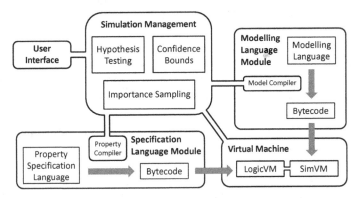

Fig. 6. The architecture of PLASMA

and the sequential hypothesis test of [27], plus an *importance sampling* engine
[16] that improves the performance when simulating rare properties. For simulating discrete and continuous time Markov models the virtual machine uses the
'method of arbitrary partial propensities' (MAPP [22,15]) that is an optimised
version of the 'direct method' of [8]. The simulation management module executes the property bytecode that, in turn, executes the model bytecode until
sufficient simulation steps are generated. In this way simulation traces contain
the minimum number of states necessary to decide a property and the simulation management ensures that the minimum number of simulation traces are
requested of the simulator.

5.1   Modeling and Checking in PLASMA

Modelling languages are built on an underlying semantics of *guarded commands*
[6] extended with stochastic rates to resolve non-determinism. These have the
form $(guard, rate, action)$, where *guard* is a logical predicate over the state of
the system which enables the command, *action* updates the state of the system
and *rate* is a function over the state of the system that returns the stochastic rate
at which an enabled command is executed. This semantics is equally applicable
when the rate is actually a probability and time plays no part.

PLASMA is designed to be language neutral, so for the present investigation
PLASMA adopts a simple chemical syntax modelling language that closely mirrors
the style of Equations (1-16). The structure of the model file follows the form:
constant initialisations, species initialisations, list of reactions. In the present
context there is an implicit assumption of *mass action kinetics* [8,7,9] and *rate*
specifies the mean of an exponential random variable that models the time between successive reaction events; non-determinism being resolved by races between realisations of the random variables of competing reactions. Reactions of
the abstract form $A + B \xrightarrow{k} C + D$ have the concrete form A + B k-> C + D with
guarded command semantics $(A > 0 \wedge B > 0, kAB, A = A - 1; B = B - 1; C = C + 1; D = D + 1)$.

PLASMA verifies properties specified in bounded linear temporal logic of the
kind described in Section 3.2. The logic accepts arbitrarily nested temporal formulae and PLASMA achieves this using a buffer to store sequences of values of
the variables of interest. When formulae are not nested, no buffer is required.
Algorithms 1 and 2 illustrate the basic notions of checking non-nested temporal
formulae, employing discrete time for clarity. Algorithm 3 is a naive implementation of a nested formula to illustrate the purpose of the buffer and how we
improve efficiency.

Algorithms 1 and 2 generate and consider states in turn, returning a result as
soon as ϕ is satisfied or not satisfied, respectively. These algorithms store nothing
and generate the minimum number of states necessary. Algorithm 3 also only
generates new states as required, but since the inner loop requires states further
into the future than the outer loop, states are stored by the inner loop for
subsequent use by the outer loop. As written, Algorithm 3 is naive because the

inner loop re-checks states that it has checked on previous iterations of the outer loop. PLASMA therefore records where the decision on the previous iteration was made and then needs only check the states after that. The case with continuous time is more complex because the length of the buffer is not known a priori (there may be an arbitrary number of steps to achieve a given time bound). PLASMA overcomes this by creating an initial buffer and then extends it as required.

Algorithm 1: $\Diamond_{\leq t}\phi$	**Algorithm 3:** $\Diamond_{\leq t_1}\Box_{\leq t_2}\phi$

for $i = 0$ **to** $i = t$ **do**
    generate $state_i$;
    if $state_i \models \phi$ **then return** $\top$
 return $\bot$
	create $buffer$ of length t_2;
	 for $i = 0$ **to** $i = t_1$ **do**
	    $inner = \top$;
	    for $j = i$ **to** $j = i + t_2$ **do**
	      if $state_j \notin buffer$ **then**
	        generate $state_j$;
	        $buffer_{j \bmod t_2} = state_j$;
	      if $state_j \models \neg\phi$ **then**
	        $inner = \bot$;
	        break

Algorithm 2: $\Box_{\leq t}\phi$	**if** $inner$ **then return** $\top$ **return** $\bot$

for $i = 0$ **to** $i = t$ **do**
    generate $state_i$;
    if $state_i \not\models \phi$ **then return** $\bot$
 return $\top$	

5.2 Rare Events

Rare events pose a challenge to simulation-based approaches, so PLASMA includes an *importance sampling* engine that makes it possible to estimate the probability of a rare property by simulating under a distribution that makes the property less rare. Given a property ϕ, with true probability γ under distribution P, the standard Monte Carlo estimator of γ is given by $\tilde{\gamma} = \frac{1}{N}\sum_{i=1}^{N} z(\omega_i)$, where ω_i is the trace of a simulation made under P and $z(\omega) \in \{0,1\}$ indicates whether $\omega \models \phi$. In general, N must be chosen significantly greater than $\frac{1}{\gamma}$ to accurately estimate γ, hence this is computationally expensive when γ is small. By contrast, the importance sampling estimator is given by $\tilde{\gamma} = \frac{1}{N}\sum_{i=1}^{N} z(\omega_i)\frac{P(\omega_i)}{Q(\omega_i)}$, where Q is ideally a distribution under which traces that satisfy ϕ are uniformly more likely and ω_i is now the trace of a simulation performed under Q. $\frac{P}{Q}$ is called the *likelihood ratio* and in a discrete event simulation can usually be calculated on the fly in constant time. Since Q is chosen to reproduce ϕ more frequently, N may be significantly less than $\frac{1}{\gamma}$. The effectiveness of importance sampling relies on finding a suitable Q.

An optimal importance sampling distribution is one under which traces that satisfy the rare property are uniformly more likely, to the exclusion of all traces that do not satisfy the property. It is possible to find such distributions by individually modifying all the transition probabilities in the system [20], however this is often intractable. PLASMA thus parametrises the distribution with a low dimensional vector of parameters applied to the rates of its guarded commands [16]. In the case of biological systems of the type considered here, this parametrisation corresponds to the rate constants of reactions.

To demonstrate the application of importance sampling to biological systems we consider a simple chemical system comprising $A + B \xrightarrow{k_1=1} C$, $C \xrightarrow{k_2=1} D$, $D \xrightarrow{k_3=1} E$. With initial conditions $A = 1000, B = 1000, C = D = E = 0$, we then consider the property $\Pr[\lozenge D \geq 470]$ that has a probability of approximately 2×10^{-10}. By multiplying the rate constants k_1, k_2, k_3 by importance sampling parameters $\lambda_1 = 1.16, \lambda_2 = 1.15, \lambda_3 = 0.69$, respectively, PLASMA is able to estimate this probability using only 1000 simulation runs (of these approximately 600 satisfy the property). The parameters were generated using the *cross-entropy* algorithm described in [16].

6 Experiments

Our first level of validation is to inspect the simulation traces to verify that they are sensible. The result from UPPAAL-SMC is displayed in Figure 7 where the ODE model yields the same (deterministic) trajectories of a pattern which repeats every 26.2 hours. The stochastic model yields an *apparently similar* but "noisy" pattern where the amplitude and periodicity are also varying. This intuitive similarity is made more formal by the frequency analysis in Section 6.1. Notice that the signal C starts at zero which allows A to reach higher amplitude

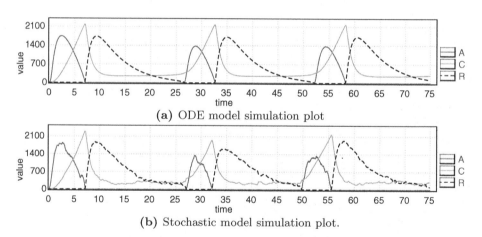

(a) ODE model simulation plot

(b) Stochastic model simulation plot.

Fig. 7. UPPAAL-SMC simulations: `simulate 1 [<=75] { A, C, R }`

than it normally would, thus we ignore the first period in our measurements. The amplitude can be measured from the plot directly for the ODE model: A – 1375, C – 2183 and R – 1717.

The amplitude is not fixed for stochastic model, and thus the distribution of probable amplitude values is estimated instead. The start of the monitoring is constrained with a variable v gaining value 1 only after 15 time units, effectively ignoring the first peaks. The results of 2000 simulations of 75 time units are shown in Fig. 8. The average amplitudes are a bit larger than in ODE model.

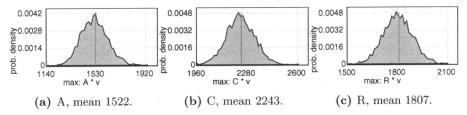

(a) A, mean 1522.   (b) C, mean 2243.   (c) R, mean 1807.

Fig. 8. Estimated amplitude: E[<=75; 2000](max: A*v,C*v,R*v)

We can also estimate periods of various signals by measuring the time distance between peaks. For this purpose we add signal peak monitor-process generated by a MITL formula: true U[<=1000] (A>1100 & true U[<=5] A<=1000), which is false unless the signal A rises above 1100 and then falls below 1000 within 5 time units. By coordinating two instances of such monitors and letting a stopwatch x run only between the two peaks we estimate the distribution of x as a period estimate. For signal C (R) we register a peak when the signal falls from 2000 to 1900 (1500 to 1400 resp.). The query then is a simple probability estimate whether the second peak is reached. Figure 9 shows estimated period with corresponding values at probability peaks. The most instances are situated around the peak value, but there are other tiny bumps on sides. The bump near zero corresponds to false positive recognition of a peak when the signal includes a saw tooth (common in stochastic simulations). The bump around 48 hours corresponds to a missed peak at 24, due to the local amplitude being too low. Interestingly there is another tiny bump at around 73 in Fig. 9b which correspond to two missed peaks in a row.

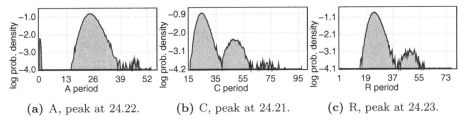

(a) A, peak at 24.22.   (b) C, peak at 24.21.   (c) R, peak at 24.23.

Fig. 9. Estimated periods: Pr[x<=100](<> secondPeak.ACCEPT)

Similarly we can estimate the phase difference between the signals as a distance between peaks of different signals. Figure 10 shows a probability density distribution of a phase difference between A and R signals, which implies that a peak in A typically leads to a peak in R within 6.21, but there might be one missed peak.

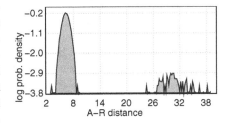

Fig. 10. Phase diff., peak at 6.21

6.1   Frequency Domain Analysis

Figures 11 and 12 compare the average frequency spectra of two variables from our deterministic and stochastic simulations. We observe that the deterministic spectra (black) tend to have sharp, well defined, peaks with discernible harmonics at high frequencies. In contrast, the spectra of stochastic simulations (red) tend to have softened peaks, few discernible high harmonics and contain an apparent continuum of frequencies. This is reflected in the reduced amplitude of these spectra relative to their deterministic counterparts: the amplitude of the original trace is effectively divided amongst many more frequencies. We note that the first three harmonics of the deterministic and stochastic spectra appear to coincide, confirming our expectation and intuition that the the two behaviours are 'similar'.

The apparent *thickness* of the red lines reflects the fact that the lines describe average spectra generated from stochastic data. Increasing N would make the lines less thick but would not change their overall form, that is derived from the frequency characteristics of the stochasticity.

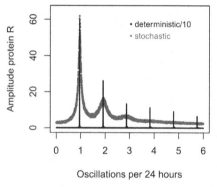
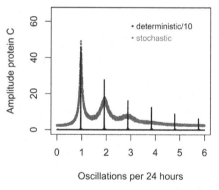

Fig. 11. Average frequency spectra of protein R. $\delta t = 2h, K = 12500$. $N = 100$ ($N = 1$) for the stochastic (deterministic) model.

Fig. 12. Average frequency spectra of protein C. $\delta t = 2h, K = 12500$. $N = 100$ ($N = 1$) for the stochastic (deterministic) model.

7   Conclusion

We have introduced and applied various advanced statistical model checking techniques to an osillatory biological system and have demonstrated their relevance to runtime verification. We have used two state of the art tools: UPPAAL-SMC and PLASMA. UPPAAL is a mature general-purpose platform based on timed automata, while PLASMA is a relatively new tool that allows domain-specific languages to describe Markov chain models.

Table 1. Tool comparison summary

Aspect	PLASMA	UPPAAL
Models	Domain specific	Stochastic hybrid automata
Semantics	DTMC/CTMC	Stochastic hybrid transition systems
Properties	MITL, rare events	(Weighted) MITL
Results	Exported data	Generic visualizations

Table 1 summarizes the aspects of both tools and shows that PLASMA is targeted for domain specific languages and the final result analysis (such as frequency analysis) is done using external tools, whereas UPPAAL provides generic features with integrated visualization of predetermined concepts. Although there are fundamental differences in the underlying semantics of the two tools, we have shown that they are united by the properties and problems of verification. In particular, frequency domain analysis and rare events are subjects of ongoing joint research.

References

1. Abelson, H., Allen, D., Coore, D., Hanson, C., Homsy, G., Knight Jr., T.F., Nagpal, R., Rauch, E., Sussman, G.J., Weiss, R.: Amorphous computing. Commun. ACM 43(5), 74–82 (2000)
2. Alur, R., Dill, D.L.: A theory of timed automata. Theor. Comput. Sci. 126(2), 183–235 (1994)
3. Barkai, N., Leibler, S.: Biological rhythms: Circadian clocks limited by noise. Nature 403, 267–268 (2000)
4. Legay, A., Delahaye, B., Bensalem, S.: Statistical Model Checking: An Overview. In: Barringer, H., Falcone, Y., Finkbeiner, B., Havelund, K., Lee, I., Pace, G., Roşu, G., Sokolsky, O., Tillmann, N. (eds.) RV 2010. LNCS, vol. 6418, pp. 122–135. Springer, Heidelberg (2010)
5. Bulychev, P.E., David, A., Larsen, K.G., Legay, A., Li, G., Poulsen, D.B., Stainer, A.: Monitor-Based Statistical Model Checking for Weighted Metric Temporal Logic. In: Bjørner, N., Voronkov, A. (eds.) LPAR-18 2012. LNCS, vol. 7180, pp. 168–182. Springer, Heidelberg (2012)
6. Dijkstra, E.W.: Guarded commands, nondeterminacy and formal derivation of programs. Commun. ACM 18(8), 453–457 (1975)
7. Gillespie, D.T.: Stochastic simulation of chemical kinetics. Annual Review of Physical Chemistry 58, 35–55 (2007)
8. Gillespie, D.T.: Exact stochastic simulation of coupled chemical reactions. Journal of Physical Chemistry 81, 2340–2361 (1977)
9. Gillespie, D.T.: Deterministic limit of stochastic chemical kinetics. The Journal of Physical Chemistry. B 113, 1640–1644 (2009)
10. Havelund, K., Roşu, G.: Synthesizing Monitors for Safety Properties. In: Katoen, J.-P., Stevens, P. (eds.) TACAS 2002. LNCS, vol. 2280, pp. 342–356. Springer, Heidelberg (2002)

11. Hérault, T., Lassaigne, R., Magniette, F., Peyronnet, S.: Approximate Probabilistic Model Checking. In: Steffen, B., Levi, G. (eds.) VMCAI 2004. LNCS, vol. 2937, pp. 307–329. Springer, Heidelberg (2004)

12. Hilborn, R.C., Erwin, J.D.: Stochastic coherence in an oscillatory gene circuit model. Journal of Theoretical Biology 253(2), 349–354 (2008)

13. Hoeffding, W.: Probability inequalities. Journal of the American Statistical Association 58, 13–30 (1963)

14. Ihekwaba, A., Sedwards, S.: Communicating oscillatory networks: frequency domain analysis. BMC Systems Biology 5(1), 203 (2011)

15. Jegourel, C., Legay, A., Sedwards, S.: A Platform for High Performance Statistical Model Checking – PLASMA. In: Flanagan, C., König, B. (eds.) TACAS 2012. LNCS, vol. 7214, pp. 498–503. Springer, Heidelberg (2012)

16. Jegourel, C., Legay, A., Sedwards, S.: Cross-Entropy Optimisation of Importance Sampling Parameters for Statistical Model Checking. In: Madhusudan, P., Seshia, S.A. (eds.) CAV 2012. LNCS, vol. 7358, pp. 327–342. Springer, Heidelberg (2012)

17. Laplante, S., Lassaigne, R., Magniez, F., Peyronnet, S., de Rougemont, M.: Probabilistic abstraction for model checking: An approach based on property testing. ACM TCS 8(4) (2007)

18. Larsen, K.G., Pettersson, P., Yi, W.: Uppaal in a nutshell. STTT 1(1-2), 134–152 (1997)

19. Purcell, O., Savery, N.J., Grierson, C.S., di Bernardo, M.: A comparative analysis of synthetic genetic oscillators. Journal of The Royal Society Interface 7(52), 1503–1524 (2010)

20. Ridder, A.: Importance sampling simulations of markovian reliability systems using cross-entropy. Annals of Operations Research 134, 119–136 (2005)

21. Roşu, G., Bensalem, S.: Allen Linear (Interval) Temporal Logic – Translation to LTL and Monitor Synthesis. In: Ball, T., Jones, R.B. (eds.) CAV 2006. LNCS, vol. 4144, pp. 263–277. Springer, Heidelberg (2006)

22. Sedwards, S.: A Natural Computation Approach To Biology: Modelling Cellular Processes and Populations of Cells With Stochastic Models of P Systems. PhD thesis, University of Trento (2009)

23. Sen, K., Viswanathan, M., Agha, G.: Statistical Model Checking of Black-Box Probabilistic Systems. In: Alur, R., Peled, D.A. (eds.) CAV 2004. LNCS, vol. 3114, pp. 202–215. Springer, Heidelberg (2004)

24. Vilar, J.M.G., Kueh, H.Y., Barkai, N., Leibler, S.: Mechanisms of noise-resistance in genetic oscillators. Proceedings of the National Academy of Sciences 99(9), 5988–5992 (2002)

25. Wald, A.: Sequential tests of statistical hypotheses. Annals of Mathematical Statistics 16(2), 117–186 (1945)

26. Younes, H.L.S.: Ymer: A Statistical Model Checker. In: Etessami, K., Rajamani, S.K. (eds.) CAV 2005. LNCS, vol. 3576, pp. 429–433. Springer, Heidelberg (2005)

27. Younes, H.L.S., Simmons, R.G.: Probabilistic Verification of Discrete Event Systems Using Acceptance Sampling. In: Brinksma, E., Larsen, K.G. (eds.) CAV 2002. LNCS, vol. 2404, pp. 223–235. Springer, Heidelberg (2002)

Behavioral Specification Based Runtime Monitors for OSGi Services

Jan Olaf Blech[1], Yliès Falcone[2], Harald Rueß[1], and Bernhard Schätz[1]

[1] fortiss GmbH, Munich, Germany
{blech,ruess,schaetz}@fortiss.org
[2] Laboratoire d'Informatique de Grenoble, Université Grenoble I, Grenoble, France
ylies.falcone@imag.fr

Abstract. Abstract constraint specifications – such as interoperability contracts – of the behavior of a system are frequently stated as requirements during early design phases. During the development process, these abstract specifications get refined until one reaches a deployable implementation. Especially in systems with components being dynamically added or replaced, it is critical that the constraints stated are met by the running system. The size of abstract constraint specifications is typically very small compared to the final implementation.

In this paper, we sketch a process, where abstract constraint specifications are used as a basis for runtime monitors and checks. These monitors and checks ensure that in cases of deviations from the original specification, the system takes compensating actions such as turning the system into a safe state. We particularly focus on systems where components can be exchanged, added or removed during runtime. We discuss a concrete application scenario: The usage of specification-based monitors for OSGi-based services in the domain of home automation.

1   Introduction

Systems with a high required level of dependability – with respect to both either safety or security – have been an important application domain for the application of formal analysis techniques. So far, this kind of systems – generally embedded systems from application domains like automotive, aerospace, or health – have traditionally been *systems with a static architecture* and a traditional design-build-commission-operate-decommission life cycle: Once the system architecture has been defined in the design phase and the properties of these components have been correctly specified, they remain unchanged through the later phases of the system life cycle. Formal analysis techniques here is mainly used to *front-load and improve the quality assurance* of the development, and thus for the validation and verification of the design. In such a context, runtime verification – i.e., observing a running system and detecting and possibly reacting to observed behaviors satisfying or violating certain properties – supports the monitoring of an implemented system or component. Monitoring is done with respect to the properties defined for this system or component during the design stage. Typical applications include debugging, verification of user-provided specifications, fault detection and recovery, security (e.g., intrusion detection).

However, with the change from classical embedded systems to cyber-physical systems – large-scale, networked systems controlling organizational as well as physical

T. Margaria and B. Steffen (Eds.): ISoLA 2012, Part I, LNCS 7609, pp. 405–419, 2012.

processes – the life-cycles of those systems – for example, a production system ranging from manufacturing automation to logistics control – have substantially changed:
Components have to be removed, added, or updated at runtime. Consequently, there
is a shift to *systems with a dynamic architecture*, accommodating the adaption of the
component structure of such systems during operation. To ensure essential properties of
those systems, of course some architectural properties have to remain invariant. These
properties are often defined in terms of interaction contracts between a component and
the system it is embedded in, defined during design time. For those kinds of systems,
a different form of runtime verification is needed, ensuring that *changes made to architecture do not violate the design*. This specifically includes the verification that the
modified/exchanged or added component respects the original contract. Thus, in this
context runtime verification is used to monitor the change of the architecture of a system, ensuring that only suitable modifications take place.

1.1   Main Research Questions

As a consequence, several research questions arise:

- Which formalisms are suitable for the requirement of specifications, behavioral
  types, or interaction contracts, that, at the same time, are expressive enough to
  describe the properties of individual components of a system needed to establish
  global and emergent properties of a system with a dynamically changing architecture? Choosing a specification formalisms with a level of expressiveness that
  exactly fits the needs of the targeted specification is paramount. There exists a spectrum of possible specification formalisms [1] that differ in terms of expressiveness.
  More expressive formalisms are often associated to less efficient monitoring algorithms. Optimal algorithms have to be chosen.
- What is a suitable analysis technique that allows to verify the conformance of a
  modified or added component to the interaction contracts imposed by the system?
- How can those formalisms and techniques be integrated into the design, implementation, and operation for monitoring properties, e.g., adaptions in systems with
  dynamically changing architectures?

In the following, we refine these challenges and suggest solutions.

1.2   Contribution

We present a vision for component-based software systems and a connected development process that aims at using behavioral specifications at runtime. Behavioral specifications are derived from requirements of the software system and its architectural
and functional specification. These specifications are used as a basis for runtime monitors for software systems and additional informative checks and search operations. The
monitors ensure that in cases of deviations from the original specification, the system
takes compensating actions such as turning the system into a safe state. Compensating
actions may themselves be derived from specifications.

We specifically discuss the proposed ideas in the context of OSGi frameworks [2] and
its bundles particularly for an Eclipse based development environment. More concretely

we exemplify some of our ideas in the domain of an OSGi based home automation framework.

1.3   Overview

Related approaches are discussed in Section 2. Our ideas for a workflow from requirements to monitors and behavioral checks at runtime of a software system are presented in Section 3. Concrete ideas and an architecture for OSGi and an integration into an Eclipse based tool-chain are described in Section 4. Section 5 presents an example from the home automation domain. Section 6 draws some conclusions.

2   Related Approaches

Specification of the behavior of OSGi-based services has also been studied in [3]. Specifications of services is mostly regarded with respect to substituting one service by another and is based on process algebra.

Behavioral types as means for behavioral checks at runtime for component based systems have been investigated in [4]. In this work, the focus is rather put on the definition of a suitable formal representation to express types and investigate their methodical application in the context of a model-based development process.

A language for behavioral specification of component-based systems aiming at object oriented systems is introduced in [5]. Compared to the requirement-based descriptions proposed in our paper, the specifications used in this work are still relatively close to an implementation.

Our behavioral specifications resemble to behavioral types for component based systems. This is studied in the context of real-time embedded systems [6] and as interface automata. Interface automata ensure the compatibility of component interfaces [7] by specifying protocols using automata. JML [8] provides assertion, pre- and postcondition based specifications for Java which can be used to describe behavior. A similar description mechanism has also been used for systems specified in synchronous dataflow languages like Lustre [9].

Runtime monitors for interface specifications of web-service in the context of a concrete e-commerce service have been studied in [10]. Behavioral conformance of web-services and corresponding runtime verification has also been investigated in [11]. Runtime monitoring for web-services where runtime monitors are derived from UML diagrams is studied in [12].

A formal approach to runtime verify the behavior of component-based systems is proposed in [13]. It is expressed in the BIP framework [14].

Runtime enforcement is also a candidate technique in our framework. So far, mainly theoretical studies have been carried out [15–17], see [18] for an overview. Runtime enforcement of safety properties was initiated with security automata [15] that are able to halt the underlying program upon a deviation from the expected behaviors. Later, edit-automata were proposed to enforce more than safety properties: by memorizing some of the events produced by the underlying system, edit-automata are able to provide some form of recovery after an error has occurred in the system. Later, previous approaches were generalized with generic enforcement monitors [19]. In these approaches, several definitions of enforcement monitoring are proposed according to how incorrect executions are modified by the monitors [18]. We shall identify the suitable definition of enforcement monitoring in the context of home automation.

3   From Behavioral Specifications to Monitors in System Development

During the development of component-based software systems requirements are typically collected at an early stage. These requirements are aggregated into a textual form or more formal descriptions.

Once an architecture has been designed, requirements can be associated with distinct components using, e.g., UML. UML diagrams can be formal enough to extract behavioral specifications of components (cf. [20]). These specifications can be used to generate monitoring code.

In a next phase, the specified system is implemented. The generated monitoring code can already be used during the implementation phase for testing purposes. It can be inserted using some instrumentation technique. Depending on the required level of observation of the underlying system, several solutions can be considered from in-house techniques to aspect-oriented techniques. In the context of OSGi services, based on Java technology, AspectJ[1] is a tried and tested technique ensuring that the interference with the implementation work is kept to a minimum, and, it provides observation means to express a wide range of properties over system executions.

For the deployed system, the monitors shall be active and observe the system's runtime behavior and take compensating actions. These compensating actions may already be stated during the requirements phase and may be generated from their formalization out of, e.g., UML state-machines, too.

3.1   Formalizing Requirements

Some work has to be done to come from informal requirements and specifications to formalized requirements for distinct components and specifications of their interactions. Semi-formal requirements may be represented by a UML diagram. Further work may have to be conducted to come to a formalism that is suitable for generating monitors or comparing formal behavior and checking for compatibility.

For our purposes, formalisms that can be used for specifying a protocol of possible system interactions are most relevant. The following formalisms are candidates:

- *Regular expressions* are equivalent to finite automata. Thus, it is possible to generate them from some forms of UML state-charts and sequence diagrams. Some abstraction steps can be necessary to transform a state-machine or a sequence diagram to a regular expression.
- *Temporal logics formulas* can be generated from sequence diagrams and other form of diagrams that specify interactions between different components.

---

[1] http://www.eclipse.org/aspectj/

– Parameterized formalisms based on the above mentioned techniques. Monitoring such formalisms is receiving a growing interest from the runtime verification community. There exist a spectrum of available formalisms associated to different monitoring algorithms and tools [1]. Generally, expressiveness comes at the price of a reduced efficiency. The input formalisms has thus to be chosen wisely to keep overhead to a minimum.

Furthermore, languages that combine regular expressions and temporal logics formulas like PSL [21] can be used. In this regard, SALT [22] is a candidate.

File-Writer Example Consider the following example for exemplifying different levels of specification:

– An informal requirement may state that a component has to open a file before it can write to it and afterwards has to close it.
– In a UML diagram this can be stated as a sequence diagram or state-machine and may involve concrete names of primitives for opening open, writing *write* and closing close.
– A regular expression as a formal representation may describe this as:

$$open.write^*.close.$$

Pre- and Post-condition Example In some cases, components may come with behavioral pre-conditions that must be met before their deployment and post-conditions that are fulfilled after their deployment provided that the pre-conditions hold. These can be specified using the languages mentioned above. For instance, consider three components A, B, and C connected to a bus. There is an order of communication that these protocols fulfill on the bus given by a regular expression:

$$(send\_A.send\_B.send\_C)^*$$

Several groups of sends can be done where A sends first, then B, then C before having another group of sends. This may serve as a pre-condition. A post-condition may ensure that D adds its messages after C and before A sends again.

$$(send\_A.send\_B.send\_C.send\_D)^*$$

Of course it would be advantageous if requirement and specification documents would already contain formalizations made in one of the languages stated above. This would make the step of transforming requirements into more formal specifications unnecessary. At this point, however, we do believe that this is only feasible for a minority of projects.

3.2   Inferring Monitors from Requirements and Specifications

At least two reasons for monitoring behaviors can be distinguished:

– *Give error messages or discover incompatibilities in order to prevent malfunctions.* Behavioral incompatibility shall be detected automatically during runtime of a system and reported to the system and its users.

- *Taking compensating actions.* In case of a detected deviation from a specification, compensating actions shall be taken automatically to minimize the effect of the deviation.

A formalism for specifications and requirements that is suitable for generating executable monitor code has to be chosen. The formalisms mentioned above are good candidates for automatically generating monitors where a state transition function updates a monitor state. In addition to this, for the described purposes, the following challenges have to be solved:

- In the case of ensuring a protocol, we are sometimes monitoring properties, where a monitor state can be distributed between different components. An appropriate implementation might require extra communication between components.
- Finding appropriate places where to inject the monitoring code (in-line monitoring) or the code used to interacts with the monitor (out-line monitoring).
- Another important aspect is to link the elements used in the specification with artifacts that will occur in the implementation. For example, a requirement that a component has to register itself to another component has to be broken down to concrete method calls. This, can already be contained in the UML diagrams.

In the case of the first two items an implementation decision between in-line and out-line monitoring has to be taken.

3.3   Integration of Monitors into the Implementation

A typical RV implementation using monitors in the regarded scenarios requires different pieces of code to be written or generated. In particular we need the following:

- Code that is used for representing and managing a monitor state. In case of out-line monitoring this code can comprise a component that realizes the actual monitor. In case-of in-line monitoring it comprises the data type definitions for the monitor state and auxiliary operations on it.
- Code that is integrated into the non-RV code for updating the monitor state. It comprises actions that trigger the updating of the monitor state. In case of out-line monitoring it comprises code for communicating with the monitor component.
- Code that is used for taking compensating actions.

Different implementation techniques have been successfully applied for monitor integration (see, e.g., [23] for .NET or AspectJ for Java).

3.4   Comparing Behavioral Specifications

While runtime monitoring checks and potentially enforces behavioral constraints in an environment where components can be dynamically composed, it is advantageous if components can inform themselves about the behavior of other components and the behavior they expect for interacting with them. Such protocols can be made available within the OSGi framework. Expected protocols may be represented using the same formalisms as for monitor generation.

The same motivation as for monitors applies here. In addition to the reasons stated in Section 3.2 components can use the formal protocol descriptions for the following purposes at runtime:

- *Search for appropriate components.* Component-based systems typically come with some kind of brokerage service that lets component search for appropriate components / services they need for performing some task. Automatic checks of compatibility is done by comparing interfaces based on primitive datatypes and their aggregation into classes, structures and arrays. Apart from this, additional descriptions may exist – for example textual – that indicates the behavior of components so that with some human interaction components can be composed in a meaningful way. Here, we are interested in extending these specifications so that components can search for required components that are compatible from a behavioral point of view – at least for some aspects – without human interaction.
- *Adapt itself to a protocol.* A component may now dynamically adapt itself to the requirements of another component. It may comprise different protocol modes that are chosen for the interaction with different implementation of another component.

The stated needs require checking compatibility of behavioral specifications. Checking compatibility can comprise:

- *Equivalence or equality checks.* Regular expressions for instance have to be transformed into a normal form. This comprises the minimization and reordering of sub-expressions in accordance with an order defined over atomic elements of the regular expression.
- *Refinement checks.* Specifications may be given at different levels of details. A refinement check performs a form of abstraction, e.g., omitting certain sub-constructs before performing an equivalence or equality check. This way one can compare behavior specified on more detailed to more abstract behavior.

Technically, the described checks can be carried out by a separate (realized as another component) or in-lined checker. A main goal for the realization of these checks is to keep them decidable and efficient. Additional tools may be involved in such as model-checkers (like SMT solvers) or theorem provers. In this case a transformation into the language of a system representation into the language of the tool is necessary (see, e.g., [24, 20] for our work on Eclipse-based implementations). Another important aspect is the scalability of the checks. A component-based system can consist of hundreds of components interacting with each other. Efficient checks of possible interactions are required.

4 An Architecture for OSGi Bundles, Behavioral Descriptions and Monitors

Here, we describe the OSGi framework and discuss the integration of the ideas described in Section 3. Furthermore, we sketch an integration into the Eclipse environment.

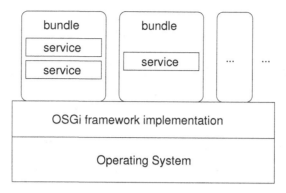

Fig. 1. OSGi framework

4.1   An Overview on OSGi

The OSGi framework is a component and service platform for Java. It allows the aggregation of services into bundles (cf. Figure 1) and provides means for dynamically configuring services, their dependencies and usages. It is used as the basis for Eclipse plug-ins but also for embedded applications including solutions for the automotive domain, home automation and industrial automation. Bundles can be installed and uninstalled during the runtime. For example, they can be exchanged by newer versions. Hence, possible interactions between bundles can in general not be determined statically. Important aspects that need to be investigated for applications in this context comprise composability – i.e., the ability to exchange a component with one or several others without changing the behavior of the system as a whole – and compositionality – i.e., when can we guarantee properties of a system that are inferred from its components (cf. [14]).

Bundles are deployed as .jar files containing extra OSGi information. Bundles generally contain a class implementing an OSGi interface that contains code for managing the bundle, e.g., code that is executed upon activation and stopping of the bundle. Upon activation, a bundle can register its services to the OSGi framework and make it available for use by other bundles. Services are technically implemented in Java. The bundle may itself start to use existing services. Services can be found using dictionary-like mechanisms provided by the OSGi framework. Typically one can search for a component with a specified Java interface.

The OSGi standard only specifies the framework including the syntactical format specifying what bundles should contain. Different implementations exist for different application domains like Equinox[2] for Eclipse, Apache Felix[3] or Knopflerfish[4]. If bundles do not depend on implementation specific features OSGi bundles can run on different implementations of the OSGi framework.

---

[2] http://www.eclipse.org/equinox/
[3] http://felix.apache.org/site/index.html
[4] http://www.knopflerfish.org/

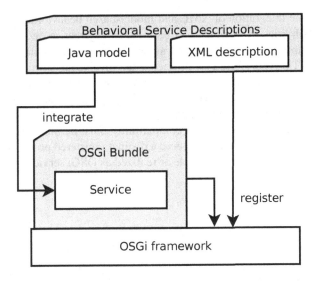

Fig. 2. Usage of XML and model based behavioral descriptions

4.2 Extending OSGi with Behavioral Descriptions

Different levels of behavioral descriptions for OSGi can be distinguished. They can all serve the purpose to ensure interoperability at an inter-bundle level, but may be described with respect to a distinct level:

- *Inter-Bundle level.* For example, some protocols may have to be fulfilled when different bundles communicate with each other. A typical Eclipse installation can start (and stop) several hundred bundles during a development session. A bundle often requires other bundles to communicates with. Hence, specifying and ensuring correctness of inter-bundle communication is important for eliminating potential incompatibilities.
- *Bundle level.* Protocols may be specified with respect to a single bundle. For example a protocol that has to be fulfilled when another bundle communicates with the specified one. Contrarily to the inter-bundle level, the specification does only describe the expected behavior of the specified bundle.
- *Service level.* More fine grained than the bundle level, the service level describes the possible behavior of an object that is registered as a service. It can describe the interplay of the different methods offered by the service or additional objects that are created and used.
- *Object level.* Compared to the service level, the object level is more implementation centric and describes the behavior of a particular object which can be a service or used by a service.
- *Method level.* The method level can describe the behavior of a particular method. For example, possible events that may be triggered. We may also provide invariants about results that are returned.

Figure 2 shows the integration of XML and model-based behavioral descriptions into OSGi. Two possibilities exist which can be realized together in one implementation: Behavioral descriptions can be registered as bundle properties upon the activation of an OSGi bundle. This is preferred for protocols that involve an entire bundle or several bundles. Another possibility is that a registered service object implements a behavioral Java interface definition. Other services can call a special method returning, e.g., a model describing the behavior of the service.

In addition, checkers for behavioral compatibility must be implemented, hence allowing to search for bundles which preserve a distinct registered protocol. Such checkers can be integrated into the bundle code or realized as OSGi services themselves.

4.3 Integration of Runtime Monitors

The code pieces described in Section 3.3 should be generated automatically using the specifications. They have to be integrated into the OSGi bundle development: Java code that is written by humans. For OSGi we can use code weaving as in aspect-oriented techniques like AspectJ in Eclipse for this integration.

4.4 Eclipse Integration of Behavioral Descriptions

Figure 3 sketches the workflow from requirements to models in Eclipse.

As a first step, informal requirements are put into a more formal format. Meta-models for describing the behavioral aspects of our services is central to handling behavioral

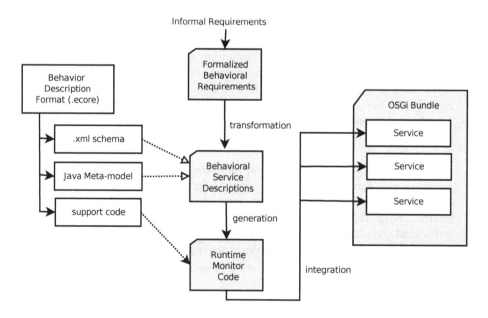

Fig. 3. From requirements to monitors in Eclipse

descriptions in Eclipse. Different meta-models can co-exist provided that some transformations between them exist. We propose the usage of an .ecore-based format for these meta-models. It allows the specification of the meta-model and the generation of a corresponding XML schema, a class structure for representing instances of behavioral specifications in Java and a variety of code support.

In the case of UML as a specification mechanism, on the implementation side, the UML2 meta-model [25] can be used. This format comes with tool support like the Papyrus tools [26] which allows the graphical editing of UML diagrams. Figure 4 shows a very simple example specification of a speed control assistant from the automotive domain using Papyrus and UML2. It serves as a basis for further refinement and automatic formal treatment and is used in [20, 27].

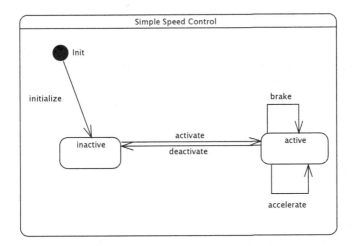

Fig. 4. A simple example specification using Papyrus

A meta-model serving as the basis for generating the monitor code has to be defined. This does not have to be the same as the one initially chosen for formalizing requirements. In the case of the UML meta-model, another meta-model that serves as the direct basis for code generation and is closer to the implementation of the monitors may be desirable. This is similar to modern compilers where a source language gets compiled to an intermediate language before it is compiled to target code. As a basis for code-generation for monitors, we suggest a format that directly reflects the property that we generate monitors for, like a format for regular expressions when regular expressions shall be monitored. Transformations between the different meta-models are required and may perform abstractions of parts that are not relevant for the generation of monitoring code. Additional information about relevant artifacts and links between specified elements and their implementation may be provided by human users and collected by another Eclipse plug-in.

Monitor code-generation and required model transformations are done using existing Java / Eclipse tools based on EMF models (e.g., ATL[5]) or a hand-written code-generation mechanism.

5   OSGi-Based Home Automation Services

We briefly describe a simple application scenario of our ideas. Figure 5 shows an example from the home automation domain similar to the one described in [28].

Our home automation OSGi-Based infrastructure comprises a central server (see Figure 5). Different bundles are running on this OSGi implementation. Physically, different components like lights, switches and sensors can be added and removed to a home network which connects them to this central server. All OSGi-Based software runs on this server and physical devices are represented by OSGi bundles and services. Each device, and in some cases each class of devices, comes with their own OSGi bundle. OSGi bundles are added, removed and exchanged during the runtime of the system. The communication between the bundles running on the server is shown in Figure 6.

Important features of this example are:

- Physical devices and their software counterparts can be added, removed and exchanged during the runtime of the system.
- The system is supposed to run for a long time (several years or more).
- Newly added devices shall not disturb the old ones.

To achieve the last one, it has to be ensured that all OSGi software components fulfill a protocol for registering their services and interacting with each other. Regarding behavioral specifications, it is desirable that components are enabled to inform each other about desired protocols. On the other hand, runtime monitors can ensure that certain requirements are indeed met: Since OSGi services correspond to real physical devices components deviating from this protocol shall be handled appropriately – e.g., shut down – as a compensating action. This is ensured by a monitor.

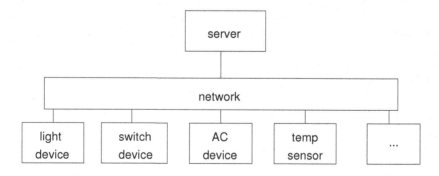

Fig. 5. A home automation infrastructure

---

[5] http://www.eclipse.org/atl/

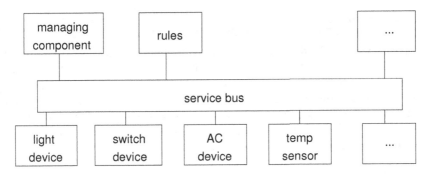

Fig. 6. Possible bundle interaction

Example Requirement Provided that the bus components offers methods *registerService* and the light components provides *on* and *off* methods as services, interaction sequences can be specified as regular expressions. Possible interaction sequences between a light component and a bus can be described using the following expression:

$$\Sigma_{\text{id}:int}(\text{id} := \text{Bus.registerService}(light).(\text{Light[id].on()} \mid \text{Light[id].off()})^*)$$

where $\Sigma_{\text{id}:int}$ is a quantifier over parameterized expressions. In this case, the expression ensures that a light is first registered and an id is returned. Only after registration the id may be used to switch a light on and off. Different service bus implementations can be available on the market. A component connected to a home automation system may not know it advance which protocol it has to fulfill. Another service bus implementation might expect the following interaction sequence with the a light component:

$$\Sigma_{\text{id}:int}(\text{id} := \text{Manager.getid()}.\text{Bus.registerService(id)}.(\text{Light[id].on()} \mid \text{Light[id].off()})^*)$$

In the case that the *light* from the first implementation is an integer constant, the interface of the two implementation of the service bus may be indistinguishable. Hence it is valuable if a newly plugged-in component is able to learn about the expected protocol and a runtime monitor is there to take compensating actions in case of deviation from the expected protocol.

Compensating actions for home automation More complex compensating actions triggered by monitors can play a role in the domain of home automation. They should be derived from specifications: for instance, given three devices: a home cinema, a light and a sensor observing a door. The movie service turns the light off when a movie is played. However, the door sensor turns the light on. Potential undesired actions can be triggered. One can imagine using an enforcer to dynamically disable actions, according to the context and some priority. We propose to enforce a correct behavior by monitoring the actions taken and taking compensating actions triggered by the monitor. In principle, the decisions taken by the components could be based on more complex behaviors, but this might result in more complex implementations.

   More complex sequences of compensating actions can be triggered by the monitor and generated using, e.g., game-based techniques that allow finding ways to leave or avoid an unsafe part of a state space as described in [29].

6 Conclusion

In this paper, we presented a vision for a deriving monitors that check requirements stated at an early phase in a software development process. Checks and monitors are used to ensure some system behaviors at runtime and report deviations triggering compensating actions. Based on this, we presented an architecture for an Eclipse-based implementation for ensuring and monitoring runtime behavior of bundles in an OSGi framework. Furthermore, we have exemplified the usage of our work for home automation.

The presented work is mostly of a conceptual and visionary nature. An implementation of the framework is subject to future work. As a first step, the choice of appropriate specification formalisms has to be fixed. It seems to be highly depending on the application domain. Here, application projects have to be undertaken to get a better understanding of the application domain. Mechanisms for deriving checks and monitors for common specification mechanisms can be developed in parallel. Complete implementations within Eclipse will contain some domain-specific parts, due to different specification mechanisms.

As a long term goal an implementation of the described framework for other component frameworks that take resource constraints – especially time: for real-time systems – into account is a goal. In that case, safety relevant aspects, for example timing properties, and the possibility for certification by authorities are more crucial and serve as motivation for this effort.

References

1. Barringer, H., Falcone, Y., Havelund, K., Reger, G., Rydeheard, D.: Quantified Event Automata: Towards Expressive and Efficient Runtime Monitors. In: Giannakopoulou, D., Méry, D. (eds.) FM 2012. LNCS, vol. 7436, pp. 68–84. Springer, Heidelberg (2012)
2. Alliance, O.: Osgi service platform core specification, Version 4.3 (2011)
3. Tchinda, H.A.M., Stouls, N., Ponge, J.: Spécification et substitution de services osgi. Technical report, Inria (2011), http://hal.inria.fr/inria-00619233
4. Arbab, F.: Abstract behavior types: a foundation model for components and their composition. Sci. Comput. Program 55, 3–52 (2005)
5. Johnsen, E.B., Hähnle, R., Schäfer, J., Schlatte, R., Steffen, M.: ABS: A Core Language for Abstract Behavioral Specification. In: Aichernig, B.K., de Boer, F.S., Bonsangue, M.M. (eds.) FMCO 2010. LNCS, vol. 6957, pp. 142–164. Springer, Heidelberg (2011)
6. Lee, E.A., Xiong, Y.: A behavioral type system and its application in ptolemy ii. Formal Asp. Comput. 16, 210–237 (2004)
7. de Alfaro, L., Henzinger, T.A.: Interface automata. In: ESEC / SIGSOFT FSE, pp. 109–120 (2001)
8. Chalin, P., Kiniry, J.R., Leavens, G.T., Poll, E.: Beyond Assertions: Advanced Specification and Verification with JML and ESC/Java2. In: de Boer, F.S., Bonsangue, M.M., Graf, S., de Roever, W.-P. (eds.) FMCO 2005. LNCS, vol. 4111, pp. 342–363. Springer, Heidelberg (2006)
9. Colaço, J.L., Pouzet, M.: Clocks as First Class Abstract Types. In: Alur, R., Lee, I. (eds.) EMSOFT 2003. LNCS, vol. 2855, pp. 134–155. Springer, Heidelberg (2003)
10. Hallé, S., Bultan, T., Hughes, G., Alkhalaf, M., Villemaire, R.: Runtime verification of web service interface contracts. IEEE Computer 43, 59–66 (2010)

11. Cao, T.D., Phan-Quang, T.T., Félix, P., Castanet, R.: Automated runtime verification for web services. In: ICWS, pp. 76–82. IEEE Computer Society (2010)
12. Gan, Y., Chechik, M., Nejati, S., Bennett, J., O'Farrell, B., Waterhouse, J.: Runtime monitoring of web service conversations. In: Proceedings of the 2007 Conference of the Center for Advanced Studies on Collaborative Research. CASCON 2007, pp. 42–57. ACM, New York (2007)
13. Falcone, Y., Jaber, M., Nguyen, T.-H., Bozga, M., Bensalem, S.: Runtime Verification of Component-Based Systems. In: Barthe, G., Pardo, A., Schneider, G. (eds.) SEFM 2011. LNCS, vol. 7041, pp. 204–220. Springer, Heidelberg (2011)
14. Sifakis, J.: A framework for component-based construction – Extended Abstract. In: Aichernig, B.K., Beckert, B. (eds.) SEFM, pp. 293–300. IEEE Computer Society (2005)
15. Schneider, F.B.: Enforceable security policies. ACM Trans. Inf. Syst. Secur. 3, 30–50 (2000)
16. Ligatti, J., Bauer, L., Walker, D.: Run-time enforcement of nonsafety policies. ACM Trans. Inf. Syst. Secur. 12 (2009)
17. Falcone, Y., Fernandez, J.C., Mounier, L.: What can you verify and enforce at runtime? STTT 14, 349–382 (2012)
18. Falcone, Y.: You Should Better Enforce Than Verify. In: Barringer, H., Falcone, Y., Finkbeiner, B., Havelund, K., Lee, I., Pace, G., Roşu, G., Sokolsky, O., Tillmann, N. (eds.) RV 2010. LNCS, vol. 6418, pp. 89–105. Springer, Heidelberg (2010)
19. Falcone, Y., Mounier, L., Fernandez, J.C., Richier, J.L.: Runtime enforcement monitors: composition, synthesis, and enforcement abilities. Formal Methods in System Design 38, 223–262 (2011)
20. Blech, J.O., Schätz, B.: Towards a formal foundation of behavioral types for UML state-machines. In: Proceedings of the 5th International Workshop UML and Formal Methods (accepted for publication, to appear, 2012)
21. Eisner, C., Fisman, D.: A Practical Introduction to PSL. Springer (2006)
22. Bauer, A., Leucker, M.: The Theory and Practice of SALT. In: Bobaru, M., Havelund, K., Holzmann, G.J., Joshi, R. (eds.) NFM 2011. LNCS, vol. 6617, pp. 13–40. Springer, Heidelberg (2011)
23. Hamlen, K.W., Morrisett, G., Schneider, F.B.: Certified in-lined reference monitoring on .NET. In: Sreedhar, V.C., Zdancewic, S. (eds.) PLAS, pp. 7–16. ACM (2006)
24. Blech, J.O., Périn, M.: Generating invariant-based certificates for embedded systems. ACM Transactions on Embedded Computing Systems (accepted for publication, 2012)
25. Object Management Group: Unified modeling language (uml), Version 2.0 (August 2005)
26. CEA LIST: Papyrus uml (2012), http://www.papyrusuml.org
27. Blech, J.O., Mou, D., Ratiu, D.: Reusing test-cases on different levels of abstraction in a model based development tool. In: Petrenko, A.K., Schlingloff, H. (eds.) MBT. EPTCS, vol. 80, pp. 13–27 (2012)
28. Koss, D., Sellmayr, F., Bauereiss, S., Bytschkow, D., Gupta, P., Schätz, B.: Establishing a smart grid node architecture and demonstrator in an office environment using the soa approach. In: Proceedings of the First International ICSE Workshop on Software Engineering Challenges for the Smart Grid. IEEE (2012)
29. Cheng, C.-H., Rueß, H., Knoll, A., Buckl, C.: Synthesis of Fault-Tolerant Embedded Systems Using Games: From Theory to Practice. In: Jhala, R., Schmidt, D. (eds.) VMCAI 2011. LNCS, vol. 6538, pp. 118–133. Springer, Heidelberg (2011)

Modelling and Decentralised Runtime Control of Self-stabilising Power Micro Grids*

Arnd Hartmanns and Holger Hermanns

Saarland University – Computer Science, Saarbrücken, Germany

Abstract. Electric power production infrastructures around the globe are shifting from centralised, controllable production to decentralised structures based on distributed microgeneration. As the share of renewable energy sources such as wind and solar power increases, electric power production becomes subject to unpredictable and significant fluctuations. This paper reports on formal behavioural models of future power grids with a substantial share of renewable, especially photovoltaic, microgeneration. We give a broad overview of the various system aspects of interest and the corresponding challenges in finding suitable abstractions and developing formal models. We focus on current developments within the German power grid, where enormous growth rates of microgeneration start to induce stability problems of a new kind. We build formal models to investigate runtime control algorithms for photovoltaic microgenerators in terms of grid stability, dependability and fairness. We compare the currently implemented and proposed runtime control strategies to a set of approaches that take up and combine ideas from randomised distributed algorithms widely used in communication protocols today. Our models are specified in MODEST, an expressive modelling language for stochastic timed systems with a well-defined semantics. Current tool support for MODEST allows the evaluation of the models using simulation as well as model-checking techniques.

1 Introduction

Political and climatical circumstances are causing a shift in electric power production around the world. While large conventional power plants dominated electric power generation up to now, the future will see a drastic increase in the number of distributed microgenerators based on renewable energy sources such as solar and wind power. Electric power grids thus move from a setting in which production was assumed fully controllable so as to always match the uncontrollable, but well-predictable consumption to a setting where the production side becomes uncontrollable, too. External influences such as changing weather conditions can imply drastically higher fluctuations in available electric power.

---

* This work has been supported by the DFG as part of SFB/TR 14 AVACS, by the DFG/NWO Bilateral Research Program ROCKS, and by the European Union FP7-ICT project MEALS, contract no. 295261.

T. Margaria and B. Steffen (Eds.): ISoLA 2012, Part I, LNCS 7609, pp. 420–439, 2012.
© Springer-Verlag Berlin Heidelberg 2012

This problem is amplified by the difficulty of centrally controlling the vast number of geographically distributed microgenerators. New solutions to the problem of matching electricity production and consumption need to be found that are suitable to overcome these new challenges.

The German power grid is a prime example where many of these future challenges are already encountered today. As a consequence of the legal framework enforced by Federal legislation over the last decades, microgenerators of photovoltaic (PV) electric power have been rolled out massively on the rooftops of end user homes all over the country. In spite of a national target growth of 1.5 gigawatt (GW) per year, the total PV generation capacity has increased from 10 GW in 2009 to 25 GW by the end of 2011. The currently estimated actual growth rate is about 1.6 GW per year [9] (despite a target growth of less than 1.1 GW). This growth creates problems, especially in areas with additional microgeneration based on wind or biogas: The Northern German energy provider EWE AG recently reported that the number of emergency situations that required manual intervention to ensure grid stability has grown from less than 1 per week in 2009 to about 1 per day in 2011 [22].

To avoid these situations in the future, improved and better coordinated diagnostic and prediction techniques as well as orchestrated demand-side mechanisms to counter critical grid and/or generation situations are needed. To develop robust and correct mechanisms that do not create unexpected instability, e.g. by introducing oscillatory behaviour, mathematically well-founded models of electric power grids and their components are needed. However, the modelling space is huge, and a precise model reflecting all components in a detailed, physically exact manner will be very complex (if at all possible), and virtually impossible to analyse. Instead, suitable abstractions need to be developed, tailored to the fragments of the system under consideration and the aspects of interest. This will be the topic of the first part of this paper, where we give an overview of the various system aspects of electric power grids, in particular of last-mile micro grids with a significant fraction of microgeneration, and the future challenges faced in such grids (Section 2). We also take a look at the modelling challenges encountered in the study of such systems, surveying different modelling and abstraction approaches suitable for different system aspects and measures (Section 3). One expressive modelling formalism that fits this scenario particularly well is MODEST, a modelling language for stochastic timed systems with a formal semantics and good tool support [6,14], which we will use in the remainder of the paper.

A central issue to ensure the stability of future power grids is proper runtime control for the increasing number of microgenerators. Due to their distributed deployment, decentralised runtime control offers several advantages over centralised management approaches. The ideal is that of a network of independent generators whose control algorithms lead to a self-stabilising system. In the second part of this paper, we thus focus on the study of runtime control algorithms for photovoltaic microgenerators as an example for the modelling and analysis of future power grids. We first introduce the concepts of the currently implemented

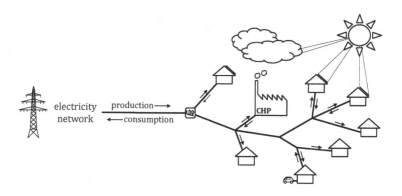

Fig. 1. Power micro grids

and proposed approaches (the former being known to introduce unwanted oscillatory effects) as well as of a potpourri of alternative approaches that take up and combine ideas from communication protocol design (Section 4). We model these approaches in MODEST and report on the results of a recent simulation study using these models [3] (Section 5).

Related work. The area of power grid modelling with formal behavioural models is gaining momentum. The most closely related work is likely the recent paper by Chen *et al.* [10], who analyse a multi-player game based on a recently proposed distributed demand-side micro grid management approach [18]. Other tangible work includes the application of probabilistic hybrid automata with distributed control to the power grid domain [21], and work on network calculus in battery buffered households [8].

2   Last Mile Power Micro Grids

The electric power grid is hierarchically structured, with a grid of long distance high voltage lines forming the top layer. At the leaves of the electric power grid hierarchy, we find the low voltage last mile which traditionally connects end consumers to the upper layers. Typically, these last miles have a tree-like structure through which electric power is distributed towards the leaves from a root. This root is a transformer, which constitutes the connection to the upper layer. Since these grids are relatively small (comprising at most a few hundred residential homes or business customers) and have a clear point of separation from the remaining grid, yet may themselves contain multiple independent microgenerators, we call these last miles *power micro grids*. Figure 1 gives a schematic overview of an exemplary power micro grid consisting of seven residential homes and a small industrial customer.

2.1   Elements of Power Micro Grids

A model of a power micro grid needs to take five central aspects into account: (1) the influence of the wide-area power grid it is connected to, (2) the local consumption of electric power, (3, 4) the grid local electric power generation—which can be further divided into (3) potential and (4) actual generation, i.e. the amount of electric power that can be produced in ideal external circumstances (such as weather and time of day), and the amount that is actually produced after control algorithms inside the generators have been applied—and finally (5) the geographic topology and capacities of the cabling inside the micro grid.

Wide-Area Connection. A power micro grid usually has a single connection point to the wide-area electric power grid. This is a transformer station that converts the network's high voltage to the grid's 400 Volt three-phase current (or 230 V per phase). Traditionally, electric power flows from large conventional 'thermal' power plants through the wide area grid into the micro grids. This infeed is controlled by grid coordinators based on predictions of the local consumption of all the micro grids [17], corrected by runtime observations. Runtime deviations must be corrected in order not to destabilise any grid. Due to the physical limitations related to the power plants in use, only a small fraction of the total generation potential can be employed for runtime adaptation. This is mainly realized with the help of pump-storage plants, where subtracting power is achieved by pumping up water, while adding power is achieved by the reverse, turning water downfall into electric power.

As part of the interconnection to the wide-area grid there is also a safety "fuse", a device that may disconnect the micro grid, intended as a preventative measure for both local events, e.g. to prevent fatal accidents when a cable is damaged during excavation works, as well as interference from the wide area grid, e.g. to prevent excessive infeed that would exceed the electric power flow capacity in the micro grid. With increasing microgeneration inside micro grids, this safety device may actually turn into a problem, for example by disconnecting the micro grid in case local overproduction exceeds the fuse specifications.

Local Consumption. At the leaves of the cabling inside the micro grid are residential homes and business customers. In the past they acted only as electric power consumers. The consumption of an individual leaf ultimately depends on a number of factors and decisions by its "inhabitants", yet it roughly follows patterns over the course of a day. Variations may be due to external influences such as temperature, influencing the electric power needed for heating or cooling. As such, consumption is uncontrollable, but predictable within certain error bounds. There is a recent trend to make consumption more controllable via so-called demand-side mechanisms [17], which intend to control the energy consumption of schedulable devices such as off-peak storage heaters and air conditioners. The decisions are to be based on electric power costs or on grid stability conditions.

Generation Potential. More and more traditional consumers at the leaves of the micro grid are turning into producer-consumers (a.k.a. "prosumers"). At certain times, they may produce more electric power than they consume. The potential output of the microgenerators installed at these leaves depends first and foremost on the type of generator: Combined heat and power plants (CHP) can essentially operate on demand, independent of external circumstances, while microgenerators based on renewable energy sources such as wind and solar power are inherently dependent on natural phenomena. These vary over time in an uncontrollable manner. Wind turbines show relatively moderate fluctuations since wind intensity usually changes only gradually; the amount of available solar power, however, can change rapidly and significantly when cloud coverage changes quickly.

Actual Generation. To avoid grid instability, consumption and production of electric power needs to be matched continuously in real time. The actual electric power emitted into the grid by a locally installed microgenerator may affect this stability. With the further increase of these sources, effective control mechanisms are needed in order to avoid over- or underprovisioning of power. Technically, it is no problem to reduce the output of all relevant types of generators—the problem is to decide when to do so, by which amount, when to switch the generators back on, and by how much. Control algorithms are thus an important aspect of future microgenerators. They are expected to have significant influence on the behaviour of future power micro grids.

Local Grid Topology. The topology and spatial layout of the micro grid in terms of cable lengths and diameters clearly impacts its behaviour. The grids have been rolled out in the past with the sole perspective of distributing power downstream, i.e. towards the leaves of the last miles. Now there might be upstream power flow in some parts of the grid. It is easy to come up with scenarios where this may result in stability violations (such as excessive voltage) inside the grid that remain unnoticed at the leaves and at the root. The proper reflection of these influences in a way that generalises to arbitrary last miles is very difficult, because it crucially depends on a specific layout.

2.2   Modelling and Abstraction Choices

Since a full model of all individual components of a power micro grid and their precise behaviour is extremely difficult to build and most probably entirely impossible to analyse, the various components have to be represented at appropriate levels of abstraction in a model. These abstractions have to be chosen carefully to make modelling and analysis feasible, yet provide sufficient information to extract reliable answers to the questions of interest from the model.

A first candidate for abstraction is the contribution of the wide-area grid. A detailed modelling of the wide-area grid is clearly out of the scope of a model focussed on just a single power micro grid, while the reverse, the impact of a single micro grid on the behaviour of the entire (e.g. European) electric power grid can be considered negligible. It is thus reasonable to represent the influence of the wide-area grid in the form of a profile, i.e. a deterministic or stochastic function mapping time to the amount of electric power provided. This is an instance of what is called a "load profile", and is itself assumed independent of what happens inside the particular micro grid. In addition, the safety fuse at the root we mentioned does not need to be explicitly modelled; instead it is present in the analysis as part of the characterisation of what "unsafe" or "unstable" states need to be avoided.

When it comes to modelling consumer behaviour, the abstraction level depends on the intended modelling purpose. If the focus is on the effects of consumer behaviour, as in a study of demand-side management mechanisms, a detailed consumer model and the explicit representation of individual consumers are obvious necessities. If this is not the focus, two choices are to be made: Should consumers be represented individually or in aggregated form (i.e. as a load profile), and how detailed does the individual or aggregated consumer model need to be? Modelling consumers individually allows the differentiation of consumer types (e.g. into households and businesses) to be represented directly. These distinctions would only lead to variations of the chosen load profile otherwise. Another fundamental question is whether to use a deterministic, stochastic or nondeterministic model of consumption. While deterministic models are often easier to analyse, they embody the risk of exhibiting or causing spurious oscillations or correlations mainly because they may ignore differences between the participants. A stochastic model typically is a good way to avoid these phenomena by assigning probabilities to different behaviours that are all considered part of the model. When it is not possible to assign probabilities to behaviours, nondeterministic models may capture all possible alternatives, but may often turn out to be hard or impossible to analyse.

The modelling spectrum on the power generation side is similar to that on the consumer side. Given a fixed set of generators of different types, a (deterministic or stochastic) load profile is a good representation of the potential generation. It can represent how the external influences on generation potential vary over time, and since a grid covers only a very restricted geographic area (of maybe 1 km^2), it can be considered constant throughout the geographic dimension, since local differences in wind or cloud cover are negligible at this resolution. With respect to actual generation, a load profile may be a good first step, but hide interesting behaviour that can result from inappropriate control algorithms. For example, the currently deployed control algorithm for PV generators in Germany can lead to oscillating behaviour in times of high potential generation once an unsafe grid state is reached (see Section 4.2). In order to study, for example, whether certain demand-side mechanisms can avoid or buffer these oscillations, one would need at least a simple behavioural model of the actual generation.

Finally, the role played by the grid topology is closely tied to the way the physical aspects of electric power are represented in the model. Intertwined differential equations or calculations with complex numbers are the norm, needed to provide nontrivial answers about frequency and voltage. They are achievable for specific layouts. A common abstraction that helps to provide valid answers on a more abstract level assumes the local grid to behave like a perfect "copper plate", thus eliminating any spacial considerations.

2.3   Properties and Challenges

As the installed microgeneration capacity increases, the effect of power micro grids on the whole network gets more significant. At the same time, as most microgenerators are based on renewable energy sources, the volatility in the micro grids' behaviour becomes an important concern. There are two core objectives of micro grid and microgenerator management: economy and stability, which are deeply intertwined, yet often conflicting interests.

Challenges. In European legislation, an electric power grid has two distinct modes of operation: *emergency operation*, where direct intervention of the grid coordinator is needed to drive the grid to a safe state, possibly impacting service levels on the consumer side, and *normal operation*, where market incentives drive the decisions of the participants. The stability of the grid is a priority concern because reliable distribution is a prerequisite for economic use of energy. However, the most economically beneficial decisions for individual participants may sometimes run counter to the goal of a stable grid. Grid instability is caused by over- or underproduction, respectively under- or overconsumption, i.e. the electric power production does not match the current consumption. It can be stabilised by suitably adjusting production, consumption, or both.

On the production side, the main issue is to avoid overproduction: While some generation technologies such as CHP are perfectly controllable, the upper limit on potential generation of renewable electric power is dependent on natural phenomena; control strategies for these microgenerators can thus only reduce production compared to their genuine potential. On the other hand, the economic interest of microgenerator owners is to feed as much energy into the grid as possible. In this sense, grid stability and production economy are conflicting interests. Control strategies on the production side, whose overriding goal is to ensure grid stability, thus have to be evaluated for efficiency and fairness in the economic sense as well.

In contrast to this, economic interests can be used as a way to guide the consumption side to a behaviour that is beneficial to stability: Over- and underproduction ideally have a direct effect on the price of electricity, which can drive demand in the desired direction. Nevertheless, the study of effective demand-side mechanisms that lead to compensation of production volatility, with or without economic aspects, is an area as widely open for research as the production side.

Properties. We propose the following set of measures to evaluate production control algorithms and demand-side mechanisms, which we collectively call *strategies*, for electric power micro grids:

- *Stability* is the ability of a strategy to keep the grid in a safe state with a minimum of oscillation between safe and unsafe states.
- *Availability* is the overall fraction of time that the grid spends in a safe state.
- *Output* measures the (total or individual, cumulative or averaged) electricity output of the relevant microgenerators, which is usually proportional to the financial rewards of the respective operators.
- *Goodput* relates output to availability: the amount of electric power a generator can add to the grid while the grid is in a safe state.
- *Quality of Service* measures negative impacts on the consumer side. While closely tied to availability, quality of service can also vary while the grid is in a safe state, for example if service reductions are used to achieve safety.
- *Fairness* is the degree to which a strategy manages to distribute adverse consequences equally among the participants. When the grid state does not allow all generators to operate at full power, for example, will each of them be allowed to provide an equal share of the allowed power generation?

3   Formal Modelling Challenges

Power micro grids are complex systems that require expressive modelling formalisms to capture the entirety of their behaviour. Even if only abstracted subsets of a micro grid shall be represented, features such as real-time behaviour and stochastics are necessary, e.g. to model delayed reactions by the grid controller and stochastic load profiles or randomised algorithms. In order to faithfully represent the precise physical behaviour of the electric components together with a discrete control strategy, a versatile modelling formalism is a necessity. A more exhaustive discussion on what kind of modelling features are needed for this problem domain can be found in [16]. However, there is an inherent tradeoff between expressivity and the analysis effort needed to compute results. Every modelling study thus needs to precisely identify the aspects to be included in the model as well as the kinds of properties to be analysed so as to make it possible to select the best matching formalism that is still sufficiently expressive.

3.1   Modest

MODEST [6] is a high-level modelling and description language for stochastic timed systems that combines expressive and powerful syntax-level features with a formal semantics in terms of stochastic timed automata (STA). Stochastic timed automata add continuous probability distributions, allowing in particular arbitrarily (e.g. uniformly or exponentially) distributed delays, to probabilistic timed automata (PTA) [19], which themselves can be seen as the orthogonal combination of timed [1] and probabilistic automata [24] (or, equivalently, Markov decision processes [23]). Other special cases of STA are generalised semi-Markov processes (GSMP) [12], which essentially constitute STA without nondeterminism, and both discrete- as well as continuous-time Markov chains (DTMCs and CTMCs). MODEST has recently been extended to support the specification of stochastic hybrid automata (SHA) models as well [13].

The key feature of MODEST that makes it attractive for electric power micro grids is that it is built around a *single-formalism, multiple-solution* approach: While expressive enough to specify SHA, most of the various well-known and extensively studied submodels can be easily identified on the syntactic level, and tool support dedicated to these submodels is available [4,5,15]. This allows a single language to be used for a wide range of models while benefiting from using restricted formalisms to achieve efficient analysis.

Syntactically, MODEST supports a process algebra-inspired compositional modelling approach. It allows smaller models to be combined into larger, more complex ones, including a parallel composition operator to specify processes or automata that perform their actions independently, subject to the classical interleaving semantics. Actions that are part of the shared alphabet of two or more processes have to be performed by all processes involved in a CSP-style synchronisation. We refer the interested reader to [6] and the MODEST TOOLSET website at

www.modestchecker.net

for details concerning the language's design and the semantics of its constructs. The website also contains further documentation, a list of MODEST-related publications as well as examples and case studies. We will use MODEST to build formal models of runtime control strategies for photovoltaic microgenerators in Section 5.

4 Decentralised Runtime Control

A major portion of the photovoltaic (PV) microgeneration capacity is mounted on the rooftops of private households, and is as such connected to the last mile. The often excessive volatility of solar production asks for a highly flexible grid management on this level. For the remainder of this paper, we therefore focus on control strategies for PV microgenerators. As outlined in the previous section, the goal of such a strategy is to reduce actual power output compared to the potential generation whenever this is necessary to maintain grid stability. Otherwise it should allow the output of as much electric power as can be generated.

Let us first take a deeper look at what constitutes a "safe state" for power (micro) grids. There are three fundamental dimensions to stability:

- In Europe, the target **frequency** is 50 Hz. If the frequency leaves the band of 49.8 to 50.2 Hz, this is a serious Europe wide phenomenon.
- In the end customer grid, the downstream customers may witness considerable **voltage** fluctuations because of upstream fluctuations in production and consumption. Deviations of more than 10 % are not tolerable.
- There are individual limits on the **capacity** of grid strands with respect to energy, i.e. the product of voltage and amperage.

The capacity limits are due to the local grid layout and the "fuse" at the connection point to the upper layers. Voltage has a direct linear dependency to production/consumption and is thus a good measure of the grid state. However, voltage changes are local phenomena, entangled with phase drifts in the last mile and intimately tied to the grid topology and the distances and cabling between producers and consumers. Therefore, the frequency is often used instead of voltage as a measure of the grid state, although frequency drifts usually affect the entire European grid and not only a specific last mile and are subject to dampening effects. An approximately linear dependency between production/consumption and frequency is known, albeit being an indirect effect of physical realities. However, it is still considered an appropriate abstraction by domain experts [20,25]. Roughly, a change in production/consumption of 15 GW approximately corresponds to a 1 Hz change in frequency in the European grid. The currently installed PV generation capacity in all of Germany (see Section 1) thus corresponds to a frequency spread of about 1.7 Hz.

4.1   Centralised vs. Decentralised Control

Photovoltaic microgenerators are difficult to manage. First, this is due to their sheer number, which leads to problems of scalability for any centralised approach. A second problem is their distributed nature: There is currently no measurement, logging and reporting infrastructure in place that enables the collection of accurate and up-to-date information about the state of the grid participants, and there is no communication infrastructure that allows safe remote control. These are two good reasons to consider highly local, decentralised and automatic grid management approaches. Additionally, decentralised approaches that do not need any transmission of information to central coordinators are inherently preferable from a privacy perspective.

The design of a highly local, highly automatic, highly decentralized, and highly flexible grid management is a challenging and pressing problem. It resembles the field of self-stabilising system (SSS) design [11]. SSS are built from a number of homogeneous systems that follow the same algorithmic pattern, with the intention that their joint execution emerges in a stable global behaviour, and can recover from transient disturbances. Compared to the setting usually considered in SSS, there are however some important differences: In a power grid, destabilisation threats must be countered within hard real time bounds. This is usually not guaranteed for SSS. On the other hand, in SSS usually no participant is considered to have knowledge about the global system state, while in a power grid, the participants do in principle have access to a joint source of localized information by measuring amperage, voltage and frequency.

4.2   Current Approaches

About 75% of the PV microgenerators rolled out so far in Germany are non-measured and cannot be remotely controlled. Since 2007, a regulation is in place that enforces a frequency-based distributed control strategy (EN 50438:2007). It stipulates that a microgenerator must shut off once the frequency is observed to overshoot 50.2 Hz. While this was initially meant as a way to stabilise the grid by cutting overproduction, it later surfaced that due to the high amount of PV generation, an almost synchronous distributed decision to take out this portion may induce a sudden frequency drop, followed by the PV generators joining back in, and so on. It hence may lead to critical Europe-wide frequency oscillations.

Due to the obvious problems that widespread use of the current rules may lead to, new requirements are being developed as part of VDE-AR-N 4105 [7]. PV generators will be required to implement the following control scheme:

- As long as the observed frequency is below 50.2 Hz, the generator may increase its output by up to 10 % of the maximum output that it is capable of per minute.
- When the observed frequency crosses the 50.2 Hz mark, the current output of the generator is saved as p_m. When the frequency f is between 50.2 and 51.5 Hz, the generator must reduce its output linearly by 40 % per Hertz relative to p_m, i.e. its output is given by the function

$$output(f) = p_m - 0.4 \cdot p_m \cdot (f - 50.2).$$

- In case the observed frequency exceeds 51.5 Hz, the generator has to be switched off immediately and may only resume production once the frequency has been observed to be below 50.05 Hz for at least one minute.

As we will see (Section 5.3), this relatively complex algorithm is designed to dampen the effect of PV generation spikes and to avoid introducing oscillatory behaviour, but not to actively steer the system towards a safe state where the frequency is below 50.2 Hz.

4.3   Probabilistic Alternatives

If we look at the PV control problem in a more abstract way, it turns out to be remarkably similar to problems solved by communication protocols in computer networks such as the Internet: Limited bandwidth (in our case, capacity of the power grid to accept produced electric power) needs to be shared between a number of hosts (in our case, generators) in a fair way. We thus consider several new control algorithms inspired by concepts from communication protocols, most of which use randomisation to break synchrony and avoid deterministic oscillations:

Additive Increase, Multiplicative Decrease: The first new control algorithm that we study is inspired by the way the Internet's Transmission Control Protocol (TCP) achieves fair usage of limited bandwidth between a number of connections: Bandwidth usage is increased in constant steps (additively), and when a message is lost (taken as an indication of buffer overflows due to congestion), it is reduced by a constant factor (multiplicatively). This *additive-increase, multiplicative-decrease* (AIMD) policy ensures that several users of the same connection eventually converge to using an equal share of the bandwidth. We directly transfer this approach to PV generators: Power output is increased in small constant steps until the frequency is measured to be above 50.2 Hz, at which point the output is multiplied by a constant factor < 1.

Frequency-dependent Probabilistic Switching: Our hypothesis is that probabilistic strategies may improve stability without requiring fine-grained modifications of the generators' power output as in AIMD. Our next controller thus always switches between full and no power output, but it does so with a certain probability that depends on the current frequency measurement with higher frequencies leading to a higher probability of switching off.

Exponential Backoff: Instead of determining the switching probability based on the current system state, we can also unconditionally switch off when the frequency exceeds the allowed value of 50.2 Hz and then wait a probabilistically chosen amount of time before again measuring and potentially switching on.

The precise scheme that we use is *exponential backoff* with *collision detection*. In the computer networks domain, this is commonly employed in CSMA/CD-based (*carrier sense multiple access* with collision detection) medium access protocols such as Ethernet: When one device connected to the shared medium (e.g. the cable) has data to send, it first *senses* the carrier to determine whether another device is currently sending. If not, it sends its data immediately. However, if the channel is occupied or if the sending is interrupted by another device starting to send as well (a collision), it waits a number of time slots before the next try. This number is sampled from a uniform distribution over a range such as $\{1, \ldots, 2^{bc}\}$, where bc, the *backoff counter*, keeps track of the number of collisions and of the number of times that the channel was sensed as occupied when this message should have been sent. The range of possible delays increases exponentially, thus the policy's name; its goal is to use randomisation to prevent two devices from perpetually choosing the same delay and thus always colliding, and to use an exponential increase in the maximum waiting time in order to adapt to the number of devices currently having data to send (again, in order to avoid continuous collisions).

The goals of exponential backoff in network protocols closely match our goals in designing a power generation control scheme: We want all generators to be able to feed power into the grid when it is not "occupied", i.e. when the frequency is below the threshold of 50.2 Hz, and we want to avoid "collisions", i.e. several generators switching on at about the same time and thus creating frequency spikes above that threshold.

Frequency-dependent Switching with Exponential Backoff: An obvious final step is to combine the frequency-dependent probabilities and the randomised delays of the previous two controllers to create one that features randomisation of both switching decisions and waiting times.

We have also considered additional algorithms and variants of those presented above; a full list with detailed explanations can be found in the accompanying technical report [2].

5   Modelling Decentralised Controllers

In order to evaluate the behaviour of the different PV generator control strategies introduced in the previous section, we build MODEST models for power micro grids that use these controllers. As our focus is on the generator control aspect, we represent the other elements of the micro grid listed in Section 2.1 as follows:

- Wide-area connection and local consumption: The influence from the upper layer power grid on our last mile as well as the local consumption within the last mile is modelled as a combined deterministic load profile.
- Generation potential: We model the "worst case" of a maximally sunny day. Each PV generator is assumed to be able to contribute the full amount of power it is capable of (given by a constant MAX) into the grid at any time.
- Local grid topology: We abstract from the physical characteristics of the grid by treating the local connections as a "copper plate" and looking only at the frequency observed. We chose this drastic abstraction due to the reasons outlined in the introduction to Section 4. By treating frequency as a local phenomenon—which it is not—we exaggerate the influence of the individual PV generators. We could easily use voltage as a reference quantity instead since the models are sufficiently abstract.

Since our focus is on effects of overproduction, we only consider the frequency range above 50 Hz, thus representing 50 Hz as frequency value 0 in our model. This value is assumed when all solar generators are switched off and there is no (= zero) influence from the wide-area connection and local consumption. We assume that adding power to the grid has a linear effect on the frequency, so we can describe the grid frequency as the sum of the generator outputs plus the in-feed from the upper layer minus the consumption.

5.1   A Model Template for Power Micro Grids

The detailed models of the control strategies all fit into the same model template shown in Figure 2. The control strategies become part of a `Generator` process, while a `LoadProfile` process represents the wide-area influence and local consumption; the entire system is finally specified as the parallel composition of G instances of `Generator` plus a single `LoadProfile` instance. This template shows a few more noteworthy modelling choices and abstractions:

Each generator repeatedly measures the grid's current frequency, uses this value to decide whether and in which way to modify its own power output, and finally update its output according to this decision. Each of these measure-update cycles takes M time units, with $D \leq M$ time units passing between the measurement and the change of power output. This delay allows us to model decision and reaction times as well as the time it actually takes for the changes made by one generator to be observed by the others. Higher values of D will thus lead to decisions being made on "older" data, while $D = 0$ implies that every change is immediately visible throughout the last mile. We have thus chosen a discrete measure-update-wait approach; an alternative is to make the generators reactive, i.e. observe the evolution of the frequency and react when relevant thresholds are crossed.

By use of the `GeneratorInit` process, each generator begins operation after a random, uniformly distributed delay in the range between 0 and M time units;

```
action init;
const int TIME_BOUND; // analysis time bound
const int G; // number of generators

// Times
const int M; // measure every M time units
const int D; // changes take D time units to take effect (D <= M)

// Frequencies (in Hz above 50.0 Hz)
const real B = 0.3; // frequency when all generators are on full power
const real MAX = B / G; // max output of a generator (contribution to frequency)
const real L = 0.1; // max sum of wide-area influence and local consumption

real input; // background generation (coming from the network), in [0, L]
real[G] output; // generator output, each in [0, MAX]

function real frequency() = input + /* sum of values in output array */;

reward r_availability; der(availability) = frequency() > 0.2 ? 0 : 1;
reward r_output; der(sumoutput) = frequency() - input;
reward r_goodput; der(goodput) = frequency() > 0.2 ? 0 : frequency() - input;

property Availability = Xmax(r_availability / TIME_BOUND | time == TIME_BOUND);
property Output = Xmax(r_output / TIME_BOUND | time == TIME_BOUND);
property Goodput = Xmax(r_goodput / TIME_BOUND | time == TIME_BOUND);

process GeneratorInit(int(0..G) id)
{
    // Generators are initially in a random state
    urgent init {= output[id] = Uniform(0, MAX) =};
    // Each generator "starts" after a random delay in [0, M]
    delay(Uniform(0, M)) Generator(id)
}

process Generator(int(0..G) id)
{
    action measure, update;
    real fm; // frequency measurement
    clock c = 0; // local clock variable

    process Measure()
    {
        measure {= fm = frequency(), c = 0 =}
    }

    /* control algorithm is modelled here */
}

process LoadProfile()
{
    /* load profile is modelled here */
}

par {
    :: GeneratorInit(0)
       /* ... */
    :: GeneratorInit(G - 1)
    :: LoadProfile()
}
```

Fig. 2. A model template for power micro grids

measurements will thus be performed asynchronously. Less realistic, but easier to analyse alternatives would be to have the generators perform their decisions in a fully synchronous manner, or at the same point of time, but in a certain order. However, we have observed that in particular the second alternative generates extreme results (e.g. for fairness) that are clearly artifacts of that abstraction.

5.2   Control Strategy Models

We now explain how to model the control strategies described in sections 4.2 and 4.3 in MODEST to fit into the template introduced above:

Current Approaches: We omit the trivial MODEST code for the simple control strategy that turns the generator off when a frequency of at least 50.2 Hz is observed and turns it to full power in all other cases. A direct implementation of the new control scheme according to VDE-AR-N 4105 is shown in Figure 3. The switch between normal and emergency mode is obvious in the model.

Probabilistic Alternatives: Figure 4 shows the model of the AIMD controller. In this case, we chose 10 % of the maximum generator output as the constant value when increasing, and $\frac{2}{3}$ as the decrease factor. The latter has shown to provide a good tradeoff between availability and goodput when we compared our analysis results (see next section) for different reduction factors. The MODEST code for the frequency-dependent probabilistic switching controller is shown in Figure 5. We have chosen a linear function over the range of $[50.0\,\text{Hz}, 50.4\,\text{Hz}]$ for the mapping from measured frequency to switch-off probability. At the critical threshold of 50.2 Hz, the probability of switching off will thus be $\frac{1}{2}$. Finally, the controller based on the exponential backoff approach can be seen in Figure 6; the combination with frequency-dependent switching is not shown because it is just a simple replacement of the **when** conditions in exponential backoff with a probabilistic alternative (**palt**) that uses the chosen probability function.

5.3   A Simulation Study

We have evaluated the different control strategies in a dedicated simulation study [3]. The properties we considered are (as outlined in Section 2.3) stability, availability versus goodput, and fairness. To evaluate stability, we evaluated the frequency traces of exemplary simulation runs with a fixed background load. Figures 7 and 8 show these traces for three of the controllers we studied, namely the on-off controller (Figure 8, left) and the controller according to VDE-AR-N 4105 (right) as well as the combination of the frequency-dependent switching controller with exponential backoff (Figure 8, left). The upper (blue) curves plot the system frequency, while the lower (red) curves show the deterministic background load we used for these runs.

The oscillatory behaviour caused by the current 50.2 Hz on-off controller is clearly visible, as are the different behavioural phases of the new strategy according to VDE-AR-N 4105. The latter clearly avoids oscillations, but does not

```
process Generator(int(0..G) id)
{
    real p_m = output[id];
    /* ...template code... */

    process NormalOperation()
    {
        alt
        {
            :: when(fm < 0.2)
                // Increase by 10% of MAX per minute
                update {= output[id] += (0.1 * MAX) / MINUTE,
                            p_m       += (0.1 * MAX) / MINUTE =};
                when urgent(c >= M) Measure()
            :: when(0.2 <= fm && fm < 1.5)
                // 40% gradient
                update {= output[id] = -0.4 * p_m * (fm - 0.2) + p_m =};
                when urgent(c >= M) Measure()
            :: when(1.5 <= fm)
                // Switch off
                EmergencySwitchOff()
        };
        when urgent(c >= D) NormalOperation()
    }

    process EmergencySwitchOff()
    {
        bool waiting;
        clock minute;

        // Switch off
        update {= output[id] = 0, p_m = 0 =};

        // Wait for frequency to be below 50.05 Hz for one minute
        do {
            :: when urgent(c >= M && !(waiting && minute >= MINUTE)) Measure();
                urgent alt {
                    :: when(fm <= 0.05 && !waiting)
                        {= waiting = true, minute = 0, c = 0 =}
                    :: when(fm <= 0.05 &&  waiting)
                        {= c = 0 =}
                    :: when(fm > 0.05)
                        {= waiting = false, c = 0 =}
                }
            :: when urgent(waiting && minute >= MINUTE) break
        }
    }

    Measure();
    when urgent(c >= D) NormalOperation()
}
```

Fig. 3. Model of the controller according to VDE-AR-N 4105

```
process Generator(int(0..G) id)
{
    /* ...template code... */

    Measure();
    when urgent(c >= D) alt {
        :: when(fm <  0.2) {= output[id] = min(MAX, output[id] + 0.1 * MAX) =}
        :: when(fm >= 0.2) {= output[id] *= 2/3 =}
    };
    when urgent(c >= M) Generator(id)
}
```

Fig. 4. Model of additive increase, multiplicative decrease of frequency

```
process Generator(int(0..G) id)
{
    /* ...template code... */

    Measure();
    when urgent(c >= D) update palt {
        :max(0, 0.4 - fm): {= output[id] = MAX =}
        :        fm       : {= output[id] = 0   =}
    };
    when urgent(c >= M) Generator(id)
}
```

Fig. 5. Model of the frequency-dependent probabilistic switching controller

```
process Generator(int(0..G) id)
{
    int bc; // backoff counter
    int backoff; // number of slots to wait till next try
    /* ...template code... */

    process Gen()
    {
        Measure();
        when urgent(c >= D) alt {
            :: when(backoff > 0) update {= backoff- =}
            :: when(backoff == 0) alt {
                :: when(fm <  0.2) {= output[id] = MAX, bc = 0 =}
                :: when(fm >= 0.2) {= output[id] = 0, bc++,
                    backoff = DiscreteUniform(0, (int)pow(2, bc)) =}
            }
        };
        when urgent(c >= M) Gen()
    }

    Gen()
}
```

Fig. 6. Model of the controller with exponential backoff

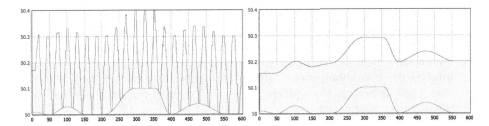

Fig. 7. Behaviour of the 50.2 Hz on-off (left) and VDE-AR-N 4105 controllers [3]

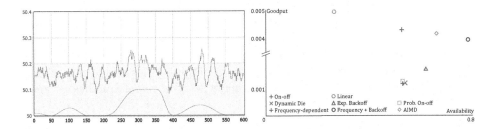

Fig. 8. Frequency-dependent control with backoff (left) and availability vs. goodput [3]

actively stabilise the grid into a safe state. As expected, the frequency-dependent controller shows a very different behaviour, which appears very erratic, but actually manages to keep the system safe for most of the simulation run. Results for the other newly proposed controllers were mixed: AIMD also works rather well and is at least fairer than its additive-decrease counterpart (as hoped), but exponential backoff alone does not manage to avoid oscillations. The graph on the right-hand side of Figure 8 compares the availability and goodput of the entire set of controllers considered in our simulation study, confirming that the combination of frequency-dependent randomisation with exponential backoff works rather well [3]. It also illustrates that taking inspiration from network protocols for distributed grid operation is indeed a promising direction.

6   Conclusion

This paper has discussed elementary mechanisms for distributed runtime control of power grids facing considerable infeed of renewable energy. We have focussed on the properties and modelling formalisms needed to describe, analyse and manage these systems in a highly flexible, highly automated, and highly decentralized manner. Another system which is highly decentralized, highly flexible and managed in a highly automated way is the Internet. As we have discussed, certain solutions that have been coined as part of Internet protocols can be adapted to serve beneficially in future distributed runtime control of power grids. This benefit might not be restricted to Internet solutions, but might more generally also materialise for some of the genuine Internet design principles, such as:

- Network neutrality and fairness: There is no discrimination in the way the network shares its capacity among its users. Ideally, the net is fair in the sense that if n users are sharing a connection, then on average each user can use about $1/n$-th of the capacity.
- Intelligent edges, dumb core: Putting intelligence into the net itself is much more cost ineffective than placing it at the edges of the networks, i.e. into the end user appliances.
- Distributed design and decentralised control: Distributed, decentralised control is not only a means to assure scalability. It also is a prime principle to protect end user privacy that would be at stake if centralised authorities would collect information for decision making.

There are a number of similarities between the Internet and the power grid, including its excessive size, its hierarchical structure, its organic growth, and its ultimately high dependability. Indeed, it seems to us that this implies a number of very good reasons why the future management of power grids should take strong inspirations from the way the Internet is managed. Our research indicates some first concrete examples of this kind.

Acknowledgments. The authors thank Pascal Berrang (Saarland University) for his assistance in carrying out the empirical studies. Mats Larrson (ABB Schweiz AG), Sebastian Lehnhoff (University of Oldenburg and OFFIS Energie), Martin Ney (Luxea GmbH), Alexandre Oudalov (ABB Schweiz AG), and Holger Wiechmann (EnBW Energie Baden-Württemberg AG) have provided insightful feedback on our findings.

References

1. Alur, R., Dill, D.L.: A theory of timed automata. Theor. Comput. Sci. 126(2), 183–235 (1994)
2. Berrang, P., Bogdoll, J., Hahn, E.M., Hartmanns, A., Hermanns, H.: Dependability results for power grids with decentralized stabilization strategies. Reports of SFB/TR 14 AVACS 83 (2012) ISSN: 1860-9821, http://www.avacs.org
3. Berrang, P., Hartmanns, A., Hermanns, H.: A comparative analysis of decentralized power grid stabilization strategies. In: Winter Simulation Conference (to appear, 2012)
4. Bogdoll, J., David, A., Hartmanns, A., Hermanns, H.: mctau: Bridging the Gap between Modest and UPPAAL. In: Donaldson, A., Parker, D. (eds.) SPIN 2012. LNCS, vol. 7385, pp. 227–233. Springer, Heidelberg (2012)
5. Bogdoll, J., Hartmanns, A., Hermanns, H.: Simulation and Statistical Model Checking for Modestly Nondeterministic Models. In: Schmitt, J.B. (ed.) MMB & DFT 2012. LNCS, vol. 7201, pp. 249–252. Springer, Heidelberg (2012)
6. Bohnenkamp, H.C., D'Argenio, P.R., Hermanns, H., Katoen, J.P.: MoDeST: A compositional modeling formalism for hard and softly timed systems. IEEE Transactions on Software Engineering 32(10), 812–830 (2006)
7. Bömer, J., Burges, K., Zolotarev, P., Lehner, J.: Auswirkungen eines hohen Anteils dezentraler Erzeugungsanlagen auf die Netzstabilität bei Überfrequenz & Entwicklung von Lösungsvorschlägen zu deren Überwindung (2011); study commissioned by EnBW Transportnetze AG, Bundesverband Solarwirtschaft e.V. and Forum Netztechnik/Netzbetrieb im VDE e.V

8. Le Boudec, J.-Y., Tomozei, D.-C.: A Demand-Response Calculus with Perfect Batteries. In: Schmitt, J.B. (ed.) MMB & DFT 2012. LNCS, vol. 7201, pp. 273–287. Springer, Heidelberg (2012)
9. Bundesnetzagentur: EEG-Vergütungssätze für Photovoltaikanlagen, `http://www.bundesnetzagentur.de/cln_1931/DE/Sachgebiete/ ElektrizitaetGas/ErneuerbareEnergienGesetz/VerguetungssaetzePVAnlagen/ VerguetungssaetzePVAnlagen/VerguetungssaetzePhotovoltaik_Basepage.html` (March 21, 2012)
10. Chen, T., Forejt, V., Kwiatkowska, M., Parker, D., Simaitis, A.: Automatic Verification of Competitive Stochastic Systems. In: Flanagan, C., König, B. (eds.) TACAS 2012. LNCS, vol. 7214, pp. 315–330. Springer, Heidelberg (2012)
11. Dolev, S.: Self-Stabilization. MIT Press (2000)
12. Haas, P.J., Shedler, G.S.: Regenerative generalized semi-Markov processes. Communications in Statistics. Stochastic Models 3(3), 409–438 (1987)
13. Hahn, E.M., Hartmanns, A., Hermanns, H., Katoen, J.P.: A compositional modelling and analysis framework for stochastic hybrid systems. Formal Methods in System Design (2012), doi: 10.1007/s10703-012-0167-z
14. Hartmanns, A.: Model-Checking and Simulation for Stochastic Timed Systems. In: Aichernig, B.K., de Boer, F.S., Bonsangue, M.M. (eds.) FMCO 2010. LNCS, vol. 6957, pp. 372–391. Springer, Heidelberg (2011)
15. Hartmanns, A., Hermanns, H.: A Modest approach to checking probabilistic timed automata. In: QEST, pp. 187–196. IEEE Computer Society (2009)
16. Hermanns, H., Wiechmann, H.: Future design challenges for electric energy supply. In: ETFA. pp. 1–8. IEEE (2009)
17. Hermanns, H., Wiechmann, H.: Demand-Response Managment for Dependable Power Grids. In: Embedded Systems for Smart Appliances and Energy Managment, Embedded Systems, vol. 3, Springer Science+Business Media, New York (2012)
18. Hildmann, H., Saffre, F.: Influence of variable supply and load flexibility on demand-side management. In: EEM 2011, pp. 63–68. IEEE Conference Publications (2011)
19. Kwiatkowska, M.Z., Norman, G., Segala, R., Sproston, J.: Automatic verification of real-time systems with discrete probability distributions. Theor. Comput. Sci. 282(1), 101–150 (2002)
20. Lehnhoff, S.: Private communication (2012)
21. Martins, J., Platzer, A., Leite, J.: Statistical Model Checking for Distributed Probabilistic-Control Hybrid Automata with Smart Grid Applications. In: Qin, S., Qiu, Z. (eds.) ICFEM 2011. LNCS, vol. 6991, pp. 131–146. Springer, Heidelberg (2011)
22. Nordwest-Zeitung: EWE spürt Wende deutlich (March 12, 2012), `http://www.nwzonline.de/Aktuelles/Politik/Hintergrund/NWZ/Artikel/ 2822057/EWE-sp%FCrt-Wende-deutlich.html`
23. Puterman, M.L.: Markov Decision Processes: Discrete Stochastic Dynamic Programming. Wiley Series in Probability and Mathematical Statistics: Applied Probability and Statistics. John Wiley & Sons Inc., New York (1994)
24. Segala, R.: Modeling and Verification of Randomized Distributed Real-Time Systems. Ph.D. thesis, MIT, Cambridge, MA, USA (1995)
25. Wiechmann, H.: Private communication (2012)

Model-Based Testing and Model Inference

Karl Meinke[1] and Neil Walkinshaw[2]

[1] School of Computer Science and Communication,
Royal Institute of Technology, 100-44 Stockholm, Sweden
karlm@nada.kth.se
[2] Department of Computer Science,
The University of Leicester, Leicester LE1 7RH, UK
nw91@le.ac.uk

1 Introduction

Model-based software testing is well established, and can be traced back to Moore's "Gedanken experiments" on finite state machines from 1956 [10]. The best known approaches involve the use of models (such as UML interaction diagrams or state machines) as the basis for selecting test inputs that seek to explore the core functionality of the system. Outputs from the test executions can subsequently be checked against the model.

The field of model-based testing complements the various model-based reasoning techniques that have arisen out of the formal methods community. The advent of efficient model-checking techniques has enabled the efficient analysis of models of software systems with respect to specific behavioral requirements. This analysis can identify counterexamples to a behavioral requirement, i.e. concrete witnesses to the failure of the requirement for a specific model. Counterexample construction gives an important and powerful new approach to test case synthesis.

Model-based testing and model checking are vulnerable to the criticism (which applies to model-based development in general) that it is generally unrealistic to expect developers to be able to design and maintain detailed systems models. This is exacerbated by agile development contexts, where requirements and implementation are constantly in flux.

To address this problem, new academic research has focussed on techniques to automatically infer models directly from systems, with only a minimal amount of human involvement. The idea of combining the two areas (model inference and testing) was first enunciated by Weyuker in 1983 [16]. Early attempts to combine testing with model inference include [2], [18] and [17].

It is only recently that the topic has become particularly popular. Notable success has been achieved in the area of testing embedded and reactive systems (including client/server systems). Here active learning algorithms for deterministic finite automata (DFA), such as Angluin's L* algorithm of [1] have been applied. Active learning is itself an important source of structural test cases, as has been shown in [15]. Moreover, active DFA learning algorithms can be combined with efficient BDD and SAT based model checkers to systematically generate test cases that explore user requirements expressed in temporal logic.

T. Margaria and B. Steffen (Eds.): ISoLA 2012, Part I, LNCS 7609, pp. 440–443, 2012.

It should be noted here that new progress in DFA learning has also been made in recent years. An extensive survey of the state of the art in active DFA learning can be found in [4]. Optimisations to the original L* learning algorithm have yielded significant improvements, in terms of the speed of model inference and the size of learned automata. Based on such progress, it is now possible to infer state space sizes of 100,000 states or more, which is sufficient to test many kinds of industrial applications.

In a field as large as software testing, much important research remains to be done. One important question is how the simple DFA models inferred from systems can be extended, say by adding control structures or data types. Such extensions are important if we are not to abstract away too much information from the system under test, thereby losing the opportunity to discover errors. However, this increase in expressiveness must be weighed against the increased computational complexity of both model inference and model checking. For many expressive models and requirements languages, model checking is known to be an undecidable problem. Besides extending expressiveness, there is a more general need to consider other types of inferred computational models besides automata.

Another important question concerns benchmarking against alternative methods of testing. There is also a great need for more practical experience with testing of real world systems and requirements. Finally, the perennial problem of coverage measurement needs further research, particularly in the context of black box testing. Here it seems that computational learning theory may be able to contribute in terms of estimating the residual probability of errors (see e.g. [6], [14],). Some of the above questions have been addressed by the contributing authors for this session, as we will discuss below.

The session on Model-based Testing and Model Inference was organised by the ISoLA 2012 program committee in order to explore the potential for interplay between these two fields. The subject matter of this session overlaps with the session on *Learning Techniques for Software Verification and Validation* also contained in this volume. The interested reader may also consult the Proceedings of ISoLA 2011, especially the session on *Machine Learning for System Construction*.

2   Overview of the Session Papers

The session consisted of four contributed papers. The paper [3] by Groz et al. considers various optimisations to Angluin's well-known L* algorithm of [1] for inferring deterministic finite automata (DFA). This learning algorithm, and its variants, have been used by several researchers to investigate automated black box testing of software systems (see e.g. [13], [9], [12], [15]). The paper considers several improvements, such as the processing of counterexamples by the learner, and more complex data type interfaces to the system under test. The specific needs of security testing are also addressed.

A contemporary topic of research in software engineering is software product lines (SPL) and product families. Meta-models for entire families must provide dimensions of variability for the specific family instances of products. This poses new challenges both for model driven development and model-based testing. The paper [5] by Kitamura et al. shows how model checking techniques can be applied to model-based testing of SPLs by using feature tree models.

The paper [11] by Lu and Mukhopadhyay considers how model checking using satisfiability modulo theories (SMT) techniques can be used for model based verification and testing of MATLAB models. The models used here are classical data flow graphs derived by abstraction and static analysis rather than computational learning.

Finally, the paper [7] by Meinke and Niu considers learning-based testing. This is an emerging paradigm for black-box requirements testing that combines incremental model inference with model checking. For further details, see the tutorial [8]. The contribution [7] presents a new incremental learning algorithm for extended Mealy automata computing over abstract data types (ADTs). Extended Mealy automata can be more effective than DFA for modeling and testing high-level software systems. The approach is based on symbolic congruence learning methods, which are dual to the tabular methods of automata inference used in Angluin's L* and similar algorithms.

We would like to thank the organisors of ISoLA 2012 for making this session possible, and of course the session authors for their valuable contributions.

References

1. Angluin, D.: Learning regular sets from queries and counterexamples. Information and Computation 75(1), 87–106 (1987)
2. Bergadano, F., Gunetti, D.: Testing by means of inductive program learning. ACM Trans. Software Engineering and Methodology 5(2), 119–145 (1996)
3. Groz, R., Irfan, M.-N., Oriat, C.: Algorithmic Improvements on Regular Inference of Software Models and Perspectives for Security Testing. In: Margaria, T., Steffen, B. (eds.) ISoLA 2012, Part I. LNCS, vol. 7609, pp. 444–457. Springer, Heidelberg (2012)
4. Howar, F.M.: Active Learning of Interface Programs. PhD thesis, Faculty of Informatics, Technical University of Dortmund (2012)
5. Kitamura, T., Do, N.T.B., Ohsaki, H., Fang, L., Yatabe, S.: Test-Case Design by Feature Trees. In: Margaria, T., Steffen, B. (eds.) ISoLA 2012, Part I. LNCS, vol. 7609, pp. 458–473. Springer, Heidelberg (2012)
6. Meinke, K.: A Stochastic Theory of Black-Box Software Testing. In: Futatsugi, K., Jouannaud, J.-P., Meseguer, J. (eds.) Algebra, Meaning, and Computation. LNCS, vol. 4060, pp. 578–595. Springer, Heidelberg (2006)
7. Meinke, K., Niu, F.: An Incremental Learning Algorithm for Extended Mealy Automata. In: Margaria, T., Steffen, B. (eds.) ISoLA 2012, Part I. LNCS, vol. 7609, pp. 488–504. Springer, Heidelberg (2012)
8. Meinke, K., Niu, F., Sindhu, M.: Learning-based software testing: a tutorial. In: Proc. Fourth Int. ISoLA Workshop on Machine Learning for Software Construction. CCIS. Springer (2011)
9. Meinke, K., Sindhu, M.A.: Incremental Learning-Based Testing for Reactive Systems. In: Gogolla, M., Wolff, B. (eds.) TAP 2011. LNCS, vol. 6706, pp. 134–151. Springer, Heidelberg (2011)

10. Moore, E.F.: Gedanken experiments on sequential machines. In: Automata Studies, Princeton, pp. 129–153 (1956)

11. Lu, Z., Mukhopadhyay, S.: Model-Based Static Code Analysis For MATLAB Models. In: Margaria, T., Steffen, B. (eds.) ISoLA 2012, Part I. LNCS, vol. 7609, pp. 474–487. Springer, Heidelberg (2012)

12. Peled, D., Vardi, M.Y., Yannakakis, M.: Black-box checking. In: Formal Methods for Protocol Engineering and Distributed Systems FORTE/PSTV, pp. 225–240. Kluwer (1999)

13. Raffelt, H., Steffen, B., Margaria, T.: Dynamic Testing Via Automata Learning. In: Yorav, K. (ed.) HVC 2007. LNCS, vol. 4899, pp. 136–152. Springer, Heidelberg (2008)

14. Walkinshaw, N.: Assessing Test Adequacy for Black-Box Systems without Specifications. In: Wolff, B., Zaïdi, F. (eds.) ICTSS 2011. LNCS, vol. 7019, pp. 209–224. Springer, Heidelberg (2011)

15. Walkinshaw, N., Bogdanov, K., Derrick, J., Paris, J.: Increasing Functional Coverage by Inductive Testing: A Case Study. In: Petrenko, A., Simão, A., Maldonado, J.C. (eds.) ICTSS 2010. LNCS, vol. 6435, pp. 126–141. Springer, Heidelberg (2010)

16. Weyuker, E.: Assessing test data adequacy through program inference. ACM Trans. Program. Lang. Syst. 5(4), 641–655 (1983)

17. Zhu, H.: A formal interpretation of software testing as inductive inference. Journal of Software testing, Verification and Reliability 6(1), 3–31 (1996)

18. Zhu, H., Hall, P., May, J.: Inductive inference and software testing. Journal of Software testing, Verification and Reliability 2(2), 3–31 (1992)

Algorithmic Improvements on Regular Inference of Software Models and Perspectives for Security Testing

Roland Groz, Muhammad-Naeem Irfan, and Catherine Oriat

LIG, Computer Science Lab
Grenoble Institute of Technology, France
Firstname.Lastname@imag.fr

Abstract. Among the various techniques for mining models from software systems, regular inference of black-box systems has been a central technique in the last decade. In this paper, we present various directions we have investigated for improving the efficiency of algorithms based on L^* in a software testing context where interactions with systems entail large and complex input domains. In particular we consider algorithmic optimizations for large input sets, for parameterized inputs, for processing counterexamples. We also present our current directions motivated by application to security testing: focusing on specific sequences, identifying randomly generated values, combining with other adaptive techniques.

1 Introduction

Regular inference, that is the derivation of an automaton model from sequences of events corresponding to a regular language, has been used for over a decade in software engineering. In particular, it has been applied to software development process ([9]), requirements engineering ([26]), model checking ([10], [33]), model based testing ([16], [29]), integration testing ([23]) and to other tasks such as component or service discovery and identification as in the Connect project ([1]). It is related to the field known as specification mining ([4]). Its development is rooted in the evolution of software development which is now well supported by tools based on models, to automate such complex tasks as software validation. But quite often, models are not available or not maintained along the development. Therefore, models have to be retrieved from software artefacts.

In this paper, we are interested in inference algorithms to support black-box testing of software systems. Testing is usually the most time consuming task of software development, and can now be supported by model based testing tools (MBT: [39]). By testing a system, we naturally get sequences of events that can be used by inference to retrieve a model. We consider that the testing process can be guided by inference needs, which means that we can use active learning techniques, as opposed to passive learning techniques where the inference is based on a predefined set of collected testing events. The advantage of active learning is that it can be much more efficient and has a lower complexity than passive learning: more accurate models can be derived with less tests.

T. Margaria and B. Steffen (Eds.): ISoLA 2012, Part I, LNCS 7609, pp. 444–457, 2012.

Therefore, most of the work on inference for black-box testing has used active learning aka learning with queries ([11]) in particular under the MAT (Minimally Adequate Teacher) paradigm and the algorithm L^* introduced by Dana Angluin ([5]). Applying L^* in the context of software testing raises several issues. Let us call SUI the System Under Inference, just as in testing a SUT refers to a System Under Test.

Output queries: Whereas L^* infers DFA as language acceptors of input words, testing is better modelled by distinguishing inputs (to the SUI from the tester) from outputs (from the SUI to the tester). Typical models used in testing are either IOTS (Input Output Transition Systems) or Mealy machines (I/O automata). Therefore we distinguish for an SUI two event sets: I as the set of input events and O as the set of output events. Although initial applications directly used L^* by defining the input alphabet A as either $A = I \times O$ ([26]) or $A = I \cup O$ ([19]), it is better to adapt the algorithm to infer directly Mealy machines as done by $L^*_{i/o}$[32] and $L_M{}^+$[37]. Consequently, instead of membership queries as in the original L^*, the system is asked output queries ([38]).

Equivalence queries: The MAT paradigm assumes an oracle can answer equivalence queries; the conjectured model is provided to the oracle and it replies either the conjecture is equivalent to the SUI or provides a counterexample, viz. a sequence of inputs for which the SUI and the conjecture provide differing answers. Since the SUI is a black-box, such an oracle is usually impossible to implement in a normal testing context. Proposed solutions either have a very high complexity, typically an exponential growth in the number of states of the SUI when using Vasilievski W-set as in [10], or yield non optimal counterexamples that impact the complexity of the inference. We address this issue in section 3.

Input structure, mapping: The most significant difference between theoretical regular inference of regular languages and software testing is that most often, exchanges with a black-box, either through the PDUs of a protocol over a network or though an API for local software testing do not have a small finite alphabet of input symbols. Interactions take the form of more complex data structures, that usually involve a main event type from a small finite set (PDU types, or API entries) complemented by parameters that may have quite complex data structures (think of an e-mail, a SOAP event, or an XML structure) and take values from very large or unbounded domains (sequences, of integers, strings...). To apply regular inference algorithms, some abstraction is required to map concrete interactions to a finite alphabet. But for converting abstract queries to concrete testing events, this mapping must work both ways. In section 2 we address the adaptation of algorithms to deal with the implications of such mappings.

Number of queries: In some contexts, inference can be done on local data either in memory or in files. This is often the case for data mining algorithms, and can be the case for white-box inference on source or binary code. However, in black-box testing, querying a system can be costly. Interfacing to a system may imply going through several layers of interface software, it can also be even slower when interacting over a network, and when the SUI is a system that may include hardware with slow reactions, as was the case for the domotics appliances used in [35] where reaction delays were to be measured in several seconds or minutes. In any case, reducing the number of queries, with typical values in thousands, is a key element to consider to design algorithms that can be used when actually testing external black-box systems.

Resetting: Active learning implies that different words from the language are submitted to the SUI. This implies that the SUI must be reset at the beginning of each test. As usual, this requires a reliable reset on the SUI. But in the case of inference, it also adds to the cost of each membership or output query; in many cases, resetting may take much more time than running the rest of the query.

Since learning from a black-box SUI is itself a testing process, how does it fit into a global testing approach? A usual objection would be that inferring a model from a flawed implementation would simply reflect the flaws in the model, so that any tests derived from the inferred model would not detect failures as the SUT would always conform to the model derived from it. In fact, it simply means that the inferred model cannot be the only oracle in the testing process. In most approaches, the inferred model is not the ultimate reference model for the SUI. Actually, the inferred model is usually an approximate conjecture of what should be a model of the system. Learning comes as one of the steps in a more global validation process.

A typical approach is incremental: testing is used to learn preliminary models which can be refined with more interactions between the models and the SUI. [29] adequately coined the phrase Learning Based Testing (LBT) to define such an iterative approach. We have actually investigated two directions for combining learning and testing into the context of integration testing for systems assembling several communicating asynchronous components that could each be modelled with automata.

- In [23], we use learning to infer models of each component in a preliminary unit testing approach. Then we use the combined models to derive integration tests to check for interactions between components.
- In [15], we infer a global model of the system, then project to local components to analyze through reachability analysis and further testing the potential integration issues, to detect in particular races that could lead to sporadic errors in specific scheduling or communication contexts.

In both cases, further testing enriches the observations which are used to refine the initial models. In fact, we use different algorithms for learning in both contexts: in the first case, we use a variant of L^*, whereas in the second case we use an algorithm based on state merging.

In this paper, we present various improvements that we have investigated to address some issues raised above. Variations on the basic inference algorithms have been proposed for more efficient inference in the software testing context. In section 2 we propose adaptations for parameterized or large input sets. In section 3, we deal with non optimal counterexamples. In section 4, we present perspectives and problems raised by the application in the context of security testing.

2   Dealing with Software Inputs

2.1   I/O Behaviour

Testing is an asymmetric process, where the tester usually has control over the queries sent to the SUI and observes the outputs from the SUI. This is why the classical regular inference algorithms that learn acceptor automata in the form of DFA have been adapted to directly infer I/O models typically Mealy machines, either with a single output for each input [37], or with multiple outputs for a single input as in [32] and [15]. Adapting the structure of observation tables to record sequences of output symbols (from the set O of outputs) rather than simply boolean membership as in L^* has been shown to greatly reduce the number of queries by an order of magnitude ([32], [37]). Two further adaptations may be useful in that context:

Filters: Initially, [19] used filters to avoid redundant queries in using L^* to learn DFA models over an alphabet made of $I \cup O$, but filters can still be meaningful to reduce the number of queries for independent events ([32]), with partial-order and symmetry filters. Another common cause for filtering is for non-complete SUI. In contexts such as asynchronous protocol testing, the SUI is assumed to be complete because it cannot prevent the tester from sending any input. However, in other contexts, only a subset of inputs may be enabled at a given state. Typically, on a Web interface with forms, only certain events might be offered.

Dictionaries: Each cell in an observation table (of L^* and other algorithms based on tables) corresponds to a query made by concatenating the label of the row with the label of the column. But since different cells could lead to the same queries, and more importantly many queries would be prefixes of longer queries, dictionaries are used to record past queries and the corresponding answers from the SUI. The learning process will also be organized to run longer queries first so that the answers to all prefixes can be filled without querying the SUI. The idea can be expanded further as in the GoodSplit algorithm ([13]).

2.2 L_1: Dealing with Large Input Sets

A first approach to deal with parameterized inputs is to consider an abstraction based on an equivalence relation that maps infinite domain values to a finite number of classes ([3]). There are some issues when the values of parameters may trigger different transitions. We will address this in the next section where we deal with parameterized (aka symbolic) machines that include guards on transitions. Here, we just consider the case where the infinite state system can actually be folded to a finite automaton by clustering inputs that trigger the same transitions into an equivalence class. There can still be many different input classes: typically, an API that would have 6 primitives, each with 4 parameters having two significant values would still lead to an input set of size 96.

The worst case complexity for the direct Mealy adaptation $L_{i/o}^*$ from [32], in terms of output queries is $O(|I|^2mn + |I|mn^2)$, where $|I|$ is the size of inputs set, m is the length of the longest counterexample provided by the oracle and n is the number of states in the learned model. The worst case complexity of $L_M{}^+$ from [37] is $O(|I|^2n + |I|mn^2)$. Even with $L_M{}^+$, the size $|I|$ of the input set is a key element of the complexity of those algorithms. In cases where the state structure of the machine is relatively simple and n is low, $|I|$ is the dominant factor. This is why we worked on a reduction of this complexity and proposed the L_1 algorithm that reduces the worst case complexity to $O(|I|mn^2)$.

The basic intuition for L_1 is that the $|I|^2$ factor in the complexity of Mealy adaptations of L^* is due to the initialization of the columns with all possible inputs. Combining these columns with the $S \cdot I$ rows that are necessary to compare the tail states of transitions from each state in S yields the $|I|^2n$ factor. This initialization is intended to provide the output for each transition starting from a state $s \in S$ on input $i \in I$ by looking at the table cell $T(s, i)$ which records this output. Actually the problem is that the structure of observation tables used by $L_{i/o}^*$ and $L_M{}^+$ only records outputs in cells.

The main idea in L_1 is to avoid such an initialization by recording separately the outputs of each transition. More precisely, an observation table in L_1 is a quadruple (S, E, L, T) where $S \subseteq I^*$ is a prefix-closed non empty finite set of access strings, which labels the rows of the observation table, $E \subseteq I^+$ is a suffix-closed finite set, which labels the columns of the observation table, for $S' = S \cup S \cdot I$, the finite function T maps $S' \times E$ to outputs O^+, and the finite function L maps $S' \setminus \{\epsilon\}$ to outputs O. The observation table rows S' are non empty and initially $S = \{\epsilon\}$ and $S \cdot I = I$. The output for the last input element for all the members of $S' \setminus \{\epsilon\}$ is recorded in L and graphically represented along the access strings S'. The columns E are initially $\emptyset$ and E augments only after processing the counterexamples.

L_1 is presented in [20]. Apart from reducing the worst case complexity, it has other advantages in practice for average complexity.

- It adds sequences to the set E used to index columns only when they contribute to distinguish states. If the input set I has a large number of elements and we initialize the columns of the observation table with I then there is strong possibility that all of the input sequences are not distinguishing strings and we have initialized the columns with too many sequences.
- Mealy adaptations of L^* use the collection of all possible inputs I for each state. While inferring models when an access string of a distinct state is

identified then its one letter extensions are added to the observation table. But for software applications valid inputs for every state are smaller than I. For L_1 the output recorded along access strings helps to identify that an access string is valid or invalid, and only valid access strings are kept in the observation table. In effect, this is a kind of prefix filter.

- L_1 adds the suffixes of the counterexample by increasing length to the columns of the observation table until the table is not closed ([21]). Since this algorithm does not initialize the columns with I and adds only those elements from I which are really required, the gain with the L_1 algorithm increases with the number of inputs for the target black-box models.

Since L_1 starts with E being an empty set, initially states are equivalent and its first conjecture will be a "daisy" machine (single state with looping transitions). This means that L_1 will only progress in state identification with equivalence queries. The use of the efficient Suffix1by1 algorithm from [21] helps to keep only shortest separating sequences and their suffixes (see section 3) in E.

Experiments have been conducted with randomly generated Mealy machines to compare L_1 with L_M^+. The results for output queries clearly show that L_1 outperforms $L_M{}^+$ in all cases, even for relatively small input sets. With input size $|I| = 10$, on the average L_1 asks 1604 output queries and $L_M{}^+$ asks 4010 output queries. There is a gain of 60% for output queries.

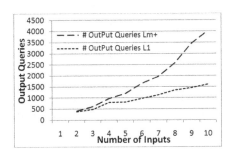

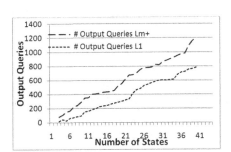

Fig. 1. $|I| \in \{2, 3 \ldots 10\}, |O| = 5$ and $n = 40$ **Fig. 2.** $|I| = 5, |O| = 7$ and $n \in \{3, 4 \ldots 40\}$

The second set of experiments is generated by fixing the size of the inputs and outputs sets, but varying the number of states. The machines are generated with inputs set size $|I| = 5$, the outputs set size $|O| = 7$ and number of states $n \in \{3, 4 \ldots 40\}$. The size of outputs set is changed to get slightly different machines as compared to the first set of experiments. Figure 2 presents the number of output queries asked by both of the algorithms. Again for this set of experiments L_1 outperforms $L_M{}^+$ even though the number of inputs is very low.

2.3   Parameterized Inputs

A second approach consists in changing the basic automaton model to infer directly extended state models where inputs and outputs can bear parameters. [24]

was a first step we made in that direction and at the same time [6] proposed another approach. Both introduced extended models with parameters and guards on transitions, but both had serious limitations: our approach was considering output parameters that could only depend on the input parameters for the same transition (the so-called PFSM model); and [6] approach was restricted to boolean domains and no propagation to output parameters.

One direction for improvement consisted in moving to better defined symbolic automata models. [30][31] connected LBT to term rewriting technologies, and the model is based on equational abstract data types. [3] defined formally the abstraction and uses symbolic Mealy Machines (SMM), extending the inference method of [7].

We followed a different track by considering that connections between parameter values could better be handled by connecting to data inference techniques that come from machine learning and data mining. Based on the restricted PFSM model, where we just have to infer output values from input values based on series of i/o couples, we first experimented with the Daikon tool [14] in [36] as had already been done for passive inference by [25].

But a drawback of those restricted models consisted in the inability to compare values in one transition with values in past transitions. For many applications, and in particular for web applications and security protocols, this is far too restrictive. A major improvement has been proposed by [17] that uses as models register automata that can store past values of parameters. In order to be able to infer accurate guards, guards are restricted to conjunctions of equalities and inequalities. Actually, this model is an acceptor for data languages, so outputs would be modelled as actions that are accepted or rejected. So in effect outputs parameter values can only be restricted to equality with previous input values.

In the framework of the SPaCIoS project (see section 4.1), we developed with Keqin Li from SAP an extension of the initial algorithm for PFSM [23]. This new algorithm uses a more general extended finite state model EFSM which extends Mealy models with parameters on inputs and outputs and variables that can store past values provided by the environment as input parameters. As for register automata, the assignments to variables are limited to past values. However, outputs are less limited. Actually, in order to be able to deal with the security protocols required by the SPaCIoS project, outputs can either be deterministic values linked to the input parameters, or non-deterministic values that can be generated by the machine (this is useful to create nonces, new session IDs etc, see section 4). The new algorithm [22] separates observations into two tables: a control table that corresponds to the usual observation table of regular inference, and a data table that has the same rows and columns but records data associations for I/O transitions.

In the same spirit as [36], we consider that we can rely on existing data mining algorithms to infer guards and I/O relations. In the incremental LBT approach, a model is always an approximation that can be refined by the next confrontation with the SUI. Data mining algorithms infer approximate relations that can also be refined by extending the corpus of observations. In the case of the experiments done for the SPaCIoS project, we used the Weka tool with various clustering algorithms depending on the type (domain) of the parameters [22]. Typically, for integer parameters we used M5P, whereas for strings we used J48 [40].

3   Processing Counterexamples

For software black-box model inference, the existence of an oracle that can answer equivalence queries is a strong assumption, which is not met in most cases. Conformance testing methods have been used ([10,28]); but such methods, especially when using the Vasilievski-Chow method comes at a high exponential cost. Random sampling as suggested by Angluin [5] and its variants [8,21,18] are heuristics to find counterexamples; these methods involve a compromise on the precision but they are easy to implement. One of the drawbacks is that they will often produce much longer counterexample than the shortest one, typically because a random walk can cycle through existing states before reaching a discriminating sequence of inputs that will separate an existing state.

The length of the counterexample is a key element of the worst-case complexity of the algorithm. Even for the mean case, it may be crippling in practice when the set E of sequences labelling columns of observation tables is suffix-closed. And the counterexample processing method plays a crucial role in this complexity.

The initial L^* algorithm [5] adds all prefixes of the counterexample to S. Rivest and Schapire [34] identified that incompatibilities in the observation table could be avoided by keeping the rows in S non equivalent. The counterexample processing method by Rivest and Schapire adds only a single distinguishing string from a counterexample CE to E. However, it may take up to $log(m)$ output queries to find such a string, where $m = |CE|$. Once CE is processed and after making the table closed a conjecture is constructed, CE may still be a counterexample for the new conjecture. Since this method does not keep the table suffix-closed, in worst case it may infer a conjecture that is not consistent with the observations. The worst case complexity of this in terms of output queries is $O(|I|^2n + |I|n^2 + nlog(m))$.

Maler and Pnueli [27] also add sequences to the indices of the columns E, but keep the table suffix-closed. Shahbaz and Groz [37] improved it by trimming from CE the longest prefix already present in the rows of the table.

Motivated by the testing context where counterexamples can be quite long when found by randomized heuristics, we found that we could keep the suffix-closure property that ensures consistency between the conjecture and the observations, while still keeping only the essential "distinguishing" part of a counterexample. The intuition is that if a counterexample string CE has useless (non distinguishing) cycles, a suffix of it will be a distinguishing sequence in reality for the state of the conjecture that has to be split and that would lay at the end of the last cycle or after it. This led us to the counterexample processing method described in figure 3.

Input: Pre-refined observation table (S, E, T), CE
Output: Refined observation table (S, E, T)

```
 1  begin
 2  |   while CE is a counterexample do
 3  |   |   for j = 2 to |CE| do
 4  |   |   |   if suffix^j(CE) ∉ E then
 5  |   |   |   |   add suffix^j(CE) to E
 6  |   |   |   |   construct the output queries for the new columns
 7  |   |   |   |   complete (S, E, T) by executing output queries
 8  |   |   |   |   if (S, E, T) is not closed then
 9  |   |   |   |   |   break for loop
10  |   |   |   |   end
11  |   |   |   end
12  |   |   end
13  |   |   make (S, E, T) closed
14  |   |   construct the conjecture M
15  |   end
16  |   return refined observation table (S, E, T)
17  end
```

Fig. 3. Counterexample Processing Suffix1by1

This method, presented in [21], has several advantages.

- Like the improvements by Rivest, Maler, Shahbaz, it keeps the rows in S inequivalent, so suppresses the consistency check of the original L^* algorithm, and reduces the size of S.
- It keeps the table suffix-closed, avoiding the inconsistencies between a conjectured model and the observation table that can result by using the method from Rivest and Schapire.
- It does not add any unnecessary element in E, since it only adds discriminating sequences (and their suffixes to keep E suffix-closed).
- Once a counterexample CE has been processed and a new conjecture has been built, CE can still be confronted to the conjecture to see if a longer suffix of it would also be a discriminating sequence for another state. This does not cost any extra testing since the outputs from the SUI for the input string CE have already been recorded.
- The worst case complexity of the algorithm is $O(|I|^2 n + |I| m n^2)$. The length of the longest suffix of a counterexample m added by Suffix1by1 to the columns E in general is smaller as compared to $L_M{}^+$. However, if the oracle provides a "smart" counterexample, such that if we drop its longest prefix which matches a row label and the remaining part of the counterexample is the smallest possible distinguishing suffix, then the m parameter is the same for Rivest and Schapire method, $L_M{}^+$ and Suffix1by1. The Suffix1by1 method is much more efficient when counterexamples are non optimal, which is the standard case in our context. And it becomes more efficient as the provided counterexamples go longer, which would be the case when conjectures

grow more accurate wrt the SUI, after a number of iterations have led to refined conjectures.

Figure 4 shows the gain of this method over the other ones for a number of inputs ($|I|$) varying from 2 to 8, with $|O| = 7$ and random machines with 40 states. The counterexamples are generated by a random walk with a uniform distribution over inputs. The number of queries is computed with the simple Mealy adaptation of L^*. Of course, this method is also integrated into L_1 with greater gains for large input sets.

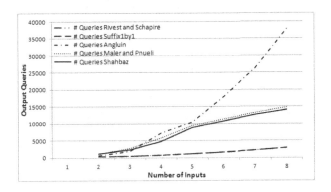

Fig. 4. $|I| \in \{2, 3 \ldots 8\}$, $|O| = 2$ and $|Q| = 40$

4 Perspectives Raised by Security Testing

4.1 SPaCIoS Project

Some of our work on inference is driven by the context of the SPaCIoS European FP7-ICT-2009 project no. 257876 [2]. SPaCIoS stands for "Secure Provision and Consumption in the Internet of Services". It uses model-checking and model-based testing to detect security flaws in (deployed) services. To that end, it uses models written in a high-level state based representation of security protocols. Model checking can detect potential violations of security goals, and testing checks whether the the potential attacks detected on models can actually be carried out on the implementations. Since models may not be available for all services or might be inaccurate, two types of model inference are considered: white-box from source code, and black-box. Figure 5 shows the overall architecture of the SPaCIoS tool and the role played by inference.

The implications for black-box inference is that it should deliver models that correspond to the typical implementations of security in services. Handwritten models exhibit only a limited number of states and few variables. Exchanges between services entities entail usually complex data, with complex coding that typically uses XML, very long strings, encrypted data, non-deterministic values, key session ids that are needed along a sequence of interactions, cookies etc.

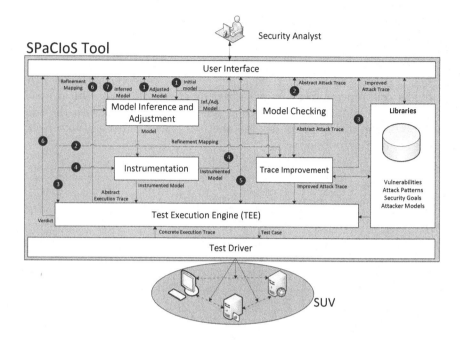

Fig. 5. SPaCIoS tool

There is also quite a distance between the abstraction of relevant data used in the model and the actual coding. But this mapping is not a specific problem for inference, and for that we can rely on the instrumentation and test execution engine that is required anyway by the MBT part to concretize tests derived from attacks on the models.

In such a context, inference of a parameterized system, including variables (registers) to record values received from a partner entity (such as session IDs, cookies etc) is essential. But there are also further needs which we discuss in the next section.

4.2 Research Directions

Dealing with Nondeterministic Values. An entity can provide fresh values (such as nonces) each time a transition is triggered. It is important to recognize that all such outputs from the black-box actually represent the same transition. So we propose a specific treatment to recognize such values, and infer models that may include this kind of data nondeterminism. This has been presented in [22].

Adjustment of Existing Specifications. As can be seen on figure 5, model inference should be used not only for getting a model "from scratch", but also to adjust preliminary models. This is similar to dealing with counterexamples or new observations to refine a model, but the initial model may have been provided tentatively by a security analyst. New observations may come from trying out attacks. The difference with counterexample processing is that the model has not been derived from an observation table. An easy workaround consists in first deriving an observation table from the model used as black-box (most inference tools anyway can work with "internal" automata). But the difference here is that some of the observations might not be consistent with the black-box. Although each observation could be cross-checked with the real black-box, it is interesting to consider optimizations to avoid redundant testing. Those optimizations should go beyond the simple ordering of queries (to avoid querying a prefix before a longer query). It can be part of an incremental refinement where observations are not systematically tested, but only when a discrepancy between the model and the SUI raises an issue in observations that came from querying the model initially.

This problem is not specific to security, but domain specific optimizations can be considered here.

Combining with Fuzzing. A test data selection strategy has to be defined for choosing parameter values to be tried out in concretizing abstract inputs. In the case of inference for security testing, it makes sense to combine with the foremost test data generation test method used to identify faulty transitions in systems, that is fuzzing. Since fuzzing implies a large number of tests, it would be inconvenient to use all the data as independent queries. The clustering approach presented in section 2.3 can be used, but it is also important to do some filtering and recognize fuzzed values that lead to new states or elicit output parameters with characteristics of interest for security testing. Typically, in [12] we consider how a combination of inference of the sort used for SPaCIoS as in [22] can be combined with fuzzing (and genetic algorithms) to identify reflected cross-site scripting attacks.

5   Conclusion

In this paper, we have presented some algorithmic improvements on Angluin-style regular inference. These improvements provide more efficient algorithms when inference is used in a software testing context: working with I/O machines rather than language acceptors, dealing with non-optimal counterexamples from randomized testing, and most importantly addressing parameterized input and output symbols and finite state models extended with parameters from unbounded domains and variables.

Our line of approach has consisted in working with adaptations of existing algorithms to make them more efficient in such a context. Testing is always an approximate and time consuming task, so improving the efficiency of the process is needed if inference is to be used more widely. Some of the research directions that we are considering in the case of security testing have been presented in section 4.2.

References

1. Connect FP7 project, https://www.connect-forever.eu/
2. SPaCIoS FP7 project, http://www.spacios.eu/
3. Aarts, F., Jonsson, B., Uijen, J.: Generating Models of Infinite-State Communication Protocols Using Regular Inference with Abstraction. In: Petrenko, A., Simão, A., Maldonado, J.C. (eds.) ICTSS 2010. LNCS, vol. 6435, pp. 188–204. Springer, Heidelberg (2010)
4. Ammons, G., Bodík, R., Larus, J.R.: Mining specifications. In: POPL, pp. 4–16 (2002)
5. Angluin, D.: Learning regular sets from queries and counterexamples. Information and Computation 2, 87–106 (1987)
6. Berg, T., Jonsson, B., Raffelt, H.: Regular Inference for State Machines with Parameters. In: Baresi, L., Heckel, R. (eds.) FASE 2006. LNCS, vol. 3922, pp. 107–121. Springer, Heidelberg (2006)
7. Berg, T., Jonsson, B., Raffelt, H.: Regular Inference for State Machines Using Domains with Equality Tests. In: Fiadeiro, J.L., Inverardi, P. (eds.) FASE 2008. LNCS, vol. 4961, pp. 317–331. Springer, Heidelberg (2008)
8. Cho, C.Y., Babic, D., Shin, E.C.R., Song, D.: Inference and analysis of formal models of botnet command and control protocols. In: ACM Conference on Computer and Communications Security, pp. 426–439 (2010)
9. Cook, J.E., Wolf, A.L.: Discovering models of software processes from event-based data. ACM Trans. Softw. Eng. Methodol. 7(3), 215–249 (1998)
10. Yannakakis, M., Peled, D., Vardi, M.Y.: Black box checking. In: Proceedings of FORTE 1999, Beijing, China (1999)
11. de la Higuera, C.: Grammatical Inference - Learning Automata and Grammars. Cambridge University Press (2010)
12. Duchène, F., Groz, R., Rawat, S., Richier, J.-L.: XSS vulnerability detection using model inference assisted evolutionary fuzzing. In: SECTEST. IEEE (2012)
13. Eisenstat, S., Angluin, D.: Learning random DFAs with membership queries: the GoodSplit algorithm. In: ZULU Workshop Organised During ICGI (2010)
14. Ernst, M.D., Perkins, J.H., Guo, P.J., McCamant, S., Pacheco, C., Tschantz, M.S., Xiao, C.: The Daikon system for dynamic detection of likely invariants. Science of Computer Programming (2006)
15. Groz, R., Li, K., Petrenko, A., Shahbaz, M.: Modular System Verification by Inference, Testing and Reachability Analysis. In: Suzuki, K., Higashino, T., Ulrich, A., Hasegawa, T. (eds.) TestCom/FATES 2008. LNCS, vol. 5047, pp. 216–233. Springer, Heidelberg (2008)
16. Hagerer, A., Hungar, H., Niese, O., Steffen, B.: Model Generation by Moderated Regular Extrapolation. In: Kutsche, R.-D., Weber, H. (eds.) FASE 2002. LNCS, vol. 2306, pp. 80–95. Springer, Heidelberg (2002)
17. Howar, F., Steffen, B., Jonsson, B., Cassel, S.: Inferring Canonical Register Automata. In: Kuncak, V., Rybalchenko, A. (eds.) VMCAI 2012. LNCS, vol. 7148, pp. 251–266. Springer, Heidelberg (2012)
18. Howar, F., Steffen, B., Merten, M.: From ZULU to RERS - Lessons Learned in the ZULU Challenge. In: Margaria, T., Steffen, B. (eds.) ISoLA 2010, Part I. LNCS, vol. 6415, pp. 687–704. Springer, Heidelberg (2010)
19. Hungar, H., Niese, O., Steffen, B.: Domain-Specific Optimization in Automata Learning. In: Hunt Jr., W.A., Somenzi, F. (eds.) CAV 2003. LNCS, vol. 2725, pp. 315–327. Springer, Heidelberg (2003)
20. Irfan, M.N., Groz, R., Oriat, C.: Improving model inference of black box components having large input test set (submitted 2012)

21. Irfan, M.N., Oriat, C., Groz, R.: Angluin style finite state machine inference with non-optimal counterexamples. In: MIIT, pp. 11–19. ACM, New York (2010)
22. Li, K., Groz, R., Hossen, K., Oriat, C.: Inferring automata with variables and nondeterministic values for testing security software (submitted 2012)
23. Li, K., Groz, R., Shahbaz, M.: Integration testing of components guided by incremental state machine learning. In: TAIC PART, pp. 59–70. IEEE Computer Society (2006)
24. Li, K., Groz, R., Shahbaz, M.: Integration Testing of Distributed Components Based on Learning Parameterized I/O Models. In: Najm, E., Pradat-Peyre, J.-F., Donzeau-Gouge, V.V. (eds.) FORTE 2006. LNCS, vol. 4229, pp. 436–450. Springer, Heidelberg (2006)
25. Lorenzoli, D., Mariani, L., Pezzè, M.: Inferring state-based behavior models. In: WODA 2006: Proceedings of the 2006 International Workshop on Dynamic Systems Analysis, pp. 25–32. ACM Press (2006)
26. Mäkinen, E., Systä, T.: Mas - an interactive synthesizer to support behavioral modelling in uml. In: ICSE 2001: Proceedings of the 23rd International Conference on Software Engineering, pp. 15–24. IEEE Computer Society, Washington, DC (2001)
27. Maler, O., Pnueli, A.: On the learnability of infinitary regular sets. Inf. Comput. 118(2), 316–326 (1995)
28. Margaria, T., Niese, O., Raffelt, H., Steffen, B.: Efficient test-based model generation for legacy reactive systems. In: IEEE International High-Level Design, Validation, and Test Workshop, pp. 95–100 (2004)
29. Meinke, K.: Automated black-box testing of functional correctness using function approximation. In: ISSTA, pp. 143–153 (2004)
30. Meinke, K.: CGE: A Sequential Learning Algorithm for Mealy Automata. In: Sempere, J.M., García, P. (eds.) ICGI 2010. LNCS, vol. 6339, pp. 148–162. Springer, Heidelberg (2010)
31. Meinke, K., Niu, F.: Learning-Based Testing for Reactive Systems Using Term Rewriting Technology. In: Wolff, B., Zaïdi, F. (eds.) ICTSS 2011. LNCS, vol. 7019, pp. 97–114. Springer, Heidelberg (2011)
32. Niese, O.: An Integrated Approach to Testing Complex Systems. PhD thesis, University of Dortmund (2003)
33. Pasareanu, C.S., Giannakopoulou, D., Bobaru, M.G., Cobleigh, J.M., Barringer, H.: Learning to divide and conquer: applying the L^* algorithm to automate assume-guarantee reasoning. Formal Methods in System Design 32(3), 175–205 (2008)
34. Rivest, R.L., Schapire, R.E.: Inference of finite automata using homing sequences. In: Machine Learning: From Theory to Applications, pp. 51–73 (1993)
35. Shahbaz, M.: Reverse Engineering Enhanced State Models of Black Box Software Components to Support Integration Testing. Phd thesis, Institut Polytechnique de Grenoble (2008)
36. Shahbaz, M., Groz, R.: Using invariant detection mechanism in black box inference. In: ISoLA Workshop on Leveraging Applications of Formal Methods (2007)
37. Shahbaz, M., Groz, R.: Inferring Mealy Machines. In: Cavalcanti, A., Dams, D.R. (eds.) FM 2009. LNCS, vol. 5850, pp. 207–222. Springer, Heidelberg (2009)
38. Shu, G., Lee, D.: Testing security properties of protocol implementations - a machine learning based approach. In: ICDCS, Toronto, Ontario, Canada (2007)
39. Utting, M., Legeard, B.: Practical Model-Based Testing - A Tools Approach. Morgan Kaufmann (2007)
40. Witten, I.H., Frank, E., Hall, M.A.: Data Mining: Practical Machine Learning Tools and Techniques, 3rd edn. Morgan Kaufmann (2011)

Test-Case Design by Feature Trees

Takashi Kitamura, Ngoc Thi Bich Do, Hitoshi Ohsaki,
Ling Fang, and Shunsuke Yatabe

National Institute of Advanced Industrial Science and Technology (AIST)
{t.kitamura,do.ngoc,hitoshi.ohsaki,fang-ling,shunsuke.yatabe}@aist.go.jp

Abstract. This paper proposes a test-case design method for black-box testing, called *"Feature Oriented Testing* (FOT)". The method is realized by applying *Feature Models* (FMs) developed in software product line engineering to test-case designs. We develop a graphical language for test-case design called *"Feature Trees for Testing* (FTT)" based on FMs. To firmly underpin the method, we provide a formal semantics of FTT, by means of test-cases derived from test-case designs modelled with FTT. Based on the semantics we develop an automated test-suite generation and correctness checking of test-case designs using SAT, as computer-aided analysis techniques of the method. Feasibility of the method is demonstrated from several viewpoints including its implementation, complexity analysis, experiments, a case study, and an assistant tool.

Keywords: black-box testing, combination testing, SAT-based analysis.

1 Introduction

In black-box testing (BBT) test cases are designed by analysing the input domain of the system under test (SUT) often according to the system's specification. The *Classification Tree Method* (CTM) [5, 9–11] is one of the-state-of-the-art test-case design methods for BBT. It is a model-based and combination testing method; i.e., test cases are designed as a visual model with a given diagram-based language, and test cases are generated automatically from such a model using combination techniques. Due to its nice characteristics as a testing method, CTM is often used in industry including automotive industries [19]. However, for a better testing method improvements can be considered from several perspectives such as its theory, higher computer-aided analysis, efficiency of automated technologies, and modelling paradigms.

Feature-Oriented Domain Analysis/Feature Models (FODA/FMs) is an analysis method for software product lines (SPLs), first proposed by Kang et al. [14]. This method takes a model-based approach; i.e., an SPL is modelled with extended and-or logical trees called "Feature Models (FMs)", which enable systematic analysis in a top-down manner, together with their graphical representations of "Feature Diagrams". In addition, useful information about the SPL can be derived by applying analysis techniques to the models. A main characteristic of FMs is its compact and visual representations by diagrams to capture SPLs as well as a

T. Margaria and B. Steffen (Eds.): ISoLA 2012, Part I, LNCS 7609, pp. 458–473, 2012.
© Springer-Verlag Berlin Heidelberg 2012

variety of analysis techniques. So far fruitful research results of FMs have been made in research and industry, including various model designs [20], semantics [3, 17, 20, 21], various analysis operations such as consistency checking, diagnosis, validations, refactoring, and so on (as summarized in [2, 17]). Also such analysis operations are carried out on various logic paradigms such as propositional logic [1, 13, 16, 22], description logic [8] or constraint programming [3] as well as algorithmic approaches [4, 23].

In this work, we propose a test-case design method by applying FMs, called "*Feature Oriented Testing* (FOT)", identified as a model-based and combination testing method for BBT. The aims of the work are three-fold: (1) to develop a test-case design language based on the model designs of FMs, which are characterized with the compact and visual representations by diagrams of extended and-or logical trees, (2) to apply rich theories of FMs to the test-case design method focusing on semantics, and (3) to apply computer-aided analysis techniques of FMs to the test-case design method, to retrieve useful information for test-case designs.

The main contributions of this paper are two-fold: (A) to realize these aims as a test-case design method, and (B) to demonstrate the method's feasibility from several viewpoints. For (A), first we analyze the requirements for developing a test-case design language, and design such a language as "*Feature Tree for Testing* (FTT)" that suits the test-case design purpose based on various designs of FMs proposed in the literature [20]. Then we build a theoretical foundation of FTT by providing its formal syntax and semantics; which makes a basis of reliability and computer-aided analysis. Further, we develop two kinds of logic-based automated analysis techniques for FTT using a SAT solver: a test-suite generation and correctness checking of test-case designs by FTT.

For (B), first feasibility is shown from the viewpoint of reliability, which is an important property as a testing method, by building formal semantics and proving the correctness of the test-case generation algorithm w.r.t. the semantics. Feasibility is demonstrated from the viewpoint of computational cost on the automated analysis, by analyzing the computational complexity and by providing experimental results. A case study is presented, where we apply FOT to test-case design for OSEK/VDX-OS (OSEK-OS), a standard real-time OS for automotives [18]. We also explain our GUI-based assistant tool for FOT. This show not only how the method can be assisted by a tool, but also some essential techniques for test-case designs of FOT using this tool.

2   A Motivating Example

Borrowing an example in [5], we design test cases for BBT for a computer vision system. As seen in Fig. 1, this system determines the size of various blocks passing the camera of the system on a belt-conveyor. Fig. 2 shows a test-case design for BBT for the system by FOT. In FOT, an FM is used to design test cases; i.e, analysis for test-case design proceeds using FTT by splitting up the input/(output) domain of the SUT with various *test-relevant aspects*, which we also refer to as *features*.

Fig. 1. Computer vision system for determining the size of building blocks

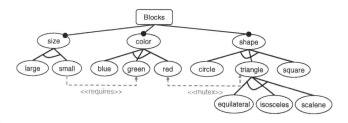

Fig. 2. A simple and small test-case design using an FTT

The analysis of the input domain, i.e., the test-case design for the SUT, proceeds in a top-down manner with its root as the input domain of SUT, which is "Blocks" here. First, "Blocks" are decomposed into features of their "size", "color" and "shape". In decompositions (decomp.), we distinguish them with two kinds of *orthogonal* and *alternative* decomp. The "block" is decomposed with an orthogonal decomp., as we regard its three sub-features are orthogonal notions. We may also call such decomp. *and-decomp.*, following the convention of and-or trees and FMs. We clarify such decomp. explicitly in the diagram by the dot on top of each feature.

Next these three decomposed sub-features are further decomposed into smaller sub-features. For example, the "size" feature is decomposed into two sub-features: "small" and "large". In this case, it is done with an *alternative* decomp., which may be also called *xor-decomp.*, by regarding the sub-features as alternatives to one another. Compositions of this kind are clarified in the diagram in the way that the edges of a decomp., are tied up with a string. Similarly, the "color" features are decomposed into "blue", "green" and "red", and "shape" into "circle", "triangle" and "square" with *alternative*-decomp. The "triangle" feature is further decomposed into "equilateral", "isosceles" and "scalene" alternatively, to design test cases in a detailed way and hence inspect the system in more details.

Besides such decomp. relations between features, which form the parent-child relations of trees, *"mutex"* and *"requires"* relations drawn globally in the tree (i.e., crossing the tree) are found in the model in Fig 2. These represent constraints between features in the tree globally, which we call *cross-tree constraints* (CTCs), to exclude nonsense or undesired test cases according to given specifications. For example, assume in the above example, the following specifications are given: (1) "There are no blocks whose color is red and whose shape is a triangle." (2) "If the size of blocks is small, then the color of the blocks is green.". Due to these specifications, it is nonsense and undesirable to prepare test cases for

Table 1. The test suite obtained from test-case design of Fig. 2

1. small, red, circle	7. small, green, square	13. small, green, isosceles
2. small, blue, circle	8. large, green, square	14. small, blue, isosceles
3. large, green, circle	9. large, green, equilateral	15. small, blue, scalene
4. small, green, circle	10. small, blue, equilateral	16. large, green, scalene
5. small, blue, square	11. small, green, equilateral	17. small, green, scalene
6. small, red, square	12. large, green, isosceles	

such cases. The CTCs clarify such nonsense test cases. The *mutex* (an abbr. for "mutually exclusive with") constraint between the "red" and "triangle" features in Fig. 2 is drawn to cover specification (1), and *requires* between the "small" to "circle" feature to cover specification (2). Note that each CTC affects all the features in the sub-tree of the features it involves. E.g., the *mutex* constraint stipulates that "red" is *mutex* not only with "triangle" but also with all the sub-features of the sub-tree: "equilateral", "isosceles" and "scalene".

The test-case design, shown as a diagram in Fig. 2, captures a set of test cases; i.e., we can obtain a set of test cases (i.e., test suite) from the diagram. Here, a test case is defined as a set of features in the tree. Table 1 shows the test suite obtained from the test-case design of Fig. 2. That is, the test suite derived from the test-case design consists of fifteen test cases; for example, test-case 1 indicates blocks whose size is "small", color is "red", is shape "circle". Roughly, test cases are derived from such test-case designs by recursively applying the following standard interpretation of and-or logical tree; i.e., all the sub-features of *and*-decomp. or its descendants have to be in any test case, and exactly one of the sub-features of *xor*-decomp. or its descendants have to be in any test case. Besides, the test cases the CTCs are applied to are excluded. The rules to derive test cases from the diagrams should be more detailed in an exact way, and we formally explain these rules in Section 4.

3   Feature Trees for Testing

This section develops a test-case design language based on FMs, called *Feature Tree for Testing* (FTT), which we regard as the *modelling language* for test-case design in FOT. First we analyze requirements for such a language as a model-based and combination testing method for BBT. According to them we design such a language as FTT based on FMs, showing its design choices. Then based on the design of FTT, the syntax and semantics of FTT are provided formally.

3.1   Requirements and Design Choices

Requirements. Though the basic idea of FTT was seen in the previous section, here we briefly summarize the requirements analysis for developing a test-case design language for our test-case design purpose of model-based and combination testing method for BBT, as follows:

1. The basic structure of FTT is designed as a *tree*; i.e., the tree structure is formed by an input-domain analysis of SUT by repeatedly decomposing it with features from the root, which facilitates systematic test-case design in a top-down manner.
2. Each decomp. of a feature (i.e., the input domain of SUT) should be distinguished by two kinds: *orthogonal decomp.*, i.e., all the sub-features are orthogonal notions to one another, and *alternative decomp.*, i.e., all the sub-features are alternative notions to one another.
3. Some kinds of constraint operators, imposed on globally (between any features crossing a tree), are equipped to exclude non-sense and undesired test cases according to given specifications.

Design Choices. We design a language for test-case design as FTT to meet the requirements based on various variants of FMs proposed in the literature [20]. By following [20] for a scheme of design choices of FMs, FTT is characterized as:

1. FTT are trees (, but not DAGs: Directed Acyclic Graphs).
2. FTT have the following two-kinds of decomp. operators:
   (a) *and*-decomp., to express *orthogonal*-decomp.
   (b) *xor*-decomp., to express *alternative*-decomp.
3. FTT have the following constraint representations drawn globally in a tree:
   (a) *requires*; if a feature f requires a feature g, the inclusion of f in a test case implies the inclusion of g in such a test case.
   (b) *mutex*; the two features related by the relation cannot be present simultaneously in a test-case.

Some other relations, often common in FMs such as "*optional*", "*or*-decomp." and "*cardinality*", are not included in FTT, since straightforward interpretations can not be given on the operators in our test-case design setting. The same is true for other relations such as "*generalization*", "*specialization*" and "*implemented-by*" found in [15]. The language design of FTT is not same as any of the FMs listed in [20], but similar to the original FM developed by Kang et al. [14]

3.2   Syntax of Feature Trees for Testing

We give a formal syntax of FTT as a basis for the formal developments:

Definition 1. *A feature tree is a tuple* $(F, r, L, \rightharpoonup, @, \xrightarrow{req}, \xleftrightarrow{mex})$ *such that*

- $(F, r, \rightharpoonup)$ *is a tree, where F is a set of features (as the nodes of a tree), r is the root, and $\rightharpoonup$ is the parent-child relation on F,*
  - *we say "feature f is the parent of g" and "g is a child of f" if $f \rightharpoonup g$,*
- $L(\subset F)$ *is a set of leaf features,*
- $@$ *is a function from $F \setminus L$ to $\{and, xor\}$,*
- $\xleftrightarrow{mex}$ *is a symmetric and irreflexive binary relation over F,*
- $\xrightarrow{req}$ *is an asymmetric and irreflexive binary relation over F.*   □

FTT are trees $(F, r, \rightharpoonup)$ extended with several notions. First FTT are a variant of and-or logical trees. We realize this with "node-based design", where each feature (i.e., node) of the tree except for leaf features is labeled with "and" or "xor". The function $@ : F \setminus L \to \{\text{and}, \text{xor}\}$, which labels each (non-leaf) features with *and* or *xor*, is equipped for this. We call features "and-feature" or "xor-feature" if it is associated with "and" and "xor" by @ respectively. Note that, due to the design, "and " and "xor"-edges shall not be mixed among the edges out-going from a feature. The two kinds of CTCs of *mutex* and *requires*, which are another extension of FTT, are expressed by the binary relations " $\overset{mex}{\leftrightarrow}$ " and " $\overset{req}{\to}$ " on F.

3.3   Semantics

An FTT captures a set of test cases. In other words, the semantics of an FTT is defined by way of a set of test cases derived from it; i.e., given an FTT, we formally understand what it means by way of a set of test cases.

Definition 2 (Pre-model). *A pre-model $M'(\in \mathcal{M}')$ of an FTT t is a subset of its features: $M' \in \mathcal{P}F$, where $\mathcal{P}X$ denotes the power set of X.*   □

Definition 3 (Model). *A model $M(\in \mathcal{M})$ of an FTT t is a pre-model that satisfies the following conditions, and is noted as $M \models' t$:*

1. *The root feature is in the model: $r \in M$,*
2. *If a feature is in a model, its parent is in the model too: $f \in M \Rightarrow \text{parent}(f) \in M$,*
3. *If an and-feature is in a model, all its children are in the model too: $f \in M \wedge @(f) = \text{and} \Rightarrow (\forall g.f \rightharpoonup g \to g \in M)$,*
4. *If an xor-feature is in a model, exactly one of its children is in the model too; $f \in M \wedge @(f) = \text{xor} \Rightarrow (\exists! g.f \rightharpoonup g \wedge g \in M)$,*
5. *The model must satisfy all formulas from the CTCs set $\Phi(= \overset{mex}{\leftrightarrow} \cup \overset{req}{\to})$: $\forall \phi \in \Phi.M \models' \phi$, where "$M \models' f \overset{mex}{\longleftrightarrow} g$" if f and g are not both in M, and "$M \models' f \overset{req}{\longrightarrow} g$" if f is in M, g is in M too.*   □

The definition of test case and test suite are given by way of the *model.*

Definition 4 (Test case and test suite). *1. A test case c is a subset of leaves: $c \in \mathcal{P}L$. 2. A test case of the model M, noted M°, is $M \cap L$. 3. A test suite s is a set of test cases: $s = \mathcal{P}c \in \mathcal{PP}L$. 4. The test suite derived from an FTT t is the set of test cases of models M satisfying t: $\llbracket t \rrbracket = \{M^\circ \mid M \models' t\}$*   □

4   SAT-Based Automated Analysis of FTT

This section explains several SAT-based automated analysis techniques of FTT, as computer-aided analysis techniques of FOT. An epoch in the research of FMs is the provision of encoding FMs to a propositional (prop.) formula, which brings many interesting logic-based analysis on FMs, often using technologies of SAT-solvers. Applying these techniques to our setting, we develop *SAT-based automated test-suite generation* and *correctness checking of test-case designs by FTT.*

Table 2. The encoding rules *trans* of an FTT into prop. formulas

	Feature model relation	Corresponding formula
(a)	r is the root feature	r
(b)	$p \rightharpoonup c_1$	$c_1 \rightarrow p$
(c)	$@(p) = and$ and $p \rightarrow c$	$p \rightarrow c$
(d)	$@(p) = xor$ and $p \rightharpoonup c_1, \cdots, p \rightharpoonup c_n$	$p \rightarrow \bigvee \begin{pmatrix} (c_1 \wedge \neg c_2 \wedge \cdots \wedge \neg c_n) \\ \cdots \\ (\neg c_1 \wedge \neg c_2 \wedge \cdots \wedge c_n) \end{pmatrix}$
(e)	$p \overset{mex}{\longleftrightarrow} q$	$\neg(p \wedge q)$
(f)	$p \overset{req}{\longrightarrow} q$	$p \rightarrow q$

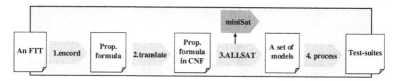

Fig. 3. The system for test-case generation

4.1 Propositional Formulas Encoding

Table 2 shows the encoding rules (*trans*) of an FTT to a prop. formula. Lemma 1 shows the rules are correct w.r.t. the semantics in Definition 4. The proof of this lemma is obvious, but it plays a critical role for guaranteeing the correctness of our automated analysis techniques.

Lemma 1. *For any FTT t, $M \models' t$ iff $M \models trans(t)$*   □

4.2 A SAT-Based Automated Test-Suite Generation

An Algorithm Design and Early Implementation. First we derive the following theorem from Lemma 1:

Theorem 1. *For any FTT t, $[\![t]\!] = \{M^\circ \mid M \models trans(t)\}$.*   □

This theorem indicates that in order to obtain the test suite of a given FTT t according to Definition 4, it suffices to follow the procedures of: (1) to derive all the models that satisfy the prop. formula encoded from the FTT t i.t.o the classical logic, and (2) to process each of the models by taking one that intersects with the leaf nodes of the FTT and (3) to take the union of the processed models. And the algorithm design follows this scheme.

The test-suite generation algorithm is displayed in Fig. 3. The input is an FTT and the output is a set of corresponding test cases (i.e., a test suite). The algorithm mainly consists of the following four components.

1. The first component encodes an FTT to a prop. formula according to the encoding rules in Table 2.

2. The second is a *conjunctive normal form* (CNF) translator, which translates a prop. formula into it in a CNF.
3. The third is an all-solutions SAT-solver (ALLSAT), inputting the encoded formula of FTT in CNF, finds all models for it. We have implemented an ALL-SAT using the blocking algorithm (which finds all models by iteratively calling a SAT solver while at each call blocking clauses which block finding a model already found is added) by extending MiniSAT[6].
4. The fourth processes a set of models obtained from the ALLSAT, by taking one that intersects with the leaf nodes of the FTT, and produces the test suite by collecting the processed models (i.e., test cases).

Computational Complexity. To analyze the complexity of the test-case generation algorithm, we analyze the complexity of each component 1-4. Given an FTT t, we denote the number of features as n.

1. The length of a formula derived by *trans* is the sum of sub-formulas by applying each rule of (a)–(f). Thus it suffices to analyze rule (d), which makes the longest sub-formula among of (a)–(f) in Table 2. The length of a sub-formula by (d) for an xor-decomp. with k-children is bound by $O(k \times k)$. Both the number of children of any feature and that of xor-decomp. in t are bound by $n - 1$. Hence the length of a formula by *trans* is bound by $O(n^2)$.
2. We have implemented an algorithm to transform a prop. formula using the standard laws of logical equivalences, and have produced a clause set that is exponential w.r.t. the size of the original formula in the worst case.
3. The SAT-problem is NP-complete, and the worst time complexity of the algorithm we use (i.e., MiniSAT[6, 12]) is $O(2^n)$ where n indicates the number of the prop. variables. Also the number of models for a given formula is bound by 2^n. Hence, the complexity of ALLSAT is bound by $2^n \times O(2^n) \in O(4^n)$.
4. The complexity of the set intersection of two sets with size k is $O(k^2)$. The number of nodes and the leaf nodes of an FTT are bound by n. There are at most 2^n models. Hence, the complexity is bound by $2^n \times O(n^2) \in O(2^n \times n^2)$.

Hence the bottleneck of the algorithm is the component of CNF-transformation and ALLSAT, whose complexity are exponential to the input FTT t.

Experimental Results. Besides the complexity analysis, we provide experimental results to show feasibility of the implementation from the viewpoint of computational cost of FOT. According to the above analysis of computational cost of the test-suite generation algorithm, we know that its bottleneck lies on computing all the models using ALLSAT, which takes exponential time w.r.t. the size of FTT. But in practice the computational cost is cheaper than the theoretical analysis. One reason is that the off-the-shelf SAT-solver we use, i.e., MiniSAT, runs faster than the above analysis. Second, the number of the models for the formula encoded from an FTT is much less than 2^n in real settings. Also, the number of test cases varies depending on the structures of FTT. The ratio of *and/xor*-decomp. and the ratio of CTCs in an FTT mainly affect the number of test cases; i.e., the more *and*-decomp. and CTCs there are in an FTT, the less test

Table 3. Experimental results

ctcr(%)		Size of an FTT (n)				
		20	30	40	50	60
0	time (s)	0.09	0.67	2.04	9.65	20.43
	# test cases	120	960	6912	19008	43200
10	time (s)	0.04	0.35	0.82	3.65	4.71
	# test cases	92	432	2464	8580	9160
20	time (s)	0.03	0.09	0.53	1.52	2.01
	# test cases	75	238	916	2710	4244
30	time (s)	0.01	0.07	0.17	0.51	0.93
	# test cases	26	120	288	880	1666
40	time (s)	0.01	0.06	0.06	0.12	0.14
	# test cases	13	45	96	122	168

cases are derived. Table 3 shows an experimental result, presenting the time and the number of test cases, where *ctcr* stands for the CTCs ratio (i.e., the ratio of CTCs w.r.t the size of FTT). The experiments were conducted on a machine with an Intel Core2 Duo CPU P8700 @2.53 GHz, 2.96 GB of RAM and Windows 7.

4.3   SAT-Based Correctness Checking of Test-Case Designs

An important class of various computer-aided analysis techniques on FMs is *correctness checking*. Generally, *correctness checking* includes *consistency checking* and detecting *dead/common* features. These notions are interpreted in the setting of test-case design as follows: an FTT, i.e., a test-case design, is *inconsistent* if no test case can be derived from it; a feature is *dead* in an FTT if it does not appear in any of the test cases of the model derived from it; and a feature is *common* in an FTT if it appears in all the test cases derived from it.

Interestingly, these analysis operations on *correctness checking* can be reduced to a simple satisfiability checking problem of a prop. formula. The *consistency of a test-case design* by a FTT can be examined by checking the satisfiability of the formula ϕ encoded from the FTT (t), i.e., $\phi = trans(t)$. Existence of a *dead* feature f in an FTT can be examined by checking the satisfiability of the formula $\phi \wedge f$; i.e., f is a *dead* feature if $\phi \wedge f$ is unsatisfiable. Similarly, existence of a *common* feature f in a model can be examined by checking the satisfiability of $\phi \wedge \neg f$; i.e., f is a *common* feature if the formula is unsatisfiable.

We have introduced these analysis operations on correctness checking of test-case designs in FOT, which help validation of test-case designs by FTT. As shown in the next section, the consistency checking, especially detecting *dead* features, are quite useful for finding defects in test-case designs since they often enter test-case designs and their existences are undesirable.

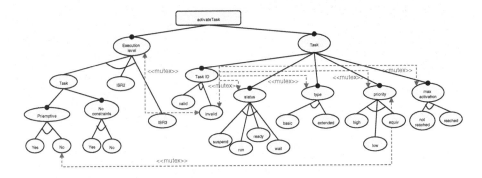

Fig. 4. A test-case design by FTT for API "activateTask" in OSEK-OS

5   A Case Study: A Test-Case Design for OSEK-OS

To demonstrate feasibility of FOT in real practice, we show a case study where we applied FOT to test case design for the OSEK-OS[18, 19], a real-time OS for automotives. Specifically, using FTT we make a test-case design for an API function "*activateTask*", which transfers a task specified with parameter "*TaskID*" from the "*suspended*" state into the "*ready*" state. We analyzed the specification [18], and made its test-case design as in Fig. 4. The figure shows the test-case design with an FTT that consists of 30 features and 6 CTCs, and 192 test cases are obtained from it.

Several observations obtained from the case-study are as follows:

1. Test-case designs with a variant of and-or tree are easily accepted by developers in practice because and-or trees are a common analysis technique and close to human thinking. Also this analysis technique using and-or trees can allow them to focus on designing test cases released from direct edits on logical formulas, which are often error-prone.
2. Efficiency of the automated analysis techniques of FOT, i.e, automated test-suite generation and correctness checking, whose experimental results are shown in Tab. 3, is practical enough in our case studies.
3. Unfortunately, FTT is not expressive enough to express any desired test suite in any settings, because test-case designs in real development are sometimes extremely detailed and beyond the expressiveness of FTT. As a result, manual arrangements of test cases such as to add, delete and modify test cases are required to cover some detailed cases. But this should not be taken as a critical defect of FOT, since CTM, which is the state-of-the-art method of test-case design for BBT often used in real developments, also inherently has this aspect of expressiveness. (See related discussions in Section 8.)
4. Detecting *dead* features for correctness checking of test-case designs by FTT is quite useful in practice. Test-case designs are often complex, and hence prone to contain deficiencies. In the test-case design in Fig. 4, the "*invalid*" and "*No*" (under "*Preemptive*") features are the *dead* features. Existence of *dead*

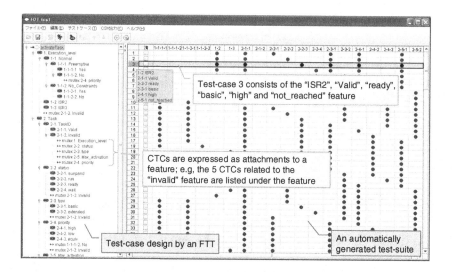

Fig. 5. The GUI tool for FOT

features indicates that some errors may be contained in the test-case design, or these *dead* features may have to be taken care of by manual arrangements.

5. Test-case designs by FTT can be used for test documentations such as a system specification for testing. These designs can also be used as communication media among developers, and as evidence for certification. The high readability of FTT, achieved by the compact and visual representation by diagrams, and by the formal semantics to unify interpretation of FTT contributes to the aspect of documentations.

6. The readability of the diagram representations of FTT can be preserved, even with many CTCs drawn all over the tree, together with the GUI-based assistant tool. We explain the tool's support for readability in the next section.

6   Tool Development

We have developed a GUI tool to assist FOT. This section will briefly explain this tool. The tool development shows not only our current status of the development of FOT, but is also essential in the test-case design method of FOT.

Describing FTT via the GUI. Fig. 5 shows the main GUI of the tool. It is separated into two panels: the left-hand-side panel where users describe and input an FTT, and the right-hand-side panel which displays the automatically generated test cases in a matrix form.

In designing test cases by describing an FTT via the GUI, several advantages ascribed to the properties of FTT become possible. First, the GUI prevents inputting illegitimate FTT w.r.t. the defined syntax in Definition 1. That is, the GUI lets users input only a legitimate FTT, which then allows them to concentrate on the logic of test-case designs. The second advantage centers on scalability w.r.t.

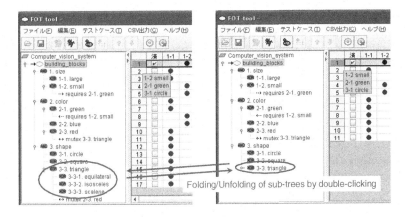

Fig. 6. The number of test-cases can be controlled by folding/unfolding sub-trees

the readability of the diagram representations of FTT. As shown in Fig. 5 in the FTT description of in the GUI, each CTC is expressed as an attachment to features involved in the description. Due to the GUI design, even with a number of CTCs, the diagram representation keeps readability.

Controlling the Number of Test Cases Flexibly. In general, the system quality guaranteed by testing and its cost is a trade-off. That is, the more the cost for detailed testing is allowed, the higher the quality of the system is guaranteed. On the other hand, the resources for testing are limited in real developments. Therefore, it is desirable for a testing method to be able to flexibly control system quality guaranteed by testing by depending on its affordable resources.

FOT is equipped with such a mechanism; i.e., it is equipped with a device to flexibly control the number of test cases. The device is realized by using a notion of abstraction on tree structures in the FTT such as folding and unfolding sub-trees. Fig. 6 demonstrates this device in the tool, using the example of the computer vision system. The left side in Fig. 6 shows the test-case design for the computer vision system in Section 2 using the tool, where 17 test cases are obtained. The number can be flexibly reduced, for instance, by abstracting the "triangle" feature by folding its sub-tree; i.e., the number of the test cases obtained from the tree whose "triangle" sub-tree is folded, can be reduced to 11.

7   Discussions and Related Work

CTM (*Classification Tree Method*) [5, 9–11] is a model-based and combination-based test-case design method for BBT; i.e., a test case is designed as a model of a tree diagram, and test cases are obtained automatically from it using a combination technique. In CTM, the model to represent a test-case design consists of the three separate description components: (1) a *"classification-tree diagram"*, which is a tree-based diagram to represent the basic structure of test-case design,

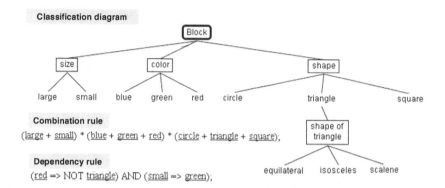

Fig. 7. Test-case design for the computer vision system in CTM

(2) *"combination rules"* to define combination rules based on the classification-tree diagram, and (3) *"dependency rules"*, written in prop. logic, to exclude nonsense test cases. Fig. 7 shows a descriptive example of a test-case design for the computer vision system using CTM to produce the same test suite in Tab. 1. FOT can be seen as a comparable test-case design method to CTM, but its advantages over CTM are the following:

The first advantage is on the modelling paradigm for test-case designs. In FOT, a test-case design is represented as an FTT in a single diagram based on *and-or logical trees*. We inherit the single and compact design of FMs, often recognized as a characteristic of FMs, in FTT, which brings higher readability. The model design of FTT requires less complex descriptions than CTM, bringing higher productivity; i.e., complex descriptions together with direct edits of the logical formula is often a main barrier preventing wider adoption of such methods in real developments. Also, the single representations of FTT achieve higher maintainability; the separate descriptions in CTM often require efforts because such changes in a description component may affect the others. Also, the model design based on *and-or trees* achieves higher availability as a common and traditional analysis technique. In fact, the model design is highly inspired by *Fault Tree Analysis* (FTA) [7], which is an established analysis technique based on and-or trees in *reliability engineering*. Also, the logic-based model of FTT facilitates the logic-based analysis in FOT.

On the other hand, theoretically CTM is more expressive than FTT. The difference lies on the expressiveness of a description device to exclude nonsense test cases: i..e, CTCs in FTT, which consists of the two operators *mutex* and *requires*, and the *dependency rules* in CTM, which deals with a full prop. formula. But from our case studies, the advantage of the expressiveness of CTM is mostly in theory. From the case studies, we learned only simple rules are needed to realize such devices, and CTCs are expressive enough for this purpose. In place of expressiveness, FTT realizes the above-mentioned nice properties such as readability, productivity, and maintainability, etc. We have mentioned in Section 6 that FTT may not be expressive enough for some settings. But this is due to the tree structure of FTT rather than due to the expressiveness of CTCs, and hence CTM also has this aspect.

Second, FOT has a formal semantics, which is missing in CTM. The semantics makes a basis for reliability by preventing the "ambiguity problem" which causes faulty developments. In addition, FOT has the advantage that due to its compact model design it can be formalized with a small set of constructs. Conciseness is not only important in a scientific sense, but also in an engineering sense since it requires less cost to learn the method and makes the method easy to extend.

Third, a SAT-based algorithm is designed and implemented for automated test-suite generation. An obvious advantage of the design is efficiency. The design can benefit from recent advances in theory and in the techniques of SAT-solvers [6]. For instance, FOT takes only about 20 seconds to generate 64200 test cases, while CTM tool[10, 11] takes 73 minutes in a similar setting. Another advantage is that the correctness of the algorithm is easy to prove as we did, making FOT more reliable; i.e., it is guaranteed the test suite generated by the algorithm is always correct (i.e., the test suite generated by the algorithm is sound and complete w.r.t a test-case design and the semantics in Definition 3.).

Fourth, FOT is equipped with several automated analysis operations for *correctness checking* for test-case designs such as *consistency checking* and detecting *dead/common* features, which are absent in CTM. These analysis operations are quite useful, and we find them in several case-studies for finding deficiencies in test-case designs by FTT, and validating test-case designs.

8   Conclusion and Future Research

Conclusion. In this paper, we have developed a test-case design method for BBT called "FOT (Feature Oriented Testing)", by applying analysis and design methods of FMs originally developed for SPLs. We designed a test-case design language as a model-based and combination testing method for BBT based on FMs. A formal semantics of FTT is developed by means of test-cases; this makes a firm underpinning of the method. Also we have develop and implemented an automated test-suite generation and correctness checking of test-case designs using SAT, as computer-aided analysis techniques of the method. Furthermore, we have demonstrated feasibility of FOT with several dimensions of implementation, analysis of computational cost, experiments, a case study, and an assistant-tool development. We have also clarified the technical and practical advances of FOT to CTM, which is the-state-of-the-art testing method for BBT.

Future Research. There are many directions for further research on the method. The first is to introduce to FOT other theories and computer-aided techniques of FMs, including refactoring, diagnosis and efficiency analysis. Another direction is to extend FOT with useful notions for test-case design such as the notion of priority. In addition, incorporating other testing methods for BBT such as combination testing methods (e.g., n-wise testing, etc) and input-domain analysis techniques (e.g., equivalent partitioning, boundary value analysis, etc) to FOT are important directions for our future research.

References

1. Batory, D.: Feature Models, Grammars, and Propositional Formulas. In: Obbink, H., Pohl, K. (eds.) SPLC 2005. LNCS, vol. 3714, pp. 7–20. Springer, Heidelberg (2005)
2. Benavides, D., Cortes, A.R., Trinidad, P., Segura, S.: A survey on the automated analyses of feature models. In: XV Jornadas de Ingenieria del Software y Bases de Datos (2006)
3. Benavides, D., Trinidad, P., Ruiz-Cortés, A.: Automated Reasoning on Feature Models. In: Pastor, Ó., Falcão e Cunha, J. (eds.) CAiSE 2005. LNCS, vol. 3520, pp. 491–503. Springer, Heidelberg (2005)
4. Cao, F., Bryant, B.R., Burt, C.C., Huang, Z., Raje, R.R., Olson, A.M., Auguston, M.: Automating feature-oriented domain analysis. In: Software Engineering Research and Practice, pp. 944–949 (2003)
5. Chen, T.Y., Poon, P.L., Tse, T.H.: An integrated classification-tree methodology for test case generation. International Journal of Software Engineering and Knowledge Engineering, 647–679 (2000)
6. Eén, N., Sörensson, N.: An Extensible SAT-solver. In: Giunchiglia, E., Tacchella, A. (eds.) SAT 2003. LNCS, vol. 2919, pp. 502–518. Springer, Heidelberg (2004)
7. Ericson, C.: Fault tree analysis - a history. In: The 17th International Systems Safety Conference (1999)
8. Fan, S., Zhang, N.: Feature Model Based on Description Logics. In: Gabrys, B., Howlett, R.J., Jain, L.C. (eds.) KES 2006. LNCS (LNAI), vol. 4252, pp. 1144–1151. Springer, Heidelberg (2006)
9. Grochtmann, M.: Test case design using classification trees. In: The International Conference on Software Testing Analysis (1994)
10. Grochtmann, M., Grimm, K., Wegener, J., Grochtmann, M.: Tool-supported test case design for black-box testing by means of the classification-tree editor. In: The 1st European International Conference on Software Testing Analysis, pp. 169–176 (1993)
11. Grochtmann, M., Wegener, J.: Test case design using classification trees and the classification-tree editor cte. In: QW (1995)
12. Impagliazzo, R., Paturi, R.: On the complexity of k-SAT. Comput. Syst. Sci. 62(2), 367–375 (2001)
13. Janota, M.: Do SAT solvers make good configurators? In: ASPL, pp. 191–195 (2008)
14. Kang, K.C., Cohen, S.G., Hess, J.A., Novak, W.E., Peterson, A.S.: Feature-oriented domain analysis (FODA) feasibility study. Technical report, Carnegie-Mellon University Software Engineering Institute (November 1990)
15. Kang, K.C., Kim, S., Lee, J., Kim, K.: FORM: a feature-oriented reuse method, annals of software engineering. Annals of Software Engineering 5, 143–168 (1998)
16. Mannion, M.: Using First-Order Logic for Product Line Model Validation. In: Chastek, G.J. (ed.) SPLC 2002. LNCS, vol. 2379, pp. 176–187. Springer, Heidelberg (2002)
17. Mendonca, M., Wsowski, A., Czarnecki, K.: SAT-based analysis of feature models is easy. In: SPLC, pp. 231–240 (2009)
18. OSEK/VDX operating system specification 2.2.3 (2005), http://www.osek-vdx.org/
19. OSEK/VDX operating system test plan, version 2.0 (1999)

20. Schobbens, P., Heymans, P., Trigaux, J., Bontemps, Y.: Generic semantics of feature diagrams. Computer Networks 51(2), 456–479 (2007)
21. Schobbens, P., Heymans, P., Trigaux, J.C.: Feature diagrams: A survey and a formal semantics. In: RE, pp. 139–148 (2006)
22. Sun, J., Zhang, H., Li, Y.F., Wang, H.H.: Formal semantics and verification for feature modeling. In: ICECCS, pp. 303–312 (2005)
23. Zhang, W., Zhao, H., Mei, H.: Binary-Search Based Verification of Feature Models. In: Schmid, K. (ed.) ICSR 2011. LNCS, vol. 6727, pp. 4–19. Springer, Heidelberg (2011)

Model-Based Static Code Analysis
for MATLAB Models

Zheng Lu and Supratik Mukhopadhyay

Department of Computer Science
Louisiana State University

Abstract. MATLAB is widely used in scientific, engineering, and numerical computations. Complex systems such as digital signal processors, process control systems, etc. are modeled in MATLAB and analyzed; C implementation of the system can be automatically generated from the validated MATLAB model. We combine static analysis techniques with model-based deductive verification using SMT solvers to provide a framework to analyze MATLAB code. The analyzer is generated by translating the collecting semantics of a MATLAB script to a formula in first order logic over multiple underlying theories. Function calls in a script can be handled by importing SMT assertions obtained by analyzing MATLAB files containing function definitions. Logical specification of the desired program behavior (rather its negation) is incorporated as a first order logic formula. An SMT-LIB formula solver treats the combined formula as a "constraint" and "solves" it. The "solved form" can be used to identify logical errors in the MATLAB model.

1 Introduction

Over the past few years, *model-driven engineering* [1] is being widely used for building complex systems. In a model-driven approach, one first develops a high-level model of the system. The model not only serves as a documentation of the system (just as a plan serves as a blueprint of a building construction) but also enables exploration of the design space, promotes understanding of the system by separating concerns, and allows validation. It can be refined in successive steps to generate code implementing the system. Several domain-specific languages have been developed to express models in different areas of systems engineering such as UML [2], Labview [3], MATLAB [4], etc. Most of these languages have only semi-formal semantics. Hence it is extremely difficult to understand complex designs and reason about their correctness.

Of late, MATLAB has become very popular among engineers and scientists performing scientific, engineering, and numerical computations. Complex systems such as digital signal processors, control systems, etc. are modeled at a high-level in MATLAB and analyzed; C implementation of the system can be automatically generated from the validated MATLAB model. Many of these systems are deployed in mission-critical environments where any malfunction can result in loss of life and/or property. Hence, it is essential that automated tools

T. Margaria and B. Steffen (Eds.): ISoLA 2012, Part I, LNCS 7609, pp. 474–487, 2012.
© Springer-Verlag Berlin Heidelberg 2012

be developed for formally verifying MATLAB models ensuring that a system performs in accordance with its requirements.

MATLAB is not a statically typed language. The standard MATLAB Workspace does not provide any tools for validating models other than manual debugging by setting breakpoints. Given the complexity of the models developed using MATLAB, manual debugging certainly can not be recommended especially if the resulting system is deployed in a mission-critical environment. One can purchase tools such as PolySpace [5] and VectorCast [6]. PolySpace performs static analysis of MATLAB code based on Abstract Interpretation techniques [7]. However, PolySpace is known to be inefficient; it has been observed that it takes several days to analyze practical models involving 100,000 lines of code [8]. Besides, PolySpace does not provide any formal language for describing properties expressing absence of deep logical errors. VectorCast provides a framework for testing models and code for embedded systems.

We combine static analysis techniques with model-based deductive verification using SMT solvers [9] to provide a framework to analyze MATLAB code. The analyzer is generated by translating the collecting semantics of a MATLAB script to a formula in first order logic over multiple underlying theories. Function calls in a script can be handled by importing SMT assertions obtained by analyzing MATLAB files containing function definitions. Logical specification of the desired program/model behavior (rather its negation) is incorporated as a first order logic formula. An SMT-LIB formula solver treats the combined formula as a "constraint" and "solves" it. The "solved form" can be used to identify logical errors in the MATLAB model. We have implemented our framework in Java with Yices [10] as the SMT solver and used it to detect logic errors in several MATLAB models obtained from [11].

2 Related Work

Techniques for system verification and validation fall into three main categories. The first category involves informal methods such as testing and monitoring [12] [13]. Such techniques scale well; they are extensively used in practice to validate systems. Traditional testing methods [14], however, are too ad hoc and do not allow for formal specification and verification of high-level logical properties that a system needs to satisfy. In the realm of mission-critical systems where exponential blow up in the number of possible situations to be dealt with is inevitable, traditional testing techniques can hardly be used to provide any amount of confidence. The second category of techniques for verification and validation involves formal methods. Traditional formal methods such as model checking [15] and theorem proving [16] are usually too heavyweight and rarely can be used in practice without considerable manual effort.

Model checking is an automatic approach to verification, mainly successful when dealing with finite state systems. It not only suffers from the infamous state explosion problem but also requires construction of a model of the system. Such a construction effort not only requires skill and ingenuity in model building but also a deep understanding of the operational semantics of the target system. Theorem proving approaches are not only labor intensive but also requires considerable skill in formal logic.

The third category of techniques for software verification and validation are static analysis [17] and abstract interpretation [7]. Static analysis refers to the technique(s) for automatically inferring a program's behavior at compile time. While static analysis tools have met with tremendous practical success and have been routinely integrated with state of the art compilers, such tools can only detect shallow and simple errors due to their lack of deductive power. For example, traditional static analysis tools cannot detect the presence of deadlocks or the violation of mutual exclusion in concurrent programs. Abstract interpretation is a technique for collecting, analyzing, and comparing the semantics of programs. It has been successful in analyzing properties of complex programs [7]. The next few paragraphs review the most successful approaches to program analysis.

2.1   Static Analysis Techniques

In recent years, much work has been done on static analysis of software. Some static analysis tools, such as Uno [18], Splint [19], Polyspace [5], Codesurfer [20], PREfix and PREfast [21], ESP [22], and PAG [23] perform lightweight data flow analysis. Coverity [24] performs data flow analysis as directed by checkers written in MetaL, a language designed to encode checking automata. Astree is a static program analyzer that is aimed at proving absence of runtime errors in embedded programs. Astree can handle only a "safe" subset of C, rather than the full C language. Also, it applies only to particular runtime errors rather than general properties of programs. Halbwachs et al [25] use linear relation analysis for discovering invariants in terms of linear inequalities among the numerical variables of a program. Their techniques have been used to validate (e.g., analyze delays) synchronous programs written in the language Lustre. Several abstractions have been considered to provide an approximate (conservative) answer to the validation problem such as widenings, convex approximations and Cartesian factoring [26]. These approximations are implemented using the polka [25] polyhedral library. Alur et al [27] have used predicate abstraction for analyzing hybrid systems. In this technique, a finite abstraction of a hybrid automaton is created a priori using the initial predicates provided by the user. Set based techniques for detecting races in relay ladder programmable logic controllers have been described in [28]. Context-sensitive analysis using deductive database techniques [29] are similar to ours. However, this technique alone is insufficient to achieve the goals we aim for due to the limited expressiveness of Datalog. Typed assembly languages [30] help detect security flaws in code. However, it is difficult to provide any insight to the developer in the event of such detection.

Verification tools for UML [31] transform UML diagrams into SMV [32] input. Specifications can be written in the branching time temporal logic CTL [15]. Doherty et. al. [33] perform kind analysis for MATLAB programs to distinguish between identifiers that denote functions and those that denote variables (e.g., array variables). Such a tool can be used as a preprocessor for an analyzer that checks for deep logical properties. Joisha and Banerjee [34] use a lattice-theoretic approach to infer types in a MATLAB program. However, their approach does not provide a framework for specifying and verifying deep logical properties. Kaufmann et. al. [35] use the first order logic theorem prover ACL2 [36] to verify Labview programs.

Tools like SofCheck Inspector [37] inspect every method of Java programs and compute their pre and post conditions. Findbugs [38] analyzes Java byte code and detects bugs due to common programming mistakes based on bug patterns. However, it is difficult to provide any meaningful insight to the developer from bugs found at the byte code level. Besides, it is difficult to provide bug patterns for deep logical errors. Fortify's [39] source code analysis engine based on verification condition generation. Boon [40] uses range analysis techniques to check for array bounds violations in C programs. However, it is not able to verify deep logical properties in MATLAB models. Klocwork provides a static analysis framework [41]. However, unlike the presented framework, their framework is not model based. In contrast our framework statically analyzes source code and tries to infer "deep" bugs. Jif [42] is a tool for guaranteeing noninterference properties in Java programs. In contrast our framework uses model-based deductive static verification to uncover bugs.

3 Preliminaries

3.1 MATLAB Features

MATLAB is a dynamically typed language. A variable in MATLAB is considered as an array by default; so every value has some number of dimensions. Variables need not be declared, they can accept any values that are assigned to them. The type of a numerical value in MATLAB is by default double. The built-in types of MATLAB can be summarized as follows:

- **double, sin**: floating point values;
- **int8, int16,int32,int64**: integer values;
- **logical**: boolean values;
- **char**: character values;

MATLAB functions are defined in .m files which have the same names as the functions. A function named comp() needs to be defined in a file with name comp.m. This file needs to be placed in the "current" directory or included in the MATLAB path. MATLAB functions can accept input arguments and output results in contrast with MATLAB scripts that can not accept any input nor generate outputs (other than printing on the workspace). MATLAB scripts are sequences of commands for simple computations and can invoke functions.

3.2 SMT-LIB Formulas and Yices

Satisfiability Modulo Theories (SMT) libraries [9] provide a framework for checking the satisfiability of first-order formulas with some background logical theories. SMT-LIB is an SMT library that provides a standard description of the background theories used in SMT systems; it gives a common input and output language for SMT solvers.

An SMT-LIB formula instance is a first-order logic formula in SMT-LIB syntax; some function and relation symbols occurring in the formula have semantic interpretations involving different types of first order structures, and SMT formula satisfiability is the problem of determining whether such a formula is satisfiable. We can consider SMT satisfiability as an instance of the Boolean satisfiability problem (SAT) in which some of the binary variables are replaced by predicates over a suitable set of variables that range over different domains. The relation/predicate symbols include linear inequalities, such as $3x + 2y - z \geqslant 0$ or equalities involving uninterpreted function symbols; for example, $f(f(u, v), v) = f(u, v)$ where f is an unspecified function of two unspecified arguments.

The predicates are classified according to the theory they belong to. For instance, linear inequalities over real variables are evaluated using the rules of the theory of linear real arithmetic; some predicates involving uninterpreted terms and function symbols are evaluated using the rules of the theory of uninterpreted functions with equality. Other theories include the theories of arrays and list structures, and the theory of bit vectors.

Yices [10] is an efficient SMT-LIB formula solver that decides the satisfiability of arbitrary formulas containing uninterpreted function symbols with equality, linear real and integer arithmetic, scalar types, recursive datatypes, tuples, records, extensional arrays, fixed-size bit-vectors, quantifiers, and lambda expressions. An example of constraints in the SMT-LIB formula syntax is given below

```
(set-logic QF_LIA)
(declare-fun x () Int)
(declare-fun y () Int)
(assert (= (+ x (* 2 y)) 20))
(assert (= (- x y) 2))
(check-sat)
```

In this example, we use the theory QF_LIA, quantifier-free linear integer arithmetic, to declare two functions which return integer values. We then assert two constraints in quantifier-free linear integer arithmetic. The satisfiability problem is to check if there exists an assignment of the functions x and y that satisfies these assertions.

4   Verification Approach

Fig 1 describes the architecture of our verification approach. The abstract collecting semantics of a MATLAB script (or a function) is a represented as a first order logic constraint in the SMT-LIB syntax. This constraint will have "holes" or "markings" corresponding to invocation of functions in the script/function which need to get interpreted. Models of functions are created from collecting

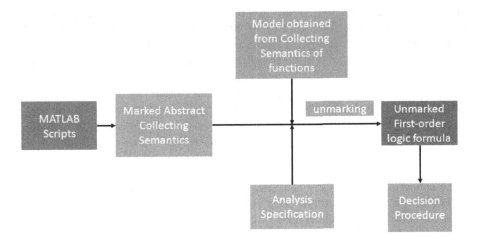

Fig. 1. Architecture of Our Verification Approach

semantics of functions described in function files (represented as first order logic constraints in the SMT-LIB syntax). These models are used to unmark the abstract collecting semantics by filling in the "holes". The negation of the property specification expressed as a formula in the SMT-LIB syntax is added to the combined constraints. The result is an "unmarked" first order logic formula that is presented to the decision procedure for satisfiability checking. We explain the steps in detail below. Let's consider the following example:

```
1 function  s=comp(d)
2 advance  =  0;
3 for  x=1:50
4       d = d+1;
5       if  d<50
6             advance  =  1/d;
7       end
8 end
9 function  bug()
10      x = 10;
11      comp(x);
12      x = -4;
13      comp(x);
```

In the example above, d is (the integer) is the formal parameter to the function comp() (call-by-value). It is incremented by 1 every time the loop executes. It is then used to determine the value of the variable **advance**. Checking whether the division operation at line 6 will cause a division-by-zero requires an interprocedural analysis to determine which values will be passed to the function comp().

In the code example, two values are passed to the function comp(). When called with x=10, d increases from 11 to 49. Line 6 will not result in a division by zero. However, when comp() is called with argument x=-4, d increases from -3 to 49. At some point, d will be equal to 0, causing a division by zero at line 6. A simple syntax check will not detect this run-time error.

We, first, generate a set of abstract constraints to describe the collecting semantics of the program (function or script), which overapproximates all the possible values for each variable. The constraints serve as an abstract intermediate representation of the code. Based on these constraints, we generate a dataflow graph of the program. The dataflow graph is used to generate SMT-LIB formulas describing the abstract collecting semantics. The abstract constraints representing the collecting semantics of the comp function are described in Figure 2; the dataflow graph of the function comp is described in Fig 3. In this figure, the integer number in each node is used to indicate the line number in the program.

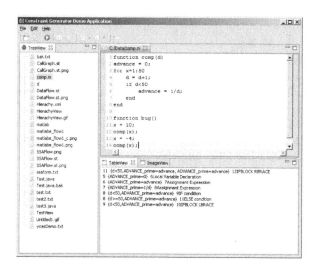

Fig. 2. Constraints

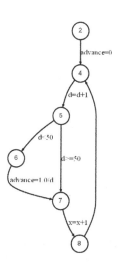

Fig. 3. Dataflow

From the dataflow graph, we create an assertion for each label. For example, the first node in the graph is advance=0, we can create (assert (= advance(0) 0)) . This indicates that advance is initialized to 0. The SMT-LIB formulas resulting from the dataflow graph in Figure 3 is shown below.

```
1 (set−logic AUFLIA)
2 (declare−fun advance (Int) Int)
3 (declare−fun d (Int) Int)
4 (assert (= advance(0) 0))
5 (assert (forall x Int) (=> (and (< x 50) (> x 2))
6     (and (and (= d(1) (+ d(0) 1))
7     (= d(x) (+ d(x−1) 1)))))
```

```
8        (and (=> (< d(1) 50) (= advance(1) (div 1 d(1))))
9             (=> (< d(x) 50)(= advance(x) (div 1 d(x))))))))
10 (check-sat)
```

For the for-loop ranging from 1 through 50, we first describe the update of d and advance in the first iteration of the loop; here d(0) represents the initial value of d, i.e., the value with which the function comp is invoked. A universal quantifier over x with domain [2, 50] is used to define the updates of d and advance during the second through the fiftieth iteration of the loop.

To detect if the program has a divide-by-zero error, we need to check if d can become zero within the for loop; this is the analysis aspect for this program. This analysis aspect is incorporated into the SMT-LIB formula characterizing the collecting semantics of the program by adding the conjunct (assert (exists x Int) (and (and (<= x 50)(>= x 1))(= d(x) 0))). The combined SMT-LIB formula was found to be satisfiable by the Yices solver indicating the program can have a division by zero error. While Yices is incomplete for quantified formulas, in most practical cases it was able to come up with a proof.

Let's consider another example in MATLAB:

```
1  if edgestop==1
2        k=K;
3        a=1;
4  elseif edgestop==2
5        k=K*(2^0.5);
6        a=1/(2*exp(-0.5));
7  elseif edgestop=='tky'
8        k=K*5^0.5;
9        a=25/32;
10 end
11 Gn=[I(1,:,:);I(1:row-1,:,:)]-I;
12 Gs=[I(2:row,:,:);I(row,:,:)]-I;
13 Ge=[I(:,2:col,:)  I(:,col,:)]-I;
14 if edgestop==1
15    Cn=1./(1+(Gn/k).^2).*a;
16    Cs=1./(1+(Gs/k).^2).*a;
17    Ce=1./(1+(Ge/k).^2).*a;
18    Cw=1./(1+(Gw/k).^2).*a;
19 elseif edgestop==2
20    Cn=exp(-(Gn/K).^2).*a;
21    Cs=exp(-(Gs/k).^2).*a;
22    Ce=exp(-(Ge/k).^2).*a;
23 end
```

In this example, there is a typical mistake that almost all the developers make. In line 22, the statement should be Cn=exp(-(Gn/k).^2).*a;; but in the program, the developer typed in the wrong variable name K. This error cannot be detected by the compiler; no error is reported at runtime either; but the program will simply spit out wrong results. Our approach can detect this problem, since we need to generate constraints to overapproximate all the possible values of each variable. In this example, if the variable edgestop is 1, the value of k is K*(2^0.5), and the value of variable Cn is exp(−(Gn/k).^2).*a. We can build the constraints as (edgestop=1) ⇒ (k=K*(2^0.5)) ∧ (Cn=exp(−(Gn/k).^2).*a). To verify the correctness of this MATLAB code, we need to set the post condition. Since the value K*(2^0.5) > K, we can set the condition Cn>exp(−(Gn/15).^2).*a; as the post condition to detect this variable misuse error. The SMT formulas are followings:

```
 1 (set−logic AUFLIA)
 2 (declare−fun edgestop () Int)
 3 (declare−fun k () Int)
 4 (declare−fun K () Int)
 5 (declare−fun Cn () Int)
 6 (declare−fun Gn () Int)
 7 (declare−fun a () Int)
 8 (declare−fun sqrt(Int))
 9 (declare−fun pow(Real Int) Real)
10 (declare−fun exp (Real) Int)
11 (define−fun div ((x Real) (y Real)) Real
12    (if (not (= y 0.0))
13        (/ x y)
14        0.0))
15 (assert (= K 15))
16 (assert (= edgestop 1))
17 (assert (=> (= edgestop 2) (= k (* K (sqrt(2)))) ))
18 (assert (=> (= edgestop 2) (= Cn exp(* (pow (div Gn k)
       2) a))))
19 (assert (=> (= edgestop 2) (> Cn exp(* (pow (div Gn K)
       2) a))))
20 (check−sat)
```

If the solver returns **sat** for the formula above, the program has a variable misuse error.

We now describe an algorithm for converting an dataflow graph of a program to SMT-LIB formulas that capture its collecting semantics. Let $\mathbb{G} = \langle \mathcal{N}, \mathcal{E} \rangle$ be the dataflow graph of the program. In this graph, each node represents a statement in the program. We represent the if and loop conditions as edge labels in the graph. We can generate SMT-LIB formulas capturing collecting semantics of the program using algorithm 1 that formalizes the intuition described above.

In this algorithm, we first visit each label in the dataflow graph to declare functions in SMT for all variables that are used in the code. Then, we visit each node to detect if there are any nodes that have children which have smaller line number than itself; such a node indicates a loop in the code. Assume that the conditions on this loop are given by $expr1 : expr2$. For each assignment statement inside this loop, we translate the statement as follows. Let d be the

---

Algorithm 1. Converting program to SMT Algorithm

---

for $e \in \mathcal{E}$ do
    if e is a simple assignment statement $VAR = EXP$ then
        Create a definition (define-fun VAR (EXP)) in SMT;
    end if
    if e is a function call statement $FUN()$ then
        Create an assertion (assert (= FUN FUN_SUMMARY));
    end if
    for $n \in \mathcal{N}$ do
        if n has two children then
            Create a conjunction of implication formula $e \rightarrow$ the children labels;
        end if
        if n has child whose line number is less than n then
            Evaluate the expression of the label from n to it's child;
            Let $exp1$ be the initial condition, $exp2$ be the end condition;
            for all the labels from the child of n to n do
                Let d be the variable in the left side of the assignment statement with *assexpr* on the right side;
                Create an assertion (assert (= d(exp1) assexpr(0))) where assexpr(0) is obtained from assexpr by replacing each variable x occurring in it by x(0);
                Create an assertion (assert forall (i Int) (=> (and (>= i exp1) (<= i exp2)
                for all the labels from the child of n to n do
                    (= d(i) assexpr(i)/(i-1)) where assexpr(i)/(i-1) represents replacing each variable x by x(i) if x has been updated in a predecessor node in the loop else by x(i-1) (obtained from use-define links)
                end for
            end for
        end if
    end for
    Provide the function summary as the function return value after the function analyzed (assert (= FUN_SUMMARY FUN_return value)).
end for

---

variable in the left side of the assignment statement with *assexpr* on the right side. We create an assertion (assert (= d(exp1) assexpr(0))) as the base condition to indicate the update of d the first time the loop is executed where assexpr(0) is obtained from assexpr by replacing each variable x occurring in it by x(0), and create an assertion (assert forall (i Int) (=> (and (>= i exp1) (<= i exp2) (= d(i) assexpr(i)/(i-1)) where assepr(i)/(i-1) represents replacing each variable x by x(i) if x has been updated in a predecessor node in the loop else by x(i-1) (obtained from use-define links) for each statement inside the loop body to express the updates in the remaining executions of the loop. If there is no loop, we can simply create assertion (assert (= VAR EXP)). To convert the `if/else` block in the code, we create a conjunction of implication formula.

Table 1. Experimental Results

GPC_timu.m	Line 113: The "if ite1 < N" block is never reached. Line 151: the statement may have division by zero error; since "k-tao-i2" can be zero.
GAconstrain.m	Line 63: The statement "if nmutationR>0" is not valid, since nmutationR is always larger than 0.
GA.m	Line 186: The if statement "if maxvalueRAND(m-m0)<maxvalueRAND(m-(m0+1))" is not valid, since m-m0 is greater than m-(m0+1). The random return value may make this condition always false.
PSK_carrier_timing_est.m	Line 178: the matrix index may be out of bound. Line 187: the statement "nco_l(k)=exp(-j*(2*pi*f0*Ts(start_diff+n+round(Kc2*err_tao(k))-8)+Kc*Uc(k)));" is not valid. It should use "fe" not "f0".
Felics.m	Line 63: the matrix index may be out of bound.
Kalman filtering.m	Line 63: The parameters in function "lmodeinitial(T,r,zx,zy,vxks,vyks,perr2)" are invalid.
TV_denoise.m	Line 37: The loop "while(i<niter)" may never terminate, since the value of variable "iflamda" is not assigned, the statement "i=i+1" may never be reached. Line 53: the statement may have division by zero error.
smooth_diffusion.m	Line 79: The statement uses a wrong parameter "K". Line 105: the function "imshow" has an invalid parameter "uint8()", since the function "uint8()" needs input.

5   Experimental Results

We implemented our analysis framework in Java (using ANTLR) with Yices as SMT solver. We analyzed the MATLAB examples including matrix computation and signal processing obtained from [11]. All the source code we verified can be found in https://tigerbytes2.lsu.edu/users/zlu5/web/MatlabExample/. Many of the examples were found to meet their specifications. However in several examples, our analysis framework found logical errors. These results are summarized in Table 1 and Table 2. All experiments were run on desktop with a Pentium dual-core CPU 2.6 GHz running Windows XP. The time needed for verification was never more than a minute.

Table 2. Experimental Results (continued)

directional_diffusion.m	Line 79: line 58: the variable "Ixy=(ESWN-ENWS)/4" maybe negative, which will lead to the program never terminate. Line 71: The variable "index" may be out bound of the matrix size. Line 72: the statement is not valid, since variable "Du(index)" has no value.
order4_diffusion.m	Line 54: the statement uses a wrong parameter; it needs to use "k" instead. Line 68: the statement "uint8(I)" uses a wrong parameter; it needs to use "It" instead.
CarLocal.m	Line 31: the statement may have division by zero error. Line 54: the statement may have division by zero error. Line 82: the "if(rec_ratio(i))>=T & rec_ratio(i)¡15)" branch may never be reached. Line 131: The parameter "I(index(1)-2" in function "imwrite" is invalid, since the parameter cannot be negative value.
FunctionChaosPredict.m	Line 38: the statement may have division by zero error. Line 73: the parameter in "roll(M+step+(j-1)*tao)" is invalid. Line 71: the "if (M-tao+step+(d-1)*tao < N+1)" block is never reached; since "M-tao+step+(d-1)*tao" is always less than N.

6   Conclusions

We have provided a deductive framework for model-based verification of complex systems. The constraint system includes all the possible values of variables; this may lead to false positives. More accurate abstract interpretation techniques are required to provide a precise analysis. In future, we need to develop patterns and good graphic user interfaces to help developers specify properties.

Acknowledgement. This research is partially supported by NSF under the grant 0965024. Any opinions, findings, and conclusions or recommendations expressed in this material are those of the author(s) and do not necessarily reflect the views of the National Science Foundation.

References

1. http://www.omg.org/mda/
2. http://www.omg.org/spec/UML/2.0/
3. http://www.ni.com/labview/
4. http://www.mathworks.com/products/matlab/
5. Polyspace, http://www.mathworks.com/products/polyspace/
6. http://www.vectorcast.com
7. Cousot, P., Cousot, R.: Abstract interpretation: a unified lattice model for static analysis of programs by construction or approximation of fixpoints. In: Proceedings of the 4th ACM SIGACT-SIGPLAN Symposium on Principles of Programming Languages, POPL 1977, pp. 238–252. ACM, New York (1977)
8. Gomes, I., Morgado, P., Gomes, T., Moreira, R.: An overview on the static code analysis approach in software development. Tech. rep., Faculdade de Engenharia da Universidade do Porto (2009)
9. Barrett, C., Stump, A., Tinelli, C.: The Satisfiability Modulo Theories Library, SMT-LIB (2010), http://www.SMT-LIB.org
10. Dutertre, B., Moura, L.D.: The yices smt solver. Tech. rep. (2006)
11. http://www.ilovematlab.cn/forum.php
12. Beizer, B.: Software testing techniques, 2nd edn. Van Nostrand Reinhold Co., New York (1990)
13. Woldman, K.I.: A dual programming approach to software testing. Master's thesis, Santa Clara University (1992)
14. Collard, J.-F., Burnstein, I.: Practical Software Testing. Springer-Verlag New York, Inc., Secaucus (2002)
15. Clarke, E., Grumberg, O., Long, D.: Model checking. In: Proceedings of the NATO Advanced Study Institute on Deductive Program Design, pp. 305–349. Springer-Verlag New York, Inc., Secaucus (1996)
16. Chang, C.-L., Lee, R.C.-T.: Symbolic Logic and Mechanical Theorem Proving, 1st edn. Academic Press, Inc., Orlando (1997)
17. Nielson, F., Nielson, H.R., Hankin, C.: Principles of Program Analysis. Springer-Verlag New York, Inc., Secaucus (1999)
18. Holzmann, G.J.: Software Analysis and Model Checking. In: Brinksma, E., Larsen, K.G. (eds.) CAV 2002. LNCS, vol. 2404, pp. 1–16. Springer, Heidelberg (2002)
19. Evans, D., Guttag, J., Horning, J., Tan, Y.: Lclint: A tool for using specifications to check code. In: ACM SIGSOFT Software Engineering Notes, vol. 19, pp. 87–96. ACM (1994)
20. Anderson, P., Reps, T.W., Teitelbaum, T., Zarins, M.: Tool support for fine-grained software inspection. IEEE Software 20(4), 42–50 (2003)
21. Evans, D., Guttag, J., Horning, J., Tan, Y.M.: Lclint: A tool for using specifications to check code. In: ACM SIGSOFT Software Engineering Notes, vol. 19, pp. 87–96. ACM (1994)
22. Das, M., Lerner, S., Seigle, M.: Esp: Path-sensitive program verification in polynomial time. In: PLDI, pp. 57–68 (2002)
23. Martin, F.: PAG – an efficient program analyzer generator. International Journal on Software Tools for Technology Transfer 2(1), 46–67 (1998)
24. Hallem, S., Chelf, B., Xie, Y., Engler, D.: A system and language for building system-specific, static analyses. In: Proceedings of the ACM SIGPLAN 2002 Conference on Programming Language Design and Implementation, pp. 69–82. ACM Press (2002)

25. Halbwachs, N., Proy, Y.-E., Roumanoff, P.: Verification of real-time systems using linear relation analysis. Formal Methods in System Design, 157–185 (1997)
26. Halbwachs, N., Merchat, D., Parent-vigouroux, C.: Cartesian Factoring of Polyhedra in Linear Relation Analysis. In: Cousot, R. (ed.) SAS 2003. LNCS, vol. 2694, pp. 355–365. Springer, Heidelberg (2003)
27. Alur, R., Dang, T., Ivancic, F.: Counterexample-guided predicate abstraction of hybrid systems. Theor. Comput. Sci. 354(2), 250–271 (2006)
28. Aiken, A., Fähndrich, M., Su, Z.: Detecting Races in Relay Ladder Logic Programs. In: Steffen, B. (ed.) TACAS 1998. LNCS, vol. 1384, pp. 184–200. Springer, Heidelberg (1998)
29. Lam, M.S., Whaley, J., Livshits, V.B., Martin, M.C., Avots, D., Carbin, M., Unkel, C.: Context-sensitive program analysis as database queries. In: PODS, pp. 1–12 (2005)
30. http://www.cs.cornell.edu/talc/
31. Beato, M.E., Barrio-Solórzano, M., Cuesta, C.E., de la Fuente, P.: Uml automatic verification tool with formal methods. Electron. Notes Theor. Comput. Sci. 127(4), 3–16 (2005)
32. http://www.cs.cmu.edu/~modelcheck/smv.html
33. Doherty, J., Hendren, L., Radpour, S.: Kind analysis for matlab. In: Proceedings of the 2011 ACM International Conference on Object Oriented Programming Systems Languages and Applications, OOPSLA 2011, pp. 99–118. ACM, New York (2011)
34. Joisha, P.G., Banerjee, P.: Correctly detecting intrinsic type errors in typeless languages such as matlab. SIGAPL APL Quote Quad 31(2), 7–21 (2000)
35. Kaufmann, M., Kornerup, J., Reitblatt, M.: Formal verification of labview programs using the acl2 theorem prover. In: Proceedings of the Eighth International Workshop on the ACL2 Theorem Prover and its Applications, ACL2 2009, pp. 82–89. ACM, New York (2009)
36. http://www.cs.utexas.edu/~moore/acl2/
37. Softcheck, http://www.sofcheck.com/products/inspector.html
38. Ayewah, N., Hovemeyer, D., Morgenthaler, J.D., Penix, J., Pugh, W.: Using static analysis to find bugs. IEEE Software 25(5), 22–29 (2008)
39. Fortify, http://www.fortify.com/
40. Wagner, D.: Static Analysis and Software Assurance. In: Cousot, P. (ed.) SAS 2001. LNCS, vol. 2126, p. 431. Springer, Heidelberg (2001)
41. Klock source code analysis for android platform, http://www.klocwork.com/news/press-releases/releases/2008/PR-2008_11_11-Source-code-analysis-for-Android.php
42. Jif: java information flow, http://www.cs.cornell.edu/jif/

An Incremental Learning Algorithm for Extended Mealy Automata

Karl Meinke and Fei Niu

School of Computer Science and Communication,
KTH Royal Institute of Technology, 100-44 Stockholm, Sweden

Abstract. We present a new algorithm ICGE for incremental learning of extended Mealy automata computing over abstract data types. Our approach extends and refines our previous research on congruence generator extension (CGE) as an algebraic approach to automaton learning. In the congruence generator approach, confluent terminating string rewriting systems (SRS) are used to represent hypothesis automata. We show how an approximating sequence R_0, R_1, ... of confluent terminating SRS can be directly and incrementally generated from observations about the loop structure of an unknown automaton A. Such an approximating sequence converges finitely if A is finite state, and converges in the limit if A is an infinite state automaton.

Keywords: algebraic automata theory, computational learning theory, finite state machine, initial algebra, Mealy automaton, string rewriting.

1 Introduction

Classical algorithms for learning a finite automaton A over a finite input alphabet (such as the L* algorithm of [2]) approach the problem of learning the state space structure of A as a partition refinement problem. In this case, the objects to be partitioned are a set of input strings for the *system under learning* (SUL) A. These act as synonyms for the unknown states. The problem is to determine which input strings denote the same states in A, from which the state transition structure of A can be inferred. Initially, one starts from the coarsest partition, in which all input strings are identified. To separate two strings $\bar{i}$ and $\bar{j}$ into distinct partition classes, it is necessary to find a suffix $\bar{k}$ such that the strings $\bar{i}\,\bar{k}$ and $\bar{j}\,\bar{k}$ generate different behaviours from A. Different learning algorithms have different methods for splitting partition classes using membership queries and equivalence queries. However, all such methods involve identifying inequalities $\bar{i} \neq \bar{j}$ between input strings.

Taking an algebraic viewpoint of this problem, one can consider the *dual approach*. Starting from the finest partition, which is equality, one can try to identify a finite set E of equations $\bar{i} = \bar{j}$ between input strings, which completely characterise the structure of A up to behavioral equivalence. This corresponds to directly learning loops and merges in the graph structure of A. The closure of E under equational inference is a finitely generated congruence $\equiv_E$ on the

T. Margaria and B. Steffen (Eds.): ISoLA 2012, Part I, LNCS 7609, pp. 488–504, 2012.

initial algebra I in the appropriate category of automata. The resulting quotient automata $H = I/ \equiv_E$, is a hypothesis automaton that is behaviorally equivalent to A. By the initiality property of I (see Section 2) every finite state automaton can be constructed in this way. This construction can also be generalised to learning an infinite state automaton which has a finitely generated congruence $\equiv_E$. The initial automaton I is related to the well known *prefix tree automaton* (see e.g. [4]).

1.1   Motivating the Congruence Generator Approach

In the congruence generator approach to automata learning, we focus on learning a finite congruence generator set. This algebraic approach has certain theoretical advantages. It clarifies the algebraic nature of the inference problem, for example by providing a framework for comparing different learning heuristics using the congruence lattice on I. It also opens up learning for more general data models, including infinite data types that give rise to infinite state automata.

The congruence generator approach also has important practical advantages for applications of automata learning such as *learning-based testing* (LBT) (see e.g. the survey [15]). LBT is an emerging paradigm for black-box requirements testing in which test cases are automatically generated as learning queries. Thus LBT is a methodology for *automated test case generation* (ATCG). In an LBT system, a model checker is used to automatically generate queries (test cases) by model checking each learned hypothesis automaton H against a user requirement *req* (such as a temporal logic formula). So LBT is also a *model-based testing method* where the models are automatically inferred hypothesis automata.

Model checker generated queries are very efficient for finding system errors. Therefore, for efficient LBT, model checker queries should be prioritised above all other types of learning queries such as membership queries, equivalence queries and random queries. This objective cannot be achieved with tabular learning algorithms such as Angluin's L* algorithm or its variants. This is because some form of behavioral data table must be completely filled in (typically by executing large numbers of membership queries) before a hypothesis automaton can even be constructed. In contrast, congruence generator based learning algorithms have no need for completed data tables, and are therefore well adapted for efficient testing. We will present experimental results that apply our new ICGE learning algorithm to LBT in Section 4.1. These results clearly illustrate the advantages of congruence generator learning methods for efficient learning-based testing.

1.2   Towards Incremental Congruence Generator Extension

In [13] we presented the CGE algorithm for learning Mealy machines based on constructing finite generator sets for congruences. The CGE algorithm uses a monotonically increasing sequence of sets Λ_i, $i = 0, 1 \dots$, of observations about an SUL A to iteratively compute a sequence R_i of congruence generator sets. Construction of each generator set R_i is by extending the empty set of generators in a consistent but greedy way to a maximal set that is consistent with Λ_i. Each generator pair $(l,\ r) \in R_i$ is represented as a *string rewriting rule* $l \to r$ over the input and output alphabets of A. Rule consistency is evaluated by rewriting (normalising) the observation set Λ_i. Unfortunately, the sequence R_i, $i = 0,\ 1\dots$, is generally *not* monotonically increasing, since the validity of a generator pair (i.e. state equation) $l \to r$ may be falsified by some new observation $O \in \Lambda_{i+j}$. Furthermore, the process of normalising Λ_i requires that R_i is a confluent and terminating string rewriting system (SRS). To achieve confluence, an efficient linear time completion algorithm for SRS was introduced in [13]. However, again because of non-monotonicity, it is not possible to perform completion in an incremental way. The CGE algorithm is therefore not incremental, and turns out to be rather inefficient for learning large automata.

In this paper we show how the problem of non-monotonicity for the validity of state equations can be overcome. We present an *incremental congruence generator extension algorithm* (ICGE), that significantly exceeds the performance of CGE. One new important observation is that we can directly generate confluent terminating SRS, and avoid completion altogether, by learning just the valid *loop rules* of A. These loop rule sets still increase non-monotonically. However, our second important observation is that they implicitly contain valid *loop rule inequalities* and these *do* increase monotonically. Therefore, there is never any need to reconsider discarded loop rules, and the learning process becomes completely incremental. By focussing on loop rules alone, we infer non-minimal hypothesis automata. However, in the limit these are always behaviorally equivalent to the SUL.

The structure of this paper is as follows. In Section 1.1, we review some incremental automata learning algorithms from the literature. In Section 2, we define basic mathematical notation including the general concept of an *extended Mealy automaton* (EMA) computing over an abstract data type (ADT). In Section 3 we review the concept of string rewriting systems (SRS) as a representation of congruence generator sets. In Section 4 we present the ICGE learning algorithm and sketch its correctness proof. In Section 5 we present some initial performance results for ICGE.

1.3   Incremental Learning Algorithms for Automata

The literature on learning algorithms for automata is extensive. Recent surveys can be found in [3], [19] and [4]. One important type of learning is *incremental learning*. Here the goal is to construct a sequence H_0, H_1, ... of hypothesis automata which are "approximations" to the SUL A using a sequence of observations O_0, O_1, ... of the behaviour of A. Each hypothesis H_i should represent a "good" hypothesis about A using all the currently available data $\Lambda_i = \{\ O_0,\ O_1,\ \dots,\ O_{k(i)}\ \}$. The number of observations $k(i+1) - k(i)$ needed between successive hypothesis constructions H_{i+1} and H_i, varies in the literature. However, the construction of H_{i+1} should build on the construction of H_i. For correctness, an incremental learning algorithm must be guaranteed to eventually produce a behaviourally equivalent hypothesis automaton given sufficient data. In this case it is said to *learn in the limit* (c.f. [7]).

For applications in software engineering such as *learning-based testing* ([14] and [16]), incremental learning is necessary for two reasons.

1. Real software systems are too large to be completely learned in practise. This is obvious for infinite state systems, and even true in practice for many finite state systems.
2. Incremental learning increases the opportunity to replace equivalence queries and membership queries by model checker generated queries related to a formal requirements specification. (C.f. the discussion in Section 1.1.) This opportunity is maximised when $k(i + 1) - k(i) = 1$.

We can compare ICGE with three other incremental learning algorithms known in the literature. In [6], an incremental version RPNI2 of the RPNI learning algorithm of [18] and [11] is presented. The RPNI2 algorithm has only a few features in common with ICGE. Most notably, both RPNI2 and CGE perform a depth first search of a lexicographically ordered state set. However, while RPNI searches the entire state space, ICGE searches only subpaths of the most recently added input sequence, sufficient to update a localised subset of loop rules. Furthermore, RPNI2 is hard-wired for DFA learning and not adaptable to learning infinite data types. Both RPNI2 and CGE can produce a new hypothesis automaton after every query, i.e. $k(i + 1) - k(i) = 1$ always.

In [20] and [16], two different incremental modifications of the ID learning algorithm of [1] have been given. Again, these are explicitly coded for DFA learning and not adaptable to infinite data types. Furthermore, both algorithms require a substantial number of new queries to produce a new hypothesis automaton, i.e. $k(i + 1) - k(i)$ is very large, typically ranging in the order of thousands to hundreds of thousands of queries.

2   Mathematical Preliminaries and Notation

We use the usual notation and terminology for strings. If Σ is an alphabet then Σ^n denotes the set of all strings of length n over Σ. The unique string of length zero is denoted by ε. We let $\Sigma^* = \cup_{n \geq 0} \Sigma^n$ and $\Sigma^+ = \Sigma^* - \{\ \varepsilon\ \}$, denote the sets of all finite strings and finite positive length strings respectively. If $\overline{\sigma} \in \Sigma$ is a finite string then $|\overline{\sigma}|$ denotes the length of $\overline{\sigma}$.

It will be helpful to have some familiarity with the theories of universal algebra, abstract data types (ADTs) and term rewriting. We use the notation and terminology of *many-sorted algebra* (see [17]). Let S be a finite set of sorts or types. An S-*sorted (ADT) signature* Σ consists of an $S^* \times S$-indexed family of sets $\Sigma = \langle \Sigma_{w,s} \mid w \in S^*,\ s \in S \rangle$. For each $s \in S$, every $c \in \Sigma_{\varepsilon,s}$ is a *constant symbol* of sort s. For any $w = s_1,\ \ldots,\ s_n \in S^+$, each $f \in \Sigma_{w,s}$ is a *function symbol* of *arity* n, *domain type* w and *codomain type* s. An S-*sorted* Σ-*algebra* A consists of particular sets, constants and functions that interpret Σ set-theoretically. Thus A has an S-indexed family of sets $A = \langle A_s \mid s \in S \rangle$, where A_s is termed a *carrier set.* For each $s \in S$ and constant symbol $c \in \Sigma_{\varepsilon,s}$, $c_A \in A_s$ is a constant, and for each $w = s_1, \ldots, s_n \in S^+$ and each $f \in \Sigma_{w,s}$, $f_A : A_{s_1} \times \ldots \times A_{s_n} \to A_s$ is a function. We let $Alg(\Sigma)$ denote the class of all Σ-algebras. The concepts of *subalgebra, minimal algebra, quotient algebra, congruence, congruence generator set, homomorphism, kernel congruence* and *isomorphism* all generalise from single-sorted to many-sorted algebras in a straightforward way by point-wise extension over S. Details can be found in [17].

Let $X = \langle X_s \mid s \in S \rangle$ be an S-indexed family of disjoint sets X_s of variables of sort s. We assume $X_s \cap \Sigma_{\varepsilon,s} = \emptyset$. The set $T(\Sigma, X)_s$ of all *terms of sort* $s \in S$ is defined inductively by: (i) $c \in T(\Sigma, X)_s$ for $c \in \Sigma_{\varepsilon,s}$, (ii) $x \in T(\Sigma, X)_s$ for $x \in X_s$, and (iii) $f(t_1, \ldots, t_n) \in T(\Sigma, X)_s$ for $f \in \Sigma_{w,s}$ $w = s_1, \ldots, s_n$ and $t_i \in T(\Sigma, X)_{s_i}$ for $1 \leq i \leq n$. We let $Vars(t)$ denote the set of all variables from X occurring in term t. Let $T(\Sigma)$ denote the S-indexed family of all *variable free* or *ground terms*. A *substitution* σ is an S-indexed family of mappings $\sigma : X \to T(\Sigma, X)$. The result of applying a substitution σ to a term $t \in T(\Sigma, X)_s$ is defined inductively in the usual way and denoted by $\sigma(t)$.

We can generalise the usual Mealy automaton model of computation from finite input and output alphabets to elements chosen from an arbitrary many-sorted algebra A, which may be finite or infinite. This gives a model of *extended Mealy automata (EMA) over an abstract data type* (ADT). These can also be defined as many-sorted algebras that simply extend the underlying ADT with one new sort *state* for states, one new constant q^0 for the initial state, and two new operations: δ for the state transition function and λ for the output function. Inputs and outputs for an EMA will typically be chosen from well known ADTs such as *int, string, array, list* etc. that provide a high level of data abstraction.

Definition 1. *An* **extended Mealy automaton signature** *(EMA signature) over an S-sorted ADT signature Σ is a four-tuple,*

$$\Sigma^{\mathrm{M}} = (S^M, \Sigma^M, input, output),$$

where $S^M = S \cup \{ state \}$ is a sort set, Σ^M is an S^M-sorted signature with $\Sigma_{w,s}^M = \Sigma_{w,s}$ for any $w \in S^*$, $s \in S$ and

$$q^0 \in \Sigma_{\varepsilon,state}^M, \ \delta \in \Sigma_{state\ input,state}^M, \ \lambda \in \Sigma_{state\ input,output}^M$$

where input, output $\in S$ are distinguished input and output sorts.

Definition 2. *Let $\Sigma^{\mathrm{M}} = (S^M, \Sigma^M, input, output)$ be an EMA signature over an S-sorted ADT signature Σ. An* **extended Mealy automaton** *A over Σ is an S^M-sorted Σ^M algebra A. If A_{state} is finite then A is termed a* **finite state EMA** *, otherwise A is termed an* **infinite state EMA**. *We let $MA(\Sigma)$ denote the class of all extended Mealy automata over Σ, i.e. the class of all Σ^M algebras. Together with all Σ^M-homomorphisms, this class forms the* **category of all EMA** *over Σ denoted by* **EMA**(Σ).

For a given EMA A as usual $q_A^0 \in A_{state}$ is the *initial state*, δ_A is the *state transition function*, and λ_A is the *output function*. We extend δ_A and λ_A inductively in the usual way to

$$\delta_A^* : A_{state} \times A_{input}^* \to A_{state}, \quad \lambda_A^* : A_{state} \times A_{input}^+ \to A_{output}.$$

Example 1. Figure 1 gives a simple example of an infinite state EMA A which computes over the integer data type. This EMA always returns the sum of the last two.integers entered. Formally, the underlying data type signature is the S-sorted signature Σ^{PA} for Peano Arithmetic on the integers, where $S = \{int\}$ and Σ^{PA} includes the usual binary addition operation $+ \in \Sigma_{int\ int,\ int}^{PA}$. For the automaton A we define $input = output = int$, $A_{int} = \mathbb{Z}$, $A_{state} = \{\ q_i \mid i \in \mathbb{Z}\ \}$ and $q_A^0 = q_0$. Also $\delta_A : A_{state} \times A_{input} \to A_{state}$ is given by $\delta_A(q_x, y) = q_y$ and $\lambda_A : A_{state} \times A_{input} \to A_{output}$ is given by $\lambda_A(q_x, y) = x +_A y$, where $+_A : A_{int} \times A_{int} \to A_{int}$ is the usual addition operation on $\mathbb{Z}$. This infinite state automaton is represented by a finite state transition diagram using a Statechart style of notation for δ_A and λ_A in Figure 1.

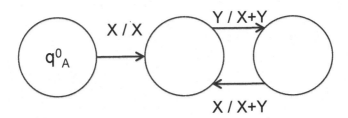

Fig. 1. A simple EMA for sequential addition

Example 2. Let $\Sigma^M = (S^M, \Sigma^M, input, output)$ be an EMA signature over an S-sorted ADT signature Σ. Define the **initial Mealy automaton** $I(\Sigma^M)$ by:

$$I(\Sigma^M)_{state} = T(\Sigma)_{input}^*, \quad I(\Sigma^M)_{output} = T(\Sigma)_{input}^+ \cup T(\Sigma)_{output}$$

and for all $s \in S$ such that $s \neq state$ and $s \neq output$, $I(\Sigma^M)_s = T(\Sigma)_s$. For any $(t_1, \dots t_n) \in T(\Sigma)_{input}^*$ and $t \in T(\Sigma)_{input}$ define

$$\delta_{I(\Sigma^M)}(\ (t_1, \dots t_n),\ t\ ) = \lambda_{I(\Sigma^M)}(\ (t_1, \dots t_n),\ t\ ) = (t_1, \dots t_n, t).$$

Also $q_{I(\Sigma^M)}^0 = \varepsilon$. The definition of $I(\Sigma^M)$ generalises the concept of a prefix tree automaton, since $I(\Sigma^M)_{state}$ is an infinite tree.

Proposition 1. $I(\Sigma^M)$ *is initial in the category* **EMA**(Σ^M), *i.e. there exists a unique homomorphism* $\phi : I(\Sigma^M) \to A$ *to every* $A \in MA(\Sigma^M)$.

Corollary 1. *Let $A \in MA(\Sigma)$ be any minimal Mealy automaton. There exists a unique epimorphism $\phi : I(\Sigma^M) \to A$ and hence $I(\Sigma^M)/\equiv^\phi \, \cong A$.*

By initiality, every minimal EMA has a unique construction (up to isomorphism) as a quotient of $I(\Sigma^M)$. The initial algebra approach to semantic constructions has been widely used elsewhere in computer science, (e.g. data type theory [8], logic programming [12]). It is also the basis of CGE automaton learning [13].

For practical learning applications, it suffices to learn an SUL A up to *behavioural equivalence*. This allows learning of both minimal and non-minimal representations of A.

Definition 3. *Let A, $B \in MA(\Sigma)$ be any minimal Mealy automata. Let $\equiv^\phi$ and $\equiv^\psi$ be the kernels of the unique epimorphisms $\phi : I(\Sigma^M) \to A$ and $\psi : I(\Sigma^M) \to B$ respectively. We say that A and B are **behaviourally equivalent** and write $A \simeq B$ if, and only if, $\equiv^\phi_{output} \, = \, \equiv^\psi_{output}$.*

Intuitively, if A and B are behaviourally equivalent then they always produce the same output sequence given the same input sequence.

Finally, observe that while congruences generally involve infinite sets of equivalence classes, their generator sets can nevertheless be finite. This can make congruence learning tractable, even for infinite state EMA.

Example 3. Let $A \in MA(\Sigma)$ be any finite state minimal EMA and let $\phi : I(\Sigma^M) \to A$ be the unique epimorphism. The kernel $\equiv^\phi$ of ϕ is finitely generated.

3   String Rewriting Systems

In this section we introduce the concept of a *string rewriting system* (SRS) as a compact representation of a congruence generator set. We rely on the notion of a *confluent terminating* SRS, which gives normal forms for state names, and a natural model of automaton simulation by *string rewriting*. String rewriting is a special case of the more general theory of term rewriting ([5], [9]), from which we borrow some important ideas and results.

Definition 4. *Let Σ be an S-sorted signature and let X be an S-indexed family of sets of variables.*
*(i) A **string rewriting rule** ρ over Σ and X (of sort $s \in S$) is a pair of strings*

$$\rho = ((l_1, \ldots, l_m), (r_1, \ldots, r_n)) \in T(\Sigma, X)^*_s \times T(\Sigma, X)^*_s$$

*where $Vars(r_i) \subseteq Vars(l_1) \cup \ldots \cup Vars(l_m)$ for $1 \leq i \leq n$. We use the more intuitive notation $l_1, \ldots, l_m \to r_1, \ldots, r_n$ to denote ρ. We say ρ is **ground** if all lhs and rhs terms are ground. A **string rewriting system** (SRS) over Σ is a set of string rewriting rules.*

(ii) Let $\rho = l_1, \ldots, l_m \to r_1, \ldots, r_n$ be a string rewriting rule and let $\bar{t}, \bar{t'} \in T(\Sigma, X)^*_s$ be any strings. We say that $\bar{t}$ **rewrites to** *$\bar{t'}$ using ρ and write $\bar{t} \xrightarrow{\rho} \bar{t'}$ if, and only if for some substitution $\sigma : X \to T(\Sigma, X)$ and suffix $\bar{t''} \in T(\Sigma, X)^*_s$:*

(a) $\bar{t} = \sigma(l_1), \ldots, \sigma(l_m) . \bar{t''}$, and

(b) $\bar{t'} = \sigma(r_1), \ldots, \sigma(r_m) . \bar{t''}$.

(iii) If R is an SRS we say that $\bar{t}$ **rewrites to** *$\bar{t'}$ using R* **in one step** *and write $\bar{t} \xrightarrow{R} \bar{t'}$ if, and only if, for some $\rho \in R$, $\bar{t} \xrightarrow{\rho} \bar{t'}$.*

(iv) We let $\xrightarrow{R^*}$ denote the reflexive transitive closure of $\xrightarrow{R}$. Then $\bar{t} \xrightarrow{R^*} \bar{t'}$ if, and only if, $\bar{t}$ **rewrites to** *$\bar{t'}$ using R* **in finitely many steps.**

(v) Define the **bi-rewriting relation** *$\xleftrightarrow{R^*}$ for any $\bar{t}, \bar{t'} \in T(\Sigma, X)^*_s$, by:*

$$\bar{t} \xleftrightarrow{R^*} \bar{t'} \iff \exists \bar{t_0} \in T(\Sigma, X)^*_s \text{ such that } \bar{t} \xrightarrow{R^*} \bar{t_0} \text{ and } \bar{t'} \xrightarrow{R^*} \bar{t_0}.$$

Notice that we only allow matching and replacement of the lhs of a rule on *prefixes* of a string. This is more restrictive than string rewriting using *semi-Thue systems*, (c.f. [5]). However, this definition suffices for simulating automata (see Definition 8 below) because of the existence of an initial state.

String rewriting means repeated application of the rules of an SRS R to a string $\bar{t}$. Since this process need not terminate, we need to find a sufficient condition for termination.

Definition 5. *(i) Let $\leq = \langle \leq_s \mid s \in S \rangle$ be an S-indexed family of well orderings $\leq_s$ on $T(\Sigma)_s$. Define the* **lexicographic ordering** *$\leq_s$ on $T(\Sigma)^n_s$ for each $s \in S$ and $n \geq 1$ inductively by:*
$t_1, \ldots, t_n \leq_s t'_1, \ldots, t'_n \iff t_1 \leq_s t'_1 \text{ or } t_1 = t'_1 \text{ and } t_2, \ldots, t_n \leq_s t'_2, \ldots, t'_n.$

(ii) Define the **short-lex ordering** *$\leq_s$ on $T(\Sigma)^*_s$ by*
$t_1, \ldots, t_m \leq_s t'_1, \ldots, t'_n \iff m < n \text{ or } m = n \text{ and } t_1, \ldots, t_m \leq_s t'_1, \ldots, t'_n.$

(iii) Let $\bar{l} \to \bar{r} \in T(\Sigma)^*_s \times T(\Sigma)^*_s$ be a ground rewrite rule. We say that $\bar{l} \to \bar{r}$ is **reducing** *(wrt. $\leq_s$) if, and only if, $\bar{r} <_s \bar{l}$.*

(iv) An SRS R is **reducing** *if, and only if, every rule $\rho \in R$ is reducing.*

Theorem 1. *Let R be a ground and reducing SRS w.r.t. a well ordering $\leq$, then R is terminating, i.e. there is no infinite rewrite sequence $\bar{t_0} \xrightarrow{R} \bar{t_1} \xrightarrow{R} \bar{t_2} \ldots$*

Proof. Follows since $\leq$ is a well ordering.

The order in which rules from an SRS are applied to rewrite a string can influence the final outcome. If the outcome never depends on this order then the SRS is termed *confluent*.

Definition 6. *Let R be an SRS.*

(i) R is **confluent** *if, and only if, for any $\bar{t}_0, \bar{t}_1, \bar{t}_2 \in T(\Sigma)^*_s$, if $\bar{t}_0 \xrightarrow{R^*} \bar{t}_1$ and $\bar{t}_0 \xrightarrow{R^*} \bar{t}_2$ then there exists $\bar{t}_3 \in T(\Sigma)^*_s$ such that $\bar{t}_1 \xrightarrow{R^*} \bar{t}_3$ and $\bar{t}_2 \xrightarrow{R^*} \bar{t}_3$.*

(ii) R is **locally confluent** *if, and only if, for any $\bar{t}_0, \bar{t}_1, \bar{t}_2 \in T(\Sigma)^*_s$, if $\bar{t}_0 \xrightarrow{R} \bar{t}_1$ and $\bar{t}_0 \xrightarrow{R} \bar{t}_2$ then there exists $\bar{t}_3 \in T(\Sigma)^*_s$ such that $\bar{t}_1 \xrightarrow{R^*} \bar{t}_3$ and $\bar{t}_2 \xrightarrow{R^*} \bar{t}_3$.*

Clearly confluence implies local confluence. The converse comes from a celebrated general result in term rewriting theory.

Lemma 1. *(Newman) Let R be a reducing SRS. Then R is locally confluent if, and only if, R is confluent.*

The problem of non-confluence is typically solved by applying a *completion algorithm* such as Knuth-Bendix completion [10] or linear time completion [13]. However, in the context of automaton learning, non-confluence can be avoided by a careful construction of SRS as we will show. For The main effect of confluence is that we obtain a unique *normal form* for every string under rewriting.

Definition 7. *Let R be a confluent reducing SRS. For any string $\bar{t} \in T(\Sigma)^*_s$ the* **normal form** *$norm_R(\bar{t})$ of $\bar{t}$ (modulo R) is the unique string obtained by rewriting $\bar{t}$ with R until termination.*

Now suppose we are given an S-sorted ADT signature Σ and a congruence $\equiv$ on the term algebra $T(\Sigma)$, so that $I = T(\Sigma)/\equiv$ represents the initial algebra semantics of some ADT specification. Consider the problem of learning an EMA A that computes over the data type I. Suppose a learning algorithm can produce a confluent SRS R representing the state equations of A inferred from a set Λ of observations about A. How can we define a canonical congruence $\equiv^{R,\Lambda}$ on the initial automaton $I(\Sigma^M)$ so that the quotient automaton $I(\Sigma^M)/\equiv^{R,\Lambda}$ represent a valid hypothesis about the unknown structure of A?

Definition 8. *Let $\Sigma^M = (S^M, \Sigma^M, input, output)$ be an EMA signature over an S-sorted ADT signature Σ. Let $\equiv$ be a congruence on the term algebra $T(\Sigma)$ associated with an ADT specification. Let $\Lambda \subseteq T(\Sigma)^+_{input} \times T(\Sigma)_{output}$ be a set of observations. Let R be any confluent SRS over Σ.*
    Define the **canonical equivalence relation** *$\equiv^{R,\Lambda}$ on $I(\Sigma^M)$ by*

$$\equiv^{R,\Lambda}_{state} = \xleftrightarrow{R^*}$$

$$\equiv^{R,\Lambda}_{output} =$$

$RST(\equiv_{output} \cup \Lambda \cup \{ \ (\bar{t} . t_0, \bar{t}' . t_0) \mid (\bar{t}, \bar{t}') \in \equiv^{R,\Lambda}_{state} \ and \ t_0 \in T(\Sigma)_{input} \ \}),$

where $RST(.)$ is the reflexive symmetric transitive closure. For all $s \in S$ if $s \neq output$ then $\equiv^{R,\Lambda}_s = \equiv_s$. Then R is **consistent** *if $\equiv^{R,\Lambda}_{output} = \equiv_{output}$.*

By Definition 8, we can compute with the equivalence classes of $\equiv_{state}^{R,\Lambda}$ by string rewriting, since $\bar{t} \equiv_{state}^{R,\Lambda} \bar{t'}$ if, and only if $norm_R(\bar{t}) = norm_R(\bar{t'})$. Thus we can simulate the quotient hypothesis automaton $I(\Sigma^M)/\equiv^{R,\Lambda}$ by string rewriting. The congruence $\equiv^{R,\Lambda}$ is canonical in the sense of making the fewest identifications of states and outputs necessary.

Proposition 2. *If R is consistent and reducing then $\equiv^{R,\Lambda}$ is the smallest congruence on $I(\Sigma^M)$ such that $R \subseteq \equiv_{state}^{R,\Lambda}$ and $\Lambda \subseteq \equiv_{output}^{R,\Lambda}$.*

Proof. Omitted

The problem of EMA learning is now reduced to construction of R from Λ.

4   Incremental CGE Learning

In this section we introduce the ICGE algorithm for incremental learning of extended Mealy automata and establish its correctness. The basic problem is to infer a sequence of hypothesis automata $H_i : i = 1, 2, \ldots$ using a sequence of observations $O_i : i = 1, 2, \ldots$ of the behavior of an unknown EMA A. Each hypothesis H_i is then constructed as a quotient automaton:

$$H_i = I(\Sigma^M)/\equiv^i .$$

Each congruence $\equiv^i$ will be represented by finite generating set R_i that is a consistent confluent terminating SRS constructed from the observation set $\Lambda_i = \{ O_1, O_2, \ldots, O_i \}$. If A is finite state then the sequence H_i finitely converges in the sense that H_n is behaviorally equivalent to A for some $n \geq 1$. Since we can identify sufficient conditions on the query set Λ_i which guarantee behavioral equivalence, then it is possible to show that the membership queries generated by ICGE satisfy this condition.

Recall that the main problem to be solved is incremental learning of the identities $\bar{t} = \bar{t'}$ between state names $\bar{t}$ and $\bar{t'}$ as string rewriting rules $\bar{t} \to \bar{t'}$. Now although inequations $\bar{t} \neq \bar{t'}$ between states are preserved by new observations, equations $\bar{t} = \bar{t'}$ are *not* preserved. So for incremental learning we must also remember which inequations have previously been established, i.e. which rewrite rules have previously been rejected as inconsistent with the observation set.

To generate confluent terminating SRS incrementally, we give up attempts to learn a minimal representation of A (i.e. a maximal congruence) and focus on learning just the loop structure of A. In general this expands the rule set size. Nevertheless, the net effect of avoiding both completion and state space minimisation (both used in the original CGE algorithm) is to achieve a significant speed-up in performance.

A loop in an SUL A can be expressed as a string rewriting rule

$$t_1, t_2, \ldots, t_{m+n} \to t_1, t_2, \ldots, t_m$$

for $n > 0$ and $m \geq 0$ and $t_i \in T(\Sigma)_{input}$. So the rhs of a loop rule is always a prefix of the lhs. In this context $t_1, t_2, \ldots, t_m$ is termed the *handle* (of length m)

and $t_{m+1}, \ldots, t_{m+n}$ is termed the *loop* (of length n). Notice that a loop rule is reducing (C.f. Definition 5) since $m + n > m$. Furthermore, no two valid loop rules can share the same lhs, which means that every loop rule set must be locally confluent and hence confluent by Lemma 2. So by restricting attention to loop rules, we obtain a confluent terminating SRS without the need for completion as in [13]. For loop rule synthesis, we consider the observation set Λ as a tree. To derive a complete set of rules, we must loop back every path in this tree (starting from the root) to a proper prefix using some loop rule.

How can we synthesize a loop rule $l \to r$ in an incremental way? We need to integrate previous negative information about invalid loop rules together with new positive information (observations). Since inequations $\bar{t} \neq \bar{t'}$ are always preserved by new observations, we can exploit a particular enumeration order of loop rules along a tree path $l = t_1, t_2, \ldots, t_k$. This order enumerates each possible rhs string r, starting from the empty prefix ϵ in order of increasing length. Thus for fixed k we consider loop rules in the order

$$t_1, t_2, \ldots, t_k \to \epsilon, \quad t_1, t_2, \ldots, t_k \to t_1, \quad t_1, t_2, \ldots, t_k \to t_1, t_2, \ldots$$

We increment k when the loop length n has decreased to 1. Once a prefix r has been rejected as inconsistent with an observation set Λ it can never become consistent with any future observation set that subsumes Λ. So this enumeration of loop rules naturally preserves negative information.

Algorithm 1 gives the procedure for revising the current SRS in the light of one new observation $O = (i_1, i_2, \ldots, i_k, o_k)$ about the SUL A. Without loss of generality, we can assume that this observation extends the set Λ of current observation by just one extra element, i.e. $i_1, i_2, \ldots, i_{k-1} \in \iota(\Lambda)$, where $\iota(\Lambda) = \{ \bar{i} \mid (\bar{i}, o) \in \Lambda \}$. Also without loss of generality, we can assume that each input datum i_j and output datum o are in normal form with respect to a congruence $\equiv$ on the underlying data type Σ. In Algorithm 1 we first compile a set B of all loop rules inconsistent with the new observation. Then for each broken rule $r \in B$, we compute a set of new loop rules that can replace r and restore consistency by calling Algorithm 2. Finally, we add self loops on all tree paths for which no loop rule applies yet. (This is necessary, since the new observation can introduce new input values $t \in T(\Sigma)_{input}$ not previously observed.)

Algorithm 2 computes a new consistent loop rule set that can replace one inconsistent loop rule $t_1, t_2, \ldots, t_{m+n} \to t_1, t_2, \ldots, t_m$. As already observed, we can inductively assume that if $t_1, t_2, \ldots, t_{m+n} \to t_1, t_2, \ldots, t_m$ is inconsistent then all of the previous loop rules

$$t_1, t_2, \ldots, t_{m+n} \to \epsilon, \quad \ldots, \quad t_1, t_2, \ldots, t_{m+n} \to t_1, t_2, \ldots, t_{m-1}$$

in the enumeration order are also inconsistent. If the search for a new loop rule reduces the loop length to one, without finding a consistent rhs, then the handle length is incremented by one and the search continues. Note that a new consistent rule set must always exist, i.e. Algorithm 2 always terminates. Finally, observe that inferring consistency of a loop rule is a simple matter of checking the

---

Algorithm 1. $ICGE(R, \Lambda, O)$

Input:
1) R, the current learned loop rule set;
2) Λ, the current observation set;
3) $O = (i_1, i_2, \ldots, i_k, o_k)$, one new SUL observation such that $i_1, i_2, \ldots, i_{k-1} \in \iota(\Lambda)$.
Output: A confluent terminating SRS $R \cup R'$ consistent with $\equiv$.

1 $B := \emptyset$
   // Find all rules in R inconsistent with new observation O
2 **foreach** $(t_1, t_2, \ldots, t_{m+n} \to t_1, t_2, \ldots, t_m) \in R$ **do**
      // Rule in contraction mode for O.
3   **if** $t_1, t_2, \ldots, t_{m+n} = i_1, i_2, \ldots, i_{m+n}$ & $(t_1, t_2, \ldots, t_m, i_{m+n+1}, \ldots, i_k, o) \in \Lambda$ & $o \neq o_k$ **then**
4        $B := B \cup \{(t_1, t_2, \ldots, t_{m+n} \to t_1, t_2, \ldots, t_m)\}$
5        $R := R - \{(t_1, t_2, \ldots, t_{m+n} \to t_1, t_2, \ldots, t_m)\}$
6   continue
      // Rule in expansion mode for O.
7   **if** $t_1, t_2, \ldots, t_m = i_1, i_2 \ldots, i_m$ & $(t_1, t_2, \ldots, t_{m+n}, i_{m+1}, \ldots, i_k, o) \in \Lambda$ & $o \neq o_k$ **then**
8        $B := B \cup \{(t_1, t_2, \ldots, t_{m+n} \to t_1, t_2, \ldots, t_m)\}$
9        $R := R - \{(t_1, t_2, \ldots, t_{m+n} \to t_1, t_2, \ldots, t_m)\}$
   // Repair the broken rules in B
10 **foreach** $r \in B$ **do**
11    $R := R \cup \text{NextConsistentLoops}(r, \Lambda)$
   // Add any missing transitions as self-loops
12 $R' := \{ (\bar{t} . t \to \bar{t}) \mid \bar{t}, t \in \iota(\Lambda), \bar{t} . t \notin \iota(\Lambda), |t| = 1, norm_R(\bar{t}) = \bar{t} \}$
13 **return** R, R'

Algorithm 2. $NextConsistentLoops(r, \Lambda)$

Input: $r = (t_1, t_2, \ldots, t_{m+n} \to t_1, t_2, \ldots, t_m)$, a loop inconsistent with Λ.
Output: A consistent rule set C replacing r in the loop enumeration order.

1 $k := m + 1$
2 **while** $k < m + n$ **do**
3   **if** Consistent($(t_1, t_2, \ldots, t_{m+n} \to t_1, t_2, \ldots, t_k)$, Λ) **then**
4   **return** $\{ (t_1, t_2, \ldots, t_{m+n} \to t_1, t_2, \ldots, t_k) \}$
5   **else**
6   k := k+1
7 $C := \emptyset$
8 **foreach** $(t_1, t_2, \ldots, t_{m+n+1}) \in \iota(\Lambda)$ **do**
9   **if** Consistent($(t_1, t_2, \ldots, t_{m+n+1} \to \epsilon)$, Λ) **then**
10       $C := C \cup \{ (t_1, t_2, \ldots, t_{m+n+1} \to \epsilon) \}$
11   **else**
12       $C := C \cup \text{NextConsistentLoops}((t_1, t_2, \ldots, t_{m+n+1} \to \epsilon), \Lambda)$
13 **return** C

---

observation set Λ. This is defined in the function $Consistent(\ (t_1, t_2, \ldots, t_{m+n} \rightarrow t_1, t_2, \ldots, t_m), \Lambda\ )$.

$$Consistent(\ (t_1, t_2, \ldots, t_{m+n} \rightarrow t_1, t_2, \ldots, t_m), \Lambda\ ) =$$

$$\begin{cases} false & \text{if there exists } p \geq 1, \ t'_1, t'_2, \ldots, t'_p \\ & (t_1, t_2, \ldots, t_m, t'_1, t'_2, \ldots, t'_p, \ o) \in \Lambda, \\ & (t_1, t_2, \ldots, t_{m+n}, t'_1, t'_2, \ldots, t'_p, \ o') \in \Lambda, \text{ such that } o \neq o' \\ true & \text{otherwise.} \end{cases}$$

Algorithm 3. $ICGELearn(A)$

Input: The system under learning A, an EMA.
Output: A consistent SRS $R \cup R'$ and observation set Λ.

1 $R := \emptyset;\ \Lambda := \emptyset$
2 **while** $True$ **do**
   // Query generation. There are two sources of query generation:
   // 1. random queries
   // 2. membership queries
3 **if** $\Lambda := \emptyset$ **then**
4     $O := (\bar{t}, output_A(\bar{t}))$ where $\bar{t} = t_1, t_2, \ldots, t_n$ is a random query of A
5 **else**
6   **let** $(l \rightarrow r) \in R$ be such that $Belief(l \rightarrow r, \Lambda)$ achieves its minimum
      over R **in let** $\bar{t}$ be the shortest suffix such that $l \cdot \bar{t} \in \Lambda$ and $r \cdot \bar{t} \notin \Lambda$ or
      $l \cdot \bar{t} \notin \Lambda$ and $r \cdot \bar{t} \in \Lambda$ **in**
7   **if** $l \cdot \bar{t} \notin \Lambda$ and $r \cdot \bar{t} \in \Lambda$ **then**
8        $O := (l \cdot \bar{t}, output_A(l \cdot \bar{t}))$
9   **else**
10       $O := (r \cdot \bar{t}, output_A(r \cdot \bar{t}))$
11    $R, R' := \text{ICGE}(R, \Lambda, O)$
12    $\Lambda := \Lambda \cup \{O\}$
13   **if** $I(\Sigma^M)/ \equiv^{R \cup R', \Lambda} \simeq A$ **then**
14   **return** $R \cup R', \Lambda$

Algorithm 3 iterates Algorithm 1 starting from the empty set of observations, $\Lambda = \emptyset$. On each iteration one new observation is added. Initially a random query is used to start the learning process. On each subsequent iteration, a membership query is generated which tests the degree of belief in the current loop rule set. This belief measure is defined below. The loop rule $l \rightarrow r$ with the least structural evidence to support it is used as the basis for the new membership query. This query appends the shortest suffix to l or r that will increase the belief value of $l \rightarrow r$ by one. Algorithm 3 terminates if, and only if, the current hypothesis automaton $I(\Sigma)/ \equiv^{R \cup R', \Lambda}$ is behaviorally equivalent to the SUL A. In Algorithm 3 we have not shown how queries generated externally by a model checker can be integrated into the learning process to replace equivalence queries. However, the basic idea is to prioritise such model checker queries above membership queries. So membership queries are only used when no model checker generated queries are available.

$$Belief(\,l \rightarrow r,\, \Lambda\,) = \begin{cases} |\{\ t_0\ |\ l \cdot t_0 \in \Lambda \text{ and } r \cdot t_0 \in \Lambda\ \}| & \text{if } l \in \Lambda, \\ -1 & \texttt{otherwise.} \end{cases}$$

This systematic belief optimising strategy for generating membership queries ensures that learning finite EMA will always terminate. This is because Algorithm 2 enumerates all possible loop rules, and systematic membership querying in Algorithm 3 will eventually reject any invalid loop rule. When the termination condition of Algorithm 3 becomes true then the current hypothesis automaton must be correct.

Theorem 2. *Let $A \in MA(\Sigma)$ be any finite state EMA over an ADT signature Σ. Then ICGELearn terminates on A.*

Proof. Omitted.

4.1   Performance Results

Below we give three types of performance results for ICGE. These are based on: (i) measuring the absolute performance of ICGE on randomly generated automata, (ii) measuring the relative performance of ICGE compared with CGE learning on random automata, and (iii) measuring the performance of ICGE applied to learning-based testing. We consider the last measure (iii) to be the most significant, since ICGE has been designed for optimal test case generation. However all three measures give some insight into algorithm performance.

Table 1. ICGE performance

State space size	Alphabet size	ICGE Queries	ICGE Time (sec)
5	2	96	0.02
15	2	2902	0.27
25	2	72001	13.2
35	2	590001	330.1
5	4	2236	0.14
5	8	60934	4.77
5	12	512501	64.4
5	16	1421501	293.9

Table 2. ICGE versus CGE : relative performance

State size	CGE/ICGE Queries	CGE/ICGE Time
5	21.8	5.7
10	237.2	11.8
20	535.8	80.7

Table 1 shows the performance of the ICGE algorithm for the task of completely learning an automaton. Although this is not the intended purpose of the algorithm, nevertheless, the results are positive. Randomly generated automata were learned with different state space and input alphabet sizes. We measured both the number of queries, and the computation time needed for convergence.

Table 2 compares the performance of ICGE with the original CGE learning algorithm on sets of randomly generated automata of different state space sizes and binary alphabets. Here we see that relative to CGE, complete learning for ICGE is improved, both in terms of the number of queries and the computation time. This improvement increases with larger state space sizes.

Table 3. Learning-based testing of the TCP/IP protocol

Requirement	Random Testing		CGE LBT		ICGE LBT	
	Queries	Time (sec)	Queries	Time (sec)	Queries	Time (sec)
Req 1	101.4	0.11	19.11	0.07	4.53	0.04
Req 2	1013.2	1.16	22.41	0.19	6.6	0.06
Req 3	11334.7	36.7	29.13	0.34	7.7	0.17
Req 4	582.82	1.54	88.14	2.45	51.1	2.31

Finally, in Table 3 we give the results of applying the ICGE algorithm to learning-based testing (LBT) of a model of the TCP/IP protocol against four linear temporal logic (LTL) requirements. This protocol model, and the definition of these requirements as temporal logic formulas, can be found in [14]. As an EMA, the TCP/IP model involves 11 states, 12 input symbols, 6 output symbols and 132 transitions. Table 3 gives the number of queries (test cases) and times needed to find an injected error, when testing the four LTL requirements which express different use cases. We compared random testing, learning-based testing using the original CGE algorithm and learning-based testing using the ICGE algorithm. Our results show that the number of queries needed to find an injected error is greatly reduced by using ICGE learning. On the other hand, the computation times are less reduced since the overhead of generating queries by model checking is high. It can even dominate the overall learning time, as can be seen with Requirement 4.

5   Conclusions

We have introduced a new algorithm ICGE for incrementally learning of extended Mealy automata over abstract data types. Our approach is based on using initial algebras and finite congruence generator sets. We use string rewriting systems to concretely represent and manipulate congruence generator sets. We have shown how this approach can be made compatible with incremental learning and hence efficient.

We acknowledge financial support for this research from the Swedish Research Council (VR), the China Scholarship Council (CSC), and the European Union under projects HATS FP7-231620 and MBAT ARTEMIS JU-269335. We also acknowledge the help of the referees in improving the presentation of this paper.

References

1. Angluin, D.: A note on the number of queries needed to identify regular languages. Information and Control 51(1), 76–87 (1981)
2. Angluin, D.: Learning regular sets from queries and counterexamples. Information and Computation 75(1), 87–106 (1987)
3. Balcazar, J.L., Diaz, J., Gavalda, R.: Algorithms for learning finite automata from queries. In: Advances in Algorithms, Languages and Complexity, pp. 53–72. Kluwer (1997)
4. de la Higuera, C.: Grammatical Inference. Cambridge University Press (2010)
5. Dershowitz, N., Jouannaud, J.-P.: Rewrite systems. In: Handbook of Theoretical Computer Science. North-Holland (1990)
6. Dupont, P.: Incremental Regular Inference. In: Miclet, L., de la Higuera, C. (eds.) ICGI 1996. LNCS (LNAI), vol. 1147, pp. 222–237. Springer, Heidelberg (1996)
7. Gold, E.M.: Language identification in the limit. Information and Control 10(5), 447–474 (1967)
8. Goguen, J.A., Meseguer, J.: Initiality, induction and computability. In: Algebraic Methods in Semantics, pp. 460–541. Cambridge University Press (1985)
9. Klop, J.W.: Term rewriting systems. In: Handbook of Logic in Computer Science, vol. 2, pp. 2–117. Oxford University Press (1992)
10. Knuth, D.E., Bendix, P.: Simple word problems in universal algebras. In: Computational Problems in Abstract Algebra, pp. 263–269. Pergamon Press (1970)
11. Lang, K.J.: Random dfa's can be approximately learned from sparse uniform examples. In: Fifth ACM Workshop on Computational Learning Theory, pp. 45–52. ACM Press (1992)
12. Lloyd, J.W.: Foundations of Logic Programming. Springer (1993)
13. Meinke, K.: CGE: A Sequential Learning Algorithm for Mealy Automata. In: Sempere, J.M., García, P. (eds.) ICGI 2010. LNCS (LNAI), vol. 6339, pp. 148–162. Springer, Heidelberg (2010)
14. Meinke, K., Niu, F.: Learning-Based Testing for Reactive Systems Using Term Rewriting Technology. In: Wolff, B., Zaïdi, F. (eds.) ICTSS 2011. LNCS, vol. 7019, pp. 97–114. Springer, Heidelberg (2011)
15. Meinke, K., Niu, F., Sindhu, M.: Learning-based software testing: a tutorial. In: Proc. Int. ISoLA Workshop on Machine Learning for Software Construction. CCIS. Springer (2012)

16. Meinke, K., Sindhu, M.A.: Incremental Learning-Based Testing for Reactive Systems. In: Gogolla, M., Wolff, B. (eds.) TAP 2011. LNCS, vol. 6706, pp. 134–151. Springer, Heidelberg (2011)
17. Meinke, K., Tucker, J.V.: Universal algebra. In: Handbook of Logic in Computer Science, vol. 1, pp. 189–411. Oxford University Press (1993)
18. Oncina, J., Garcia, P.: Inferring regular languages in polynomial update time. In: Pattern Recognition and Image Analysis. Series in Machine Perception and Artificial Intelligence. World Scientific (1992)
19. Parekh, R., Honavar, V.: Grammar inference, automata induction and language acquisition. In: Handbook of Natural Language Processing, Marcel Dekker (2000)
20. Parekh, R.G., Nichitiu, C., Honavar, V.G.: A Polynomial Time Incremental Algorithm for Learning DFA. In: Honavar, V.G., Slutzki, G. (eds.) ICGI 1998. LNCS (LNAI), vol. 1433, pp. 37–49. Springer, Heidelberg (1998)

Learning Techniques
for Software Verification and Validation

Corina S. Păsăreanu[1,2] and Mihaela Bobaru[1,2]

[1] Carnegie Mellon Silicon Valley, NASA Ames, Moffett Field, CA, USA
[2] NASA Jet Propulsion Laboratory, Pasadena, CA, USA

Learning techniques are being used increasingly to improve software verification and validation activities. For example, automata learning techniques have been used for extracting behavioral models of software systems, e.g. [8]. These models can serve as formal documentation of the software and they can be verified using automated tools or used for model-based testing. Automata learning techniques have also been used for automating compositional verification, e.g. [3], for building abstractions of software behavior in the context of symbolic or parameterized model checking, e.g. [9] or for the automatic inference and security analysis of botnet protocols, e.g. [1]. This Special Track aims at bringing together researchers and practitioners working on the integration of learning techniques in verification and validation activities for software systems. The Special Track is part of the 2012 International Symposium on Leveraging Applications of Formal Methods, Verification, and Validation (ISoLA).

The track includes five presentations. The first four papers address automata learning and present various techniques for learning different kinds of automata. The last paper has a different focus, as it studies the relationship between machine learning and automated testing. All the presentations have been reviewed by the track chairs.

The first presentation, "Learning Stochastic Timed Automata from Sample Executions" [7], addresses learning techniques for generalized semi-Markov processes, an important class of stochastic systems which are generated by stochastic timed automata. A novel methodology for learning this type of stochastic timed automata is presented from sample executions of a stochastic discrete event system. Apart from its theoretical interest in the machine learning area, the presented algorithm can be used for quantitative analysis and verification in the context of model checking. This paper also presents a Matlab toolbox for the learning algorithm and a case study of the analysis for a multi-processor system scheduler with uncertainty in tasks duration.

The second presentation, "Learning Minimal Deterministic Automata from Inexperienced Teachers" [6], addresses extensions of a prominent learning algorithm, namely Angluin's L*, which allows to learn a minimal deterministic automaton using membership and equivalence Queries addressed to a Teacher. In many applications, a teacher may be unable to answer some of the membership queries because parts of the object to learn are not completely specified, not observable, or it is too expensive to resolve these queries, etc. The extensions allow such queries to be answered inconclusively. In this paper, the authors

T. Margaria and B. Steffen (Eds.): ISoLA 2012, Part I, LNCS 7609, pp. 505–507, 2012.

survey different algorithms to learn minimal deterministic automata in this setting in a coherent fashion. Moreover, new modifications and improvements for these algorithms are presented, prompted by recent developments.

The third presentation, "Model Learning and Test Generation for Event-B Decomposition" [2], addresses the Event-B formal method for reliable systems specification and verification, which uses model refinement and decomposition as techniques to scale the design of complex systems. The presentation improves previous work by the authors, which proposed an iterative approach for test generation and state model inference based on a variant of the same Angluin's learning algorithm, that integrates well with the notion of Event-B refinement. The authors extend the method to work also with the mechanisms of Event-B decomposition. Two types of decomposition, shared-events and shared-variables, are considered and the generation of a global test suite from the local ones is proposed. The implementation of the method is evaluated on publicly available Event-B decomposed models.

The fourth presentation, "Inferring Semantic Interfaces of Data Structures" [5], shows how to fully automatically infer semantic interfaces of data structures on the basis of systematic testing. The semantic interfaces are a generalized form of Register Automata (RA), comprising parameterized input and output, allowing to model control- and data-flow in component interfaces concisely. Algorithmic key to the automated synthesis of these semantic interfaces is the extension of an active learning algorithm for Register Automata to explicitly deal with output. The algorithm is evaluated on a complex data structure, a stack of stacks, the largest of which is learned in 20 seconds with less than 4000 membership queries, resulting in a model with roughly 800 nodes. In contrast, even when restricting the data domain to just four values, the corresponding plain Mealy machine would have more than 10 to the power of 9 states and presumably require billions of membership queries.

The last presentation, "Learning-Based Test Programming for Programmers" [4], studies a diverse array of approaches to applying machine learning for testing. Most of these efforts tend to share three central challenges, two of which had been often overlooked. First, learning-based testing relies on adapting the tests generated to the program being tested, based on the results of observed executions. This is the heart of a machine learning approach to test generation. A less obvious challenge in many approaches is that the learning techniques used may have been devised for problems that do not share all the assumptions and goals of software testing. Finally, the usability of approaches by programmers is a challenge that has often been neglected. Programmers may wish to maintain more control of test generation than a "push button" tool generally provides, without becoming experts in software testing theory or machine learning algorithms. In this paper the authors consider these issues, in light of their experience with adaptation-based programming as a method for automated test generation.

References

1. Cho, C.Y., Babic, D., Shin, E.C.R., Song, D.: Inference and analysis of formal models of botnet command and control protocols. In: ACM Conference on Computer and Communications Security, pp. 426–439 (2010)
2. Dinca, I., Ipate, F., Stefanescu, A.: Model Learning and Test Generation for Event-B Decomposition. In: Margaria, T., Steffen, B. (eds.) ISoLA 2012, Part I. LNCS, vol. 7609, pp. 539–553. Springer, Heidelberg (2012)
3. Giannakopoulou, D., Pasareanu, C.S.: Special issue on learning techniques for compositional reasoning. Formal Methods in System Design 32(3), 173–174 (2008)
4. Groce, A., Fern, A., Erwig, M., Pinto, J., Bauer, T., Alipour, A.: Learning-Based Test Programming for Programmers. In: Margaria, T., Steffen, B. (eds.) ISoLA 2012, Part I. LNCS, vol. 7609, pp. 572–586. Springer, Heidelberg (2012)
5. Howar, F., Isberner, M., Jonsson, B.: Inferring Semantic Interfaces of Data Structures. In: Margaria, T., Steffen, B. (eds.) ISoLA 2012, Part I. LNCS, vol. 7609, pp. 554–571. Springer, Heidelberg (2012)
6. Leucker, M., Neider, D.: Learning Minimal Deterministic Automata from Inexperienced Teachers. In: Margaria, T., Steffen, B. (eds.) ISoLA 2012, Part I. LNCS, vol. 7609, pp. 524–538. Springer, Heidelberg (2012)
7. de Matos Pedro, A., Crocker, P.A., de Sousa, S.M.: Learning Stochastic Timed Automata from Sample Executions. In: Margaria, T., Steffen, B. (eds.) ISoLA 2012, Part I. LNCS, vol. 7609, pp. 508–523. Springer, Heidelberg (2012)
8. Raffelt, H., Steffen, B., Berg, T., Margaria, T.: Learnlib: a framework for extrapolating behavioral models. STTT 11(5), 393–407 (2009)
9. Vardhan, A., Viswanathan, M.: LEVER: A Tool for Learning Based Verification. In: Ball, T., Jones, R.B. (eds.) CAV 2006. LNCS, vol. 4144, pp. 471–474. Springer, Heidelberg (2006)

Learning Stochastic Timed Automata
from Sample Executions

André de Matos Pedro[1], Paul Andrew Crocker[2], and Simão Melo de Sousa[3],[*]

[1] University of Minho, Braga, Portugal
pg15753@alunos.uminho.pt
[2] IT - Instituto de Telecomunicações, University of Beira Interior, Covilhã, Portugal
crocker@ubi.pt
[3] LIACC - Laboratório de Inteligência Artificial e Ciência de Computadores,
University of Beira Interior, Covilhã, Portugal
desousa@ubi.pt

Abstract. Generalized semi-Markov processes are an important class of stochastic systems which are generated by stochastic timed automata. In this paper we present a novel methodology to learn this type of stochastic timed automata from sample executions of a stochastic discrete event system. Apart from its theoretical interest for machine learning area, our algorithm can be used for quantitative analysis and verification in the context of model checking. We demonstrate that the proposed learning algorithm, in the limit, correctly identifies the generalized semi-Markov process given a structurally complete sample. This paper also presents a Matlab toolbox for our algorithm and a case study of the analysis for a multi-processor system scheduler with uncertainty in task duration.

1 Introduction

Stochastic processes are commonly used as an approach to describe and make a quantitative evaluation of more abstract models which may be described by a high-level specification. When a model is evaluated we can use it for the design phase and subsequently make an implementation. However, even if a model is validated this does not imply that the implementation is in conformity with the model. This is normally due to bugs in the implementation, wrong interpretation of the model, or possibly, wrong approximations in the construction of the stochastic model. Unfortunately techniques for discovering these errors such as testing are unlikely to be sufficient due to the difficulty of achieving a complete or total coverage.

This paper is concerned with how these models can be derived from sample executions provided by an implementation in order to verify them. There are several learning algorithms for learning probabilistic and stochastic languages [3,13,20], including a learning algorithm for continuous-time Markov processes (CTMP) [19], but there is no algorithm in the case of processes that do not hold

---

[*] This work was supported in part by the FCT CANTE project (Ref^a PTPC/EIA-CCO/101904/2008).

T. Margaria and B. Steffen (Eds.): ISoLA 2012, Part I, LNCS 7609, pp. 508–523, 2012.

the Markov property such as *generalized semi-Markov processes* (GSMP) [10]. Thus, the learning of stochastic timed automata covered in this paper falls in the category of language identification [2,17,1]. For most of the methods in this category, the identified stochastic languages are inferred from a set of sample executions, i.e., these samples are a particular multi-set of the original language to identify, and the inference has as target the identification of the language in the limit, i.e., if the number of samples tends towards infinity then the learned language will converge to the original language that generated the sample [11]. Learning of stochastic languages essentially follows a common method, firstly establishing an equivalent relation between the states, then constructing a prefix tree from samples provided by the original stochastic language, and lastly describing an algorithm for the merge of equivalent states which is called *state merge*.

In this paper, we address the problem of learning generalized semi-Markov processes that are the most known extensive stochastic processes when lifetimes can be governed by any continuous probabilistic distributions [7]. From classical Markov processes, exponential probability distributions are not sufficient to model the lifetime of a product such as an electronic component [16] or even model a computer process [12]. The use of generalized semi-Markov processes may cover a wider set of problems however they are more complex and analytically intractable.

1.1   Contribution of the Paper

The learning algorithm we shall present infers a GSMP model from a given set of trajectories and therefore must be capable of inferring the model by running the deployed system in a test phase and of learning trajectories according to the observed distributions. The learned stochastic timed automaton that is generated by a GSMP is a model that can be used by existing statistical model-checkers [15,23,22,5] and by the existing performance evaluation tools for further analysis and thereby ultimately helping to find bugs in the post-implementation phase. Learning algorithm for GSMP may also potentially be used to perform automatic verification for stochastic discrete event systems.

In addition we also establish the correctness of our algorithm. We ensure that, in the limit, when the samples grow infinitely the learned model converges to the original model. Thus, a set of conditions like the definition of inclusion of a prefix tree in a GSMP have to be ensured as well as the definition of probability measure of paths.

1.2   Structure of the Paper

In section 2 some preliminary definitions are given in order to establish the learning algorithm detailed in section 3. In section 4 we demonstrate the correctness of our algorithm. In section 5, the tool and a practical application are presented. In the final section 6 we give our conclusions and discuss directions for further work.

2   Preliminaries

In order to formulate the next notations we describe the concept of finite path that is established by a prefix,

$$\sigma_{\leq\tau} = \{s_0, \langle e_1, t_1 \rangle, s_1, \langle e_2, t_2 \rangle, ..., s_k, \langle e_{k+1}, t_{k+1} \rangle\}$$

based on the infinite sequence $\sigma = \{s_0, \langle e_1, t_1 \rangle, s_1, \langle e_2, t_2 \rangle, \cdots\}$ of a GSMP, where s_k is a state, e_k is an event, t_k is the holding time of the event e_k, and $\tau = \sum_{i=1}^{k+1} t_i$ is the path duration upon k. A set of paths with prefix p is denoted by $Path(p)$, where p shall be $\sigma_{\leq\tau}$. Some notation will now be introduced to describe the structure of the algorithm. The definitions are based on symbol ('$\|$') that symbolizes a path with respect to an element of a particular set (of states $\mathcal{X}$, of events $\mathcal{E}$ or of holding times $\mathcal{G}$) and brackets ('[';']') a sequential identification, as follows: $\sigma\|_{\mathcal{X}}[s, i]$ is the ith state of the state sequence that begins in state s, $\sigma\|_{\mathcal{E}}[s, i]$ is the ith event of the event sequence that begins in state s, $\sigma\|_{\mathcal{G}}[s, i]$ is the ith holding time of the event sequence ($\sigma\|_{\mathcal{E}}[s, i]$) that begin in s state, $\eta(\sigma\|_{\mathcal{E}}[s, i]) = \sigma\|_{\mathcal{X}}[s, i - 1]$ is a function that returns the state associated to an event e_i, $\varepsilon(\sigma\|_{\mathcal{X}}[s, i]) = \sigma\|_{\mathcal{E}}[s, i + 1]$ is a function that given a state of a path returns its associated event, and $\delta(\sigma\|_{\mathcal{E}}[s, i]) = \sigma\|_{\mathcal{G}}[s, i]$ is a function that given an event $\sigma\|_{\mathcal{E}}[s, i]$ returns its holding time $\sigma\|_{\mathcal{G}}[s, i]$. A sequence of events $\langle e_1, e_2, e_3, \ldots, e_k \rangle$ produced by the prefix tree that accepts the prefix $\sigma_{\leq\tau}$ is denoted by $\sigma_{\leq\tau}\|_{\mathcal{E}}$.

A *prefix tree* (denoted Pt) that has an acceptor $Path(\sigma_{\leq\tau})$ (a set of paths with prefix $\sigma_{\leq\tau}$), is a tree

$$Pt(Path(\sigma_{\leq\tau})) = (\mathcal{F}, \mathcal{Q}, \rho, \varrho, \delta)$$

where $\mathcal{F}$ is a set of leaf nodes of the prefix tree (i.e., $\mathcal{F} = Path(\sigma_{\leq\tau}\|_{\mathcal{E}})$), $\mathcal{Q}$ is the set of nodes of the prefix tree composed by the sequence of events from $Path(\sigma_{\leq\tau}\|_{\mathcal{E}})$ (i.e., $\mathcal{Q}$ represents all accepted sequences in the prefix tree), $\rho : \mathcal{Q} \to [0, 1]$ is the function that associate the expectation value for each node $n \in \mathcal{Q}$, $\varrho : \mathcal{Q} \to \mathbb{R}_{\geq 1} \times ... \times \mathbb{R}_{\geq 1}$ is the function that associate each node with a n-tuple of clock values, and $\delta : \mathcal{Q} \to \mathcal{Q} \cup \bot$ is the transition function which have the following definition, $\delta(s, \lambda) = s$ where λ is the empty string and s is the reference point (where all samples are measured), $\delta(s, e) = \bot$ if $\delta(s, e)$ is not defined, and $\delta(s, xe) = \delta(\delta(s, x), e)$, where $x \in \mathcal{Q}$ and $e \in \mathcal{E}$, $\delta(s, xe) = \bot$ if $\delta(s, x) = \bot$ or $\delta(\delta(s, x), e)$ is undefined.

A *generalized semi-Markov process* is a stochastic process $\{X(t)\}$ with state space X, generated by a *stochastic timed automaton* (sta, for short),

$$sta = (\mathcal{X}, \mathcal{E}, \Gamma, p, p_0, G)$$

where $\mathcal{X}$ is a finite state space, $\mathcal{E}$ is a finite event set, $\Gamma(x)$ is a set of feasible or enabled events, defined for every $x \in \mathcal{X}$, with $\Gamma(x) \subseteq \mathcal{E}$, $p(x'; x, e')$ is a state transition probability (x' to x given event e') defined for every $x, x' \in \mathcal{X}$ and $e' \in \mathcal{E}$ such that $\forall e' \notin \Gamma(x) p(x'; x, e') = 0$, $p_0(x)$ is the probability mass function (*pmf*) $Pr[X_0 = x]$, $x \in \mathcal{X}$ of the initial state X_0, and finally $G = \{G_i : i \in \mathcal{E}\}$ is a stochastic clock structure where G_i is a cumulative distribution function (*cdf*) for each event $i \in \mathcal{E}$.

The probability measure μ for a *cylinder set* composed by a prefix $\sigma_{\leq\tau}$, $C\left(\sigma_{\leq\tau}, \langle E_k, Y_k^* \rangle, X_k, ..., X_{n-1}, \langle E_n, Y_n^* \rangle, X_n\right)$ accordingly to [23], can be defined recursively as

$$\mu(C(\sigma_{\leq\tau}, \langle E_k, Y_k^* \rangle, X_k, ..., \langle E_n, Y_n^* \rangle, X_n)) = P_e(s'; \sigma_{\leq\tau}) \cdot H_e(t; \cdot, \sigma_{\leq\tau}) \cdot$$
$$\mu(C(\sigma_{\leq\tau} \oplus (\langle e, t \rangle, s'), \langle E_{k+1}, Y_{k+1}^* \rangle, X_{k+1}, ..., X_{n-1}, \langle E_n, Y_n^* \rangle, X_n))$$

where the recursive base case is $\mu(C(s_0, \langle E_1, Y_1^* \rangle, X_1, ..., \langle E_n, Y_n^* \rangle, X_n)) = 1$, $P_e(s'; \sigma_{\leq\tau})$ is the next-state probability transition matrix given an event e, and $H_e(t; \cdot, \sigma_{\leq\tau})$ is the density function of triggering the event e upon t time units. The enabled events in a state race to trigger first, the event that triggers first causes a transition to a state $s' \in \mathcal{X}$ according to the next-state probability matrix for the triggering event. The GSMP is considered as analytically intractable and the probability measure formulation is not at all intuitive.

3   Learning Stochastic Timed Automata

We shall now present a novel algorithm for learning GSMP from sample executions (fully detailed in [6,7]), where the GSMP are processes generated by stochastic timed automata. In order to ensure the correctness of our algorithm, we define first an inclusion relation between the prefix tree and the *sta*. Next, we define the similarity relation between the states, and lastly we describe the algorithm for the merge of compatible states which is commonly called *state merge*.

3.1   The Inclusion Relation and the State Relation

Before introducing the definitions (1) and (2), we need to define two auxiliary functions to simplify the notation of the relation between paths and the prefix tree, as follows:

- $\tau(s, x)$ gives the set of feasible events of a given event sequence x from a prefix tree $Pt(Path(\sigma_{\leq\tau}))$, $\{y \in \mathcal{E} \mid \delta(\delta(s, x), y) \neq \bot\}$, for instance, from a set of sequences $\{x\,a, x\,b, ...\}$ we get $\{a, b, ...\}$, and
- $\nu(\sigma\|_{\mathcal{X}}[s, i])$ maps a state $\sigma\|_{\mathcal{X}}[s, i]$ to u, where $u \in \mathcal{Q}$ is a sequence of events accepted by the prefix tree $Pt(Path(\sigma_{\leq\tau}))$.

One says that a prefix tree $Pt(Path(\sigma_{\leq\tau}))$ is a particular case of a GSMP, or in other words a *sta*. However, only the relation between the data structures is ensured with this definition, we shall need to establish a correction of the state merge algorithm as well (as we will see later).

Definition 1. *The prefix tree* $Pt(Path(\sigma_{\leq\tau})) = (\mathcal{F}, \mathcal{Q}, \rho, \varrho, \delta)$, *denoted Ptsta, for a set of multiple paths* $Path(\sigma_{\leq\tau})$ *is a particular* sta,

$$Ptsta(Path(\sigma_{\leq\tau})) = (\mathcal{X}, \mathcal{E}, \Gamma, p, p_0, G)$$

where $\mathcal{X} = \mathcal{Q}$; $\mathcal{E}$ *is the set of single and unique events in the* $\mathcal{F}$ *set;* $\Gamma(s_i) = \tau(s, \nu(s_i))$; $p(s'; s, e^*) = 1$ *if* $\delta(\nu(s), e^*) \neq \bot$ *and* $\nu(s') \neq \bot$, *otherwise*

$p(s'; s, e^*) = 0$; $p_0(s) = 1$; and G is a set of distributions estimated by sample clocks associated on each event, given by the function ϱ.

The $Ptsta(Path(\sigma_{\leq\tau}))$ is a GSMP consistent with the sample in $Path(\sigma_{\leq\tau})$. For all paths with prefix $\sigma_{\leq\tau}$ there exists a corresponding execution in the GSMP that produces the same path.

Now, we introduce the notion of a stable equivalence relation that establishes the similarity between states. This relation, that is applied statistically, allows the creation of a more abstract model from a set of paths $Path(\sigma_{\leq\tau})$. The size of the model at each equivalence between states is reduced.

Definition 2. *Let* $\mathcal{M} = (\mathcal{X}, \mathcal{E}, \Gamma, p, p_0, G)$ *be a sta, a relation* $R \subseteq \mathcal{X} \times \mathcal{X}$ *is said to be a* stable relation *if and only if any* s, s' *have the following three properties,*

$$|\Gamma(s)| = |\Gamma(s')| \tag{1}$$

there is a one to one correspondence f *between* $\Gamma(s)$ *and* $\Gamma(s')$,

$$\text{if } \exists e \in \mathcal{E} \text{ and } \exists n \in \mathcal{X} \text{ such that } p(n; s, e) > 0, \text{ then} \tag{2}$$
$$\exists n' \in \mathcal{X} \text{ such that } p(n'; s', f(e)) > 0, \ G(s, e) \sim G(s', f(e)), \text{ and } (n, n') \in R$$

and

$$\text{if } \exists e \in \mathcal{E} \text{ and } \exists n, n' \in \mathcal{X} \text{ such that } n \neq n' , \ p(n; s, e) > 0 \text{ and} \tag{3}$$
$$p(n'; s, e) > 0 \text{ then } p(n; s, e) \approx p(n; s', e) \text{ and } p(n'; s, e) \approx p(n'; s', e)$$

where $|\Gamma(s)|$ *is the number of active events in the state* s, p *is a probabilistic transition function,* G *is a probability distribution function, and the tilde* $(\sim)$ *and double tilde* $(\approx)$ *notations denote "with same distribution" and "with same probability" respectively. Two states* s *and* s' *of* $\mathcal{M}$ *are said equivalent* $s \equiv s'$ *if and only if there is a stable relation* R *such that* $(s, s') \in R$.

A concrete example is now described for the application of the definition (2). For instance, suppose that we have $|\Gamma(s)| = |\Gamma(s')| = 2$, $\Gamma(s) = \{a, b\}$, and $\Gamma(s') = \{c, d\}$. The equation (1) is trivially satisfied, i.e., the feasible event set have the same size. However, the equation (2) and (3) are not trivially satisfied. To be satisfied we need to conclude that $G(s, a) \sim G(s', c)$ and $G(s, b) \sim G(s', d)$, or $G(s, a) \sim G(s', d)$ and $G(s, b) \sim G(s', c)$ is true, if $G(s, a) \sim G(s, b)$, $G(s, a) \sim G(s', c)$ or $G(s, a) \sim G(s', d)$ then $p(n; s, a) \approx p(n'; s', b)$, $p(n; s, a) \approx p(n'; s', c)$, $p(n'''; s, a) \approx p(n'''; s', d)$ respectively, otherwise a test for two Bernoulli distributions p is not necessary [3], and all states reachable by s and all states reachable by s' must also form a stable relation, i.e., the next states of (s, s') also have to satisfy these three properties.[1]

3.2   Testing Statistically the Similarity of States

The similarity test follows the same scheme of algorithms RPNI [17] and ALER-GIA [3], except for: the compatible function which incorporates a different

---

[1] In the definition (2) the real event identifiers are not necessary but we need to know that the sets of feasible events have associated for each event the same distribution.

Algorithm 1: Testing statistically the similarity of states (T3S)

input : A set of paths with prefix $\sigma_{\leq \tau}$, $Path(\sigma_{\leq \tau})$, and a type I error α between $[0; 1]$.
output: A *sta* $\mathcal{M}$.

$\mathcal{M} = Ptsta(\texttt{scheduler\_estimator}(Path(\sigma_{\leq \tau}), Pt(Path(\sigma_{\leq \tau}))))$;   `// See definition (1)`
$attempt \leftarrow 1$;
while $attempt > 0$ **do**
   $attempt \leftarrow 0$;
   $\mathcal{C} \leftarrow \texttt{clusterize}(\mathcal{M})$;
   for $n \leftarrow 1$ **to** $|\mathcal{C}|$ **do**
      for $k \leftarrow 1$ **to** $|\mathcal{C}^n|$ **do**
         $x \leftarrow k + 1$;
         while $\mathcal{C}^{n,x} \neq \mathcal{C}^{n,|\mathcal{C}^n|}$ **do**
            if $\texttt{is\_active}(\mathcal{C}^{n,x})$ **then**
               if $\texttt{similar}(\mathcal{C}^{n,k}, \mathcal{C}^{n,x}, \alpha)$ **then**
                  $\texttt{dmerge}(\mathcal{M}, \mathcal{C}^{n,k}, \mathcal{C}^{n,x}, \cdot, \cdot)$;
                  $\texttt{inactivate}(\mathcal{C}^{n,x})$;
                  $attempt \leftarrow attempt + 1$;
            $x \leftarrow x + 1$;

$\mathcal{M} = \texttt{infer\_distributions}(\mathcal{M})$;

---

statistical test structure, there is an estimator for unknown new clocks, and there is an event distribution estimator.

The algorithm 1 together with the auxiliary functions , , and establish a new methodology to learn GSMP, which are processes that hold a semi-Markov property. We call the presented solution *model identification in the limit*.

The algorithm 1 has notations associated to the ordered set of clusters and also between these cluster elements, as follows:

- the set of n ordered clusters $\mathcal{C}$, classified by events, are denoted by $\mathcal{C}^n$, and
- $\mathcal{C}^{n,k}$ is the kth element of cluster $\mathcal{C}^n$, for each $1 \leq n \leq |\mathcal{C}|$ and $1 \leq k \leq |\mathcal{C}^n|$.

The clustering function `clusterize` produces groups of elements $\mathcal{C}$ with a selection based on the feasible event set $\tau(s\cdot)$ for each state $s\cdot$ of $\mathcal{M}$, where $\mathcal{M}$ at first attempt is equal to $Ptsta(Pt(Path(\sigma_{\leq \tau})))$. The `is_active` and `inactivate` functions allow that only the prefix tree nodes that were not merged are used, and the function `similar` tests the similarity between two feasible event sets $\tau(\mathcal{C}^{n,k})$ and $\tau(\mathcal{C}^{n,x})$.

The *testing statistically the similarity of states* (T3S) algorithm is subdivided in three blocks. The first block is composed by a `clusterize` function that clusters the states with an equal active event set (the function τ). The `clusterize` function establishes a plain static equivalence between states, nevertheless we need to establish a while cycle with $attempt > 0$ to cover the other cases such as when `dmerge` changes the clock samples of the similar states. With this `clusterize` function we guarantee equation 1, which says that only states with event sets of the same size can be merged.

In the second block we use the `similar` function to test when two states are similar. This function is defined as and it uses the Kolmogorov-Smirnov test [8, p. 552] to decide if two empirical probabilistic distributions are equal. It verifies whether there exists a one to one correspondence of events between two active event sets through a statistical equivalence. If there is a correspondence for all events of an active event set, the equation 2 is satisfied. Lastly, the algorithm 1

Function: `scheduler_estimator`$(Path(\sigma_{\leq\tau}), Pt(Path(\sigma_{\leq\tau})))$

input : A $Path(\sigma_{\leq\tau})$ with initial state s, and a $Pt(Path(\sigma_{\leq\tau}))$.
output: The $Pt(Path(\sigma_{\leq\tau}))$ with replaced old clocks by original values of clocks.

for $n \leftarrow 1$ to $|Path(\sigma_{\leq\tau})|$ do
  for $l \leftarrow 2$ to $|\sigma^n|$ do
    for $x \leftarrow 0$ to $l - 1$ do   // Decrement p
      $p \leftarrow l - x$;
      if $\sigma^n\|_{\mathcal{E}}[s, l] \notin \tau(\nu(\sigma^n\|_{\mathcal{X}}[s, p]))$ and $|\tau(\nu(\sigma^n\|_{\mathcal{X}}[s, p]))| \leq 1$ and
      $\sigma^n\|_{\mathcal{E}}[s, p] = \sigma^n\|_{\mathcal{E}}[s, l]$ then break;
    if $p > 1$ then $p \leftarrow p + 1$;
    if $\sigma^n\|_{\mathcal{X}}[s, p] \neq \sigma^n\|_{\mathcal{X}}[s, l]$ then
      Val $\leftarrow 0$;
      for $t \leftarrow p$ to l do   // Estimating
        Val $\leftarrow$ Val $+ \sigma^n\|_{\mathcal{G}}[s, t]$;
        if $\sigma^n\|_{\mathcal{X}}[s, t] = \sigma^n\|_{\mathcal{X}}[s, l]$ then break;
      `replace`$(Pt(Path(\sigma_{\leq\tau})), \nu(\sigma^n\|_{\mathcal{X}}[s, l]),$ Val$)$;

---

merges the equal states by the function composed by equation 7. It initializes the construction of the *sta*. This function defined according to the equation 7 solves the problem of non-deterministic merge of states when two states have the same set of events.

Inferring the State Age Structure. The considered stochastic process, the GSMP, requires a state age memory [4,10]. This state age structure, normally identified as a scheduler, allows the use of different continuous distributions for each inter-event time, i.e., the inter-event times between events of a GSMP are not equal. This is not true in CTMP where all inter-event times follow an exponential distribution. The scheduling of events is a data structure that allows the calculation of the next event to be triggered.

We introduce the notion of scheduler estimation in order to calculate the history of clock values for each event. Thus, we reconstruct values sampled from new clocks to estimate the events distribution of the model that produces those executions. For instance, suppose that we have two events a and b that can be triggered in a state s_0, where s_0 is the initial state of the model, and there are two random variables $X_a \sim E(0.2)$ and $X_b \sim W(1, 0.1)$ associated to each event. The events a and b begin labeled as new clock and therefore two samples are given by random variables, respectively, X_a and X_b. Given the samples $x_a = 1.2$ and $x_b = 0.5$ from their respective distributions, the event b wins. Next, the clock value of event b is subtracted and is stored with value $1.2 - 0.5 = 0.7$ and a new clock is sampled to b. Then, the event a wins with value 0.7 versus the event b with new clock 1.4. Therefore we can calculate the original value of the event a from the produced sample execution $\{s_0, (b, 0.5), s_1, (a, 0.7), \cdot\}$ adding inter-event times between a and b, $0.5 + 0.7 = 1.2$. So, we can say that the value sampled in state s_0 to the event a has the value 1.2, which is true. Although this scheme can be extended recursively to any finite sample execution, we need to clearly identify the new and old clocks for any path. In order to check the definition (2), only the new clock samples are suitable to predict the distributions associated to each event i. The estimation process happens essentially due to the existence of the map function ν (defined in 3.1).

The function has a particular notation of order in a set of paths $Path(\sigma_{\leq \tau})$ with prefix $\sigma_{\leq \tau}$ that is described, as follows: σ^n is the nth path $Path(\sigma_{\leq \tau})$, where $0 < n \leq |Path(\sigma_{\leq \tau})|$, and $\sigma^{n,l}$ is the lth piecewise of path n, where $0 < l \leq |\sigma^n|$, where symbols ('|') denotes the size of a variable that is between these symbols. We explain in the following how function estimates original sample clock values. First, the algorithm begins by traversing each path of sample executions set in a bottom-up order to know if the current event can be triggered by a clock with a label "new clock" or an "old clock". In this step, we know that an old clock is valid when the successor nodes have this event activated, otherwise it is as "inactive clock". The algorithm goes to the predecessor node of the current node recursively, always in one sample execution, until we have found a possible inactive clock. When an inactive clock is found for the current event, in state $s^{\cdot}$, this implies that this event e cannot be in $\tau(s^{\cdot})$, which is an active event set for a state $s^{\cdot}$. Therefore, even in the worst case, the first state (s_0) of the sample execution can always be found. Given this element we can reconstruct the original clock value by the sum of the values between the found state $(s^{\cdot}$ or $s_0)$ and the current state. Lastly, we replace the old clock value by the estimated original clock value.

Establish the Similarity Test of States. The similarity between two active event sets Γ_1 and Γ_2 within the type I error α is solved by the function . Thus, the Kolmogorov-Smirnov test (K-S test) [8, p. 552] is applied to test if two distributions are or are not the same (i.e., compare two empirical cumulative distribution functions). Let $\{X_n\}_{n \geq 1}$ and $\{Y_n\}_{n \geq 1}$ be two independent successions of independent real random variables with common distribution functions, respectively F_1 and F_2. The K-S test allows testing two hypothesis,

$$H_0 : F_1(x) = F_2(x), \text{ for all } x \in \mathbb{R} \text{ against} \tag{4}$$
$$H_1 : F_1(x) \neq F_2(x), \text{ for some } x \in \mathbb{R}$$

using the statistical test,

$$T_{n_1,n_2} = \sqrt{\frac{n_1 n_2}{n_1 + n_2}} \sup_{x \in \mathbb{R}} |F_{n_1}(x) - F_{n_2}(x)| \tag{5}$$

where F_{n_1} and F_{n_2} denotes respectively the empirical distribution functions associated to the samples $(X_1, ..., X_{n_1})$ and $(Y_1, ..., Y_{n_2})$. The random variable T_{n_1,n_2} converges to the Kolmogorov distribution whose values are tabled in [8, p. 555]. For a significance level α we reject H_0 when the observed value $\widehat{T}_{n_1,n_2}$ of the test statistic for the particular samples $(x_1, ..., x_{n_1})$ and $(y_1, ..., y_{n_2})$ exceeds the value K_α, with $G(k_\alpha) = 1 - \alpha$. The two empirical cumulative distributions F_{n_1} and F_{n_2} are estimated using the function $\mathcal{T}$. This function estimates the distribution from a set of sample clocks and is defined, as follows:

$$\mathcal{T}_n(x) = \frac{clock \ value \ of \ z_1, z_2, ..., z_n \ that \ are \leq x}{N} \tag{6}$$

where x is the threshold of the cumulative function, and z_i for all events $i \in D$ and $D \subseteq \mathcal{E}$ are the sample clock values.

Function: $\mathtt{similar}(s',s'',\alpha)$

input : Two states s_1 and s_2, and a type I error α.
output: Boolean, *true* if it is similar, or otherwise *false*.

$\Gamma_1 \leftarrow \tau(s_1);\ \Gamma_2 \leftarrow \tau(s_2);$
if $|\Gamma_1| \neq |\Gamma_2|$ **then** return *false*;
for each e_1 in Γ_1 **do**
$\quad$ **while** $|\Gamma_2| > 0$ **do**
$\quad\quad$ $e_2 \leftarrow \mathtt{get}(\Gamma_2);$
$\quad\quad$ $F_{n_1} = \mathcal{T}(\varrho(s_1 e_1));\ F_{n_2} = \mathcal{T}(\varrho(s_2 e_2));$
$\quad\quad$ **if** $\sqrt{\frac{n_1 n_2}{n_1+n_2}}\ \sup\limits_x |F_{n_1}(x) - F_{n_2}(x)| > K_\alpha$ **then**
$\quad\quad\quad$ **if** $\mathtt{similar}(\delta(s_1 e_1), \delta(s_2 e_2), \alpha) \neq true$ **then**
$\quad\quad\quad\quad$ return *false*;
$\quad\quad\quad$ continue;
$\quad\quad$ $\mathtt{put}(\Gamma_2, e_2);$

for each e_1, e_2 in Γ_1 such that $s_1\, e_1 \sim s_1\, e_2$ **do**
$\quad$ **if** $|\varrho(s_1\, e_1) - \varrho(s_1\, e_2)| > \sqrt{\frac{1}{2}\log\frac{2}{\alpha}}\left(\frac{1}{\sqrt{n_1}} + \frac{1}{\sqrt{n_2}}\right)$ **then**
$\quad\quad$ return *false*;

if $|\Gamma_2| < 1$ **then** return *true*; **else** return *false*;

The function   begins by comparing two feasible event sets Γ_1 and Γ_2. The comparison is made by establishing a one to one relation between events in feasible sets. If the relationship between events is complete then the states are similar and so it allows equation 2 to be checked. Another particularity in this algorithm is when two events have the same 'id' in the feasible event set, for two states respectively. This indicates that the event is triggered as e but there are different probabilities in the transition probability matrix. To solve this, we construct a hypothesis test for two Bernoulli distributions using Hoeffding bounds [3] in order to know if the occurrence probabilities are the same (i.e., satisfies equation 3). This method is similar to the one described in [13]. The method checks if the means $\varrho(s_1\, e_1)$ and $\varrho(s_1\, e_2)$ of two Bernoulli distributions are statistically different or not.

The Deterministic Merge Function. The existence of equal feasible event sets $(\Gamma(s) = \Gamma(s'))$ creates a non deterministic choice when merged. This problem can be solved applying a deterministic merge function, as follows:

$$\text{While } \exists s, x \in \mathcal{Q} \text{ and } \exists e \in E \text{ such as } s', s'' \in \sigma(s, x\, e),\ merge(s', s'') \qquad (7)$$

The merge shall be made recursively until no more non-deterministic event transitions occur. In the T3S algorithm this is named as $\mathtt{dmerge}$ function. We describe with a brief example the application of the equation 7. Let two non-deterministic transitions from s_1 and s_2 labeled with same event e, $\tau(s, x\, \nu(s_0)) = \{e\}$ and $\tau(s, x\, \nu(s_0')) = \{e\}$ respectively. Supposing that we merge s_0 in s_0' we get a new non-deterministic choice between s_1 and s_1' until to the end of the paths. Therefore, we need to apply the merge recursively until there are only deterministic choices.

Inferring Event Distributions Using Maximum Likelihood. And now, to conclude the learning method, we need to introduce the concept of distribution discriminant and its selection criteria. Given a prefix tree with all the similar

---

Function: `infer_distributions` ($\mathcal{M}$)

---

input : A deterministic *sta* $\mathcal{M}$.
output: A deterministic *sta* $\mathcal{M}$ with associated random variables and those distributions.

for each n **in** Q such that $removed[n] = 0$ **do**
$\quad$ **for each** e **in** $\tau(s, n)$ **do**
$\quad\quad$ $G_e \leftarrow \int_0^\infty arg \max\limits_{f_d \in \mathcal{D}} \{ln\,[\mathcal{L}_d(\varrho[n\,e])]\};$

---

states merged, we need to estimate the parameters of each empirical distribution of each event that best fits the sample data. For this, the maximum likelihood estimator (MLE) and selection criteria, such as maximum log likelihood, are needed [9]. In order to test the validity of the selection model, a goodness of fit test could be applied (e.g., $\mathcal{X}^2$).

We present the function that estimates the distribution parameters using the maximum likelihood estimator (MLE) for continuous distributions such as: Exponential, Weibull and Log-Normal. However, there are other continuous distributions, such as: Rayleigh, Normal (with non negative part), that we have not described in detail in this paper, but that can be applied in this estimator. The *log likelihood* $\mathcal{L}_d$ of a distribution f_d is defined by

$$ln\,[\mathcal{L}_d\,(\theta \mid x_1, ..., x_n)] = \sum_{i=0}^{n} ln\,[f_d\,(x_i \mid \theta)] \qquad (8)$$

where θ is the set of parameters for a distribution f_d, and $x_1, ..., x_n$ are samples to be measured. MLE of f_d is composed by the maximization of likelihood function $\mathcal{L}_d$ with respect to the set of parameters θ which are parameters used in the following criterion. The *maximum log likelihood criterion* selects the model that best fits the data from the different estimations of distributions with maximum likelihood [9]. This selection criteria is defined by the maximum value of the calculated log likelihood, i.e.,

$$ln\,[\mathcal{L}_{dm}] > max\,\{\forall d \in \mathcal{D}\ \text{s.t.}\ d \neq dm\ \text{then}\ ln\,[\mathcal{L}_d]\} \qquad (9)$$

where D is a set of distributions in analysis, and $ln\,[\mathcal{L}_d]$ the log likelihood of distribution d. The distribution with maximum likelihood is denoted by $dm \in \mathcal{D}$. So, we need two or more distributions to make a decision. Note that distributions of set $\mathcal{D}$ are distributions with a parameter or a set of parameters estimated by using the MLE method. By this means we estimate the distribution that, in the limit, is more similar to the distribution that produce these samples to learn.

4 Model Identification in the Limit

The correctness argument for the proposed learning algorithm can be defined in terms of *correct model identification*. For such, we need to show that the produced GSMP is similar to the model that was used to generate the samples. There are therefore three conditions or clauses for correct model identification:

1. the prefix tree constructed by sample executions provided by a GSMP, $Pt(Path(\sigma_{\leq\tau}))$, is also a GSMP.

2. the sample executions to learn have the minimal information necessary to form the model.
3. the $Pt(Path(\sigma_{\leq\tau}))$ with state merge, in the limit, converges to one similar model that identifies $Path(\sigma_{\leq\tau})$.

Since the definition 1 is correct by construction and assuming a structurally complete sample, the correctness of the learning algorithm depends essentially on the correctness of the state merge procedure. From definition 1 the first clause is ensured and therefore only the other two clauses need to be guaranteed. For the second clause, we need to ensure that the sample executions to learn form a *structurally complete sample* (SCS). This is known as the problem of insufficient data training and when this occurs it is obviously impossible to learn the model that produces an incomplete set of sample executions. For the third clause, we need to ensure that, in the limit, the error of merging two non equivalent states tends to zero. Note that the error of merging two non equivalent states is guaranteed by the K-S test. With these three clauses satisfied, we can prove that the model that is learned by the algorithm, in the limit, and behaves as the original.

Ensuring a Structurally Complete Sample. Commonly used methods to achieve a structurally complete sample, like reachability analysis, are not enough when the model is not known. In this case acquiring a SCS is a big challenge. The selection of termination probability for a sample execution can be used as a method to achieve a SCS in known and unknown models. However, the probability measure of a path from an unknown model is not trivially assured.

A SCS is a sample composed by a set of paths that explores every possible transition and every reachable state. This structure solves a common problem known as *insufficient data training* to learn a model, i.e., only with paths of infinite size can one guarantee that for any model, the learned model eventually converges to an equivalent. With a SCS, we ensure that the minimum information needed to learn a model from sample executions is achieved. In order to ensure that a set of paths relying on SCS, we introduce a termination probability p_t as a solution. The simulation technique is described, as follows: 1) simulate the SDES M, 2) terminate when probability measure of a path $\sigma_{\leq\tau}$ of execution is less than p_t, i.e., $\mu(C(\sigma_{\leq\tau}, \langle E_k, Y_k^* \rangle, X_k, ..., \langle E_n, Y_n^* \rangle, X_n)) < p_t$, and 3) apply recursively the steps 1 and 2 to generate more sample executions. We simply note that the solution method based on termination probability has weaker correctness guarantees than reachability analysis. It also places a greater responsibility on the user, who has to choose a good value for p_t. The automatic achievement of p_t is not trivial.

The State Merge Error, in the Limit, Converges to Zero. Assuming that the first two correctness clauses are satisfied then the learning algorithm can only make errors when testing the similarity between two states. In addition, the errors α and β between two event distributions of the K-S test are defined, as follows:

. α is the type I error of H_0 be rejected, where in fact H_0 should not be rejected, and

. β is the type II error of H_1 be accepted, where in fact H_1 should be rejected.

Hence this means that the state merge errors α_s and β_s are defined by the multiplication of the errors made in the comparison of each event distribution $\alpha_s = \prod_{i=1}^{k} \alpha_i$ and $\beta_s = \prod_{i=1}^{k} \beta_i$, where k is the number of similar events. Moreover, the model errors α^* and β^* are equal to the multiplication of the error α_s and β_s used for each state merged $\alpha^* = \prod_{i=1}^{n} \alpha_s[i]$ and $\beta^* = \prod_{i=1}^{n} \beta_s[i]$, where n is the number of merged states. We present, in the following, two propositions about the bounds of type II error.

Proposition 1. *Suppose the Kolmogorov-Smirnov test for two samples with size n_1 e n_2 respectively, and a significance level α. For sufficiently large samples, i.e., when $n_1 \to \infty$ and $n_2 \to \infty$, β tends to zero.*

In the following we present a sketch of the proof. The proof of this proposition is based on the following facts: by the theorem of Glivenko-Cantelli when H_0 is true and n_1 and n_2 tend to infinity, $\sup_{x \in \mathbb{R}} |F_{n_1}(x) - F_{n_2}(x)|$ converges certainly to zero. So, from the uniqueness of the limit, when H_0 is true and $n_1 \to \infty$, $n_2 \to \infty$, we have that $\sqrt{\frac{n_1 n_2}{n_1 + n_2}} \sup_{x \in \mathbb{R}} |F_{n_1}(x) - F_{n_2}(x)|$ tends certainly to $+\infty$. Therefore, in the validity of H_1, the probability of rejecting H_0 tends to 1, which was to be demonstrated.

It is known that the convergence of k-S test is exponential [24]. Moreover, the reader can find a detailed account to β error boundaries and correctness arguments as presented here in [14].

Proposition 2. *If the type II error β, in the limit, for the K-S test converges to zero, a multiplication of the type II error $\prod_{i=1}^{k} \beta_i$, in the limit, also tends to zero.*

This proposition is trivially satisfied. Given the limit law of multiplication, we know that the $\lim_{x \to a} f(x) \cdot g(x) = \lim_{x \to a} f(x) \cdot \lim_{x \to a} g(x)$. Then, because $f(x) = g(x)$, the limit is maintained.

5   Tool and Proof of Concept

The implementation of the learning algorithm is the basis of the *SDES toolbox*, that allows the learning and analysis of a set of case studies, such as: task schedulers, land mobile satellite communication systems, and network traffic model estimation. In order to illustrate the learning process, we use as an example a scheduler for a multi-processor system and show how the proposed method can learn a model that can be used for further analysis.

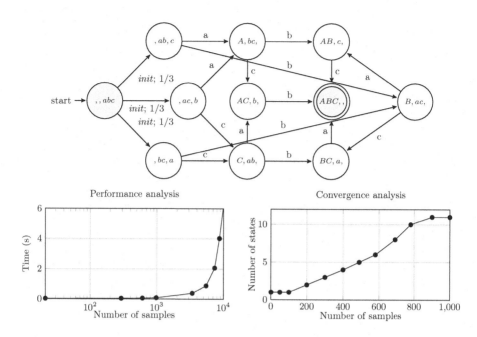

Fig. 1. Learning GSMP of a multi-processor system scheduler with uncertainty

SDES Toolbox. We have developed a SDES toolbox[2] in C and C++ language that implements the presented learning approach. The toolbox was developed to analyze and learn generalized semi-Markov processes. It also supports the model description by an event-driven language that can be directly used as the input model language to a GSMP model checker [21].

Stochastic Analysis of a Scheduler for a Multi-processor System. An optimal scheduler design for a multi-processor system with uncertainty in task duration is difficult to achieve and a significant challenge [18]. In figure 1, we present the model from which it is possible to derive, statistically, answers about the worst case sequence and the optimal case sequence of a two-processor scheduler system. In this system there are two processors that can run two tasks at the same time. Supposing that there are three tasks $\{a, b, c\}$, only two tasks can be run at the same time and the other one only when one of the tasks is finished. The model of this system has eleven states which describe the state of the two processors and tasks at any given time. The scheduler can initially make three choices, (a, b), (a, c), or (b, c). The event *init* of the model, representing these choices is: $p([, ab, c]; [, , abc], init) = \frac{1}{3}$, $p([, ac, b]; [, , abc], init) = \frac{1}{3}$, and $p([, bc, a]; [, , abc], init) = \frac{1}{3}$ respectively. These choices bind the time (i.e., worst and optimal) of the execution for these three tasks. If we have a scheduler that is completely random (i.e., the probability of events $\{ab, ac, bc\}$ are equiprobable) then we select the path with maximum probability which means that it

---

[2] Available from http://sourceforge.net/projects/t3s-tool/

is the better sequence. Thus, if we have a scheduler that begins with the optimal tasks then we will have an optimal scheduler for these tasks. However, we need to distinguish two situations, as follows: if only exponential distributions are used then the choice is easy, the rate of distribution identifies the order (the lower expected value is the more probable), but if on the other hand we have different continuous distributions then the ordering selection is not so trivial. This will be the case for this example that our method will solve. Namely using the distributions $init : T_{init} \sim Exponential(1)$, $a : T_a \sim Weibull(0.1, 1)$, $b : T_b \sim Exponential(0.4)$, and $c : T_c \sim Log\text{-}Normal(0, 0.25)$, respectively.

Given the sample executions that form a SCS, we have compared the performance and convergence of our algorithm given an increasing number of sample executions, see figure 1. We can see in the convergence graph that for one thousand sample executions, the model converges into a model with same number of states. According to the correctness of our learning algorithm, we have guaranteed that if the umber of samples grows infinitely then the model converges to the original model. Notice that in fact in this example we verify that the model learnt by our algorithm with approximately nine hundred sample executions has the same event language of the original model. This experiment was made on a machine with an *Intel Core 2 Duo CPU T7500 @ 2.2Ghz* processor with *4Gb* of memory. An interesting point in this model is that the path with the greatest probability to occur is the optimal case execution and the path with the lowest probability is the worst case execution, when we have a random scheduler.

6   Conclusion and Future Work

To the best of our knowledge, this is the first learning algorithm that is able to cope with GSMP learning of deployed stochastic discrete event systems for which we do not know the model before-hand. The learning algorithm can be used to verify the deployed systems using existing probabilistic model-checking tools. We also have developed a toolbox for Matlab that applies the techniques described in this paper. We have shown with our experiment that this type of model is really capable and scalable. We can use it not only for the analysis of a computer system but also to verify or test it. However, one of the limitations of our work is that it may not scale up for systems having large stochastic timed automata. Development of techniques that allow the approximate verification while the model is learned may be the solution.

Acknowledgments. We would like to thank to Ana Paula Martins for the very constructive discussions about the statistical properties of the proposed T3S algorithm.

References

1. Bollig, B., Habermehl, P., Kern, C., Leucker, M.: Angluin-style learning of nfa. In: Proceedings of the 21st International Joint Conference on Artifical Intelligence, IJCAI 2009, San Francisco, CA, USA, pp. 1004–1009. Morgan Kaufmann Publishers Inc. (2009)

2. Bollig, B., Katoen, J.-P., Kern, C., Leucker, M., Neider, D., Piegdon, D.R.: libalf: The Automata Learning Framework. In: Touili, T., Cook, B., Jackson, P. (eds.) CAV 2010. LNCS, vol. 6174, pp. 360–364. Springer, Heidelberg (2010)

3. Carrasco, R.C., Oncina, J.: Learning deterministic regular grammars from stochastic samples in polynomial time. RAIRO (Theoretical Informatics and Applications) 33, 1–20 (1999)

4. Cassandras, C.G., Lafortune, S.: Cassandras and Stephane Lafortune. In: Introduction to Discrete Event Systems. Springer-Verlag New York, Inc., Secaucus (2006)

5. David, A., Larsen, K.G., Legay, A., Mikučionis, M., Wang, Z.: Time for Statistical Model Checking of Real-Time Systems. In: Gopalakrishnan, G., Qadeer, S. (eds.) CAV 2011. LNCS, vol. 6806, pp. 349–355. Springer, Heidelberg (2011)

6. de Matos Pedro, A.: Learning and testing stochastic discrete event systems. Master's thesis, Universidade do Minho, Portugal (December 2011)

7. de Matos Pedro, A., de Sousa, S.M.: Learning generalized semi-markov processes: From stochastic discrete event systems to testing and verification. Technical Report DCC-2012-01, Department of Computer Science, University of Porto (2012)

8. DeGroot, M.H.: Probability and Statistics, 2nd edn. Addison Wesley (1989)

9. Dey, A.K., Kundu, D.: Discriminating among the log-normal, weibull, and generalized exponential distributions. IEEE Transactions on Reliability 58(3), 416–424 (2009)

10. Glynn, P.W.: A gsmp formalism for discrete event systems. Proceedings of The IEEE 77, 14–23 (1989)

11. Mark Gold, E.: Language identification in the limit. Information and Control 10(5), 447–474 (1967)

12. Harchol-Balter, M., Downey, A.B.: Exploiting process lifetime distributions for dynamic load balancing. ACM Trans. Comput. Syst. 15, 253–285 (1997)

13. Kermorvant, C., Dupont, P.: Stochastic Grammatical Inference with Multinomial Tests. In: Adriaans, P.W., Fernau, H., van Zaanen, M. (eds.) ICGI 2002. LNCS (LNAI), vol. 2484, pp. 149–160. Springer, Heidelberg (2002)

14. Klotz, J.: Asymptotic efficiency of the two sample Kolmogorov-Smirnov test. Journal of the American Statistical Association 62(319), 932–938 (1967)

15. Legay, A., Delahaye, B., Bensalem, S.: Statistical Model Checking: An Overview. In: Barringer, H., Falcone, Y., Finkbeiner, B., Havelund, K., Lee, I., Pace, G., Roşu, G., Sokolsky, O., Tillmann, N. (eds.) RV 2010. LNCS, vol. 6418, pp. 122–135. Springer, Heidelberg (2010)

16. Lu, M.-W., Wang, C.J.: Weibull data analysis with few or no failures. In: Pham, H. (ed.) Recent Advances in Reliability and Quality in Design, pp. 201–210. Springer, London (2008)

17. Parekh, R., Honavar, V.: Learning dfa from simple examples. Machine Learning 44(1/2), 9–35 (2001)

18. Pinedo, M.L.: Scheduling: Theory, Algorithms, and Systems, 3rd edn. Springer Publishing Company, Incorporated (2008)

19. Sen, K., Viswanathan, M., Agha, G.: Learning continuous time markov chains from sample executions. In: Proceedings of the The Quantitative Evaluation of Systems, First International Conference, pp. 146–155. IEEE Computer Society Press, Washington, DC (2004)

20. Wei, W., Wang, B., Towsley, D.: Continuous-time hidden Markov models for network performance evaluation. Perform. Eval. 49, 129–146 (2002)

21. Younes, H.L.S.: Ymer: A Statistical Model Checker. In: Etessami, K., Rajamani, S.K. (eds.) CAV 2005. LNCS, vol. 3576, pp. 429–433. Springer, Heidelberg (2005)

22. Younes, H.L.S., Clarke, E.M., Zuliani, P.: Statistical verification of probabilistic properties with unbounded until. In: SBMF, pp. 144–160 (2010)

23. Lorens, H., Younes, S.: Verification and planning for stochastic processes with asynchronous events. PhD thesis, Pittsburgh, PA, USA (2004)

24. Yu, C.S.: Pitman efficiencies of Kolmogorov-Smirnov test. The Annals of Mathematical Statistics 42(5), 1595–1605 (1971)

Learning Minimal Deterministic Automata from Inexperienced Teachers

Martin Leucker[1] and Daniel Neider[2]

[1] Institute for Software Engineering and Programming Languages,
University of Lübeck, Germany
[2] Lehrstuhl für Informatik 7, RWTH Aachen University, Germany

Abstract. A prominent learning algorithm is Angluin's L* algorithm, which allows to learn a minimal deterministic automaton using so-called membership and equivalence queries addressed to a teacher. In many applications, however, a teacher might be unable to answer some of the membership queries because parts of the object to learn are not completely specified, not observable, it is too expensive to resolve these queries, etc. Then, these queries may be answered inconclusively. In this paper, we survey different algorithms to learn minimal deterministic automata in this setting in a coherent fashion. Moreover, we provide modifications and improvements for these algorithms, which are enabled by recent developments.

1 Introduction

In recent years, automata learning techniques have gained a lot of interest in the field of verification. In this application domain, often some form of abstract system or some invariant is needed within the verification process, which may be learned using such techniques. Prominent applications are compositional verification, in which an abstraction of a component is essential, or verification of infinite state systems by means of invariants. See [8] for further typical applications of learning techniques for verification tasks.

In simple words, the nature of automata learning techniques is to identify some automaton based on samples. More specifically, the general goal of automata learning algorithms is to identify an automaton, usually of minimum size, that conforms to an a priori fixed but unknown automaton. In general, two types of learning algorithms for automata can be distinguished, so-called *passive* and *active* algorithms. Passive algorithms get a fixed set of examples and compute a minimal conforming automaton. Active algorithms may use additional queries to the underlying system to improve the learning process. In this paper, we mainly focus on active learning algorithms.

A popular setup for actively learning automata is that of Angluin's L* algorithm [1] in which a so-called *learner* identifies a minimal deterministic finite automaton for a regular language L with the help of a so-called *teacher* that may be consulted with *membership* and *equivalence queries*. A membership query

T. Margaria and B. Steffen (Eds.): ISoLA 2012, Part I, LNCS 7609, pp. 524–538, 2012.

clarifies whether a given word is in the language in question while an equivalence query answers whether an automaton currently proposed by the learner is correct or not. In the latter case, a counter-example showing the difference of the two languages is returned.

In Angluin's setting, a teacher answers membership queries either positively or negatively. In many application scenarios, however, parts of the automaton to learn are not completely specified or not observable so that the corresponding information is not available, or it may be just too expensive to resolve these queries, etc. Then, queries may be answered inconclusively, by *don't know* (or *don't care*), denoted by ?. Moreover, in this context the goal is often more relaxed in the sense that no longer a (not necessarily unique) automaton has to be learned that coincides with some language L but one that accepts a superset of a language L_1 but has an empty intersection with a language L_2. This setup is faced, e.g., when verifying that some system with behavior given by L_1 does not violate a safety property given by behaviors L_2. Then, any superset L of L_1 having an empty intersection with L_2 proves the intended goal, regardless whether the words that are neither in L_1 nor in L_2 are accepted or not.

In this paper, we survey different algorithms to learn minimal deterministic automata that are designed to work with such an *inexperienced* teacher in a coherent fashion. Moreover, we provide modifications and improvements for these algorithms, which are enabled by recent developments.

More precisely, we review three different types of algorithms in the setting of learning with an inexperienced teacher. All algorithms maintain a set of sample words, which give partial information on the automaton in question. The general idea of the algorithms shown in Section 3 and 4 is to perform a loop of deriving a minimal automaton conforming to the sample and checking by means of an equivalence query whether the desired automaton is already found. If not, a corresponding counter-example is added to the sample. Here, inconclusive answers by the teacher are resolved to either $+$ (accepting) or $-$ (rejecting) to actually obtain a minimal automaton.

In Section 3, we study a family of algorithms that make use of at most equivalence queries but do not employ any membership queries. The main idea of these algorithms is to formulate the problem of finding a minimal conforming automaton as a constraint satisfaction problem, which in turn may be solved either directly, or, as described here, using SAT encodings and corresponding SAT solvers. In Section 4, we look in which way membership queries may be used to improve the learning process. The idea here is to use membership queries to round off a corresponding sample before performing an equivalence query.

The algorithm described in Section 5 uses a different approach. Roughly speaking, it learns a Moore machine with three outputs $(+, -, ?)$ using a straightforward adaption of Angluin's L^* algorithm. It classifies samples in L_1 as $+$, in L_2 as $-$, or those neither in L_1 nor L_2 as ?. Thus, inconclusive answers are treated as a special output rather than a placeholder. However, before performing an equivalence query, the information collected so far is used to derive an automaton by treating the words classified as ? as unspecified.

We summarize the main features of the algorithms, discuss their strengths and weaknesses and their preferable application area in Section 6.

2 Learning from Inexperienced Teachers

Let us first introduce definitions and notations used throughout this paper and the learning scenario we are going to study.

Words, Languages and Finite Automata. Let Σ be a finite *alphabet*. A *word* is a finite sequence $w = a_1 \ldots a_n$ of symbols $a_i \in \Sigma$. The empty sequence is called the *empty word* and denoted by ε. The *length* $|w|$ of a word w is the number of its symbols. For two words $u = a_1 \ldots a_n$ and $v = b_1 \ldots b_m$, let the word $uv = a_1 \ldots a_n b_1 \ldots b_m$ be the *concatenation* of u and v.

The set Σ^* is the set of all words over the alphabet Σ. A set $L \subseteq \Sigma^*$ is called a *language*. For a language $L \subseteq \Sigma^*$, the set of all *prefixes* of words in L is the set $\mathrm{Pref}(L) = \{u \in \Sigma^* \mid \exists v \in \Sigma^* : uv \in L\}$. The concatenation of two languages $L, L' \subseteq \Sigma^*$ is the language $L \cdot L' = LL' = \{uv \mid u \in L, v \in L'\}$.

A *deterministic finite automaton (DFA)* is a tuple $\mathcal{A} = (Q, \Sigma, q_0, \delta, F)$ where Q is a finite, nonempty set of states, Σ is the input alphabet, $q_0 \in Q$ is the initial state, $\delta : Q \times \Sigma \to Q$ is the transition function and $F \subseteq Q$ is the set of final states. A *run* of $\mathcal{A}$ from state $q \in Q$ on some word $w = a_1 \ldots a_n \in \Sigma^*$ is a sequence $q_1, \ldots, q_{n+1}$ such that $q_1 = q$ and $q_{i+1} = \delta(q_i, a_i)$ for $i = 1, \ldots, n$; we also write $\mathcal{A} : q \xrightarrow{w} q_{n+1}$ for short. A word w is *accepted* by $\mathcal{A}$ if $\mathcal{A} : q_0 \xrightarrow{w} q$ with $q \in F$. The *language accepted by* $\mathcal{A}$ is the set $L(\mathcal{A}) = \{w \in \Sigma^* \mid \mathcal{A} : q_0 \xrightarrow{w} q, q \in F\}$. A language $L \subseteq \Sigma^*$ is called *regular* if there exists a DFA $\mathcal{A}$ such that $L = L(\mathcal{A})$. The *size* $|\mathcal{A}|$ of a DFA $\mathcal{A}$ is the number of its states. Finally, it is well known that for every regular language L there exists a unique minimal DFA $\mathcal{A}_L$ such that $L = L(\mathcal{A}_L)$.

Learning from Inexperienced Teachers. In Angluin's original setting [1], a *learner* learns a regular *target language* $L \subseteq \Sigma^*$ over an a priori fixed alphabet Σ from a *teacher*. Thereby, the learner can pose two different types of queries: *membership* and *equivalence* queries. On membership queries, the learner proposes a word $w \in \Sigma^*$ and the teacher checks whether $w \in L$ and replies "yes" or "no" accordingly. On equivalence queries, on the other hand, the learner conjectures a regular language, typically given as a DFA $\mathcal{A}$. The teacher checks if $L = L(\mathcal{A})$ and replies either "yes" or a *counter-example* $w \in L \Leftrightarrow w \notin L(\mathcal{A})$ as a witness that L and $L(\mathcal{A})$ are different.

In [1], Angluin presents an algorithm, called L^*, to learn the (unique) minimal automaton for a target language L in the setting described above. The runtime of the algorithm and the number of queries posed are polynomial in the size of the minimal automaton $\mathcal{A}_L$ and the length of the longest counter-example returned by the teacher.

The setting we study in this paper is a generalization of Angluin's setting. We assume that the teacher is *inexperienced* and answers some of the queries inconclusively. This is formalized in the definition below.

Definition 1 (Inexperienced Teacher). *An inexperienced teacher has access to two disjoint (but not necessary regular) languages $L_1, L_2 \subseteq \Sigma^*$ and answers membership and equivalence queries as follows.*

- *On a membership query on $w \in \Sigma^*$, the teacher answers "yes" if $w \in L_1$, "no" if $w \in L_2$, and "don't care" (or "don't know", "maybe", etc.), denoted by "?", in any other case.*
- *On an equivalence query on a DFA $\mathcal{A}$, the teacher checks whether $L_1 \subseteq L(\mathcal{A})$ and $L(\mathcal{A}) \cap L_2 = \emptyset$. If $\mathcal{A}$ satisfies these properties, then the teacher returns "yes"; in this case, we call $\mathcal{A}$ feasible. Otherwise, the teacher returns a counter-example $w \in L_1 \cap (\Sigma^* \setminus L(\mathcal{A}))$ or $w \in L_2 \cap L(\mathcal{A})$.*

Note that this setting is in fact a generalization since we obtain Angluin's original setting if we consider regular languages $L_1 \subseteq \Sigma^*$ and set $L_2 = \Sigma^* \setminus L_1$.

The task of the learner is the following.

Definition 2 (Learning from Inexperienced Teachers). *Given an inexperienced teacher, the task of the learner is to find a minimal feasible DFA using membership and equivalence queries as in Definition 1.*

In other words, the task of the learner is to come up with a DFA that accepts at least L_1 and whose language has an empty intersection with L_2. Analogous to Angluin's algorithm, the learner has to learn a feasible DFA of minimal size. Note, however, that there is no longer a unique (minimal) feasible DFA to learn since their behavior on "don't cares" is unspecified. Intuitively, this is what makes the learning task difficult.

To implement an inexperienced teacher, the languages L_1, L_2 have to belong to language classes that allow the teacher to answer membership and equivalence queries. However, even if a teacher can be implemented, a feasible DFA might not exist. Consider, for instance, the class of context-free languages and let $L_1 = \{a^n b^n \mid n \in \mathbb{N}\}$ and $L_2 = \{a, b\}^* \setminus L_1$. Then, any feasible DFA would have to accept exactly L_1, which is not possible since L_1 is not a regular language.

Even worse, decidability of the question whether there exists a feasible DFA depends on the language classes L_1 and L_2 are taken from. A complete characterization of language classes for which the question is decidable is still missing, but we observe the following.

Observation. *Let $L_1, L_2 \subseteq \Sigma^*$ be two disjoint languages.*

- *If L_1 and L_2 are both regular languages, then there always exists a feasible DFA, e.g., any DFA accepting exactly L_1 (cf. Section 5).*
- *If L_1 and L_2 are deterministic pushdown languages or visibly pushdown languages, then it is unknown whether the decision problem is decidable.*
- *Already if L_1 and L_2 are nondeterministic context-free languages, the decision problem is undecidable.*

The latter point can be seen by a simple reduction from the problem to decide whether a (nondeterministic) context-free language is regular. Hence, all algorithms described in the remainder of this paper, except those in Section 5, are necessarily semi algorithms: they learn a feasible DFA if one exists.

3   Learning without Membership Queries

Let us begin by describing two approaches in which the learner only uses equivalence queries. Although such a setting seems a bit artificial, there are situations in which one might want to avoid membership queries, e.g., because they are much more expensive to answer than equivalence queries.

3.1   Naive Enumeration

Given an inexperienced teacher, a feasible DFA can already be learned in the following easy, yet inefficient way. Since the class of DFAs over a fixed alphabet can be enumerated according to their size, it is enough to pose an equivalence query on each DFA one after another. Once the teacher returns "yes", the learner halts and outputs this DFA. Since the DFAs are enumerated with respect to their size, this procedure yields a smallest feasible DFA if one exists.

This approach shows that minimal feasible DFAs can already be learned using only equivalence queries without the additional information of counter-examples. This means that counter-examples and membership queries can only be used (and should be used) to enhance the performance of the learning process. A first improvement is described next.

3.2   Counter-Example Guided Learning

Clearly, discarding the counter-examples as done in the naive enumeration is inefficient. A better way is to rule out DFAs that contradict knowledge already obtained from previous counter-examples. To this end, a learner can use the following idea, which is among others described in [8].

The learner maintains a *sample* $\mathcal{S} = (S^+, S^-)$ consisting of two finite sets $S^+, S^- \subseteq \Sigma^*$ of words. In every iteration, the learner constructs a minimal DFA that is *consistent* with the sample, i.e., a minimal DFA $\mathcal{A}$ such that $S^+ \subseteq L(\mathcal{A})$ and $S^- \cap L(\mathcal{A}) = \emptyset$. This DFA is then used on an equivalence query. If the teacher answer "yes", then the learner has found a feasible DFA and terminates. If the teacher returns a counter-example w, the learner adds w either to S^- or S^+ depending on whether $w \in L(\mathcal{A})$. Then, it repeats this procedure.

It is not hard to verify that this learner will never construct the same DFA twice and that it will never conjecture a DFA smaller than the DFA of the previous iteration. Hence, because all feasible DFAs are consistent with any sample obtained from the teacher this way, the learner eventually finds a smallest feasible DFA if one exists.

Thus, it is left to provide a technique that allows to find a minimal DFA consistent with a given sample. Note, however, that this task is not only performed by the counter-example guided learner, but also by the learning algorithm in Section 4. Hence, it is worth spending some time on such techniques.

3.3 Computing Minimal Consistent DFAs

The task of computing a minimal DFA consistent with a given sample is hard: Gold [5] showed that the corresponding decision problem "Given a sample S and $k \in \mathbb{N}$. Does a DFA with k states consistent with S exist?" is NP-complete. Nevertheless, several methods have been proposed. We present the most significant three next.

Bierman and Feldmann's Approach. Bierman and Feldmann were among the first to study the problem of finding a minimal DFA consistent with a given sample [3]. Their approach is also the prototype of all techniques we describe here and works as follows.

Let a sample $S = (S^+, S^-)$ over Σ be given. Bierman and Feldmann's idea is to consider the runs of a (minimal) consistent DFA $\mathcal{A}$ on the words in $S^+ \cup S^-$ (and their prefixes of course). To this end, let S_u be the state that $\mathcal{A}$ reaches after reading a word $u \in \mathrm{Pref}(S^+ \cup S^-)$. Since we do not know $\mathcal{A}$, we think of S_u as a variable and define constraints that allow to derive a consistent DFA from the values of the variables S_u. This leads to the following *constraint-satisfaction-problem* $\mathrm{CSP}(S)$ comprising the set of constraints

$$\{S_u = S_{u'} \rightarrow S_{ua} = S_{u'a} \mid ua, u'a \in \mathrm{Pref}(S^+ \cup S^-)\} \tag{1}$$

$$\{S_u \neq S_{u'} \mid u \in S^+, u' \in S^-\}. \tag{2}$$

The first type of constraints states that whenever a DFA reaches the same state after reading u and u', then it also reaches the same state after reading the next input symbol a, i.e., after reading ua and $u'a$. The second type states that two words that are classified contrary can never lead to the same state.

Let $\mathcal{D}(\mathrm{CSP}(S))$ be the domain of $\mathrm{CSP}(S)$ consisting of all variables S_u. A *model* of $\mathrm{CSP}(S)$ is mapping $\Gamma: \mathcal{D}(\mathrm{CSP}(S)) \rightarrow \mathbb{N}$ fulfilling the constraints over $\mathbb{N}$. Moreover, $\mathrm{CSP}(S)$ is *solvable* over $[n] = \{0, \dots, n-1\}$ if there exists a model such that every variable ranges in $[n]$. From a model Γ of $\mathrm{CSP}(S)$ with range $[n]$ we can construct a DFA $\mathcal{A}_\Gamma = ([n], \Sigma, q_0, \delta, F)$ with n states: $q_0 = S_\varepsilon$, $\delta(i, a) = j$ if a $ua \in \mathrm{Pref}(S^+ \cup S^-)$ exists such that $S_u = i$ and $S_{ua} = j$, and $F = \{i \mid \exists u \in S^+: S_u = i\}$. Note that $\mathcal{A}_\Gamma$ is well defined since δ is well defined due to constraints (1). An induction over the length of the inputs of $\mathcal{A}_\Gamma$ using the constraints (1) and (2) shows that $\mathcal{A}_\Gamma$ is indeed a DFA consistent with S.

Assigning a different value for every variable S_u trivially solves $\mathrm{CSP}(S)$. Thus, a solution with a minimal range exists and yields a minimal consistent DFA. This is summarized in the following lemma.

Lemma 1 (Biermann and Feldman [3]). *For a sample S, a model Γ of $CSP(S)$ with minimal range yields a minimal DFA $\mathcal{A}_\Gamma$ consistent with S.*

A model for $\mathrm{CSP}(S)$ with minimal range can be found in various ways: for instance, Oliveira and Silva [9] develop an explicit search algorithm using backtracking techniques, one can use generic CSP solvers, and also SMT solvers are able to solve CSPs.

A SAT-Based Approach. Grinchtein, Leucker, and Piterman [6] propose to translate the CSP from above into an equivalent satisfiability problem of *propositional formulae over Boolean variables (SAT)*. As there exist highly-optimized off-the-shelf solver for such problems, this approach can solve reasonable large problems effectively.

Their key idea is to construct a Boolean formula $\varphi_{\mathcal{S},n}$ for some natural number $n \geq 1$ that is satisfiable if and only if there exists a DFA with n states that is consistent with $\mathcal{S}$. Moreover, $\varphi_{\mathcal{S},n}$ can be used to derive a minimal consistent DFA. Although n is not known in advance, one can use a binary search to find the minimal value for n.

The formula $\varphi_{\mathcal{S},n}$ ranges over Boolean variables $x_{u,i}$ for $u \in \mathrm{Pref}(S^+ \cup S^-)$ and $i \in [n]$. The meaning is that if $x_{u,i}$ is set to **true**, then the unknown DFA reaches the state i after reading the word u. Hence, each variable S_u of the CSP from above is encoded unary by the variables $x_{u,0}, \ldots, x_{u,n-1}$. To make this encoding work, one has to make sure that for every $u \in \mathrm{Pref}(S^+ \cup S^-)$ exactly one variable $x_{u,i}$ set to **true**. The following constraints ensure this.

$$\bigwedge_{u \in \mathrm{Pref}(S^+ \cup S^-)} \ \bigvee_{i \in [n]} x_{u,i} \tag{i}$$

$$\bigwedge_{u \in \mathrm{Pref}(S^+ \cup S^-)} \ \bigwedge_{i,j \in [n], i<j} \neg x_{u,i} \vee \neg x_{u,j} \tag{ii}$$

It is left to translate constraints (1) and (2) of CSP($\mathcal{S}$). This is done by constraints (iii) and (iv) below. Note that constraints (i) to (iv) are written in conjunctive normal form since this is the standard format for most SAT solvers.

$$\bigwedge_{ua,u'a \in \mathrm{Pref}(S^+ \cup S^-)} \ \bigwedge_{i,j \in [n]} \begin{matrix} (\neg x_{u,i} \vee \neg x_{u',i} \vee x_{ua,j} \vee \neg x_{u'a,j}) \wedge \\ (\neg x_{u,i} \vee \neg x_{u',i} \vee \neg x_{ua,j} \vee x_{u'a,j}) \end{matrix} \tag{iii}$$

$$\bigwedge_{u \in S^+, u' \in S^-} \ \bigwedge_{i \in [n]} \neg x_{u,i} \vee \neg x_{u',i} \tag{iv}$$

Let $\varphi_{\mathcal{S},n}$ be the conjunction of the constraints (i) to (iv). We observe that $\varphi_{\mathcal{S},n}$ consists of $\mathcal{O}(mn)$ variables and $\mathcal{O}(m^2n^2)$ clauses where $m = |\mathrm{Pref}(S^+ \cup S^-)|$. As before, one can use a model Γ of $\varphi_{\mathcal{S},n}$, i.e., an evaluation of the variables that satisfies $\varphi_{\mathcal{S},n}$, to derive a DFA $\mathcal{A}_\Gamma$. It is not hard to verify that $\mathcal{A}_\Gamma$ is a DFA with n states that is consistent with $\mathcal{S}$. This leads to the following lemma.

Lemma 2 (Grinchtein, Leucker, and Piterman [6]). *For a sample $\mathcal{S}$ and $n \in \mathbb{N}$, a model Γ of $\varphi_{\mathcal{S},n}$ yields a DFA $\mathcal{A}_\Gamma$ with n states that is consistent with $\mathcal{S}$. A binary search can be used to find the smallest n for which $\varphi_{\mathcal{S},n}$ is satisfiable and, thus, a minimal DFA consistent with $\mathcal{S}$.*

Grinchtein, Leucker, and Piterman also propose a slightly different encoding in which each variable S_u of the CSP is encoded binary using $\log n$ Boolean variables. Although this encoding has only $\mathcal{O}(m \log n)$ variables and $\mathcal{O}(m^2 n \log n)$ clauses, they observe that the unary encoding performs better in their experiments. Moreover, they list further, small optimizations that reduce the search space of the resulting CSP and SAT encoding. We refer to [6] for further details.

An Improved SAT-Based Approach. Heule and Verwer [7] suggest a modification of Grinchtein, Leucker, and Piterman's unary encoding, which introduces additional auxiliary variables, but typically has less clauses. Heule and Verwer's approach is to encode the unknown DFA directly into the formula using the auxiliary variables $d_{i,a,j}$ and f_i for $i, j \in [n]$, $a \in \Sigma$. The meaning is that if $d_{i,a,j}$ is set to $\mathtt{true}$, then the unknown DFA contains the transition $\delta(i, a) = j$. Moreover, if f_i is set to $\mathtt{true}$, then i is a final state.

The constraints on the variables $d_{i,a,j}$, f_i, and $x_{u,i}$ now have to express two things. First, the variables $d_{i,a,j}$ have to encode a deterministic function. More precisely, constraints (I) ensure that for each state i and input symbol a there exists at least one outgoing transition whereas constraints (II) assure that there is at most one. Second, the variables $x_{u,i}$ have to encode valid runs with respect to the transition function defined by $d_{i,a,j}$. This means that some state is reached after reading u (cf. constraints (III)). Moreover, $x_{ua,j}$ has to be set to $\mathtt{true}$ if the unknown DFA reaches state i after reading u, i.e., $x_{u,i}$ is set to $\mathtt{true}$, and there exists the transition $\delta(i, a) = j$, i.e., $d_{i,a,j}$ is set to $\mathtt{true}$ (cf. constraints (IV)). Finally, words from S^+ have to lead to accepting states while words from S^- have to lead to rejecting states (cf. constraints (V)).

$$\bigwedge_{i\in[n]} \bigwedge_{a\in\Sigma} \bigvee_{j\in[n]} d_{i,a,j} \tag{I}$$

$$\bigwedge_{i\in[n]} \bigwedge_{a\in\Sigma} \bigwedge_{j,j'\in[n],j<j'} (\neg d_{i,a,j} \vee \neg d_{i,a,j'}) \tag{II}$$

$$\bigwedge_{u\in\mathrm{Pref}(S^+\cup S^-)} \bigvee_{i\in[n]} x_{u,i} \tag{III}$$

$$\bigwedge_{ua\in\mathrm{Pref}(S^+\cup S^-)} \bigwedge_{i,j\in[n]} (\neg x_{u,i} \vee \neg d_{i,a,j} \vee x_{ua,j}) \tag{IV}$$

$$\left(\bigwedge_{u\in S^+} \bigwedge_{i\in[n]} (\neg x_{u,i} \vee f_i) \right) \wedge \left(\bigwedge_{u\in S^-} \bigwedge_{i\in[n]} (\neg x_{u,i} \vee \neg f_i) \right) \tag{V}$$

Let $\psi_{S,n}$ be the conjunction of the constraints (I) to (V). From a model Γ of $\psi_{S,n}$ it is straight-forward how to derive a DFA $\mathcal{A}_\Gamma = ([n], \Sigma, q_0, \delta, F)$: $q_0 = i$ for the unique $i \in [n]$ such that $x_{\varepsilon,i}$ is set to $\mathtt{true}$, $\delta(i, a) = j$ if $d_{i,a,j}$ is set to $\mathtt{true}$, and $F = \{i \in [n] \mid f_i \text{ is set to } \mathtt{true}\}$. Again, an induction over the length of input words shows that $\mathcal{A}_\Gamma$ is in fact consistent with the sample S, and we obtain a result analogous to Lemma 2.

In total, $\psi_{S,n}$ comprises $\mathcal{O}(mn + n^2|\Sigma|)$ variables and $\mathcal{O}(n^3|\Sigma| + mn^2)$ clauses. If n is much smaller than m, which is typically the case, then this encoding is in fact smaller than Grinchtein, Leucker, and Piterman's unary and binary encoding and performs better in the experiments in [7]. However, if the number of words in a sample is small but a minimal consistent DFA has many states, then Heule and Verwer's encoding degenerates. Therefore, the choice which encoding to prefer should depend on the specific situation. We refer to [7] for details.

4   Learning with Membership Queries

Whenever possible, membership queries should be used to improve the learning process. To this end, Grinchtein, Leucker, and Piterman [6] proposed a combination of the approach described in the previous section and that of Angluin's L^* algorithm. Let us first recall the basic details of L^*.

Angluin's learning algorithm [1] is designed for learning a regular language, $L \subseteq \Sigma^*$, by constructing a minimal DFA $\mathcal{A}$ such that $L(\mathcal{A}) = L$. The learner maintains a prefix-closed set $U \subseteq \Sigma^*$ of prefixes, which are candidates for identifying states, and a suffix-closed set $V \subseteq \Sigma^*$ of suffixes, which are used to distinguish such states. The sets U and V are increased when needed during the execution. The learner makes membership queries for all words in $(U \cup U\Sigma)V$, and organizes the results into a *table* $T \colon (U \cup U\Sigma) \to (V \to \{+, -\})$, which maps each $u \in (U \cup U\Sigma)$ to a mapping $T(u) \colon V \to \{+, -\}$ where "+" represents accepted and "−" not accepted. In [1], each function $T(u)$ is called a *row*. In every iteration, the L^* algorithm makes the table closed and consistent:

- A table T is *closed* if for all $u \in U$, $a \in \Sigma$ there is a $u' \in U$ such that $T(ua) = T(u')$. If this is not the case, the algorithm adds ua to U.
- A table T is *consistent* if $T(u) = T(u')$ implies $T(ua) = T(u'a)$ for $u, u' \in U$. If a table is not consistent, then there is a $v \in V$ such that $T(uav) \neq T(u'av)$, and the algorithm adds av to V.

Once the table is both closed and consistent, the learner constructs a hypothesized DFA $\mathcal{A} = (Q, \Sigma, q_0, \delta, F)$, where $Q = \{T(u) \mid u \in U\}$ is the set of distinct rows, q_0 is the row $T(\varepsilon)$, δ is defined by $\delta(T(u), a) = T(ua)$, and $F = \{T(u) \mid u \in U, T(u)(\varepsilon) = +\}$. $\mathcal{A}$ is then submitted as an equivalence query. If the answer is "yes", the learning procedure is finished. Otherwise, the returned counter-example and all of its prefixes are added to U. Then, subsequent membership queries are performed in order to make the new table closed and consistent producing a new hypothesized DFA, etc.

In our setting, queries are no longer answered by either "yes" or "no", but also by "don't care", denoted by ?. Therefore, Grinchtein, Leucker, and Piterman adapt Angluin's algorithm. The idea of a table is kept but now, for every $u \in (U \cup U\Sigma)$, a row is a mapping $T(u) \colon V \to \{+, -, ?\}$. For $u, u' \in (U \cup U\Sigma)$, two rows $T(u)$ and $T(u')$ are said to *look similar*, denoted by $T(u) \equiv T(u')$, if for all $v \in V$, $T(u)(v) \neq ?$ and $T(u')(v) \neq ?$ implies $T(u)(v) = T(u')(v)$. Otherwise, $T(u)$ and $T(u')$ are called *obviously different*. A table T is

- *weakly closed* if for each $u \in U$, $a \in \Sigma$ there is a $u' \in U$ such that $T(ua) \equiv T(u')$, and
- *weakly consistent* if $T(u) \equiv T(u')$ implies $T(ua) \equiv T(u'a)$.

Grinchtein, Leucker, and Piterman's algorithm is sketched in Figure 1. It works like the L^* algorithm, but uses the weak versions of closedness and consistency. However, the problem is that extracting a DFA from a weakly closed and weakly consistent table is no longer immediate. Their solution is to turn a weakly closed and weakly consistent table into a sample $\mathcal{S} = (S^+, S^-)$ where $S^+ = \{uv \mid u \in U, v \in V, T(u)(v) = +\}$ and $S^- = \{uv \mid u \in U, v \in V, T(u)(v) = -\}$. Then, one of the approaches presented in Section 3.3 can be applied to derive a minimal DFA that is consistent with the data in the table.

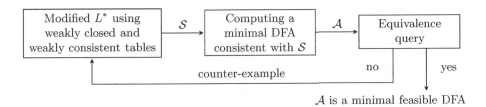

Fig. 1. Grinchtein, Leucker, and Piterman's learning algorithm [6]

Using similar arguments as in Section 3.2, it is not hard to verify that Grinchtein, Leucker, and Piterman's algorithm terminates if there exists a feasible DFA: the learner will never construct the same conjecture twice and two consecutive conjectures will never decrease in size. Moreover, since all feasible DFAs are always consistent with the data in the table and the learner conjectures only minimal DFAs, it will eventually find a smallest feasible DFA. Let us summarize this with the following lemma.

Lemma 3 (Grinchtein, Leucker, and Piterman [6]). *Let an inexperienced teacher be given. If a feasible DFA exists, the learner in Figure 1 terminates eventually and returns a minimal feasible DFA.*

Finally, note that the approach presented in this section shares many similarities with the one presented in [6]. However, there a more involved learning procedure has been elaborated since the underlying problem is different from the problem studied here.

5   An Improved Algorithm for Regular L_1, L_2

Chen et al. [4] consider an improved algorithm of learning from inexperienced teachers for a special case. Their setting differs from Definition 1 in two aspects.

- Both languages L_1 and L_2 have to be regular.
- Rather than equivalence queries, the learner is allowed to ask *containment queries* on a DFA $\mathcal{A}$ of the following types: $L_1 \subseteq L(\mathcal{A})$, $L(\mathcal{A}) \subseteq L_1$, $L_2 \subseteq L(\mathcal{A})$, $L(\mathcal{A}) \subseteq L_2$. The teacher returns either "yes" or a counter-example.

Note that equivalence queries can be "simulated" by containment queries, but the latter provide more information about L_1 and L_2 than ordinary equivalence queries. Moreover, note that here a feasible DFA always exists (e.g., a DFA accepting exactly L_1).

Chen et al. introduce so-called *3-valued DFAs (3DFA)* as succinct representations of the information gathered during the learning process. A 3DFA $\mathcal{C} = (Q, \Sigma, q_0, \delta, \text{Acc}, \text{Rej}, \text{Dont})$ is basically a finite automaton (or a Moore machine) whose states are partitioned into accepting, rejecting and don't care states. In this context, a word $u \in \Sigma^*$ is accepted if $\mathcal{A}\colon q_0 \xrightarrow{u} q$ with $q \in \text{Acc}$, rejected if $\mathcal{A}\colon q_0 \xrightarrow{u} q$ with $q \in \text{Rej}$, and a don't care word if $\mathcal{A}\colon q_0 \xrightarrow{u} q$ with $q \in \text{Dont}$. Moreover, let $\mathcal{C}^+ = (Q, \Sigma, q_0, \delta, \text{Acc} \cup \text{Dont})$ denote the DFA where accepting and don't care states become final states and let $\mathcal{C}^- = (Q, \Sigma, q_0, \delta, \text{Acc})$ be the DFA where only accepting states are final. Finally, a DFA $\mathcal{A}$ is called *consistent with a 3DFA* $\mathcal{C}$ if $\mathcal{A}$ accepts all words that $\mathcal{C}$ accepts and rejects all words that $\mathcal{C}$ rejects, i.e., $L(\mathcal{C}^-) \subseteq L(\mathcal{A})$ and $L(\mathcal{A}) \subseteq L(\mathcal{C}^+)$.

Chen et al.'s idea is to interweave the learning of a 3DFA with a minimization procedure that takes a 3DFA and computes a minimal consistent DFA. The learning part is carried out by a slight modification of Angluin's L^* algorithm [1] adapted to the 3-valued setting (since the changes are only minor, we call it L^* though). The minimization procedure can be any procedure that takes a 3DFA and produces a minimal consistent DFA. Chen et al., e.g., use an algorithm for minimizing incompletely specified sequential switching circuits [10]. Thus, the minimization procedure is a black-box for which various algorithms can be utilized. Note, however, that minimizing 3DFAs in this sense is hard (the corresponding decision problem whether a consistent DFA with $k \geq 1$ states exists is NP-complete).

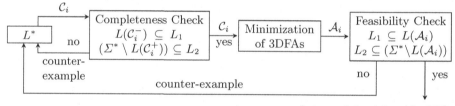

Fig. 2. Chen et al.'s learning algorithm (figure taken from [4])

Figure 2 sketches Chen et al.'s learning algorithm. During the learning process, the L^* algorithm generates conjecture 3DFAs $\mathcal{C}_i$, which generalize the data learned so far. $\mathcal{C}_i$ is given to the minimization routine, which returns a minimal DFA $\mathcal{A}_i$ consistent with $\mathcal{C}_i$. The learner then conducts containment queries to check whether $\mathcal{A}_i$ is feasible. It terminates if the teacher returns "yes". If the teacher returns a counter-example w, then $\mathcal{C}_i$ classifies w incorrectly (since $\mathcal{A}_i$ is consistent with $\mathcal{C}_i$) and the learner passes w back to the L^* algorithm. However, before a 3DFA can be given to the minimization procedure, it has to be checked if $\mathcal{C}_i$ is *complete* with respect to L_1 and L_2, i.e., $L(\mathcal{C}_i^-) \subseteq L_1$ and $(\Sigma^* \setminus L(\mathcal{C}_i^+)) \subseteq L_2$. This is necessary to assure that a conjecture 3DFA does not rule out any (and, hence, also not a minimal) feasible DFA. Two containment queries are used to check whether a 3DFA is complete. Also here, a counter-example obtained from the completeness check indicates that $\mathcal{C}_i$ is still incorrect.

Since the L^* algorithm generates conjectures of increasing size, the hope is that a feasible DFA is found early in the learning process. In the worst case, however, the L^* algorithm learns the unique minimal 3DFA $\mathcal{C}_{L_1,L_2}$ that characterizes L_1 and L_2 exactly, i.e., $L(\mathcal{C}_{L_1,L_2}^-) = L_1$ and $(\Sigma^* \setminus L(\mathcal{C}_{L_1,L_2}^+)) = L_2$, which is then minimized. Since any feasible DFA is consistent with $\mathcal{C}_{L_1,L_2}$, the minimization of $\mathcal{C}_{L_1,L_2}$ yields a minimal feasible DFA. The 3DFA $\mathcal{C}_{L_1,L_2}$ has the size $|\mathcal{B}_1 \times \mathcal{B}_2|$ where $\mathcal{B}_i$ is the minimal DFA accepting L_i, $i = 1, 2$, and $\mathcal{B}_1 \times \mathcal{B}_2$ is the product of $\mathcal{B}_1$ and $\mathcal{B}_2$ defined in the usual way. Thus, Chen et al.'s learner asks $\mathcal{O}(|\mathcal{B}_1 \times \mathcal{B}_2|^2 + |\mathcal{B}_1 \times \mathcal{B}_2|m)$ membership and $\mathcal{O}(|\mathcal{B}_1 \times \mathcal{B}_2|)$ containment queries where m is the length of the longest counter-example. Note, however, that this also means that there are $\mathcal{O}(|\mathcal{B}_1 \times \mathcal{B}_2|)$ calls to the minimization procedure. This is summarized in the following lemma.

Lemma 4 (Chen et al. [4]). *Given an inexperienced teacher for regular languages L_1, L_2 that is able to answer containment queries, the learner in Figure 2 always terminates and returns a minimal feasible DFA. It asks $\mathcal{O}(|\mathcal{B}_1 \times \mathcal{B}_2|^2 + |\mathcal{B}_1 \times \mathcal{B}_2|m)$ membership queries, $\mathcal{O}(|\mathcal{B}_1 \times \mathcal{B}_2|)$ containment queries, and calls the minimization procedure $\mathcal{O}(|\mathcal{B}_1 \times \mathcal{B}_2|)$ times.*

One might be tempted to generalize Chen et al.'s algorithm to the setting of Definition 1. This, however, seems difficult—if it is possible at all. If, on the one hand, the teacher answers equivalence queries rather than containment queries, then a completeness check is no longer possible and one might miss minimal feasible DFAs. On the other hand, if L_1, L_2 are no more regular languages, then the algorithm is not guaranteed to terminate since there might no longer exist a 3DFA $\mathcal{C}_{L_1,L_2}$ that can be learned eventually.

Finally, let us sketch Chen et al.'s adaptation of Angluin's L^* algorithm. Their adaptation is straight-forward and extends the observation table to a mapping $T \colon (U \cup U\Sigma) \to (V \to \{+, -, ?\})$, which allows to store "don't care" entries and is filled at need using membership queries. Rather than in Section 4, $?$ entries are treated as ordinary "output symbols".

Everything else stays basically the same as in Angluin's original algorithm. A *row* $u \in (U \cup U\Sigma)$ is the mapping $T(u)$, and two rows $u, u' \in (U \cup U\Sigma)$ are equal if $T(u) = T(u')$, i.e., $T(u)(v) = T(u')(v)$ for all $v \in V$. The table is *closed* if for all $u \in U$, $a \in \Sigma$ there is a $v \in U$ such that $T(ua) = T(v)$; if this is not the case, then the learner adds ua to U. The table is *consistent* if for all $u, u' \in U$ with $T(u) = T(u')$ and $a \in \Sigma$ we have $T(ua) = T(u'a)$; if this is not the case, then there is a $v \in S$ such that $T(uav) \neq T(u'av)$, and the teacher adds av to V. Once T is closed and consistent, the learner constructs a 3DFA $\mathcal{C} = (Q, \Sigma, q_0, \delta, \text{Acc}, \text{Rej}, \text{Dont})$ with $Q = \{T(u) \mid u \in U\}$, $q_0 = T(\varepsilon)$, $\delta(T(u), a) = T(ua)$, and $\text{Acc} = \{T(u) \mid u \in U, T(u)(\varepsilon) = +\}$, $\text{Rej} = \{T(u) \mid u \in U, T(u)(\varepsilon) = -\}$, and $\text{Dont} = \{T(u) \mid u \in U, T(u)(\varepsilon) = ?\}$. Then, the learner asks containment queries on the DFAs $\mathcal{C}^+$ and $\mathcal{C}^-$. If the teacher returns a counter-example w, then the learner adds $\text{Pref}(\{w\})$ to U and continues. Otherwise, the learner terminates. Using the same proofs as in [1]

Table 1. An overview over learning algorithms that work with inexperienced teachers

Algorithm	Section	Setting and Properties
Naive enumeration	3.1	No membership queries, equivalence queries without counter-examples
Counter-example guided learning	3.2	No membership queries; calls a subprocedure to compute minimal consistent DFAs
Grinchtein, Leucker, and Piterman's learner [6]	4	Most general setting; calls a subprocedure to compute minimal consistent DFAs
Chen et al.'s learner [4]	5	L_1, L_2 have to be regular, containment instead of equivalence queries; polynomial number of queries; calls a subprocedure to minimize 3DFAs

adapted to the 3-valued setting (cf. [4]), one can show that this learner eventually terminates and learns the (unique) minimal 3DFA $\mathcal{C}_{L_1,L_2}$.

An Improvement for Large Feasible DFAs. If all feasible DFAs are large, then Chen et al.'s learner has the drawback that many (expensive) minimizations have to be performed during the learning process. In such a situation, we propose the following much simpler and more direct approach.

1. Learn $\mathcal{C}_{L_1,L_2}$ using Chen et al.'s adapted L^* learning algorithm.
2. Minimize $\mathcal{C}_{L_1,L_2}$ to obtain a minimal feasible DFA.

Although this algorithm also poses at least the same number of membership and containment queries as Chen et al.'s, it makes only one call to the (expensive) minimization procedure. However, there is a trade-off between one call to the minimization procedure with a big 3DFA and many calls with potentially much smaller 3DFAs. Finally, note that this approach also works if the teacher cannot answer containment queries, but allows equivalence queries.

6   Conclusion

We considered the task of learning minimal DFAs from inexperienced teachers. An inexperienced teacher has access to two disjoint languages $L_1, L_2 \subseteq \Sigma^*$ and may answer queries inconclusively: it returns "yes", "no", or "don't care" on membership queries and checks whether a conjecture DFA $\mathcal{A}$ satisfies $L_1 \subseteq L(\mathcal{A})$ and $L_2 \cap L(\mathcal{A}) = \emptyset$ on equivalence queries. Although there can in general only exist semi-algorithms for this task, we surveyed several techniques successfully applied in practice. Table 1 gives a brief overview.

The simplest (and most inefficient) learner naively enumerates all DFAs with respect to their size, successively asks the teacher for equivalence, and terminates once a feasible DFA is found (cf. Section 3.1). This approach is useful if membership queries are unwanted, unavailable, or it is simply too expensive to answer them. Moreover, the naive learner does not need counter-examples, which allows to employ it even in situations where a teacher can only check a conjecture for equivalence but cannot return counter-examples.

In situations where no membership queries are available but the teacher returns counter-examples on equivalence queries, the counter-example guided learner should be used (cf. Section 3.2). The idea of this learner is to maintain a sample consisting of two finite sets of positively and negatively classified counter-examples and to produce only such conjectures that are minimal and consistent with the sample. The counter-example guided learner calls an external algorithm to compute minimal consistent DFAs in a black-box fashion, thus, allowing to experiment with different techniques. Note, however, that finding a minimal consistent DFA is a computationally hard task.

In Section 3.3, we surveyed three techniques to compute minimal DFAs that are consistent with a given sample. The first, due to Bierman and Feldmann [3], uses a CSP to encode accepting and rejecting runs of the unknown minimal DFA on the sample. A model for this CSP can then be used to derive a minimal consistent DFA. The second technique, due to Grinchtein, Leucker, and Piterman [6], translates Bierman and Feldmann's CSP into an equivalent SAT formula. Finally, the third technique, due to Heule and Verwer [7], is a modification of Grinchtein, Leucker, and Piterman's encoding and yields good results in cases where consistent DFAs are small. According to the experiments in [6], SAT-based techniques seem to be more efficient than CSP-based. The choice between both SAT-based techniques, however, heavily depends on the particular setting: if it is a priori known that small consistent DFAs exist, then Heule and Verwer's technique should be used (according to Heule and Verwer's experiments [7]). If, on the other hand, all consistent DFAs are big, then Heule and Verwer's encoding blows up and Grinchtein, Leucker, and Piterman's approach should be preferred.

Whenever possible, membership queries should be used to guide and improve the learning process. In Section 4, we described Grinchtein, Leucker, and Piterman's learning algorithm [6] that works in the most general learning scenario. Their algorithm is similar to the counter-example guided learner, but additionally uses membership queries to accelerate the learning process. Analogous to Angluin's L^* algorithm, Grinchtein, Leucker, and Piterman's algorithm maintains the learned data in a table, which has been adapted to handle "don't care" entries. Once enough data has been gathered, the learner extracts the data from the table into a sample and uses one of the techniques described in Section 3.3 to compute minimal consistent DFA. Again, the technique to compute minimal consistent DFAs might be exchanged for a better fit in particular situations.

If the languages L_1 and L_2 are both regular and the teacher is able to answer containment queries, then the learning task becomes much easier and Chen et al.'s learner [4] can be employed (cf. Section 5). The idea of this learning algorithm is to learn 3DFAs rather than DFAs and to minimize these 3DFAs before the teacher is consulted. Chen et al.'s learner asks only polynomially many queries, but calls a computationally expensive minimization procedure before every feasibility check. Note that the learner uses the minimization procedure in a black-box fashion, which allows to try different techniques. In situations where feasible DFAs are big, we developed a more direct algorithm that needs only one call to the minimization procedure and also works if the teacher answers equivalence rather than containment queries.

Finally, let us briefly comment on the fact that we estimated the number of queries necessary to learn a feasible DFA only for the special case of Chen et al.'s learning algorithm. The reason for this is that this question in its whole generality is still a matter of ongoing research. Similar to [2], we would like to prove (or disprove) that there exists an algorithm that learns a minimal feasible DFA from inexperienced teachers using only a polynomial number of queries. So far, the best bound we can give is the following. If we fix an alphabet Σ, two languages $L_1, L_2 \subseteq \Sigma^*$ and assume that a feasible DFA $\mathcal{A}$ exists, say of size n, then there are at most $n^{\mathcal{O}(n)}$ DFAs of size n or less. Hence, the naive algorithm terminates at least after constructing this number of conjectures. This bound is also valid for both the counter-example guided learner and Grinchtein, Leucker, and Piterman's algorithm since the size of two consecutive conjectures does not decrease in either cases. Although the techniques used in [2] look promising, it is not clear if and how they can be applied to learning from inexperienced teachers.

References

1. Angluin, D.: Learning regular sets from queries and counterexamples. Inf. Comput. 75(2), 87–106 (1987)
2. Angluin, D.: Negative results for equivalence queries. Machine Learning 5, 121–150 (1990)
3. Biermann, A.W., Feldman, J.A.: On the synthesis of finite-state machines from samples of their behavior. IEEE Transactions on Computers C 21(6), 592–597 (1972)
4. Chen, Y.-F., Farzan, A., Clarke, E.M., Tsay, Y.-K., Wang, B.-Y.: Learning Minimal Separating DFA's for Compositional Verification. In: Kowalewski, S., Philippou, A. (eds.) TACAS 2009. LNCS, vol. 5505, pp. 31–45. Springer, Heidelberg (2009)
5. Gold, E.M.: Complexity of automaton identification from given data. Information and Control 37(3), 302–320 (1978)
6. Grinchtein, O., Leucker, M., Piterman, N.: Inferring Network Invariants Automatically. In: Furbach, U., Shankar, N. (eds.) IJCAR 2006. LNCS (LNAI), vol. 4130, pp. 483–497. Springer, Heidelberg (2006)
7. Heule, M., Verwer, S.: Exact DFA Identification Using SAT Solvers. In: Sempere, J.M., García, P. (eds.) ICGI 2010. LNCS, vol. 6339, pp. 66–79. Springer, Heidelberg (2010)
8. Leucker, M.: Learning Meets Verification. In: de Boer, F.S., Bonsangue, M.M., Graf, S., de Roever, W.-P. (eds.) FMCO 2006. LNCS, vol. 4709, pp. 127–151. Springer, Heidelberg (2007)
9. Oliveira, A.L., Silva, J.P.M.: Efficient algorithms for the inference of minimum size dfas. Machine Learning 44(1/2), 93–119 (2001)
10. Paull, M., Unger, S.: Minimizing the number of states in incompletely specified sequential switching functions. IRE Transactions on Electronic Computers (3), 356–367 (1959)

Model Learning and Test Generation
for Event-B Decomposition

Ionut Dinca, Florentin Ipate, and Alin Stefanescu

University of Pitesti, Department of Computer Science
Str. Targu din Vale 1, 110040 Pitesti, Romania
{ionut.dinca,alin.stefanescu}@upit.ro, florentin.ipate@ifsoft.ro

Abstract. Event-B is a formal method for reliable systems specification and verification, which uses model refinement and decomposition as techniques to scale the design of complex systems. In previous work, we proposed an iterative approach for test generation and state model inference based on a variant of Angluin's learning algorithm, which integrates well with the notion of Event-B refinement. In this paper, we extend the method to work also with the mechanisms of Event-B decomposition. Two types of decomposition, i.e. shared-events and shared-variables, are considered and the generation of a global test suite from the local ones is proposed at the end. The implementation of the method is evaluated on publicly available Event-B decomposed models.

1 Introduction

Event-B [1] is a formal method for reliable systems specification and verification, which was introduced about ten years ago and was tuned up in several industrial-academic projects. Event-B models are a type of abstract state machines in which a set of global variables are changed by so called events. When the guard of an event is satisfied, its action code can executed having an effect on the global variables. The main modeling approach in Event-B relies on the notion of refinement, i.e., the modeler starts with an abstract model which is iteratively enriched and concretized by capturing more and more features of the system to be specified. Each refinement step is accompanied by formal proofs for properties of interest for the system. As the complexity of the model increases, so does the difficulty the proof obligations and verification tasks. One powerful method to address this situation is to decompose a larger model into smaller sub-models which can be further refined and analyzed independently [2,3]. There are two main types of decomposition: shared events style [4,5] and shared variables style [6,7]. In the former, the communication and consistency between sub-models is realized via shared events, while in the latter this is done via shared variables.

The current efforts of further developing Event-B are concerted in a large European project, DEPLOY[1], which also includes industrial partners from the embedded and business applications domains (Bosch, Siemens, SAP, SSF).

---

[1] European FP7 project (2008-2012): http://www.deploy-project.eu

T. Margaria and B. Steffen (Eds.): ISoLA 2012, Part I, LNCS 7609, pp. 539–553, 2012.
© Springer-Verlag Berlin Heidelberg 2012

The main platform supporting Event-B, called Rodin [8], is an extensible Eclipse-based tool offering different capabilities such as model refinement, model decomposition, theorem-proving, and model-checking. Complementing the formal verification, *test generation* from Event-B is a recent topic of interest backed by concrete requirements from industry.

Essentially, in order to generate test suites for an Event-B model one has to first construct an equivalent automaton and then apply one of the many finite state based test generation techniques existing in the literature [9,10]. However, as the states of this equivalent automaton are given by the combinations of the model global variables, this may lead to the well-known state explosion problem. In order to address such issue, in our previous work, we have developed an automata learning and test generation approach [11], implemented in a Rodin plug-in [12], that constructs a finite state *approximation* and an associated test suite for an Event-B model. The core of the method relies on a variant of Angluin's algorithm [13] adapted to finite cover automata [14]. A finite cover automaton (CA)[15] represents an approximation of the system which only considers sequences of length up to an established upper bound ℓ. Crucially, the size of the cover automaton, which normally depends on ℓ, can be significantly lower than the size of the exact automaton model. A powerful (conformance) test suite, including appropriate test data, is obtained as a by-product of the learning algorithm. Last but not least, the whole procedure can be applied incrementally, allowing the reuse of the learned model and test cases from the abstract to the more concrete levels of refinement.

The main contribution of this paper is an extension of the above method that integrates not only the Event-B refinement mechanism, but also the different Event-B decomposition styles. More precisely, for decomposition, we investigate the generation of CAs for the sub-models by reusing information via projections from the global model. Also vice-versa, for the recomposition operation we can reuse the information from the CAs of the sub-models for the construction of a CA for the global model. Conformance test suites are also generated alongside. Finally, an integrated approach involving both refinements and (de)compositions in an Event-B development chain is proposed.

The paper is structured as follows. The next section presents prerequisites from formal languages and automata theory. Section 3 shortly recalls the previous work on automata learning for Event-B and Section 4 introduces the extension of this work to Event-B decomposition and recomposition operators. Section 5 provides experiments on publicly available Event-B models, while Section 6 concludes the paper.

2   Preliminaries

In this section we provide theoretical prerequisites on finite automata, cover automata and product automata, together with their accepted languages.

Finite Automata - General Concepts. We start by introducing some classic definitions from automata theory.

A *deterministic finite automaton (DFA)* M is a tuple (A, Q, q_0, F, h), where: A is the finite *input alphabet*; Q is the finite *set of states*; $q_0 \in Q$ is the *initial state*; $F \subseteq Q$ is the *set of final states*; h is the *next-state*, $h : Q \times A \longrightarrow Q$. A DFA is usually described by a *state-transition diagram*. The next-state function h can be naturally extended to a function $h : Q \times A^* \longrightarrow Q$, where $A^* := \bigcup_{i \geq 0} A^i$. A state $q \in Q$ is called *reachable* if there exists $s \in A^*$ such that $h(q_0, s) = q$. M is called *reachable* if all states of M are reachable.

Given $q \in Q$, the set L_M, called the *language accepted by* M, is defined by $L_M = \{s \in A^* \mid h(q_0, s) \in F\}$. A DFA M is called *minimal* if any DFA that accepts L_M has at least the same number of states as M. A classic results states that there exists a unique (up to a renaming of the state space) minimal DFA that accepts a given regular language [16].

Now let us also introduce the concept of *deterministic finite cover automaton* (DFCA). Informally, a DFCA of a finite language U, as defined by Câmpeanu et al. [15], is a DFA that accepts all sequences in U and possibly other sequences that are longer than any sequence in U.

In this paper we use a slightly more general concept, as defined in [14]: given a finite language $U \subseteq A^*$ and a positive integer ℓ that is greater than or equal to the length of the longest sequence(s) in U, a *deterministic finite cover automaton (DFCA)* of U w.r.t. ℓ is a DFA M that accepts all sequences in U and possibly other sequences that are longer than ℓ, i.e. $L_M \cap A[\ell] = U$, where $A[\ell] := \bigcup_{0 \leq i \leq \ell} A^i$. A DFCA M of U w.r.t. ℓ is called *minimal* if any DFCA of U w.r.t ℓ has at least the same number of states as M. Note that, unlike the case in which the acceptance of the exact language is required, the minimal DFCA is not necessarily unique (up to a renaming of the state space) [14].

Naturally, a DFA that accepts a finite language U is also a DFCA of U w.r.t. any $\ell \geq \|U\|$. Consequently, the number of states of a minimal DFCA of U w.r.t. ℓ will not exceed the number of states of the minimal DFA accepting U. Furthermore (and more importantly from the point of view of practical applications), the size of a minimal DFCA of U w.r.t. ℓ can be much smaller than the size of the minimal DFA that accepts U [14].

Product Automata and Projections - General Concepts. We now provide a couple of definitions and results for product automata and languages. This is a prerequisite for the setting of decomposed Event-B models that we present later on. To simplify the presentation, we only consider the case the two automata, but the definitions and the results hold also for more than two automata.

We start by describing formally the product of two automata synchronizing on their common input symbols. First of all, since the two automata have different input alphabets A_1 and A_2, their transition function is extended to the whole set of symbols $A = A_1 \cup A_2$ using the following definition. Given DFA $M = (B, Q, q_0, F, h)$ and $B \subset A$ we define the DFA $Ext_A(M) = (A, Q, q_0, F, h')$ by: for every $q \in Q$ and $a \in A$, $h'(q, b) = h(q, b)$ if $b \in B$ and $h'(q, a) = q$ if $a \in A \setminus B$.

When the two automata operate on the same input alphabet, their product can be described in a traditional fashion, as follows:

Definition 1. *Let* $M_1 = (A, Q_1, q_{01}, F_1, h_1)$ *and* $M_2 = (A, Q_2, q_{02}, F_2, h_2)$ *be two DFAs. Then we define the DFA* $M_1 \times M_2 = (A, Q, q_0, F, h)$ *by:* $Q = Q_1 \times Q_2$, $q_0 = (q_{01}, q_{02})$, $F = F_1 \times F_2$ *and for every* $q_1 \in Q_1$, $q_2 \in Q_2$, $a \in A$, $h((q_1, q_2), a) = (h_1(q_1, a), h_2(q_2, a))$.

Thus, for two DFAs M_1 and M_2 over alphabets A_1 and A_2, we denote by $M_1 \parallel M_2 := Ext_A(M_1) \times Ext_A(M_2)$ the *product automaton* over alphabet $A = A_1 \cup A_2$ capturing the synchronization on common symbols of M_1 and M_2. This is similar to the standard synchronization of labeled transition systems used in the literature (see e.g. [17]).

The languages accepted by product automata are characterized by the so-called *product languages*. For their definition, we first need the notion of *projection*. Given a sequence $s \in A^*$ and $A_1 \subset A$, the projection of s on A_1, denoted by $proj_{A_1}(s)$, is the sequence obtained from s by removing all symbols not in A_1. For a language $L \subseteq A^*$, $proj_{A_1}(L) = \{proj_{A_1}(s) \mid s \in L\}$. Now, we can define the notion of *product language*:

Definition 2. *Let* A_1 *and* A_2 *be two alphabets, not necessarily disjoint, and* $A := A_1 \cup A_2$. *Then, a language* $L \subseteq A^*$ *is called a* product language *(over* A_1 *and* A_2) *if and only if there exist two languages* $L_1 \subseteq A_1^*$ *and* $L_2 \subseteq A_2^*$ *such that*

$$L = \{w \in A^* \mid proj_{A_1}(w) \in L_1 \text{ and } proj_{A_2}(w) \in L_2\}.$$

Moreover, there exist also a useful result (see e.g. [18]) proving that a product language is always the product of its projections, i.e. languages L_1 and L_2 in the previous definition can be replaced by $proj_{A_1}(L)$ and $proj_{A_2}(L)$, respectively. Finally, the expected result relating the languages of product automata with product languages says that:

Proposition 1. *[18] The class of regular product languages coincides with the class of languages accepted by products of DFAs.*

Corollary 1. *For a finite alphabet* $A := A_1 \cup A_2$, *let* $L \subseteq A^*$ *be a regular product language, and* M_1 *and* M_2 *be two DFAs for* $proj_{A_1}(L)$ *and* $proj_{A_2}(L)$, *respectively. Then,* $L = L_{M_1 \parallel M_2}$.

Since any finite language is also a regular language, Corollary 1 holds also when L is a finite product language. Therefore, we can easily derive:

Corollary 2. *For a finite alphabet* $A := A_1 \cup A_2$, *let* $U \subseteq A^*$ *be a finite product language and* ℓ *a positive bound (larger than the size of any word in* U). *If* M_1 *and* M_2 *are two DFCAs w.r.t.* ℓ *for* $proj_{A_1}(U)$ *and* $proj_{A_2}(U)$, *then* $M_1 \parallel M_2$ *is a DFCA w.r.t.* ℓ *for* U.

3 Cover Automata Based Learning and Test Generation for Event-B

In this section we present the main elements of the approach proposed in [11], that can incrementally construct a series of finite state approximations and corresponding test suites for a series of Event-B refined models. Before that, we need to provide the basic elements of Event-B.

A Short Introduction to Event-B. Event-B [1] is a formal methodology having its mathematical foundations rooted in set theory and first order logic. A Event-B specification consists of a static part called *context* and a dynamic part called *machine*. A context defines a set of datatypes as carrier sets, constants and axioms that relate the constants to the carrier sets. A machine will be specified by a set of global *variables* and a set of *events*, which are the first-class citizens of the formalism. Moreover, a set of *invariants* captures the properties of the specified system. Proof obligations solved (automatically or manually) by the supporting platform will ensure that the invariants are always true, i.e. both before and after the execution of any event.

An event is an element consisting of a set of *local parameters*, a *guard* and an *action* code. An event *evt* has the following general form:

$$evt \; \widehat{=} \; \textbf{any } t \textbf{ where } G(t, v) \textbf{ then } S(v, t) \textbf{ end.} \tag{1}$$

Above, t is a set of local parameters, v is a set of global variables appearing in the event, G is a predicate over t and v, called the guard, and $S(v, t)$ represents a substitution. If the guard of an event is false, the event cannot occur and is called disabled. The substitution S modifies the values of the global variables in the set v. It can use the old values from v and the parameters from t. For example, an event that adds a number i smaller than 9 to a global variable n, in case n is greater than 15, is modeled as:

$$increment \; \widehat{=} \; \textbf{any } i \textbf{ where } i \in \mathbb{N} \wedge i < 9 \wedge n > 15 \textbf{ then } n := n + i \textbf{ end.}$$

The semantics of an Event-B model is based on the execution of its events. First of all, a special event called *Initialisation*, which does not have a guard, is executed; usually, its action will set initial values to the global variables. Then, in a loop, all the guards of the events are evaluated and the set of enabled events is established. From them, one event is nondeterministically chosen and its action is executed, some of the variables being updated. The process then iterates. Note that the state space of the model is not explicit, but is implicitly given by the evolving values of the variables.

Given an Event-B model, *a test case* can be defined as a sequence of events. This can be either positive, if it corresponds to a feasible (i.e. executable) path through the Event-B model, or negative, otherwise. The feasibility of a test case implies the existence of appropriate *test data* for the events, i.e. an appropriate initialization of the global variables and suitable values for the local parameters, such that all the guards of the events in the sequence are satisfied. Furthermore, a *test suite* is by definition a collection of test cases.

Given an Event-B model Z having its set of events denoted by E, we can define the language of Z to be the set of feasible sequences over E, i.e.

$$L(Z) := \{w \in E^* \mid w \text{ is feasible in } Z\}.$$

Note that $L(Z)$ is not regular in general, since one can easily simulate a two-counter machine in Event-B, so the formalism is Turing-complete [16]. However, we can naturally obtain a regular subset by considering only a finite subset of $L(Z)$, namely the sequences of length up to a bound ℓ, i.e. $L(Z, \ell) := L(Z) \cap E[\ell]$.

Finally, the *refinement in Event-B* is a mechanism of constructing a series of more abstract models before reaching a very detailed one. For instance, in a refinement step, new variables and new events can be introduced and the existing events can be made more concrete with the assumption (that must be formally proved) that the concrete guard is not weaker than the abstract one (i.e. the concrete guard logically implies the abstract one) [1].

Incremental Model Learning Based on Cover Automata. In [11] we present an automata learning and test generation procedure for Event-B: given an Event-B model Z and a positive bound ℓ, we produce a DFCA M for $U :=$ $L(Z, \ell)$ and an associated test suite. The procedure can be iteratively used for a series of model refinements.

The core of the procedure is based on a modification of Angluin's learning algorithm [14] that is specialized to finite languages, and that is more efficient than the original Angluin's algorithm, called L^*, for regular languages [13].

In a similar but not trivial way, in [14] we extend Angluin's work by proposing an algorithm, called L^ℓ, for learning a DFCA. Given an unknown finite set $U \subseteq A^*$ and a known integer ℓ that is greater than or equal to the length of the longest sequence(s) in U, the L^ℓ algorithm will construct a minimal DFCA of U w.r.t. ℓ. Analogously to L^*, the L^ℓ algorithm uses membership and language equivalence queries to find the automaton in polynomial time.

The L^ℓ algorithm constructs two sets: S, a non-empty, prefix-closed set of sequences and W, a non-empty, suffix-closed set of sequences. Additionally, S will not contain sequences longer than ℓ and W will not contain sequences longer than $\ell - 1$, i.e. $S \subseteq A[\ell]$ and $W \subseteq A[\ell - 1]$. The algorithm keeps an *observation table*, which is a mapping T from a set of finite sequences to $\{0, 1, -1\}$. The sequences in the table are formed by concatenating each sequence of length at most ℓ from the set $S \cup SA$ with each sequence from the set W. Thus, the table can be represented by a two-dimensional array with rows labeled by elements of $(S \cup SA) \cap A[\ell]$ and columns labeled by elements of W. The function T : $((S \cup SA) \cap A[\ell])W \longrightarrow \{0, 1, -1\}$ is defined by $T(u) = 1$ if $u \in U$, $T(u) = 0$ if $u \in A[\ell] \setminus U$ and $T(u) = -1$ if $u \notin A[\ell]$. The values 0 and 1, respectively, are used to indicate whether a sequence is contained in U or not. However, only sequences of length less than or equal to ℓ are of interest. For the others, an extra value, -1, is used. Similar to the L^* algorithm, two properties of the observation table are defined: *consistency* and *closedness*.

The algorithm starts with $S = W = \{\epsilon\}$. It periodically checks the consistency and closedness properties and extends the table accordingly using membership queries. When both conditions are met, the DFA $M(S, W, T)$ corresponding to the table is constructed and it is checked whether the language L accepted by $M(S, W, T)$ satisfies $L \cap A[\ell] = U$. If this language query fails, a counterexample t is produced, the table is expanded to include t and all its prefixes and the consistency and closedness checks are performed once more. Eventually, the language query will succeed and the algorithm will return a minimal DFCA of U w.r.t. ℓ.

The iterative procedure of the algorithm for Event-B is shortly presented below. The technical details can be found in [11]. The main idea is that we evolve the observation table based on previous versions of it, by reusing existing information whenever possible. In particular, for the Event-B refinement, the observation tables of the refined model is not generated from scratch, but from the table of the abstract model that is refined, so unlike the original L^ℓ algorithm, the procedure does not start with empty S, W and T, but with some initial values S_0, W_0 and T_0, which reflect the current knowledge about the DFCA model. An important observation is that, for efficiency reasons, in the recalculation of the observation table only a part of the previous information is sufficient, viz. $S_{min} \subseteq S$ and $W_{min} \subseteq W$, which satisfy certain properties: they are a proper state cover and strong characterization set, respectively (see [11] for definitions).

For the first execution of the procedure, the initial sets S_0 and W_0 are based on an initial estimation of the states of the model. In the worst case (when no initial estimation is available), we take $S_0 = \{\epsilon\}$, $W_0 = \{\epsilon\} \cup E$, where E is the set of events. Note that the alphabet A from L^ℓ above is now the set E. When the procedure has been applied at least once, previous information can be reused. If the model is not totally accurate and needs to be improved, we can distinguish the different reasons for that:

- **Case 1:** the Event-B model has been modified or augmented due to changes in the requirements.
- **Case 2:** the Event-B model has not been changed but the associated DFCA is deemed to be insufficient for testing purposes. In this case, the upper bound ℓ is increased according to the existing testing needs and the procedure is executed once more for the new value of ℓ.
- **Case 3:** the existing Event-B model has been refined and extra detail has been added (using the Event-B refinement). In this case, information from the abstract model can be reused in the computation of the refined model.

A test suite TS can be derived from the observation table as follows:

$$TS := \{t \in E^* \mid t \in ((S \cup SE) \cap E[\ell])W \text{ such that } T(t) = 1\}. \tag{2}$$

Note that we only take positive test cases into account in TS. However, we could also use the existing information about infeasible sequences, i.e. T(t)=0, to generate negative tests, if such a testing requirement exists. Moreover, in (2) we usually take S and W to be the sets S_{min} and W_{min} mentioned above. Furthermore, the test cases from TS are provided with the test data that prove their feasibility. The test data is obtained during the construction of the observation table T, because the membership queries, i.e. feasibility checks, are implemented using a dedicated set-based constraint solver for Event-B, which also returns the values of variables and local parameters for a given feasible sequence. As discussed in [11], TS will constitute a conformance test suite for the Event-B model modulo the bound ℓ (the ℓ-bounded behavior of the model). Such a test suite is more powerful than test suite based on simple state or transition coverage criteria since it covers all states and all transitions of the equivalent automaton and also checks each state and the initial and destination states of each transition. Conformance testing is especially relevant in the embedded systems domain.

4   Model Learning for Event-B Decomposition

4.1   Event-B Decomposition Styles

There are two main decomposition styles in Event-B: shared-events [4,5] and shared-variables [6,7]. Other variants such as *atomicity decomposition* [4,19] or *modularization* [20,3] also exist, but we do not address them in this paper for the following reasons. Since the atomicity decomposition is in fact a special case of refinement, our method in [11] works for it out-of-the-box. On the other hand, modularization defines a different approach to decomposition that reuses a sub-model in several other models using interface specifications, so we leave its investigation to the future (moreover, there is some yet to be solved integration issues between the modularization plug-in and the Event-B constraint solver that we use).

Shared Events Decomposition. In the case of shared events decomposition, an Event-B model is decomposed into several sub-models such that all its events and variables are distributed over the local models. As the name suggests, the local sets of events may have common events (shared events). However, the local sets of variables are disjoint, i.e. the partition of the variables will determine the structure of the decomposition. The left hand side of Fig. 1 presents a minimalistic example of shared events decomposition. At the top, we have a global model Z with three events $\{ev_A, ev_B, ev_C\}$ and two global variables $\{var_1, var_2\}$. The lines between the events and variables suggests the dependencies between them, e.g $ev_A - var_1$ means that var_1 appears in the guard or/and action of ev_A. Assume that the modeler chose to distribute the variables over two sub-models: the first one, denoted Z_1, takes over var_1, and the second, Z_2, takes over var_2. Then, the events are distributed to Z_1 and Z_2 according to the distribution of the variables, so Z_1 has ev_A and ev_B as events (because they depend on var_1) and similarly, Z_2 has ev_B and ev_C as events. In this case, ev_B is a shared event for Z_1 and Z_2.

However, there is a technical issue to be solved for ev_B; the fact that ev_B depends on both var_1 and var_2, while the local models contain only one of the variables. This means that the local events corresponding to ev_B, denoted in Fig. 1 by ev_{B_1} and ev_{B_2}, will only be restricted versions of ev_B that only depend on var_1 and var_2, respectively. So, for the decomposition to be possible, ev_B should have such a form that "separates" the use of var_1 and var_2 in its guards and actions. This is a task for the modeler that should design the Event-B specification in this way as a preparation step for decomposition (refinement may be use in previous modeling steps to achieve this goal). Below, we present ev_B, ev_{B_1}, and ev_{B_2} using the general form of an event in (1):

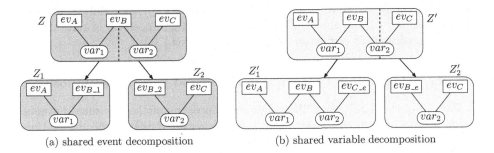

(a) shared event decomposition   (b) shared variable decomposition

Fig. 1. The shared event vs. shared variable decomposition styles

$$ev_B \; \hat{=} \; \textbf{any } t, t_1, t_2 \textbf{ where } G_1(t, t_1, var_1) \wedge G_1(t, t_2, var_2)$$
$$\textbf{then } S_1(var_1, t, t_1); S_2(var_2, t, t_2) \textbf{ end.}$$
$$ev_{B\_1} \; \hat{=} \; \textbf{any } t, t_1 \textbf{ where } G_1(t, t_1, var_1) \textbf{ then } S_1(var_1, t, t_1) \textbf{ end.}$$
$$ev_{B\_2} \; \hat{=} \; \textbf{any } t, t_2 \textbf{ where } G_2(t, t_2, var_2) \textbf{ then } S_2(var_2, t, t_2) \textbf{ end.}$$

Above, we see that ev_B has a set of local parameters t, t_1, t_2, a guard that is the conjunction of two guards using var_1 and var_2 separately, and also an action that can be split into two actions that do not mix the two global variables. The local events will then only use the parts of the guards and actions that refer to their corresponding global variable. Without going into details, it is also important to observe the existence of the common local parameter t, which can be used for passing data between ev_{B_1} and ev_{B_2}. This makes the shared event decomposition suitable for specifying distributed systems communicating via message-passing [19]. Finally, we mention also the fact that the decomposition mechanism is correct in the sense of Event-B refinement [1], by proving specific proof obligations (e.g. deadlock freedom) and putting restrictions on the subsequent refinements of the shared events in the local sub-models.

The decomposition operation induces the inverse operation of *composition*, for which a dedicated Rodin plug-in exists [21]. It takes a input two models Z_1 and Z_2 that may have events with the same name and constructs a composed model Z (look at Fig. 1 bottom-up). Z is obtained by putting together the variables and events Z_1 and Z_2, taking care that the local shared events are merged by concatenating their guards and actions following the same scheme as for ev_{B_1}, ev_{B_2}, and ev_B above.

Shared Variables Decomposition. Let us also touch upon the shared variables decomposition, using the exemplification on the right of Fig. 1. In this case, we partition the set of events and then distribute the variables. If we partition the events of Z' into $\{ev_A, ev_B\}$ and $\{ev_C\}$, due to the variables dependences, the sub-models Z'_1 and Z'_2 have the variables $\{var_1, var_2\}$ and $\{var_2\}$, so they share variable var_2. However, since sub-models have in fact two copies of the shared variable, they need to learn the changes made to the shared variable in the other sub-models. This is implemented adding so-called *external* events. For instance, in addition to its "native" event ev_C, Z'_2 will also include an external event ev_{B_e} that is a restricted version of ev_B, that only simulates its effect on var_2. Note that the shared variables decomposition is suitable for the specification and verification of parallel programs [7].

4.2   Learning and Test Generation for Shared Events Decomposition

In the rest of the paper, we will present our approach only for the shared events decomposition. We can do this without loss of generality based on the observation that, for our purposes, the shared variables decomposition can be reduced to the shared event decomposition as follows. Suppose Z' is decomposed using shared variables into Z'_1 and Z'_2 and the decomposition is based on the partition of set of events E of Z' into E_1 and E_2 Assume that $E_{11} \subseteq E_1$ is the set of external events for Z_1 and $E_{21} \subseteq E_2$ the set of external events for Z_2. Then, if we duplicate the shared variables and consider each of the two Event-B components to work on its own copy (the definition of the shared variables ensures that they process the two copies identically), the shared variables decomposition can be transformed into a shared events decomposition of Z' into sub-models with set of events $E'_1 = E_1 \cup E_{21}$ and $E'_2 = E_2 \cup E_{12}$, respectively.

Before we proceed, we establish a formal relation between Event-B decomposition and the theory of product languages from Section 2. The proofs of the theoretical results can be found in the long version of our paper [22].

Lemma 1. *Let Z be an Event-B model, which is decomposed into Z_1 and Z_2. Then, for any w sequence of events in Z, w is feasible if and only if, $proj_1(w)$ and $proj_2(w)$ are both feasible in Z_1 and Z_2, respectively.*

Using Lemma 1 and Definition 2 for product languages, we can show that:

Proposition 2. *Let Z be an Event-B model, which can be decomposed into Z_1 and Z_2. Then, the language of Z, $L(Z)$, is a product language over $E := E_1 \cup E_2$, where E_1 are the events of Z_1 and E_2 are the events of Z_2.*

As an immediate corollary, the result holds also when we impose a bound ℓ, i.e. $L(Z, \ell)$ is also a product language, so Corollary 2 can be applied.

Next we now show how our learning and test generation method can be applied to the two operations of decomposition and composition.

Approach for Decomposition. Let Z be an Event-B model and E the set of events of Z. We assume that Z is decomposed, using the shared events scheme, into models Z_1 and Z_2 with event sets E_1 and E_2, respectively. Given a bound ℓ, our goal is to obtain DFCAs and associated test suites for Z, Z_1, and Z_2. Although one can apply the method in Section 3 directly and separately on Z, Z_1, and Z_2, we would like to improve the process by reusing information.

We assume that we have a DFCA M and a test suite TS for Z. Then, the DFCA learning procedure for Z_1 will not start with $S_1 = \{\epsilon\}$, as when no previous model is available, but with the set $S_1 = \{proj_1(s) \mid s \in S_{min}\}$, where S_{min} is the proper state cover derived from the DFCA model of Z. The set

W_1 is initialized with $E_1 \cup \{\epsilon\}$. Similarly for Z_2. We could also to start with a projection of the set W obtained for Z (i.e. $W_1 = \{proj_1(s) \mid s \in W_{min}\}$), but, this may not improve performance since W usually contains only singletons [11].

With this input, the learning procedure may not produce a correct DFCA M_1 for Z_1 from the beginning and more iterations may be needed. The reason is that, even though Lemma 1 ensures that a feasible path in Z is projected to a feasible path in Z_1, the projection S_1 may not be rich enough to cover all the states of M_1. This can be understood from the fact that, in general, there is no concrete relation between the sizes of a minimal DFA of a regular language $L \subseteq A^*$ and of the minimal DFA of its projection on a sub-alphabet $A' \subset A$. Thus, the size of a minimal DFA accepting the projection $proj_{A'}(L)$ can be smaller, equal to, or even exponentially larger than the size of the minimal DFA accepting L [23]. The same holds even when L is a finite language. Moreover, in the specific case of Event-B decomposition, the DFCAs of the sub-models may be larger not only because of the effects of the projections just mentioned, but also because there might exist more feasible paths in the projections due to the weakened guards of the shared events, with the effect that the DFCAs for the local sub-models have more states. However, our experiments showed that our choice of S_1 will speed up the learning procedure, generating richer DFCAs in less time compared to the procedure of learning an DFCA for Z_1 from scratch.

Approach for Composition. The inverse operation to decomposition is that of composition [21,5]. Given two models Z_1 and Z_2 with event sets E_1 and E_2, one can construct an Event-B model Z that synchronizes on the shared events.

There are several ways in which we can construct a global DFCA model and/or a test suite for Z from Z_1 and Z_2 or their DFCAs:

1. Construct Z and then apply the techniques of [11] to derive a DFCA and a test suite associated to Z. In this case, there is no reuse of information from Z_1 and Z_2.
2. Construct the two DFCAs M_1 and M_2 for Z_1 and Z_2 and then construct the product $M_1 \parallel M_2$, minimize it and denote it M_{min}. Then, construct a test suite TS from the minimal DFCA M_{min} using the W-method adapted to bounded testing [10]. For every test sequence s for M_{min}, the test data generation process will check if $proj_1(s)$ and $proj_2(s)$ are test sequences for M_1 and M_2, respectively. If this is the case, the test data values for $proj_1(s)$ and $proj_2(s)$ will be reused. This variant is sound due to Corollary 2.
3. Construct only a global test suite TS from the local test suites TS_1 and TS_2 by composing individually the test cases, i.e. $TS := \{t \in E^* \mid proj_1(t) \in TS_1 \text{ and } proj_2(t) \in TS_2\}$. (Optionally, apply a symmetry reduction by only keeping traces in TS that are not equivalent modulo swapping of independent events.)
4. Construct directly a DFCA for the composed model Z without applying the composition of Z_1 and Z_2, nor the product of M_1 and M_2. This is done by applying a learning algorithm for global sequences of events (of length up to ℓ) and answering the global membership queries via answering the local membership queries for the projections (this is sound because of Lemma 1).

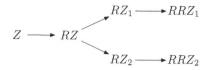

Fig. 2. A sample of decomposition flow

The first two proposals above are correct, i.e. the obtained automata are DFCAs with respect to $L(Z, \ell)$, while the last two are heuristics that in our experiments produced reasonable results, even though they are in general only approximations.

Approach for Integrated Process. Finally, let us sketch how the above proposals can be integrated in our incremental, refinement based, model learning and test generation strategy presented in [11].

Figure 2 describes a typical incremental development in Event-B involving decomposition. There, RZ, which is a refinement of Z, is decomposed into RZ_1 and RZ_2, which are further refined into RRZ_1 and RRZ_2. For this example, our approach will first construct a DFCA model for Z, which will be reused in the construction of a DFCA for RZ. RZ will constitute the basis for the construction of the DFCAs for RZ_1 and RZ_2 starting the learning procedure with the projections as previously explained. The DFCAs for RZ_1 and RZ_2 will, in turn, be reused in the construction of the final models, for RRZ_1 and RRZ_2. These latter models are used to produce a DFCA model and tests for the overall system by one of the methods proposed for the composition operator.

5   Experiments

We implemented the methods for decomposition presented in this paper, extending our Rodin plug-in that previously only addressed refinement [12]. The experiments were conducted on a Windows 7 Professional 64-bit machine with an Intel Core i7 2.80GHz (8 CPUs) processor and 12 GB of RAM.

For the benchmark, we investigated all the publicly available Event-B models involving decomposition from the DEPLOY repository[2]. From the total of eight found models, we could not use two of them because they involved some advanced data types that were not yet supported by the Event-B constraint solver deployed for the membership queries. From the rest of six models, the first three use shared events and the last three use shared variables. Their dimensions are presented in Table 1. The first column gives their name together with a reference. The second column gives the evolution of the models by the operations of refinement and decomposition in a similar fashion to Fig. 2. The '/' symbol represents a refinement step, while '{' depicts a decomposition. For instance, for BepiColombo_SE, there are three refinement steps $m_0/m_1/m_2/m_3$, followed by a decomposition of m_3 into m_4 and m_5; then, m_4 is further refined to m_6 and m_7. The third and forth

---

[2] http://deploy-eprints.ecs.soton.ac.uk

Table 1. The dimensions of 6 models from DEPLOY repository (development process, no. of events and no. of variables)

Subject	Development process	No. events $(m_0/m_1...)$	No. variables $(m_0/m_1...)$
BepiColombo_SE from [19]	$m_0/m_1/m_2/m_3 \left\{ \begin{array}{l} m_4/m_6/m_7 \\ m_5 \end{array} \right.$	$6/11/13/17 \left\{ \begin{array}{l} 15/19/23 \\ 10 \end{array} \right.$	$5/10/12/16 \left\{ \begin{array}{l} 12/16/20 \\ 4 \end{array} \right.$
UpdateMaster_SE from [3]	$m_0/m_1/m_2 \left\{ \begin{array}{l} m_3/m_5/m_7 \\ m_4/m_6/m_8 \end{array} \right.$	$5/6/6 \left\{ \begin{array}{l} 4/5/5 \\ 4/6/6 \end{array} \right.$	$4/5/5 \left\{ \begin{array}{l} 4/6/6 \\ 3/8/8 \end{array} \right.$
Monitor_SE from [3]	$m_0/m_1/m_2 \left\{ \begin{array}{l} m_3/m_6/m_9 \\ m_4/m_7/m_{10} \\ m_5/m_8/m_{11} \end{array} \right.$	$7/7/7 \left\{ \begin{array}{l} 7/5/5 \\ 4/6/6 \\ 4/6/6 \end{array} \right.$	$4/6/6 \left\{ \begin{array}{l} 2/4/4 \\ 2/3/3 \\ 2/3/3 \end{array} \right.$
Monitor_SV from [3]	$m_0/m_1/m_2 \left\{ \begin{array}{l} m_3/m_6/m_9 \\ m_4/m_7 \\ m_5/m_8/m_{10} \end{array} \right.$	$7/11/11 \left\{ \begin{array}{l} 9/11/11 \\ 10/10 \\ 7/7/9 \end{array} \right.$	$4/4/4 \left\{ \begin{array}{l} 2/5/5 \\ 3/4 \\ 3/4/6 \end{array} \right.$
QResponse_SV	$m_0/m_1/m_2/m_3/m_4 \left\{ \begin{array}{l} m_5 \\ m_6 \\ m_7 \end{array} \right.$	$2/3/4/5/5 \left\{ \begin{array}{l} 3 \\ 5 \\ 3 \end{array} \right.$	$2/3/5/7/9 \left\{ \begin{array}{l} 4 \\ 7 \\ 4 \end{array} \right.$
FindP_SV from [7]	$m_0 \left\{ \begin{array}{l} m_1/m_3/m_4/m_5 \\ m_2 \end{array} \right.$	$6 \left\{ \begin{array}{l} 4/5/6/6 \\ 4 \end{array} \right.$	$5 \left\{ \begin{array}{l} 3/4/5/6 \\ 3 \end{array} \right.$

columns provide the corresponding numbers of events and global variables for the models. For example, BepiColombo starts at m_0 with 6 events and 5 global variables, increases its complexity via refinement to m_3 which exhibits 17 events and 16 variables, and ends up having 23 events and 20 variables for the last refinement m_7 of one of the sub-models.

Note that the search space in BepiColombo case can be very large. E.g. the third refinement m_3 of BepiColombo has 17 events, so for $\ell := 8$ the number of possible sequences or tests of length up to 8 is 17^8 which is almost equal to $7 \cdot 10^9$. Moreover, to this complexity we have to add the computation time for test data for the generated test cases. The constraint solver performing this task need to address a search space implied by 16 global variables of type *Set* and 17 local parameters appearing in the events.

In our experiments, we checked the feasibility of our approach and the scalability of the implementation, by performing the steps for the integrated process at the end of the previous section, i.e. we incrementally construct DFCAs for the refinement and decomposition from abstract model to more concrete levels, combining the (integration) tests at the end using a method for composition. Due to space constraints, we provide the tables with experimental results only in the extended version of our paper [22]. However, we report a successful generation of DFCAs and test suites within reasonable time (max. 6 minutes) for sufficiently high values of ℓ (up to 13 for smaller models). Moreover, the experiments confirmed that the reuse improves the quality of the generated DFCAs (i.e. more states compared to learning from scratch) and reduces the computation time in many cases.

6 Conclusions

In this paper, we presented a method for automata learning and test generation that can be applied along the specification process of Event-B. We focused on the mechanism of decomposition, because this is an important way of dealing with the large models that may occur in industrial practice. Our approach makes use of the advantages of cover automata and its soundness is based on the theory of product languages. In the future, we will continue to improve the prototype e.g. by a better (UI) integration with decomposition and composition plug-ins [2,21] and extend its use to the modularization plug-in [20]. We will also investigate the quality of the generated test suites using mutation testing techniques.

In the end, we mention a couple of related papers, even though they solve different problems in different settings. First, we are not aware of any work that generates test cases for Event-B decomposed models, see e.g. [24] and the references therein. An idea of using model projections combined with automata learning for black-box testing of components is presented in [25]. Our relation between learning and conformance test suite is similar to the one presented in [26]. Learning is also used for the generation of communicating automata [27,28] and for compositional verification of system components [17].

Acknowledgments. This work was supported by project DEPLOY, FP7 EC grant no. 214158, and Romanian National Authority for Scientific Research (CNCS-UEFISCDI) grant no. PN-II-ID-PCE-2011-3-0688 (project MuVet) and grant no. 7/05.08.2010.

References

1. Abrial, J.-R.: Modeling in Event-B – System and Software Engineering. Cambridge University Press (2010)
2. Silva, R., Pascal, C., Son Hoang, T., Butler, M.: Decomposition tool for Event-B. Softw., Pract. Exper. 41(2), 199–208 (2011), Plug-in webpage: `http://wiki.event-b.org/index.php/Event_Model_Decomposition`
3. Son Hoang, T., Iliasov, A., Silva, R., Wei, W.: A survey on Event-B decomposition. ECEASST 46, 1–15 (2011)
4. Butler, M.: Decomposition Structures for Event-B. In: Leuschel, M., Wehrheim, H. (eds.) IFM 2009. LNCS, vol. 5423, pp. 20–38. Springer, Heidelberg (2009)
5. Silva, R., Butler, M.: Shared Event Composition/Decomposition in Event-B. In: Aichernig, B.K., de Boer, F.S., Bonsangue, M.M. (eds.) FMCO 2010. LNCS, vol. 6957, pp. 122–141. Springer, Heidelberg (2011)
6. Abrial, J.-R.: Event model decomposition. Technical Report 626, ETH Zurich (May 2009)
7. Hoang, T.S., Abrial, J.-R.: Event-B Decomposition for Parallel Programs. In: Frappier, M., Glässer, U., Khurshid, S., Laleau, R., Reeves, S. (eds.) ABZ 2010. LNCS, vol. 5977, pp. 319–333. Springer, Heidelberg (2010)
8. Abrial, J.-R., Butler, M., Hallerstede, S., Hoang, T.S., Mehta, F., Voisin, L.: Rodin: an open toolset for modelling and reasoning in Event-B. STTT 12(6), 447–466 (2010), Tool available online at: `http://sourceforge.net/projects/rodin-b-sharp`
9. Lee, D., Yannakakis, M.: Principles and methods of testing finite state machines – A survey. Proc. of the IEEE 84(8), 1090–1123 (1996)
10. Ipate, F.: Bounded sequence testing from deterministic finite state machines. Theoret. Comput. Sci. 411(16-18), 1770–1784 (2010)

11. Ipate, F., Dinca, I., Stefanescu, A.: Model learning and test generation using cover automata (submitted, 2012)
12. Dinca, I., Ipate, F., Stefanescu, A.: Learn and Test for Event-B – A Rodin Plugin. In: Derrick, J., Fitzgerald, J., Gnesi, S., Khurshid, S., Leuschel, M., Reeves, S., Riccobene, E. (eds.) ABZ 2012. LNCS, vol. 7316, pp. 361–364. Springer, Heidelberg (2012), Plug-in webpage: http://wiki.event-b.org/index.php/MBT_plugin
13. Angluin, D.: Learning regular sets from queries and counterexamples. Inf. Comput. 75(2), 87–106 (1987)
14. Ipate, F.: Learning finite cover automata from queries. Journal of Computer and System Sciences 78, 221–244 (2012)
15. Câmpeanu, C., Sântean, N., Yu, S.: Minimal cover-automata for finite languages. Theoret. Comput. Sci. 267(1-2), 3–16 (2001)
16. Hopcroft, J.E., Motwani, R., Ullman, J.D.: Introduction to Automata Theory, Languages, and Computation, 3rd edn. Addison-Wesley (2006)
17. Pasareanu, C.S., Giannakopoulou, D., Bobaru, M.G., Cobleigh, J.M., Barringer, H.: Learning to divide and conquer: applying the L^* algorithm to automate assume-guarantee reasoning. Formal Methods in System Design 32(3), 175–205 (2008)
18. Thiagarajan, P.S.: A Trace Consistent Subset of PTL. In: Lee, I., Smolka, S.A. (eds.) CONCUR 1995. LNCS, vol. 962, pp. 438–452. Springer, Heidelberg (1995)
19. Salehi Fathabadi, A., Rezazadeh, A., Butler, M.: Applying Atomicity and Model Decomposition to a Space Craft System in Event-B. In: Bobaru, M., Havelund, K., Holzmann, G.J., Joshi, R. (eds.) NFM 2011. LNCS, vol. 6617, pp. 328–342. Springer, Heidelberg (2011)
20. Iliasov, A., Troubitsyna, E., Laibinis, L., Romanovsky, A., Varpaaniemi, K., Ilic, D., Latvala, T.: Supporting Reuse in Event B Development: Modularisation Approach. In: Frappier, M., Glässer, U., Khurshid, S., Laleau, R., Reeves, S. (eds.) ABZ 2010. LNCS, vol. 5977, pp. 174–188. Springer, Heidelberg (2010), http://wiki.event-b.org/index.php/Modularisation_Plug-in
21. Poppleton, M.: The Composition of Event-B Models. In: Börger, E., Butler, M., Bowen, J.P., Boca, P. (eds.) ABZ 2008. LNCS, vol. 5238, pp. 209–222. Springer, Heidelberg (2008), http://wiki.event-b.org/index.php/Parallel_Composition_using_Event-B
22. http://tinyurl.com/isola12-with-appendix – extended version of our paper
23. Jirásková, G., Masopust, T.: State Complexity of Projected Languages. In: Holzer, M. (ed.) DCFS 2011. LNCS, vol. 6808, pp. 198–211. Springer, Heidelberg (2011)
24. Julliand, J., Stouls, N., Bué, P.-C., Masson, P.-A.: Syntactic Abstraction of B Models to Generate Tests. In: Fraser, G., Gargantini, A. (eds.) TAP 2010. LNCS, vol. 6143, pp. 151–166. Springer, Heidelberg (2010)
25. Shahbaz, M., Li, K., Groz, R.: Learning and Integration of Parameterized Components Through Testing. In: Petrenko, A., Veanes, M., Tretmans, J., Grieskamp, W. (eds.) TestCom/FATES 2007. LNCS, vol. 4581, pp. 319–334. Springer, Heidelberg (2007)
26. Berg, T., Grinchtein, O., Jonsson, B., Leucker, M., Raffelt, H., Steffen, B.: On the Correspondence Between Conformance Testing and Regular Inference. In: Cerioli, M. (ed.) FASE 2005. LNCS, vol. 3442, pp. 175–189. Springer, Heidelberg (2005)
27. Bollig, B., Katoen, J.-P., Kern, C., Leucker, M.: Learning communicating automata from MSCs. IEEE Trans. Software Eng. 36(3), 390–408 (2010)
28. Bohlin, T., Jonsson, B., Soleimanifard, S.: Inferring Compact Models of Communication Protocol Entities. In: Margaria, T., Steffen, B. (eds.) ISoLA 2010, Part I. LNCS, vol. 6415, pp. 658–672. Springer, Heidelberg (2010)

Inferring Semantic Interfaces of Data Structures*

Falk Howar[1], Malte Isberner[1], Bernhard Steffen[1],
Oliver Bauer[1], and Bengt Jonsson[2]

[1] Technical University Dortmund, Chair for Programming Systems,
Dortmund, D-44227, Germany
`{falk.howar,malte.isberner,steffen,oliver.bauer}@cs.tu-dortmund.de`
[2] Dept. of Information Technology, Uppsala University, Sweden
`bengt.jonsson@it.uu.se`

Abstract. In this paper, we show how to fully automatically infer *semantic interfaces* of data structures on the basis of systematic testing. Our semantic interfaces are a generalized form of Register Automata (RA), comprising parameterized input and output, allowing to model control- and data-flow in component interfaces concisely. Algorithmic key to the automated synthesis of these semantic interfaces is the extension of an active learning algorithm for Register Automata to explicitly deal with output. We evaluated our algorithm on a complex data structure, a "stack of stacks", the largest of which we could learn in merely 20 seconds with less than 4000 membership queries, resulting in a model with rougly 800 nodes. In contrast, even when restricting the data domain to just four values, the corresponding plain Mealy machine would have more than 10^9 states and presumably require billions of membership queries.

1   Introduction

With the increased use of external libraries and (web-)services, mining behavioral interfaces of black-box software components gains practical and economical importance. Automata learning techniques [3] have therefore successfully been employed for inferring behavioral interfaces of software components [1], such as data structures.

Most of these algorithms come with the limitation of being restricted to finite input alphabets, which hinders adequate treatment of parameterized actions whose parameter values often range over infinite domains. Apart from the infinite structure of possible input actions, another issue is raised by the influence of data on the control flow. As a simple example, consider a set-style data structure: Upon insertion of a new element, the effect in terms of control flow will naturally depend on whether this element is already contained in the set, or not. Such behavior cannot be modeled adequately by "classical" automata models such

---

* This work was partially supported by the European Union FET Project CON-
NECT: Emergent Connectors for Eternal Software Intensive Networked Systems
(`http://connect-forever.eu/`).

T. Margaria and B. Steffen (Eds.): ISoLA 2012, Part I, LNCS 7609, pp. 554–571, 2012.

as DFAs or Mealy machines. What is required are *semantic interfaces*, which transparently reflect the behavioral influence of parameters at the interface level.

In this paper, we show how to efficiently overcome these limitations by generalizing our approach for inferring register automata [6,11] models, which are designed for symbolically dealing with parameterized input, to also capture parameterized output. This extension, which is similar in guise to the extension of finite automata learning to the learning of Mealy machines, allows us to fully automatically infer semantic interfaces solely on the basis of systematic testing. Although this extension is technically quite straightforward, its impact is dramatic: Our Register Mealy Machines

- express the data structures' behavior concisely and faithfully, at a level ideal even for manual inspection,
- the inference of RMMs does not require any prerequisites like manual abstraction, a real bottleneck for "classical" learning of practical systems, and
- RMMs can be learned much more efficiently than both Register Automata and plain Mealy machines at some predefined level of abstraction.

In the evaluation section of this paper, we will discuss data structures whose complexity reaches far beyond the state of the art [1,9], the largest of which would comprise more than 10^9 states as a plain Mealy machine for an abstract data domain of just four values. In contrast, the RMM model—which is semantically richer—has only 781 nodes, *independently* of the size of the data domain, and is learned fully automatically in approximately 20 seconds using only 9 equivalence queries!

Related work. Synthesis of component interfaces has been a research interest for the past decade. Presented approaches fall into three classes described in [15].

First, *Client-side Static Analysis* uses a static analysis of source code using the component of which a model is to be inferred. The approach described in [15] mine Java code to infer common sequences of method calls.

Second, *Component-side Static Analysis* uses a static analysis on the component itself. In [1] an approach is presented that generates behavioral interface specifications for Java classes by means of predicate abstraction and active learning. Another approach uses counterexample guided abstraction refinement (CEGAR) [10] instead of active learning in order to derive a regular model from the Boolean program obtained by predicate abstraction.

Finally, *Dynamic Analysis* infers interface models from actual program executions. The authors of [2] present an approach for inferring probabilistic finite state automata (PFSA) describing a components' interface using a variant of the k-tail algorithm [5] for learning finite state automata from positive examples. In [12] behavioral models are inferred from program traces obtained through monitoring using passive automata learning. The influence of data values on the behavior is inferred with an invariance detector [8]. The authors of [7] use a combination of component-side static analysis, identifying side-effect free methods (so-called *inspectors*), which are then used to identify states of the component. These states are explored systematically in a dynamic analysis.

All static-analysis methods rely on access to source-code, either of the component or of code using the component. Only dynamic analysis can deal with black-box systems. Most of the dynamic approaches, on the other hand, use passive learning and are thus limited to (possibly small) sets of observed concrete executions. In case some functionality of a component is not executed, it will not be captured in the inferred model. In contrast, our approach does not depend on the quality of preexisting observations as it uses active automata learning to interact with black-box components and produce a model in an "active" dynamic analysis.

Outline. This paper is organized as follows. In the following section, we will introduce the modeling formalism of Register Mealy Machines. We will develop an active learning algorithm for our new formalism in Section 3, highlighting the key ideas and differences compared to Register Automata learning. The practical impact of our algorithm is discussed in Section 4 by evaluating it on a number of examples. Finally, Section 5 concludes the paper, giving an outlook on both extensions and more elaborate case studies.

2   Modeling Data Structures

As discussed above, in many real systems data parameters of inputs influence the behavior of the system. In order to represent such systems as finite models, storing and comparing data values has to be made explicit in the automaton representation. In this section we will present a Register Automaton model that allows for modeling data in outputs and discuss how such an automaton can be reconstructed from its semantics.

2.1   Register Mealy Machines

Let $\mathcal{D}$ be an unbounded domain of data values which can be compared for equality, and Σ be a set of *parameterized input symbols*, each with a fixed arity (i.e., number of arguments it takes from $\mathcal{D}$). A *data input* is a pair $(a, \bar{d})$, where $a \in \Sigma$ is the *base symbol* with arity k, and $\bar{d} = \langle d_1, \ldots, d_k \rangle$ is a sequence of data values from $\mathcal{D}$. In the following, we will use the more intuitive notation $a(d_1, \ldots, d_k)$ instead of $(a, \bar{d})$. We write $a^{\mathcal{D}}$ for the set of all data inputs with base symbol a and data values from $\mathcal{D}$, and $\Sigma^{\mathcal{D}}$ for the set of all data inputs with base symbols in Σ. Sequences of data inputs are *data words*, for given Σ and $\mathcal{D}$ the set of all data words is denoted by $\mathcal{W}_{\Sigma,\mathcal{D}} = \left(\Sigma^{\mathcal{D}}\right)^*$, and $\mathcal{W}_{\Sigma,\mathcal{D}}^+ = \mathcal{W}_{\Sigma,\mathcal{D}} \setminus \{\varepsilon\}$ for the set of all non-empty data words. For a data word w, let $Acts(w)$ be the sequence of parameterized input symbols in w and $Vals(w)$ be the sequence of data values in w (from left to right). Let then $ValSet(w)$ denote the set of distinct data values in $Vals(w)$. Data words are concatenated just like plain words.

Let now a *symbolic input* be a pair $(a, \bar{p})$, of a parameterized input a of arity k and a sequence of symbolic parameters $\bar{p} = \langle p_1, \ldots, p_k \rangle$. Especially when depicting automaton models, we will use the more intuitive notation $a(p_1, \ldots, p_k)$.

Let further $X = \langle x_1, \ldots, x_m \rangle$ be a finite set of *registers*. A *guard* is a propositional formula of equalities and negated equalities over symbolic parameters and
registers of the form

$$G ::= G \wedge G \mid G \vee G \mid p_i = p_j \mid p_i \neq p_j \mid x_i = p_j \mid x_i \neq p_j \mid true,$$

where *true* denotes the atomic predicate that is always satisfied. A parallel *assignment* is a partial mapping $\sigma : X \to X \cup P$ for a set S of formal parameters.
Finally, a *symbolic output* is a pair $(o, \bar{r})$, of a parameterized output o of arity k
and a sequence of *symbolic references* $\bar{r} = \langle r_1, \ldots, r_k \rangle$, where $r_i \in X \cup P$.

Definition 1 (Register Mealy Machine). *A* Register Mealy Machine *(RMM)
is a tuple* $\mathcal{M} = (\Sigma, \Omega, L, l_0, X, \Gamma)$, *where*

- *Σ is a finite set of parameterized inputs,*
- *Ω is a finite set of parameterized outputs,*
- *L is a finite set of locations,*
- *$l_0 \in L$ is the initial location,*
- *X is a finite set of registers,*
- *Γ is a finite set of transitions, each of which is of form $\langle l, (a, \bar{p}), g, (o, \bar{r}), \sigma, l' \rangle$,
  where l is the source location, l' is the target location, $(a, \bar{p})$ is a symbolic
  input, g is a guard, $(o, \bar{r})$ is a symbolic output, and σ is a parallel assignment.*   □

Let us describe how an RMM $\mathcal{M} = (\Sigma, \Omega, L, l_0, X, \Gamma)$ processes data words. A
valuation, denoted by ν, is a (partial) mapping from X to $\mathcal{D}$. A *state* of $\mathcal{M}$ is a
pair $\langle l, \nu \rangle$ where $l \in L$ and ν is a valuation. The *initial state* is the pair of initial
location and empty valuation $\langle l_0, \emptyset \rangle$.

A *step* of $\mathcal{M}$, denoted by $\langle l, \nu \rangle \xrightarrow{(a,\bar{d})/(o,\bar{d}')} \langle l', \nu' \rangle$, transfers $\mathcal{M}$ from $\langle l, \nu \rangle$ to
$\langle l', \nu' \rangle$ on input $(a, \bar{d})$ if there is a transition $\langle l, (a, \bar{p}), g, (o, \bar{r}), \sigma, l' \rangle \in \Gamma$ such that

1. g is satisfied by $\bar{d}$ and ν, i.e., if it becomes true when replacing all p_i by d_i
   and all x_i by $\nu(x_i)$, and
2. ν' is the updated valuation, where $\nu'(x_i) = \nu(x_j)$ whenever $\sigma(x_i) = x_j$, and
   $\nu'(x_i) = d_j$ whenever $\sigma(x_i) = p_j$.

When performing the above step, $\mathcal{M}$ generates an output $(o, \bar{d}')$, where $\bar{d}'$ is
obtained from $\bar{r} = \langle r_1, \ldots, r_k \rangle$ by adequate substitution of the references, i.e.,
$d_i' = d_j$ if $r_i = p_j$, and $d_i' = \nu(x_j)$ if $r_i = x_j$. Note that this means that $\bar{r}$ refers
to the *old* valuation rather than the updated one.

A *run* of $\mathcal{M}$ over a data word $(a_1, \bar{d}_1) \ldots (a_k, \bar{d}_k)$ is a sequence of steps

$$\langle l_0, \emptyset \rangle \xrightarrow{(a_1,\bar{d}_1)/(o_1,\bar{d}_1')} \langle l_1, \nu_1 \rangle \ldots \langle l_{k-1}, \nu_{k-1} \rangle \xrightarrow{(a_k,\bar{d}_k)/(o_k,\bar{d}_k')} \langle l_k, \nu_k \rangle.$$

The output data word produced during this run is $(o_1, \bar{d}_1') \ldots (o_k, \bar{d}_k')$.

An RMM $\mathcal{M}$ is called *deterministic* if every data word in $\mathcal{W}_{\Sigma, \mathcal{D}}^+$ has exactly
one run in $\mathcal{M}$. For the remainder of this paper, we will assume RMMs to be
deterministic.

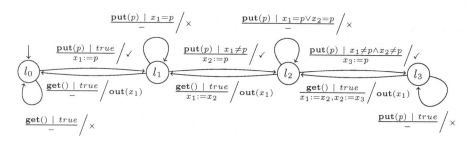

Fig. 1. RMM for a FIFO-set with a capacity of 3

Example 1. At this point, we introduce our running example, which aligns with the field of application we envision for our technique: inferring semantic interfaces of data structures. Consider a collection data structure that allows storing a bounded number of data values, which combines aspects of both a queue and a set: when retrieving values from the collection, FIFO semantics apply. However, like in a set, it is not possible to store the same value twice; doing so will have no effect. For insertion and retrieval, the interface offers the input actions **put**(p) and **get**(). The response upon **put** is ✓ or ×, signaling whether or not the collection was modified. A **get** operation is either answered by **out**(x), with x being the value that is returned, or × if the collection is empty.

An RMM of this data structure is depicted in Fig. 1 for a capacity of three. A transition $\langle l, (a, \bar{p}), g, (o, \bar{r}), \sigma, l' \rangle$ is represented by an arrow between l and l', with the label $\frac{a(\bar{p}) \mid g}{\sigma} / o(\bar{r})$. □

2.2 Register Mealy Machine Semantics

Let us now define the semantics of RMMs. Register Mealy Machines are *trans-ducers*, consuming inputs and producing outputs. Technically speaking, an RMM realizes a function from $\mathcal{W}^+_{\Sigma, \mathcal{D}}$ to $\mathcal{W}^+_{\Omega, \mathcal{D}}$. Since we further assume that an output symbol is emitted every time an input symbol is read (and only then) and since data outputs may only contain data values that have previously occurred in the input data word the *semantics* of an RMM $\mathcal{M}$ can be expressed as a function $[\![\mathcal{M}]\!] \colon \mathcal{W}^+_{\Sigma, \mathcal{D}} \to \Omega^{\mathcal{D}}$, with $[\![\mathcal{M}]\!](w)$ being the *last* output symbol that was emitted in the run of $\mathcal{M}$ over $w \in \mathcal{W}^+_{\Sigma, \mathcal{D}}$.

Since a Register Mealy Machine $\mathcal{M}$ can test data values in parameters only against values in registers (and not against constants), the function $[\![\mathcal{M}]\!]$ is closed under permutations on the data domain in the following sense: For all permu-tations π on $\mathcal{D}$ it holds that $[\![\mathcal{M}]\!](\pi(w)) = \pi([\![\mathcal{M}]\!](w))$. This property fits the context of data structures very well: the behavior and output depend on the or-dering in which data arises in the data structure while not depending on concrete values.

This closedness under permutations on $\mathcal{D}$ can be leveraged when inferring RMM models: it will be sufficient to use one word to represent an infinite number of equivalent words. Let $w \simeq w'$ if $Acts(w) = Acts(w')$ and $\pi(w) = w'$ for some permutation π on $\mathcal{D}$. Let $[w]_\sim$ be the set of all words $w' \simeq w$, i.e., words that can be derived from w by some π, and let $\overline{w}$ be the canonical representative word for $[w]_\sim$ in which the data values from $\mathcal{D}$ occur in some fixed order in $Vals(\overline{w})$. Since $[\![\mathcal{M}]\!]$ is closed under permutation, $[\![\mathcal{M}]\!](w) = \pi([\![\mathcal{M}]\!](\overline{w}))$ for $w = \pi(\overline{w})$.

When constructing RMM models from a system under learning (SUL), we will use test cases, i.e., canonical data words, to infer the semantics of a SUL and then construct an RMM from it. While the first step is covered in the next section, the remainder of this section will focus on how to derive an RMM model from a function $S: \mathcal{W}_{\Sigma,\mathcal{D}}^+ \rightarrow \Omega^\mathcal{D}$ with the properties discussed above. In particular, it will be discussed how locations, registers and assignments, and guarded transitions of an RMM can be constructed from a function S.

From semantics to locations. In classical Mealy machine learning, words are recognized as leading to the same state if they have the same residual semantics [16], i.e., the same output for all suffixes. This requirement has to be loosened slightly, since we have to abstract from concrete data values while still respecting (in-)equalities between data values.

Definition 2. *Words $u, u' \in \mathcal{W}_{\Sigma,\mathcal{D}}$ are equivalent wrt. S, denoted by $u \equiv_S u'$, iff for some permutation π on $\mathcal{D}$*

$$S(u \cdot v) = \pi^{-1}(S(u' \cdot \pi(v))) \quad \forall v \in \mathcal{W}_{\Sigma,\mathcal{D}}^+. \qquad \square$$

Definition 2 is a straightforward adaption of the well-known Nerode relation for regular languages. The permutation on $\mathcal{D}$ helps abstracting from concrete data values and focusing on the flow of data values. In an RMM for S, locations will correspond to equivalence classes of $\equiv_S$.[1]

Classes of $\equiv_S$ can be distinguished by suffixes: According to Definition 2 there is at least one suffix $v \in \mathcal{W}_{\Sigma,\mathcal{D}}^+$ for $u \not\equiv_S u'$ such that for all permutations π on $\mathcal{D}$ it holds that $S(u \cdot v) \neq \pi^{-1}(S(u' \cdot \pi(v)))$.

In our running example, the two data words ε and $\mathbf{put}(1)$ are not equivalent. They can be distinguished by the suffix $\mathbf{get}()$ for all permutations π:

$$S(\varepsilon \cdot \pi(\mathbf{get}())) = \times \neq \pi(\mathbf{out}(1)) = \pi(S(\mathbf{put}(1)\mathbf{get}())).$$

In this particular case π is not essential for distinguishing locations. The different behavior is observable at the level of output symbols already. However, to establish, e.g., the equivalence of words $\mathbf{put}(1)$ and $\mathbf{put}(1)\mathbf{get}()\mathbf{put}(2)$ the permutation on $\mathcal{D}$ is mandatory.

From semantics to registers. Considering a prefix u and a suffix v, there are two observations from which one might conclude that, in the state reached by u, a value from u has to be stored in a register:

---

[1] We will not introduce a location for every class of $\equiv_S$ as is discussed at the end of Section 2.2.

1. A data value occurring in the output equals a data value in u.
2. The output depends on the equality of data values in u and v.

The set of *memorable* data values in u is denoted by $mem(u)$. Memorable data values have to be stored in registers of an RMM. In order to identify memorable data values in the prefix, we will replace data values in the suffix and observe the effect.

In particular, it is important to observe what happens if equalities between data values in the prefix and in the suffix are eliminated: Let $d \in ValSet(u) \cap ValSet(v)$ and $d' \in \mathcal{D} \setminus ValSet(uv)$. Let further $\pi \colon \mathcal{D} \to \mathcal{D}$ be a transposition of d and d', i.e., a permutation exchanging d and d' and leaving all other data values untouched. Applying π to v yields the suffix $\pi(v)$ with all occurrences of d replaced by d'.

Now, the data value d is memorable in u if $\pi(S(uv)) \neq S(u \cdot \pi(v))$: In such a case either $ValSet(S(u \cdot \pi(v)))$ still contains a data value d (first case), or an equality between an occurrence of d in both u and v was meaningful, leading to the changed output (second case).

Considering our FIFO set, in **put**(1) the argument is memorable, as can be proven either by the suffix **get**() (yielding **out**(1)) or by the suffixes **put**(1) and **put**(2), yielding outputs $\times$ and $\checkmark$.

From semantics to transitions. In an RMM, transitions are guarded by logic formulas over binary (in-)equalities between registers and symbolic parameters. Assume a data word u with memorable data values $mem(u)$ for some semantics S. Then, the transitions for some input symbol a originating in the location reached by u in the RMM for S can be derived from the set $\{u\} \times a^{\mathcal{D}}$ of a-continuations of u in two steps. In the first step we construct many *atomic* transitions, each describing exactly one combination of equalities between parameters of a and memorable data values of u, i.e., one atomic transition per class $[u \cdot (a, \bar{d})]_{\sim}$. In a second step, we will group these transitions depending on the location they lead to.

Let $\kappa_u \colon mem(u) \to X$ be an arbitrary injective function determining in which registers the memorable data values of a prefix u are to be stored in the RMM for S. Then, for some word $u \cdot (a, \bar{d})$ we can construct a transition, where

- the classes of u and $u \cdot (a, \bar{d})$ wrt. $\equiv_S$ determine the source and target location of the transition,
- the guard describes exactly the equalities of data values in $u \cdot (a, \bar{d})$, i.e., for $d_i \in \bar{d}$ and $d \in mem(u)$ there will be the atomic proposition $\kappa(d) = p_i$ in the guard if $d = d_i$, and the proposition $\kappa(d) \neq p_i$ otherwise, and
- the assignment will be determined using κ_u and $\kappa_{u \cdot (a, \bar{d})}$.

Since S is closed under permutations on $\mathcal{D}$ this will result in a finite number of transitions, bounded by the number of combinations of possible equalities between parameters of a and the (finitely many) memorable data values in u.

In the second step we will group all a-transitions that (1) lead to the same location and (2) have compatible assignments, i.e., where corresponding memorable data values are stored in identical registers.

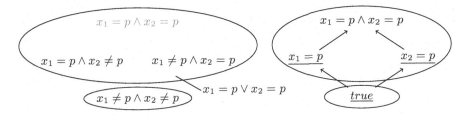

Fig. 2. Grouping atomic transition guards for the **put**-transitions originating from l_2 in Fig. 1 (left) and corresponding poset of conjunctions of equalities; minimal elements underlined for all transitions (right)

Figure 2 (left) shows an example of how atomic transitions can be grouped for the **put**-transitions originating from l_2 of the FIFO-set from Figure 1. The atomic guard $x_1 \neq p \wedge x_2 \neq p$ corresponds to the **put**-transition to l_3. The other atomic guards are grouped by the reflexive **put**-transition. The guard $x_1 = p \wedge x_2 = p$ is colored gray in the figure as it does not occur in the RMM: In our example location l_2 can never be reached with identical values in x_1 and x_2. However, since the guard is not accessible, we can add the case to any transition, resulting in the abstract guard $x_1 = p \vee x_2 = p$

Now, we can construct an RMM for some function S: the locations are determined by the classes of $\equiv_S$, registers and assignments are determined using the memorable data values and the guards of abstract transitions are obtained by grouping atomic transitions. However, when inferring RMM models in the next section, we will use two interrelated optimizations.

First, we do not introduce a location for every class of $\equiv_S$ but merge compatible locations as is described in [6] to obtain exponentially smaller models in some cases. Intuitively, we group locations that only appear to be different because in one location data values in two registers are identical, resulting in fewer memorable data values and inequivalence wrt. $\equiv_S$.

Second, we do not use all atomic transitions but only certain "representative" ones. In [6,11] it is shown that one can introduce a partial order on the set of atomic guards and that it is sufficient to use the minimal elements (wrt. to this partial order) in the domain of each transition. The basic idea is shown in Figure 2: Removing the in-equalities from each atomic guard (in the left) results in a partially ordered set (by implication), which is shown in the right of the figure. Representative elements are underlined.

During inference this will allow for an approach reminding of interval stacking, adding one "representative" atomic case at a time.

3   Inferring RMM Models

In this section, we want to discuss the key ideas of adapting automata learning techniques to Register Mealy Machines. Our algorithm is based on the one for inferring Register Automata as presented in [11]. As usual in active learning, we will assume a teacher answering two kinds of queries:

- *membership queries* (MQs), which query the reaction of the *system under learning* (SUL) for a given input word,
- *equivalence queries* (EQs), which check if a constructed hypothesis correctly models the target system, and if not, return a counterexample exposing a deviation in the behavior of the target system from the behavior predicted by the hypothesis.[2]

According to this two kind of queries the learning algorithm can be divided into two phases: *hypothesis construction*, during which the learner poses membership queries until it has enough information to consistently construct a hypothesis, and *hypothesis verification*, where an equivalence query is posed and the counterexample—if existent—is handled accordingly.

3.1   Inferring Residuals from Test Cases

Before we describe the two phases of the algorithm, let us briefly consider how membership queries can be used to infer residuals, which will be one cornerstone of our algorithm. As discussed in the previous section, residuals are essential for constructing an automaton from a semantic function. The main problem here is to represent or infer an infinite (partial) residual with finitely many test cases.

Thus, first of all, instead of considering all data words, we can focus on canonical data words as discussed early in Section 2.2. In the examples we will use $\mathcal{D} = \mathbb{N}$ and $<$ as a total order on $\mathbb{N}$. In our running example, the data words **put**(1)**put**(1) and **put**(1)**put**(2) are canonical while **put**(2)**put**(1) and **put**(1)**put**(3) are not.

Then, for a function $S\colon \mathcal{W}^+_{\Sigma,\mathcal{D}} \to \Omega^{\mathcal{D}}$, a (canonical) data word u, and a set $V \subset \Sigma^+$ of sequences of inputs symbols (so-called *suffix patterns*), let the *partial residual* of u wrt. S and V be a mapping S^u_V from $\mathcal{W}^+_{\Sigma,\mathcal{D}}$ to $\Omega^{\mathcal{D}}$ s.t.

$$S^u_V(v) \;=\; S(uv) \qquad \text{for } v \text{ with } Acts(v) \in V.$$

The mapping S^u_V can be represented finitely using canonical words. In a partial residual, memorable data values may be identified using the approach discussed in the previous section. Let $mem_V(u)$ denote the (subset of) memorable data values of u identified by S^u_V.

Now, we need a means of comparing partial residuals algorithmically in order to derive locations. The main problem here is that the finite representations of partial residuals for words u, u' with differently many distinct data values will have domains of different sizes. In order to compare such partial residuals, we will restrict their domains.

In [11], we have shown that the domain of the finite representation of S^u_V can be restricted since the future behavior after u for suffixes from V only depends

---

[2] In true black-box scenarios, equivalence queries cannot be realized. Several approaches have been proposed to approximate equivalence queries (e.g., [4]).

on data values from $mem_V(u)$ (by construction of $mem_V(u)$). In particular, the domain can be restricted to the set of suffixes v with $Acts(v) \in V$ for which (1) uv is canonical and (2) where data values that are shared between prefix and the suffix are from $mem_V(u)$. The size of this new domain depends only on V, which will be uniform for all prefixes in our algorithm and on the size of $mem_V(u)$.

In fact, for $u \equiv_P u'$ we will have $|mem_V(u)| = |mem_V(u')|$ and there will exist a permutation π on $\mathcal{D}$ such that for all suffixes v from the restricted domain of S_V^u the word $\pi(v)$ is in the (restricted) domain of $S_V^{u'}$ and $\pi(S_V^u(v)) = S_V^{u'}(\pi(v))$, denoted by $S_V^u \equiv_V S_V^{u'}$.

We can now formulate our learning algorithm for RMMs.

3.2   Hypothesis Construction

As usual in active learning, the algorithm uses a table for organizing observations. An *observation table* is a tuple $\langle U, V, T \rangle$, where $U \subset \mathcal{W}_\mathcal{D}$ is a prefix-closed set of data words (the *prefixes*), the set $V \subset \Sigma^+$ contains sequences of parameterized symbols (the *suffix patterns*), and T maps prefixes u from U to their partial residuals S_V^u.

The learning algorithm will maintain a special set $U_s \subset U$ of *access sequences* (to locations in the SUL) and for all $u \in U_s$ there will at least be the canonical word $ua^\perp$ in U. There, $ua^\perp$ denotes the canonical word from $\{u\} \times a^\mathcal{D}$ which has no additional equalities between data values and corresponds to the *true* case in Figure 2.

As usual, in order to be able to construct a well-defined hypothesis, we require the observation table to be *closed*, meaning that every prefix in $U \setminus U_s$ has a matching counterpart in U_s. By matching we here mean that for $u \in U \setminus U_s$ there is a prefix $u' \in U_s$ with $S_V^u \equiv_V S_V^{u'}$. This can be achieved by subsequently adding prefixes violating this requirement to U_s.

In addition, we also require an observation to be *register consistent*, as defined in [11]: For a prefix ua, we require all of its memorable data values which also occur in u to be memorable for the prefix u as well, guaranteeing well-defined register assignments along the transitions of the hypothesis. This can be achieved by subsequently extending the set of suffix patterns. In case a data value d from u is proven to be memorable in ua by the suffix pattern $\bar{v}$, we extend the observation table by $Acts(a) \cdot \bar{v}$, which will prove d memorable in u.

Now, constructing a hypothesis RMM $\mathcal{H}$ from an observation table turns out to be rather straightfoward. Similar to L^*, prefixes in U_s identify locations in $\mathcal{H}$. Transitions in the hypothesis are constructed as follows from prefixes $ua \in U$, with $u \in \mathcal{W}_{\Sigma, \mathcal{D}}$, $a \in \Sigma^\mathcal{D}$:

1. The *destination* is the location for $u' \in U_s$ with $T[u'] \equiv_V T[ua]$ due to some permutation π on $\mathcal{D}$, transforming $T[ua]$ to $T[u']$ (where $ua = u'$ in case $ua \in U_s$).
2. *Guards* are derived by analyzing which data values in a equal data values in u. As prefixes are minimal words in the realm of a transition, none of these

equalities are accidental and have to be expressed in the guard. The missing inequalities and other atomic cases are added in a post-processing step once all transitions are created (cf. Section 2.2).

3. For *assignments*, one has to copy the contents of the registers (corresponding data values in $mem_V(u)$) as well as the parameter values (corresponding to data values in $mem_V(ua) \setminus mem_V(u)$) to the target registers (concrete registers are determined using π from step 1).

4. *Outputs* can be derived from analyzing the equalities of the values occurring in the output symbol. If the data value in question is in $mem_V(u)$, then a register is used, and the respective parameter of the input symbol a otherwise.

Once a hypothesis RMM is constructed from the observation table, an equivalence query can be used to determine if the hypothesis is a model of the system under learning, already.

3.3   Hypothesis Verification

In case a hypothesis is not equivalent to the system under learning, an equivalence query will return a counterexample. Handling counterexamples in our case is a much more involved task than in L^*, where each counterexample gives rise to at least one additional state in the hypothesis. In contrast, when inferring RMMs, the obtained growth can be in any of three dimensions. A counterexample can:

1. prove a data value to be memorable, leading to the introduction of a new register;
2. disprove a permutation which is used for matching the target location of a transition. If no alternative permutation accomplishing this can be found, this leads to the creation of a new location;
3. prove an abstract transition too coarse, leading to a new minimal representative word and thus a new transition.

When a counterexample is returned, all of the above cases have to be investigated accordingly. We refer to [11] for technical details of the approach. The construction presented there can be extended to RMMs straightfowardly. We here just state a variant of the resulting theorem.

Theorem 1. *From a counterexample w with $[\![\mathcal{H}]\!](w) \neq [\![SUL]\!](w)$ a prefix u and a suffix v can be derived such that either*

1. *u is in U_s and the suffix pattern $Acts(v)$ witnesses a new memorable data value in u,*
2. *u is in $U \setminus U_s$ and the suffix pattern $Acts(v)$ disproves the permutation used in the table to show $T[u] \equiv_V T[u']$ for some $u' \in U_s$*
3. *$u = u' \cdot (a, \bar{d}) \notin U$, where $u' \in U_s$, the prefix u is a new unknown minimal canonical word for some transition.*   □

Thus, a counterexample will lead to progress in one of the three dimensions when extending the observation table accordingly.

Algorithm 1 L^*_{RMM}

Input: A set of parameterized input symbols Σ
Output: An RMM model $\mathcal{H}$ with $[\![\mathcal{H}]\!] = [\![SUL]\!]$

1:	$U_s := \{\varepsilon\}$	▷ *Initialize observation table*
2:	$U := U_s \cup \{a^\perp \mid a \in \Sigma\}$	▷ *Use one "base-case" per input*
3:	$V := \Sigma$	▷ *Use inputs as suffix patterns*
4:	**loop**	
5:	**repeat**	
6:	$T :=$ compute_residuals(U, V)	▷ *Fill table using MQs, cf. Section 3.1*
7:	**if** $\langle U, V, T \rangle$ not closed **then**	
8:	Let u in $U \setminus U_s$ s.t. $\forall u' \in U_s$. $T[u] \not\equiv_V T[u']$	▷ *New access seq.*
9:	$U_s := U_s \cup \{u\}$	▷ *Extend prefixes*
10:	$U := U \cup \{ua^\perp \mid a \in \Sigma\}$	▷ *by "base cases"*
11:	**end if**	
12:	**if** $\langle U, V, T \rangle$ not register-consistent **then**	
13:	Let $ua \in U$, and $|Acts(a)| = 1$ s.t. for $d \in ValSet(u) \setminus ValSet(a)$:	
14:	- d is memorable in $T[ua]$ proven by $\bar{v} \in V$	
15:	- d is *not* memorable in $T[u]$	▷ *To make d memorable in u:*
16:	$V := V \cup \{Acts(a) \cdot \bar{v}\}$	▷ *Extend suffixes accordingly*
17:	**end if**	
18:	**until** $\langle U, V, T \rangle$ is closed **and** register-consistent.	
19:	$\mathcal{H} :=$ construct_hypothesis(U, V, T)	▷ *cf. Section 3.2*
20:	$ce := EQ(\mathcal{H})$	▷ *Perform equivalence query*
21:	**if** $ce = {}'OK'$ **then**	
22:	**return** $\mathcal{H}$	▷ *Done!*
23:	**end if**	
24:	$(u, v) :=$ decompose(ce)	▷ *cf. Theorem 1*
25:	**if** $u \in U$ **then**	
26:	$V := V \cup \{Acts(v)\}$	▷ *New remapping, location, or assigment*
27:	**else**	
28:	$U := U \cup \{u\}$	▷ *New guarded transition*
29:	**end if**	
30:	**end loop**	

3.4   The L^*_{RMM} Algorithm

Put together, this results in Algorithm 1. Lines 1-3 initialize the observation table. The set U_s contains the prefix ε, reaching the initial location. The remaining prefixes are the canonical words representing the *true* cases (cf. Figure 2) for transitions from the initial location. As usual in active learning of Mealy machines, the set of suffix patterns is initialized using the input alphabet.

Hypothesis construction is covered in lines 5-19: First, in line 6 partial residuals are computed as described in Section 3.1. Then, the observation table is checked for closedness (lines 7-11) and for register consistency (lines 12-17). This is repeated until a hypothesis can be constructed from the observation table (line 19) as discussed in Section 3.2.

The second phase, hypothesis verification, begins in line 20 with performing an equivalence query. If no counterexample is returned the algorithm terminates successfully with the last hypothesis (line 22). Otherwise, the counterexample is analyzed as described in Section 3.3. In case the obtained prefix is in the set of prefixes, the obtained suffix will be used as the basis for a new suffix pattern (line 26). In case the prefix is unknown, it will be added to the set of prefixes (line 28).

As discussed in the previous section, this leads to progress in one of three dimensions: new locations (or at least less permutations), new register assignments, or new guarded transitions. Progress achieved in any of the three dimensions is strictly monotonic. The idea for proving convergence is the same as in [11]: the model is monotonically refined only when this is observed to be necessary, thus the hypothesis can never exceed the level of refinement of the (finite) model of the target system. However, since the algorithm is guaranteed to make progress after each equivalence query, a finite number certainly suffices.

The wost case complexity in terms of membership queries and equivalence queries of L^*_{RMM} is the same as in the case of inferring RAs [11] (in the worst case the outputs in an RMM encode only acceptance and rejection). Instead of restating the result here, we will show in the next section that the RMM approach will outperform the RA approach on many concrete examples.

4   Experimental Evaluation

We have implemented the algorithm outlined in this paper on top of Learn-Lib [14], our framework for active automata learning. We conducted several experiments to demonstrate the efficiency of our algorithm. Note that for all of the experiments we conducted, we used a cache, preventing membership queries for the same words to be posed twice.

In a first series of experiments, we employed our algorithm for learning models of small container data structures: a stack, a queue, and a (FIFO-)set with fixed capacities. All those data structures expose two input actions: **put** of arity one, and **get** without any parameters. The semantics of **put** and **get** is the same as the one in our running example (cf. Fig. 1 for the example RMM of a FIFO-set with a capacity of three). The queue and the stack allow storing the same object multiple times, while the set can only store distinct elements.

For assessing the efficiency of our algorithm, we considered two different approaches that can be employed in order to infer models of such data structures: We used a classical active learning algorithm, treating the data structure as an ordinary Mealy machine. In this case, it was necessary to restrict the size of the (visible) data domain in order to gain a finite representation. For a stack with a capacity of two and $\mathcal{D} = \{1, 2\}$, this is exemplarily displayed in the left of Fig. 3. In the experiments we used $n + 1$ as size of the data domain for data structures of capacity n. This allows to observe the behavior of the data structures in the case where all registers store different values. The additional "new" data value is used as data parameter. We have used *symmetry reduction*, i.e., normalizing the

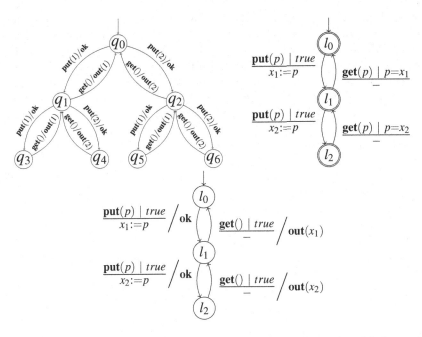

Fig. 3. Three variants of modeling a stack with a capacity of two: As a Mealy machine with a sample data domain $\mathcal{D} = \{1, 2\}$ (left), as a prefix-closed Register Automaton (right), or as a Register Mealy Machine (middle). Unsuccessful operations (e.g., reflexive transitions) and sink locations are omitted in all three models.

Table 1. Experimental results for inferring register automata models from data structures using various algorithms

Name	Mealy ($|\mathcal{D}| = n + 1$)		Mealy w/ sym.red.		RA [11][3]			RMM		
	$|Q|$	MQs	EQs	MQs	EQs	$|L|$	MQs	EQs	$|L|$	MQs	EQs
Stack (1)	3	30	0	16	0	3	35	2	2	10	0
Stack (2)	13	252	1	52	1	4	135	4	3	18	0
Stack (3)	85	2,833	3	232	3	5	554	6	4	38	1
Stack (4)	781	39,996	4	890	4	6	2,998	8	5	53	2
Queue (4)	781	39,996	4	890	4	6	2,711	5	5	76	2
FIFO-Set (4)	206	9,484	2	128	2	6	1,566	15	5	129	12

order of data values occurring in an input word as described in [13], to reduce the number of queries when inferring plain Mealy machine models.

We also compared our algorithm to an alternative way of representing output in systems with data: by modeling them as Register Automata, i.e., acceptors,

---

[3] The algorithm infers a complete model also containing a sink, hence the greater number of locations compared to our new algorithm.

and considering the (prefix-closed) data language of all valid combinations of input symbols with the respective data values in the output. This is detailed in the right of Fig. 3 for the case of a stack: here, the input symbol **get** also has a parameter, and transitions are only valid if the provided data value matches the one in the output. This resembles a common way of encoding Mealy machines as (prefix-closed) DFA. For inferring these models, we used the algorithm presented in [11]. The difference between an RA model and an RMM model is apparent in the figure: While in the RMM model (middle) transitions have outputs with data values, these outputs have to be encoded as guarded transitions in the RA model.

The results of this evaluation series are displayed in Tab. 1. Our novel algorithm impressively outperforms the alternative approaches in all but one cases. When looking at the series of stacks with growing capacities, it is particularly striking that, while the number of membership queries for learning RAs grows quickly, there is only moderate growth for the inference of RMMs. As was analyzed in [11], handling counterexamples in order to infer guards is a task with an exponential worst-case complexity in the number of registers, as numerous combinations of (in-)equalities between parameter values have to be considered. When modeling the component as an RMM, however, memorable data values are provided by output symbols without any additional effort. Apart from this improvement in terms of efficiency, our algorithm also produces a much more intuitive model. In the case of the FIFO set of size 4, on the other hand, inferring plain Mealy machines using symmetry reduction is as efficient as inferring RMMs. This is due to the fact that for the FIFO set guards have to be inferred, which is expensive.

Table 2. Impact of the size of $\mathcal{D}$ on model and algorithmic complexity when inferring classical Mealy machine models of a stack with a capacity of 4

$|\mathcal{D}|$	$|Q|$	w/o sym.red. MQs	EQs	w/ sym.red. MQs	EQs
1	5	32	2	32	2
2	31	486	4	277	4
3	121	3,072	4	657	4
4	341	12,710	4	854	4

Considering the plain Mealy machines, one notices the rather large state space. This is due to the fact that, since Mealy machines are data-unaware, each possible combination of data values results in a different state (as can also be seen in Fig. 3). Further, to faithfully relate data values in both input and output in a Mealy machine, it would be necessary to have at least as many different data values as can be distinguished by the component. This leads to an exponential growth of the state space (and thus complexity in terms of membership queries), as can be seen in Tab. 2, where both the size of the state space and the query complexity are displayed for growing values of $|\mathcal{D}|$ and a fixed capacity of 4.

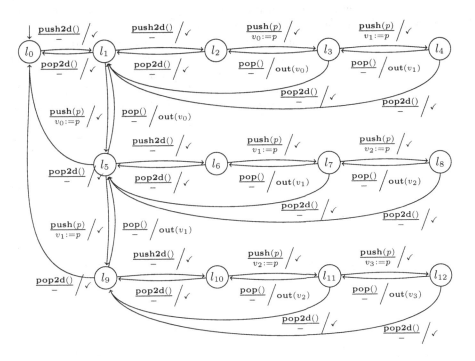

Fig. 4. RMM for a 2-dimensional stack of overall capacity 4. Operations **push2d** and **pop2d** operate the outer stack while **push** and **pop** operate the inner stacks. Unsuccessful operations (i.e., reflexive transitions) are omitted.

As with increasing capacities more data values are needed to observe the behavior exhaustively, one easily sees that this becomes intractable very quickly. Symmetry reduction helps to reduce the number of membership queries, but does not solve the issues regarding the large state space.

We conducted a second series of experiments in order to analyze the behavior of our algorithm on more complex data structures. For this, we chose a two-dimensional data structure, a *stack of stacks*. The interface exposes operations **push2d, pop2d, push, pop**, the former two operating on the (outer) "stack of stacks", the latter two on the (inner) stack (of plain values) currently at the top: **push2d()** puts an additional stack on top of the outer stack (as long as this does not violate capacity restrictions), and **pop2d()** removes this stack. On the other hand, **push**(p) pushes a value onto the current inner stack, while **pop()** outputs and removes the top value of the inner stack. The capacity of the inner stacks is denoted by m, while n denotes the capacity of the outer stack. The experimental results can be found in Tab. 3.

The inferred RMM model for the case $m = n = 2$ is shown in Figure 4: From the initial location a **push2d()** in required to make the first inner stack accessible. The transitions between locations l_1, l_5, and l_9 are operations on the first inner stack. From each of these locations a **push2d()** will lead to a subgraph, describing actions on the second inner stack – relative to the state (contents) of the first inner stack.

For this series of experiments we did not compare our algorithm to alternative approaches as this would certainly be a vain endeavor: Considering the stack for $m = 4, n = 4$ (thus capable of holding in total 16 elements), the state space of a Mealy machine with $|\mathcal{D}| = 4$ would have significantly more than $4^{16} = 2^{32}$ states, which is several orders of magnitude higher than the number of *membership queries* alone required by our algorithm. In particular, we tested this for $n = 3, m = 3, |\mathcal{D}| = 3$, where the unfolded Mealy machine has 65,641 states, compared to 3,910 membership queries for inferring the respective RMM. Further, when increasing any of these values, it was not possible to unfold the model in reasonable time any more.

We did not measure time in our experiments, as we deem the complexity in terms of membership queries the more relevant result. However, even these complex models could be inferred rather quickly with our tool, not exceeding 20 seconds even for $n = 4, m = 4$. This is by far lower than the time required to unfold the RMM in order to obtain a plain Mealy machine, even for $|\mathcal{D}| = 2$.

Table 3. Experimental results for inferring a two-dimensional stack with outer capacity n and inner capacity m

m	$|L|$	$n = 2$ MQs	EQs	$|L|$	$n = 3$ MQs	EQs	$|L|$	$n = 4$ MQs	EQs
1	7	160	1	15	470	3	31	1,142	5
2	13	373	2	40	1,596	5	121	5,126	5
3	21	744	3	85	3,910	6	341	16,454	6
4	31	1,283	5	156	8,551	9	781	44,589	9

5   Conclusions and Future Work

In this paper we have presented a new method for generating semantic (i.e., data-aware) interfaces for black-box components. Our approach is based on an extension of active automata learning for Register Automata, allowing us to deal with data values in inputs and outputs. Although this extension is technically quite straightforward, its impact is dramatic: The complexity of our "stack of stacks" examples is far beyond the reach of the state of the art in interface synthesis: our largest example, whose RMM has only 781 states, *independently* of the size of the data domain and is learned fully automatically in 20 seconds using only 9 equivalence queries, would lead to more than 10^9 states for an abstract data domain of just four values!

Currently, we are investigating the limitations of the RMM technology. In particular, we are investigating whether this technology is sufficient to satisfy the real time requirements of the CONNECT project, where component interfaces must be learned fully automatically at run time, a requirement considered a true bottleneck up to now.

References

1. Alur, R., Cerný, P., Madhusudan, P., Nam, W.: Synthesis of interface specifications for Java classes. In: POPL, pp. 98–109 (2005)
2. Ammons, G., Bodík, R., Larus, J.R.: Mining specifications. In: POPL, pp. 4–16 (2002)
3. Angluin, D.: Learning Regular Sets from Queries and Counterexamples. Information and Computation 75(2), 87–106 (1987)
4. Berg, T., Grinchtein, O., Jonsson, B., Leucker, M., Raffelt, H., Steffen, B.: On the Correspondence Between Conformance Testing and Regular Inference. In: Cerioli, M. (ed.) FASE 2005. LNCS, vol. 3442, pp. 175–189. Springer, Heidelberg (2005)
5. Biermann, A.W., Feldman, J.A.: On the Synthesis of Finite-State Machines from Samples of Their Behavior. IEEE Trans. Comput. 21, 592–597 (1972)
6. Cassel, S., Howar, F., Jonsson, B., Merten, M., Steffen, B.: A Succinct Canonical Register Automaton Model. In: Bultan, T., Hsiung, P.-A. (eds.) ATVA 2011. LNCS, vol. 6996, pp. 366–380. Springer, Heidelberg (2011)
7. Dallmeier, V., Lindig, C., Wasylkowski, A., Zeller, A.: Mining object behavior with ADABU. In: Proceedings of the 2006 International Workshop on Dynamic Systems Analysis, WODA 2006, pp. 17–24. ACM, New York (2006)
8. Ernst, M.D., Perkins, J.H., Guo, P.J., McCamant, S., Pacheco, C., Tschantz, M.S., Xiao, C.: The Daikon system for dynamic detection of likely invariants. Science of Computer Programming 69(1-3), 35–45 (2007)
9. Ghezzi, C., Mocci, A., Monga, M.: Synthesizing Intentional Behavior Models by Graph Transformation. In: ICSE 2009, Vancouver, Canada (2009)
10. Henzinger, T.A., Jhala, R., Majumdar, R.: Permissive interfaces. In: ESEC/SIG-SOFT FSE, pp. 31–40 (2005)
11. Howar, F., Steffen, B., Jonsson, B., Cassel, S.: Inferring Canonical Register Automata. In: Kuncak, V., Rybalchenko, A. (eds.) VMCAI 2012. LNCS, vol. 7148, pp. 251–266. Springer, Heidelberg (2012)
12. Lorenzoli, D., Mariani, L., Pezzè, M.: Automatic generation of software behavioral models. In: ICSE 2008, pp. 501–510. ACM (2008)
13. Margaria, T., Raffelt, H., Steffen, B.: Knowledge-based relevance filtering for efficient system-level test-based model generation. Innovations in Systems and Software Engineering 1(2), 147–156 (2005)
14. Raffelt, H., Steffen, B., Berg, T., Margaria, T.: LearnLib: a framework for extrapolating behavioral models. Int. J. Softw. Tools Technol. Transf. 11(5), 393–407 (2009)
15. Shoham, S., Yahav, E., Fink, S., Pistoia, M.: Static specification mining using automata-based abstractions. In: ISSTA 2007, pp. 174–184. ACM, New York (2007)
16. Steffen, B., Howar, F., Merten, M.: Introduction to Active Automata Learning from a Practical Perspective. In: Bernardo, M., Issarny, V. (eds.) SFM 2011. LNCS, vol. 6659, pp. 256–296. Springer, Heidelberg (2011)

Learning-Based Test Programming
for Programmers

Alex Groce, Alan Fern, Martin Erwig, Jervis Pinto,
Tim Bauer, and Amin Alipour

School of Electrical Engineering and Computer Science
Oregon State University, Corvalis, OR

Abstract. While a diverse array of approaches to applying machine learning to testing has appeared in recent years, many efforts share three central challenges, two of which are not always obvious. First, learning-based testing relies on adapting the tests generated to the program being tested, based on the results of observed executions. This is the heart of a machine learning approach to test generation. A less obvious challenge in many approaches is that the learning techniques used may have been devised for problems that do not share all the assumptions and goals of software testing. Finally, the usability of approaches by programmers is a challenge that has often been neglected. Programmers may wish to maintain more control of test generation than a "push button" tool generally provides, without becoming experts in software testing theory or machine learning algorithms, and with access to the full power of the language in which the tested system is written. In this paper we consider these issues, in light of our experience with adaptation-based programming as a method for automated test generation.

1 Introduction

The combination of machine learning (ML) and software/hardware correctness is now well-established as a fruitful intersection. In some cases, learning is used to aid complete verification: in these approaches, the stochastic nature of most machine learning is incidental. The learning is either by nature complete (e.g., using Angluin's algorithm [1] to learn a bounded finite state machine [2–4]) or intended to help produce an effective abstraction for model checking [5–7][1]. While the learning in some of these cases may not be guaranteed to reach a correct answer, it is easy to determine if the current answer is satisfactory: namely, when an abstraction produces either a proof of correctness or a valid counterexample, the current learned hypothesis is in no need of further refinement. Additionally, in these settings, the "user" for machine learning is a essentially a model

---

[1] In some cases, abstraction learning uses SAT to solve for a "perfect" hypothesis over current information, rather than a traditional ML algorithm; the approach is nonetheless learning, as it features an inductive bias and may be modified in response to future "training set" examples. The connection between CEGAR [8] and active learning is intuitively clear.

T. Margaria and B. Steffen (Eds.): ISoLA 2012, Part I, LNCS 7609, pp. 572–586, 2012.

checking algorithm; a human user of adaptive model checking or a learning-assisted Counterexample Guided Abstraction Refinement (CEGAR) [8] system need not even be aware that learning is taking place "underneath the hood", and is highly unlikely to have useful knowledge for improving the effectiveness of learning. Moreover, because a "correct" answer can be mechanically checked, there is typically no need for a user to assess the effectiveness of the learning algorithm.

Another large body of recent work at the intersection of ML and system reliability, however, has focused on learning to produce an effective test suite for a program, whether by genetic/evolutionary techniques [9, 10] or by reinforcement learning [11, 12]. In these cases, learning is obviously not expected to be complete (there is no final, "correct" test suite), and evaluating the effectiveness of testing techniques is notoriously difficult, since testing is typically applied to precisely those systems where complete verification is not feasible, the set of all faults for realistic systems is seldom if ever known, and coverage and other metrics of test suite quality are of varied and difficult-to-predict effectiveness [13–16]. In these cases, therefore, a human user often must assess the effectiveness of an "answer" provided by an ML algorithm, without a general mechanical means for evaluating its value. Moreover, even automated testing is usually much less of a "black box" approach than model checking, and the user is likely to want to or need to influence the choices made by a search or learning algorithm, or tune its heuristics or reward structure.

Efforts where the machine learning is directed towards testing a program, must therefore address a set of *three* potential core challenges:

1. First, learning-based testing is inspired by the idea of using machine learning to adapt the set of tests run to the Software Under Test (SUT): the learning problem is to choose new inputs based on the behavior observed on past inputs. Obviously, this problem is recognized and addressed by all learning/search-based testing approaches: proposing a solution to this problem defines the field! This problem is essentially equivalent to the core problem in ML for verification — the application of machine learning to a computational problem.

2. Second, in some cases, the learning techniques proposed may make assumptions that do not (quite) match the aims of software testing. In particular, for reinforcement-learning (RL) [17] based techniques, the goal of maximizing total coverage can lead to formulations of reward that do not naturally fit the usual RL assumptions.

3. Finally, programmers often want to experience the benefits of automated test generation without completely abandoning part of their test effort to a "black box" that is given, e.g., a set of method calls and input types, or a numeric input range, and produces tests. Effective random testing tools for complex system software, for example, are often highly engineered artifacts with special-casing, test case filtering, human-designed feedback, and hand-written specifications written in a standard programming language [18, 19]. In fact, random testing's popularity among programmers (even among those

who might be more inclined to prove programs correct, such as Haskell users [20]) is likely due to the combination of ease of use, effectiveness, and control that it provides programmers. The "interface" to random testing's core test-generation approach is simply a method for producing a pseudo-random number, which is provided as a standard library by all popular programming languages. The gap between test programming and "normal" programming in random testing essentially vanishes, and the only "tool" that must be understood is, typically, a small set of API calls.

In this paper, we discuss our experiences with these three challenges, in the context of one ML-based approach to software testing based on adaptation-based programming (ABP) [21]. Rather than new technical contributions or experimental results, the primary aim of this paper is to bring the second and third challenges of ML-based testing to the attention of other researchers and practitioners. We first briefly introduce ABP-based testing [12], then discuss the problems of adapting testing to learning (Section 2), adapting learning to testing (Section 3), and adapting test programming to programmers (Section 5), primarily focusing on the latter two, less widely recognized, challenges.

1.1 Adaptation-Based Programming

Adaptation-based programming (ABP) [21, 22] is a novel approach to programming that allows a programmer to exploit reinforcement learning (RL) [17] to "implement" difficult algorithms. Rather than writing code to compute a value, the programmer simply asks an ABP-library to "suggest" a value, given a context (the context is the formulation of the current state of the system). The programmer then rewards the ABP library based on how good the suggestion is. The ABP-library uses a reinforcement learning algorithm to attempt to optimize expected reward.

RL is an approach to the problem of learning controllers that maximize expected reward in controllable stochastic transition systems. Such a system can be imagined as a graph of control points with rewards possibly observed on transitions. Each control node has an associated set of actions that influence (perhaps only probabilistically) the transition taken. An optimum controller for such a system is one that selects actions at all control points such that total reward is maximized. Program-like structures annotated with control points are isomorphic to Semi-Markov Decision Processes (SMDPs), widely used models of controllable stochastic systems [23, 24]. The details of SMDP theory are not essential to understand ABP: what is important is that there are well-known RL algorithms for learning policies (action choices based on a context indicating the control point) for SMDPs based on repeated interactions and rewards.

As an example, to program tic-tac-toe in ABP, a programmer would allow the ABP library to suggest a move (e.g. a number 1-9 indicating a board position) based on the current board state (perhaps a string, e.g. 'X-XO-OO-X'),

```
playGame():
  ABP.beginEpisode();
  while (!gameOver()) {
    context = boardState();
    move(ABP.suggest(boardState()));
    if (victory())
      ABP.reward();
    opponentMove();
  ABP.endEpisode()
```

Fig. 1. Pseudo-code for ABP-style Tic-Tac-Toe

and provide a positive reward if the move proposed resulted in a win (see Figure 1 for pseudo-code). Each game would constitute one "episode" of learning, since moves in previous games have no influence on reward for future games. Initially, behavior of the ABP-based player would be essentially random. Over time, however, the adaptive process (the library's encapsulation of all it has learned about the problem using RL) should improve its play; for a simple game like tic-tac-toe this might only take a small number of iterations. A key point is that the programmer need not be aware of the concept of SMDPs underlying this adaptation to the reward function. The programmer only needs to be able to generate a good description of the current state and a reasonable evaluation of choices made.

The ABP library referred to in this paper, available for download on the web [25], makes use of a popular reinforcement learning algorithm called $SARSA(\lambda)$ [17]. At the heart of $SARSA(\lambda)$ is the notion of a Q value defined as follows: at adaptive A, the Q value of context c and action a ($Q_A(c, a)$) is the expected sum of rewards seen by executing a in c and following the optimal policy thereafter. Learning these Q values allows us to pick actions optimally since the best action is simply the one with the largest Q value. The $SARSA(\lambda)$ algorithm learns Q values from experience. This is done by executing the learning algorithm for a number of episodes during which it updates the Q values at every (*context, action*) pair that is encountered. The algorithm follows an ϵ-greedy explore-exploit policy which means that the best action is chosen (i.e. exploited) with probability $(1 - \epsilon)$ while an action is chosen randomly (i.e. explored) with the remaining ϵ probability. The library uses a small (typical) value of 0.1 for ϵ. Finally, the value of λ ($\in [0, 1]$) controls the extent to which a particular action is given credit for future rewards. A large value of λ updates an action's Q value with rewards that occur long after the action is taken whereas a small value of λ only updates the Q value with rewards seen immediately after the action is taken. Our ABP library sets λ to the moderately high value of 0.75, allowing test coverage that only results from a complex combination of operations to be effectively taken into account.

```
import abp.*;
...
public enum TestOp implements java.io.Serializable
    INSERT,REMOVE,FIND;
    public static final Set<TestOp> AllVals =
      unmodifiableSet(EnumSet.allOf(TestOp.class));
...
  AdaptiveProcess test = AdaptiveProcess.init();
  HashSet<String> states = new HashSet<String>(); // Store all states visited
  Adaptive<String,TestOp>opChoice =
    test.initAdaptive(String.class,TestOp.class);
  Adaptive<String,TestVal>valChoice =
    test.initAdaptive(String.class,TestVal.class);
  for (int i = 0; i < NUM_ITERATIONS; i++) {
    SUT = new SplayTree(); // Create an empty container at beginning of each test case
    Oracle = new BinarySearchTree(); // Empty oracle container
    String context = SUT.toString();
    // The context/state is simply a linearization of the SplayTree
    for (int j = 0; j < M; j++) {
      TestOp o = opChoice.suggest(context, TestOp.AllVals);
      // Used just like pseudo-random number generator
      TestVal v = valChoice.suggest(context, TestVal.AllVals).ordinal();
      Object r1, r2;
      switch (o) {
      case INSERT:
        r1 = SUT.insert(v);
        r2 = Oracle.insert(v);
        break;
      case REMOVE:
        r1 = SUT.remove(v);
        r2 = Oracle.remove(v);
        break;
      case FIND:
        r1 = SUT.find(v);
        r2 = Oracle.find(v);
        break;
      }
      assert ((r1 == null && r2 == null) || r1.equals(r2)); // Behavior should match
      context = SUT.toString(); // Update the context
      if (!states.contains(context)) { // Is this a new state?
        states.add(context);
        test.reward(1000); // Good work, AdaptiveProcess test, you found a new state!
      }
    }
    test.endEpisode();
  }
```

Fig. 2. Adaptation-Based Programming: a Simple Example

1.2   ABP-Based Testing

The key insight of ABP-based testing is that a programmer can take a similar approach to generating tests for a program with a clear API or other stateful input-definition. Rather than selecting moves in a game, she lets the ABP library select methods to call and parameters for the selected method calls for the program being tested (the SUT). In practice, the programmer essentially writes a random testing harness, replacing calls to a pseudo-random number generator with calls to the ABP library's **suggest** method, using, e.g., a string representation (via **toString**) of the SUT's current state as a context. Each test sequence (from container initialization until we begin a new test on a new container) constitutes an episode. Figure 2 shows an example ABP test harness for a **SplayTree** class, using a binary search tree (a simpler to implement library with equivalent functionality) as an oracle. Notice that the ABP-based testing harness is just a standard Java program, making calls to a library implemented in Java. No special compilation or execution environment is involved; conceptually, the ABP library's interface is only slightly more complex than that of a typical pseudo-random number generator. Note that the use of methods with a single integer parameter is simply an accident of the example; an Adaptive (action variable) can be based on any finite type (though, as in pure random testing, we might expect poor results when the size of the domain is too large). The key question is now: what can the programmer reasonably use as a reward, in order to "encourage" the adaptive process to thoroughly test the SplayTree code?

The example provides a concrete clue to the general answer. After each test step, the harness checks to see if the current SUT state has been previously seen during testing. If not, it adds it to the set of visited states and *rewards the ABP library for exposing new behavior of the SUT*. In other words, the programmer can provide *rewards based on increases in test coverage*. It is easy to augment coverage instrumentation to not only record statement/branch/path coverage, but to signal an appropriate reward for new coverage. This gives the ABP's adaptive process an optimization goal that the programmer can hope will correlate with effective testing, with little additional complexity over that required in computing coverage in the first place. Initially, in the absence of experience, ABP chooses randomly, effectively duplicating random testing. However, after the adaptive process has observed a few rewards, the learned policy will, with high probability (about 90% of the time), take the actions with maximum predicted reward, and only choose randomly 10% of the time. This alternation between exploiting what has been learned and exploring with random actions ensures that testing is likely to improve over time but that exploration is never abandoned.

Note that in some sense this approach to rewards is "abusing" the basis of RL: the objective function is changing with each episode, in that the probabilities of reward for certain actions in certain states is decreasing with time. The adaptive process will *only* receive a reward for its first exploration of a new coverage element, whether that element is a statement, a branch, a shape, a path, or a predicate valuation. This approach to reward derives from typical methods for evaluating software test suites: for any coverage metric, the "score" for a suite is typically based on treating the suite as a "hitting set" for the coverage targets: in typical usage, if suite A takes 100% of all program branches precisely once each and suite B covers 90% of all branches, but takes each branch 10 times, we simply say that suite A "has better branch coverage." Even using a set of coverages (including path, branch, and statement) as in our framework only complicates this essential fact: repeated exploration is not considered valuable, in and of itself. In the usual RL setting, e.g., game playing or planning, reaching a goal in future episodes is just as good as reaching it the first time — e.g., there is no penalty for winning a game in the same state as in a previous game. This property of rewards is known as stationarity. Experimental results [12] indicate that this unusual reward structure does not prevent the ABP library from learning a policy that, over time, improves test suite coverage. Informally, we can think of this setting as playing a game against an opponent who never "falls for" the same trick twice — but exploring strategies similar to those that recently proved successful increases the chance of finding a new way to win.

Out experimental results indicate that ABP can be effective for testing, at least for container classes and an HTML parser, even with no tuning of the RL algorithm to the problem, and no programmer tuning of the contexts used or reward structure beyond a naive combination of string linearizations and "off-the-shelf" coverage metrics.

2 Adapting Testing to Learning

The previous section of this paper presents one approach to the problem of adapting testing to learning. Many other approaches are possible, but all are essentially applications of some learning or search algorithm to the problem of test generation, and in this sense typical of much applied machine learning research. The nature and importance of this problem is widely understood. We do believe that one aspect of this problem (related to the generally difficult problem of evaluating test suites) may merit further attention, but must delay the discussion of this idea (in Section 4) until after we place it in the context of adapting learning to testing.

3 Adapting Learning to Testing

ML-based testing has mostly applied off-the-shelf techniques to the problem of software testing. While using ML as a "black-box" is a good start, it unfortunately treats software testing as "just another domain." This is in contrast to much work in the ML community, where learning algorithms are often developed to leverage the structure of a problem, particularly for those with significant applications. Such a learning algorithm can be expected to perform far better than a more general one. The problem of testing software is of sufficient importance to warrant a learning algorithm explicitly designed for it. Therefore, in this section, we attempt to identify the specific characteristics of software testing, viewed as a class of learning problems. We use the gained insight to propose extensions to the existing ABP-based testing framework followed by sketching an outline of RL algorithms that might be better suited for our purpose.

3.1   Assessment of ABP-Based Software Testing

In section 1.2, we briefly described how the current use of the ABP system violates one of the fundamental assumptions of the underlying RL algorithm, namely, the stationarity of the reward signal. The assumption of stationarity means that the expected reward we get for being in a particular context c does not depend on how many times we have visited a context. However, this is clearly violated in the software testing setting, where the reward for being in a context, will typically decrease each time the context is re-visited. At the extreme, if a context corresponds exactly to a program state, then the reward would often be zero after the first visit, depending on the kind of coverage considered.

However, despite the non-stationarity, positive experimental results indicate that the learner can still use the feedback to improve testing performance. In order to understand this behavior, it is useful to note that each context c used in software testing actually represents an entire class of program states. It appears that this fact leads to a useful form of generalization that the ABP system is able to exploit. In particular, if a context is visited for the first time and results in a positive reward, then the ABP system will tend to estimate that the context will have a positive reward in the future. This is a good assumption when that context describes a set of unique but similar program states that will each generate rewards on the first visit. In this situation, the ABP system will tend to bias the exploration of the program executions toward such promising contexts.

$$Q_{t+1}(c, a) = Q_t(c, a) + \alpha z(r_t) \tag{1}$$

Of course, after visiting a context many times, we can expect that the positive rewards will become rare. Unfortunately, this is where the ABP system will run into difficulty. The value estimates maintained by the ABP system, which are used to select its actions, are averages of observed reward sequences (see Equation 1). It can take significant time for this average to track the change in reward for a context and in the meantime the ABP system will continually explore the now exhausted context, wasting program executions. Eventually the system will learn that the previously attractive contexts are exhausted and then explore more promising areas. It is easy to imagine situations where this type of behavior can lead an ABP-based system to perform worse than random testing. In particular, this will happen when the early positive impact of ABP's biased exploration does not counteract the later inefficiencies resulting from slowly realizing a context is no longer rewarding. In what follows, we propose a number of simple extensions to the current ABP system that might allow it to better leverage this insight.

3.2 Dealing with Non-stationarity

One approach to dealing with non-stationarity is to use a more refined context. For example, if we augment a given context with the counts of how many times we've visited the context, then the reward signal will appear to be much more stationary. However, there is a serious drawback to this "solution." The number of possible contexts would increase substantially and this would reduce the ABP system's ability to generalize, which was one of our main hypothesized reasons for the ABP system's current success. Thus, simply increasing the scope of the context does not appear to address the fundamental issue.

Another approach would be to adjust the way that the system updates the Q-values $Q_A(c, a)$, which estimate the value of taking action a in context c for adaptive A. Recall that these values are used to select an action to execute in a given context. Currently, after each program trajectory, these values are updated as a moving average of past rewards and the newly observed reward. As mentioned above, this averaging process can be quite slow with respect to realizing that a previously good Q-value is now bad. A solution would be to place more weight on the newly observed rewards in the update equations. This is certainly a reasonable engineering approach to the problem, that deserves further investigation. However, there is no clear principle for selecting the particular weighting scheme, which is likely to vary from problem to problem, leading to robustness concerns.

A more principled approach would be to explicitly define a non-stationary reward model that makes sense for software testing and to modify the RL algorithms to take that model into account. In particular, this reward model should encode the notion that subsequent visits to a newly discovered context are likely to produce a reward pattern that tends to decrease toward. Working out the technical details of this approach is an interesting research problem and would suggest new update mechanisms that would actively try to estimate non-stationary changes and correct Q-value estimates accordingly.

The last observation raises an interesting question: Is learning online, as we do here, the best way to apply RL to software testing? A fundamentally different approach is training offline on a diverse set of programs which has the potential of improving generalization between contexts. Furthermore, training offline produces a useful policy that can be applied off-the-shelf to testing a SUT which is desirable since its performance can be carefully evaluated before deployment and optimized for efficiency. This approach requires a carefully engineered context encoding for an SUT (perhaps by ML experts) which seems feasible. For instance, we may include features that compute counts of the number of new states seen from a given (*context, action*) pair, number of visits since the last reward was seen, and so on. It opens the door to using efficient feature vector representations which typically achieve better generalization compared to the current tabular approach. If required, we may even have different contexts corresponding to fundamental differences in search spaces.

3.3   Monte-Carlo Tree Search

The ABP approach has so far focused on controlling exploration by biasing random walks according to continually adapting Q-value estimates. There are, however, other approaches for exploration developed in the machine learning (and more generally, the AI) field, that also deserve attention. One particularly promising class of algorithms is known as Monte-Carlo Tree Search (MCTS) [26], which has demonstrated tremendous success in recent years, most famously for its major advances in computer Go [27]. In the context of software testing, MCTS can be viewed as a way of building a tree of program executions in a way that is biased toward more promising areas of the tree. Each iteration of MCTS would correspond to selecting a program execution, where the actions at adaptives are selected in a way that attempts to balance exploration with exploitation of actions that look more promising based on past executions. One of the key contributors to the recent success of MCTS is the use of modern rules for managing this explore/exploit tradeoff in a theoretically rigorous way that works well in practice.

MCTS seems well-suited for testing software since any good adaptive method of testing software within a time budget should perform a careful exploration of an unknown search space. It is easy to modify the existing ABP library so that MCTS could be run under the hood rather than RL, with no noticeable difference to the tester with respect to writing the adaptive test program. However, like RL, MCTS also assumes the search problem involves stationary rewards. Thus, an interesting research direction is to consider variants of MCTS that capture its strengths while taking into account the non-stationary nature of the software testing search problems. As for RL, there are a variety of starting points for doing this, the most promising of which is to explicitly build a model of non-stationary reward into an MCTS algorithm, which continually tries to estimate the non-stationarity and account for that in its explore/exploit behavior.

4   Adapting Testing to Learning, Revisited

One mitigation of the problem of non-stationary reward is to abandon the typical software testing evaluation of test suites as hitting sets. While re-visits of coverage entities should almost certainly be de-valued according to some discount function, considering one execution of a branch in a test suite to be just as effective for testing as multiple executions is not particularly intuitive. Certainly, when evaluating randomly-generated suites in terms of fault detection, test engineers prefer suites that detect a fault multiple times to suites that only detect a fault once, on the grounds that the later method has a high probability of not detecting the fault at all [28]. Model checking heuristics based on structural coverage have used such a discounted (rather than binary) approach successfully [29, 30]. Note that this approach, to our knowledge not applied in learning-based approaches to date, only reduces the non-stationarity of the reward, rather than completely removing it. We do not believe that considering a suite that executes one branch 1,000 times "just as good as" a suite that executes 1,000 branches once is wise, so some discount for revisits is clearly required.

5   Adapting Test Programming to Programmers

It seems rather obvious that a program can be tested only after it has been written. This view can easily lead to the assumption that test cases for a program also have to be created after it has been been written. This perspective leads to a decoupling of testing from programming, which has the danger of making testing seem more like an optional part, something that can be left out. In a sense, this is the point of view taken by testing approaches that take as input a program, its input structure, and possibly a specification, and output a set of tests, whether this generation is based on machine learning or some other technique.

That testing can be integrated well with programming has been impressively demonstrated by the QuickCheck tool for Haskell [20]. QuickCheck provides an easy way for a programmer to generate random values of almost any predefined or user-defined type. The programmer implements tests by writing Haskell functions that represent properties to be checked. These properties can then be tested using the automatically generated data. The fact that tests for Haskell code are written as Haskell functions as well as the fact that automatic test data generation is also expressed within the program to be tested leads to a testing system that is tightly integrated into the language that is to be tested.

Specifically, QuickCheck is a *domain-specific language* for testing. A domain-specific language (DSL) offers notations and abstractions that are designed to work in a specific application domain [31]. DSLs can be implemented in quite different ways. Most importantly, we can distinguish between *external* and *internal* DSLs. An external DSL is implemented as a stand-alone product, which means that it has complete control over the syntax of the DSL, which is one of the major advantages of external DSLs. On the other hand, the implementation of an external DSL is usually quite complex and often difficult to adapt. In contrast, an internal DSL is implemented as an extension of an existing language (called the *host language*) and uses constructs of the host language as part of its syntax. Internal DSLs are also called domain-specific *embedded* languages (DSELs) [32]. DSELs are easier to implement and adapt since they can reuse much of the infrastructure of the host language. For example, all functionality for arithmetic or string processing is immediately available whereas these have to be reimplemented in an external DSL. QuickCheck is a DSEL in Haskell and it depends crucially on the fact that it has direct access to Haskell code. It is hard to imagine a version of QuickCheck implemented as an external DSL, which would essentially have to re-implement a significant part of, if not all of, the Haskell language.

We find ourselves in a quite similar situation for ABP. While QuickCheck is a tool for deriving properties of a program, ABP is a tool for changing programs. It is in a sense a metaprogramming tool. But much like QuickCheck, ABP needs access to the program it is supposed to adapt — which is precisely what the Java ABP library provides, a language embedded in Java that offers constructs to produce adaptive Java programs.

The combination of ABP with testing further leverages the integration into the host language and makes it possible to base the adaptation process of test cases on information obtained directly from the program to be tested during the testing process itself. In particular, in contrast to test-generation approaches that operate as external tools, ABP-based testing can "talk to" the program being tested (and its host language) with great ease, letting programmers assert as much or as little control over the testing process as with random testing. This gives programmer some extremely useful abilities:

- A context in ABP can be anything that can be computed by the SUT or by auxiliary functions in the host language. In our container class experiments, "system state" was produced by simply calling toString, abstracting the result with a simple string-processing function written in Java, and merging in some single-test coverage results.
- The reward in ABP can, again, be computed by arbitrary code. It can make complex context-sensitive evaluations of test fitness easy by directly inspecting system state. There is no need to express desirable properties of the system's behavior in any language other than that of the implementation itself.
- Similarly, if programmers wish to introduce new coverage metrics that generalize to more than one program, they can program these instrumentations in Java itself, making use of reflection. Our own implementation uses automatic instrumentation to compute path coverage based on Java-coded branch and statement coverage provided by CodeCover [33].
- A programmer can "override" ABP when needed — if certain behaviors in rare states are known to lead to known faults, for example, a hand-coded choice function can be used in place of the ABP suggestion.
- Contracts/properties can be implemented directly in SUT terms, without the need to learn a new property language.
- ABP-based testing, as noted before, "looks like" simple random testing (or generalized unit testing) to a large extent, and does not require a programmer to leave the "comfort of home" by changing languages or running an external tool.

In a sense, ABP-based testing has some similarities to the approach to checking C code introduced in version 4.0 of the SPIN model checker [34, 35]. The ability to directly call C code, check properties, and bias model checking exploration based on C-language constructs made it much easier to model check large, complex C programs in SPIN [36, 37]. C served as a "DSEL" for SPIN's PROMELA language; in our case, we are similarly describing a search problem, with the added advantage of not requiring programmers to switch between two languages (SPIN and PROMELA): testing and tested code are both written in Java, and have the same language of discourse.

In short, the realization of ABP as a DSEL is crucial in feeding test-relevant program information into the adaptation process, and it is this language design decision which contributes significantly to the style of ABP-based testing that makes it into an interesting new opportunity for programmers.

6   Conclusions

While the use of machine learning (and related AI approaches) in testing has already proved fruitful, we believe that the full potential of this combination can only be reached when research efforts move beyond formulating testing problems as machine learning problems to consider two additional aspects that distinguish learning-based test generation from the use of machine learning in model checking:

- First, while off-the-shelf ML/AI approaches may work well for testing, many of the most effective uses of ML involve leveraging the structure of a unique problem domain with new machine learning algorithms specially suited for the nature of the problem at hand.
- Second, the adaptation of learning-based testing by users outside the research community may be greatly speeded by placing test generation in a context that such users already understand: namely, the language in which they are developing the Software Under Test. Such an approach not only makes using ML to produce tests more appealing to programmers; it also gives test generation systems access to programmer knowledge and the full power of the implementation language, which may improve the quality of the tests generated.

In particular, the second point brings us to the title of this paper. We have come to believe that it may be fruitful to think of learning-based test generation not so much as "generation" which implies a completely automatic process without human control but as *test programming* where a human test engineer/domain expert makes use of algorithmic techniques to ease the task of *programming* a highly effective method for generating tests. ABP systems (in conjunction with automated coverage tools) can in this light be seen simply as libraries, albeit more sophisticated and powerful than most, for helping programmers write programs to accomplish their tasks. It may be possible to (mostly) remove the human programmer from testing; we do not know if it is altogether wise.

References

1. Angluin, D.: Learning regular sets from queries and counterexamples. Information and Computation 75, 87–106 (1987)
2. Cobleigh, J.M., Giannakopoulou, D., Păsăreanu, C.S.: Learning Assumptions for Compositional Verification. In: Garavel, H., Hatcliff, J. (eds.) TACAS 2003. LNCS, vol. 2619, pp. 331–346. Springer, Heidelberg (2003)
3. Groce, A., Peled, D., Yannakakis, M.: Adaptive Model Checking. In: Katoen, J.-P., Stevens, P. (eds.) TACAS 2002. LNCS, vol. 2280, pp. 357–370. Springer, Heidelberg (2002)
4. Peled, D., Vardi, M.Y., Yannakakis, M.: Black box checking. In: FORTE, pp. 225–240 (1999)
5. Brady, B., Bryant, R.E., Seshia, S.A.: Learning conditional abstractions. In: Proceedings of the IEEE International Conference on Formal Methods in Computer-Aided Design (FMCAD), pp. 116–124 (October 2011)

6. Gupta, A., Clarke, E.M.: Reconsidering CEGAR: Learning good abstractions without refinement. In: International Conference on Computer Design, pp. 591–598 (2005)
7. Chaki, S., Clarke, E., Groce, A., Strichman, O.: Predicate Abstraction with Minimum Predicates. In: Geist, D., Tronci, E. (eds.) CHARME 2003. LNCS, vol. 2860, pp. 19–34. Springer, Heidelberg (2003)
8. Clarke, E., Grumberg, O., Jha, S., Lu, Y., Veith, H.: Counterexample-Guided Abstraction Refinement. In: Emerson, E.A., Sistla, A.P. (eds.) CAV 2000. LNCS, vol. 1855, pp. 154–169. Springer, Heidelberg (2000)
9. McMinn, P.: Search-based software test data generation: A survey. Software Testing, Verification, and Reliability 14, 105–156 (2004)
10. Andrews, J., Li, F., Menzies, T.: Nighthawk: A two-level genetic-random unit test data generator. In: Automated Software Engineering, pp. 144–153 (2007)
11. Veanes, M., Roy, P., Campbell, C.: Online Testing with Reinforcement Learning. In: Havelund, K., Núñez, M., Roşu, G., Wolff, B. (eds.) FATES/RV 2006. LNCS, vol. 4262, pp. 240–253. Springer, Heidelberg (2006)
12. Groce, A.: Coverage rewarded: Test input generation via adaptation-based programming. In: IEEE/ACM International Conference on Automated Software Engineering, pp. 380–383 (2011)
13. Frankl, P.G., Weiss, S.N.: An experimental comparison of the effectiveness of branch testing and data flow testing. IEEE Transactions on Software Engineering 19, 774–787 (1993)
14. Frankl, P.G., Iakounenko, O.: Further empirical studies of test effectiveness. In: International Symposium on Foundations of Software Engineering, pp. 153–162 (1998)
15. Lyu, M.R., Huang, Z., Sze, S.K.S., Cai, X.: An empirical study on testing and fault tolerance for software reliability engineering. In: International Symposium on Software Reliability Engineering, pp. 119–126 (2003)
16. Cai, X., Lyu, M.R.: The effect of code coverage on fault detection under different testing profiles. In: International Workshop on Advances in Model-Based Testing, pp. 1–7 (2005)
17. Sutton, R., Barto, A.: Reinforcement Learning: an Introduction. MIT Press (1998)
18. Groce, A., Holzmann, G., Joshi, R.: Randomized differential testing as a prelude to formal verification. In: International Conference on Software Engineering, pp. 621–631 (2007)
19. Yang, X., Chen, Y., Eide, E., Regehr, J.: Finding and understanding bugs in C compilers. In: Programming Language Design and Implementation, pp. 283–294 (2011)
20. Claessen, K., Hughes, J.: QuickCheck: a lightweight tool for random testing of haskell programs. In: International Conference on Functional Programming, pp. 268–279 (2000)
21. Bauer, T., Erwig, M., Fern, A., Pinto, J.: Adaptation-based programming in Java. In: ACM SIGPLAN Workshop on Partial Evaluation and Program Manipulation, pp. 81–90 (2011)
22. Pinto, J., Fern, A., Bauer, T., Erwig, M.: Robust learning for adaptive programs by leveraging program structure. In: International Conference on Machine Learning and Applications, pp. 943–948 (2010)
23. Andre, D., Russel, S.: State abstraction for programmable reinforcement learning agents. In: National Conference on Artificial Intelligence (2002)
24. Mahadevan, S.: Agent reward reinforcement learning: Foundations, algorithms, and empirical results. Machine Learning 22(1), 159–195 (1996)

25. Fern, A., Pinto, J., Bauer, T.: Adapatation-based programming library in Java, http://groups.engr.oregonstate.edu/abp/
26. Browne, C., Powley, E., Whitehouse, D., Lucas, S., Cowling, P., Rohlfshagen, P., Tavener, S., Perez, D., Samothrakis, S., Colton, S.: A survey of monte carlo tree search methods. IEEE Transactions on Computational Intelligence and AI in Games 4(1), 1–43 (2012)
27. Gelly, S., Silver, D.: Achieving master level play in 9× 9 computer go. In: Proceedings of the AAAI on Artificial Intelligence, pp. 1537–1540 (2008)
28. Andrews, J.H., Groce, A., Weston, M., Xu, R.G.: Random test run length and effectiveness. In: Automated Software Engineering, pp. 19–28 (2008)
29. Groce, A., Visser, W.: Model checking Java programs using structural heuristics. In: International Symposium on Software Testing and Analysis, pp. 12–21 (2002)
30. Groce, A., Visser, W.: Heuristics for model checking Java programs. Software Tools for Technology Transfer 6(4), 260–276 (2004)
31. Fowler, M.: Domain-Specific Languages. Addison-Wesley Professional (2010)
32. Hudak, P.: Building Domain-Specific Embedded Languages. ACM Computing Surveys 28(4es), 196–196 (1996)
33. Codecover - an open-source glass-box testing tool., http://codecover.org/
34. Holzmann, G.J., Joshi, R.: Model-Driven Software Verification. In: Graf, S., Mounier, L. (eds.) SPIN 2004. LNCS, vol. 2989, pp. 76–91. Springer, Heidelberg (2004)
35. Holzmann, G.J.: The SPIN Model Checker: Primer and Reference Manual. Addison-Wesley Professional (2003)
36. Groce, A., Holzmann, G., Joshi, R., Xu, R.G.: Putting flight software through the paces with testing, model checking, and constraint-solving. In: International Workshop on Constraints in Formal Verification, pp. 1–15 (2008)
37. Holzmann, G., Joshi, R., Groce, A.: Model driven code checking. Automated Software Engineering 15(3-4), 283–297 (2008)

LearnLib Tutorial: From Finite Automata to Register Interface Programs

Falk Howar[1], Malte Isberner[2], Maik Merten[2], and Bernhard Steffen[2]

[1] Carnegie Mellon University, Silicon Valley Campus,
Mountain View, CA
falk.howar@tu-dortmund.de
[2] Technical University Dortmund, Chair for Programming Systems,
Dortmund, D-44227, Germany
{malte.isberner,maik.merten,steffen}@cs.tu-dortmund.de

1 Motivation

In the past decade, active automata learning, an originally merely theoretical enterprise, got attention as a method for dealing with black-box or third party systems. Applications ranged from the support of formal verification, e.g. for assume guarantee reasoning [4], to usage of learned models as the basis for regression testing. In the meantime, a number of approaches exploiting active learning for validation [17,20,6,7,2,1] emerged.

Today, active automata learning is on the verge of becoming a valuable asset in bringing formal methods to systems lacking formal descriptions (e.g., the huge class of legacy systems): This edition of ISoLA alone features a track on active learning in formal verification [16], one on model-based testing and model inference [12], this tutorial, and is co-located with the STRESS summer school,[1] where active automata learning is part of the curriculum.

In particular when dealing with black-box systems, i.e., systems that can be observed, but for which no or little knowledge about the internal structure or even their intent is available, *active* automata learning can be considered as a key technology due to its test-based approach to model inference. However, the test-based interaction introduces a number of challenges when using active automata learning to infer models of real word systems, which have been summarized in [21]:

A: Interacting with Real Systems
The interaction with a realistic target system comes with two problems. The technical problem of establishing an adequate interface that allows one to apply test cases for realizing so-called membership queries, and a conceptual problem of bridging the gap between the abstract learned model and the concrete runtime scenario.

B: Membership Queries
Whereas small learning experiments typically require only a few hundred membership queries, learning realistic systems may easily require several orders of magnitude more.

---

[1] http://info.santoslab.org/event/stress2012

T. Margaria and B. Steffen (Eds.): ISoLA 2012, Part I, LNCS 7609, pp. 587–590, 2012.

C: Reset

Active learning requires membership queries to be independent. Whereas this is no problem for simulated system, this may be quite problematic in practice.

D: Parameters and Value Domains

Active learning classically is based on abstract communication alphabets. Parameters and interpreted values are only treated to an extent expressible within the abstract alphabet. In practice, this typically is not sufficient, not even for systems as simple as communication protocols, where, e.g., increasing sequence numbers must be handled, or where authentication requires matching user/password combinations.

E: Equivalence Queries

Equivalence queries compare a learned hypothesis model with the target system for language equivalence and, in case of failure, return a counterexample exposing a difference. In practice, equivalence queries will have to be approximated using membership queries. Methods from conformance testing have been suggested as approximations but are in general too expensive to be feasible for industry scale applications.

The tutorial discusses all these issues along a number of practical examples. In particular, using the LearnLib [19,18,15,13], a flexible automata learning framework, it provides hands-on experience on

- Challenge A: It is discussed how test drivers can be created for the LearnLib. Starting with the construction of application-specific test drivers by hand, it is discussed how a generic test driver can be employed by means of configuration. This configuration can be (semi-)automatically created by analysis of the target system's interface [14].
- Challenge E: Here we illustrate how a more global view of the learning process that more closely coalesces the two intertwined learning phases of model construction and model validation improves both, intuition and efficiency. This approach was applied successfully as part of the winning contribution of the ZULU competition [5,9] where it clearly dominated other methods of searching for counterexamples.
- Challenge D: Here two approaches are discussed and applied [22], alphabet abstraction refinement [10], and the explicit treatment of data flow using the more powerful modeling format of register automata [3,8,22].

Participants are invited to experience the impact of all these methods on their own laptop using their own LearnLib installation.[2]

References

1. Aarts, F., Schmaltz, J., Vaandrager, F.W.: Inference and Abstraction of the Biometric Passport. In: Margaria, Steffen [11], pp. 673–686

---

[2] http://www.learnlib.de

2. Bohlin, T., Jonsson, B.: Regular Inference for Communication Protocol Entities. Technical report, Department of Information Technology, Uppsala University, Schweden (2009)

3. Cassel, S., Howar, F., Jonsson, B., Merten, M., Steffen, B.: A Succinct Canonical Register Automaton Model. In: Bultan, T., Hsiung, P.-A. (eds.) ATVA 2011. LNCS, vol. 6996, pp. 366–380. Springer, Heidelberg (2011)

4. Cobleigh, J.M., Giannakopoulou, D., Păsăreanu, C.S.: Learning Assumptions for Compositional Verification. In: Garavel, H., Hatcliff, J. (eds.) TACAS 2003. LNCS, vol. 2619, pp. 331–346. Springer, Heidelberg (2003)

5. Combe, D., de la Higuera, C., Janodet, J.-C.: Zulu: An Interactive Learning Competition. In: Yli-Jyrä, A., Kornai, A., Sakarovitch, J., Watson, B. (eds.) FSMNLP 2009. LNCS, vol. 6062, pp. 139–146. Springer, Heidelberg (2010)

6. Hagerer, A., Hungar, H., Niese, O., Steffen, B.: Model Generation by Moderated Regular Extrapolation. In: Kutsche, R.-D., Weber, H. (eds.) FASE 2002. LNCS, vol. 2306, p. 80. Springer, Heidelberg (2002)

7. Hagerer, A., Margaria, T., Niese, O., Steffen, B., Brune, G., Ide, H.-D.: Efficient Regression Testing of CTI-Systems: Testing a Complex Call-center Solution. Annual Review of Communication, Int.Engineering Consortium (IEC) 55, 1033–1040 (2001)

8. Howar, F., Steffen, B., Jonsson, B., Cassel, S.: Inferring Canonical Register Automata. In: Kuncak, V., Rybalchenko, A. (eds.) VMCAI 2012. LNCS, vol. 7148, pp. 251–266. Springer, Heidelberg (2012)

9. Howar, F., Steffen, B., Merten, M.: From ZULU to RERS – Lessons Learned in the ZULU Challenge. In: Margaria, Steffen [11], pp. 687–704

10. Howar, F., Steffen, B., Merten, M.: Automata Learning with Automated Alphabet Abstraction Refinement. In: Jhala, R., Schmidt, D. (eds.) VMCAI 2011. LNCS, vol. 6538, pp. 263–277. Springer, Heidelberg (2011)

11. Margaria, T., Steffen, B. (eds.): ISoLA 2010, Part I. LNCS, vol. 6415. Springer, Heidelberg (2010)

12. Meinke, K., Walkinshaw, N.: Model-based Testing and Model Inference. In: Margaria, T., Steffen, B. (eds.) ISoLA 2012, Part I. LNCS, vol. 7609, pp. 440–443. Springer, Heidelberg (2012)

13. Merten, M., Howar, F., Steffen, B., Cassel, S., Jonsson, B.: Demonstrating Learning of Register Automata. In: Flanagan, C., König, B. (eds.) TACAS 2012. LNCS, vol. 7214, pp. 466–471. Springer, Heidelberg (2012)

14. Merten, M., Isberner, M., Howar, F., Steffen, B., Margaria, T.: Automated Learning Setups in Automata Learning. In: Margaria, T., Steffen, B. (eds.) ISoLA 2012, Part I. LNCS, vol. 7609, pp. 591–607. Springer, Heidelberg (2012)

15. Merten, M., Steffen, B., Howar, F., Margaria, T.: Next Generation LearnLib. In: Abdulla, P.A., Leino, K.R.M. (eds.) TACAS 2011. LNCS, vol. 6605, pp. 220–223. Springer, Heidelberg (2011)

16. Pasareanu, C., Bobaru, M.: Learning Techniques for Software Verification and Validation. In: Margaria, T., Steffen, B. (eds.) ISoLA 2012, Part I. LNCS, vol. 7609, pp. 505–507. Springer, Heidelberg (2012)

17. Peled, D., Vardi, M.Y., Yannakakis, M.: Black Box Checking. Journal of Automata, Languages and Combinatorics 7(2), 225–246 (2002)

18. Raffelt, H., Steffen, B.: LearnLib: A Library for Automata Learning and Experimentation. In: Baresi, L., Heckel, R. (eds.) FASE 2006. LNCS, vol. 3922, pp. 377–380. Springer, Heidelberg (2006)

19. Raffelt, H., Steffen, B., Berg, T., Margaria, T.: LearnLib: A Framework for Extrapolating Behavioral Models. Int. J. Softw. Tools Technol. Transf. 11(5), 393–407 (2009)
20. Shahbaz, M., Li, K., Groz, R.: Learning Parameterized State Machine Model for Integration Testing. In: Proc. 31st Annual Int. Computer Software and Applications Conf., vol. 2, pp. 755–760. IEEE Computer Society, Washington, DC (2007)
21. Steffen, B., Howar, F., Merten, M.: Introduction to Active Automata Learning from a Practical Perspective. In: Bernardo, M., Issarny, V. (eds.) SFM 2011. LNCS, vol. 6659, pp. 256–296. Springer, Heidelberg (2011)
22. Steffen, B., Howar, F., Isberner, M.: Active Automata Learning: From DFAs to Interface Programs and Beyond. In: ICGI 2012 (2012)

Automated Learning Setups
in Automata Learning[*]

Maik Merten[1], Malte Isberner[1], Falk Howar[1],
Bernhard Steffen[1], and Tiziana Margaria[2]

[1] Technical University Dortmund, Chair for Programming Systems,
Dortmund, D-44227, Germany
{maik.merten,malte.isberner,falk.howar,steffen}@cs.tu-dortmund.de
[2] University Potsdam, Chair for Service and Software Engineering,
Potsdam, D-14482, Germany
margaria@cs.uni-potsdam.de

Abstract. Test drivers are an essential part of any practical active
automata learning setup. These components to accomplish the translation of abstract learning queries into concrete system invocations while
managing runtime data values in the process. In current practice test
drivers typically are created manually for every single system to be
learned. This, however, can be a very time-consuming and thus expensive
task, making it desirable to find general solutions that can be reused.

This paper discusses how test drivers can be created for LearnLib, a
flexible automata learning framework. Starting with the construction of
application-specific test drivers by hand, we will discuss how a generic
test driver can be employed by means of configuration. This configuration
is created manually or (semi-)automatically by analysis of the target
system's interface.

1   Introduction

In recent years, automata learning has been employed to create formal models of real-life systems, such as electronic passports [1], telephony systems [5,7],
web applications [14,15], communication protocol entities [3], and malicious networked agents [4]. The wide scope of application areas gives testimony on the
universality of the automata learning approach.

However, challenges remain regarding the construction of application-specific
learning setups. A major obstacle for widespread deployment of active automata
learning is the effort needed to design and implement application-fit learning setups. This involves determining a suitable form of abstraction and finding ways to
manage concrete runtime data that influences the behavior of the target system.
In [16], the combined effort for constructing an application-specific abstraction
and a test driver is estimated to have consumed approximately 27% of the total

---

[*] This work was partially supported by the European Union FET Project CON-
NECT: Emergent Connectors for Eternal Software Intensive Networked Systems
(http://connect-forever.eu/).

T. Margaria and B. Steffen (Eds.): ISoLA 2012, Part I, LNCS 7609, pp. 591–607, 2012.

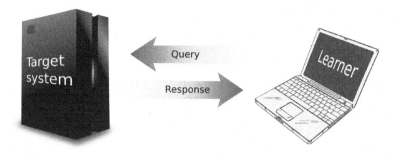

Fig. 1. High-level overview on an active learning setup

effort of analyzing an embedded system from the application area of automotive systems.

Learning aims at inferring an abstract model of the SUL. While the chosen abstraction has influence on the expressiveness of the final learned model, dealing with concrete runtime data is an immediate concern when interacting with reactive systems where communication often is dependent on concrete data values previously transferred. For example, a system guarded by an authorization system may transport a security token to the client on login, which then has to be included in any interaction with protected system areas.

In order to support the full communication of the learner with the SUL, the learning setup has to translate abstract learning queries into concrete requests to the target system. These concrete requests may have to be outfitted with data values. In automata learning, the building block facilitating the translation is a so-called mapper [8]. In this paper we show how to manually create test drivers that include mapper functionality, and discuss how a reconfigurable and reusable test driver can be set up by means of interface analysis.

2   Active Automata Learning

In active automata learning, models of a target system—here denoted as *SUL* (*System Under Learning*)—are created by active interaction and by reasoning on the observed output behavior. This is done by constructing *queries*, which are sequences of *input symbols* from an alphabet that represents actions executable on the SUL, and answering these queries by means of actual execution. A high-level overview of the structure of an active automata learning setup is provided in Figure 1.

There exists a variety of different active learning algorithms that interrogate the SUL in the described fashion. A selection of algorithms, complete with corresponding infrastructure, is provided with LearnLib [13,11], a versatile automata learning framework available free of charge at http://learnlib.de.

Fig. 2. A possible data dependency between method calls

3   A Running Example

In this paper, we will discuss the construction of test drivers along the example of a fictional e-commerce application where users can log in, retrieve a list of products, add products to their shopping cart, and finally buy its contents. This example has been implemented as web service exposing a WSDL interface and thus offers a standardized and networked way of interaction. Following methods are exposed:

- openSession expects user credentials and returns an authentication token. Conversely, destroySession invalidates a specified session and the associated shopping cart.
- getAvailableProducts returns a list of available products.
- addProductToShoppingCart expects an authentication token identifying a user session and adds a provided product to the associated shopping cart. Conversely, the emptyShoppingCart primitive empties the shopping cart of a specified session. The method getShoppingCart returns a representation of the session's shopping cart, with references to all products it contains.
- buyProductsInShoppingCart will purchase the contents of the shopping cart associated with the provided session.

When interacting with this example system, the following challenges have to be addressed, and we will refer to these challenges when demonstrating ways to establish application-fit learning setups:

Data dependencies: To be able to learn this system, the learning setup needs to deal with the data dependencies between methods. For instance, most actions require a valid authentication token which is provided by the openSession primitive. However, this method again is dependent on data values, namely valid login credentials, which have to be provided beforehand. This situation is illustrated in Figure 2.

Dependencies on substructures: Merely filling in parameters with runtime values is not sufficient to interact with this system. For instance, the addProductToShoppingCart method expects a single product to be provided. The getAvailableProducts method provides a collection of fitting data values, but the returned data structure cannot be directly used as a parameter value for addProductToShoppingCart, that expects only a single data value, as illustrated in Figure 3. Determining a fitting valuation for this parameter requires a basic

Fig. 3. A data dependency involving a singular value out of a collection of values

understanding of the application's data structures, accompanied by means to execute basic operations on these data structure such as, e.g., isolating single data values out of a collection of values.

These two forms of dependencies imply a required, but not sufficient order on method calls. For instance, the method **buyProductsInShoppingCart** needs a valid session identifier to conclude a purchasing transaction, implying that the method **openSession** needs to be called beforehand. However, this alone is not sufficient, as empty shopping carts cannot be purchased, which is a behavioral aspect arising from the stateful nature of the system that cannot be determined by data dependency analysis alone. Active automata learning, however, is able to fill in these state-dependent behavioral traits.

In the following we discuss an architecture for test drivers that enables dealing with these challenges.

4   Test Drivers and Mappers in Active Automata Learning

In most real-life automata learning applications, learning alphabets impose an abstraction on the actual interaction with the SUL. For instance, a sequence of several concrete input symbols of the SUL may be combined into one single abstract symbol that represents a single use case.

Consequently, as the active automata learning procedure has to procure the production of observable system output, these abstract learning alphabets have to be translated into concrete system alphabets, i.e., alphabets composed of inputs the target system can process. Conversely, the concrete system output has to be translated into abstract output symbols that fit the intended model structure.

In practice, this two-way translation process can be handled by a test driver, which can be integrated seamlessly into LearnLib's modular framework. Figure 4 shows a component-wise view onto such a test driver, embedded within a learning setup. In this figure, the following core components are visible:

– A *mapper* is responsible for bridging the gap between abstract and concrete alphabets, i.e., the mapper is responsible for the translation of learning queries composed of abstract input symbols into queries composed of concrete system inputs. For parameterized symbols, the mapper also determines fitting parameter valuations and inserts these data values accordingly. Referring to the running example, the mapper concretely invokes the **openSession**

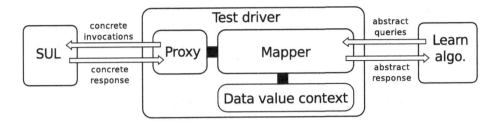

Fig. 4. General architecture of a test driver for active automata learning

action on the SUL with fitting credentials whenever an abstract symbol such as "login" is encountered. The concrete return value of this method, which differs for every invocation, needs to be abstracted to gather reproducible observations. This can be done, e.g., by emitting an output symbol that merely denotes invocation success or failure.

- The *data value context* supports the mapper whenever parameterized actions have to be translated. Many interactions with SULs require parameter values, e.g., login procedures need preset credentials that do not change during learning, while subsequent actions may require an authentication token determined at runtime. The data value context manages such concrete values from the application's data value domain, which is a prerequisite for overcoming both data-related challenges outlined in Section 3. Data values are fetched and updated according to requests issued by the mapper component during concretization and abstraction steps. During concretization data values are fetched from the data value context and used by the mapper for parameterized invocations. Consequently, when abstracting from concrete return values, the mapper will generate a fitting abstract output symbol, but will also issue a request to the data value context to store the concrete data value for future reference. In the running example, the `openSession` action returns an authentication token whose concrete value needs to be stored for methods such as `addProductToShoppingCart`.

- The *proxy* is a component that directly interfaces with the SUL, maintains a connection and thus serves as the funnel to direct learning queries to the target system. Responses of the target system are collected by the proxy and transferred into concrete output symbols subsequently processed by the mapper component. The main purpose of the proxy thus is to facilitate interaction with the SUL by means of a unified invocation mechanism (e.g., simple Java methods), abstracting from the underlying invocation technology (such as, e.g, SOAP, RMI or CORBA). For systems with an interface description in a standardized format such as WSDL, fitting proxy objects can often be generated fully automatically by employing connector generation tools for that standardized format. The example application falls within this category: it exposes a WSDL interface that can be converted into invocable code by a tool that emits a Java class encapsulating the remote invocation mechanics.

Providing these three components can be a major bottleneck when preparing real-life learning scenarios. This effort includes thoughtful construction of the involved abstraction layers and implementation of the according translation mechanisms, i.e., the construction of a fitting mapper.

5   Manual Construction of Test Drivers and Setups

In LearnLib, any components that answer learning queries need to implement the MembershipOracle interface. A test driver implemented according to this interface possesses one single method processQuery providing system output in response to system input, i.e., it generates output for learning queries.

Figure 5 shows a manually created test-driver for the example system described in Section 3. For reasons of simplicity, not all actions available on the target system are implemented in this test driver. Regarding the core components of the test driver, the following implementations can be observed:

- The *mapper* is implemented using hardwired abstraction and concretization steps, e.g., by invoking the openSession method of the target system when the abstract input symbol "login" is encountered. In the code example, the mapping between abstract symbols and concrete invocations is realized employing simple if statements (lines 20 to 26). In a similarly coarse fashion system output is abstracted as "ok" if no error was signaled, as "error" otherwise (lines 26 and 30 respectively). In effect this means that both the abstract input alphabet ("login", "getProducts", and "addProduct") and the abstract output alphabet ("ok" and "error") are fixed, as is the mapping from the abstract input alphabet to the concrete system invocations (methods openSession, getAvailableProducts and addProductToShoppingCart). Note that this particular test driver does not support any additional symbols: for instance, to actually conclude a purchase, it would have to be extended accordingly.
- The variables session and products in the processQuery method (lines 11 and 12) are used as a *data-value context* to resolve *data dependencies*. The former is employed to store the invocation result of the openSession method, the latter stores a collection of product information returned by getAvailableProducts. The credentials for the openSession method (line 21) are hardcoded strings which were determined beforehand.

  As described in Section 3 on the challenge of *dependencies on substructures*, direct use of runtime data as parameter valuations is not always sufficient. This is visible in line 25, where the addProductToShoppingCart action is invoked. There, the second parameter is instantiated using the products variable. However, instead of passing the whole collection of products as parameter, a single value is selected (in this case always the first element). This constitutes an operation upon a data structure previously returned by the application, which involves a basic understanding of the organization of the affected data structure.

```
1  public class TestDriver implements MembershipOracle {
2
3    private ShopSystem system = new ShopSystem ();
4
5    @Override
6    public Word processQuery (Word query) throws LearningException {
7      // output word collecting system reaction
8      Word output = new WordImpl ();
9
10     // variable to store authentication token
11     Session session;
12     Product[] products;
13
14     for (int i = 0; i < query.size (); ++i) {
15       // retrieve current symbol from query
16       Symbol inputsym = query.getSymbolByIndex (i);
17
18       try {
19         // act on system according to abstract symbol
20         if (inputsym.toString ().equals ("login")) {
21           session = system.openSession ("username", "password");
22         } else if (inputsym.toString ().equals ("getProducts")) {
23           products = system.getAvailableProducts ();
24         } else if (inputsym.toString ().equals ("addProduct")) {
25           system.addProductToShoppingCart (session, products[0]);
26         }
27
28         // no error
29         output.addSymbol (new SymbolImpl ("ok"));
30
31       } catch (Exception e) {
32         // error signalled via system exception
33         output.addSymbol (new SymbolImpl ("error"));
34       }
35     }
36
37     return output;
38   }
39 }
```

Fig. 5. A manually created test-driver

– The *proxy* in this example is provided in the form of the `system` variable (line 3), which contains a reference to an object directly exposing the SUL's methods, e.g., an object generated from the system's WSDL interface description. This object encapsulates interacting with the SUL by means of network messages, shielding the test driver developer from interaction details such as maintaining a network connection and assembling, e.g., SOAP (Simple Object Access Protocol) messages. Thus the proxy object enables interaction with the target system by means of simple method invocations, as is done in lines 21, 23 and 25.

Clearly, hand-tailoring fitting test drivers for more complex systems can quickly become a bothersome, time-consuming (and thus expensive) task. To make matters worse, such test drivers are not reusable for any other system than for the original SUL and offer only limited flexibility even when considering a single system, because each adaption necessitates code changes.

The following sections will discuss how the setup effort can be dramatically reduced, to the point of approaching fully automated construction and execution of learning setups.

6   Constructing Learning Setups by Interface Analysis

Key to automated instantiation of learning setups is the development of flexible, configurable test drivers. Such a test driver was developed for LearnLib, which can operate on a wide range of systems [12]. It is structured as follows:

– The *mapper* translates abstract input symbols into concrete Java method invocations of the proxy. The return values are stored in the data value context as named variables. Abstract output symbols named after these variables are returned on success. If, e.g., the proxy signals a system exception, an abstract error symbol is emitted instead. In contrast to the manually constructed test driver discussed in Section 5 the abstraction function is not hard coded, but configurable.
– As *data value context* a JavaScript context is employed. It can not only store named variables to resolve *data dependencies*, and also allows the execution of data retrieval operations, such as isolating single data values from complex data structures such as collections to resolve the challenge of *dependencies on substructures*. The data value context is also employed to store predefined data values such as login credentials.
– The *proxy* is a Java object upon which methods are invoked employing the Java reflection API. While in Section 5 the proxy object was hardcoded in the test driver, the configurable test driver is designed to generate a proxy object at runtime from an interface description and subsequently use it for system invocation. This is currently implemented for WSDL, employing the `wsimport` utility, so it suffices to provide only an URL to the interface description.

When employing such a test-driver, fitting configurations must be determined for the mapper, the proxy generation and the data value context. This boils down to the questions of how to construct an alphabet, how to locate to the SUL's interface description, and how to manage live data values necessary to drive interaction with the target system. The questions can be answered by interface analysis, as illustrated in the following.

6.1 Constructing the Alphabet

Most APIs are structured with some sense of abstraction in mind. In fact, a major purpose of well-designed APIs is the abstraction from the underlying implementation details, offering application features in a structured and meaningful way.

When documenting how to interact with a target system, the abstraction level imposed by the design of the system's API is a natural abstraction level of the model that is to be created for documentation purposes. Thus, an alphabet can be constructed in a straightforward way:

- Every *method* in the API can be translated into an abstract symbol of the learning alphabet. The runtime semantics of these abstract learning symbols is the concrete invocation of the corresponding method exposed by the API.
- *Parameters* of API methods are handled by parameterizing the abstract learning symbols of parameterized interface methods. At runtime, fitting valuations have to be retrieved from the data value context and included in the concrete system invocations. Data values can be stored in named variables in the data value context. Parameters in abstract learning symbols subsequently refer to these variable names.
- *Return values* can be abstracted according to the return type, i.e., the abstract output symbol merely denotes that a data value of a specific type has been returned. The concrete live data values are delivered to the data value context and stored in variables named after the corresponding return types. In effect this means that only one data value per data type can be stored, a limitation which precludes, e.g., the possibility of invoking actions that require two distinct values of the same type. For systems that employ a single data type to encode data values with distinct purposes (e.g., if all data values are encoded as character strings) this limitation can severely restrict the ability to interact with the SUL, necessitating a refined approach for output abstraction. As demonstrated for learning Register Automata, it is possible to determine the exact set of data values that have to be memorized [6].

In case of standard Java interfaces, the necessary analysis steps can easily be done using the class reflection scheme that is part of the Java platform. Cross-platform interface description formats can usually be parsed by specialized tools in a comparable fashion.

6.2   Interfacing with the Target System

The configurable test driver includes a component to generate a proxy object from interface descriptions, which is currently implemented for WSDL interface descriptions. The `wsimport` tool employed generates a Java class that exposes the methods defined in the interface description and handles all networked communication with the SUL, abstracting from the underlying protocol details. Thus, from the perspective of the test driver, proxy objects generated by `wsimport` are merely normal Java objects, with methods that can be invoked dynamically at runtime by the Java reflection mechanism. Apart from WSDL web services (such as the discussed example system) this approach is also feasible for other remote invocation technologies, such as CORBA, for which similar code generation tools exist.

6.3   Managing Live Data Values

Method calls in interfaces often depend on parameters that are instantiated with runtime data. For example, a method may produce data values that are consumed by a consecutive method call. This is easy to witness in the example e-commerce scenario of Section 3, where one API method produces an authentication token that has to be provided by other methods of the system (a situation illustrated in Figure 2). This sort of data dependency must be satisfied with live data values determined at runtime. To be able to solve this problem with no or little manual intervention, such data dependencies must be determined automatically. In the following, a solution is sketched:

- In case of interfaces with strongly typed data, data dependencies can only exist in alignment with the type concept, i.e., a value returned by one method can only be provided as input parameter for another method if the return value type equals (or is a subtype of) the parameter type. Consequently, no data dependencies have to be assumed outside of the type hierarchy. In the example sketched above, one method may produce a sequence of values, each typed as "Product", which can subsequently be consumed by another method. Thus the former is a potential producer of viable data values for the latter.

  This type of analysis is bound to be impractical if the interface is specified over a depleted type system. For instance, many web services encode all or most data values as simple character strings. From the perspective of the type system thus any data values could apply "anywhere", devoid of any semantic meaning.

- If no data type concept is present (or if a depleted type concept is employed as described above), the syntactic analysis over data types can be replaced or augmented by a testing phase in which active interaction with the target system determines which return values are fitting input for parameters of subsequent method calls. This, in effect, means that static analysis of a strong type system is replaced by a training phase to determine a type system regarding interoperability of method calls. A tool for performing this kind of analysis on WSDL interfaces is `StrawBerry` [2].

Once the relation between methods and involved data types has been determined, the data flow induced by data dependencies can easily be realized by allocating one variable in the data value context per data type. Parameter values can be retrieved according to the parameter type and return values can be stored according to the returned data type. This scheme can be implemented with a data value context that in essence is a map containing data values associated with keys corresponding to the involved data types.

It is easy to see how simple data dependencies over single data values can be handled in this fashion.

However, the *dependencies on substructures* challenge described in Section 3 eludes this simple treatment as shown in Figure 3, where one method provides a sequence of values, while the other method consumes single values. This means that merely providing the returned sequence as parameter value is not an option. While it is possible to detect this situation during in-depth type analysis, a conventional map data structure is not a fitting implementation for the data value context, as simple operations such as isolation of single data values out of data value sequences are needed. The same problem occurs when only a single attribute of a complex data type has to be provided as an argument to another method call.

For this reason the data value context of the reconfigurable test driver employs a scriptable JavaScript context that can execute arbitrary program statements on stored data values, such as, e.g., "`elementof(collection)`", which retrieves one single data value out of a collection, and also supports the common dot notation for accessing attributes and methods of complex types. These statements are included in the abstract parameterized learning symbols and are evaluated as provided by the mapper component that inspects symbols of the abstract learning alphabet as part of the mapping process.

6.4   Employing Semantic Analysis

In Section 6.3, type analysis was employed to determine data-flow between invocations of the SUL. For cases where the type system of the interface description was nondescript or even missing, a testing phase was proposed to experimentally determine data dependencies between method invocations.

Any such testing procedure, however, may yield unsatisfactory results, depending on the complexity of inter-method data dependencies and the employed coverage criteria used during the testing phase. Thus data dependencies may be missed, causing the construction of incomplete system models in the subsequent active learning phase.

Due to the limitations of pure syntactical interface analysis, which can detect false data dependencies if generic data types are used as parameters and return types, and test-based analysis of data dependencies, which can miss data dependencies if testing is not thorough enough, an alternative approach is desirable.

602 M. Merten et al.

One such approach is based on explicitly specifying the semantical concepts of parameters and return values in a way that is independent of the type system. For WSDL, an extension called *Semantic Annotations for WSDL* (SAWSDL) has been proposed [17]. Using SAWSDL, data occurring in the interface description—not only on the level of formal parameters, but also for attributes of complex types—can be annotated with a reference to a concept in an Ontology. A common example is distinguishing the semantic concepts of the username and password parameters of a login operation, which usually are both strings, even in case of depleted type systems. Using an OWL reasoner like Pellet,[1] also more complex relations like subclassing and inferring class membership can be realized.

This approach crucially relies on semantic annotations (and a corresponding ontology) being available, an assumption which is false for most third-party web services. Despite allowing the most fine-grained inference of data dependencies, we will therefore not detail this approach here any further, as its applicability to real-world use cases is limited.

7 The Setup Interchange Format

The result of the analysis steps is stored in an interchange format, which is parsed to instantiate an actual learning setup. This format includes the following information:

- A location of the target system
- An instance pool of predetermined data values (such as credentials)
- A description of the alphabet, i.e., a list of methods that are to be invoked
- For every method information the symbolic names of parameters and return values

Such of a setup description file concerned with learning the example WSDL e-commerce application is presented in Figure 6.

The location of the target system is provided in Line 2, which denotes a URL from which to retrieve the WSDL interface descriptor. From this descriptor, tools such as `wsimport` can fully automatically generate Java proxy classes, which can be employed by a configurable test driver to facilitate SUL invocations.

Lines 3 to 6 specify an instance pool of two string values which represent authentication credentials for the target system. By their very nature, such values have to be provided beforehand, i.e., have to be present in the instance pool.

The provided credentials are utilized in Lines 8 to 18, where a symbol for the `openSession` method of the SUL is defined. This method is parameterized, expecting the credentials previously defined for the instance pool. The execution result is stored in a variable as defined in Line 17.

The method `getAvailableProducts`, defined in lines 20 to 23, is simpler in comparison, as no parameters are expected. The most sophisticated symbol declaration is the one of `addProductsToShoppingCart`, where the second

---

[1] http://clarkparsia.com/pellet

```
 1 <learnsetup>
 2 <serviceurl>http://vulpis.cs.tu-dortmund.de:9000/ecommerceservice?wsdl
     </serviceurl>
 3 <provided>
 4  <object name="username" type="string">username</object>
 5  <object name="password" type="string">password</object>
 6 </provided>
 7 <symbols>
 8  <symbol name="openSession">
 9   <parameters>
10    <parameter>
11     <alternative>username</alternative>
12    </parameter>
13    <parameter>
14     <alternative>password</alternative>
15    </parameter>
16   </parameters>
17   <return>session</return>
18  </symbol>
19  ...
20  <symbol name="getAvailableProducts">
21   <parameters />
22   <return>productArray</return>
23  </symbol>
24  ...
25  <symbol name="addProductToShoppingCart">
26   <parameters>
27    <parameter>
28     <alternative>session</alternative>
29    </parameter>
30    <parameter>
31     <alternative selector="elementOf" field="item">productArray
        </alternative>
32     <alternative selector="elementOf" field="items">shoppingCart
        </alternative>
33    </parameter>
34   </parameters>
35   <return>session</return>
36  </symbol>
37 </symbols>
38 </learnsetup>
```

Fig. 6. Example of a setup description file for automated setup instantiation

method parameter can retrieve valuations from two different named variables: productArray, which is returned by the getAvailableProducts symbol, or shoppingCart, which is provided by a symbol not visible in the chosen excerpt of the setup descriptor. Each of those two variables indeed provides collections of values of the required type Product, whereas the method parameter only expects a single Product object. Thus the elementOf selector is applied onto the respective fields of the data structures, retrieving a singular data value.

8   Usage in LearnLib

The main class for interfacing the above description of learning setup in a Learn-Lib application is the class LearnConfig. Upon construction it receives the XML file name, and provides the deduced information, such as the learning alphabet, in a form compatible with the LearnLib API.

Figure 7shows how such an automatically generated test driver is used in a LearnLib scenario. In lines 1–2, the LearnConfiguration object is created from the path name of a learning setup descriptor. For interfacing the target system (which is assumed to be a web service), a dynamic proxy object of type WSDL-DynamicProxy is instantiated (line 3). The purpose of this object is to provide a simple interface for invoking operations by name, which is achieved by generating proxy classes using the wsimport tool from the WSDL description of the service.

```
1  LearnConfiguration config
2     = new LearnConfiguration(new FileInputStream("learnsetup.xml"));
3  DynamicProxy proxy = new WSDLDynamicProxy(config.getServiceURL());
4  MembershipOracle mqOracle
5     = new ProxyOracle(config.getContextSeed(), proxy, ERROR, ERROR);
6
7  LearningAlgorithm learner = new Angluin();
8  learner.setAlphabet(config.getAlphabet());
9  learner.setOracle(mqOracle);
10
11 for(;;) {
12    learner.learn();
13    Automaton hypothesis = learner.getResult();
14    // ...
15 }
```

Fig. 7. Using an automatically generated test driver for a webservice in LearnLib

As has been noted in Section 5, a component answering queries has to implement the MembershipOracle interface. In our scenario, this is the ProxyOracle (lines 4–5). This oracle translates symbols of a special form to invocations on the proxy object. The LearnConfiguration method getAlphabet() (line 8) provides a learning alphabet which consists of symbols of the required form.

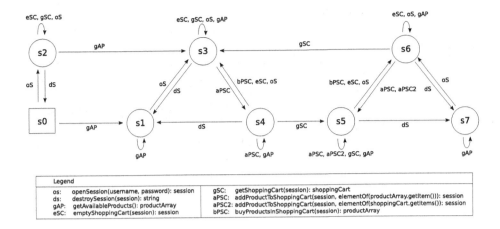

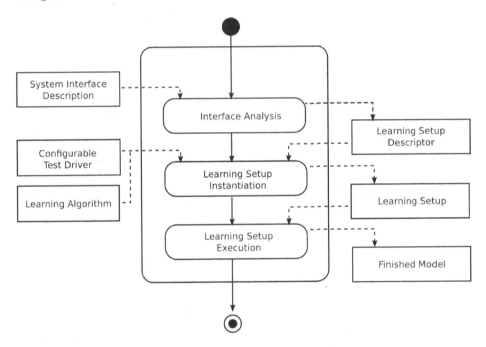

Fig. 8. Learned model of an e-commerce application, learned with the setup descriptor of Figure 6

Fig. 9. Overall workflow for (semi-)automated active automata learning

The single symbols are created from the setup description in the fashion sketched in Section 7. Having instantiated a membership oracle along with a compatible learning alphabet, learning can be performed in the usual fashion with an arbitrary learning algorithm such as Angluin's L^*.

Figure 8 shows the result of executing a learning setup with the presented configuration. The result of executing a learning setup with the presented configuration is shown in Figure 8. This model reveals properties of the system's behavior, for instance how to finally place an order (which requires a non-empty shopping cart), which is useful behavioral information when trying to interact with the system.

The overall workflow for active automata learning within the presented framework, formalized in XPDD [9], is shown in Figure 9: on the left hand side input artifacts are visualized (e.g., the SUL's interface description), while on the left hand side output artifacts are visible (most importantly the learned model). If all processing steps (shown in the center of the figure) are automated, complete learning setups can be instantiated and executed without manual intervention.

9   Conclusion

Test drivers with mapper functionality are essential components of pretty much every active learning setup involving real-life systems that react according to data generated at runtime.

In this paper we presented how to manually create application-specific data-aware test drivers for LearnLib, an extensible framework for automata learning. This is a straightforward process for systems of limited size, supported by the component-based approach of the LearnLib library.

For large-scale application and to create flexible learning setups, however, the approach of hand-crafting test-drivers is of limited appeal. Thus we presented a general architecture and concrete implementation of a reconfigurable test driver. The setup configuration for this test driver is generated by means of interface analysis, either conducted manually or (preferably) by automated means.

By introducing means to automatically generate setup descriptions, it is expected that automata learning becomes a much less laborious process, making adoption for real-life scenarios routinely feasible.

References

1. Aarts, F., Schmaltz, J., Vaandrager, F.W.: Inference and Abstraction of the Biometric Passport. In: Margaria, Steffen [10], pp. 673–686
2. Bertolino, A., Inverardi, P., Pelliccione, P., Tivoli, M.: Automatic synthesis of behavior protocols for composable web-services. In: van Vliet, H., Issarny, V. (eds.) ESEC/SIGSOFT FSE, pp. 141–150. ACM (2009)
3. Bohlin, T., Jonsson, B., Soleimanifard, S.: Inferring compact models of communication protocol entities. In: Margaria, Steffen [10], pp. 658–672
4. Bossert, G., Hiet, G., Henin, T.: Modelling to Simulate Botnet Command and Control Protocols for the Evaluation of Network Intrusion Detection Systems. In: Proceedings of the 2011 Conference on Network and Information Systems Security, La Rochelle, France, pp. 1–8 (June 2011)

5. Hagerer, A., Hungar, H., Margaria, T., Niese, O., Steffen, B., Ide, H.-D.: Demonstration of an Operational Procedure for the Model-Based Testing of CTI Systems. In: Kutsche, R.-D., Weber, H. (eds.) FASE 2002. LNCS, vol. 2306, pp. 336–340. Springer, Heidelberg (2002)

6. Howar, F., Steffen, B., Jonsson, B., Cassel, S.: Inferring Canonical Register Automata. In: Kuncak, V., Rybalchenko, A. (eds.) VMCAI 2012. LNCS, vol. 7148, pp. 251–266. Springer, Heidelberg (2012)

7. Hungar, H., Margaria, T., Steffen, B.: Test-based model generation for legacy systems. In: Proceedings of International Test Conference, ITC 2003, October 2-30, vol. 1, pp. 971–980 (2003)

8. Jonsson, B.: Learning of Automata Models Extended with Data. In: Bernardo, M., Issarny, V. (eds.) SFM 2011. LNCS, vol. 6659, pp. 327–349. Springer, Heidelberg (2011)

9. Jung, G., Margaria, T., Wagner, C., Bakera, M.: Formalizing a Methodology for Design- and Runtime Self-Healing. In: IEEE International Workshop on Engineering of Autonomic and Autonomous Systems, pp. 106–115 (2010)

10. Margaria, T., Steffen, B. (eds.): ISoLA 2010, Part I. LNCS, vol. 6415. Springer, Heidelberg (2010)

11. Merten, M., Howar, F., Steffen, B., Cassel, S., Jonsson, B.: Demonstrating Learning of Register Automata. In: Flanagan, C., König, B. (eds.) TACAS 2012. LNCS, vol. 7214, pp. 466–471. Springer, Heidelberg (2012)

12. Merten, M., Howar, F., Steffen, B., Pellicione, P., Tivoli, M.: Automated Inference of Models for Black Box Systems Based on Interface Descriptions. In: Margaria, T., Steffen, B. (eds.) ISoLA 2012, Part I. LNCS, vol. 7609, pp. 79–96. Springer, Heidelberg (2012)

13. Merten, M., Steffen, B., Howar, F., Margaria, T.: Next Generation LearnLib. In: Abdulla, P.A., Leino, K.R.M. (eds.) TACAS 2011. LNCS, vol. 6605, pp. 220–223. Springer, Heidelberg (2011)

14. Raffelt, H., Margaria, T., Steffen, B., Merten, M.: Hybrid test of web applications with webtest. In: TAV-WEB 2008: Proceedings of the 2008 Workshop on Testing, Analysis, and Verification of Web Services and Applications, pp. 1–7. ACM, New York (2008)

15. Raffelt, H., Merten, M., Steffen, B., Margaria, T.: Dynamic testing via automata learning. Int. J. Softw. Tools Technol. Transf. 11(4), 307–324 (2009)

16. Shahbaz, M., Shashidhar, K.C., Eschbach, R.: Iterative refinement of specification for component based embedded systems. In: ISSTA, pp. 276–286. ACM (2011)

17. W3C. Semantic Annotations for WSDL and XML Schema. Technical report (2007), http://www.w3.org/TR/sawsdl/

The RERS Grey-Box Challenge 2012:
Analysis of Event-Condition-Action Systems

Falk Howar[1], Malte Isberner[2], Maik Merten[2],
Bernhard Steffen[2], and Dirk Beyer[3]

[1] Carnegie Mellon University, Mountain View, USA
[2] TU Dortmund, Germany
[3] University of Passau, Germany

Abstract. The goal of the RERS Grey-Box Challenge is to evaluate the effectiveness of various verification and validation approaches on Event-Condition-Action (ECA) systems, which form a specific class of systems that are important for industrial applications. We would like to bring together researchers from all areas of software verification and validation, including theorem proving, model checking, program analysis, symbolic execution, and testing, and discuss the specific strengths and weaknesses of the different technologies.

Keywords: Program Analysis, Model Checking, Verification, Model-Based Testing, Competition, Event-Condition-Action System.

1 Motivation

Event-Condition-Action (ECA) Systems are omnipresent in industrial practice. Notable applications include programmable logic controllers (PLCs) [1], active databases [20], and web-service composition [4]. Moreover, they are the basis of the increasingly popular rule-based systems [16], which can be regarded as de-facto standard for dealing with permissions and access control, and ECAs are promoted as a means for realizing compliant business processes on top of rule engines like Drools [9] or JRules [8].

The popularity of this rule architecture comes from its apparent simplicity: one can add and change the functionality simply by adding and removing rules. However, this simplicity has its price: it is extremely difficult to understand and control the global implications of these apparently simple changes. It is almost impossible to manually find out if there are side-effects, whether the new rule is executed at all, if the whole rule system behaves deterministically, or if the system does actually terminate—to name only a few problems.

Modern verification techniques make it possible to automatically answer many of those questions. However, treating ECA systems is challenging for almost all verification and validation approaches, because there is little control structure to hook on to. The inherent structure of ECA systems (causalities, conflicts, dependencies, etc.) needs therefore to be inferred from their data-flow alone.

T. Margaria and B. Steffen (Eds.): ISoLA 2012, Part I, LNCS 7609, pp. 608–614, 2012.

To obtain an overview over the various techniques, and to compare the techniques on a common set of problems, we have set up a grey-box challenge.

The RERS[1] Grey-Box Challenge at ISoLA 2012 proceeds in two parts:

- an offline part, where the contestants have two months to analyze all benchmark systems and to carefully prepare their results, and
- an online part during ISoLA, where the contestants have to prepare their results between the opening on Sunday, October 14th, 2012 and the presentation session on Thursday, October 18th, 2012, in the morning.

Everybody who is interested in the verification of ECA systems is invited to apply his/her techniques to the ECA setting. The aim is to reveal, compare, and combine the specific strengths of the various verification techniques, be they manual, tool-supported, or fully automated, for treating this peculiar but nevertheless practically highly important kind of systems.

Springer sponsors a 500 Euro gift certificate for Springer books for the best solutions, and the teams with the best solutions in their categories will be invited for an STTT Special Section summarizing the results of the challenge, and, in particular, presenting the most advanced solutions.

The RERS Grey Box Challenge at ISoLA 2012 is the first of a series of events in which we aim at successively refining the 2012 challenge scenario in order to specifically discuss current strengths and limitations, and to exchange implementations, algorithms, ideas, and visions. In particular, during the challenge meeting at ISoLA 2012 it is planned to discuss the profile of the 2013 challenge held in fall in Mountain View as a satellite of ASE 2013. The third RERS challenge is planned to be part of ISoLA's 10th anniversary in 2014.

2   Characteristics of the Challenge

The challenge is very special. On the one hand, it is fully 'white-box'—the full Java/C code is available. On the other hand, it has a black-box character—ECA code is particularly unstructured, not easy to analyze.

It will therefore be interesting to see how well, e.g., program-analysis techniques and model checking, perform in comparison with black-box techniques like model-based testing, and how these techniques may be profitably combined. We are therefore particularly looking forward to contributions based on tools that comprise one or the combination of many of the following technologies:

- program analysis and verification [22],
- symbolic execution [18],
- software model checking [12, 17],

---

[1] The name RERS originally was an acronym for *R*egular *E*xtrapolation of *R*eactive *S*ystems. Although the name remained the same, the challenge itself has evolved towards a broader focus, addressing a variety of techniques for analyzing and inferring the behavior of reactive systems.

- statistical model checking [6],
- model-based testing [10],
- inference of invariants [14],
- automata learning [2, 23],
- run-time verification [19], and
- monitoring [15].

Of course, this list is not meant to be exhaustive. Rather we want to encourage everybody to approach this challenge with all the available means and ideas, and people are welcome to join effort and to approach the problem in heterogeneous teams.

3   Challenge Setup and Rules

Contestants are confronted with a number of ECA systems given in both Java and C, ranging from structurally simple and small to structurally complex and large, as well as corresponding collections of properties to be checked against these systems, which fall into two categories:

Reachability Properties: Some assignments to internal state variables correspond to erroneous states, which cause the system to fail with a specific error code. Not all of those error states are reachable, and the goal is to check which of these states can in fact be reached (it is not expected to also provide a sequence of inputs reaching them). Those errors come in the form of either an `IllegalStateException` (Java) or a failed assertion (C), along with a specific error label. Each individual such reachability problem is evaluated and ranked exactly in the same fashion as the behavioral properties.

Behavioral Properties: An execution trace of the ECA system consists of a sequence of inputs and outputs, each from a finite alphabet. For each of the systems, a file `properties.txt` is provided, containing a set of 100 properties for which the contestants have to check whether they are satisfied by all traces, or if there are traces that violate them (it is not expected to also provide these traces). The properties are given both as an LTL formula and a textual description. For example, (G ! oU) means that output U does never occur. In other words, the expression states that it is not possible—by any sequence of input events—to make the system produce an output action U.

To allow an intuitive mapping from LTL expressions to textual descriptions, the properties to be checked are closely adhering to the patterns in property specifications identified by Dwyer et al. [13]

In LTL formulas, the atomic propositions correspond to input and output symbols, where the prefix i is used for input and o is used for output symbols, to allow a clear distinction.[2]

The LTL formulas are given in a standard syntax, making use of the following temporal operators:

---

[2] The more common prefixes ? and ! for inputs and outputs, respectively, cause confusion with the unary negation operator !.

- **X**ϕ (next): ϕ has to hold after the next step
- **F**ϕ (eventually): ϕ has to hold at some point in the future (or now)
- **G**ϕ (globally): ϕ has to hold always (including now)
- ϕ**U**ψ (until): ϕ has to hold until ψ holds (which eventually occurs)
- ϕ**WU**ψ (weak until): ϕ has to hold until ψ holds (which does not necessarily occur)
- ϕ**R**ψ (release): ϕ has to hold until ψ held in the previous step.

Additionally, the boolean operators & (conjunction), | (disjunction) and ! (negation) are used.

In order to better reflect the multiple facets of the grey-box challenge, there will be two kinds of rankings:

- A purely numeric ranking, according to the percentage of correctly verified properties, providing a true *competition*. In order to express ones confidence in own verification results, one can assign to each verification result a confidence weight from 0 to 9. In case of a correct answer, the weight value is added to the overall score of the contestant. Otherwise, twice the weight value is subtracted.
- A conceptual ranking, according to the employed (combination of) methods, emphasizing the *challenge* character. In this category, solutions will be reviewed and ranked by the challenge team. Due to the possible variety of methods, there may be several winners in this category.

4   How to Proceed

We have set up the challenge problems for Java and C almost identically. The main difference is that input and output symbols are given as strings in the Java setting, and as plain integers in the C setting (an explicit request from the community). Despite this difference, one can proceed exactly in the same fashion, e.g.:

- For solving the implicit problems, a tool might analyze the code for error/exception/assertion labels. Each such label that occurs in the code defines a reachability problem, which can be solved with the method of the contestant's choice. There are no limitations.
- The explicit problems, even if reminding of typical model-checking problems, may also be dealt with in any fashion, e.g. data-flow analysis, symbolic execution, testing, learning, (statistical) model checking, run-time methods, etc.
- The challenge is free-style. The contestant's are allowed to patch the code in any way, but the validity has, of course, to be stated according to the original problems.
- One should first concentrate on the problems and properties that one can master well. There is no need to give an answer to all problems. Of course, the more problems one can tackle, the more points one may be able to win, but be aware: wrong answers have a large penalty!

– The weighting scheme gives a way to express personal confidence in the
obtained results, e.g., if one has found a path to some error and is convinced
that this is indeed feasible, then one should weight it with confidence level 9.
A liveness property, or stating that certain errors do not occur, is of course
more risky.

Concerning the second form of ranking, the team needs to write a short summary
of the chosen approach, the encountered hurdles, the solutions, and the obtained
results. In these summaries, honesty, e.g., also concerning weaknesses/limitations
of the employed methods, is important. Our challenge aims at profiling the various approaches and methods, which in particular means that weaknesses need
to be identified. Of course, we are also very interested in new ideas and solutions
that were motivated by the challenge.

The challenge starts with nine categories of ECA systems of varying complexity. After an initial phase of four weeks, three further problems of higher
complexity will be added, specifically tailored to differentiate the participating
competitors.

5   Relation to Other Challenges and Competitions

Competition and challenge events are well-understood in the community as an
effective means for technology evaluation and exchange, for revealing the state
of the art in a tangible fashion, and to stimulate robust tool implementations.
Notable examples range over various fields such as software verification [5], SAT
and SMT solving [3, 11], planning [25], quantified boolean formulas [21], hardware model checking [7], or theorem proving [24]. All of those events impact the
development pace and the quality of the competing software tools; results from
theory are almost instantly transferred to practical tool implementations.

Of the mentioned events, the Competition on Software Verification (SV-
COMP) [5] at TACAS is thematically closest to the RERS Grey-Box Challenge,
even though it is complementary in the following respects:

– The RERS Challenge focuses on a very specific program pattern, but considers complex properties, and allows competitors to employ arbitrary means,
both in terms of hardware and in terms of software.
– In contrast, SV-COMP focuses mainly on reachability problems to be solved
on a given platform under clearly defined frame conditions, but with strongly
varying program structures.

This difference characterizes SV-COMP as a pure competition with a clear ranking, which contrasts the RERS Challenge, whose frame conditions make it difficult to define a global ranking. This is why we have two rankings, one which is
purely numerical, simply based on a 'multiple choice' test which may be solved
'free-style', and one where the approach taken, the underlying ideas, and the
concrete realization are evaluated by the challenge team.

Acknowledgement. We would like to thank Rustan Leino and Jaco van de Pol for their helpful comments, and Maren Geske for her assistance in implementing the challenge infrastructure.

References

[1] Almeida, E.E.: Event-Condition-Action Systems for Reconfigurable Logic Control. IEEE Transactions on Automation Science and Engineering 4(2), 167–181 (2007)

[2] Angluin, D.: Learning Regular Sets from Queries and Counterexamples. Information and Computation 75(2), 87–106 (1987)

[3] Balint, A., Belov, A., Järvisalo, M., Sinz, C.: SAT Challenge 2012. In: SAT (2012), http://baldur.iti.kit.edu/SAT-Challenge-2012/index.html

[4] Benatallah, B., Sheng, Q.Z., Dumas, M.: The Self-Serv Environment for Web Services Composition. IEEE Internet Computing 7(1), 40–48 (2003)

[5] Beyer, D.: Competition on Software Verification (SV-COMP). In: Flanagan, C., König, B. (eds.) TACAS 2012. LNCS, vol. 7214, pp. 504–524. Springer, Heidelberg (2012), http://sv-comp.sosy-lab.org/

[6] Bianco, A., de Alfaro, L.: Model Checking of Probabilistic and Nondeterministic Systems. In: Thiagarajan, P.S. (ed.) FSTTCS 1995. LNCS, vol. 1026, pp. 499–513. Springer, Heidelberg (1995)

[7] Biere, A., Heljanko, K., Seidl, M., Wieringa, S.: HWMCC 2012. In: FMCAD (2012), http://fmv.jku.at/hwmcc12/

[8] Boyer, J., Mili, H.: IBM WebSphere ILOG JRules. In: Agile Business Rule Development, pp. 215–242. Springer (2011)

[9] Browne, P.: JBoss Drools Business Rules. Packt Publishing, Birmingham (2009)

[10] Broy, M., Jonsson, B., Katoen, J.-P., Leucker, M., Pretschner, A. (eds.): Model-Based Testing of Reactive Systems. LNCS, vol. 3472. Springer, Heidelberg (2005)

[11] Bruttomesso, R., Cok, D., Griggio, A.: SMT-COMP 2012. In: IJCAR (2012), http://smtcomp.sourceforge.net/2012/

[12] Clarke, E.M., Grumberg, O., Peled, D.: Model Checking. MIT Press (2001)

[13] Dwyer, M.B., Avrunin, G.S., Corbett, J.C.: Patterns in Property Specifications for Finite-State Verification. In: Boehm, B.W., Garlan, D., Kramer, J. (eds.) ICSE, pp. 411–420. ACM (1999)

[14] Ernst, M.D., Cockrell, J., Griswold, W.G., Notkin, D.: Dynamically Discovering Likely Program Invariants to Support Program Evolution. IEEE Transactions on Software Engineering 27(2), 99–123 (2001)

[15] Havelund, K., Roşu, G.: Monitoring Java Programs with Java PathExplorer. Electronic Notes in Theoretical Computer Science 55(2), 200–217 (2001); RV 2001, Runtime Verification (in connection with CAV 2001)

[16] Hayes-Roth, F.: Rule-Based Systems. Commun. ACM 28(9), 921–932 (1985)

[17] Holzmann, G.J., Smith, M.H.: Software Model Checking: Extracting Verification Models from Source Code. Software Testing, Verification and Reliability 11(2), 65–79 (2001)

[18] King, J.C.: Symbolic Execution and Program Testing. Commun. ACM 19(7), 385–394 (1976)

[19] Leucker, M., Schallhart, C.: A Brief Account of Runtime Verification. Journal of Logic and Algebraic Programming 78(5), 293–303 (2009)

[20] McCarthy, D., Dayal, U.: The Architecture of an Active Database Management System. In: Proceedings of the 1989 ACM SIGMOD International Conference on Management of Data, SIGMOD 1989, pp. 215–224. ACM, New York (1989)

[21] Narizzano, M.: QBFEVAL (2012), http://www.qbflib.org/index_eval.php

[22] Nielson, F., Nielson, H.R., Hankin, C.: Principles of Program Analysis. Springer-Verlag New York, Inc., Secaucus (1999)

[23] Steffen, B., Howar, F., Merten, M.: Introduction to Active Automata Learning from a Practical Perspective. In: Bernardo, M., Issarny, V. (eds.) SFM 2011. LNCS, vol. 6659, pp. 256–296. Springer, Heidelberg (2011)

[24] Sutcliffe, G., Suttner, C.: The State of CASC. AI Communications 19(1), 35–48 (2006), http://www.cs.miami.edu/~tptp/CASC/

[25] Vaquero, T.S., Fratini, S.: ICKEPS – International Competition on Knowledge Engineering for Planning and Scheduling. In: ICAPS (2012), http://icaps12.poli.usp.br/icaps12/ickeps

Author Index